MW00835243

MATHEMATICAL METHODS FOR FOREIGN EXCHANGE

A Financial Engineer's Approach

MATHEMATICAL METHODS
FOR FOREIGN EXCHANGE

A Financial Engineer's Approach

ALEXANDER LIPTON

DEUTSCHE BANK, USA

World Scientific
Singapore • New Jersey • London • Hong Kong

Published by

World Scientific Publishing Co. Pte. Ltd.

P O Box 128, Farrer Road, Singapore 912805

USA office: Suite 1B, 1060 Main Street, River Edge, NJ 07661

UK office: 57 Shelton Street, Covent Garden, London WC2H 9HE

British Library Cataloguing-in-Publication Data
A catalogue record for this book is available from the British Library.

MATHEMATICAL METHODS FOR FOREIGN EXCHANGE
A Financial Engineer's Approach

ISBN 981-02-4615-3
ISBN 981-02-4823-7 (pbk)

This book is printed on acid-free paper.

Printed in Singapore by World Scientific Printers

This Book is Dedicated

To Marsha

*The importance of money essentially flows from it
being a link between the present and the future.*

John Maynard Keynes

*Money and currency are very strange things.
They keep on going up and down and no one knows why;
If you want to win, you lose, however hard you try.*

Gilles li Muisis

Preface

This book is devoted to some mathematical problems encountered by the author in his capacity as a mathematician turned financial engineer at Bankers Trust and Deutsche Bank. The exposition is restricted mainly to problems occurring in the foreign exchange (forex) context not only due to the fact that it is the author's current area of responsibility but also because mathematical methods of financial engineering can be described more vividly when the exposition is centered on a single topic. Studying forex is interesting and important because it is the grease on the wheels of the world economy. Besides, while the meaning of some financial instruments is difficult to comprehend without prior experience, everyone who has ever travelled abroad has had to exchange currencies thus acquiring direct experience of such concepts as spot forex rate, bid-ask spread, transaction costs (in the form of commissions), etc. At the same time, the reader who acquires working knowledge of the material presented in this book should be able to handle efficiently most of the problems occurring in equity markets and some of the problems relevant for fixed income markets.

If one were to choose just one word in order to characterize financial markets, that word would be *uncertainty* since it is their dominant feature. Some investors consider uncertainty a blessing, while others think it a curse, yet both groups participate in the intricate inner workings of the markets. The fact that foreign exchange rates (relative prices of different currencies), as well as prices of bonds (government or corporate obligations to repay debts) and stocks (claims on future cash flows generated by companies) are random and financial investments are risky was realized long ago and has been a source of fascination for economists, mathematicians, speculators, philosophers, and moralists, not to mention laymen.

Due to the random nature of financial markets, trying to predict future prices of individual financial instruments makes little sense. However, one can introduce so-called derivative instruments (the name indicates that their

ix

prices are derived from the prices of some underlying financial instruments, namely, currencies, bonds, stocks, credits, etc.), which can be used in order to cope with financial risks and uncertainties. Alternatively, one can develop optimal investment strategies in the presence of uncertainty which are based on diversification and creation of portfolios of different instruments which are less risky than individual instruments. In the present book we show how to value derivatives and construct optimal portfolios in the forex context by using modern mathematical methods.

This book is devoted to various problems which financial engineers face in the market place and gives a detailed account of mathematical methods necessary for their solution. Even though the exposition is presented from a financial engineer's prospective, the author tried his best to expose all the necessary details. At the same time, mathematical rigor as such was not high on the author's priority list. In particular, most of the results are not formulated as theorems and lemmas since this traditional format is not adequate for the purposes of the present exposition. We start with a brief survey of relevant mathematical concepts. After that we present an in-depth discussion of discrete-time models of forex. We distinguish between single-period and multi-period models. In both cases the corresponding models are too stylized to be of practical importance but they do allow the reader to understand some of the issues which occur in more complicated situations. For this reason, and because of their aesthetic appeal, these models deserve a careful study. We analyze conditions which guarantee that a particular model is financially reasonable and show how to price derivatives and solve the optimal investment problem for such models. Once discrete-times models are mastered, we switch our attention to more practically useful continuous-time models. We describe in detail a variety of models, starting with the standard Black-Scholes model and ending with rather involved stochastic volatility models with a special emphasis on practical aspects. We then show how to price derivatives and solve the optimal investment problem in the continuous setting.

Recently, several very good (and some not so good) books dealing with various aspects of financial engineering were published. The author hopes that the present book can complement the existing literature on the subject and will be useful to the reader in more than one way. In fact, when deciding whether to write this book, he followed the advice of Franz Kafka who once said "Such books as make us happy, we could, if need be, write ourselves".

In the process of writing this book the author enjoyed help, advice, and support of various individuals. First and foremost, he is grateful to his wife Marsha, father Yefim, mother Eugenia, and daughter Rachel. Next, he is also deeply grateful and much indebted to his fellow quants, especially to Christopher Berry, Stewart Inglis, and William McGhee, as well as to Peter Carr, Brian Davidson, Vladimir Finkelstein, Ken Garbade, Arvind Hariharan, Tom Hyer, Andrew Jacobs, Bin Li, Dmitry Pugachevsky, Eric Reiner, and Paul Romanelli. Last but not least, he greatly benefited from the interactions with a group of outstanding managers and traders including Hal Herron, Dan Almeida, Jim Turley, Kevin Rodgers, Matt Desselberger, Perry Parker, and Andrew Baxter.

Reasonable efforts were made to publish reliable information. However, in a book like this one typing and other errors are unavoidable. The author and the publisher do not assume any responsibility or liability for the validity of the information presented in this book and for the consequences of its use or misuse. The book represents only the personal views of the author and does not necessarily reflect the views of Deutsche Bank, its subsidiaries or affiliates.

Finally, a few words about the epigraphs. J. M. Keynes needs no introduction. The Abbot Gilles li Muisis of Tournai lived in the fourteenth century. His wonderful verse is quoted by P. S. Lewis in *"Later Medieval France"* and by B. W. Tuchman in *"A Distant Mirror"*.

Alexander Lipton
New York and London
March 2001.

Contents

Part I

Introduction

Chapter 1

Foreign exchange markets

1.1 Introduction

They say that money never sleeps. The truth of this statement is apparent to anyone who has even passing familiarity with the inner workings of the world financial markets. Perhaps, the best confirmation can be found in the foreign exchange (forex) markets because of their depth, versatility and transparency. The sheer size of forex markets is mind boggling: the daily turnover is about $1.5 trillion. Changes in foreign exchange rates (FXRs) (i.e., relative prices of different currencies) are caused by both deep structural shifts in the respective economies and a variety of less fundamental factors. These changes have a profound impact on the world economy at large. An adequate formalism for studying the dynamics of FXRs has been developed by a number of researchers over the last thirty years. In addition to explaining the qualitative behavior of FXRs, this formalism can be used in order to develop consistent pricing of various derivative instruments, such as forwards, calls, puts, etc., whose value depends on the value of the underlying FXRs. By necessity this formalism is probabilistic in nature and requires a solid grasp of several mathematical disciplines for its efficient usage. In the present book we use these to solve a number of fundamental problems of financial engineering, such as derivative pricing, asset management, etc.

This Chapter is organized as follows. In Section 2 we give the a brief overview of the historic development of financial engineering. In Section 3 we discuss properties of forex as an asset class. In Section 4 we describe properties of spot FXRs. In Section 5 we introduce and discuss derivatives in the forex context. In Section 6 we give relevant references to the literature.

1.2 Historical background

In different disguises, problems of financial engineering have been discussed since classical times in a variety of sources stretching from Plato's Dialogues to the Old and New Testaments. Many illustrious noble houses in Medieval Italy made their fortunes by astute dealings in money lending and foreign exchange. An intimate relation between money lending (fixed income in modern language) and money changing (foreign exchange) was used by Italian bankers collectively known as the Lombards, in order to circumvent the church prohibition on charging interest on loans. They lent money in one currency and received it back in another one with the FXR artificially lowered to accommodate the interest. The blossoming of the Netherlands in the seventeenth century is, at least partly, due the introduction of new financial instruments such as forward contracts, calls and puts, etc. The rise of the British Empire resulted in further advances in finance, particularly, on the fixed income side. The economic growth in the United States was facilitated by the unprecedented growth of the financial system, especially, by the introduction of limited liability companies.

The modern development of financial engineering starts with the work of the French mathematician Louis Bachelier who, in the year 1900, published the now famous memoir entitled *"Theorie de la spéculation"*. Bachelier's achievements are remarkable in several respects. To mention just one, he developed (before Einstein and others) the first theory of Brownian motion which he used in order to quantify the evolution of stock prices. In modern terms, Bachelier assumed that the stock price follows an arithmetic Brownian motion and, consequently, is distributed normally at any given time. He derived the pricing formulas for call and put options on such stocks. However, since Bachelier's theory predicted that stock prices can become negative and because of the sheer complexity of its mathematical apparatus, the theory was neglected by the mainstream economists for more than fifty years.

Fundamental contributions to modern financial engineering were made in the 1950s by several authors. Arrow (1953) and Debreu (1959) extended the existing economic models by incorporating uncertainty and showed how to solve the corresponding asset allocation problem. Modigliani and Miller (1958) proved that the financial structure of the firm, i.e., the firm's choice between equity and debt financing, does not affect its value. The method of financial arbitrage they used turned out to be even more useful than the theorem itself and became the method of choice for generations of financial engineers. Finally,

Markowitz (1959) developed the mean-variance portfolio selection theory.

In the 1960s financial engineering continued to grow rapidly. In particular, Sprenkle (1961), Boness (1964), and Samuelson (1965) proposed a more adequate description of the stock price evolution by assuming that this price follows the geometrical Brownian motion and, consequently, is distributed lognormally which guarantees its positivity. Although they obtained a closed form formula for pricing options on lognormally distributed stocks, this formula was difficult to use in practice because it contained too many free parameters, namely, the volatility of the stock, and the growth rates of the stock and option. In the meantime, Sharpe (1964), Lintner (1965), and Mossin (1966) extended the Markowitz theory and created the so-called capital asset pricing model (CAPM).

The major breakthrough was achieved the early 1970s when Black and Scholes (1973) and Merton (1973) discovered a consistent pricing formula for stock options depending on the volatility of the underlying stock and the riskless interest rate at which the money can be borrowed overnight (rather than the growth rates of the underlying stock and option). The Black-Scholes-Merton pricing methodology is based on the idea of dynamic hedging of derivatives which allows the seller of an option to become indifferent to the changes in the underlying stock price. In order to hedge himself, the seller of an option has to maintain positions in both stock and bond and to adjust them dynamically when the stock price changes. For their discovery Scholes and Merton were awarded the Nobel Prize for Economics in 1997 (Black died in 1995). The Black-Scholes formula instantly became extremely popular among practitioners and academics alike, and within a few years helped to create a multi-trillion dollar market in financial derivatives, currently estimated at $65 trillion. (The impact of Black-Scholes discovery on financial markets is a great example of the influence of mathematics on society at large.)

Many important contributions to financial engineering were made after publication of the seminal papers by Black and Scholes and Merton. For instance, Merton himself and later Rubinstein and Reiner (1991), used the well-known method of images in order to price the so-called barrier options which disappear when the price of the underlying hits a predetermined barrier. Black (1976) derived the formula for the valuation of options on futures. Ross (1976) developed the arbitrage-pricing theory (APT) as an alternative to CAPM. Margrabe (1978) valued the right to exchange one risky asset for another (via an elegant application of the principle of homogeneity). Harrison and Kreps (1979) and Harrison and Pliska (1981) developed an approach to pricing and hedging of derivatives which complements the one developed by Black and Scholes and Merton. They showed that the price of an option (provided that it is hedged appropriately), can be written as the expectation (with respect to the so-called risk-neutral probability measure) of its discounted payoff at maturity. In probabilistic terms, they showed that the discounted value of an option is a martingale so that options can be priced via probabilistic methods (which complement partial differential equations methods originally used by Black-Scholes). Mathematical aspects of this approach were elucidated by Delbaen and Schachermayer (1994). Garman and Kohlhagen (1983) extended the Black-Scholes valuation formula in order to incorporate options on forex.

Although the original approach to problems of financial engineering was predominantly analytical, numerical methods necessary to solve more complicated problems were developed as well. The earliest were the so-called binomial, explicit finite difference, and Monte Carlo methods introduced by Cox, Ross and Rubinstein (1979), Schwartz (1977) and Brennan and Schwartz (1978), and Boyle (1977), respectively. Although these methods were very intuitive, they were not sufficiently refined and could not price certain derivatives accurately. In a due course they were complemented by the implicit finite difference method which became the method of choice for solving more advanced problems.

In spite of its many successes, the Black-Scholes formula is too idealized and does not capture certain features of the market. The most important of those features are the non-lognormal distribution of the underlying stock prices, transaction costs, liquidity, and discontinuous nature of trading. When this formula is used in practice, different volatilities are used to price options with different strikes which gives rise to the so-called volatility skew (in equity markets) and smile (in forex markets). Appropriate modifications of the Black-Scholes paradigm which would account for skews and smiles observed in actual markets is a major challenge which is only partly met at present.

It proved to be more difficult to model fixed income derivatives, such as bond options, caps, floors, etc., than forex and equity derivatives. This disparity is due to the fact that the dynamics of the underlying short term interest rate (or the bond price) is much more complicated than the forex and stock dynamics and cannot be approximated by the geometrical Brownian motion. (Indeed, empirical observations suggest that interest rates are mean-reverting, while, by definition, bond prices exhibit the so-called pull-to-par property and approach bond's notional value at maturity). In addition, one has to deal with bonds of all maturities (the so-called yield curve) at once. Vasicek (1977) was the first to propose an analytically tractable model taking into account the mean reversion property of the instantaneous interest rate and the pull-to-par property. He assumed that the interest rate follows the Ornstein-Uhlenbeck process and obtained analytical expressions for prices of bonds and bond options. However, Vasicek model is not without some limitations; namely, it cannot be fitted sufficiently accurately to the market data, and it allows interest rates to become negative, i.e., it suffers from the same difficulty as the original Bachelier model for equities. While the first drawback is easy to rectify, as was done by Hull and White (1990), the second one is an inherited feature of the model and cannot be helped. In order to guarantee the positivity of interest rates one needs to use other stochastic processes with mean reversion, such as the Feller square-root process used by Cox, Ingersoll and Ross (1985), or the log-Ornstein-Uhlenbeck process used Black and Karasinski (1991). An alternative idea of dealing with fixed income derivatives is based on studying the yield curve in its entirety, as described by Heath, Jarrow and Morton (1992) and Brace, Gatarek and Musiela (1997) in continuous and discrete settings, respectively. In spite of the progress made by the above mentioned authors and many others, an adequate versatile model for pricing and hedging of fixed income derivatives is still missing.

1.3   Forex as an asset class

As was mentioned earlier, the daily turnover of forex markets is approximately $1.5 trillion. The majority of transactions with foreign exchange are executed from London and New York (about 1/3 and 1/5 of the total, respectively), as well as Tokyo, Singapore, Frankfurt, Zurich, etc. Market participants include governments, banks, international corporations, mutual and hedge funds, and individual investors. With increasing globalization of the world financial system, the role of forex as an important asset class in its own right on a par with more traditional equity and fixed income instruments becomes more and more apparent. Indeed, it is necessary to have an exposure to forex in order to be able to invest in the global markets and create a well-balanced portfolio.

When investors based in a particular country put their money in domestic bonds and equities, they are not (directly) affected by the forex rate fluctuations and all the uncertainties they have to face are domestic in nature. However, if they decide to invest their money in foreign bonds and equities, they first have to convert the domestic currency (say US dollars) into the foreign currency (say euros) at the deterministic spot rate in order to purchase foreign securities, and then, at some time in the future, they have to convert the foreign currency generated by these securities into the domestic currency (at the unknown rate prevailing at that time). Thus, investors have to deal with uncertainties both at home and overseas, and, in addition, with changes in forex rate. Nonetheless, foreign investments can generate returns which are so attractive that additional risks are worth taking.

For simplicity we consider only investments in domestic and foreign fixed income instruments. In order to quantify uncertainties associated with these investments, we need to know the prices of domestic and foreign zero coupon bonds, i.e., the price in dollars (euros) at time $t = 0$ of the obligation to pay one dollar (euro) at time T in the future. We denote the price of the domestic and foreign bonds maturing at time T by $B^0_{0,T}$ and $B^1_{0,T}$, respectively. Assuming that the bond prices are deterministic (this is a strong assumption which is made in order to simplify the exposition), we can represent the bond prices at time t as

$$B^0_{t,T} = \frac{B^0_{0,T}}{B^0_{0,t}}, \qquad B^1_{t,T} = \frac{B^1_{0,T}}{B^1_{0,t}}.$$

In addition, we need to know the forex rate S_t, i.e., the number of dollars one needs to pay at time t in exchange for one euro. The dimension of S_t is dollar/euro. In contrast to bond prices which are deterministic in our simplified framework, the forex rate is random, so that its value at some future time T is uncertain. We use the domestic bond as a benchmark for measuring the rate of return on different investments. It is clear that the relative rate of return on investment in domestic bonds is zero. The relative rate of return on investment in foreign bonds is

$$\hat{r} = \frac{B^0_{0,T} S_T}{B^1_{0,T} S_0} - 1. \tag{1.1}$$

It can be both positive and negative. Thus, in order to achieve relative rates of return above zero, domestic investors have to put some of their money overseas.

For simplicity, in this chapter we assume that

$$B^0_{t,T} = e^{-r^0(T-t)}, \qquad B^1_{t,T} = e^{-r^1(T-t)},$$

where r^0 and r^1 are constant domestic and foreign interest rates, respectively.

1.4   Spot forex

Perhaps the simplest transaction in the forex market is the exchange of two currencies at the (fluctuating) spot rate prevailing at the time of the exchange. As a rule, all exchanges are conducted through middlemen called market makers, rather than directly between two interested parties, which explains the so-called bid-ask spread, i.e., the difference between the lower rate at which the foreign currency can be sold to market makers and the higher rate at which it can be bought from them. (This concept will be familiar to anyone who has exchanged currency abroad.) Depending on the particular currency pair, the rate is agreed upon today while the actual transfer takes place either in two business days (US dollar/yen, euro/US dollar, pound/US dollar) or in one business day (US dollar/Canadian dollar). Instantaneous FXRs (as well as stock and bond prices) are determined by market forces (through the "invisible hand" envisioned by Adam Smith) and reflect their intrinsic values, as well as considerations of supply and demand. FXRs constantly fluctuate around their moving equilibrium values. Their most important characteristics are rates of return on investments in foreign currency (yearly, monthly, daily, hourly, etc.). Rates of return are random and have to be treated via statistical methods for studying time series. To give the reader an idea of what can be expected, we just mention that the distribution of daily returns for the foreign exchange rate USD/DEM over a period of ten years from 1986 to 1996 has volatility 0.11, skewness -0.1, kurtosis 5, and no daily deviations exceeded five standard deviations, while for the S&P 500 Index over the same period the distribution of returns has volatility 0.16, skewness -5, kurtosis 111, and that one (five) daily deviation (deviations) exceeded ten (five) standard deviations. The distribution of daily returns for the FXR is reasonably close to Gaussian, while for the S&P 500 Index the corresponding distribution is strongly non-Gaussian. In most cases it is not necessary to explain the observed FXRs and rates of return on investments in foreign currencies in fundamental terms; the main objective is to develop a model for pricing derivative instruments in terms of the underlying ones and to solve the asset management problem. Even though, in general, the distribution of the daily returns for underlying instruments is non-Gaussian, it is frequently assumed to be Gaussian for practical purposes. Surprisingly, more often than not, this approach produces satisfactory results.

Typical behavior of FXRs is illustrated in Figure 1.1.

1.5 Derivatives: forwards, futures, calls, puts, and all that

Exchange of currencies at spot rates serves only the most obvious and the most immediate needs of market participants. Their more sophisticated needs are met by derivative instruments. The basic types of forex and equity derivatives are forward and futures contracts, and calls and puts; their fixed income counterparts are known as forward rate agreements, Euros, caps, and floors.

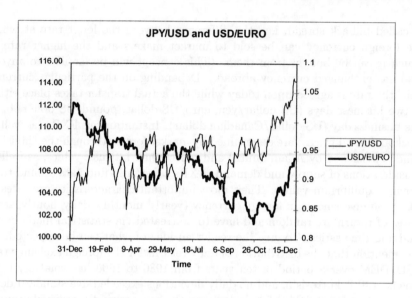

Figure 1.1: The behavior of JPY/USD (left scale) and USD/Euro (right scale) over a representative one-year period. (From 12/31/99 to 12/31/2000.)

In a nutshell, a forward (and to a large degree futures) contract on a financial instrument imposes an obligation on the buyer (seller) to buy (sell) this instrument for a predetermined strike price at a predetermined maturity time. The settlement either occurs at maturity (forward contracts) or continuously (futures contracts). Theoretically, one of the parties has to pay an upfront premium in order to enter into a forward contract with a given strike. However, in practice, the strike is determined in such a way that the initial value of the claim is zero, so that entering into a forward contract does not require any initial investment from the parties involved. The party that buys (sells) an instrument forward expects its price to be above (below) the predetermined price at maturity. Broadly speaking, the forward and futures prices are expectations of the spot price of the corresponding instrument at maturity (with respect to appropriate probability measures). Finding the correct forward FXR is one of the basic problems of financial engineering. It is remarkable that this rate can be determined without knowing any details about the behavior of the underlying FXR *per se*.

Options on a financial instrument are different from forward and futures contracts because they give the buyer of an option the right to buy (call) or to sell (put) the underlying instrument and impose on the seller of an option the obligation to sell (call) or to buy (put) this instrument at a predetermined strike price at maturity (European options) or at any moment between the inception of the option and its maturity (American options). Since the buyer of an option receives a right and its seller accepts an obligation, options have to be purchased for an upfront premium with the subsequent settlement at (or before) maturity. The buyer of an option cannot lose more than the premium paid, while the losses of the seller can, in certain cases, be unlimited. The holder of a call (put) option will benefit from the rise (fall) of the price of the underlying instrument. Knowing prices of forward and futures contracts, and calls and puts with different strikes and maturities, we can obtain detailed probabilistic information about the future spot price of the underlying. Pricing and risk-managing derivatives is one of the most important objectives of financial engineering which we discuss in detail below. We emphasize that it is necessary for market makers to know fair prices of derivatives because they need to quote these prices (with bid-ask spread) before being told if they are going to be a seller or a buyer of the corresponding derivative. This situation is not dissimilar to the one discussed in the old mathematical problem: how two persons should divide a cake in such a way that each one receives a piece which is perceived to be greater or equal to half the cake. The answer is that the first person (the market maker) divides the cake in two parts, while the second person (the investor) chooses the part which he thinks is bigger. [1] The way the market maker earns a living is via the bid-ask spread. Under normal circumstances the fair price is sandwiched between the bid and ask prices. There are at least three reasons for an investor to buy a derivative instrument: (A) for protection against unfavorable forex changes; (B) for leveraging his market views; (C) for speculation.

We consider forward contracts and European calls and puts, which are called plain vanilla instruments, and denote the prices of these claims at time t for the spot FXR equal S by $FO(t, S, T, K)$, $C(t, S, T, K)$, $P(t, S, T, K)$, where the second pair of arguments emphasizes their dependence on the strike K and maturity T. When $t = T$ we have

$$FO(T, S, T, K) = S - K, \tag{1.2}$$

$$C(T, S, T, K) = \max\{S - K, 0\} \equiv (S - K)_+, \tag{1.3}$$

---

[1] The reader is encouraged to solve a similar problem for N persons.

$$P(T, S, T, K) = \max\{K - S, 0\} \equiv (K - S)_+, \qquad (1.4)$$

respectively. Here and below $x_+ = \max\{x, 0\}$. It is clear that for a forward contract the payoff can be both positive and negative while for calls and puts it is always positive, so that forwards can be both assets and liabilities while calls and puts are always assets for the buyer who cannot lose more than the option premium. For a forward contract, we need to find the strike K such that $FO(0, S, K, T) = 0$, while for calls and puts strikes are defined externally. Payoffs (1.2) - (1.4) are shown in Figure 1.2

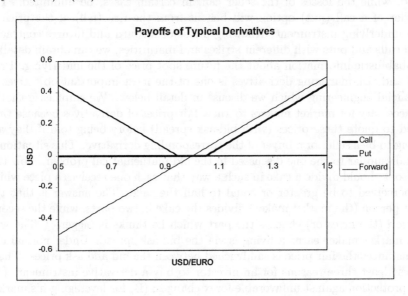

Figure 1.2: Representative payoffs of the call, put, and forward contract.

Even without knowing much about the dynamics of the underlying FXR we can say a lot about the valuation of forwards, calls and puts. First, we can find the fair forward strike K, which we denote by $F_{0,T}$. If we sell a forward contract, we agree to deliver one unit of foreign currency at maturity in exchange for $F_{0,T}$ units of domestic currency. To avoid the exposure to random fluctuation of the FXR, we have to buy one foreign zero coupon bond maturing at T. Accordingly, we have to borrow $e^{-r^1 T} S_0$ units of domestic currency which we need to repay in the amount of $e^{-r^1 T} S_0 / e^{-r^0 T}$ at time T. At maturity our bond produces one unit of foreign currency which we deliver to the buyer and receive $F_{0,T}$ units of domestic currency which we have to pay back to the lender of domestic currency, so that

$$F_{0,T} = e^{(r^0 - r^1)T} S_0. \tag{1.5}$$

This important relation, known as the *interest rate parity theorem*, establishes the fair forward FXR because of the perfect reversibility of the entire procedure which we used to establish it. (This reversibility is similar, in more than one respect, to the reversibility in thermodynamics.) We emphasize that the forward FXR depends only on the spot FXR, and domestic and foreign bond prices. A foreign currency is called a discount currency if $B_{0,T}^1 < B_{0,T}^0$, and a premium currency otherwise. For discount currencies the forward FXR is lower than the spot one, while for premium currencies the opposite is true. The reader should think about this seemingly simple statement at some length because it is not obvious. For an arbitrary (nonequilibrium) strike, we can write

$$FO(t, S, T, K) = e^{-r^1(T-t)} S - e^{-r^0(T-t)} K.$$

Comparison of expressions (1.1), (1.5) shows that if a domestic investor uses the forward FXR rather than the spot FXR for repatriating his profits at time T, the rate of return on foreign investment becomes deterministic and vanishes. (No pain, no gain.)

We use the forward rate $F_{0,T}$ in order to classify calls and puts. We say that calls and puts with $K = F_{0,T}$ are at the money forward (ATMF), calls (puts) with $K < F_{0,T}$ ($K > F_{0,T}$) are in the money forward (ITMF), while calls (puts) with $K > F_{0,T}$ ($K < F_{0,T}$) are out of the money forward (OTMF).

To find the bounds for the price of calls and puts we can use the comparison principle for two portfolios which says that the portfolio which pays more at maturity should be more expensive at any time t before maturity. It is clear that the portfolio consisting of a European call with strike K and of K domestic bonds pays at maturity no less than a portfolio consisting of a foreign bond. This is true at any time t before maturity. At the same time the portfolio consisting of a call pays at maturity no more than the portfolio consisting of one unit of foreign currency. Accordingly, we can conclude that

$$\left(e^{-r^1(T-t)} S - e^{-r^0(T-t)} K \right)_+ \le C(t, S, T, K) \le S. \tag{1.6}$$

Similarly,

$$\left(e^{-r^0(T-t)} K - e^{-r^1(T-t)} S \right)_+ \le P(t, S, T, K) \le K. \tag{1.7}$$

It is interesting to note that in the special case when $e^{-r^1(T-t)} = 1$ (so that the foreign interest rates is equal to zero) we have

$$(S - K)_+ \leq C(t, S, T, K) \leq S,$$

i.e., the call price never falls below its intrinsic value. Similarly, when $e^{-r^0(T-t)} = 1$ (so that the domestic interest rates is equal to zero) the put price does not fall below its intrinsic value,

$$(K - S)_+ \leq P(t, S, T, K) \leq K.$$

It is easy to establish relations between European calls and puts. It follows from contract definition that at maturity we have

$$C(T, S, T, K) - P(T, S, T, K) = S - K = FO(T, S, T, K). \qquad (1.8)$$

The pricing problem for European options is linear, i.e., any linear combination of its solutions is a solution, too. Accordingly, equation (1.8) is valid for any t, so that

$$C(t, S, T, K) - P(t, S, T, K) = e^{-r^1(T-t)}S - e^{-r^0(T-t)}K.$$

This relation is known as *put-call parity*.

In addition to put-call parity there exists one more important relation between calls and puts which we call put-call symmetry. The buyer of a call has the right to buy one euro (the notional amount) at the rate of K dollars/euro. Alternatively, he has the right to sell K dollars at the rate of $1/K$ euros/dollar. The right to buy euros is worth $C^0(0, S, T, K)$ dollars. (Here and below we use superscripts to show the currency in which the corresponding option is valued.) The right to sell dollars is worth $KP^1(0, 1/S, T, 1/K)$ euros. Since buying euros is equivalent to selling dollars the corresponding amounts have to coincide once they are expressed in the same currency (domestic, say). Accordingly,

$$C^0(0, S, T, K) = SKP^1\left(0, \frac{1}{S}, T, \frac{1}{K}\right).$$

This relation expresses put-call symmetry. Since C^0 and P^1 are homogeneous functions of degree one, we can rewrite the above relation in the form

$$C^0(0, S, T, K) = P^1(0, K, T, S),$$

which is probably more elegant but definitely less useful. To switch from P^0 to P^1 one needs to interchange the domestic and foreign interest rates, $r^0 \to r^1$, $r^1 \to r^0$.

American calls and puts are determined by the same terminal payoffs as their European counterparts but can be executed at any time between the inception and maturity of the option; their prices are denoted by $C'(t, S, T, K)$, $P'(t, S, T, K)$. Since American options can be executed at any time t, $0 \leq t \leq T$, their prices cannot fall below their intrinsic values, additionally, they are always more expensive that the corresponding European options. Accordingly,

$$\max\{(S-K)_+, C(t, S, T, K)\} \leq C'(t, S, T, K) \leq S, \tag{1.9}$$

$$\max\{(K-S)_+, P(t, S, T, K)\} \leq P'(t, S, T, K) \leq K. \tag{1.10}$$

When $e^{-r^1(T-t)} = 1$, the prices of American and European calls coincide,

$$C(t, S, T, K) = C'(t, S, T, K),$$

when $e^{-r^0(T-t)} = 1$, the prices of American and European puts coincide,

$$P(t, S, T, K) = P'(t, S, T, K).$$

We cannot expect that *put-call parity* is preserved for American options since the early exercise feature destroys linearity. Instead, weaker inequalities can be proved, namely

$$e^{-r^1(T-t)}S - K \leq C'(t, S, T, K) - P'(t, S, T, K) \leq S - e^{-r^0(T-t)}K.$$

At the same time *put-call symmetry* is preserved since both the pricing equations and the constraints are invariant with respect to switching countries:

$$C'^0(0, S, T, K) = SKP'^1\left(0, \frac{1}{S}, T, \frac{1}{K}\right).$$

This formula expresses the symmetry between a euro call (i.e. the right to buy euros) and a dollar put (i.e. the right to sell dollars). This relation becomes more transparent when we take into account the fact that dollars grow at the domestic risk-free rate r^0, while euros grow at the foreign risk-free rate r^1.

It is difficult to say more about option prices without constructing an adequate model for the behavior of S. We discuss different possibilities throughout the book.

Certain linear combinations of European calls and puts with the same maturity are particularly popular in the market place. These are strangles, straddles, and risk reversals which are discussed in Chapter 9.

In addition to options mentioned above, several others are important in the forex context. The reason is that European and American calls and puts can be rather expensive, so that their cheaper versions can be attractive to investors.

One popular way of making them cheaper, is to take a view on the distribution of the future FXR and to finance the purchase of one option by selling another one. For instance, an investor who thinks that the foreign currency will be traded above a certain level K_1 but below some other level K_2, where $K_1 < K_2$, can buy a call with strike K_1 and sell a call with strike K_2, thus creating the so-called call spreads with payoffs of the form

$$
\text{payoff} = \begin{cases} 0, & S < K_1 \\ S - K_1, & K_1 \leq S < K_2 \\ K_2 - K_1, & K_2 \leq S \end{cases} .
$$

Another approach is to add various barrier features to ordinary calls and puts. For instance, a down-and-out call (up-and-out put) disappears if the FXR hits a certain level below (above) the strike level. Even though the corresponding option provides less protection than its European or American analogue, it can be attractive to investors having specific market views, or those who can adjust to low (high) FXRs. Other options with mild barrier features which are frequently traded in practice are the so-called timers and faders (also known as time trades) with payoffs depending on the amount of time the FXR spends above (or below) a certain barrier.

In addition, there are many investors whose needs are better served by the so-called lookback calls (puts) which give the buyer the right to buy (sell) foreign currency at the best FXR observed between the inception and maturity of the corresponding option, and Asian options which give the right to buy or sell currency at the average FXR. We also study the so-called passport options. In contrast to all other options considered in this book, passport options are written on the trading account rather than on the underlying FXR. The buyer of such an options has the right to keep all the profit and is compensated for any loss generated by buying and selling a specific amount of foreign currency between the inception of the option and its maturity. Passport options require active participation of the buyer in the trading process, so that their value depends not only on the evolution of the FXR but also on the buyer's strategy. Barrier, lookback, Asian, and passport options are examples of the so-called path-dependent options whose payoff depends on the entire trajectory of the FXR between the inception and maturity of an option rather than on the terminal value of the FXR. Since it is more difficult to price and hedge such options, below we spend considerable effort in order to show how it can be done.

Yet another class of path-dependent options which gained popularity in the past few years includes the so-called volatility and variance swaps and options on realized volatility and variance. As their name suggests, these options are written on the volatility or variance of returns on foreign currency. For example, the buyer of a variance swap receives some fixed amount and has to pay the realized variance of returns on foreign currency multiplied by some notional amount. Since all other options depend on volatility, options on volatility are interesting not only in their own right but also as important hedging instruments for a portfolio of options.

1.6 References and further reading

The key original contributions mentioned in this chapter are as follows (in alphabetical order): Arrow (1971), Bachelier (1900), Black (1976), Black, Derman and Toy (1990), Black and Karasinski (1991), Black and Scholes (1973), Boness (1964), Boyle (1977), Brace, Gatarek and Musiela (1997), Brennan and Schwartz (1978), Cox, Ingersoll and Ross (1985), Cox, Ross and Rubinstein (1979), Debreu (1959), Delbaen and Schachermayer (1994), Garman and Kohlhagen (1983), Harrison and Kreps (1979), Harrison and Pliska (1981), Heath, Jarrow and Morton (1992), Ho and Lee (1986), Hull and White (1990), Lintner (1965), Margrabe (1978), Markowitz (1990), Merton (1973), Modigliani and Miller (1958), Mossin (1966), de Pinto (1771), Ross (1976), Rubinstein and Reiner (1991), Samuelson (1965), Schwartz (1977), Sharpe (1985), Sprenkle (1961), and Vasicek (1977). Details on empirical distributions of returns of forex and other asset classes are discussed by many authors, for example, by Duffie and Pan (1997). An overview of the subjects covered in this chapter can be found in Lipton-Lifschitz (1999), and Lipton (2000 a).

There are many (some would say too many) books on financial engineering. Here are the books which the present author finds particularly useful for his purposes: Avellaneda and Laurence (2000), Baxter and Rennie (1996), Dixit and Pindyck (1994), Dothan (1990), Duffie (1996), Cox and Rubinstein (1985), Fama and Miller (1972), Huang and Litzenberger (1988), Hull (2000), Hunt and Kennedy (2000), Ingersoll (1987), Jarrow and Rudd (1983), Karatzas and Shreve (1998), Lamberton and Lapeyre (1996), Luenberger (1998), Malkiel (1990), Merton (1990), Musiela and Rutkovsky (1997), Nielsen (2000), Pliska (1997), Shimko (1992), Shiryaev (1999), Wilmot *et al.* (1993), Wilmott *et al.* (1995), and Zang (1997).

Part II

Mathematical preliminaries

Chapter 2

Elements of probability theory

2.1 Introduction

In this chapter we introduce the basic definitions and concepts of probability theory and describe some of the results which are needed in order to appreciate the theory of discrete- and continuous-time processes, and, by implication, the dynamics of FXRs.

Specifically, we introduce random experiments with finite and infinite elementary outcomes, aggregate elementary outcomes into (sigma) algebras of nonelementary outcomes, define frequential probabilities of different outcomes and construct probability spaces associated with random experiments. Next, we define random variables on such spaces and introduce the techniques which are needed to handle such variables efficiently. We give a few examples of random variables which are particularly useful in the financial engineering context.

The chapter is organized as follows. In Section 2 we introduce probability spaces and discuss their basic properties. In Section 3 we describe random variables on probability spaces. In Section 4 we study convergence of sequences of random variables and briefly discuss limit theorems for sums of independent random variables. References to the literature are given in Section 5.

21

2.2 Probability spaces

We start with the concept of a *random experiment* which is characterized by the conditions under which it is conducted and its possible elementary outcomes (which we also call elementary events). We assume that the conditions of the experiment are reproducible, so that, in principle, it can be repeated as many times as desired. This assumption is conceptually very important since it allows us to develop probability theory based on the so-called frequential interpretation of probabilities. The classical examples of such experiments are coin tossing, dice rolling, roulette spinning, throwing a needle on a checker board, etc.

Traditionally, the set of all elementary events is denoted by Ω and its elements by $\omega, \omega', \omega_1$, etc. All other legitimate events can be considered as subsets of Ω, i.e., as unions of elementary events. An experiment is called finite if there is a finite complete set of elementary events, otherwise it is called infinite. When Ω contains infinitely many points it has "too many" subsets and some of them have truly pathological properties, so that they do not represent legitimate events.

Two legitimate events are particularly important - the certain event Ω and the impossible event $\varnothing$, which are the union and the complement of all legitimate events, respectively. For any event $\mathfrak{a}$ we introduce the complementary event $\bar{\mathfrak{a}}$ which occurs whenever $\mathfrak{a}$ does not occur, $\bar{\mathfrak{a}} = \Omega\backslash\mathfrak{a}$. We say that an event $\mathfrak{a}$ implies an event $\mathfrak{b}$ if $\mathfrak{b}$ occurs whenever $\mathfrak{a}$ occurs, the corresponding notation is $\mathfrak{a} \subset \mathfrak{b}$. It is clear that an event $\mathfrak{a}$ is elementary if for any event $\mathfrak{b}$, $\mathfrak{a}$ implies either $\mathfrak{b}$ or $\bar{\mathfrak{b}}$. For any two events $\mathfrak{a}, \mathfrak{b}$ we introduce the event $\mathfrak{a} \bigcup \mathfrak{b}$ which is called the union (sum) of $\mathfrak{a}, \mathfrak{b}$ and occurs when either $\mathfrak{a}$ or $\mathfrak{b}$ occur, the event $\mathfrak{a} \bigcap \mathfrak{b}$ which is called the intersection (product) of $\mathfrak{a}, \mathfrak{b}$ and occurs when both $\mathfrak{a}$ and $\mathfrak{b}$ occur, and the event $\mathfrak{a}\backslash\mathfrak{b}$ which occurs whenever $\mathfrak{a}$ occurs and $\mathfrak{b}$ does not . Events $\mathfrak{a}, \mathfrak{b}$ are incompatible if the event $\mathfrak{a} \bigcap \mathfrak{b}$ is impossible.

We denote the set of legitimate events by $\mathfrak{U}$. In order to use the probabilistic techniques to the full extent we have to make sure that $\mathfrak{U}$ is closed with respect to the logical operations such as "either" and "or" introduced above. We say that $\mathfrak{U}$ is an algebra of events if: (A) $\Omega \in \mathfrak{U}$, (B) if $\mathfrak{a} \in \mathfrak{U}$ then $\bar{\mathfrak{a}} \in \mathfrak{U}$ as well, (C) if $\mathfrak{a} \in \mathfrak{U}$ and $\mathfrak{b} \in \mathfrak{U}$, then $\mathfrak{a} \bigcup \mathfrak{b} \in \mathfrak{U}$. It is easy to show that $\varnothing \in \mathfrak{U}$, and $\mathfrak{a} \bigcap \mathfrak{b} \in \mathfrak{U}$. We say that $\mathfrak{U}$ is a sigma algebra if it has all the properties of an algebra, and, in addition, contains infinite unions of elements from $\mathfrak{U}$, so that

$$\bigcup_{n=1}^{\infty} \mathfrak{a}_n \in \mathfrak{U},$$

provided that $a_n \in \mathfrak{U}$. For infinite experiments we deal exclusively with sigma algebras of events. For experiments with a finite number of outcomes the concepts of algebra and sigma algebra are equivalent. For such experiments it is natural to identify $\mathfrak{U}$ with the set of all subsets of Ω. If Ω contains K elements, then $\mathfrak{U}$ contains 2^K elements.

For every family of subsets $\mathfrak{G}$ we let $\mathfrak{G}'$ be the extension of $\mathfrak{G}$ which contains all elements $\mathfrak{g}$ and their complements $\bar{\mathfrak{g}}$. We denote by $\mathfrak{U}(\mathfrak{G})$ the sigma algebra such that every element $\mathfrak{u}$ of this algebra is either a union of certain elements $\mathfrak{g}_1, ..., \mathfrak{g}_\Lambda$ of the set $\mathfrak{G}'$ or a complement of such union. We say that $\mathfrak{U}(\mathfrak{G})$ is generated by $\mathfrak{G}$.

A set of events $\mathfrak{c}_1, ..., \mathfrak{c}_I$ is called a partition of Ω (a complete set of events) if any two events $\mathfrak{c}_i, \mathfrak{c}_{i'}$ are incompatible and

$$\bigcup_{i=1}^{I} \mathfrak{c}_i = \Omega.$$

Example 2.1. *Rolling a dice is a classical finite random experiment. In this experiment, the set of elementary events Ω contains six elements $\{\omega_1, ..., \omega_6\}$ which are distinguished by the outcome of the rolling. (Below we index events starting with 0, however, here we start with 1 for obvious reasons.) The set of all possible outcomes U contains $2^6 = 64$ events which are unions of elementary events. For instance, an elementary event is: the outcome is 5, while a nonelementary event is: the outcome is odd.*

Example 2.2. *Observing daily domestic returns on investments in foreign bonds is a typical infinite random experiment. The corresponding set Ω coincides with the real axis $\mathbb{R}$, elementary events $\omega, \omega', ...,$ are points in $\mathbb{R}$. We restrict ourselves to the so-called Borel sigma algebra $\mathfrak{B}$ of Borel sets in $\mathbb{R}$ which is generated by the closed intervals $a_0 \leq x_0 \leq b_0$. This sigma-algebra contains all closed and open sets in $\mathbb{R}$, and many other sets, too. In fact, it is rather difficult to construct an example of a set which does not belong to $\mathfrak{B}$, however, such sets do exist. More generally, when we are interested in returns on investments in different currencies, we consider the K-dimensional Euclidean space $\mathbb{R}^K$. The corresponding Borel sigma algebra $\mathfrak{B}^K$ is generated by the family $\mathfrak{G}^K$ of closed K-dimensional parallelograms defined by the inequalities $a_k \leq x_k \leq b_k$, $k = 0, ..., K-1$.*

Once the space of elementary events is introduced, we can define probabilities of both elementary and nonelementary events. We understand the probability of an event frequentially. In other words, we repeat our experiment many times in a row (under the same conditions) and count the number of times the event occurs (we call the corresponding experiments successful).

The frequency of this event is the ratio of the number of successful experiments to the total number of experiments. It has been established experimentally that the frequency of a particular event approaches a certain limiting value (sandwiched between 0 and 1) when the number of trials goes to infinity. This value can be called the (frequential) probability of the event in question.

In order to introduce the concept of probability without contradictions and in agreement with our frequential interpretation, we have to respect the following axioms of probability. For every event $a \in \mathfrak{U}$ we can define its probability $P(a)$ in such a way that:

$$0 \leq P(a) \leq 1;$$

$$P\left(a \bigcup b\right) = P(a) + P(b) \quad \text{if} \quad a \bigcap b = \varnothing;$$

$$P(\Omega) = 1.$$

When Ω is infinite, we require, in addition, that

$$P\left(\bigcup_{n=1}^{\infty} u_n\right) = \sum_{n=1}^{\infty} P(u_n) \quad \text{provided that} \quad u_n \bigcap u_{n'} = \varnothing. \tag{2.1}$$

We call $P(a)$ a probability measure on $\mathfrak{U}$ and consider it as a function from $\mathfrak{U}$ to $\mathbb{R}_+$. It is clear that there are many possible probability measures on $\mathfrak{U}$. We leave it to the reader to deduce the following properties of probability:

$$P(\varnothing) = 0, \quad P(\bar{a}) = 1 - P(a), \quad P\left(a \bigcup b\right) = P(a) + P(b) - P\left(a \bigcap b\right).$$

Thus, the probability of every observable event is sandwiched between 0 and 1, with probabilities of the impossible event and the certain event equal to 0 and 1 respectively. Property (2.1) expresses the so-called sigma additivity of probabilities. (The fact that $\mathfrak{U}$ is a sigma-algebra rather than an algebra becomes important at this stage.)

For finite experiments we have K possible elementary outcomes and any other outcome can be presented as a union of elementary outcomes. We denote the probabilities of elementary outcomes ω_k by p_k, $k = 0, ..., K - 1$. The probability of an outcome

$$a = \bigcup_{l=0}^{L-1} \omega_{k_l},$$

where $(k_0, ..., k_{L-1})$ is a subset of $(0, ..., K)$, is

$$P(\mathfrak{a}) = \sum_l p_{k_l} = \sum_k p_k \chi_{\mathfrak{a}}(\omega_k),$$

where $\chi_{\mathfrak{a}}(\omega)$ is the characteristic function of the event $\mathfrak{a}$, $\chi_{\mathfrak{a}}(\omega) = 1$ if $\omega \in \mathfrak{a}$, and $\chi_{\mathfrak{a}}(\omega) = 0$ if $\omega \notin \mathfrak{a}$.

Example 2.3. *For dice rolling the probabilities of all elementary outcomes ω_k are equal to 1/6 (by symmetry). Accordingly, the probability of getting an odd number as an outcome is $1/2 = 1/6 + 1/6 + 1/6$.*

A very important extension of the concept of probability is the concept of conditional probability. Consider an event $\mathfrak{b}$ such that $P(\mathfrak{b}) > 0$. We define the conditional probability of an event $\mathfrak{a}$ with respect to the event $\mathfrak{b}$ as follows

$$P(\mathfrak{a}|\mathfrak{b}) = \frac{P(\mathfrak{a} \cap \mathfrak{b})}{P(\mathfrak{b})}.$$

The conditional probability shows how often the event $\mathfrak{a}$ occurs if in a sequence of experiments we consider only experiments where the event $\mathfrak{b}$ occurs. It is clear that

$$P\left(\mathfrak{a} \cap \mathfrak{b}\right) = P(\mathfrak{a}|\mathfrak{b}) P(\mathfrak{b}) = P(\mathfrak{b}|\mathfrak{a}) P(\mathfrak{a}),$$

$$P(\mathfrak{a}|\mathfrak{b}) = \frac{P(\mathfrak{b}|\mathfrak{a}) P(\mathfrak{a})}{P(\mathfrak{b})}.$$

provided that $P(\mathfrak{a}) > 0$.

Two events $\mathfrak{a}, \mathfrak{b}$ are independent if

$$P\left(\mathfrak{a} \cap \mathfrak{b}\right) = P(\mathfrak{a}) P(\mathfrak{b}),$$

or, equivalently, if

$$P(\mathfrak{a}|\mathfrak{b}) = P(\mathfrak{a}), \qquad P(\mathfrak{b}|\mathfrak{a}) = P(\mathfrak{b}).$$

Two partitions $\mathfrak{c}_1, ..., \mathfrak{c}_I$ and $\mathfrak{d}_1, ..., \mathfrak{d}_J$ are independent if for every i, j,

$$P\left(\mathfrak{c}_i \cap \mathfrak{d}_j\right) = P(\mathfrak{c}_i) P(\mathfrak{d}_j).$$

If events $\mathfrak{c}_1, ..., \mathfrak{c}_I$ form a complete set and $P(\mathfrak{c}_i) > 0$, we have

$$P(\mathfrak{a}) = \sum_{1 \le i \le I} P(\mathfrak{a}|\mathfrak{c}_i) P(\mathfrak{c}_i).$$

This formula is known as the total probability formula. Its sister formula is known as Bayes's formula which states

$$P(c_i|a) = \frac{P(a|c_i)P(c_i)}{\sum_{1 \le i \le I} P(a|c_i)P(c_i)}.$$

This formula which plays an outstanding role in statistics and many other areas allows us to find the probability that the event c_n is observed in the experiment provided that we know that the event a has been observed.

Example 2.4. *Consider two partitions of Ω of the form*

$$c_1 = \{\omega_1, \omega_2\}, \quad c_2 = \{\omega_3, \omega_4\}, \quad c_3 = \{\omega_5, \omega_6\},$$
$$\mathfrak{d}_1 = \{\omega_1, \omega_3, \omega_5\}, \quad \mathfrak{d}_2 = \{\omega_2, \omega_4, \omega_6\}.$$

Their elements have probabilities of $1/3$ and $1/2$, respectively. These partitions are independent. For the event $a = \{\omega_4, \omega_5, \omega_6\}$ whose probability is $1/2$, the conditional probabilities are

$$P(a|c_1) = 0, \quad P(a|c_2) = \frac{1}{2}, \quad P(a|c_3) = 1,$$

while the total probability and Bayes's formulas yield

$$P(a) = 0 \cdot \frac{1}{3} + \frac{1}{2} \cdot \frac{1}{3} + 1 \cdot \frac{1}{3} = \frac{1}{2}, \quad P(c_2|a) = \frac{(1/2) \cdot (1/3)}{(1/2)} = \frac{1}{3}.$$

Now we can define a finite probability space $\{\Omega, \mathfrak{U}, P\}$ which is a triple consisting of the finite space of elementary outcomes Ω, the algebra of all possible outcomes $\mathfrak{U}$ (which is the set of all subsets of Ω), and the probability measure P on $\mathfrak{U}$. An infinite probability space is a triple $(\Omega, \mathfrak{U}, P)$, where Ω is the infinite space of elementary outcomes, $\mathfrak{U}$ is a sigma algebra of legitimate events and P is a probability measure.

2.3   Random variables

Scalar random variables on a finite probability space are simply functions of the set of elementary events Ω. They assign numerical values to individual elementary events, or, equivalently, map Ω onto the real axis $\mathbb{R}^1$. Whenever possible, we use Greek letters such as ξ in order to denote random variables. A random variable ξ can have no more than K distinct values (where K is the number of elementary events), we denote these values by $y_0, ..., y_{L-1}$, where

$L \leq K$, and without loss of generality assume that $y_0 < ... < y_{L-1}$. It is clear that every random variable generates a complete partition of Ω into sets c_l, where c_l is the level set of ξ, i.e., the union of all elementary events ω such that $\xi(\omega) = y_l$. We denote the algebra generated by this partition by $\mathfrak{U}_\xi$. By using the probability measure, which is an attribute of the corresponding probability space, we can define the probabilities $\pi_l = P\{\xi = y_l\} = P(c_l)$. We define the modes of a finite random variable ξ as its most probable values y_l. If there is only one mode the corresponding random variable is called unimodal, otherwise it is called multimodal.

Consider now random variables on an infinite probability space defined by the triple $(\Omega, \mathfrak{U}, P)$. We define a scalar random variable on such a space as a $\mathfrak{U}$-measurable function from Ω to $\mathbb{R}$ such that preimages of all Borel sets in $\mathbb{R}$ belong to the corresponding sigma-algebra $\mathfrak{U}$. For every set $\mathfrak{u}$ we can consider its indicator function $\chi_\mathfrak{u}(\omega)$. This indicator function is a random variable if and only if $\mathfrak{u} \in \mathfrak{U}$. The space of random variables considered as functions on Ω is rich enough to be closed with respect to standard mathematical operations such as addition, multiplication, etc.

A vector random variable is a mapping from Ω onto $\mathbb{R}^N$, $\boldsymbol{\xi} = \left(\xi^1, ..., \xi^N\right)$, where ξ^n are scalar random variables.

In order to describe a scalar random variable ξ in quantitative terms we introduce its cumulative distribution function. Since the open interval $-\infty \leq x < x_0$ is a Borel set, its preimage is an element of the sigma algebra $\mathfrak{U}$. Accordingly, we can define the cumulative distribution function (c.d.f.) $F_\xi(x_0)$ as follows

$$F_\xi(x_0) = P\{\omega : \xi(\omega) < x_0\}.$$

It is clear that

$$F_\xi(x_0 \to -\infty) \to 0, \qquad F_\xi(x_0 \to \infty) \to 1.$$

If $F_\xi(x_0)$ is an absolutely continuous function of its argument, we can define the probability density function (p.d.f.) $f_\xi(x_0)$ such that

$$F_\xi(x_0) = \int_{-\infty}^{x_0} f_\xi(x_0')\, dx_0'.$$

For random variables on finite probability spaces the c.d.f. F_ξ on $\mathbb{R}^1$ can be written as

$$F_\xi(x) = \sum_{y_l < x} \pi_l = \sum_l \pi_l\left[1 - \theta(y_l - x)\right],$$

where $\theta(x)$ is the Heaviside function, $\theta(x) = 1$ when $x \geq 0$, $\theta(x) = 0$ when $x < 0$. It is clear that $F_\xi(x)$ is a piecewise constant function which is continuous from the left, it has jumps of magnitude π_l at $x = y_l$. The corresponding p.d.f. has the form

$$f_\xi(x) = \sum_l \pi_l \delta(x - y_l),$$

where $\delta(x)$ is the Dirac delta function.

We can use the distribution function in order to define some key numerical characteristics of a scalar random variable such as its moments $\mathbb{M}_k$,

$$\mathbb{M}_k\{\xi\} = \int_\Omega \xi^k(\omega) P(d\omega) = \int_{-\infty}^\infty x^k dF_\xi(x) = \int_{-\infty}^\infty x^k f_\xi(x) \, dx,$$

where the second and third integrals are understood in the Stieltjes and Lebesgue sense, respectively. (For practical purposes they can be replaced by the Riemann integral.) Central moments $\overline{\mathbb{M}}_k$ are defined as moments of the shifted random variable $\bar\xi = \xi - \mathbb{M}_1\{\xi\}$.

The most important quantitative characteristics of a given random variable which are known as its expectation $\mathbb{E}\{\xi\}$, variance $\mathbb{V}\{\xi\}$, volatility $\sigma\{\xi\}$, skewness $\gamma_3\{\xi\}$, and kurtosis $\gamma_4\{\xi\}$, are defined as follows:

$$
\begin{aligned}
\mathbb{E}\{\xi\} &= \mathbb{M}_1\{\xi\}, \quad \mathbb{V}\{\xi\} = \overline{\mathbb{M}}_2\{\xi\}, \quad \sigma\{\xi\} = (\mathbb{V}\{\xi\})^{1/2}, \\
\gamma_3\{\xi\} &= \overline{\mathbb{M}}_3\{\xi\} / (\sigma\{\xi\})^3, \quad \gamma_4\{\xi\} = \overline{\mathbb{M}}_4\{\xi\} / (\sigma\{\xi\})^4 - 3.
\end{aligned}
$$

We can interpret $\mathbb{E}\{\xi\}$ as the average value of ξ observed in a sequence of independent identical experiments, and $\sigma\{\xi\}$ as a measure of deviation of ξ from $\mathbb{E}\{\xi\}$. In particular, if $\sigma\{\xi\} = 0$, then ξ is constant. Skewness and kurtosis characterize the degree of deviation of the distribution of ξ from the ubiquitous Gaussian distribution for which (as we will see shortly) they are equal to zero.

We define a random variable η which is a function of a random variable ξ, $\eta = h(\xi)$, in a natural way:

$$\eta(\omega) = h(\xi(\omega)).$$

Assuming for simplicity that h is differentiable and monotonously increasing, we can represent the c.d.f. F_η and p.d.f. f_η as

$$F_\eta(x) = F_\xi\left(h^{-1}(x)\right),$$

$$f_\eta(x) = \frac{f_\xi\left(h^{-1}(x)\right)}{h'\left(h^{-1}(x)\right)}.$$

More generally, if h is not monotonous, we have

$$f_\eta(x) = \sum_{i=1}^{I} \frac{f_\xi\left(h_i^{-1}(x)\right)}{\left|h'\left(h_i^{-1}(x)\right)\right|},$$

where $h_i^{-1}(x)$ are the preimages of x. The corresponding $F_\eta(x)$ is defined by integration.

These formulas show how to construct a random variable ξ with given F_ξ, f_ξ in terms of a random variable η which is uniformly distributed on the interval $[0,1]$:

$$\xi = F_\xi^{-1}(\eta).$$

The distribution functions for η have the form

$$F_\eta(x) = x\theta(x)\theta(1-x) + \theta(x-1),$$

$$f_\eta(x) = \theta(x)\theta(1-x).$$

When h is a convex function of its argument, $h'' \geq 0$, it is easy to prove the so-called Jensen inequality:

$$\mathbb{E}\{h(\xi)\} \geq h(\mathbb{E}\{\xi\}).$$

Indeed, $h(x)$ can be expanded in a Taylor series of the form

$$h(x) = h(\mathbb{E}\{\xi\}) + h'(\mathbb{E}\{\xi\})(x - \mathbb{E}\{\xi\}) + \frac{1}{2}h''(\theta_x)(x - \mathbb{E}\{\xi\})^2,$$

where θ_x is an appropriate intermediate point depending on x, and $h''(\theta_x) \geq 0$ due to convexity. Accordingly,

$$\mathbb{E}\{h(\xi)\} = h(\mathbb{E}\{\xi\}) + \frac{1}{2}\int h''(\theta_x)(x - \mathbb{E}\{\xi\})^2 dF_\xi(x) \geq h(\mathbb{E}\{\xi\}).$$

We now discuss the linearization procedure. Let

$$Y = G(X),$$

where X, Y are random variables. Then we can approximate Y as follows

$$
\begin{aligned}
Y &= G\left(\mathbb{E}\{X\} + X - \mathbb{E}\{X\}\right) \\
&= G_0 + G_1\left(X - \mathbb{E}\{X\}\right) + \frac{1}{2}G_2\left(X - \mathbb{E}\{X\}\right)^2 + ...,
\end{aligned}
$$

where

$$
G_0 = G\left(\mathbb{E}\{X\}\right), G_1 = G_X\left(\mathbb{E}\{X\}\right), G_2 = G_{XX}\left(\mathbb{E}\{X\}\right),
$$

and dots stand for higher-order terms. Simple approximate formulas can be obtained for $\mathbb{E}\{Y\}$, $\mathbb{V}\{Y\}$, when the linear approximation is used:

$$
\mathbb{E}\{Y\} = G_0,
$$

$$
\mathbb{V}\{Y\} = G_1^2 \mathbb{V}\{X\}.
$$

More accurate formulas based on the quadratic approximation have the form

$$
\mathbb{E}\{Y\} = G_0 + \frac{1}{2}G_2\mathbb{V}\{X\}, \tag{2.2}
$$

$$
\mathbb{V}\{Y\} = G_1^2\mathbb{V}\{X\} + \frac{1}{4}G_2\left(\overline{\mathbb{M}}_4\{X\} - \left(\mathbb{V}\{X\}\right)^2\right) + G_1 G_2 \overline{\mathbb{M}}_3\{X\}. \tag{2.3}
$$

Formulas (2.2), (2.3) are rather useful in many situations occurring in practice. In the financial engineering literature they are loosely called convexity formulas.

Example 2.5. *Consider the random variable ξ on the space Ω of the form*

$$
\xi\left(\omega_k\right) = |k - 3|.
$$

This variable assumes four distinct values $0, 1, 2, 3$ with probabilities $1/6$, $1/3$, $1/3$, $1/6$, respectively. Its cumulative probability distribution is

$$
F_\xi\left(x\right) = 1 - \frac{1}{6}\theta\left(-x\right) - \frac{1}{3}\theta\left(1 - x\right) - \frac{1}{3}\theta\left(2 - x\right) - \frac{1}{6}\theta\left(3 - x\right).
$$

Accordingly,

$$
\mathbb{E}\{\xi\} = \frac{3}{2}, \quad \sigma\{\xi\} = \sqrt{\frac{11}{12}}, \quad \gamma_3\{\xi\} = 0, \quad \gamma_4\{\xi\} = -\frac{114}{121}.
$$

The variable ξ is bimodal. Its modes are $1, 2$.

Example 2.6. *The standard normal (or Gaussian) variable ξ takes values on the entire real line. It has the c.d.f. $F_\xi(x)$ and p.d.f. $f_\xi(x)$ of the form*

$$F_\xi(x) = \int_{-\infty}^{x} \frac{e^{-(x')^2/2}}{\sqrt{2\pi}} dx' \equiv \mathfrak{N}(x),$$

$$f_\xi(x) = \frac{e^{-x^2/2}}{\sqrt{2\pi}} \equiv \mathfrak{n}(x).$$

Straightforward calculation yields

$$M_k\{\xi\} = \int_{-\infty}^{\infty} x^k \frac{e^{-x^2/2}}{\sqrt{2\pi}} dx = \begin{cases} 0, & k \text{ is odd} \\ 1 \cdot 3 \ldots \cdot (k-1), & k \text{ is even} \end{cases}$$

Accordingly,

$$\mathbb{E}\{\xi\} = 0, \quad \sigma\{\xi\} = 1, \quad \gamma_3\{\xi\} = 0, \quad \gamma_4\{\xi\} = 0.$$

When ξ is the standard normal variable we use the notation $\mathfrak{N}(x)$, $\mathfrak{n}(x)$ for $F_\xi(x), f_\xi(x)$, and write $\xi \sim \mathfrak{N}(0,1)$. If $\xi \sim \mathfrak{N}(0,1)$, then $\xi' = \sigma\xi + \mu$ is a normal variable. It takes values on the entire real line and has the p.d.f. of the form

$$f_{\xi'}(x) = \frac{1}{\sigma} \mathfrak{n}\left(\frac{x-\mu}{\sigma}\right).$$

Below we use the notation $\xi' \sim \mathfrak{N}(\mu, \sigma^2)$ for the corresponding ξ'. It is easy to check that $\mathbb{E}\{\xi'\} = \mu$, $\mathbb{V}\{\xi'\} = \sigma^2$, etc. If $\xi \sim \mathfrak{N}(\mu, \sigma^2)$, then $\eta = \exp(\xi)$ is called a lognormal variable. It takes values on the positive semi-axis. The corresponding f_η is

$$f_\eta(x) = \frac{1}{\sigma x} \mathfrak{n}\left(\frac{\ln x - \mu}{\sigma}\right).$$

A simple calculation yields

$$
\begin{aligned}
\mathbb{M}_k \{\eta\} &= \int_0^\infty x^k \frac{e^{-(\ln x - \mu)^2/2\sigma^2}}{\sqrt{2\pi\sigma^2}} \frac{dx}{x} \\
&= \int_{-\infty}^\infty \frac{e^{-(y-\mu)^2/2\sigma^2 + ky}}{\sqrt{2\pi\sigma^2}} dy \\
&= e^{\mu k + k^2 \sigma^2/2} \int_{-\infty}^\infty \frac{e^{-((y-\mu)/\sigma - k\sigma)^2/2}}{\sqrt{2\pi\sigma^2}} dy \\
&= e^{\mu k + k^2 \sigma^2/2}.
\end{aligned}
$$

We leave it to the reader an exercise to show that

$$
\begin{aligned}
\mathbb{E}\{\eta\} &= e^{\mu+\sigma^2/2}, \quad \sigma\{\eta\} = e^{\mu+\sigma^2/2}\sqrt{e^{\sigma^2}-1}, \\
\gamma_3\{\eta\} &= \left(e^{\sigma^2}+2\right)\sqrt{e^{\sigma^2}-1}, \quad \gamma_4\{\eta\} = e^{4\sigma^2} + 2e^{3\sigma^2} + 3e^{2\sigma^2} - 6.
\end{aligned}
$$

The p.d.f.'s $f_\xi(x)$ and $f_\eta(x)$ for $\xi = N(0,1)$ and $\eta = \exp(\xi)$ are shown in Figure 2.1.

Example 2.7. *The Poisson distribution is a discrete distribution of the form*

$$
P(\xi = k) = \begin{cases} 0, & k < 0 \\ e^{-\theta}\theta^k/k!, & k \geq 0 \end{cases},
$$

where $\theta > 0$ is a free parameter and k is an integer. A simple calculation shows that

$$
\begin{aligned}
\mathbb{E}\{\xi\} &= \theta, \quad \sigma\{\xi\} = \sqrt{\theta}, \\
\gamma_3\{\xi\} &= 1/\sqrt{\theta}, \quad \gamma_4\{\xi\} = 1/\theta.
\end{aligned}
$$

Consider now a vector random variable $\boldsymbol{\xi} = \left(\xi^1, ..., \xi^N\right)$. For such a variable we can define the (joint) c.d.f. $F_{\boldsymbol{\xi}}(\mathbf{x})$ according to

$$
F_{\boldsymbol{\xi}}(\mathbf{x}) = P\left\{\omega : \xi^1(\omega) < x^1, ..., \xi^N(\omega) < x^N\right\}.
$$

We can use the joint c.d.f. function in order to define marginal c.d.f.'s

$$
F_{\xi^n}(x^n) = F_{\boldsymbol{\xi}}(\infty, ..., x^n, ..., \infty),
$$

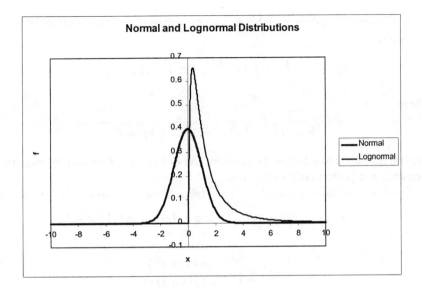

Figure 2.1: P.d.f.'s for the standard normal variable $\xi \sim \mathfrak{N}(0, 1.0)$ and the lognormal variable $\eta = \exp(\xi)$.

which can be considered as c.d.f.'s for the nth component ξ^n. The p.d.f. is defined as follows

$$F_\xi(\mathbf{x}) = \int_{-\infty}^{x^1} ... \int_{-\infty}^{x^N} f_\xi(\mathbf{x}') \, d\mathbf{x}'.$$

For a vector random variable on a finite probability space we have

$$F_\xi(\mathbf{x}) = \sum_{y_{l_1}^1 < x^1, ..., y_{l_N}^N < x^N} \pi_{l_1, ..., l_N},$$

$$f_\xi(\mathbf{x}) = \sum_{y_{l_1}^1 < x^1, ..., y_{l_N}^N < x^N} \pi_{l_1, ..., l_N} \delta\left(x^1 - y_{l_1}^1\right) ... \delta\left(x^N - y_{l_1}^N\right),$$

where

$$\pi_{l_1, ..., l_N} = P\left(\xi^1 = y_{l_1}^1, ..., \xi^N = y_{l_N}^N\right).$$

For a vector random variable $\boldsymbol{\xi}$, we can define mixed moments of order K as follows

$$\mathbb{M}_{\mathbf{k}}\{\boldsymbol{\xi}\} = \int \cdots \int \left(x^1\right)^{k_1} \ldots \left(x^N\right)^{k_N} dF_{\xi^1,\ldots,\xi^N}(\mathbf{x}),$$

where

$$\mathbf{k} = (k_1,\ldots,k_N), \quad k_1 + \ldots + k_L = K.$$

Central moments are defined by analogy. As before, the first and second order moments are particularly important.

For two random variables ξ^1, ξ^2, we define their covariance and correlation

$$\mathrm{cov}\left\{\xi^1,\xi^2\right\} = \overline{\mathbb{M}}_{1,1}\left\{\xi^1,\xi^2\right\} = \mathbb{E}\left\{\xi^1\xi^2\right\} - \mathbb{E}\left\{\xi^1\right\}\mathbb{E}\left\{\xi^2\right\},$$

$$\rho\left\{\xi^1,\xi^2\right\} = \frac{\mathrm{cov}\left\{\xi^1,\xi^2\right\}}{\sigma\left\{\xi^1\right\}\sigma\left\{\xi^2\right\}}.$$

It is clear that $-1 \le \rho \le 1$. When $\rho = \pm 1$, we have

$$\xi^2 - \mathbb{E}\left\{\xi^2\right\} = \beta\left(\xi^1,\xi^2\right)\left(\xi^1 - \mathbb{E}\left\{\xi^1\right\}\right),$$

where

$$\beta\left(\xi^1,\xi^2\right) = \pm\sigma\left\{\xi^2\right\}/\sigma\left\{\xi^1\right\},$$

so that ξ^1 and ξ^2 are linearly dependent. Broadly speaking, the correlation ρ is one of the measures of the degree of linear dependence between ξ^1 and ξ^2. When $\rho = 0$, ξ^1, ξ^2 are called uncorrelated.

Example 2.8. *The most important example of the vector random variable is the standard N-component normal variable $\xi = \left(\xi^1,\ldots,\xi^N\right)$, where ξ^n are independent normal variables. We denote this variable by $\xi \sim \mathfrak{N}(\mathbf{0},\mathcal{I})$, where I is the $N \times N$ identity matrix. The corresponding p.d.f. is*

$$f_\xi(\mathbf{x}) = \frac{e^{-|\mathbf{x}|^2/2}}{\sqrt{(2\pi)^N}}.$$

More generally, the N-component normal variable is $\xi = \left(\xi^1,\ldots,\xi^N\right)$, where ξ^n are correlated normal variables. We denote this variable by $\xi \sim \mathfrak{N}(\boldsymbol{\mu},C)$, *where* $\mu = (\mu^n)$ *is the N-component vector of expectations, while* $C = (C^{mn})$ *is the* $N \times N$ *matrix of covariations. The corresponding p.d.f. is*

$$f_\xi(\mathbf{x}) = \frac{\exp\left(-C^{-1}(\mathbf{x} - \mu) \cdot (\mathbf{x} - \mu)/2\right)}{\sqrt{(2\pi)^N \det C}}.$$

A simple calculation yields

$$\mathbb{E}\{\xi^n\} = \mu^n, \quad \operatorname{cov}\{\xi^m, \xi^n\} = C^{mn}.$$

By using the joint p.d.f. f_{ξ^1, ξ^2} for two random variables ξ^1, ξ^2, we can find the p.d.f. for the scalar function $h(\xi^1, \xi^2)$, such as their sum, difference, product, ratio, etc. For instance, $f_{\xi^1 + \xi^2}$ is

$$f_{\xi^1 + \xi^2}(x) = \int_{-\infty}^{\infty} f_{\xi^1, \xi^2}(x - y, y)\, dy.$$

Sums and other scalar functions of several random variables can be defined in a similar way. If the corresponding densities do not exist, the situation becomes more involved.

Consider a certain event $\mathfrak{a}$ with $P(\mathfrak{a}) > 0$ and a random variable ξ. We can define the conditional c.d.f.

$$F_\xi(x|\mathfrak{a}) = \frac{P(\{\xi < x\} \bigcap \mathfrak{a})}{P(\mathfrak{a})},$$

and the corresponding conditional p.d.f.

$$f_\xi(x|\mathfrak{a}) = \frac{dF_\xi(x|\mathfrak{a})}{dx},$$

if the derivative exists. The random variable ξ is independent of $\mathfrak{a}$ provided that

$$F_\xi(x|\mathfrak{a}) = F_\xi(x).$$

For instance, if $\boldsymbol{\xi} = (\xi^1, \xi^2)$ is a vector random variable with the p.d.f. $f_\xi(x^1, x^2)$, then the p.d.f. for ξ^1 conditioned on $\xi^2 = x^2$ can be written as

$$f_{\xi^1}(x^1 | \xi^2 = x^2) = \frac{f_\xi(x^1, x^2)}{f_{\xi^2}(x^2)}.$$

The conditional c.d.f. $F_\xi(x|\mathfrak{a})$ is used in order to define conditional moments of ξ, and, in particular, its conditional expectation,

$$\mathbb{E}\{\xi|\mathfrak{a}\} = \int_{-\infty}^{\infty} x dF_\xi(x|\mathfrak{a}) = \frac{1}{P(\mathfrak{a})} \int_\mathfrak{a} \xi(\omega) P(d\omega).$$

For expectations, the analogue of the total probability formula, which is called the total expectation formula, has the form

$$\mathbb{E}\{\xi\} = \sum_i \mathbb{E}\{\xi|\mathfrak{c}_i\} P(\mathfrak{c}_i).$$

Here events $\mathfrak{c}_1, ..., \mathfrak{c}_I$ form a complete set and $P(\mathfrak{c}_i) > 0$.

For a given random variable ξ and a partition $\mathfrak{c}_1, ..., \mathfrak{c}_I$ we can define a new random variable $\mathbb{E}\{\xi|\mathfrak{U}_\mathfrak{c}\}$ which is called the conditional expectation of ξ with respect to the algebra $\mathfrak{U}_\mathfrak{c}$ generated by the corresponding partition as follows

$$\mathbb{E}\{\xi|\mathfrak{U}_\mathfrak{c}\}(\omega) = \mathbb{E}\{\xi|\mathfrak{c}_i\} \quad \text{when} \quad \omega \in \mathfrak{c}_i.$$

We emphasize that in this way we obtain a nontrivial random variable, which, by definition, is constant on every set $\mathfrak{c}_i$, besides, for every set $\mathfrak{C} \subset \mathfrak{U}_\mathfrak{c}$ we have

$$\int_\mathfrak{C} \xi(\omega) P(d\omega) = \int_\mathfrak{C} \mathbb{E}\{\xi|\mathfrak{U}_\mathfrak{c}\}(\omega) P(d\omega).$$

In particular, the total conditional expectation formula can be written as

$$\mathbb{E}\{\xi\} = \mathbb{E}\{\mathbb{E}\{\xi|\mathfrak{U}_\mathfrak{c}\}\}.$$

Example 2.9. *For the random variable ξ and partition $\mathfrak{c}_1, \mathfrak{c}_2, \mathfrak{c}_3$, we have*

$$\mathbb{E}\{\xi|\mathfrak{U}_\mathfrak{c}\}(\omega_k) = \begin{cases} 3/2, & k = 1, 2 \\ 1/2, & k = 3, 4 \\ 5/2, & k = 5, 6 \end{cases},$$

$$\mathbb{E}\{\mathbb{E}\{\xi|\mathfrak{U}_\mathfrak{c}\}\} = \frac{3}{2} \cdot \frac{1}{3} + \frac{1}{2} \cdot \frac{1}{3} + \frac{5}{2} \cdot \frac{1}{3} = \frac{3}{2} = \mathbb{E}\{\xi\}.$$

For a given event $\mathfrak{a}$ we can define a random variable $\chi_\mathfrak{a}(\omega)$, where $\chi_\mathfrak{a}$ is the corresponding characteristic function. Its conditional expectation with respect to the algebra generated by a partition $\mathfrak{c}_1, ..., \mathfrak{c}_I$, which we denote by $\mathbb{E}(\chi_\mathfrak{a}|\mathfrak{U}_\mathfrak{c})$, is called conditional probability of $\mathfrak{a}$ with respect to $\mathfrak{c}_1, ..., \mathfrak{c}_I$. By using this random variable, we can rewrite the total probability formula as follows

$$P(\mathfrak{a}) = \mathbb{E} \left\{ \mathbb{E} \left\{ \chi_\mathfrak{a} | \mathfrak{U}_\mathfrak{c} \right\} \right\}.$$

We say that the event $\mathfrak{a}$ is independent of the partition $\mathfrak{c}_1, ..., \mathfrak{c}_I$ if the corresponding random variable $\mathbb{E} \left\{ \chi_\mathfrak{a} | \mathfrak{U}_\mathfrak{c} \right\}$ is constant,

$$\mathbb{E} \left\{ \chi_\mathfrak{a} | \mathfrak{U}_\mathfrak{c} \right\} = P(\mathfrak{a}).$$

Two random variables ξ^1, ξ^2 are independent if the corresponding algebras $\mathfrak{U}_{\xi^1}, \mathfrak{U}_{\xi^2}$ are independent. The joint distribution function for independent random variables can be factorized as follows

$$F_{\xi^1, \xi^2} \left(x^1, x^2 \right) = F_{\xi^1} \left(x^1 \right) F_{\xi^2} \left(x^2 \right).$$

It is obvious that independent random variables are uncorrelated but the opposite is not necessarily true.

In general, random variables $\xi^1, ..., \xi^N$ are mutually independent if

$$F_{\xi^1, ..., \xi^N} \left(x^1, ..., x^N \right) = F_{\xi^1} \left(x^1 \right) ... F_{\xi^N} \left(x^N \right).$$

For studying sums of independent random variables and many other purposes, it is very convenient to use the so-called characteristic functions (the Fourier transforms) of random variables. The characteristic function $\Phi_\xi(\varsigma)$ of a scalar random variables ξ has the form

$$\Phi_\xi(\varsigma) = \int_{-\infty}^{\infty} e^{i\varsigma x} dF_\xi(x).$$

For vector random variables the definition is analogous.

Example 2.10. *It is easy to find the characteristic function for the normal distribution by completing the squares:*

$$\Phi(\varsigma) = \int \frac{e^{i\varsigma x - x^2/2}}{\sqrt{2\pi}} dx = e^{-\varsigma^2/2}. \tag{2.4}$$

The moments $\mathbb{M}_k(\xi)$ of a random variable ξ can be expressed in terms of the derivatives of its characteristic function as follows

$$\mathbb{M}_k(\xi) = (-i)^k \Phi_\xi^{(k)}(0).$$

The following properties of characteristic functions are particularly important for us:

(A) If random variables ξ^1, ξ^2 are perfectly correlated so that $\xi^2 = a\xi^1 + b$, then

$$\Phi_{\xi^2}(\varsigma) = e^{ib\varsigma} \Phi_{\xi^1}(a\varsigma).$$

(B) If random variables ξ^1, ξ^2 are independent, then

$$\Phi_{\xi^1 + \xi^2}(\varsigma) = \Phi_{\xi^1}(\varsigma) \Phi_{\xi^2}(\varsigma).$$

(C) In general, if random variables $\xi^1, ..., \xi_M$ are independent, then

$$\Phi_{\xi^1 + ... + \xi^M}(\varsigma) = \Phi_{\xi^1}(\varsigma) ... \Phi_{\xi^M}(\varsigma).$$

2.4   Convergence of random variables and limit theorems

There are different definitions of convergence of a sequence of random variables ξ_n to a random variable ξ. We say that ξ_n converges to ξ almost certainly and write

$$\xi = \text{ac-lim } \xi_n,$$

if there is a set $\mathfrak{N} \subset \mathfrak{U}$ of measure zero, $P(\mathfrak{N}) = 0$, such that for all $\omega \notin \mathfrak{N}$ we have

$$\xi_n(\omega) \to \xi(\omega).$$

We say that ξ_n converges to ξ stochastically or in probability,

$$\xi = \text{st-lim } \xi_n,$$

if for every $\varepsilon > 0$ we have

$$P\{\omega : |\xi_n(\omega) - \xi(\omega)| > \varepsilon\} \to 0.$$

Finally, we say that ξ_n converges to ξ in distribution,

$$\xi = \text{dist-lim } \xi_n,$$

if for every continuous bounded function $g(x)$ we have

$$\int_{\mathbb{R}^K} g(x)\, dF_{\xi_n}(x) \to \int_{\mathbb{R}^K} g(x)\, dF_{\xi}(x).$$

It is relatively easy to see that almost certain convergence implies stochastic convergence which, in turn, implies convergence in distribution.

When we define Ito's integral and for other purposes we use the concept of mean square convergence. We that ξ_n converges to ξ in mean square,

$$\xi = \text{ms-lim } \xi_n,$$

if

$$\mathbb{E}\left\{ |\xi_n - \xi|^2 \right\} \to 0.$$

We can use the above definitions in order to describe the limiting behavior of sums

$$S_n = \xi_1 + \dots + \xi_n,$$

of independent identically distributed (i.i.d.) scalar random variables $\xi_n \sim \xi$.

Assuming that the expectation of ξ_n is finite, we can prove the so-called strong law of large numbers which states that

$$\text{ac-lim } \frac{S_n}{n} = \mu,$$

where $\mu = \mathbb{E}\{\xi_n\}$.

The manner of convergence of S_n/n to μ is described by law of the iterated logarithm, provided that ξ_n have finite variance $\mathbb{V}\{\xi_n\} = \sigma^2$. This law states that with probability one

$$\left\{ \begin{array}{c} \text{lim-sup} \\ \text{lim-inf} \end{array} \right\} \frac{S_n - n\mu}{\sqrt{2n \ln(\ln n)}} = \left\{ \begin{array}{c} \sigma \\ -\sigma \end{array} \right\}.$$

Thus, asymptotically the deviations of $S_n - n\mu$ from zero grow parabolically.

The central limit theorem provides further information on the behavior of the normalized variables

$$\eta_n = \frac{S_n - n\mu}{\sigma \sqrt{n}}.$$

In its simplest form this theorem states that

$$\text{dist-lim } \eta_n \sim \mathfrak{N}(0,1),$$

where $\mathfrak{N}(0,1)$ is the standard normal variable, or, explicitly,

$$\lim P\{\eta_n < x\} = \mathfrak{N}(x).$$

We emphasize that the appearance of the normal distribution in the above formulas is due to the fact that ξ_n have finite volatility. When this assumption is violated, non-normal distributions become important.

The universality of the normal distribution is easy to understand. It has the same origin as the fact that in a small neighborhood of an extremum all (nondegenerate) functions can be approximated by parabolas. By using properties of characteristic functions we obtain

$$\Phi_{\eta_n}(\varsigma) = \left(\Phi_\xi \left(\frac{\varsigma}{\sqrt{n}\sigma} \right) \exp\left(-\frac{i\mu\varsigma}{\sqrt{n}\sigma} \right) \right)^n.$$

In view of equation (2.4), all we need to do is to show that

$$\Phi_{\eta_n}(\varsigma) \to \exp\left(-\frac{\varsigma^2}{2} \right) \quad \text{when} \quad n \to \infty.$$

To this end we expand the product $\Phi_\xi(\varsigma/\sqrt{n}\sigma) \exp(-i\mu\varsigma/\sqrt{n}\sigma)$ in a Taylor series at zero and retain the first three terms:

$$\Phi_\xi \left(\frac{\varsigma}{\sqrt{n}\sigma} \right) \exp\left(-\frac{i\mu\varsigma}{\sqrt{n}\sigma} \right) = \left(1 + \frac{i\mu\varsigma}{\sqrt{n}\sigma} - \frac{(\mu^2+\sigma^2)\varsigma^2}{2n\sigma^2} + \dots \right)$$

$$\times \left(1 - \frac{i\mu\varsigma}{\sqrt{n}\sigma} - \frac{\mu^2\varsigma^2}{2n\sigma^2} + \dots \right)$$

$$= 1 - \frac{\varsigma^2}{2n} + \dots.$$

Accordingly,

$$\Phi_{\eta_n}(\varsigma) = \left(1 - \frac{\varsigma^2}{2n} + \dots \right)^n \to \exp\left(-\frac{\varsigma^2}{2} \right) \quad \text{when} \quad n \to \infty.$$

It is useful to analyze the asymptotic behavior of η_n for sufficiently large (but finite) n in more detail. Let us assume that higher-order moments $\mathbb{M}_k\{\xi\}$,

$k = 3, 4, ...$, exist and the function $|\Phi_\xi(\varsigma)|^\nu$, for some $\nu \geq 1$, is integrable. Then f_{η_n} exists for $n \geq \nu$ and for $n \to \infty$

$$f_{\eta_n}(x) = \left(1 + n \sum_{k=3}^{K} \frac{P_k(x)}{n^{k/2}}\right) \mathfrak{n}(x) + o\left(\frac{1}{n^{K/2-1}}\right), \qquad (2.5)$$

uniformly in x. Here $P_k(x)$ are polynomials of degree k which depend only on $\mathbb{M}_1\{\xi\}, ..., \mathbb{M}_k\{\xi\}$. Occasionally, expansion (2.5) is called the Edgeworth expansion for f_{η_n}.

The first two polynomials P_3, P_4 have the form

$$P_3(x) = \frac{\gamma_3}{6} H_3(x), \qquad P_4(x) = \frac{\gamma_3^2}{72} H_3(x) + \frac{\gamma_4}{24} H_4(x),$$

where $H_k(x)$ are the Hermite polynomials. Recall that these polynomials are defined as follows

$$H_k(x) = (-1)^k \frac{d^k \mathfrak{n}(x)/dx^k}{\mathfrak{n}(x)}.$$

The first five polynomials have the form

$$H_0(x) = 1, \quad H_1(x) = x, \quad H_2(x) = x^2 - 1,$$
$$H_3(x) = x^3 - 3x, \quad H_4(x) = x^4 - 6x^2 + 3.$$

These polynomials have many interesting properties. Here we just mention one useful property: the Fourier transform of the product

$$f(x) = H_k(x)\mathfrak{n}(x) = (-1)^k d^k \mathfrak{n}(x)/dx^k, \qquad (2.6)$$

has the form

$$\begin{aligned} f(x) \to \Phi(\varsigma) &= \int_{-\infty}^{\infty} e^{i\varsigma x} H_k(x)\mathfrak{n}(x)\, dx \\ &= \int_{-\infty}^{\infty} e^{i\varsigma x} d^k \mathfrak{n}(x)/dx^k\, dx \\ &= (i\varsigma)^k e^{-\varsigma^2/2}. \end{aligned}$$

Thus, in the ς-space product (2.6) has a simpler form than in the x-space. We can rewrite relation (2.5) as follows

$$f_{\eta_n}(x) = \left(1 - \left(\frac{\gamma_3}{6n^{1/2}} + \frac{\gamma_3^2}{72n}\right)\frac{d^3}{dx^3} + \frac{\gamma_4}{24n}\frac{d^4}{dx^4} + ...\right)\mathfrak{n}(x).$$

When expectations of ξ are finite, but their variances are not, the limiting distribution of their normalized sums has complicated properties. For example, if ξ_n is a sequence of i.i.d. random variables with symmetric slowly decaying p.d.f.'s such that

$$f_\xi(x) = f_\xi(-x), \qquad f_\xi(x) \sim \frac{c}{|x|^{1+\alpha}},$$

where $0 < \alpha < 2$, then the distributions of the normalized variables $\eta_n = S_n/n^\alpha$ converge to a distribution with characteristic function

$$\Phi(\varsigma) = \exp\left(-d|\varsigma|^\alpha\right).$$

2.5   References and further reading

The material covered in this chapter is standard. It is discussed by many authors. We can refer the interested reader to the following excellent books: Feller (1968), Korolyk *et al.* (1985), Stirzaker(1994), Sveshnikov (1978).

Chapter 3

Discrete-time stochastic engines

3.1 Introduction

By using the results discussed in the previous chapter as a starting point, we can describe the properties of the "stochastic engines" needed in order to construct discrete-time models of forex in single- and multi-period markets. These engines which are called binomial and multinomial Bernoulli processes are well-known in probability theory and have been tested in a variety of situations occurring in physics, biology, operational research, game theory, etc.

A single-period binomial Bernoulli process can be thought of as a single coin tossing deciding the outcome of an experiment. A multi-period process is simply a sequence of several independent tossings which is considered as a single experiment. In the multinomial version the number of possible outcomes of an individual trial is greater than two (for instance, one can think of a roulette spinning).

One can argue that the interpretation of Bernoulli processes in gambling terms, although colorful, is somewhat restrictive. For our purposes it is more convenient to think of these processes as one-dimensional and multi-dimensional random walks. This is a tribute to the long tradition established in the physics literature. In financial framework, Bernoulli processes describe sequences on returns on investments in risky financial instruments, for example, in foreign bonds.

Beyond any doubt, the multi-period binomial Bernoulli process is the most important and versatile construction of probability theory with the multinomial process coming a close second. In particular, we can obtain the Wiener and Poisson processes (which play the role of "stochastic engines" for the continuous time market models) as limiting cases of the binomial Bernoulli process with the number of trials going to infinity and the probability of success in an individual trial either kept fixed (Wiener processes) or being reduced to zero in such a way that the expected number of successes is kept fixed (Poisson processes).

In this chapter we deal with the most general properties of Bernoulli processes, their further properties are studied in the financial context in the subsequent chapters as required.

The chapter is organized as follows. In Section 2 we define time series and discuss their properties. In Section 3 we study binomial stochastic engines (Bernoulli processes) in single- and multi-period settings. In Section 4 we briefly discuss multinomial stochastic processes. Relevant references are given in Section 5.

3.2   Time series

We define a scalar time series in a finite probability space as a family of scalar random variables $\xi(t)$ or ξ_t depending on a discrete time parameter $t \in I = \{0, 1, ...\}$. By fixing a particular elementary event ω we obtain a sample path or trajectory $\xi(t; \omega)$ or $\xi_t(\omega)$ which is a function from I to $\mathbb{R}$, or, in other words, a scalar function of a discrete scalar argument. A vector time series is a family of N-component random variables $\boldsymbol{\xi}_t$ depending on $t \in I$. For given ω the series $\boldsymbol{\xi}_t(\omega)$ is a function from I to $\mathbb{R}$, or, in other words, a vector function of a discrete scalar argument. We assume that trajectories describe a sequence of positions of a material particle and think about time series in terms of random walks. Without loss of generality we identify elementary outcomes ω with individual trajectories, so that the set Ω consists of all possible trajectories of our particle.

We describe the flow of information associated with a time series available at time t by introducing filtrations in the space Ω. We identify all the trajectories which coincide up to (and including) time t. Subsets of equivalent trajectories form a partition $\mathfrak{G}_t$ of the space of elementary events Ω; elements of this partition are denoted by $\mathfrak{g}_{t,i}$. Next, we construct the algebra $\mathfrak{F}_t$ with elements $\mathfrak{f}_{t,i}$ by using the partition $\mathfrak{G}_t$ as a foundation. Elements of this algebra are unions or complements of unions of $\mathfrak{g}_{t,i}$. Algebras $\mathfrak{F}_t$ are ordered as follows

$$\mathfrak{F}_t \subset \mathfrak{F}_{t'}, \quad t < t',$$

they form a filtration on the space Ω. It is clear that $\mathfrak{F}_0$ contains just two sets, namely the set Ω and $\emptyset$ since trajectories are indistinguishable at time 0. The algebra $\mathfrak{F}_T$ consists of all the subsets of the space of Ω, including all individual elementary events ω_l since at time T all trajectories are different; if the total number of individual trajectories is L, then the total number of different elements in $\mathfrak{F}_T$ is 2^L.

By using the concept of filtration we can define stopping times as scalar random variables ς with $T+2$ values $\{0, ..., T, \infty\}$ such that for every $t, 0 \leq t \leq T$ the set of elementary events satisfying the condition $\varsigma(\omega) = t$ is an element of the algebra $\mathfrak{F}_t$. This definition suggests that we can decide whether or not $\varsigma(\omega) = t$ for a given trajectory ω by observing its behavior up to and including time t.

Example 3.1. *In the space of random walk trajectories $y_t(\omega)$ the function $\varsigma(\omega) = \min\{t, y_t(\omega) \geq \lambda\}$ is a stopping time (for a given ω its value is infinite if all $y_t(\omega)$ are less than λ), while the function $\varsigma(\omega) = \max\{t, y_t(\omega) \geq \lambda\}$ is obviously not.*

We can use the filtration $\mathfrak{F}_t$ in order to define important special classes of time series. We choose a certain time $0 < t < T$ and observe the values of the time series until time t. Accordingly, we know the partition $\mathfrak{G}_t$ of Ω which we can extend to the algebra $\mathfrak{F}_t$. For every time $t' > t$ we can define the random variable $\mathbb{E}\{\xi_{t'}|\mathfrak{F}_t\}$ which is the expectation of $\xi_{t'}$ conditional on the information available at time t. As we know, this random variable is automatically compatible with the partition $\mathfrak{G}_t$ in a sense that it is constant on its elements. We say that a random time series is a martingale if for all t, t', $t \leq t'$ the following conditions are satisfied

$$\mathbb{E}\{|\xi_t|\} < \infty,$$

$$\mathbb{E}\{\xi_{t'}|\mathfrak{F}_t\} = \xi_t.$$

It is called a supermartingale and a submartingale if the equality $=$ is replaced by the inequalities $\leq$ and $\geq$ respectively. We will see later that random processes possessing the martingale property play an outstanding role in financial engineering. The martingale property expresses in mathematical terms the idea of a fair game. If ξ_t represents some financial variable, such as the wealth of a representative investor, then its discounted expected value in the future should be equal to its present value.

We can also define time series possessing the so-called Markov property which we call Markov time series. For the Markov series we have

$$P\left\{\xi_{t'} \in B' | \mathfrak{F}_t\right\} = P\left\{\xi_{t'} \in B' | \xi_t = x\right\},$$

where B' is a suitable subset in $\mathbb{R}^N$, and $t \leq t'$. Thus, the probability of $\xi_{t'}$ belonging to B' depends solely on the value of ξ_t, rather than on the entire trajectory $\{\xi_0, \xi_1, ..., \xi_t\}$. It is clear that the future behavior of a Markov time series is independent on its past behavior provided that its present state is known, or, in other words, such a series "tends to forget" about its own history. To put it differently, the entire relevant history of a Markovian time series is collapsed into its current state.

Scalar (vector) Markov chains are Markov time series such that for all t possible values of ξ_t belong to the same discrete subset $Z \subset \mathbb{R}$ $(Z \subset \mathbb{R}^N)$ which we call the phase space. For Markov chains we can define transition probabilities (t.p.) as follows

$$P\left(t, x, t', x'\right) = P\left\{\xi_{t'} = x' | \xi_t = x\right\},$$

where $x, y \in Z$. By counting all trajectories starting at t, x and finishing at t'', x'', we can derive the celebrated Chapman-Kolmogoroff equation for Markov chains which can be written as

$$P\left(t, x, t'', x''\right) = \sum_{x' \in Z} P\left(t, x, t', x'\right) P\left(t', x', t'', x''\right),$$

where t' is sandwiched between t and t'', $t \leq t' \leq t''$. A Markov chain is uniform provided that $P\left(t, x, t', x'\right)$ depends only on the time difference $t' - t$ rather that individual times t, t'. In this case we use the notation $P\left(\tau, x, x'\right)$ for the t.p.[1]

3.3   Binomial stochastic engines for single- and multi-period markets

To start with, we consider single-period markets. As a stochastic engine for such markets we can use the single-period Bernoulli process. In the binomial case this process has two possible outcomes $\{0, 1\}$ with probabilities p_k, $p_0 +$

---

[1] Here and below we slightly abuse the notation and use the same symbol to denote two different t.p.'s which depend on four and three arguments, respectively.

$p_1 = 1$. Depending on the circumstances, these outcomes can be interpreted in many different ways.

The classical interpretation of a trial is as a single coin tossing, with outcomes 0 and 1 corresponding to heads and tails, respectively. In general, the coin is not fair, so that the probabilities of heads p_0 and tails p_1 are not equal to each other. For the fair coin $p_0 = p_1 = 1/2$. One can also think of the possible outcomes as changes of the capital of a gambler who bets a dollar on the outcome of the coin tossing and assume that if the outcome is 0 the gambler loses and his wealth decreases by one, when the outcome is 1 he wins and his wealth increases by one. Originally the Bernoulli process was invented in order to describe games of chance (hence the coin tossing terminology), and, in particular, to solve the famous gambler's ruin problem. Later it found numerous applications in physics, mathematics, and, as we will see in a due course, financial engineering. For our purposes it is useful to consider a particle on the line and identify outcomes 0 and 1 of a Bernoulli trial with its unit shifts in the negative and positive directions, respectively. Alternatively, we can think of outcomes as possible returns on an uncertain investment.

The discrete random variable ξ which describes the location of the particle after the trial has two possible values, ± 1, and

$$P(\xi = -1) = p_0, \qquad P(\xi = 1) = 1 - p_0 = p_1.$$

We say that ξ has the binomial distribution with parameters $(1, p_0, p_1)$. The corresponding cumulative distribution function is

$$F_\xi(x) = \begin{cases} 0, & x \leq -1 \\ p_0, & -1 < x \leq 1 \\ 1, & 1 < x \end{cases}.$$

If $p_0 \neq p_1$, the mode of ξ is equal to $\operatorname{sign}(p_1 - p_0)$, otherwise, there are two modes, $x = \pm 1$. The characteristic function of ξ is

$$\Phi(\varsigma) = p_0 e^{-i\varsigma} + p_1 e^{i\varsigma}. \tag{3.1}$$

The moments of ξ are

$$\mathbb{M}\left\{\xi^k\right\} = (-1)^k p_0 + p_1,$$

Its expectation and variance are

$$\mathbb{E}\{\xi\} = p_1 - p_0, \qquad \mathbb{V}\{\xi\} = 4p_0 p_1.$$

In the symmetric case $p_0 = p_1 = 1/2$ and

$$\mathbb{E}\{\xi\} = 0, \quad \mathbb{V}\{\xi\} = 1.$$

For multi-period markets we use the binomial Bernoulli process with T independent trials, or, equivalently, a T-period simple random walk on the line. This process describes a sequence of T independent trials each with two outcomes $\{0, 1\}$. Traditionally, these trials are thought of as tossings of the same coin. In general, the coin is not fair, so that $p_0 \neq p_1$. A typical outcome can be encoded as a word of the form $\omega = \{\kappa_1...\kappa_T\}$, where $\kappa_t = 0, 1$, for example, $\omega = \{10011...1\}$. There are 2^T outcomes in total. We can think of ω as a binary representation of the integer

$$\hat{\omega} = \sum_{t=1}^{T} \kappa_t 2^{t-1}.$$

The interpretation of the process which is most useful for our purposes is in terms of the random walk on the line. Consider a particle which is initially located at the origin and after each trail moves by one unit of length in the positive or negative direction depending to the outcome of the trial. The interval of time between trials is one unit of time. For every sequence $\omega = \{\kappa_1...\kappa_T\}$ we introduce the sequence $\omega' = \{x_1, ..., x_T\}$, where $x_t = 2\kappa_t - 1$, describes the corresponding moves of the particle. We also consider the sequence $\omega'' = \{y_0, y_1, ..., y_T\}$, where $y_0 = 0$, and $y_t = \sum_{t'=1}^{t} x_{t'}$ is the position of our particle after t trials, and draw the broken line passing through the points (t, y_t) which represents the trajectory of the particle in the (t, y) plane. Figuratively speaking, the trajectory of a random walk describes movements of a heavily drunk person. The possible positions of the particle in the (t, y)-plane form a triangular lattice (or tree). Since the trajectory uniquely defines individual movements, we use the same symbol ω for all the three sequences $\{\kappa_1...\kappa_T\}$, $\{x_1, ..., x_T\}$, $\{y_0, y_1, ..., y_T\}$. We denote a particular trajectory by ω_l, and the space of these trajectories by Ω. Here $0 \leq l \leq L - 1$, where $L = 2^T$ is the total number of all possible trajectories. Thus, Ω is our space of elementary events. This space can be represented graphically as a recombining tree, see Figure 3.1.

We endow Ω with the probability measure P as follows

$$P(\omega_l) = p_0^{\chi_0(\omega_l)} p_1^{\chi_1(\omega_l)}, \tag{3.2}$$

where $\chi_0 = \chi_0(\omega_l)$ and $\chi_1 = \chi_1(\omega_l)$ are the total numbers of zeroes and ones for a given trajectory ω_l. This formula makes sense because individual trials

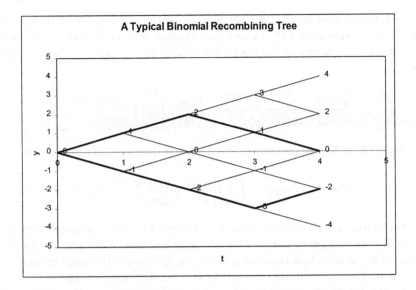

Figure 3.1: A typical four-period binomial recombining tree in the (t, y)-plane. Two representative trajectories are shown in boldface.

governing the movements of our particle are independent. It is clear that

$$\chi_0 + \chi_1 = T, \quad \chi_1 - \chi_0 = y_T,$$

where y_T is the terminal location of the particle. For the so-called symmetric random walks such that $p_0 = p_1 = 1/2$ all trajectories have equal probability, namely,

$$P(\omega_l) = \frac{1}{2^T}.$$

Consider two sequences of Bernoulli trials of length T with probabilities p_0, p_1, and q_0, q_1, respectively. Both sequences have the same space of trajectories Ω. However, the corresponding probability measures are different. For the first sequence $P(\omega)$ is given by formula (3.2), for the second one $Q(\omega)$ is given by

$$Q(\omega_l) = q_0^{\chi_0(\omega_l)} q_1^{\chi_1(\omega_l)}.$$

We emphasize that there is a change of measure on the space of trajectories which transforms P into Q. To find this transformation explicitly, we evaluate the ratio Q/P (which is called the Radon-Nikodym derivative of Q with respect to P):

$$\frac{Q\left(\omega_l\right)}{P\left(\omega_l\right)} = \frac{q_0^{\chi_0(\omega_l)} q_1^{\chi_1(\omega_l)}}{p_0^{\chi_0(\omega_l)} p_1^{\chi_1(\omega_l)}} = \left(\frac{q_0 q_1}{p_0 p_1}\right)^{T/2} \left(\frac{q_1 p_0}{q_0 p_1}\right)^{y_T/2}.$$

Thus, by changing the probability of a given trajectory according to the rule

$$P\left(\omega_l\right) \to Q\left(\omega_l\right) = \left(\frac{q_0 q_1}{p_0 p_1}\right)^{T/2} \left(\frac{q_1 p_0}{q_0 p_1}\right)^{y_T/2} P\left(\omega_l\right),$$

we transform the measure P into the measure Q. We emphasize that this transformation depends only on the terminal location of the particle $y_T\left(\omega_l\right)$, rather than on the whole trajectory. Thus, by appropriately changing measures we can alter the probabilities of positive and negative moves of the particle. In particular, we can always make its random walk symmetric. Below we study the important Cameron-Martin-Girsanov transformation of Wiener processes which is a natural extension of the above construction for the continuous case.

The probability of the event

$$\Omega_{t_0 t_1} = \left\{\omega : \chi_0\left(\omega_l\right) = t_0, \chi_1\left(\omega_l\right) = t_1\right\},$$

where $t_0 + t_1 = T$, can be found via a simple combinatorics. It is given by the binomial distribution with parameters (T, p_0, p_1),

$$P\left(\chi_0\left(\omega_l\right) = t_0, \chi_1\left(\omega_l\right) = t_1\right) = \frac{T!}{t_0! t_1!} p_0^{t_0} p_1^{t_1} = C_{t_0}^T p_0^{t_0} p_1^{t_1}, \qquad (3.3)$$

where

$$C_{t_0}^T = C_{t_1}^T = \frac{T!}{t_0! t_1!},$$

$C_{t_0}^T$ is called the binomial coefficient equal to the number of different choices of t_0 (or, equivalently, t_1) objects out of a set of T objects.

One very important issue which we need to address is the distribution of the random variable y_T. Since

$$y_T\left(\omega\right) = \chi_1\left(\omega\right) - \chi_0\left(\omega\right) = 2\chi_1\left(\omega\right) - T = T - 2\chi_0\left(\omega\right),$$

y_T belongs to the set $\Xi_{[-T,T]} = \{-T, -T+2, ..., T-2, T\}$ which contains $T+1$ elements. We can use formula (3.3) in order to show that

$$P(y_T = v) = C^T_{(T-v)/2} p_0^{(T-v)/2} p_1^{(T+v)/2},$$

$$F_{y_T}(x) = \begin{cases} 0, & x \leq -T \\ \displaystyle\sum_{v \in [-T,t]} C^T_{(T-v)/2} p_0^{(T-v)/2} p_1^{(T+v)/2}, & t < x \leq t+2 \\ 1, & T > x \end{cases}.$$

If $(T+1) p_0$ is not an integer, y_T has a unique mode given by

$$\Lambda = T - 2\left[(T+1) p_0\right] \sim (p_1 - p_0) T,$$

where $[x]$ denotes the integer part of x, otherwise, it has two modes, Λ and $\Lambda + 2$.

Since y_T is the sum of T identical independent variables x_t each with the characteristic function given by equation (3.1), its characteristic function can be written as

$$\Phi_{y_T}(\varsigma) = \left(p_0 e^{-i\varsigma} + p_1 e^{i\varsigma}\right)^T.$$

Once the characteristic function of y_T is determined, its moments can be found according to the general recipe,

$$M\{y_T^k\} = (-i)^k \Phi^{(k)}(0).$$

By using this formula for $k = 1, 2$ we obtain the expectation and variance of y_T

$$\mathbb{E}\{y_T\} = (p_1 - p_0) T, \quad \mathbb{V}\{y_T\} = 4 p_0 p_1 T.$$

Thus, the most probable values of y_T belong to an interval of order $\sqrt{T}$ centered at the point $(p_1 - p_0) T$, i.e., in the vicinity of the mode. In particular, for symmetric walks we have

$$\mathbb{E}\{y_T\} = 0, \mathbb{V}\{y_T\} = T,$$

so that the corresponding values are likely to be located on an interval of order $\sqrt{T}$ centered at zero.

A typical binomial distribution with parameters $T = 20, p_1 = 5/8$, is shown in Figure 3.2. This figure confirms the fact that probabilities of the extreme

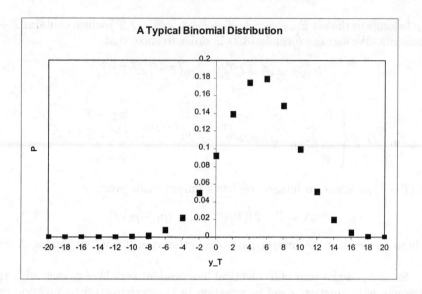

Figure 3.2: A typical binomial distribution for $T = 20$, $p_0 = 3/8$, $p_1 = 5/8$. Its mode is located at $y_T = 6$.

values $y_T = \pm T$ are negligible, while the most likely values of y_T are centered around its mode $y_T \sim (p_1 - p_0)\, T$.

For modest values of T the binomial distribution is relatively simple. However, for large values of T its computation becomes rather involved. Fortunately, in this case we can use general results concerning the behavior of sums of independent random variables to describe the distribution of y_T. The strong law of large numbers yields

$$\text{ac-}\lim_{T \to \infty} \frac{y_T}{T} = p_1 - p_0.$$

The law of the iterated logarithm shows that asymptotically

$$-\sqrt{8 p_0 p_1 T \ln(\ln T)} \le y_T - (p_1 - p_0)\, T \le \sqrt{8 p_0 p_1 T \ln(\ln T)}.$$

Finally, the central limit theorem, which, in the special case of a random walk is known as the integral De Moivre-Laplace theorem allows one to approximate the behavior of the binomial probabilities in the interval

$$I_{AB} = \{v|\, (p_0 - p_1)\, T + A\sqrt{4 p_0 p_1 T} \le v \le (p_1 - p_0)\, T + B\sqrt{4 p_0 p_1 T}\},$$

outside of which they are negligible. Here A, B, are fixed numbers, and $A < B$.

De Moivre-Laplace theorem. *For any A, B we have*

$$\lim_{T \to \infty} \sum_{v \in I_{A,B}} P_v = \int_A^B \frac{e^{-z^2/2}}{\sqrt{2\pi}} dz = \mathfrak{N}(B) - \mathfrak{N}(A).$$

In particular,

$$\lim_{T \to \infty} \sum_{v \in I_{A,\infty}} P_v = \mathfrak{N}(-A), \qquad \lim_{T \to \infty} \sum_{v \in I_{-\infty,B}} P_v = \mathfrak{N}(B).$$

The De Moivre-Laplace theorem can be used in practice provided that $p_0 p_1 > 9/T$, and $p_0, p_1 > 1/(T+1)$. Thus, if probability of success is kept fixed when T becomes large, the distribution of the random variable

$$\eta_T = (y_T - (p_1 - p_0) T) / \sqrt{4 p_0 p_1 T}$$

asymptotically approaches the Gaussian distribution. That is why this distribution naturally appears in most financial models with no jumps.

One more possibility deserves mentioning. Suppose that we consider a series of trials of fixed known length T and assume that the probability of success in each individual trial is of order $1/T$. The Poisson limit theorem shows that the corresponding binomial distribution approaches the Poisson distribution.

Poisson theorem. *If p_1 explicitly depends on T in such a way that*

$$p_1 T \to \theta \quad \text{when} \quad T \to \infty,$$

then

$$P\left(\chi_0(\omega_l) = t_0, \chi_1(\omega_l) = t_1\right) \to e^{-\theta} \frac{\theta^{t_1}}{t_1!},$$

where $t_0 + t_1 = T$, and

$$P\left(y_T = v\right) \to e^{-\theta} \frac{\theta^{(T+v)/2}}{((T+v)/2)!}.$$

The Poisson theorem can be called the limit theorem for rare events. The corresponding distribution naturally appears in financial models which take jumps into account.

We mention some other properties of random walks which are observed for an arbitrary long time. Assume that a particle starts at $y_0 = 0$. The probability that the particle returns to zero, i.e., that $y_T = 0$ for some T, is equal to $1 - |p_1 - p_0|$. Thus, for a symmetric walk this probability is equal to one, while for an asymmetric walk it is less than one. For a symmetric walk we denote by $\tau_1, \tau_2, \ldots$ successive times when the particle returns to zero. It can be shown that τ_i are independent random variables such that $\mathbb{E}\{\tau_i\} = \infty$. Moreover, the time until the Nth return grows as N^2, while the total number of returns occurring between 0 and T is proportional to $\sqrt{T}$. Thus, in general, $\tau_n \gg 1$. Because of that, the distribution of the occupational times $\vartheta_{0,2T}^{(+)}$ which the particle spends on the positive semi-axis has very peculiar properties. It can be shown that the random variable $\vartheta_{0,2T}^{(+)}/2T$ which represents the fraction of time the particle spends on the positive semi-axis is asymptotically distributed according to the so-called arcsine law,

$$P\left(\frac{\vartheta_{0,2T}^{(+)}}{2T} < \alpha\right) \sim \frac{2}{\pi}\arcsin\sqrt{\alpha},$$

where $0 \leq \alpha \leq 1$. Thus, an "intuitively obvious" hypothesis that $\vartheta_{0,2T}^{(+)}/2T$ is a unimodal random variable and its mode is $1/2$, so that the particle spends roughly one-half of its time on the positive semi-axis, is not confirmed by a rigorous analysis. In fact, the random variable in question is bimodal, and its modes are 0 and 1. By using the arcsine law we can show that the probability that the particle spends more than 9760 (9930) moments of time out of 10000 on the positive semi-axis is approximately equal to 0.2 (0.1), (i.e., one out of five (ten) random walks has this property,) however strange it sounds. If we return to the original interpretation of the random walk as a game of chance, we can conclude that when the coin is fair, it is very unlikely that a gambler is mediocre, it is much more likely that he is either very good or very bad. The same conclusion is true for investors (if one assumes that their actions are truly random and not affected by experience and smarts): there are very few mediocre investors, the majority of investors are either very good or very bad.

In the usual way we can define the filtration $\mathfrak{F}_t$ which is consistent with the random walk by extending the partition $\mathfrak{G}_t$ with elements consisting of trajectories coinciding up to time t. A relatively straightforward calculation yields

$$\mathbb{E}\{y_{t'}|\mathfrak{F}_t\} = y_t + (p_1 - p_0)(t' - t).$$

Thus, a random walk is a martingale when it is symmetric, $p_0 = p_1 = 1/2$, it is a supermartingale when $p_1 < p_0$ and a submartingale when $p_0 > p_1$. In the symmetric case the expected position of the particle at time t' is its position at time t. Thus, a gambler who accumulated y_t dollars as a result of t tossing of a fair coin should expect that his fortune on average stays the same if he continues to play further. Likewise, a physicist observing movements of a particle which can move in the positive and negative direction with equal probability expects the average position of the particle to be fixed. For an arbitrary random walk we can assign equal probabilities to the original trajectories of the particle thus making its position a martingale. This change of measure approach, which is deceptively simple for the problem in question, turns to be rather useful in many problems of financial engineering.

It is easy to see that binomial random walks describing movements of a particle are Markov chains with the phase space Z consisting of integers in $\mathbb{R}$. Suppose that at time t our particle is located at a point v. By inspection of the tree describing the random walk, we conclude that its subsequent movements depend only on v, so that the random walk posses the Markov property. It is clear that the movements of the particle from time t until the final time T are described by a random walk starting at $x = v$ for the period of $\tau = T - t$. The latter random walk is a uniform shift of the walk starting at $x = 0$. Thus, we can write the corresponding t.p. in the form

$$P\left(\tau, x, x'\right) = \begin{cases} C^{\tau}_{(\tau-x'+x)/2} p_0^{(\tau-x'+x)/2} p_1^{(\tau+x'-x)/2}, & x' - x \in \Xi_{[-\tau,\tau]} \\ 0, & x' - x \notin \Xi_{[-\tau,\tau]} \end{cases}.$$

In particular,

$$P\left(1, x, x'\right) = \begin{cases} p_1, & x' = x+1 \\ p_0, & x' = x-1 \\ 0, & |x' - x| > 1 \end{cases}.$$

It is easy to check that these t.p.'s satisfy the Chapman-Kolmogoroff equation.

3.4 Multinomial stochastic engines

In the multinomial case the number of possible outcomes of a single Bernoulli trial is $K > 2$; these outcomes are distinguished by the subscripts $\{0, ..., K-1\}$, their probabilities are $p_0, ..., p_{K-1}$, $\sum p_k = 1$. A typical outcome of a sequence of T trials is a word of the form $\omega = \{\kappa_1, ..., \kappa_T\}$, where κ_t is an integer between 0 and $K - 1$. The total number of different events (outcomes) is $L = K^T$, they are denoted by ω_l, $l = 0, ..., L - 1$. For a particular event ω_l we denote by

$\chi_k(\omega_l)$ the total number of trials which result in the kth outcome. It is clear that

$$\sum_{0 \le k \le K-1} \chi_k(\omega_l) = T.$$

The probability of the event ω_l is

$$P(\omega_l) = \prod_{0 \le k \le K-1} p_k^{\chi_k(\omega_l)}.$$

The probability of the event $\Omega_{t_0 \dots t_{K-1}}$ defined by the conditions $\chi_k(\omega_l) = t_k$, where $\sum t_k = T$, is given by the multinomial distribution with parameters $(T, p_0, \dots, p_{K-1})$,

$$P\left(\chi_0(\omega_l) = t_0, \dots, \chi_{K-1}(\omega_l) = t_{K-1}\right) = \frac{T!}{\prod_{0 \le k \le K-1} t_k!} \prod_{0 \le k \le K-1} p_k^{t_k}.$$

We can identify the outcomes of a trinomial Bernoulli trial with movements of the particle on the line, if we assume that in addition to moving in the positive and negative directions, the particle can also stay in place. In the multinomial case with arbitrary $K > 2$ the trial can be thought of as a roulette spin, say. However, for special values of K, namely for $K = 2^\kappa$, we can identify the outcomes with movements of the particle on the integer lattice Z^κ in the κ-dimensional space $\mathbb{R}^\kappa$. In financial terms we can interpret these movements as returns on bonds denominated in several different currencies (which can be correlated).

In the trinomial case the corresponding ξ has three possible values $1, -1, 0$, with probabilities p_0, p_1, p_2. We leave it to the reader to determine the corresponding distribution function, etc.

In the quadrinomial case we deal with a two-dimensional random walk. The particle can move to the right and up, right and down, left and up, and left and down in the plane. Initially the particle is at $(0,0)$. The location of our particle after the trial is governed by the vector random variable $\boldsymbol{\xi} = \left(\xi^1, \xi^2\right)$, where ξ^1, ξ^2 are binomial random variables (which, in general, are correlated). Possible movements in the plane and represented by the vectors $(1,1)$, $(-1,1)$, $(1,-1)$, $(-1,-1)$, their probabilities are $p_{1,1}, p_{0,1}, p_{1,0}, p_{0,0}$. In the symmetric case these probabilities are equal to $1/4$. It is clear that in the symmetric case the random variables ξ^1, ξ^2 are independent. More generally, these variables are independent if $p_{\mu,\nu} = p'_\mu p''_\nu$, where p', p'' are some binomial probabilities. The computation of the covariation and correlation between ξ^1 and ξ^2 for the general single-period two-dimensional walk is left to the reader as a useful exercise.

A two-dimensional random walk is a Markov chain with the phase space Z being the set of vectors with integer components in $\mathbb{R}^2$. We leave it to the reader as a very instructive exercise to find the corresponding t.p.'s and the distribution of the terminal value $\mathbf{y}_T = \left(y_T^1, y_T^2\right)$ of a random walk starting at the point $(0, 0)$ at time 0.

3.5   References and further reading

The reader can find further details in the following books: Feller (1968), Karlin and Taylor (1975), Korolyk *et al.* (1985), Stirzaker(1994), Sveshnikov (1978).

3.5 References and further reading

Chapter 4

Continuous-time stochastic engines

4.1 Introduction

In this chapter we describe the mathematical apparatus which is needed for our investigation of continuous-time markets with a particular emphasis on the stochastic engines which are used as sources of randomness in continuous time. We define random processes on infinite probability spaces as families of random variables depending on a continuous parameter which we interpret as time. We introduce finite-dimensional distributions associated with a random process and formulate Kolmogoroff's fundamental theorem which shows that without loss of generality we can consider random processes on the space of $\mathbb{R}^K$-valued functions on an interval of the real axis. We define the so-called Markov random processes which have the property that the future states are independent of the past states provided that the present state is known. We discuss the t.p.'s and transition probability density functions (t.p.d.f.'s) associated with Markov processes and formulate the Chapman-Kolmogoroff equation which restricts possible choices of t.p.'s. Next we introduce diffusion processes which are Markov processes with sufficiently regular trajectories and discuss Kolmogoroff's backward and the Fokker-Planck forward equations which govern the t.p.d.f.'s for diffusion processes. We emphasize their duality which is particularly important for such tasks of financial engineering as model calibration. As examples of diffusion processes we discuss the so-called Wiener processes which are continuous-time limits of Bernoulli processes with fixed probabilities of success. Even though a rigorous description of such processes is somewhat involved, it is easier to deal with them than with Bernoulli processes. We interpret Wiener processes in terms of a Brownian (random) walk of a particle on the real axis. Since knowing properties of Wiener processes is necessary in order to obtain an adequate description of markets with continuously evolving FXRs, we expose the key features of such processes in detail. In particular, we show how to construct the corresponding functional probability space and endow it with an appropriate filtration which is used in order to describe the flow of information revealed during the observation of the movements of a Brownian particle. We calculate the t.p.d.f.'s for Wiener processes as well as some other useful distributions associated with such processes. We also discuss the martingale property of the Brownian motion. Next, we study Poisson processes which are continuous-time limits of Bernoulli processes with decaying probabilities of success. We also refer to Poisson processes as jump-diffusions. Such processes are used to describe markets with discontinuous FXRs which cannot be done by using Wiener processes alone since trajectories of the latter processes are continuous. We use the stochastic engines in order to define stochastic integrals and stochastic differential equations (SDEs) which are needed in order to construct financially relevant stochastic processes such as arithmetic and geometric Brownian motions and Bessel processes out of Wiener and Poisson processes. We discuss in detail Ito's lemma and the Meyer-Tanaka formula. Both are used on numerous occasions below. We briefly discuss some general properties of SDEs such as existence and uniqueness of solutions and then introduce some special classes of SDEs which are particularly useful for the purposes of financial engineering including linear SDEs in the narrow and broad sense. We also describe the reduction method which allows us to reduce complicated SDEs to a simple form. We show that solutions of SDEs can be considered as diffusions and derive the corresponding backward and forward equations for their t.p.d.f.'s. We finish the chapter with a brief discussion of various numerical methods which can be used in order to solve SDEs and the associated forward and backward Kolmogoroff equations.

The chapter is organized as follows. In Section 2 we define stochastic processes which are continuous time counterparts of time series. In Section 3 we introduce and study Markov processes which form a special class of stochastic processes which are particularly important for our purposes. In Section 4 we study diffusions which are Markov processes whose trajectories are regular. Sections 5 and 6 are devoted to Wiener and Poisson processes which are used later as "stochastic engines" for continuous time markets. In Section 7 we study stochastic differential equations (SDEs) which are used in order to construct new stochastic processes from the standard Wiener processes as well as partial differential equations (PDEs) which describe the corresponding t.p.d.f.'s. In Section 8 we show how to solve linear SDEs which form a very important special class of SDEs. In Section 9 we study SDEs driven by combined Wiener and Poisson processes. In Section 10 we describe various method for analytical solution of PDEs. In Section 11 we describe methods which are used for their numerical solution. In Section 12 we study methods used for numerical solution of SDEs. We give relevant references in Section 13.

4.2 Stochastic processes

We define a *scalar stochastic (or random) process* as a family of scalar random variables $\xi(t)$ or ξ_t depending on a continuous time parameter t varying on an interval $I = [t_0, t_1]$ which can be semi-infinite. We define a sample path (trajectory) of a random process $\xi_t(\omega)$ in the same way as before, such a path is a function from I to $\mathbb{R}$, i.e., a scalar function of a continuous scalar argument.

Recall that with a random variable we associate a distribution function. Similarly, with a random process we associate finite-dimensional distributions which are defined as follows

$$F_{t_1}\left(x^1\right) = P\left\{\xi_{t_1} \leq x^1\right\},$$

$$F_{t_1,t_2}\left(x^1, x^2\right) = P\left\{\xi_{t_1} \leq x^1, \xi_{t_2} \leq x^2\right\},$$

etc., where times $t_1, ..., t_n, ...$ are chosen in the increasing order. Finite-dimensional distributions have to satisfy the *compatibility condition*:

$$F_{t_1,...,t_m,...t_n}\left(x^1, ..., x^m, \infty, ..., \infty\right) = F_{t_1,...,t_m}\left(x^1, ..., x^m\right).$$

A random process is called *stationary* if

$$F_{t_1+t,...,t_n+t}\left(x^1, ..., x^n\right) = F_{t_1,...,t_n}\left(x^1, ..., x^n\right), \tag{4.1}$$

i.e., if its distribution functions are invariant with respect to time shifts. The vector case is studied by analogy.

Kolmogoroff's fundamental theorem states that for every family of finite-dimensional distributions which satisfies the compatibility condition there is a probability space and a stochastic process having this family of distributions. Moreover, we can choose as a space of events Ω the set of all functions $\omega(t)$ from I to $\mathbb{R}$, assume that the corresponding sigma algebra $\mathfrak{U}$ is generated by the so-called cylinder sets $\mathfrak{g}$ of the form

$$\mathfrak{g} = \left\{\omega : \omega(t_1) \in B_1, ..., \omega(t_n) \in B_n\right\},$$

where B_n are Borel sets in $\mathbb{R}$ and assign probabilities $P(\mathfrak{g})$ to these sets in accordance with the given family of distributions,

$$P\{\omega : \omega(t_1) < x^1, ..., \omega(t_n) < x^n\} = F_{t_1,...,t_n}(x^1, ..., x^n).$$

For a function $\omega(t)$ the value of the corresponding stochastic processes $\xi_t(\omega)$ at time t is the value of this function,

$$\xi_t(\omega) = \omega(t).$$

This construction shows that in dealing with stochastic processes we can restrict ourselves to functional spaces. To put it another way, without loss of generality we can restrict ourselves to probability spaces whose elements are functions from I to $\mathbb{R}$. We say that two processes ξ_t and ξ'_t on the same functional space are versions of each other if for every t they coincide with probability one. The celebrated Kolmogoroff's theorem shows that for every process such that the expectation of the increment $|\xi_{t'} - \xi_t|$ decays sufficiently rapidly when $t' \to t$, so that

$$|\xi_{t'} - \xi_t|^\alpha \leq K |t - t'|^{1+\beta}, \qquad \alpha, \beta, K > 0, \tag{4.2}$$

there is an equivalent process with continuous trajectories. In this case we can restrict Ω to be the space of continuous functions on I. The reader is warned, however, that on occasion continuous functions have rather pathological properties.

In order to describe the flow of information associated with a given random process we first define the set $\mathfrak{G}_t$ of cylinder sets of the form

$$\mathfrak{g} = \{\omega : \omega(t_1) \in B_1, ..., \omega(t_n) \in B_n\},$$

where $0 \leq t_1 < t_2... < t_n \leq t$, and then introduce the sigma algebra $\mathfrak{F}_t$ generated by $\mathfrak{G}_t$. The corresponding sigma algebras are ordered as follows

$$\mathfrak{F}_t \subseteq \mathfrak{F}_{t'}, \qquad t \leq t'.$$

We say that these sigma algebras form a filtration generated by the random process $\xi(t)$. This filtration can be used in order to define martingales, super- and submartingales. The corresponding definitions for random processes are the same as for time series. A random process is called a martingale if

$$\mathbb{E}\{|\xi_t|\} < \infty, \qquad t \in I,$$

$$\mathbb{E}\left\{\xi_{t'}|\mathfrak{F}_t\right\} = \xi_t.$$

It is called super (sub) martingale if the equality = is replaced by the inequalities $\leq$ and $\geq$, respectively.

The characteristic function of a stochastic process is defined as follows

$$\Phi\left(t,\varsigma\right) = \mathbb{E}\left\{e^{i\varsigma\xi_t}\right\} = \int_{-\infty}^{\infty} e^{i\varsigma x}dF_t\left(x\right).$$

The covariation and correlation function of a stochastic process such that $\mathbb{E}\left\{|\xi_t|^2\right\} < \infty$, $t \in I$, are given by

$$\Psi\left(t_1,t_2\right) = \mathbb{E}\left\{\left(\xi_{t_1} - \mathbb{E}\left\{\xi_{t_1}\right\}\right)\left(\xi_{t_2} - \mathbb{E}\left\{\xi_{t_2}\right\}\right)\right\},$$

$$\tilde{\Psi}\left(t_1,t_2\right) = \frac{\mathbb{E}\left\{\left(\xi_{t_1} - \mathbb{E}\left\{\xi_{t_1}\right\}\right)\left(\xi_{t_2} - \mathbb{E}\left\{\xi_{t_2}\right\}\right)\right\}}{\sqrt{\mathbb{E}\left\{\left(\xi_{t_1} - \mathbb{E}\left\{\xi_{t_1}\right\}\right)^2\right\}\mathbb{E}\left\{\left(\xi_{t_2} - \mathbb{E}\left\{\xi_{t_2}\right\}\right)^2\right\}}}.$$

Similarly, we define a vector stochastic process as a family of N-component random variables $\boldsymbol{\xi}_t = \left(\xi_t^1, ..., \xi_t^N\right)$. For such processes the above constructions and definitions can be extended without difficulty.

4.3 Markov processes

Deterministic dynamical systems are said to have the Markov property when their future states are independent of their past states provided that their present state is known. It is possible to extend this property to stochastic dynamical systems whose behavior is described by stochastic processes on an interval $I = [0, T]$, where T can be infinite. We already know that in order to describe the flow of information associated with a particular stochastic process we need to construct the filtration $\mathfrak{F}_t$ associated with this process and condition all probabilities on this filtration. We say that a scalar stochastic process ξ_t has the Markov property if

$$P\left\{\xi_{t'} \in B'|\mathfrak{F}_t\right\} = P\left\{\xi_{t'} \in B'|\xi_t\right\},$$

where $0 \leq t \leq t' \leq T$ and B' is a Borel set in $\mathbb{R}$. Such processes are called Markov processes. Broadly speaking, this is the only class of processes used in this book.

For Markov processes we can define the so-called t.p.'s $P(t, x, t', B')$ as follows

$$P(t, x, t', B') = P\{\xi_{t'} \in B' | \xi_t = x\}.$$

T.p.'s have several useful properties. For instance, for fixed t, x, t' they define a probability measure on $\mathbb{R}$. Another property, which is very important for us, is the fact that for all times $t \le t' \le t'' \le T$, Borel sets B'' and almost all x they satisfy the Chapman-Kolmogoroff equation which states that

$$P(t, x, t'', B'') = \int_{\mathbb{R}^N} P(t, x, t', dx') P(t', x', t'', B''). \qquad (4.3)$$

We can always modify the t.p.'s in such a way that the above equation is satisfied for all x. Equation (4.3) is a mathematical expression of the fact that trajectories starting at a point x at time t and finishing in a set B'' at time t'' do so by visiting intermediate points x' at time t'. The initial condition for this equation is

$$P(t, x, t, B) = \chi_B(x),$$

where, as usual, $\chi_B(.)$ is the characteristic function of a set.

In view of definition (4.1) we define homogeneous Markov processes as processes with stationary t.p.'s such that

$$P(t, x, t', B') = P(t' - t, x, B'),$$

so that t.p.'s depend only on the interval of time between observations $\tau = t' - t$, rather than the moments t, t' when these observations are made. For homogeneous Markov processes the Chapman-Kolmogoroff equation can be written as follows

$$P(t'' - t, x, B'') = \int_{\mathbb{R}^N} P(t' - t, x, dx') P(t'' - t', x', B'').$$

We say that the t.p. P has t.p.d.f. p if

$$P(t, x, t', B') = \int_{B'} p(t, x, t', x') dx'.$$

In terms of t.p.d.f.'s the Chapman-Kolmogoroff equation can be written as

$$p(t, x, t'', x'') = \int_{\mathbb{R}^N} p(t, x, t', x') p(t', x', t'', x'') dx'. \qquad (4.4)$$

The corresponding homogeneous equation has the form

$$p\left(t'' - t, x, x''\right) = \int_{\mathbb{R}^N} p\left(t' - t, x, x'\right) p\left(t'' - t', x', x''\right) dx'.$$

Example 4.1. *The principal example of a Markov process with continuous trajectories is the ubiquitous scalar Wiener process W_t. This process is characterized by its nonrandom initial value $W_0 = 0$ and the stationary t.p.d.f.*

$$p\left(\tau, x, x'\right) = \frac{e^{-\left(x' - x\right)^2 / 2\tau}}{\sqrt{2\pi\tau}} \equiv H\left(\tau, x' - x\right). \tag{4.5}$$

It is easy to verify that this t.p.d.f. satisfies the Chapman-Kolmogoroff equation. Moreover, by using Kolmogoroff's condition (4.2), one can show that trajectories of W_t are continuous. As we will see shortly, these trajectories are nowhere differentiable. For fixed t the scalar random variable W_t is distributed normally, $W_t \sim \mathfrak{N}(0, t)$. For historic reasons the function $H(\tau, x)$ is called the one-dimensional heat kernel.

The extension of the above definitions and results to the vector case is straightforward. For instance, the vector Chapman-Kolmogoroff equation can be written in the form

$$P\left(t, \mathbf{x}, t'', \mathfrak{B}''\right) = \int_{\mathbb{R}^N} P\left(t, \mathbf{x}, t', d\mathbf{x}'\right) P\left(t', \mathbf{x}', t'', \mathfrak{B}''\right),$$

where $\mathfrak{B}''$ is a Borel set in $\mathbb{R}^N$.

Example 4.2. *The principal example of a vector Markov process with continuous trajectories is the standard N-component Wiener processes $W_t = \left(W_t^1, ..., W_t^N\right)$, where W_t^n are independent scalar Wiener processes. The corresponding t.p.d.f. is*

$$p\left(\tau, \mathbf{x}, \mathbf{x}'\right) = \frac{e^{-\left|\mathbf{x}' - \mathbf{x}\right|^2 / 2\tau}}{\left(2\pi\tau\right)^{N/2}} = H\left(\tau, \mathbf{x}' - \mathbf{x}\right). \tag{4.6}$$

For fixed t the vector random variable W_t has an N-dimensional normal distribution, $W_t \sim \mathfrak{N}(\mathbf{0}, \mathcal{I}t)$, where I is the $N \times N$ identity matrix. The function $H(\tau, x)$ is called the N-dimensional heat kernel.

4.4 Diffusions

In principle, trajectories of Markov processes can have rather peculiar properties. Diffusion processes form a special class of Markov processes such that all the trajectories are continuous and have other useful properties. (Markov processes with continuous trajectories which are not diffusions do exist.) They model a great many physically and financially important phenomena from Brownian motion of small particles in water, to propagation of heat in solids, to evolution of FXRs for major currency pairs. For simplicity, we consider Markov processes with t.p.d.f.'s.

A scalar Markov process is called a diffusion provided that the following conditions are satisfied

$$\lim_{t' \to t} \left[\frac{1}{t' - t} \int_{|x' - x| < \upsilon} \left\{ \begin{array}{c} (x' - x) \\ (x' - x)^2 \\ (x' - x)^3 \end{array} \right\} p\,(t, x, t', x')\, dx' \right] = \left\{ \begin{array}{c} b\,(t, x) \\ a\,(t, x) \\ 0 \end{array} \right\}.$$

(4.7)

If a particle moves from (t, x) to (t', x'), then the drift coefficient $b\,(t, x)$ and the diffusion coefficient $a\,(t, x)$ measure the regular velocity and the degree of stochasticity of its motion, respectively.

It turns out that for diffusion processes t.p.d.f.'s are completely determined by the drift $b\,(t, x)$ and diffusion $a\,(t, x)$. Moreover, one can derive the so-called Kolmogoroff's backward and Fokker-Planck forward partial differential equations (PDEs) for $p\,(t, x, t', x')$.

In order to derive the Fokker-Planck forward PDE we multiply the Chapman-Kolmogoroff equation by an arbitrary smooth function $\Psi\,(x'')$ vanishing outside of a certain domain and integrate the product with respect to x'' to get:

$$\int p\,(t, x, t'', x'')\, \Psi\,(x'')\, dx'' - \int p\,(t, x, t', x')\, dx' \int p\,(t', x', t'', x'')\, \Psi\,(x'')\, dx'' = 0.$$

(4.8)

Next, we expand $\Psi\,(x'')$ in the second integral in a Taylor series centered at x',

$$\Psi\,(x'') = \Psi\,(x') + \Psi_{x'}\,(x')\,(x'' - x') + \frac{1}{2}\Psi_{x'x'}\,(x')\,(x'' - x')^2 + \dots,$$

keep the first three terms and rewrite equation (4.8) as

$$\int p\,(t, x, t'', x'')\, \Psi\,(x'')\, dx'' - \int p\,(t, x, t', x')\, \Psi\,(x')\, dx'$$

$$- \int p\,(t, x, t', x') \left(\int p\,(t', x', t'', x'')\,(x'' - x')\, dx'' \right) \Psi_{x'}\,(x')\, dx'$$

$$- \frac{1}{2} \int p\,(t, x, t', x') \left(\int p\,(t', x', t'', x'')\,(x'' - x')^2\, dx'' \right) \Psi_{x'x'}\,(x')\, dx' = 0.$$

Thus,

$$\int \left(p\left(t,x,t'',y\right) -p\left(t,x,t',y\right) \right) \Psi \left(y\right) dy-\int p\left(t,x,t',x'\right)$$

$$\times \quad \left\{ \int p\left(t',x',t'',x''\right) \left(x''-x'\right) dx''\Psi_{x'}\left(x'\right) \right.$$

$$\left. +\frac{1}{2}\int p\left(t',x',t'',x''\right) \left(x''-x'\right)^{2} dx''\Psi_{x'x'}\left(x'\right) \right\} dx'=0,$$

where y is a dummy variable. We divide the above equation by $t''-t'$, let $t''\rightarrow t'$, and use conditions (4.7) to obtain

$$\int p_{t'}\left(t,x,t',x'\right) \Psi \left(x'\right) dx'-\int p\left(t,x,t',x'\right)$$

$$\times \quad \left\{ b\left(t',x'\right) \Psi_{x'}\left(x'\right) +\frac{1}{2}a\left(t',x'\right) \Psi_{x'x'}\left(x'\right) \right\} dx'=0.$$

Finally, integration by parts yields

$$\int \left\{ p_{t'}\left(t,x,t',x'\right) +\left(b\left(t',x'\right) p\left(t,x,t',x'\right) \right)_{x'} \right.$$

$$\left. -\frac{1}{2}\left(a\left(t',x'\right) p\left(t,x,t',x'\right) \right)_{x'x'} \right\} \Psi \left(x'\right) dx'=0.$$

Since $\Psi \left(x\right)$ is arbitrary, this equation implies that $p\left(t,x,t',x'\right)$ as a function of t',x' satisfies the forward Fokker-Plank PDE:

$$p_{t'}\left(t,x,t',x'\right) -\frac{1}{2}\left(a\left(t',x'\right) p\left(t,x,t',x'\right) \right)_{x'x'} +\left(b\left(t',x'\right) p\left(t,x,t',x'\right) \right)_{x'} =0. \tag{4.9}$$

The initial condition is

$$p\left(t,x,t'\rightarrow t,x'\right) =\delta \left(x'-x\right),$$

where, as usual, $\delta \left(.\right)$ is the Dirac delta function.

Straightforward integration by parts shows that as a function of t,x the t.p.d.f. $p\left(t,x,t',x'\right)$ satisfies the backward Kolmogoroff equation:

$$p_{t}\left(t,x,t',x'\right) +\frac{1}{2}a\left(t,x\right) p\left(t,x,t',x'\right)_{xx} +b\left(t,x\right) p\left(t,x,t',x'\right)_{x} =0. \tag{4.10}$$

The final condition is

$$p\left(t \rightarrow t', x, t', x'\right) = \delta\left(x - x'\right).$$

Since the backward and forward equations govern the behavior of the same t.p.d.f. they are called dual.

For financial applications we need to consider more general dual backward and forward equations, namely:

$$p_t\left(t, x, t', x'\right) + \frac{1}{2} a\left(t, x\right) p\left(t, x, t', x'\right)_{xx} \qquad (4.11)$$
$$+ \quad b\left(t, x\right) p\left(t, x, t', x'\right)_x - c\left(t, x\right) p\left(t, x, t', x'\right) = 0,$$

$$p\left(t \rightarrow t', x, t', x'\right) = \delta\left(x - x'\right), \qquad (4.12)$$

and

$$p_{t'}\left(t, x, t', x'\right) - \frac{1}{2}\left(a\left(t', x'\right) p\left(t, x, t', x'\right)\right)_{x'x'}$$
$$+ \quad \left(b\left(t', x'\right) p\left(t, x, t', x'\right)\right)_{x'} + c\left(t', x'\right) p\left(t, x, t', x'\right) = 0,$$

$$p\left(t, x, t' \rightarrow t, x'\right) = \delta\left(x' - x\right),$$

where $c > 0$. These equations can be interpreted in probabilistic terms. To do so, we start with a process ξ_t with the diffusion coefficient a and drift coefficient b and construct a new process $\tilde{\xi}_t$ by killing ξ_t at a certain random stopping (killing) time ζ,

$$\tilde{\xi}_t = \begin{cases} \xi_t, & t < \zeta \\ \maltese, & t > \zeta \end{cases}.$$

Here $\maltese \notin \mathbb{R}$ is an artificial "coffin" state. If we assume that killing occurs at the rate c, i.e.,

$$\lim_{t' \rightarrow t}\left[\frac{1}{t' - t}\left(1 - P\left(t, x, t', \mathbb{R}\right)\right)\right] = c\left(t, x\right),$$

then the corresponding backward and forward equations for the t.p.d.f. have the form (4.11), (4.12), respectively.

Due to the linearity of the general final value problem

$$U_t\left(t, x\right) + \frac{1}{2} a\left(t, x\right) U_{xx}\left(t, x\right) + b\left(t, x\right) U_x\left(t, x\right) - c\left(t, x\right) U\left(t, x\right) = 0, \quad (4.13)$$

$$U\left(T,x\right)=u\left(x\right),$$

we can represent its solution in the form

$$U\left(t,x\right)=\int_{\mathbb{R}}p\left(t,x,T,\xi\right)u\left(\xi\right)d\xi. \tag{4.14}$$

Similarly, the solution of the initial value problem

$$V_t\left(t,x\right)-\frac{1}{2}\left(a\left(t,x\right)V\left(t,x\right)\right)_{xx}+\left(b\left(t,x\right)V\left(t,x\right)\right)_x+c\left(t,x\right)U\left(t,x\right)=0,$$

$$V\left(0,x\right)=v\left(x\right),$$

can be written as

$$V\left(t,x\right)=\int_{\mathbb{R}^N}p\left(0,\xi,t,x\right)v\left(\xi\right)dx.$$

In the PDE literature p is called Green's function for the above problems.

On several occasions below we need to solve inhomogeneous backward problems of the form

$$U_t\left(t,x\right)+\frac{1}{2}a\left(t,x\right)U_{xx}\left(t,x\right)+b\left(t,x\right)U_x\left(t,x\right)-c\left(t,x\right)U\left(t,x\right)=W\left(t,x\right),$$

$$U\left(T,x\right)=u\left(x\right),$$

and similar forward problems. This task can be accomplished via Duhamel's principle. This principle (which can be proved by direct substitution) states that

$$U\left(t,x\right)=\int_{\mathbb{R}}p\left(t,x,T,\xi\right)u\left(\xi\right)d\xi-\int_t^T\int_{\mathbb{R}}p\left(t,x,t',\xi\right)W\left(t',\xi\right)dt'd\xi.$$

For homogeneous killed diffusions with $p\left(t,x,t',x'\right)=p\left(\tau,x,x'\right)$, where $\tau=t'-t$, $a\left(t,x\right)=a\left(x\right)$, $b\left(t,x\right)=b\left(x\right)$, $c\left(t,x\right)=c\left(t\right)$, the backward and forward equations assume the form

$$p_\tau\left(\tau,x,x'\right)-\frac{1}{2}a\left(x\right)p_{xx}\left(\tau,x,x'\right) \tag{4.15}$$
$$-\quad b\left(x\right)p_x\left(\tau,x,x'\right)+c\left(x\right)p\left(\tau,x,x'\right)=0,$$

and

$$p_\tau\left(\tau, x, x'\right) - \frac{1}{2}\left(a\left(x'\right) p\left(\tau, x, x'\right)\right)_{x'x'} \tag{4.16}$$
$$+ \quad \left(b\left(x'\right) p\left(\tau, x, x'\right)\right)_{x'} + c\left(x'\right) p\left(\tau, x, x'\right) = 0,$$

respectively. Both of them are forward parabolic equations augmented with the initial condition

$$p\left(0, x, x'\right) = \delta\left(x - x'\right). \tag{4.17}$$

When the coefficients a, b, c are constant, we can write $p\left(\tau, x, x'\right)$ as $p\left(\tau, y\right)$, where $y = x' - x$. The initial value for $p\left(\tau, y\right)$ is

$$p_\tau\left(\tau, y\right) - \frac{1}{2}a p_{yy}\left(\tau, y\right) + b p_y\left(\tau, y\right) + cp\left(\tau, y\right) = 0,$$

$$p\left(0, y\right) = \delta\left(y\right). \tag{4.18}$$

We can associate with a homogeneous diffusion the so-called *natural scale density* $\mathsf{s}\left(x\right)$, *speed measure* $\mathsf{m}\left(x\right)$ and *killing measure* $\mathsf{k}\left(x\right)$ as follows:

$$\mathsf{s}\left(x\right) = \exp\left\{-\int^x 2b\left(y\right)/a\left(y\right) dy\right\},$$

$$\mathsf{m}\left(x\right) = \frac{\exp\left\{\int^x 2b\left(y\right)/a\left(y\right) dy\right\}}{a\left(x\right)},$$

$$\mathsf{k}\left(x\right) = \frac{c\left(x\right)\exp\left\{\int^x 2b\left(y\right)/a\left(y\right) dy\right\}}{a\left(x\right)}.$$

By using these quantities, we represent equations (4.15), (4.16), in the so-called self-adjoint form

$$\mathsf{m}\left(x\right) p_\tau\left(\tau, x, x'\right) - \frac{1}{2}\frac{\partial}{\partial x}\left(\frac{1}{\mathsf{s}\left(x\right)}\frac{\partial}{\partial x}p\left(\tau, x, x'\right)\right) + \mathsf{k}\left(x\right) p\left(\tau, x, x'\right) = 0, \tag{4.19}$$

$$\mathsf{m}\left(x'\right) q_\tau\left(\tau, x, x'\right) - \frac{1}{2}\frac{\partial}{\partial x'}\left(\frac{1}{\mathsf{s}\left(x'\right)}\frac{\partial}{\partial x'}q\left(\tau, x, x'\right)\right) + \mathsf{k}\left(x'\right) q\left(\tau, x, x'\right) = 0, \tag{4.20}$$

where

$$q\left(\tau, x, x'\right) = \frac{p\left(\tau, x, x'\right)}{\mathsf{m}\left(x'\right)}.$$

These equations show that the modified t.p.d.f. $q\left(\tau, x, x'\right)$ is a symmetric function of its arguments.

Example 4.3. *In this example we treat the scalar Wiener process as a diffusion process. Since this process is homogeneous, we know that $p = p\left(\tau, x, x'\right)$, $a = a\left(x\right)$, $b = b\left(x\right)$. The killing rate is zero, $c\left(x\right) = 0$. Straightforward calculation which is left to the reader as an exercise shows that $a\left(x\right) = 1$, $b\left(x\right) = 0$. Thus, both the backward and forward problems reduce to the standard heat equation*

$$p_\tau - \frac{1}{2}p_{xx} = 0, \tag{4.21}$$

supplied with the initial condition

$$p\left(0, x, x'\right) = \delta\left(x - x'\right).$$

The corresponding natural scale density, speed and killing measures are constant, $\mathsf{s}\left(x\right) = 1$, $\mathsf{m}\left(x\right) = 1$, $\mathsf{k}\left(x\right) = 0$.

So far, we considered processes which take values on the entire real line. Often, it is necessary to consider processes taking values on the interval $\mathcal{I} = \left(e_1, e_2\right)$, where $-\infty \leq e_1 < e_2 \leq \infty$. The boundaries can appear due to singularities in coefficients a, b, c or be introduced for other reasons. When the process $\tilde{\xi}$ reaches the boundaries of the interval $\mathcal{I}$ it is necessary to augment PDEs (4.19), (4.20) with appropriate boundary conditions. A very detailed classification of the boundary points is due to Feller. To be concrete, we consider the left boundary e_1. In general, a diffusion process can exhibit different types of behavior at e_1. The simplest possibility is that the process never reaches the value e_1. In this case, no boundary conditions at $x = e_1$ are needed and the corresponding point is called natural. Alternatively, the diffusion process can reach the value e_1 with positive probability. In this case two possibilities have to be distinguished: (A) the boundary point e_1 absorbs the process, so that no boundary conditions can be imposed there; (B) the process behaves like the standard diffusion in the vicinity of e_1, so that different boundary conditions can be imposed there. The corresponding boundary is called an exit in case (A) and regular in case (B). In order to classify the boundaries, we choose an arbitrary point x inside the interval $\mathcal{I}$. The left boundary point e_1 is called entrance if

$$J_{11} = \int_{e_1}^{x} \left(\int_{y}^{x} \mathsf{s}(z)\,dz \right) (\mathsf{m}(y) + \mathsf{k}(y))\,dy < \infty,$$

and exit if

$$J_{12} = \int_{e_1}^{x} \left(\int_{y}^{x} (\mathsf{m}(z) + \mathsf{k}(z))\,dz \right) \mathsf{s}(y)\,dy < \infty.$$

For the right boundary point the definition is analogous. The process can reach an exit boundary and can be started at an entrance boundary. The boundary point is called regular if it is both exit and entrance, and natural if it is neither exit nor entrance.

Example 4.4. *We consider the standard Wiener process on the semi-infinite interval* $(0, \infty)$. *We already know that the Kolmogoroff and Fokker-Planck equations have the same form (4.21). Since we consider these equations on the half-axis, we have to augment them with appropriate boundary conditions. By definition,* $\mathsf{s}(x) = 1$, $\mathsf{m}(x) = 1$, $\mathsf{k}(x) = 0$. *For the left end point* $e_1 = 0$ *both integrals* J_{11}, J_{12} *are clearly finite, so that this point is regular. For the right end point* $e_2 = \infty$, *both integrals* J_{21}, J_{22} *are infinite, so that this point is natural. Accordingly, we have to impose only one boundary condition at* $e_1 = 0$. *There are several possibilities. The Wiener process can be: (A) reflected at zero*

$$p_{x'}(\tau, x, 0) = 0; \tag{4.22}$$

(B) killed at zero,

$$p(\tau, x, 0) = 0; \tag{4.23}$$

(C) killed elastically at zero,

$$p_{x'}(\tau, x, 0) = \alpha p(\tau, x, 0). \tag{4.24}$$

In the first case the process is immediately returned back to the interval $(0, \infty)$, *in the second case it is terminated as soon as it reaches zero, finally, in the third case a combination of the above occurs. It is easy to find the corresponding t.p.d.f.'s in the first and second case by the method of images. In the case of reflecting boundary we represent* $p(\tau, x, x')$ *as a sum*

$$p(\tau, x, x') = H(\tau, x - x') + H(\tau, x + x'),$$

which guarantees that p solves equation (4.21) and satisfies boundary conditions (4.22). For the killing boundary we write $p(\tau, x, x')$ as a difference

$$p(\tau, x, x') = H(\tau, x - x') - H(\tau, x + x'),$$

which guarantees that p solves equation (4.21) and satisfies boundary conditions (4.23). The case of elastic killing (4.24) is more complex and will be studied later in the specific financial context.

Example 4.5. *We consider the so-called Bessel process with*

$$a(x) = 1, \quad b(x) = \frac{(1 - 2\nu)}{2x}, \quad c(x) = 0.$$

It is natural to consider such a process on the semi-infinite interval $(0, \infty)$. The corresponding Kolmogoroff equation is

$$p_\tau - \frac{1}{2}p_{xx} - \frac{(1 - 2\nu)}{2x}p_x = 0.$$

The expression in parenthesis is the radial part of the Laplace operator in $2(1 - \nu)$ dimensional space. The natural scale density and the speed measure are

$$\mathsf{s}(x) = x^{-(1-2\nu)}, \quad \mathsf{m}(x) = x^{(1-2\nu)}.$$

For the left boundary we have (for simplicity we assume that $\nu \neq 1$)

$$
\begin{aligned}
J_{11} &= \int_0^x \left(\int_y^x z^{-(1-2\nu)} dz \right) y^{1-2\nu} dy \\
&= \frac{1}{2\nu} \int_0^x (x^{2\nu} - y^{2\nu}) y^{1-2\nu} dy \\
&= \left(\frac{x^{2\nu} y^{2-2\nu}}{2\nu(2 - 2\nu)} - \frac{y^2}{4\nu} \right) \Big|_0^x,
\end{aligned}
$$

so that

$$
J_{11} \begin{cases} < \infty, & \text{if } \nu < 1 \\ = \infty, & \text{if } \nu \geq 1 \end{cases}.
$$

Similarly,

$$
J_{12} \begin{cases} < \infty, & \text{if } \nu > 0 \\ = \infty, & \text{if } \nu \leq 0 \end{cases}.
$$

Thus, 0 is an entrance-not-exit boundary when $\nu \leq 0$, exit-not-entrance boundary when $\nu \geq 1$, and a regular boundary when $0 < \nu < 1$. The right boundary is always natural.

Consider now a N-component Markov process. Such a process is called a killed diffusion provided that

$$\lim_{t' \to t} \left[\frac{1}{t' - t} \left(1 - P\left(t, \mathbf{x}, t', \mathbb{R}^N\right) \right) \right] = c\left(t, \mathbf{x}\right),$$

$$\lim_{t' \to t} \left[\frac{1}{t' - t} \int_{|\mathbf{x}' - \mathbf{x}| < v} \left\{ \begin{array}{l} (x'^n - x^n) \\ (x'^m - x^m)(x'^n - x^n) \\ |\mathbf{x}' - \mathbf{x}|^3 \end{array} \right\} p\left(t, \mathbf{x}, t', \mathbf{x}'\right) d\mathbf{x}' \right]$$

$$= \left\{ \begin{array}{l} b^n\left(t, \mathbf{x}\right) \\ a^{mn}\left(t, \mathbf{x}\right) \\ 0 \end{array} \right\}.$$

The Kolmogoroff's backward problem for $p\left(t, \mathbf{x}, t', \mathbf{x}'\right)$ with the arguments $t', \mathbf{x}'$ fixed (and suppressed for brevity) has the form

$$p_t\left(t, \mathbf{x}\right) + \frac{1}{2} \sum_{m,n=1}^{N} a^{mn}\left(t, \mathbf{x}\right) p_{x^m x^n}\left(t, \mathbf{x}\right)$$

$$+ \quad \sum_{n=1}^{N} b^n\left(t, \mathbf{x}\right) p_{x^n}\left(t, \mathbf{x}\right) - c\left(t, \mathbf{x}\right) p\left(t, \mathbf{x}\right) = 0,$$

$$p\left(t \to t', \mathbf{x}, t', \mathbf{x}'\right) \to \delta\left(\mathbf{x} - \mathbf{x}'\right).$$

The Fokker-Planck forward problem for $p\left(t, \mathbf{x}, t', \mathbf{x}'\right)$ with the arguments $t, \mathbf{x}$ fixed (and suppressed for brevity) has the form

$$p_{t'}\left(t', \mathbf{x}'\right) - \frac{1}{2} \sum_{m,n=1}^{N} \left(a^{mn}\left(t', \mathbf{x}'\right) p\left(t', \mathbf{x}'\right)\right)_{x'^m x'^n}$$

$$+ \quad \sum_{n=1}^{N} \left(b^n\left(t', \mathbf{x}'\right) p\left(t', \mathbf{x}'\right)\right)_{x'^n} + c\left(t', \mathbf{x}'\right) p\left(t', \mathbf{x}'\right) = 0,$$

$$p\left(t, \mathbf{x}, t' \to t, \mathbf{x}'\right) \to \delta\left(\mathbf{x}' - \mathbf{x}\right).$$

For homogeneous diffusions with $p\left(t, \mathbf{x}, t', \mathbf{x}'\right) = p\left(\tau, \mathbf{x}, \mathbf{x}'\right)$, where $\tau = t' - t$, and

$$a^{mn}\left(t, \mathbf{x}\right) = a^{mn}\left(\mathbf{x}\right), \quad b^n\left(t, \mathbf{x}\right) = b^n\left(\mathbf{x}\right), \quad c\left(t, \mathbf{x}\right) = c\left(\mathbf{x}\right),$$

the backward and forward equations assume the form

$$p_\tau\left(\tau, \mathbf{x}'\right) - \frac{1}{2} \sum_{m,n=1}^{N} \left(a^{mn}\left(\mathbf{x}'\right) p\left(\tau, \mathbf{x}'\right)\right)_{x'^m x'^n}$$

$$+ \sum_{n=1}^{N} \left(b^n\left(\mathbf{x}'\right) p\left(\tau, \mathbf{x}'\right)\right)_{x^n} + c\left(\mathbf{x}'\right) p\left(\mathbf{x}'\right) = 0,$$

and

$$p_\tau\left(\tau, \mathbf{x}\right) - \frac{1}{2} \sum_{m,n=1}^{N} a^{mn}\left(\mathbf{x}\right) p_{x^m x^n}\left(\tau, \mathbf{x}\right)$$

$$- \sum_{n=1}^{N} b^n\left(\mathbf{x}\right) p_{x^n}\left(\tau, \mathbf{x}\right) + c\left(\mathbf{x}\right) p\left(\mathbf{x}\right) = 0,$$

respectively. Both of them are forward parabolic equations.

By using the t.p.d.f. p which is also called Green's function, we can represent solutions of the problems

$$U_t\left(t, \mathbf{x}\right) + \frac{1}{2} \sum_{m,n=1}^{N} a^{mn}\left(t, \mathbf{x}\right) U_{x^m x^n}\left(t, \mathbf{x}\right) \tag{4.25}$$

$$+ \sum_{n=1}^{N} b^n\left(t, \mathbf{x}\right) U_{x^n}\left(t, \mathbf{x}\right) - c\left(t, \mathbf{x}\right) U\left(t, \mathbf{x}\right) = 0,$$

$$U\left(T, \mathbf{x}\right) = u\left(\mathbf{x}\right),$$

and

$$V_t\left(t, \mathbf{x}\right) - \frac{1}{2} \sum_{m,n=1}^{N} \left(a^{mn}\left(t, \mathbf{x}\right) V\left(t, \mathbf{x}\right)\right)_{x^m x^n} \tag{4.26}$$

$$+ \sum_{n=1}^{N} \left(b^n\left(t, \mathbf{x}\right) V\left(t, \mathbf{x}\right)\right)_{x^n} + c\left(t, \mathbf{x}\right) U\left(t, \mathbf{x}\right) = 0,$$

$$V\left(0,\mathbf{x}\right)=v\left(\mathbf{x}\right),$$

in the form

$$U\left(t,\mathbf{x}\right)=\int_{\mathbb{R}^{N}}p\left(t,\mathbf{x},T,\boldsymbol{\xi}\right)u\left(\boldsymbol{\xi}\right)d\boldsymbol{\xi},$$

$$V\left(t,\mathbf{x}\right)=\int_{\mathbb{R}^{N}}p\left(0,\boldsymbol{\xi},t,\mathbf{x}\right)v\left(\boldsymbol{\xi}\right)d\boldsymbol{\xi}.$$

4.5   Wiener processes

Scalar Wiener processes which are the most important stochastic engines for continuous-time financial models have several important properties. They were introduced in Section 4.3 as examples of Markov processes. The t.p.d.f. for such processes is given by formula (4.5). Trajectories of Wiener processes are continuous. For the standard Wiener process starting at zero, $W_0 = 0$, we have

$$P\left\{W_{t_1}\in B_1,...,W_{t_N}\in B_N\right\} \tag{4.27}$$

$$=\int_{B_1}...\int_{B_N}H\left(t_1,x_1\right)H\left(t_2-t_1,x_2-x_1\right)$$

$$\times...\times H\left(t_N-t_{N-1},x_N-x_{N-1}\right)dx_1...dx_N,$$

where $t_0 = 0 < t_1 < t_2... < t_N = T$, and $H\left(t,x\right)$ is the one-dimensional heat kernel. This formula defines a probability measure P on the space Ω of continuous functions on the interval $[0,T]$.

Formula (4.27) shows that the Wiener process has independent normally distributed increments, i.e., that random variables W_{t_1}, $W_{t_2}-W_{t_1}$, ..., are independent normal variables $\mathfrak{N}\left(0,t_1\right)$, $\mathfrak{N}\left(0,t_2-t_1\right)$, ... In fact, this property defines the Wiener process. Symbolically,

$$W_{t'}-W_t\sim\sqrt{t'-t}. \tag{4.28}$$

More formally,

$$\mathbb{E}\left\{W_{t'}-W_t\right\}=0,$$

$$\mathbb{E}\left\{\left(W_{t'}-W_t\right)^2\right\}=t'-t. \tag{4.29}$$

One more useful formula which is used below is

$$\mathbb{E}\left\{|W_{t'} - W_t|\right\} = \sqrt{\frac{2(t'-t)}{\pi}}.$$ (4.30)

The characteristic function of the Wiener process is given by

$$\Phi(t, \varsigma) = e^{-t\varsigma^2/2},$$

while its covariation and correlation functions have the form

$$\Psi(t_1, t_2) = \mathbb{E}\left\{W_{t_1} W_{t_2}\right\} = \min\{t_1, t_2\},$$

$$\tilde{\Psi}(t_1, t_2) = \frac{\mathbb{E}\left\{W_{t_1} W_{t_2}\right\}}{\sqrt{\mathbb{E}\left\{W_{t_1}^2\right\} \mathbb{E}\left\{W_{t_2}^2\right\}}} = \min\left\{\sqrt{\frac{t_1}{t_2}}, \sqrt{\frac{t_2}{t_1}}\right\}.$$

The Wiener process W_t is a martingale, and so is the process $W_t^2 - t$. Levy's theorem states that every continuous scalar process ξ_t, such that ξ_t and $\xi_t^2 - t$ are martingales, is a Wiener process.

The Wiener process has important symmetry properties which show that the processes

$$W_t^{sym} = -W_t, \quad \text{(symmetry)},$$

$$W_t^{sca} = \sqrt{c} W_{t/c}, \quad \text{(scaling)},$$

$$W_t^{inv} = \begin{cases} 0, & t = 0 \\ tW_{1/t}, & t > 0 \end{cases}, \quad \text{(inversion)},$$

$$W_t^{ref} = \begin{cases} W_t, & t \leq T \\ 2W_T - W_t, & t \geq T \end{cases}, \quad \text{(reflection)},$$ (4.31)

are Wiener processes as well. In equation (4.31) T is a stopping time.

Due to the fact that the increments of the Wiener process are independent, we can use the strong law of large numbers and show that

$$\text{ac-lim} \frac{W_t}{t} = 0.$$

The behavior of the Wiener process can be described more precisely by the law of the iterated logarithm which states that asymptotically W_t oscillates between two parabolas,

$$\left\{ \begin{array}{c} \lim\sup_{t\to\infty} \\ \lim\inf_{t\to\infty} \end{array} \right\} \frac{W_t}{\sqrt{2t\ln(\ln t)}} = \left\{ \begin{array}{c} 1 \\ -1 \end{array} \right\}.$$

For small t we can use the scaling properties of the Wiener process and the law of iterated logarithm to get

$$\left\{ \begin{array}{c} \lim\sup_{t\to 0} \\ \lim\inf_{t\to 0} \end{array} \right\} \frac{W_t}{\sqrt{2t\ln(\ln 1/t)}} = \left\{ \begin{array}{c} 1 \\ -1 \end{array} \right\}.$$

Since a similar relation describes the behavior of the increment $W_{t'} - W_t$, we can conclude that trajectories of W_t are nowhere differentiable and have unbounded variation on any interval $[t, t']$, i.e.,

$$\lim_{N\to\infty} \sum_{n=1}^{N} |W_{t_n} - W_{t_{n-1}}| \to \infty,$$

where $t_0 = t < t_1 < t_2 ... < t_N = t'$. However, their quadratic variation is finite,

$$\lim_{N\to\infty} \sum_{n=1}^{N} |W_{t_n} - W_{t_{n-1}}|^2 = t' - t.$$

An important characteristic of a scalar Wiener process is the so-called Levy's local time $\lambda_{0,t}(y)$ at time t and level y which is defined as follows

$$\lambda_{0,t}(y) = \lim_{\varepsilon\to 0} \frac{1}{2\varepsilon} \int_0^t \chi_{[0,\varepsilon]}(|W_s - y|)\, ds,$$

where χ_ε is the characteristic function of the interval $[0, \varepsilon]$. The local time increases only when the value of W_s is equal to y. For fixed t, y the p.d.f. for the random variable $\lambda_{0,t}(y)$ has the form

$$f_{\lambda_{0,t}(y)}(x) = \left\{ \begin{array}{ll} 0, & x < 0 \\ 2H(t, x + |y|), & x \geq 0 \end{array} \right.,$$

its c.d.f. is given by

$$F_{\lambda_{0,t}(y)}(x) = \left\{ \begin{array}{ll} 0, & x < 0 \\ 2\mathfrak{N}\left(\frac{x+|y|}{\sqrt{t}}\right), & x \geq 0 \end{array} \right. . \tag{4.32}$$

Another useful quantity associated with the Wiener process is the so-called occupational time $\vartheta_{0,t}(B)$ which the Wiener process spends in a domain B. This quantity is defined by

$$\vartheta_{0,t}(B) = \int_0^t \chi_B(W_s)\,ds.$$

The occupational time and the local time are related as follows

$$\vartheta_{0,t}(B) = \int_B \lambda_{0,t}(y)\,dy.$$

The distribution of the occupational time for the positive semi-axis $B = (0, \infty)$ is governed by the celebrated Levy's arcsine law which states that the cumulative distribution function for $\vartheta_{0,t}((0, \infty))$ has the form

$$F_{\vartheta_{0,t}((0,\infty))}(s) = \frac{2}{\pi}\arcsin\sqrt{\frac{s}{t}}, \tag{4.33}$$

where $0 \le s \le t$.

We discuss other characteristics of Wiener processes such as the distribution of their extrema and the joint distribution of extrema and values in Chapter 13 when we price barrier options. We show how to derive important formulas (4.32), (4.33) in Chapter 13 as part of our study of path-dependent options.

Scalar Wiener processes with drift are deterministic functions of the standard Wiener processes,

$$W_t^{(\mu)} = \mu t + W_t.$$

For fixed t we have $W_t^{(\mu)} \sim \mathfrak{N}(\mu t, t)$. Such processes are supermartingales when $\mu < 0$ and submartingales when $\mu > 0$. Their t.p.d.f.'s have the form

$$p(\tau, x, x') = \frac{e^{-(x'-x-\mu\tau)^2/2\tau}}{\sqrt{2\pi\tau}} = H(\tau, x' - x - \mu\tau),$$

so that

$$P\left\{W_{t_1}^{(\mu)} \in B_1, ..., W_{t_N}^{(\mu)} \in B_N\right\} \tag{4.34}$$

$$= \int_{B_1} ... \int_{B_N} H(t_1, x_1 - \mu t_1)\, H(t_2 - t_1, x_2 - x_1 - \mu(t_2 - t_1))$$

$$\times ... \times H(t_N - t_{N-1}, x_N - x_{N-1} - \mu(t_N - t_{N-1}))\,dx_1...dx_N.$$

This formula defines a probability measure $P^{(\mu)}$ on the space Ω of continuous functions on the interval $[t, t']$.

The properties of $W_t^{(\mu)}$ are broadly similar to the properties of W_t. Moreover, by changing the measure on the space Ω of continuous real-valued functions on the interval $[0, T]$, we can transform $W_t^{(\mu)}$ into the standard Wiener process. Of course, in view of our treatment of random walks in Section 3.3, such a possibility does not come as a real surprise. The exact adjustment is described by the following theorem.

Cameron-Martin-Girsanov theorem. *Consider a Brownian motion with drift $W_t^{(\mu)}$ and denote by Ω the space of its trajectories. Let $P^{(\mu)}$ be the measure on this space defined by equation (4.34). Choose a finite time interval $[0, T]$. Put*

$$M_t = \exp\left(-\mu W_t - \frac{1}{2}\mu^2 t\right), \qquad 0 \le t \le T.$$

and define a new measure Q on the space of trajectories by

$$dQ(\omega) = M_T(\omega)\, dP^{(\mu)}(\omega) = \exp\left(-\mu W_T - \frac{1}{2}\mu^2 T\right) dP^{(\mu)}(\omega),$$

or, equivalently,

$$\frac{dQ(\omega)}{dP^{(\mu)}(\omega)} = M_T(\omega).$$

Then $W_t^{(\mu)}$ is a standard Wiener process with respect to the new measure Q.

The transformation $P^{(\mu)} \to Q$ is called the Girsanov transformation of measures. The quotient $dQ(\omega)/dP^{(\mu)}(\omega)$ is called the Radon-Nikodym derivative of Q with respect to $P^{(\mu)}$.

It is easy to understand the meaning of this theorem. Since

$$\sum_{n=1}^{N} \frac{(x_n - x_{n-1} - \mu(t_n - t_{n-1}))^2}{2(t_n - t_{n-1})} = \sum_{n=1}^{N} \frac{(x_n - x_{n-1})^2}{2(t_n - t_{n-1})} - \mu x_N + \frac{\mu^2 t_N}{2},$$

provided that $x_0 = 0$, $t_0 = 0$, we can immediately conclude that

$$P\left\{W_{t_1}^{(\mu)} \in B_1, ..., W_{t_N}^{(\mu)} \in B_N\right\} = e^{-\mu X_N + \mu^2 t_N/2} P\left\{W_{t_1} \in B_1, ..., W_{t_N} \in B_N\right\},$$

which is precisely the statement of the theorem.

It is useful to look at the Girsanov transformation from the PDE viewpoint. The problem for the t.p.d.f. $p(\tau, y)$ is

$$p_\tau(\tau, y) - \frac{1}{2}p_{yy}(\tau, y) + \mu p_y(\tau, y) = 0,$$

$$p(0, y) = \delta(y).$$

We introduce the transformed t.p.d.f. $q(\tau, y)$ according to

$$p(\tau, y) = e^{\mu y - \mu^2 \tau/2} q(\tau, y),$$

and obtain the following problem for $q(\tau, y)$:

$$q_\tau(\tau, y) - \frac{1}{2}q_{yy}(\tau, y) = 0,$$

$$q(0, y) = \delta(y).$$

Thus, q is the t.p.d.f. for the standard Wiener process.

The N-component Wiener process is a collection of independent scalar Wiener processes, $\mathbf{W}_t = (W_t^1, ..., W_t^N)$. Their properties can easily be deduced from the properties of scalar components. An intricate nuance is that the law of the iterated logarithm has the form

$$\left\{ \begin{array}{c} \lim\sup_{t\to\infty} \\ \lim\inf_{t\to\infty} \end{array} \right\} \frac{|\mathbf{W}_t|}{\sqrt{2t\ln(\ln t)}} = \left\{ \begin{array}{c} 1 \\ -1 \end{array} \right\}.$$

The fact that there is no prefactor $\sqrt{N}$ in this formula indicates that different components of W_t become large at different times. For $\mathbf{W}_t$ the t.p.d.f. has the form (4.6).

Typical trajectories of Wiener processes without and with drift are shown in Figures 4.1, 4.2.

4.6   Poisson processes

A scalar Poisson process has nonnegative integer values. In the financial engineering context such processes are used for modeling prices of financial instruments which exhibit jumps. In the physical world they are used for describing

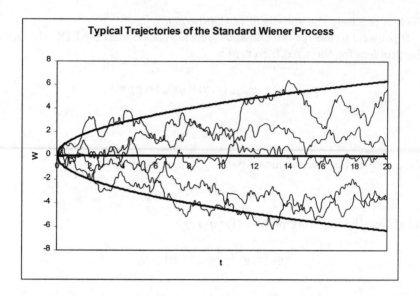

Figure 4.1: Typical trajectories of the standard Wiener process without drift. The limiting curves $W = \pm\sqrt{2t}$ and the mean $W = 0$ are shown in boldface.

various discrete random events such as the number of customer orders received by a retailer, the number of radioactive particles registered by a physical devise, etc. In a typical experiment the number of events is described by a Poisson process if the following three conditions are satisfied: (A) The number of events which occurred on the interval $[t, t + \tau]$ is independent on the number of events which occurred on the interval $[0, t]$; (B) The probability of exactly one event occurring on the interval $[t, t + \tau]$ is proportional to τ with the coefficient of proportionality λ, $\lambda\tau + o(\tau)$; (C) The probability of more than one event occurring on the interval $[t, t + \tau]$ is $o(\tau)$. In this case the random quantity ξ_t representing the total number of events which occurred on the interval $[0, t]$ is a Poisson process. The finite-dimensional distributions of such a process are defined by the formula

$$P\left\{\xi_{t_1} = k_1, \xi_{t_2} = k_2, ..., \xi_{t_N} = k_N\right\}$$

$$= \begin{cases} \prod_{n=1}^{N} e^{-\lambda(t_n - t_{n-1})} \dfrac{[\lambda(t_n - t_{n-1})]^{k_n - k_{n-1}}}{(t_n - t_{n-1})!}, & \text{if } k_1 \leq k_2 \leq ... \leq k_N \\ 0, & \text{in all other cases} \end{cases}.$$

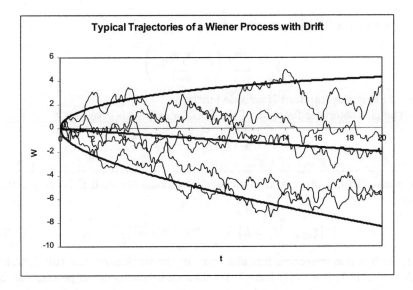

Figure 4.2: Typical trajectories of a Wiener process with drift $\mu = -0.1$. The limiting curves $W = \mu t \pm \sqrt{2t}$ and the mean $W = \mu t$ are shown in boldface.

where $t_0 = 0 < t_1 < t_2 ... < t_N = T$. Here λ is the parameter of the process which determines the average number of events occurring on the interval $[0, t]$:

$$\lambda = \frac{\mathbb{E}\{\xi_t\}}{t}.$$

The process ξ_t is stationary and has independent increments. These increments have Poisson distribution:

$$P\{\xi_\tau = k\} = P\{\xi_{t+\tau} - \xi_t = k\} = e^{-\lambda\tau}\frac{(\lambda\tau)^k}{k!}.$$

We consider a sequence of i.i.d. random variables $\eta_1, \eta_2, ...$, having the exponential distribution with parameter λ:

$$f_\eta(x) = \begin{cases} \lambda e^{-\lambda x}, & x \geq 0 \\ 0, & x < 0 \end{cases},$$

and construct a Poisson process as follows:

$$\xi_t = \sum_{n=1}^{\infty} \theta \left(t - \sum_{m=1}^{n} \eta_m \right).$$

Here $\theta(x)$ is the standard Heaviside function.

The characteristic function of the Poisson process is given by

$$\Phi(t, \varsigma) = e^{\lambda t (e^{i\varsigma} - 1)}.$$

We can extend the above definition and consider nonstationary Poisson processes. Such a process has independent increments with Poisson distribution:

$$P\{\xi_{t+\tau} - \xi_t = k\} = e^{-(\lambda_{t+\tau} - \lambda_t)} \frac{(\lambda_{t+\tau} - \lambda_t)^k}{k!}. \tag{4.35}$$

Here λ_t is a nondecreasing function of t. In the stationary case this function is $\lambda_t = \lambda t$. If λ_t is strictly increasing, then an inhomogeneous process can be made homogeneous by a simple change of time. Consider an inhomogeneous process defined on the interval $[0, \infty]$ by equation (4.35). Assuming that the function λ_t is increasing, we introduce on the interval $[\lambda_0, \lambda_\infty]$ the inverse function μ_t such that $\lambda_{\mu_t} = t$, and define a new process on this interval according to the rule $\tilde{\xi}_t = \xi_{\mu_t}$. A simple calculation yields

$$\begin{aligned}
P\left\{\tilde{\xi}_{t+\tau} - \tilde{\xi}_\tau = k\right\} &= P\left\{\xi_{\mu_{t+\tau}} - \xi_{\mu_t} = k\right\} \\
&= e^{-(\lambda_{\mu_{t+\tau}} - \lambda_{\mu_t})} \frac{\left(\lambda_{\mu_{t+\tau}} - \lambda_{\mu_t}\right)^k}{k!} \\
&= e^{-\tau} \frac{\tau^k}{k!},
\end{aligned}$$

provided that $\lambda_0 \leq t < t+\tau \leq \lambda_\infty$. Thus, $\tilde{\xi}_t$ is the standard stationary Poisson process with parameter 1.

A vector Poisson process has the form $\boldsymbol{\xi}_t = \left(\xi_t^1, ..., \xi_t^N\right)$, where ξ_t^n are scalar Poisson processes.

4.7   SDE and Mappings

For the purposes of financial engineering we need to map Wiener and Poisson processes which are the principal "stochastic engines" for continuous-time markets onto financially observable quantities. This can be done via stochastic differential equations.

Recall that a typical ordinary differential equation (ODE) can be written is several equivalent forms, namely,

$$\frac{dx_t}{dt} = b(t, x_t), \qquad x_0 \text{ is given,} \tag{4.36}$$

$$dx_t = b(t, x_t)\, dt, \qquad x_0 \text{ is given,} \tag{4.37}$$

$$x_t = x_0 + \int_0^t b(s, x_s)\, ds. \tag{4.38}$$

According to Picard's existence theorem in a sufficiently small neighborhood of the point $(0, x_0)$ the evolution of x_t is deterministic and is completely specified by the initial condition x_0, provided that b is a continuous function that satisfies the Lipschitz condition

$$|b(t, x) - b(t, y)| \leq L\,|x - y|.$$

We can introduce stochasticity into the picture by generalizing equations (4.36), (4.37), and (4.38) as follows:

$$\frac{dx_t}{dt} = b(t, x_t) + \sigma(t, x_t)\,\varpi_t, \qquad x_0 \text{ is given,} \tag{4.39}$$

$$dx_t = b(t, x_t)\, dt + \sigma(t, x_t)\, dW_t, \qquad x_0 \text{ is given,} \tag{4.40}$$

$$x_t = x_0 + \int_0^t b(s, x_s)\, ds + \int_0^t \sigma(s, x_s)\, dW_s, \tag{4.41}$$

where ϖ_t is the so-called white noise formally defined as the derivative of the standard Wiener process with respect to time,

$$\varpi_t = dW_t / dt.$$

Solutions of stochastic differential equations (SDEs) (4.39), (4.40), (4.41) exhibit sufficient randomness to describe the continuous evolution of FXRs and other financially relevant quantities. In situations when jumps are important, we need to incorporate Poisson process into our framework. The coefficients

b and σ are called the drift and volatility of the process x_t. An SDE is called autonomous if b and σ are time-independent.

The first generalization, which is due to Langevin is much less straightforward than the other two because of the highly irregular properties of the white noise and we do not consider it here. An obvious difficulty with formalizing the concept of SDEs written either in the differential form (4.40), or the integral form (4.41) is that W_s is so irregular that dW_s does not exist in the usual sense. Equation (4.28) suggests that, broadly speaking, $dW_s \sim \sqrt{ds}$. To illustrate the implications of this fact, we consider two integrals

$$I_{0,T} = \int_0^T f(s)\, dW_s,$$

where $f(t)$ is a nonrandom function, and

$$\tilde{I}_{0,T} = \int_0^T W_s dW_s.$$

Let $t_0 = 0, t_1, ..., t_{k-1}, t_K = T$ be a uniform partition of the interval $[0, T]$ into K subintervals, $t_k = kT/K$, and τ_k be some intermediate points, $t_{k-1} \leq \tau_k \leq t_k$. The first integral can be understood in the usual Riemann-Stieltjes sense

$$I_{0,T} = \lim_{K \to \infty} I_{0,T}^K,$$

where

$$I_{0,T}^K = \sum_{k=1}^K f(\tau_k) \left(W_{t_k} - W_{t_{k-1}} \right),$$

as can be expected. This integral is independent of the choice of intermediate points τ_i. However, this is not the case for the second integral. We have

$$\tilde{I}_{0,T} = \lim_{K \to \infty} \tilde{I}_{0,T}^K,$$

where

$$
\begin{aligned}
\tilde{I}_{0,T}^K &= \sum_{k=1}^K W_{\tau_k} \left(W_{t_k} - W_{t_{k-1}} \right) \\
&= \frac{1}{2} W_T^2 - \frac{1}{2} \sum_{k=1}^K \left(W_{t_k} - W_{t_{k-1}} \right)^2 + \sum_{k=1}^K \left(W_{\tau_k} - W_{t_{k-1}} \right)^2 \\
&\quad + \sum_{k=1}^K \left(W_{t_k} - W_{\tau_k} \right) \left(W_{\tau_k} - W_{t_{k-1}} \right).
\end{aligned}
$$

By using equation (4.29) and the fact the process W_t has independent increments, we obtain

$$
\begin{aligned}
\underset{K\to\infty}{\text{ms-lim}}\tilde{I}^K_{0,T} &= \frac{1}{2}W^2_T - \frac{1}{2}\lim_{K\to\infty}\sum^K_{k=1}(t_k - t_{k-1}) \\
&\quad + \lim_{K\to\infty}\sum^K_{k=1}(\tau_k - t_{k-1}) \\
&= \frac{1}{2}W^2_T - \frac{1}{2}T + \lim_{K\to\infty}\sum^K_{k=1}(\tau_k - t_{k-1}).
\end{aligned}
$$

It is obvious that the corresponding limit depends of the choice of τ_k. For instance, if we follow Ito and choose τ_k in a nonanticipating manner, $\tau_k = t_{k-1}$, we get

$$
\tilde{I}_{0,T} \overset{\text{Ito}}{=} \frac{1}{2}W^2_T - \frac{1}{2}T. \tag{4.42}
$$

On the other hand, if we choose τ_k according to Stratonovich, $\tau_k = (t_k + t_{k-1})/2$, we get

$$
\tilde{I}_{0,T} \overset{\text{Stratonovich}}{=} \frac{1}{2}W^2_T.
$$

Stratonovich's stochastic integrals have many nice properties. However, below we always use Ito's integrals because they are based on choosing the integrand in the nonanticipating way and are better suited for the purposes of financial engineering. There are relatively simple rules for transforming Ito's integrals into Stratonovich's integrals and *vice versa*.

Inspired by the above example, we define the general Ito's integral as a mean-square limit of nonanticipating integrals over step functions

$$
\begin{aligned}
I_{0,T} &= \int^T_0 f(s,\omega)\,dW_s(\omega) \\
&= \underset{K\to\infty}{\text{ms-lim}}\sum^K_{k=1}f(t_{k-1},\omega)\left(W_{t_k}(\omega) - W_{t_{k-1}}(\omega)\right),
\end{aligned}
$$

where ω is a particular trajectory (realization) of the Wiener process and $W_s(\omega)$ is its value at time s. It is clear that I is a random variable on Ω.

Due to the nonanticipating choice of intermediate points τ_k, $I_{0,t}$ is a martin-gale as function of t, so that

$$\mathbb{E}\left\{I_{0,t'}|\mathfrak{F}_t\right\} = I_{0,t},$$

where $\mathfrak{F}_t$ is the filtration generated by the Wiener process W_t. The martingale property is arguably the single most important property of Ito's integrals.

Below we understand an SDE as an integral equation (4.41) (with integra-tion performed according to Ito). The differential equation (4.40) is considered as a short-hand notation for the integral equation (4.41).

Conditions guarantying existence and uniqueness of solutions of SDE (4.41) are the Lipschitz condition

$$|b\left(t,x\right) - b\left(t,y\right)| + |\sigma\left(t,x\right) - \sigma\left(t,y\right)| \leq C\left|x-y\right|,$$

which guarantees that the coefficients of the SDE are sufficiently smooth, and the growth condition

$$|b\left(t,x\right)|^2 + |\sigma\left(t,x\right)|^2 \leq C\left(1 + |x|^2\right),$$

which guarantees that the coefficients grow at most linearly when $x \to \infty$. When these conditions are violated, solutions can have undesirable properties, for instance, they can blow up in finite time or even instantaneously. (This is not just a theoretical possibility, the blow up does occur when one solves the so-called Heath-Jarrow-Morton equations describing the dynamics of forward interest rates in fixed income.)

Since the rules of Ito's integration deviate from the familiar rules of classical analysis, so do the rules of Ito's differentiation. These are expressed by the celebrated Ito's lemma.

Scalar Ito's lemma. *Let x_t be a scalar stochastic process with stochastic differential of the form*

$$dx_t = b\left(t,x_t\right)dt + \sigma\left(t,x_t\right)dW_t,$$

where the coefficients are sufficiently regular. If $f\left(t,x\right)$ is a continuous func-tions with continuous derivatives f_t, f_x, f_{xx}, then the process $f\left(t,x_t\right)$ also has stochastic differential and

$$\begin{aligned} df\left(t,x_t\right) &= \left[f_t\left(t,x_t\right) + b\left(t,x_t\right)f_x\left(t,x_t\right) + \frac{1}{2}a\left(t,x_t\right)f_{xx}\left(t,x_t\right)\right]dt \\ &\quad + \sigma\left(t,x_t\right)f_x\left(t,x_t\right)dW_t, \end{aligned}$$

where $a(t,x) = \sigma^2(t,x)$. *Below we call* $a(t,x)$ *the diffusion coefficient.*

Heuristically, Ito's lemma can be understood as a second-order Taylor expansion formula based on the following multiplication rule

$$dt \cdot dt = 0, \quad dt \cdot dW_t = 0, \quad dW_t \cdot dW_t = dt.$$

For two processes x^1, x^2 governed by SDEs (4.41) the product rule consistent with Ito's calculus reads

$$d(x^1 x^2) = x^1 dx^2 + x^2 dx^1 + \sigma^1 \sigma^2 dt.$$

Example 4.6. *If we choose* $x_t = W_t$ *and* $f(t,x) = x^2/2$, *we get*

$$d\left[\frac{1}{2}W_t^2\right] = \frac{1}{2}dt + W_t dW_t,$$

so that

$$I_{0,t} = \int_0^t W_s dW_s = \frac{1}{2}W_t^2 - \frac{1}{2}t,$$

in agreement with formula (4.42).

Ito's lemma for scalar processes can be used provided that $f(t,x)$ can be differentiated ones with respect to t and twice with respect to x. Since in many situations interesting in the financial engineering context these conditions are violated, it is important to understand how this lemma can be extended. The best known extension is given by the so-called Meyer-Tanaka formula which covers the case when

$$f(x) = \max(x - y, 0) \equiv (x - y)_+,$$

where y is a given constant, or, more generally, when $f(x)$ is the difference of two convex functions. In the simplest case this formula can be written as

$$d(x_t - y)_+ = \theta(x_t - y)\, dx_t + \frac{1}{2}\lambda_{0,t}(y), \tag{4.43}$$

where $\lambda_{0,t}(y)$ is the local time for the process x_t at y.

Solutions of SDEs represent new stochastic processes generated by the standard Wiener process. These processes are martingales provided that $b = 0$. It can be shown that these processes are diffusions, so that they can be described in terms of the t.p.d.f.'s. The corresponding Kolmogoroff's backward and Fokker-Planck forward equations $p(t, x, t', x')$ have the form (4.10), (4.9) with a, b being the diffusion and drift, respectively.

In a typical financial engineering context we have to evaluate the conditional expectation

$$U(t, x) = \mathbb{E}\{f(x_T) \,|\, x_t = x\}, \tag{4.44}$$

for a given function $f(x)$. It can be shown that $U(t, x)$ solves the equation

$$U_t(t, x) + \frac{1}{2} a(t, x) U_{xx}(t, x) + b(t, x) U_x(t, x) = 0, \tag{4.45}$$

supplied with final condition

$$U(T, x) = f(x). \tag{4.46}$$

Thus, we can either compute the corresponding expectation (4.44) directly or solve the problem (4.45), (4.46) (if necessary, numerically).

If killing (or discounting) is important the expectation assumes the form

$$U(t, x) = \mathbb{E}\left\{ f(x_T) \exp\left(-\int_t^T c(s, x_s)\, ds \right) \bigg|\, x_t = x \right\}, \tag{4.47}$$

where $c(t, x) \geq 0$. The corresponding backward problem is

$$U_t(t, x) + \frac{1}{2} a(t, x) U_{xx}(t, x) + b(t, x) U_x(t, x) - c(t, x) U(t, x) = 0, \tag{4.48}$$

$$U(T, x) = f(x).$$

Formula (4.47) is known as the Feynman-Kac formula. It should be compared with formula (4.14).

Vector SDEs can be written in the differential form

$$d\mathbf{x}_t = \mathbf{b}(t, \mathbf{x}_t)\, dt + \sigma(t, \mathbf{x}_t)\, d\mathbf{W}_t,$$

or in the integral form

$$\mathbf{x}_t = \mathbf{x}_0 + \int_0^t \mathbf{b}(s, \mathbf{x}_s)\, ds + \int_0^t \sigma(s, \mathbf{x}_s)\, d\mathbf{W}_s.$$

Here $\mathbf{x}_t$ is a M-component stochastic process, $\mathbf{W}_t$ is the standard N-component Wiener process, $\mathbf{b}(s, \mathbf{x})$ is a M-component drift vector, and $\sigma(t, \mathbf{x})$ is a $M \times N$ volatility matrix. The corresponding integrals are defined by analogy with the scalar case.

It is not difficult to extend Ito's lemma to the vector case.

Vector Ito's lemma. *If* $\mathbf{x}_t$ *is a M-component vector stochastic process with stochastic differential of the form*

$$d\mathbf{x}_t = \mathbf{b}\left(t, \mathbf{x}_t\right) dt + \sigma\left(t, \mathbf{x}_t\right) d\mathbf{W}_t,$$

and $f\left(t, \mathbf{x}\right)$ *is a sufficiently smooth function, then* $f\left(t, \mathbf{x}_t\right)$ *also has stochastic differential and*

$$df\left(t, \mathbf{x}_t\right) = \left[f_t\left(t, \mathbf{x}_t\right) + \sum_m b^m\left(t, \mathbf{x}_t\right) f_{x^m}\left(t, \mathbf{x}_t\right) \right.$$

$$+ \frac{1}{2} \sum_{m,m'} a^{mm'}\left(t, \mathbf{x}\right) f_{x^m x^{m'}}\left(t, \mathbf{x}_t\right) \Bigg] dt$$

$$+ \sum_{m,n} \sigma_n^m\left(t, \mathbf{x}_t\right) f_{x^m}\left(t, \mathbf{x}_t\right) dW^n\left(t\right),$$

where $a\left(t, \mathbf{x}\right) = \sigma\left(t, \mathbf{x}_t\right) \cdot \sigma^T\left(t, \mathbf{x}_t\right)$ *is a* $M \times M$ *matrix,*

$$a^{mm'}\left(t, \mathbf{x}\right) = \sum_n \sigma_n^m\left(t, \mathbf{x}\right) \sigma_n^{m'}\left(t, \mathbf{x}\right).$$

The corresponding heuristic multiplication rule is

$$dt \cdot dt = 0, \quad dt \cdot dW_t^n = 0, \quad dW_t^n \cdot dW_t^{n'} = \delta^{nn'} dt,$$

where $\delta^{nn'}$ is the Kroneker's delta symbol.

Backward and forward parabolic equations associated with vector SDEs have the form (4.25), (4.26).

In general, solving vector SDEs is more difficult than solving their scalar counterparts and requires a lot of ingenuity. Below we solve such equations on a case by case basis as need arises.

4.8   Linear SDEs

In this section we consider linear SDEs which very frequently appear in financial engineering problems. Scalar SDEs linear in the broad sense have the form

$$dx_t = \left(\beta_0 + \beta_1 x_t\right) dt + \left(\sigma_0 + \sigma_1 x_t\right) dW_t,$$

where $\beta_0, \beta_1, \gamma, \delta$ are scalar functions of time, their vector counterparts have the form

$$d\mathbf{x}_t = (\boldsymbol{\beta}_0 + \beta_1 \mathbf{x}_t)\, dt + (\sigma_0 + \sigma_1 \mathbf{x}_t)\, d\mathbf{W}_t$$

where $\boldsymbol{\beta}_0, \beta_1, \sigma_0, \sigma_1$, are vector, matrix, matrix and tensor functions of time, respectively. Scalar and vector SDEs linear in the narrow sense have the form

$$dx_t = (\beta_0 + \beta_1 x_t)\, dt + \sigma_0 dW_t,$$

$$d\mathbf{x}_t = (\boldsymbol{\beta}_0 + \beta_1 \mathbf{x}_t)\, dt + \sigma_0 d\mathbf{W}_t,$$

respectively.

Surprisingly enough, even in the scalar case general linear SDEs cannot be solved explicitly. At the same time, an explicit solution for scalar SDEs linear in the narrow sense can easily be found.

We start with the following SDE linear in the narrow sense

$$dx_t = \beta_0 dt + \sigma_0 dW_t,$$

where β_0, β are constant parameters. This equation describes the arithmetic Brownian motion. Its solution is a Wiener process with drift starting at x_0,

$$x_t = x_0 + \beta_0 t + \sigma_0 W_t.$$

For time-dependent β_0, γ the corresponding solution is

$$x_t = x_0 + \int_0^t \beta_0(s)\, ds + \int_0^t \sigma_0(s)\, dW_s.$$

The arithmetic Brownian motion plays an important role in financial engineering where it is used to model the dynamics of returns on risky investments. For fixed t the random variable x_t is distributed normally,

$$x_t \sim \mathfrak{N}\left(x_0 + \beta_0 t, \sigma_0^2 t\right).$$

The process x_t is a martingale, supermartingale, and submartingale when $\beta_0 = 0$, $\beta_0 \le 0$, $\beta_0 \ge 0$, respectively.

The geometric Brownian motion is described by the following scalar SDE which is linear in the broad sense:

$$dx_t = \beta_1 x_t dt + \sigma_1 x_t dW_t. \tag{4.49}$$

We introduce

$$y_t = \ln\left(\frac{x_t}{x_0}\right),$$

and use Ito's lemma to get the following equation for y_t:

$$dy_t = \left(\beta_1 - \frac{1}{2}\sigma_1^2\right) dt + \sigma_1 dW_t.$$

Accordingly,

$$y_t = \left(\beta_1 - \frac{1}{2}\sigma_1^2\right) t + \sigma_1 W_t,$$

$$x_t = x_0 \exp\left(\left(\beta_1 - \frac{1}{2}\sigma_1^2\right) t + \sigma_1 W_t\right). \tag{4.50}$$

Equation (4.49) is extremely important in the financial context since it describes the evolution of prices of risky assets, and, in particular, FXRs. The fact that it has an explicit solution explains why so many problems of financial engineering can be solved in the closed form. Since y_t is distributed normally, x_t is distributed lognormally,

$$\ln x_t \sim \mathfrak{N}\left(\ln x_0 + \left(\beta_1 - \frac{1}{2}\sigma_1^2\right) t, \sigma_1^2 t\right).$$

Typical trajectories of a lognormal process are shown in Figure 4.3.

Another important scalar linear SDE describes the so-called Ornstein-Uhlenbeck (OU) process. This SDE has the form

$$dx_t = (\beta_0 - \beta_1 x_t) dt + \sigma_0 dW_t,$$

where $\beta_1 > 0$. Its deterministic counterpart has the form

$$dx_t = (\beta_0 - \beta_1 x_t) dt.$$

The solution of the above equation is

$$x_t = \frac{\beta_0}{\beta_1} + e^{-\beta_1 t}\left(x_0 - \frac{\beta_0}{\beta_1}\right),$$

it describes the transition of x_t from its initial value x_0 to its asymptotic value β_0/β_1. The corresponding time scale is $1/\beta_1$. We solve the Ornstein-Uhlenbeck

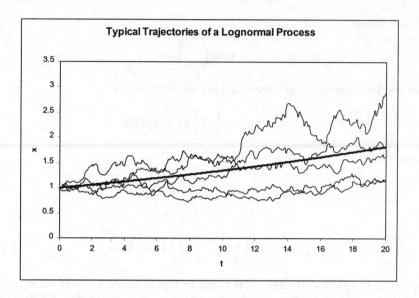

Figure 4.3: Typical trajectories of a lognormal process with $x_0 = 1$, $\beta_1 = 0.03$, $\sigma = 0.1$. The exponential trajectory $x = \exp(\beta_1 t)$ is shown in boldface.

equation via the method of variation of constants. Namely, we represent x_t in the form $x_t = e^{-\beta_1 t} y_t$ and verify that y_t follows the arithmetic Brownian motion,

$$dy = \beta_0 e^{\beta_1 t} dt + \sigma_0 e^{\beta_1 t} dW_t.$$

Accordingly,

$$y_t = x_0 + \frac{\beta_0 \left(e^{\beta_1 t} - 1 \right)}{\beta_1} + \int_0^t \sigma_0 e^{\beta_1 s} dW_s,$$

$$x_t = \frac{\beta_0}{\beta_1} + e^{-\beta_1 t} \left(x_0 - \frac{\beta_0}{\beta_1} \right) + \int_0^t \sigma_0 e^{-\beta_1 (t-s)} dW_s.$$

Thus, for fixed t the corresponding x_t is normal,

$$x_t \sim \mathfrak{N} \left(\frac{\beta_0}{\beta_1} + e^{-\beta_1 t} \left(x_0 - \frac{\beta_0}{\beta_1} \right), \frac{\sigma_0^2 \left(1 - e^{-2\beta_1 t} \right)}{2\beta_1} \right)$$

The corresponding stochastic process is called mean-reverting since its behavior is determined by two competing trends, namely, the deterministic attraction to the asymptotic level β_0/β_1 and the stochastic repulsion from this level. We emphasize that the variance of x_t does not become infinite when $t \to \infty$ (in sharp contrast with the standard Wiener process). The limiting random variable x_∞ has the form

$$x_\infty \sim \mathfrak{N}\left(\frac{\beta_0}{\beta_1}, \frac{\sigma_0^2}{2\beta_1}\right).$$

Trajectories of a typical Ornstein-Uhlenbeck process are shown in Figure 4.4.

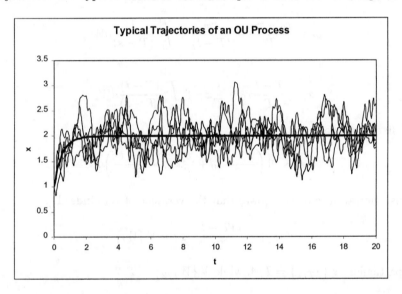

Figure 4.4: Typical trajectories of an Ornstein-Uhlenbeck process with $x_0 = 1$, $\beta_0 = 4$, $\beta_1 = 2$, $\sigma = 0.6$. The deterministic trajectory corresponding to $\sigma = 0$ is shown in boldface.

Brownian bridges form a particular subclass of Ornstein-Uhlenbeck processes with time dependent coefficients for which the emphasis is shifted from the mean reversion to exact fixing of their value x_T at time T. The corresponding SDE describing such bridges has the form

$$dx_t = \frac{x_T - x_t}{T - t}dt + dW_t. \tag{4.51}$$

It is clear that $x_{t \to T} \to x_T$. To solve equation (4.51) we use the same technique as before and introduce

$$y_t = \frac{x_t}{T - t}.$$

Ito's lemma yields the following SDE for y:

$$dy_t = \frac{x_T}{(T - t)^2} dt + \frac{1}{(T - t)} dW_t.$$

Thus, y_t is a Wiener process with drift. Accordingly,

$$y_t = \frac{x_0 - x_T}{T} + \frac{x_T}{(T - t)} + \int_0^t \frac{1}{(T - s)} dW_s,$$

$$x_t = \frac{T - t}{T} x_0 + \frac{t}{T} x_T + \int_0^t \frac{(T - t)}{(T - s)} dW_s.$$

For fixed t we have

$$x_t \sim \mathfrak{N} \left(\frac{T - t}{T} x_0 + \frac{t}{T} x_T, \frac{t(T - t)}{T} \right).$$

Thus, the variance of x_t is lower that the variance of W_t. Indeed

$$\mathbb{V} \{ x_t \} = \frac{t(T - t)}{T} < t = \mathbb{V} \{ W_t \}.$$

In particular, $\mathbb{V} \{ x_{T/2} \} = T/4$, while $\mathbb{V} \{ W_{T/2} \} = T/2$.

4.9   SDEs for jump-diffusions

It is very useful to extend the definition of stochastic processes described by SDEs by including jumps into the picture. A scalar SDEs governing the evolution of stochastic processes with jumps (which are called jump-diffusions) can be written in the form

$$dx_t = b(t, x_t) dt + \sigma(t, x_t) dW_t + j(t, x_t) y dN_t, \tag{4.52}$$

where W_t, N_t are standard Wiener and Poisson processes which are assumed to be independent. The intensity of the Poisson process N_t (i.e., the average number of jumps per unit time) is λ. The random variable y describes the magnitude of the jump when it occurs. Its p.d.f. is denoted by ϕ_y. As before, equation (4.52) is understood as a short-hand for the following integral relation

$$x_t = x_0 + \int_0^t b\,(t, x_t)\, dt + \int_0^t \sigma\,(t, x_t)\, dW_t + \sum_{n=1}^{N_t} j\,(t, x_t)\, y_n,$$

where y_n are i.i.d. random variables with the p.d.f. ϕ_y.

It can be shown that under mild constraints on the coefficients of equation (4.52) its solutions are right-continuous and left-bounded for any t. For jump-diffusions the following version of Ito's lemma holds.

Scalar Ito's lemma with jumps. *Let x_t be a right-continuous left-bounded scalar stochastic process with stochastic differential of the form*

$$dx_t = b\,(t, x_t)\, dt + \sigma\,(t, x_t)\, dW_t + j\,(t, x_t)\, y\, dN_t,$$

where the coefficients are sufficiently regular. If $f\,(t, x)$ is a continuous functions with continuous derivatives f_t, f_x, f_{xx}, then the process $f\,(t, x_t)$ also has stochastic differential and

$$df\,(t, x_t) = \left[f_t\,(t, x_{t-}) + b\,(t, x_{t-})\, f_x\,(t, x_{t-}) + \frac{1}{2} a\,(t, x_{t-})\, f_{xx}\,(t, x_{t-}) \right] dt$$
$$+ \sigma\,(t, x_{t-})\, f_x\,(t, x_{t-})\, dW_t + \left[f\,(t, x_{t-} + j\,(t, x_{t-})\, y) - f\,(t, x_{t-}) \right] dN_t,$$

where x_{t-} stands for the value of the process x_t just before the jump occurs.

For jump-diffusions the Feynman-Kac formula states that the expectation

$$U\,(t, x) = \mathbb{E}\left\{ f\,(x_T) \exp\left(-\int_t^T c\,(s, x_s)\, ds \right) | x_t = x \right\},$$

where $c\,(t, x) \geq 0$ solves the non-local partial integro-differential equation (PIDE) of the form

$$U_t\,(t, x) + \tfrac{1}{2} a\,(t, x)\, U_{xx}\,(t, x) + b\,(t, x)\, U_x\,(t, x) - c\,(t, x)\, U\,(t, x)$$
$$+ \lambda \int_{-\infty}^{\infty} \left[U\,(t, x + j\,(t, x)\, y) - U\,(t, x) \right] d\phi_y\,(y) = 0,$$

supplied with the standard final condition

$$U\,(T, x) = f\,(x).$$

The final value problem for PIDEs is usually more complex than the corresponding problem for PDEs due to its non-locality. However, it is shown below that in several interesting cases it can be solved explicitly.

4.10   Analytical solution of PDEs

4.10.1   Introduction

Analytical solution of the PDEs of financial engineering is a challenging task. Problems which can be solved analytically are not only interesting in their own right but also serve as useful benchmarks for other problems which can only be solved numerically. There are many methods which can be used for solving parabolic equations analytically. In this section we discuss three methods which are repeatedly used below. Other methods which are used less frequently, are introduced when they are needed for a specific application.

4.10.2   The reduction method

Consider a process which is governed by the SDE:

$$dS_t = b(t, S_t)dt + \sigma(t, S_t)dW_t,$$

and is killed at the rate $c(t, S_t)$. The corresponding backward Kolmogoroff equation with killing is

$$V_t(t, S) + \frac{1}{2}a(t, S) V_{SS}(t, S) + b(t, S) V_S(t, S) - c(t, S) V(t, S) = 0, \quad (4.53)$$

where $a(t, S) = \sigma^2(t, S)$.[1] The main idea of the reduction method is to transform this equation into the simplest possible form, preferably, into the standard backward heat equation, or, more generally, to the Bessel equation, by using changes of independent and dependent variables. In probabilistic terms it means that we transform a given killed stochastic process into a known stochastic process.

Reducibility to the Wiener process

First, we derive conditions on the coefficients of the backward parabolic equation which guarantee that it is reducible to the standard backward heat equation

$$U_\vartheta(\vartheta, X) + \frac{1}{2}U_{SS}(\vartheta, X) = 0,$$

---

[1] When we discuss the reduction method, we change our standard notation in order to make connections with specific problems considered in Chapter 10 more transparent.

by virtue of the following transformations:

$$U\left(\vartheta, X\right) = e^{-\mathtt{A}(t,S)} V\left(t, S\right), \quad \vartheta = \mathtt{B}\left(t\right), \quad X = \mathtt{C}\left(t, S\right). \tag{4.54}$$

The change of dependent variable yields the equation for $U\left(t, S\right)$,

$$U_t + \frac{1}{2} a U_{SS} + \tilde{b} U_S - \tilde{c} U = 0,$$

where

$$\tilde{b} = a\mathtt{A}_S + b,$$

$$\tilde{c} = - \left(\mathtt{A}_t + \frac{1}{2} a \left(\mathtt{A}_{SS} + \mathtt{A}_S^2 \right) + b\mathtt{A}_S \right) + c.$$

Here we use the relations

$$\partial_S e^{\mathtt{A}} = e^{\mathtt{A}} \left(\partial_S + \mathtt{A}_S \right),$$

$$\partial_S^2 e^{\mathtt{A}} = e^{\mathtt{A}} \left(\partial_S^2 + 2\mathtt{A}_S \partial_S + \mathtt{A}_{SS} + \mathtt{A}_S^2 \right),$$

$$\partial_t e^{\mathtt{A}} = e^{\mathtt{A}} \left(\partial_t + \mathtt{A}_t \right).$$

The change of independent variables yields the equation for $U\left(\vartheta, X\right)$,

$$U_\vartheta + \frac{1}{2} \frac{a\mathtt{C}_S^2}{\mathtt{B}_t} U_{XX} + \frac{\mathtt{C}_t + a\mathtt{C}_{SS}/2 + \tilde{b}\mathtt{C}_S}{\mathtt{B}_t} U_X - \frac{\tilde{c}}{\mathtt{B}_t} U = 0.$$

Here we use the relations

$$\partial_S = \mathtt{C}_S \partial_X, \quad \partial_S^2 = \mathtt{C}_S^2 \partial_X^2 + \mathtt{C}_{SS} \partial_X, \quad \partial_t = \mathtt{B}_t \partial_\vartheta + \mathtt{C}_t \partial_X.$$

It is important to emphasize that the derivatives of $\mathtt{B}, \mathtt{C}$ are taken with respect to the original variables t, S rather than the modified variables ϑ, X. In order to obtain the heat equation we have to impose the following reducibility conditions:

$$\frac{a\mathtt{C}_S^2}{\mathtt{B}_t} = 1,$$

$$C_t + \frac{1}{2}aC_{SS} + (aA_S + b)C_S = 0, \tag{4.55}$$

$$A_t + \frac{1}{2}a\left(A_{SS} + A_S^2\right) + bA_S - c = 0. \tag{4.56}$$

By using the first condition we can rewrite the other two as follows

$$C_t + \frac{1}{2}aC_{SS} + bC_S + P\sigma A_S = 0,$$

$$A_t + \frac{1}{2}aA_{SS} + bA_S - c + \frac{1}{2}aA_S^2 = 0,$$

where $P = \sqrt{B_t}$. The first reducibility condition yields

$$C(t, S) = P(t)I(t, S) + Q(t), \tag{4.57}$$

where

$$I(t, S) = \int d\zeta/\sigma(t, \zeta).$$

We introduce

$$\Omega = -A_S$$

differentiate equation (4.56) with respect to S and obtain

$$\Omega_t + \left(\frac{1}{2}a\left(\Omega_S - \Omega^2\right) + b\Omega + c\right)_S = 0. \tag{4.58}$$

We use equations (4.55), (4.57) to get

$$\begin{aligned}
\Omega &= \frac{(PI + Q)_t + P(aI_{SS}/2 + bI_S)}{P\sigma} \\
&= \frac{P_t I}{P\sigma} + \frac{I_t}{\sigma} + \frac{Q_t}{P\sigma} - \frac{\sigma_S}{2\sigma} + \frac{b}{\sigma^2},
\end{aligned}$$

thus obtaining the reducibility condition written in terms of the coefficients $a = \sigma^2, b, c$ and two arbitrary functions of time P, Q. We emphasize that condition (4.58) is constructive since it not only guarantees that the reduction is possible, but also shows how it can be achieved.

To illustrate the efficiency of condition (4.58) we show how to use it to prove the well-known Bluman theorem. This theorem deals with the reducibility of the killed Wiener process to the standard Wiener process, or, to put it differently, the reducibility of the equation

$$V_t + \frac{1}{2}V_{SS} - cV = 0,$$

to the standard backward heat equation. In the case in question we have $a = 1, b = 0$, so that

$$\vartheta = \mathrm{B}(t) = \int \mathrm{P}^2(t)\, dt,$$

$$X = \mathrm{C}(t, S) = \mathrm{P}(t)\, S + \mathrm{Q}(t),$$

$$\Omega = \frac{C_t + C_{SS}/2}{\mathrm{P}} = \frac{\mathrm{P}_t}{\mathrm{P}} S + \frac{\mathrm{Q}_t}{\mathrm{P}}.$$

Accordingly, the reducibility condition can be written in the form

$$\left(\left(\frac{\mathrm{P}_t}{\mathrm{P}}\right)_t - \frac{\mathrm{P}_t^2}{\mathrm{P}^2}\right) S + \left(\left(\frac{\mathrm{Q}_t}{\mathrm{P}}\right)_t - \frac{\mathrm{P}_t \mathrm{Q}_t}{\mathrm{P}^2}\right) + c_S = 0. \qquad (4.59)$$

For solvability of this equation, it is necessary and sufficient that

$$
\begin{aligned}
c &= -\frac{1}{2}\left(\left(\frac{\mathrm{P}_t}{\mathrm{P}}\right)_t - \frac{\mathrm{P}_t^2}{\mathrm{P}^2}\right) S^2 - \left(\left(\frac{\mathrm{Q}_t}{\mathrm{P}}\right)_t - \frac{\mathrm{P}_t \mathrm{Q}_t}{\mathrm{P}^2}\right) S - R \\
&= \frac{1}{2}\mathrm{P}\left(\frac{1}{\mathrm{P}}\right)_{tt} S^2 - \mathrm{P}\left(\frac{\mathrm{Q}_t}{\mathrm{P}^2}\right)_t S + R,
\end{aligned}
$$

where R is an arbitrary function of time (on a par with P, Q). Thus, a Wiener process killed at the rate

$$c = \frac{1}{2}\alpha(t) S^2 + \beta(t) S + \gamma(t),$$

is equivalent to the standard Wiener process. To carry out the corresponding reduction for a given c we have to find P, Q. For a given quadratic c equation (4.59) yields the following linear equations for $1/\mathrm{P}$ and Q_t:

$$(1/\mathrm{P})_{tt} - \alpha/\mathrm{P} = 0, \qquad \left(\mathrm{Q}_t/\mathrm{P}^2\right)_t + \beta/\mathrm{P} = 0.$$

Bluman's theorem has interesting applications in the fixed income context which will be described elsewhere.

Reducibility to the Bessel process

We now study conditions under which a diffusion can be reduced to a Bessel process of order ν, or, equivalently, equation (4.53) can be reduced to the backward parabolic equation of the form [2]

$$U_\vartheta(X, \vartheta) + \frac{1}{2}U_{XX}(X, \vartheta) + \frac{1 - 2\nu}{2X}U_X(X, \vartheta) = 0.$$

Conditions guaranteeing that a diffusion is reducible to the Bessel process via transformations (4.54) have the form

$$\frac{a\mathsf{C}_S^2}{\mathsf{B}_t} = 1,$$

$$\frac{\mathsf{C}_t + \frac{1}{2}a\mathsf{C}_{SS} + (a\mathsf{A}_S + b)\,\mathsf{C}_S}{\mathsf{B}_t} = \frac{1 - 2\nu}{2\mathsf{C}},$$

$$\mathsf{A}_t + \frac{1}{2}a\left(\mathsf{A}_{SS} + \mathsf{A}_S^2\right) + b\mathsf{A}_S - c = 0.$$

By using the first condition, we rewrite the second and the third conditions as

$$\mathsf{C}_t + \frac{1}{2}a\mathsf{C}_{SS} + b\mathsf{C}_S + \mathsf{P}\sigma\mathsf{A}_S = \frac{(1 - 2\nu)\,\mathsf{P}^2}{2\mathsf{C}},$$

$$\mathsf{A}_t + \frac{1}{2}a\mathsf{A}_{SS} + b\mathsf{A}_S - c + \frac{1}{2}a\mathsf{A}_S^2 = 0.$$

As before C has the form (4.57), while the reducibility condition has the form (4.58). However, the expression for Ω is different,

$$
\begin{aligned}
\Omega &= \frac{(\mathsf{P}I + \mathsf{Q})_t + \mathsf{P}\,(aI_{SS}/2 + bI_S)}{\mathsf{P}\sigma} - \frac{(1 - 2\nu)\,\mathsf{P}}{2\,(\mathsf{P}I + \mathsf{Q})\,\sigma} \\
&= \frac{\mathsf{P}_t I}{\mathsf{P}\sigma} + \frac{I_t}{\sigma} + \frac{\mathsf{Q}_t}{\mathsf{P}\sigma} - \frac{\sigma_S}{2\sigma} + \frac{b}{\sigma^2} - \frac{(1 - 2\nu)\,\mathsf{P}}{2\,(\mathsf{P}I + \mathsf{Q})\,\sigma}.
\end{aligned}
$$

---

[2] This equation describes the propagation of heat from a spherically symmetric source in the $(2 - 2\nu)$-dimensional space.

4.10.3 The Laplace transform method

A typical initial value problem associated with a scalar stationary process on the entire real axis which is governed by an autonomous SDE with drift $b(X)$ and volatility $\sigma(X)$ and killed at a rate $c(X)$ can be written in the form

$$\mathsf{m}(X)\,U_\tau(\tau,X) - \frac{1}{2}\frac{\partial}{\partial X}\left(\frac{1}{\mathsf{s}(X)}\frac{\partial}{\partial X}U(\tau,X)\right) + \mathsf{k}(X)\,U(\tau,X) = 0, \quad (4.60)$$

$$U(0,X) = u(X), \qquad (4.61)$$

where $\mathsf{s}(X)$, $\mathsf{m}(X)$, $\mathsf{k}(X)$ are the natural scale density, and speed and killing measures.

The Laplace transform method is very well suited for solving the above problem. The Laplace transform is defined as follows

$$U(\tau,X) \to \Theta(\lambda,X) = \int_0^\infty e^{-\lambda\tau}U(\tau,X)\,d\tau.$$

By using the standard properties of the Laplace transform we can derive the equation for $\Theta(\lambda,X)$:

$$\lambda\mathsf{m}(X)\,\Theta(\lambda,X) - \frac{1}{2}\frac{\partial}{\partial X}\left(\frac{1}{\mathsf{s}(X)}\frac{\partial}{\partial X}\Theta(\lambda,X)\right) + \mathsf{k}(X)\,\Theta(\lambda,X) = \mathsf{m}(X)\,u(X).$$

Thus, $\Theta(\lambda,X)$ solves the inhomogeneous ODE which is much easier to handle than the original PDE for $U(\tau,X)$. In many cases of practical interest $\Theta(\lambda,X)$ can be found explicitly. The major difficulty, however, is in the evaluation of the inverse Laplace transform

$$\Theta(\lambda,X) \to U(\tau,X) = \frac{1}{2\pi i}\int_{c-i\infty}^{c+i\infty} e^{\lambda\tau}U(\tau,X)\,d\tau,$$

where c is a suitably chosen real number. The numerical inversion of the Laplace transform is an ill-posed operation which causes serious problems when it is performed in practice. However, in some cases it can be suitably regularized. Moreover, in some cases the inversion can be done analytically.

It is easy to extend the Laplace transform method to cover the case when the process X is considered on the interval $[e_1, e_2]$, rather than on the entire axis.

4.10.4 The eigenfunction expansion method

The eigenfunction expansion method complements the Laplace transform method. In many cases the former method is much more efficient than the latter and leads to more tractable formulas.

The method is particularly useful for studying the case when X is considered on a finite interval $[e_1, e_2]$ with regular end points. To be concrete we assume that the process X is killed at e_1, e_2, so that

$$U(\tau, e_1) = U(\tau, e_2) = 0. \qquad (4.62)$$

In a nutshell the method can be summarized as follows. First, we use separation of variables are consider particular solutions of equation (4.60) of the form

$$U_\mu(\tau, X) = e^{-\mu\tau} U_\mu(X).$$

We assume that these particular solutions satisfy boundary conditions (4.62). In general, these solutions do not satisfy initial condition (4.61). Substitution of this expression in equation (4.60) and boundary conditions (4.62) yields the so-called spectral problem for $U_\mu(X)$:

$$-\mu \mathrm{m}(X) U_\mu(X) - \frac{1}{2} \frac{\partial}{\partial X} \left(\frac{1}{\mathrm{s}(X)} \frac{\partial}{\partial X} U_\mu(X) \right) + \mathrm{k}(X) U_\mu(X) = 0, \qquad (4.63)$$

$$U_\mu(e_1) = U_\mu(e_2) = 0. \qquad (4.64)$$

This problem is homogeneous. It has nontrivial (nonzero) solutions only for some special values of μ which are called eigenvalues of the problem, the corresponding solutions $U_\mu(X)$ (which are defined up to a multiplicative constant) are called eigenvectors. The set of all eigenvalues is called the spectrum of the problem (4.63), (4.64). Multiplying equation (4.63) by $U_\mu^*(X)$, where the superscript asterisk * denotes the complex conjugation, and integrating by parts we get

$$\mu = \frac{\int_{e_1}^{e_2} \left\{ \frac{1}{2\mathrm{s}(X)} \left| \frac{\partial}{\partial X} U_\mu(X) \right|^2 + \mathrm{k}(X) |U_\mu(X)|^2 \right\} dX}{\int_{e_1}^{e_2} \mathrm{m}(X) |U_\mu(X)|^2 dX}.$$

Thus, μ is real and nonnegative, so that, without loss of generality, we can assume that $U_\mu(X)$ is real. Moreover, it is easy to check that eigenfunctions corresponding to different eigenvalues μ, μ' are orthogonal with respect to the measure $\mathsf{m}(X)$, i.e.,

$$\int_{e_1}^{e_2} \mathsf{m}(X) U_\mu(X) U_{\mu'}(X) \, dX = 0.$$

When the coefficients $\mathsf{s}(X)$, $\mathsf{m}(X)$, $\mathsf{k}(X)$ are well-behaved the spectrum of the problem is purely discrete and consist of an infinite number of isolated eigenvalues. These eigenvalues are denoted by $\mu_1, ..., \mu_n, ...$, where $\mu_1 ... < \mu_n < ...$, while the corresponding eigenvectors are denoted by $U_1(X), ..., U_n(X), ...$ We assume that $U_n(X)$ are normalized as follows

$$\int_{e_1}^{e_2} \mathsf{m}(X) U_n(X) U_n(X) \, dX = \delta_{nn'}, \tag{4.65}$$

where $\delta_{nn'}$ is the Kronecker delta, $\delta_{nn'} = 0$, $n \neq n'$, $\delta_{nn} = 1$. The general solution of equation (4.60) has the form

$$U(\tau, X) = \sum_{n=1}^{\infty} e^{-\mu_n \tau} v_n U_n(X),$$

where v_n are arbitrary coefficients. In order to satisfy initial condition (4.61) we have to choose these coefficients in such a way that

$$u(X) = \sum_{n=1}^{\infty} v_n U_n(X).$$

We leave it to the reader as an exercise to show that

$$v_n = \int_{e_1}^{e_2} u(X) U_n(X) \, dX.$$

(Hint: use normalization conditions (4.65).) Thus, the solution of the initial-boundary value problem can be represented in the form

$$U(\tau, X) = \sum_{n=1}^{\infty} e^{-\mu_n \tau} \left(\int_{e_1}^{e_2} u(X) U_n(X) \, dX \right) U_n(X).$$

Consider, for example, the standard Wiener process W_t killed at the end points e_1, e_2, where $-\infty < e_1 < e_2 < \infty$. The corresponding spectral problem has the form

$$-\mu U_\mu(X) - \frac{1}{2} \frac{\partial^2 U_\mu(X)}{\partial X^2} = 0,$$

$$U_\mu(e_1) = U_\mu(e_2) = 0.$$

It has nontrivial solutions when

$$\mu = \mu_n = \frac{n^2\pi^2}{2(e_2 - e_1)^2}.$$

The corresponding normalized eigenvectors are

$$U_n(X) = \sqrt{\frac{2}{(e_2 - e_1)}} \sin\left(\frac{n\pi}{(e_2 - e_1)}(X - e_1)\right).$$

Accordingly, the solution of the initial value problem is

$$
\begin{aligned}
U(\tau, X) =\ & \sqrt{\frac{2}{(e_2 - e_1)}} \sum_{n=1}^{\infty} \exp\left(-\frac{n^2\pi^2}{2(e_2 - e_1)^2}\tau\right) \\
& \times v_n \sin\left(\frac{n\pi}{(e_2 - e_1)}(X - e_1)\right),
\end{aligned}
$$

where

$$v_n = \sqrt{\frac{2}{(e_2 - e_1)}} \int_{e_1}^{e_2} u(X) \sin\left(\frac{n\pi}{(e_2 - e_1)}(X - e_1)\right) dX,$$

is the Fourier sine coefficient of $u(X)$. In particular, when

$$u(X) = \delta(X - Y), \quad e_1 < Y < e_2,$$

the corresponding solution $U(\tau, X, Y)$ represents the t.p.d.f. for the Wiener process killed at the end points. We have

$$
\begin{aligned}
U(\tau, X, Y) =\ & \frac{2}{(e_2 - e_1)} \sum_{n=1}^{\infty} \exp\left(-\frac{n^2\pi^2}{2(e_2 - e_1)^2}\tau\right) \\
& \times \sin\left(\frac{n\pi(X - e_1)}{(e_2 - e_1)}\right) \sin\left(\frac{n\pi(Y - e_1)}{(e_2 - e_1)}\right).
\end{aligned}
$$

4.11   Numerical solution of PDEs

4.11.1   Introduction

It was mentioned above on several occasions that parabolic PDEs which are important in the financial context are also important in many other areas of science and engineering. Since such PDEs can be solved analytically only in exceptional situations, a lot of concentrated effort was devoted by scientists and engineers for designing efficient numerical algorithms for solving parabolic PDEs. There are many different approaches to solving PDEs stretching form finite differences, to finite elements, to methods of lines, Monte Carlo, boundary elements, etc. Finite difference methods have firmly established themselves as the most versatile and powerful methods for solving "standard" parabolic problems. They can be used to solve both one- and multi-dimensional Kolmogoroff and Fokker-Planck equations, however, when the dimension exceeds four, their efficiency rapidly deteriorates and Monte Carlo methods become dominant. In this section we briefly explain how to solve parabolic problems via the method of finite differences.

4.11.2 Explicit, implicit, and Crank-Nicolson schemes for solving one-dimensional problems

We start with the one-dimensional case. To be specific, we consider equation (4.13) which is a backward Kolmogoroff equation for a killed diffusion. The key idea is to convert the original PDE into a system of algebraic equations. This is done by replacing the (t, X)-plane by a grid

$$t_m = mk, \qquad X_n = X_{\min} + nh,$$

where k is the step size in the t direction and h is the step size in the X direction,

$$k = \frac{T}{M}, \qquad h = \frac{X_{\max} - X_{\min}}{N}.$$

and approximating $U(t, X)$ by a set of values $\tilde{U}_{m,n}$, $U(t, X) \approx \tilde{U}_{m,n}$. The values $X_{\min}, X_{\max}$ are either the smallest and largest X-values of interest (if the stochastic process is considered on the entire axis), or the boundary values (if this process is considered on the interval $[e_1, e_2]$). Next, the derivatives ∂_t and ∂_X are approximated by finite differences. There are several possibilities, and, depending on which one is chosen, different schemes are produced. Since equation (4.13) is backward in nature, we use backward differences in the t variable and approximate ∂_t as:

$$U_t(t, X)|_{t=t_m, X=X_n} \approx \frac{\tilde{U}_{m,n} - \tilde{U}_{m-1,n}}{k} + O(k). \qquad (4.66)$$

Whenever possible, we use central differences in the X variable and approximate $\partial_X, \partial^2_{XX}$ as

$$U_X(t,X)\,|_{t=t_m,X=X_n} = \frac{\tilde{U}_{m,n+1} - \tilde{U}_{m,n-1}}{2h} + O\left(h^2\right) \qquad (4.67)$$

$$\equiv \frac{1}{2h}\mathcal{E}\tilde{U}_{m,n} + O\left(h^2\right),$$

$$U_{XX}(t,X)\,|_{t=t_m,X=X_n} = \frac{\tilde{U}_{m,n+1} - 2\tilde{U}_{m,n} + \tilde{U}_{m,n-1}}{h^2} + O\left(h^2\right) \quad (4.68)$$

$$\equiv \frac{1}{h^2}\mathcal{F}\tilde{U}_{m,n} + O\left(h^2\right),$$

where $\mathcal{E}, \mathcal{F}$ are central difference operators of the form

$$\mathcal{E}\tilde{U}_{m,n} = \tilde{U}_{m,n+1} - \tilde{U}_{m,n-1},$$
$$\mathcal{F}\tilde{U}_{m,n} = \tilde{U}_{m,n+1} - 2\tilde{U}_{m,n} + \tilde{U}_{m,n-1}.$$

When the drift term is large compared with the diffusion term, it might be necessary to use either a forward or a backward approximation for U_X (depending on the direction of the drift).

The easiest way to solve equation (4.13) numerically is via an explicit scheme. The corresponding equations are

$$\tilde{U}_{m-1,n} = \tilde{U}_{m,n} + \frac{v}{2}a_{m,n}\mathcal{F}\tilde{U}_{m,n} + \frac{hv}{2}b_{m,n}\mathcal{E}\tilde{U}_{m,n} - h^2 v c_{m,n}\tilde{U}_{m,n}, \qquad (4.69)$$

where $a_{m,n} = a(t_m, X_n)$, etc. Here is the ratio

$$v = \frac{k}{h^2},$$

which is a very important characteristics of the grid. Equations (4.69) are solved by marching backward in m starting with $\tilde{U}_{M,n} = u(X_n)$. The values $\tilde{U}_{m,0}$ and $\tilde{U}_{m,N}$ are supplied by the boundary conditions. The main drawback of the explicit scheme is that the time spacing often has to be very small in order for the scheme to be stable. Roughly speaking, the explicit scheme is stable when

$$v \sim 1.$$

Thus, the explicit scheme is simple but inefficient. In view of equations (4.66)-(4.68) it is first-order accurate in t and second-order accurate in X.

To overcome the need for very small time steps we can use an implicit scheme and average the values of spacial derivatives evaluated at times t_m and t_{m-1}. The corresponding scheme is

$$\tilde{U}_{m-1,n} - \frac{\theta v}{2}a_{m-1,n}\mathcal{F}\tilde{U}_{m-1,n} - \frac{\theta h v}{2}b_{m-1,n}\mathcal{E}\tilde{U}_{m-1,n} + \theta h^2 v c_{m-1,n}\tilde{U}_{m-1,n}$$
$$= \tilde{U}_{m,n} + \frac{(1-\theta)v}{2}a_{m,n}\mathcal{F}\tilde{U}_{m,n} + \frac{(1-\theta)h v}{2}\mathcal{E}\tilde{U}_{m,n} - (1-\theta)h^2 v c_{m,n}\tilde{U}_{m,n},$$

$$(4.70)$$

where θ is an arbitrary weight sandwiched between 0 and 1. When $\theta = 0$ we recover the explicit scheme. When $\theta = 1$ we obtain the fully implicit scheme.

To move one time step backward we need to solve the tridiagonal system of linear equations for $\tilde{U}_{m-1,n}$. Although several methods of linear algebra are available for solving this system efficiently, its solution is still relatively expensive. However, since the implicit scheme is usually unconditionally stable (provided that θ is sufficiently close to one) it can be used with large time spacing which compensates for the difficulties associated with individual steps.

In general, an implicit scheme is first-order accurate in t and second-order accurate in X. When $\theta = 1/2$ equation (4.70) describes the celebrated Crank-Nicolson scheme which is second-order accurate in both t and X. The higher accuracy of the latter scheme compared to other implicit schemes is due to the fact that Crank-Nicolson approximate ∂_t by a central difference with respect to the middle point $(m + 1/2)\,k$. At present, this scheme is considered to be the best one for solving "standard" one-dimensional parabolic equations.

Typical finite difference schemes are shown in Figure 4.5.

4.11.3   ADI scheme for solving two-dimensional problems

Consider the two-dimensional backward parabolic equation for the unknown function $U(t, X^1, X^2)$ defined in a rectangular domain $\{e_1^1 \le X^1 \le e_2^1, e_1^2 \le X^2 \le e_2^2\}$. For convenience, we write it explicitly:

$$U_t(t, X^1, X^2) + \frac{1}{2}a^{11}(t, X^1, X^2)U_{X^1 X^1}(t, X^1, X^2)$$

$$+ \quad a^{12}(t, X^1, X^2)U_{X^1 X^2}(t, X^1, X^2) + \frac{1}{2}a^{22}(t, X^1, X^2)U_{X^2 X^2}(t, X^1, X^2)$$

$$+ \quad b^1(t, X^1, X^2)U_{X^1}(t, X^1, X^2) + b^2(t, X^1, X^2)U_{X^2}(t, X^1, X^2)$$

$$- \quad c(t, X^1, X^2)U(t, X^1, X^2) = 0,$$

$$U(T, X^1, X^2) = u\left(X^1, X^2\right),$$

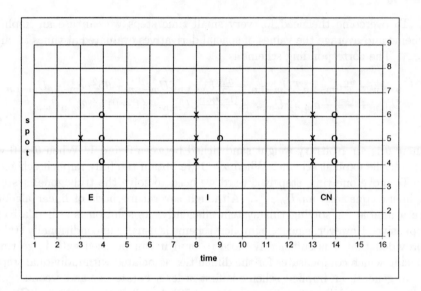

Figure 4.5: Explicit (E), implicit (I), and Crank-Nickolson (CN) finite differencing schemes for solving a backward Kolmogoroff equation.

$$U\left(t,e_1^1,X^2\right) = u_1^1\left(t,X^2\right), \quad U\left(t,e_2^1,X^2\right) = u_2^1\left(t,X^2\right),$$
$$U\left(t,X^1,e_1^2\right) = u_1^2\left(t,X^1\right), \quad U\left(t,X^1,e_2^2\right) = u_2^2\left(t,X^1\right).$$

Our objective is to derive a stable, accurate and fast algorithm for solving this evolutionary problem for $0 < t < T$, $e_1^1 < X^1 < e_2^1$, $e_1^2 < X^2 < e_2^2$. Under normal circumstances we discard explicit schemes because they require too many time steps in order to guarantee their stability, and implicit schemes because they are too computationally cumbersome. It turns out that there exists an attractive alternative which is known as the alternating direction implicit (ADI) scheme.

Without going into details, we now describe the ADI scheme. For simplicity we assume that the computational domain is the unit square, i.e., $e_1^1 = e_1^2 = 0$, $e_2^1 = e_2^2 = 1$. If this is not the case, an additional stretching and shifting of the independent variables is necessary. We discretize t and X^i, $i = 1, 2$, as follows

$$t = mk, \quad X^i = n^i h, \quad 0 \le m \le M, \quad 0 \le n \le N, \quad k = M/T, \quad h = 1/N.$$

The values $U\left(t_m, X_{n^1}^1, X_{n^2}^2\right)$ are denoted by $\tilde{U}_{m,n^1,n^2}$. The coefficients $a^{11}, \ldots, c$ turn into the matrices $a_{m,n^1,n^2}^{11}, \ldots, c_{m,n^1,n^2}$. As before, the ratio $v = k/h^2$ is an important characteristics of the grid. For stable explicit schemes we have to have $v \sim 1$ which makes them exceedingly slow. On the other hand, for the ADI method this restriction is no longer needed.

To discretize the differential operators in the governing equation we introduce the following central difference operators

$$\mathcal{I}\tilde{U}_{m,n^1,n^2} = \tilde{U}_{m,n^1,n^2}$$

$$\mathcal{E}^1\tilde{U}_{m,n^1,n^2} = \tilde{U}_{m,n^1+1,n^2} - \tilde{U}_{m,n^1-1,n^2},$$

$$\mathcal{E}^2\tilde{U}_{m,n^1,n^2} = \tilde{U}_{m,n^1,n^2+1} - \tilde{U}_{m,n^1,n^2-1},$$

$$\mathcal{F}^1\tilde{U}_{m,n^1,n^2} = \tilde{U}_{m,n^1+1,n^2} - 2\tilde{U}_{m,n^1,n^2} + \tilde{U}_{m,n^1-1,n^2},$$

$$\mathcal{F}^2\tilde{U}_{m,n^1,n^2} = \tilde{U}_{m,n^1,n^2+1} - 2\tilde{U}_{m,n^1,n^2} + \tilde{U}_{m,n^1,n^2-1},$$

$$\mathcal{F}^{12}\tilde{U}_{m,n^1,n^2} = \tilde{U}_{m,n^1+1,n^2+1} + \tilde{U}_{m,n^1-1,n^2-1}$$
$$- \tilde{U}_{m,n^1+1,n^2-1} - \tilde{U}_{m,n^1-1,n^2+1},$$

where $1 \leq n^1, n^2 \leq N - 1$. In terms of these composite operators we can rewrite the evolutionary problem as follows

$$\left(\mathcal{I} - \frac{v}{4}a_{m-1}^{11}\mathcal{F}^1\right)\left(\mathcal{I} - \frac{v}{4}a_{m-1}^{22}\mathcal{F}^2\right)\tilde{U}_{m-1,n^1,n^2}$$

$$= \left[\left(\mathcal{I} + \frac{v}{4}a_m^{11}\mathcal{F}^1\right)\left(\mathcal{I} + \frac{v}{4}a_m^{22}\mathcal{F}^2\right)\right.$$

$$\left. + \frac{v}{4}a_m^{12}\mathcal{F}^{12} + \frac{hv}{2}b_m^1\mathcal{E}^1 + \frac{hv}{2}b_m^2\mathcal{E}^2 - h^2vc_m\right]\tilde{U}_{m,n^1,n^2}$$

$$\tilde{U}_{M,n^1,n^2} = \tilde{u}_{n^1,n^2},$$

$$\tilde{U}_{m-1,0,n^2} = \tilde{u}_{m-1,0,n^2}^1, \quad \tilde{U}_{m-1,N,n^2} = \tilde{u}_{m-1,N,n^2}^1,$$

$$\tilde{U}_{m-1,n^1,0} = \tilde{u}_{m-1,n^1,0}^2, \quad \tilde{U}_{m-1,n^1,N} = \tilde{u}_{m-1,n^1,N}^2,$$

where

$$\tilde{u}_{n^1,n^2} = u\left(X_{n^1}^1, X_{n^2}^2\right), \quad \tilde{u}_{m,0,n^2}^1 = u_1^1\left(t_m, X_{n^2}^2\right), \quad \text{etc.}$$

The idea of the ADI method can be formulated as follows. We want to introduce an intermediate variable $\tilde{U}^*$ and rewrite the discretized governing equation as a sequence of two equations affecting the X^1 and X^2 directions separately. Specifically, we split the governing equation as

$$\left(\mathcal{I} - \frac{\upsilon}{4}a_{m-1}^{11}\mathcal{F}^1\right)U^* = \left[\mathcal{I} + \frac{\upsilon}{4}a_m^{11}\mathcal{F}^1 + \frac{\upsilon}{2}a_m^{22}\mathcal{F}^2 + \frac{\upsilon}{4}a_m^{12}\mathcal{F}^{12}\right.$$
$$\left. + \frac{h\upsilon}{2}b_m^1\mathcal{E}^1 + \frac{h\upsilon}{2}b_m^2\mathcal{E}^2 - h^2\upsilon c_m\right]\tilde{U}_m,$$

$$\left(\mathcal{I} - \frac{\upsilon}{4}a_{m-1}^{22}\mathcal{F}^2\right)\tilde{U}_{m-1} = \tilde{U}^* - \frac{\upsilon}{4}a_m^{22}\mathcal{F}^2\tilde{U}_m.$$

The corresponding initial and boundary conditions are

$$\tilde{U}_{M,n^1,n^2} = \tilde{u}_{n^1,n^2},$$

$$\tilde{U}_{0,n^2}^* = \left(\mathcal{I} - \frac{\upsilon}{4}a_{m-1}^{22}\mathcal{F}^2\right)\tilde{u}_{m-1,0,n^2}^1 + \frac{\upsilon}{4}a_m^{22}\mathcal{F}^2\tilde{u}_{m,0,n^2}^1,$$
$$\tilde{U}_{N,n^2}^* = \left(\mathcal{I} - \frac{\upsilon}{4}a_{m-1}^{22}\mathcal{F}^2\right)\tilde{u}_{m-1,N,n^2}^1 + \frac{\upsilon}{4}a_m^{22}\mathcal{F}^2\tilde{u}_{m,N,n^2}^1,$$

$$\tilde{U}_{m-1,n^1,0} = \tilde{u}_{m-1,n^1,0}^2, \quad \tilde{U}_{m-1,n^1,N} = \tilde{u}_{m-1,n^1,N}^2.$$

Thus, instead of solving the full two-dimensional problem we can solve a sequence of one-dimensional problems similar to the ones considered in the previous subsection.

Since a two-factor difference equation can be factorized into a product of one-factor difference equations in many different ways, there are many different versions of the ADI method. The one presented above had been chosen for its robustness.

4.12 Numerical solution of SDEs

4.12.1 Introduction

A viable alternative to solving PDE (4.48) in order to find the conditional expectation of $f(x_T)$, is to solve SDE (4.40) for different realizations of the Wiener process and to use the Feynman-Kac formula to perform the averaging. In this section we discuss some of the methods which can be used for this purpose. In particular, we derive the so-called first-order accurate Milstein approximation scheme for stochastic differential equations (SDEs).

4.12.2   Formulation of the problem

Consider a SDE for the unknown vector function $\mathbf{x}_t$:

$$d\mathbf{x}_t = \mathbf{b}(t, \mathbf{x}_t)dt + \sigma(t, \mathbf{x}_t)d\mathbf{W}_t,$$

where x is the M-component vector of unknowns, b is the M-component vector of drifts, σ is the $M \times N$-component matrix of volatilities, and $\mathbf{W}_t$ is the N-component vector of uncorrelated Brownian motions. In components this equation can be written as

$$dx_t^m = b^m(t, x_t^1, \ldots, x_t^M)dt + \sigma^{mn}(t, x_t^1, \ldots, x_t^M)dW_t^n,$$

where $1 \leq m \leq M$, $1 \leq n \leq N$. Here and below the standard summation rule over repeated indices is used. As usual, we can rewrite the evolution equation in the integral (Ito) form. Our objective is to derive a stable, accurate and fast approximation for solving this SDE on the interval $0 < t < T$. We divide this interval into L subintervals, of length $k = T/L$ and evaluate the solution at points $t_l = lk$, $l = 0, \ldots, L$. We denote by $\tilde{\mathbf{x}}_l$ the values of the approximate solution at t_l. Before plunging into devising approximation schemes, we have to agree on the way of measuring their efficiency. Partly the corresponding measure depends on the reason for solving the SDE in the first place. If we need to know the behavior of the trajectories as such, (when we evaluate barrier options, say), we have to use the so-called strong convergence measure. When we are interested in the behavior of the trajectories on average, for example, when we evaluate simple European options, we can use the much cruder weak convergence measure instead.

We say that $\tilde{\mathbf{x}}$ is a strong approximation of $\mathbf{x}$ of order γ if

$$E[\|\mathbf{x}_T - \tilde{\mathbf{x}}_L\|] = O(k^\gamma),$$

and a weak approximation of order γ if

$$|E[g(\mathbf{x}_T) - g(\tilde{\mathbf{x}}_L)]| \leq O(k^\gamma).$$

Here g is a more or less arbitrary smooth function. It is clear that the strong convergence implies that $\tilde{\mathbf{x}}_L$ approximates $\mathbf{x}_T$ pointwise, while the weak convergence means that $\tilde{\mathbf{x}}_L$ approximates $\mathbf{x}_T$ on average. As usual, the strong convergence implies the weak one but not *vice versa*.

4.12.3   The Euler-Maruyama scheme

The simplest and the most popular approximation scheme is the Euler-Maruyama scheme borrowed from the theory of deterministic ordinary differential equations. This scheme simply states that

$$\tilde{x}_{l+1} = \tilde{x}_l + k\mathbf{b}(t_l, \tilde{x}_l) + \sqrt{k}\sigma(t_l, \tilde{x}_l)\boldsymbol{\xi},$$

where $\boldsymbol{\xi}$ is the N-component vector of independent $\mathfrak{N}(0,1)$ random variables. This scheme is too simple to be efficient. Indeed, it is easy to see that its strong order of convergence is $\gamma = 0.5$, while its weak order of convergence is $\gamma = 1$. As usual, this scheme can be unstable.

4.12.4 The Milstein scheme

It was realized by Milstein long ago that more sophisticated schemes are needed in order to capture fine details of the behavior of trajectories. It is natural to derive such schemes using the integral form of the evolution equation. For the exact trajectory we can easily establish the following approximate relations

$$x_{t_{l+1}}^m = x_{t_l}^m + \int_{t_l}^{t_{l+1}} b^m\left(s, \mathbf{x}_s\right) ds + \int_{t_l}^{t_{l+1}} \sigma^{mn}\left(s, \mathbf{x}_s\right) d\mathbf{W}_s^n$$

$$\approx x_{t_l}^m + kb^m(t_l, \mathbf{x}_{t_l}) + \sqrt{k}\sigma^{mn}(t_l, \mathbf{x}_{t_l})\xi^n + \sigma^{ij}(t_l, \mathbf{x}_{t_l})\frac{\partial \sigma^{mn}}{\partial x^i}(t_l, \mathbf{x}_{t_l})\mathcal{I}^{jn}$$

where

$$\mathcal{I}^{kn} = \int_{t_l}^{t_{l+1}} (W_s^k - W_{t_l}^k) dW_s^n.$$

At this stage it is natural to replace the exact trajectory $\mathbf{x}_t$ by the approximate trajectory $\tilde{\mathbf{x}}_t$ and write the approximation scheme in the form

$$\tilde{x}_{l+1}^m \approx \tilde{x}_l^m + kb^m(t_l, \tilde{x}_l) + \sqrt{k}\sigma^{mn}(t_l, \tilde{x}_l)\boldsymbol{\xi}_n + \sigma^{ij}(t_l, \tilde{x}_l)\frac{\partial \sigma^{mn}}{\partial \tilde{x}^i}(t_l, \tilde{x}_l)\mathcal{I}^{jn},$$

It is clear that this scheme is a natural extension of the standard Euler scheme. It can be shown that its order of strong convergence $\gamma = 1$.

The main difficulty in applying the Milstein scheme in practice is the need to evaluate the integrals $\mathcal{I}^{jn}$. Diagonal integrals can be found explicitly as follows

$$\mathcal{I}^{nn} = \int_{t_l}^{t_{l+1}} (W_s^n - W_{t_l}^n) dW_s^n = \int_0^k \tilde{W}_s^n d\tilde{W}_s^n = \frac{1}{2}[(\tilde{W}_k^n)^2 - k] = \frac{1}{2}k[(\xi^n)^2 - 1],$$

where $\tilde{W}_s^n = W_s^n - W_{t_i}^n$. Unfortunately, this is not true for nondiagonal integrals. One can try to obtain an approximate expressions for these integrals by using the so-called Karhunen-Loeve, or random Fourier series, expansion of the underlying Brownian motions. Once the processes $\tilde{W}_s^j$ and $\tilde{W}_s^n$ are expanded in Fourier series and terms of order $p+1$ and above are dropped (here p is an integer controlling the quality of approximation) one can represent the approximate value $\mathcal{I}^{jn;p}$ of the integral $\mathcal{I}^{jn}$ as

$$\mathcal{I}^{jn;p} = \frac{j}{2}\left\{\xi^j\xi^n + \frac{\sqrt{2}}{\pi}\sum_{r=1}^{p+1}\rho_r(\zeta^{j,r}\xi^n - \zeta^{n,r}\xi^j)\right.$$
$$\left. +\frac{1}{\pi}\sum_{r=1}^{p}\frac{1}{r}(\zeta^{j,r}\eta^{n,r} - \zeta^{n,r}\eta^{j,r})\right\}$$

where

$$\rho_r = 1/r, \ r = 1,\ldots,p, \ \rho_{p+1} = \sqrt{\pi^2/6 - \sum_{r=1}^{p}1/r^2} = \sqrt{\sum_{r=p+1}^{\infty}1/r^2},$$

and ξ, ν, ζ are independent $\mathfrak{N}(0,1)$ variables. In general one should choose p to be of order $1/k$ for achieving meaningful approximations for the integrals $\mathcal{I}^{jn}$. This is the reason why the Milstein method is so difficult to use for multidimensional SDEs (as opposed to one-dimensional SDEs which can be studied with ease).

Consider the standard geometrical Brownian motion with constant parameters described by the scalar linear SDE of the form

$$dx = \beta_1 x dt + \sigma_1 x dW.$$

The Euler scheme can be written as

$$\tilde{x}_{l+1} = \tilde{x}_l(1 + \beta_1 k + \sigma_1\sqrt{k}\xi).$$

This scheme is too crude to be of practical value. However, in the case in question the corresponding Milstein scheme can be easily implemented as well. The corresponding scheme yields

$$\tilde{x}_{l+1} = \tilde{x}_l\left(1 + \left(\beta_1 + \frac{1}{2}\sigma_1^2(\xi^2 - 1)\right)k + \sigma_1\sqrt{k}\xi\right), \tag{4.71}$$

so that the value of $\tilde{x}$ at T can be written as

$$\tilde{x}_L = x_0 \prod_{l=0}^{L-1} \left(1 + \left(\beta_1 + \frac{1}{2}\sigma_1^2(\xi_l^2 - 1) \right) k + \sigma_1\sqrt{k}\xi_l \right).$$

It is interesting to compare this formula with the one obtained via the logarithmic change of variables. The evolution of $y_t = \ln(x_t/x_0)$ is governed by the scalar linear SDE of the form

$$dy = (\beta_1 - \frac{1}{2}\sigma_1^2)dt + \sigma_1 dW.$$

For this equation both the Euler and Milstein schemes yield

$$y_{l+1} = y_l + \left(\beta_1 - \frac{1}{2}\sigma_1^2 \right) k + \sigma_1\sqrt{k}\xi, \qquad (4.72)$$

$$y_L = \left(\beta_1 - \frac{1}{2}\sigma_1^2 \right) T + \sigma_1\sqrt{\frac{T}{L}} \sum_{l=0}^{L-1} \xi_l,$$

$$\tilde{x}_L = x_0 \exp\left(\left(\beta_1 - \frac{1}{2}\sigma_1^2 \right) T + \sigma_1\sqrt{\frac{T}{L}} \sum_{l=0}^{L-1} \xi_l \right).$$

It is clear that schemes (4.71), and (4.72) correctly describe the drift term while the naively applied Euler-Maruyama scheme does not.

4.13 References and further reading

Original sources for this chapter are the following papers: Beam and Warming (1980), Cameron and Martin (1945), Crank and Nicolson (1947), Feynman (1948), Girsanov (1962), Ito (1944), Kolmogoroff (1931), Langevin (1908), Maruyama (1955), Milstein (1974), Peaceman and Rachford (1955), Uhlenbeck and Ornstein (1930).

The reader can find a lot of useful information on various topics covered in this chapter in the following books: Arnold (1974), Bertoin (1996), Bluman and Kumei (1989), Borodin and Salminen (1996), Churchill and Brown (1987), Durrett (1996), Feller (1971), Gihman and Skorohod (1972), Ito and McKean (1965), Karazas and Shreve (1991), Karlin and Taylor (1981), Kevorkian

(1993), Kloeden and Platen (1992), Korolyk *et al.* (1985), Lévy (1948), Milstein (1995), Mitchell and Griffiths (1980), Morse and Feschbach (1953), Morton and Mayers (1994), Oksendal (1992), Press *et al.* *(1992)*, Rogers and Williams (1987), Smith (1985), Strikwerda (1989), Sveshnikov (1978), Tikhonov and Samarskiji (1963), Tavella and Randall (2000), Zolotarev (1986), Zwilliger (1989).

Part III

Discrete-time models

Chapter 5

Single-period markets

5.1 Introduction

In this chapter we study simple but surprisingly deep problems of financial engineering in the context of single-period markets. We consider such markets as collections of different countries each with its own currency. Every country is characterized by its interest rate. Relative values of different currencies are characterized by forex rates. Investors based in different countries can invest money either domestically (in the domestic money market account (MMA) and bonds), or abroad (in the foreign MMAs and bonds). In order to be specific we describe things from the standpoint of investors based in a particular country which is called domestic, all other countries are called foreign. We introduce forex rates with respect to the domestic currency which show the number of units of the domestic currency one needs to pay for one unit of the foreign currency. If the so-called cross rates, i.e., forex rates between two foreign currencies are required, they can be found as ratios of the corresponding domestic rates. We observe the market twice, at $t = 0$ (today) and $t = 1$ (at maturity), where the unit of time is chosen as appropriate. At $t = 0$ the state of the market, which is characterized solely by the exchange rates, is known. At $t = 1$ the market is characterized by the amount of money accumulated in domestic and foreign MMAs and the exchange rates; it can be in one of the K possible states which are determined by outcomes of a random experiment, their objective probabilities are $p_0, ..., p_{K-1}$, the corresponding probability measure is P. (In other words, the state of the market is determined by a K-nomial Bernoulli trial.)

Domestic investors can make investments in the domestic money market account and bonds which are nonrisky in relative terms (but can be both nonrisky and risky in absolute terms), and risky investments in foreign money market accounts and bonds. Even in this simple context the objectives of a financial engineer are manifold. To start with, it is necessary to decide how to compare the value of a portfolio today and at maturity. It turns out that it is most natural to use the value of the MMA for this purpose. Next, it is necessary to find conditions which guarantee that the market does not allow arbitrage, or, in other words, that the choice of the present and future FXRs is such that it is not possible to make a certain investment gain exceeding the gain on the investment in the money market account. We show that the market does not allow arbitrage if current FXRs are expectations of the future FXRs with respect to a certain probability measure Q which assigns probabilities $q_0, ..., q_{K-1}$ to the corresponding outcomes. This probability measure which is known as the risk-free measure plays an outstanding role in many situations. In general, the risk-free and objective probability measures are not directly related. Once the risk-free measure is constructed, pricing of options becomes straightforward since the present value of an option is simply the expected value of its payoff at maturity expressed in terms of the domestic MMA. It is shown however, that the risk-neutral pricing of options makes sense only if they are hedged and an appropriate amount of foreign currency is bought or sold by the seller of an option. For investment purposes one needs to use the objective probability measure.

The chapter is organized as follows. In Section 2 we study a very simple case of the binomial single-period two-country market with nonrisky MMAs and show how to solve the corresponding forex problem. In Section 3 we consider the binomial model with risky MMAs and give the reader a first taste of possible difficulties. In Section 4 we describe an idealized world market in its generality and formulate the forex problem. In Section 5 we derive relevant economic constraints on the relative FXRs which guarantee that this market is logically consistent. Then we show how these constraints can be formulated in the language of linear algebra and construct the FXRs by virtue of the theorem of the alternative and two theorems of the separating hyperplane. In Section 6 we define complete and incomplete markets and show how to price contingent claims in terms of underlying assets. Section 7 is devoted to elementary portfolio theory with forex treated as an asset class. In Section 8 we solve the optimal investment problem for a representative investor in our market. In Section 9 we discuss the equilibrium approach to finding the FXRs. References are given in Section 10.

5.2 Binomial markets with nonrisky investments

We emphasized on several occasions above that values of FXRs and the corresponding derivative instruments evolve in time in a random fashion. This is true for all financial instruments with the notable exception of cash which has constant absolute value (but looses its relative value over time due to inflation) and MMA investment which has constant relative value (but increasing absolute value). Accordingly, in order to model the evolution of an idealized market we have to come up with an appropriate source of uncertainty and decide how to compare the value of one currency unit today and its future value as well as the relative values of two different currencies. In this section we study the simplest example.

We consider an idealized single period binomial market. In our model we consider two countries - the domestic country and the foreign country which are distinguished by the superscripts 0 and 1, respectively. We develop our theory from the standpoint of investors residing in the domestic country. For concreteness we call the domestic and foreign currencies the dollar and euro, respectively. The length of the period of observation is one unit of time (one year, say). We assume that in each country investors can put their money into nonrisky MMAs and that the relative value of the currencies is characterized by some FXR. We assume that at time $t = 0$ the FXR (i.e., the number of dollars which one needs to pay to buy one euro) is S_0^{01}. It is obvious that

$$S_0^{10} = \frac{1}{S_0^{01}}.$$

Whenever possible, we suppress the superscripts and use the simplified notation S_0 rather than S_0^{01}. As a source of uncertainty we use a single Bernoulli experiment with two outcomes (a coin tossing) which determines one of the two possible states of the market distinguished via the subscripts 0 and 1, respectively. The probabilities of these states are denoted by p_0, p_1, $p_0 + p_1 = 1$. We do not assume that our coin is fair, so that, in general, the probabilities p_0 and p_1 are different. At time $t = 1$ one unit of currency invested in the corresponding MMA is worth

$$A^{\nu} = (1 + r^{\nu}), \quad \nu = 0, 1,$$

units of currency regardless of the state of the world (here r^{ν} is the interest rate in the corresponding country), while the FXR has two possible values

$$S_1^{01} = \left(S_{1,0}^{01}, S_{1,1}^{01} \right),$$

with $S_{1,0}^{01} < S_{1,1}^{01}$, say, so that for domestic investors in state 0 euro is cheaper that in state 1. Here and below the first subscript corresponds to time and the second subscript to state of the market. The corresponding simplified notation is

$$S_1 = (S_{1,0}, S_{1,1}).$$

Thus, in both states of the world the values of the MMAs are the same while the values of FXR are different, so that FXR is a random variable. We require that $r^\nu \geq 0$, i.e., that money generates interest (otherwise nobody is going to invest in MMAs).

In order to construct a useful market model we need to solve two comparison problems. First, we need to compare the values of one unit of currency paid at $t = 0$ and $t = 1$, respectively. (It is clear that a dollar today is better than a dollar tomorrow.) Second, we need to compare relative values of different currencies paid at the same time. The first problem is solved by using the MMA to measure all other cash flows in the corresponding currency, the second one is solved by using the FXR. We say that the MMA is used as a numeraire.

For domestic investors there are two venues for investing their money: (A) they can put it into the dollar MMA at $t = 0$ and receive it back with interest at $t = 1$; (B) they can convert their dollars into euros at the spot FXR S_0 at $t = 0$, invest euros thus acquired into the euro MMA, and convert the accumulated funds into dollars at time $t = 1$ at the uncertain rate S_1. Accordingly, in the domestic market there are certain and uncertain investments. One dollar invested in the domestic MMA at $t = 0$ is worth A^0 dollars at $t = 1$, one euro invested in the foreign MMA is worth S_0 dollars at $t = 0$, at $t = 1$ it is worth A^{01} dollars, where

$$A^{01} = \left(A_0^{01}, A_1^{01} \right),$$

$$A_k^{01} = \left(1 + r^1 \right) S_{1,k},$$

with probabilities p_0, p_1, respectively. Foreign investors have to consider the quantities A^1, A^{10} which are defined in an obvious way.

Absolute dollar rates of return on investments in the euro MMA are

$$\varrho_k^{01} = \frac{\left(1 + r^1 \right) S_{1,k}}{S_0} - 1, \quad k = 0, 1.$$

In order to compute relative rates of return we use the domestic MMA rate of return and discount all future currency cash flows. This is a logical step which takes into account the natural expansion of the market. We have

$$\hat{A}^0 = \frac{A^0}{A^0} = 1,$$

$$\hat{A}^{01} = \frac{A^{01}}{A^0} = \left(\hat{A}_0^{01}, \hat{A}_1^{01} \right),$$

$$\hat{A}_k^{01} = \frac{\left(1 + r^1 \right) S_{1,k}}{\left(1 + r^0 \right)}.$$

Here and below we use carets to denote relative values. It is clear that the relative rate of return on dollars invested in the domestic MMA is zero. The relative rate of return on dollars invested in the euro MMA is

$$\hat{\varrho}_k^{01} = \frac{\left(1 + r^1 \right) S_{1,k}}{\left(1 + r^0 \right) S_0} - 1.$$

We cannot choose the relative rates of return on foreign investments arbitrarily. We require that the following condition is satisfied:

$$\hat{\varrho}_0^{01} < 0 < \hat{\varrho}_1^{01}, \tag{5.1}$$

and similarly for $\hat{\varrho}^{10}$. This condition guarantees that risky investment in euros can produce results which can be both better and worth that the non-risky investment in dollars. If this condition is violated, then shrewd investors can arbitrage the market, or, in other words, generate a certain profit at time $t = 1$ without putting any money at risk at time $t = 0$. Suppose, for example, that $\hat{\varrho}_0^{01} > 0$, so that investing in euros is always better than investing in dollars. Then at $t = 0$ investors can borrow dollars, convert them in euros and put euros in the foreign MMA. At time $t = 1$ they sell euros for dollars, return dollars (with interest) to the bank and are left with a positive profit. The equality $\hat{\varrho}_0^{01} = 0$ is impossible as well because the above strategy will never produce loss and can produce profit. Since all the transactions in our idealized market are reversible, the inequality $\hat{\varrho}_1^{01} \leq 0$ is impossible either. We conclude that conditions (5.1) have to be satisfied and call them the no-arbitrage conditions.

By using the no-arbitrage conditions we can introduce the so-called domestic risk-neutral probabilities $q_0^0, q_1^0, 0 < q_0^0, q_1^0 < 1$, (which are not directly related to the real world probabilities p_0, p_1), in such a way that the expected relative rate of return on the foreign investment is zero,

$$\begin{aligned} q_0^0 + q_1^0 &= 1, \\ q_0^0 \hat{\varrho}_0^{01} + q_1^0 \hat{\varrho}_1^{01} &= 0. \end{aligned} \tag{5.2}$$

A simple calculation yields

$$q_k^0 = (-1)^k \frac{(1+r^1) S_{1,1-k} - (1+r^0) S_0}{(1+r^1)(S_{1,1} - S_{1,0})}. \tag{5.3}$$

By using the definitions of the rates of return on foreign currency, we can show that the expectation with respect to the risk-neutral probability measure of the relative value of the foreign investment at time $t = 1$ is equal to its value at $t = 0$,

$$q_0^0 \hat{A}_{1,0}^{01} + q_1^0 \hat{A}_{1,1}^{01} = S_0,$$

or, symbolically,

$$\mathbb{E}_{Q^0} \left\{ \hat{A}_1^{01} \right\} = S_0.$$

Equivalently, we can write this relation in the form

$$\mathbb{E}_{Q^0} \left\{ \frac{(1+r^1) S_1}{(1+r^0)} \right\} = S_0.$$

We will see shortly that a similar relation is valid for contingent claims, too. Yet another equivalent relation is

$$\mathbb{E}_{Q^0} \left\{ \hat{\varrho}^{01} \right\} = 0,$$

i.e., on average, investing in euros is equivalent to investing in dollars (with respect to the risk-neutral measure). In general,

$$\mathbb{E}_P \left\{ \hat{\varrho}^{01} \right\} \equiv \hat{R}^{01} > 0,$$

since domestic investors expect to be compensated for the risks they assume by holding euros.

It should be emphasized that, in general, the risk-neutral probabilities for foreign investors, Q^1, are different from the ones for domestic investors, Q^0. The computation of Q^1, which is left to the reader as an exercise, yields

$$Q^1 = (q_0^1, q_1^1) = \left((1 + \hat{\varrho}_0^{01}) q_0^0, (1 + \hat{\varrho}_1^{01}) q_1^0 \right), \tag{5.4}$$

$$\begin{aligned}
q_k^1 &= (-1)^k \frac{S_{1,k}^{01}}{S_0^{01}} \frac{\left((1+r^1) S_{1,1-k}^{01} - (1+r^0) S_0^{01} \right)}{(1+r^0)(S_{1,1}^{01} - S_{1,0}^{01})} \\
&= (-1)^k \frac{(1+r^0) S_{1,1-k}^{10} - (1+r^1) S_0^{10}}{(1+r^0)(S_{1,1}^{10} - S_{1,0}^{10})},
\end{aligned}$$

where we use the reciprocity of the FXRs. By using the Radon-Nikodym derivative N^{10} of Q^1 with respect to Q^0, such that

$$N^{10} = \left(\frac{q_0^1}{q_0^0}, \frac{q_1^1}{q_1^0}\right) = \left(\frac{S_{1,0}}{F}, \frac{S_{1,1}}{F}\right) = \left(n_0^{10}, n_1^{10}\right),\qquad(5.5)$$

we can represent expectations of random variables with respect to Q^1 in terms of their expectations with respect to Q^0,

$$\mathbb{E}_{Q^1}\{X\} = \mathbb{E}_{Q^0}\{N^{10}X\}.$$

Example 5.1. *We consider a two-country market with nonrisky investments over a period of one year. The states of this market are described by the following table*

	p	r^0	r^1	S_0^{01}	S_1^{01}
ω_0	0.6	0.06	0.04	0.9	0.8
ω_1	0.4	0.06	0.04	0.9	1.0

(5.6)

Our immediate objective is to find the corresponding rates of return, risk-neutral measures, etc. A simple algebra yields

	$\hat{\varrho}^{01}$	q^0	q^1	N^{10}
ω_0	-0.128	0.413	0.361	0.872
ω_1	0.090	0.587	0.639	1.090

The corresponding binomial market is shown in Figure 5.1.

Our market is a playground for a host of idealized investors who are allowed to invest and borrow money in both domestic and foreign markets. A domestic investor can borrow dollars in order to purchase euros (long euro), and borrow euros in order to buy dollars (short euro). Investors going long expect the market to end up in the state 1 since they plan to sell euros at $t = 1$, pay their debt to the bank and make a profit, while investors going short expect the market to end up in the state 0 since at time $t = 1$ they plan to buy back euros, repay their debt and keep a portion of the money they generated by selling euros at time $t = 0$. Even in our idealized world domestic investors have to protect themselves from market uncertainties. They can achieve this goal by using the principles of financial engineering.

The simplest instruments which can be used for streamlining cash flows are (zero coupon) bonds. A buyer of a bond (with the face value of one) pays

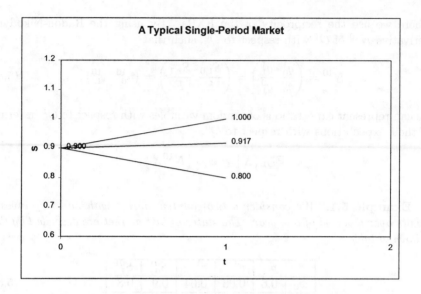

Figure 5.1: The no-arbitrage binomial market described by Table 5.6. In addition to spot FXRs the forward FXR given by equation (5.10) is shown.

some money in the beginning of the period in exchange for the unconditional obligation of a seller to return one unit of currency in the end of the period. We denote the bond prices (in appropriate currencies) by B^0, B^1.

In order to insulate themselves from FXR swings, investors can enter into a forward contract which is an agreement between a buyer and a seller to pay (receive) K (more precisely, K^{01}) dollars at maturity is exchange for one euro. Usually, the strike K is chosen in such a way that the initial value of the contract is zero. The corresponding strike which is denoted by F (more precisely, F^{01}) is called the forward FXR.

Alternatively, investors can buy calls (puts) which give them the right (but not the obligation) to buy (or sell) one euro at or below (at or above) a certain rate K^{01}.

The payoffs of bonds, forward contracts, calls, and puts at $t = 1$ are

$$B(1, S_1) = 1,$$
$$FO(1, S_1) = S_1 - K,$$
$$C(1, S_1) = (S_1 - K)_+,$$
$$P(1, S_1) = (K - S_1)_+.$$

Here and below $V(t, S)$ stands for the value of a derivative contract as a function of calendar time and spot. Occasionally, we use a more elaborated notation. For instance, when we want to emphasize that we are dealing with a domestic contingent claim, we write $V^0(t, S)$. Finding fair prices of bonds, forward contracts, calls, and puts at $t = 0$ is one of the fundamental objectives of financial engineering. These are typical examples of derivative pricing problems. As we will see shortly, knowing the real-world probability P is not important for solving these problems since the corresponding prices depend on the risk-neutral probability Q^0. Another fundamental problem which can be formulated and solved in our idealized framework, is how to invest in dollars and euros in order to receive a desired (expected) return on the investment with the lowest possible risk. As we will see below, the solution of the latter problem depends on both Q^0 and P.

Since the return on investment in the MMA is certain, the bond is trivial to value. Its price has the form

$$B^0 = \frac{1}{(1 + r^0)} = \mathbb{E}_{Q^0} \left\{ \frac{1}{(1 + r^0)} \right\}.$$

In the present model investment in a bond is equivalent to investment in the MMA. In more general models this is not the case. By the same token we can evaluate the foreign bond

$$B^1 = \frac{1}{(1 + r^1)} = \mathbb{E}_{Q^1} \left\{ \frac{1}{(1 + r^1)} \right\}.$$

We leave it to the reader as an exercise to check that

$$B^1 = \mathbb{E}_{Q^0} \left\{ \frac{(1 + \hat{\varrho}^{01})}{(1 + r^1)} \right\}.$$

In order to find the fair price of a forward contract we can argue as follows. Consider the problem from the standpoint of a seller of a forward contract who agrees to deliver one euro at $t = 1$ in exchange for F^{01} dollars regardless of the state of the market. The seller of the contracts expect that the FXR will go down but has to protect himself from the possibility of the FXR going up. In order to be protected, he has to create a replicating portfolio for a forward contract by investing Δ^0 and Δ^1 in the dollar and euro MMAs, respectively. [1] At $t = 0$ the replicating portfolio is worth zero,

$$\Delta^0 + \Delta^1 S_0 = 0, \tag{5.7}$$

---

[1] Positive (negative) Δ's mean investing to (borrowing from) the MMAs, or, equivalently, buying (selling) bonds.

while at $t = 1$ its discounted value coincides with the discounted payoff of a forward contract,

$$\Delta^0 + \Delta^1 \frac{(1+r^1) S_{1,0}}{(1+r^0)} = \frac{S_{1,0} - F}{(1+r^0)}, \tag{5.8}$$

$$\Delta^0 + \Delta^1 \frac{(1+r^1) S_{1,1}}{(1+r^0)} = \frac{S_{1,1}^{01} - F}{(1+r^0)}. \tag{5.9}$$

Equations (5.7) - (5.9) have to be solved with respect to Δ^0, Δ^1, F. The corresponding solution is

$$\Delta^0 = -\frac{S_0}{(1+r^1)},$$

$$\Delta^1 = \frac{1}{(1+r^1)},$$

$$F = \frac{(1+r^0) S_0}{(1+r^1)}. \tag{5.10}$$

Relation (5.10) is the simplest form of the interest rate parity theorem which we discussed in Section 1.5. This theorem plays an important role in forex theory. If $r^0 > r^1$, then the domestic currency is called the discount currency since its value in the future is going to decline, if $r^0 < r^1$, the domestic currency is called the premium currency. Currently the dollar is the discount currency with respect to the euro. By using the definition of the risk-neutral probabilities, we can rewrite the interest rate parity theorem in the following equivalent form,

$$F = \mathbb{E}_{Q^0} \{S_1\}.$$

There is no discounting in this formula since it relates cash flows paid at the same time, namely, at $t = 1$. The no-arbitrage condition can be written as

$$S_{1,0} < F < S_{1,1}.$$

It is clear that the hedging strategy for the buyer of a forward contract is opposite to the one for the seller. The above construction illustrates two important facts: (A) it is possible to establish a rational forward price of the foreign currency without knowing the actual future states of the market or their probabilities; (B) in order to eliminate the impact of randomness on the outcome of the contract at $t = 1$ both buyers and sellers have to hedge themselves at $t = 0$ by creating the so-called replicating portfolios. At this stage the reader can ask why investors would enter into a forward contract at all if they can replicate it directly. The answer is that liquidity constraints, bid-ask spreads and other market imperfections make forward contracts attractive instruments.

Let us now find the fair price $C_0 \equiv C(0, S_0)$ for a call with strike K. We assume that $S_{1,0} < K < S_{1,1}$, so that there is true optionality in the problem. Depending on the relation between K and F we distinguish at-the-money forward (ATMF) ($K = F$), in-the-money forward (ITMF) ($K < F$), and out-of-the-money forward (OTMF) ($K > F$) calls. As before, we consider the problem from the seller's viewpoint. His objective is to create a replicating portfolio which has the same payout as a call by investing Δ^0 in dollars and Δ^1 in euros. At time $t = 0$ the value of the portfolio coincides with the initial price of a call, so that

$$\Delta^0 + \Delta^1 S_0 = C_0.$$

At time $t = 1$ the situation is as follows. If the market is in state 0 the buyer is not going to exercise the option since FXR is below the strike. Accordingly, from the seller's prospective,

$$\Delta^0 + \Delta^1 \frac{(1 + r^1) S_{1,0}}{(1 + r^0)} = 0.$$

In state 1 the buyer exercises his option, so that, from the seller's prospective the situation is as follows

$$\Delta^0 + \Delta^1 \frac{(1 + r^1) S_{1,1}}{(1 + r^0)} = \frac{(S_{1,1} - K)}{(1 + r^0)}.$$

(Recall that we use the factor $(1 + r^0)$ in order to discount all domestic cash flows.) The objective of the seller is to charge the price C_0 and to choose hedges Δ^0, Δ^1 in such a way that the above equations are satisfied. The corresponding solution has the form

$$\Delta^0 = -\frac{S_{1,0} (S_{1,1} - K)}{(S_{1,1} - S_{1,0})(1 + r^0)},$$

$$\Delta^1 = \frac{(S_{1,1} - K)}{(S_{1,1} - S_{1,0})(1 + r^1)},$$

$$C_0 = \frac{(F - S_{1,0})(S_{1,1} - K)}{(S_{1,1} - S_{1,0})(1 + r^0)} \qquad (5.11)$$

$$= \frac{\mathbb{E}_{Q^0}\{S_1 \mid S_1 > K\}}{(1 + r^0)} - \frac{KQ^0\{S_1 > K\}}{(1 + r^0)},$$

where $Q^0\{S_1 > K\}$ is the probability of the FXR S_1 being above the strike level K. It is clear that $C_0 > 0$, by virtue of the no-arbitrage condition. We see that $\Delta^0 < 0$ and $0 < \Delta^1 < 1/(1 + r^1)$, so that borrowing is necessary to execute the hedging strategy. Since all the transactions are reversible, the buyer can agree to pay C_0 for a call since at this price he can make his profit or loss (P&L) zero regardless of the state of the market provided that he sells Δ^1 euros at $t = 0$ and invests Δ^0 dollars in the dollar MMA. Equation (5.11) shows that C_0 is the difference between the discounted expected values of two transactions which occur only if the spot rate S is above the strike rate K: (A) the exchange of one euro for S dollars, (B) the exchange of one euro for K dollars. In one form or the other this decomposition appears in every model we use to evaluate a call option. Equation (5.11) can be rewritten in the form which is manifestly symmetric with respect to the switch between the domestic and foreign markets:

$$C_0 = \frac{S_0 Q^1\{1/K > 1/S_1\}}{(1 + r^1)} - \frac{KQ^0\{S_1 > K\}}{(1 + r^0)}.$$

By using the risk-neutral probabilities we can represent the price of a call at $t = 0$ as its discounted expected price at $t = 1$,

$$C_0 = q_0^0 \frac{C_{1,0}}{(1 + r^0)} + q_1^0 \frac{C_{1,1}}{(1 + r^0)} = \mathbb{E}_{Q^0}\left\{\frac{C_1}{(1 + r^0)}\right\},$$

where

$$C_1 = (C_{1,0}, C_{1,1}) = (0, S_{1,1} - K),$$

is the intrinsic call price at maturity.

By the same token as before, we can find the price of the put. Omitting the corresponding algebra (which is straightforward) we simply present the answer

$$P_0 = q_0^0 \frac{P_{1,0}}{(1 + r^0)} + q_1^0 \frac{P_{1,1}}{(1 + r^0)} = \mathbb{E}_{Q^0}\left\{\frac{P_1}{(1 + r^0)}\right\},$$

where

$$P_1 = (P_{1,0}, P_{1,1}) = (K - S_{1,0}, 0),$$

is the intrinsic put price. In order to hedge himself the seller of a put option has to sell foreign currency and invest proceeds in the domestic MMA.

By subtracting P_0 from C_0 (with the same strike) we obtain

$$
\begin{aligned}
C_0 - P_0 &= \mathbb{E}_{Q^0}\left\{\frac{C_1 - P_1}{(1+r^0)}\right\} = \mathbb{E}_{Q^0}\left\{\frac{S_1 - K}{(1+r^0)}\right\} \\
&= \frac{S_0}{(1+r^1)} - \frac{K}{(1+r^0)} = B^1 S_0 - B^0 K \\
&= B^0\left(F - K\right).
\end{aligned}
$$

This very important relation between C, P is called put-call parity. The importance of put-call parity has been appreciated by investors already in the seventeenth century and used for both speculation and hedging ever since.

In addition to put-call parity there exists one more important relation between calls and puts known as put-call symmetry. Since the right to buy one euro (the notional amount) at the rate of K^{01} dollars/euro which is worth $C^0\left(0, S_0^{01}, 1, K^{01}\right)$ dollars is equivalent to right to sell K^{01} dollars at the rate of $1/K^{01}$ euros/dollar which is worth $K^{01}P^1\left(0, 1/S_0^{01}, 1, 1/K^{01}\right)$ euros, we have the following relation between prices of dollar calls (in dollars) and euro puts (in euros):

$$
C^0\left(0, S_0^{01}, 1, K^{01}\right) = S_0^{01} K^{01} P^1\left(0, \frac{1}{S_0^{01}}, 1, \frac{1}{K^{01}}\right).
$$

Here and below we use the detailed notation $C^0\left(t, S_t^{01}, T, K^{01}\right)$ for the price of the domestic call maturing at time T and having the strike K^{01}, and similar notation for the foreign put. We leave it to the reader as an exercise to check this relation directly by evaluating C_0^0 and P_0^1 via the risk-neutral valuation principle using Q^0 and Q^1, respectively. Since prices of securities are homogeneous functions of degree one, we can rewrite the above equation as

$$
C^0\left(0, S_0^{01}, 1, K^{01}\right) = P^1\left(0, K^{01}, 1, S_0^{01}\right).
$$

Example 5.2. *We now consider the market introduced in Example 5.1 and evaluate all the derivative instruments discussed in this section and find the corresponding hedges. Specifically we consider the domestic bond, forward contract, and ITMF call and OTMF put with strike $K = 0.85$. In addition we* *check put-call parity. We use the relevant formulas and obtain*

	B^0	F	C	P	$C - P$	$B^0(F - K)$
V_0	0.943	0.917	0.083	0.020	0.063	0.063
Δ^0	0.943	-0.865	-0.566	0.236	*	*
Δ^1	0.000	0.962	0.721	-0.240	*	*

We leave it to the reader as an exercise to price the corresponding contingent claims from the foreign investor viewpoint and to verify put-call symmetry.

In the framework of our simple model we can also illustrate the idea of calibration. We say that the model is calibrated properly if it generates option prices which agree with the market data. Thus, for given S_0, r^0, r^1, we need to choose $S_{1,k}$ in such a way that no-arbitrage condition (5.1) is satisfied, and the model reproduces some given option prices. It is natural to calibrate the model to the ATMF call (or put) price which we denote by η. Since we have two FXRs at our disposal, the model has one degree of freedom. We eliminate this degree of freedom by assuming that the model is geometrically centered at the forward FXR as follows

$$\sqrt{S_{1,0}S_{1,1}} = F.$$

We can represent the forward call price $\check{\eta} = \left(1 + r^0\right)\eta$ as

$$\check{\eta} = \frac{(F - S_{1,0})(S_{1,1} - F)}{(S_{1,1} - S_{1,0})}.$$

This relation allows us to express $S_{1,1}$ in terms of $S_{1,0}$ as follows

$$S_{1,1} = \frac{\check{\eta}S_{1,0} - (F - S_{1,0})F}{\check{\eta} - (F - S_{1,0})}.$$

We substitute this expression into the centering condition, solve the corresponding quadratic equation and find $S_{1,0}, S_{1,1}$:

$$S_{1,0} = \frac{F(F - \check{\eta})}{F + \check{\eta}}, \quad S_{1,1} = \frac{F(F + \check{\eta})}{F - \check{\eta}}. \tag{5.12}$$

This procedure makes sense provided that $F > \check{\eta}$. The latter inequality which is equivalent to (5.1) has to be satisfied since otherwise the market can be arbitraged.

We can represent the value V_0 of an arbitrary derivative instrument with the payoff $V_1 = (V_{1,0}, V_{1,1})$ as

$$V_0 = \mathbb{E}_{Q^0}\left\{\frac{V_1}{(1 + r^0)}\right\}. \tag{5.13}$$

This is the key formula of derivative pricing theory which, in one form or the other, appears throughout this book. It is the mathematical expression of the risk-neutral valuation principle. Everyone who sees the above formula for the first time is invariably struck by the fact that the fair price of a contingent claim is independent on the actual probabilities of different states of the market. This independence is due to the fact that both the seller and the buyer of the option can hedge themselves perfectly which allows them to agree on a fair price of a derivative *relative* to the price of the foreign currency. One should also recall that the forward FXR is independent on these probabilities as well.

Formula (5.13) perfectly expresses the relative nature of derivative pricing and exploits this nature to its fullest extend. However, it leaves unanswered the intriguing question of finding the underlying FXR *per se*.

We now consider the most important special case of our binomial model. Namely, we assume that

$$S_{1,0} = \frac{(1+r^0)(1-\sigma)}{(1+r^1)} S_0, \quad S_{1,1} = \frac{(1+r^0)(1+\sigma)}{(1+r^1)} S_0,$$

where the meaning of the parameter σ will become clear shortly. We have

$$q_0^0 = q_1^0 = \frac{1}{2},$$

so that the risk-neutralized coin which is used to generate uncertainty in the model is fair. The variance of relative returns on dollar invested in euros is

$$\mathbb{V}\{\hat{\varrho}\} = \frac{1}{2}(1-\sigma)^2 + \frac{1}{2}(1+\sigma)^2 - 1 = \sigma^2.$$

Thus, σ is the volatility of the rate of return in the foreign MMA (or bond). We can represent the value of a contingent claim at $t = 0$ in the form

$$V_0 = \frac{1}{2}\frac{V_{1,0}}{(1+r^0)} + \frac{1}{2}\frac{V_{1,1}}{(1+r^0)}.$$

To draw some interesting conclusions we further assume that the period of observation is sufficiently short so that the ordering of the relevant parameters is as follows

$$r^0 \sim r^1 \sim \sigma^2 \ll \sigma \ll 1.$$

Provided that there is a sufficiently smooth function $\tilde{V}(t, S_t)$ such that

$$\tilde{V}(0, S_0) = V_0, \quad \tilde{V}(1, S_{1,k}) = V_{1,k},$$

we can rewrite the above relation as

$$\tilde{V}(0, S_0) = \frac{1}{2} \frac{\tilde{V}(1, S_{1,0})}{(1+r^0)} + \frac{1}{2} \frac{\tilde{V}(1, S_{1,1})}{(1+r^0)},$$

or, equivalently, as

$$\tilde{V}(0, S_0) = \frac{1}{2} \frac{\tilde{V}\left(1, \left(1+r^0\right)\left(1-\sigma\right) S_0 / \left(1+r^1\right)\right)}{(1+r^0)}$$
$$+ \frac{1}{2} \frac{\tilde{V}\left(1, \left(1+r^0\right)\left(1+\sigma\right) S_0 / \left(1+r^1\right)\right)}{(1+r^0)}.$$

We expand the terms on the r.h.s. of the above equation in the Taylor series and drop all the terms smaller than r^0, r^1, σ^2. As a result, we obtain

$$\frac{\tilde{V}\left(1, \left(1+r^0\right)\left(1 \pm \sigma\right) S_0 / \left(1+r^1\right)\right)}{(1+r^0)}$$
$$\approx \tilde{V}(0, S_0) + \tilde{V}_t(0, S_0) + \tfrac{1}{2}\sigma^2 S_0^2 \tilde{V}_{SS}(0, S_0)$$
$$+ \left(\pm\sigma + \left(r^0 - r^1\right)\right) S_0 \tilde{V}_S(0, S_0) - r^0 \tilde{V}(0, S_0).$$

By using these expressions we obtain the partial differential equation (PDE) for pricing derivative securities, namely,

$$\tilde{V}_t + \frac{1}{2}\sigma^2 S^2 \tilde{V}_{SS} + \left(r^0 - r^1\right) S \tilde{V}_S - r^0 \tilde{V} = 0.$$

This equation which will appear in this book on numerous occasions is the celebrated Black-Scholes equation of option theory as adapted by Garman and Kohlhagen to the forex context. In a due course we will give its derivation in the continuous setting. It is truly remarkable that is appears already in our extremely simplified model.

We can calibrate our simple model to a given ATMF call price η. We can write η as

$$\eta = \frac{\left(\left(1+r^0\right)\left(1+\sigma\right) S_0 / \left(1+r^1\right) - \left(1+r^0\right) S_0 / \left(1+r^1\right)\right)}{2\left(1+r^0\right)} = \frac{\sigma S_0}{2\left(1+r^1\right)}.$$

Thus, in order to calibrate the model we have to choose

$$\sigma = \frac{2\left(1+r^1\right)\eta}{S_0}. \tag{5.14}$$

In a different disguise equation (5.14) appears in the continuous-time setting where it gives a rough estimate for the value of ATMF calls and puts (which is a measure of FXR volatility since, if FXR is deterministic, their value is zero). We emphasize that even though this model does not satisfy the centering condition exactly, this condition is still satisfied approximately.

In the framework of our simple binomial model we briefly discuss the role of transaction costs in option pricing. We assume that currency exchange involves a bid-ask spread, so that investors who buy a euro (a dollar) have to pay $S^{01,a} = (1+\theta) S^{01}$ dollars ($S^{10,a} = (1+\theta)/S^{01}$ euros) for it (the ask rate), while investors who sell a euro (a dollar) receive $S^{01,b} = (1-\theta) S^{01}$ dollars ($S^{10,b} = (1-\theta)/S^{01}$ euros) for it (the bid rate). The arithmetic average of the bid and ask rates is the spot rate,

$$\frac{S^b + S^a}{2} = S.$$

In the presence of the bid-ask spread currency exchange is no longer a reversible operation. Indeed, an investor selling a dollar for euros at the bid rate and immediately using euros to buy back dollars at the ask rate reduces his capital by a factor of $(1-\theta)/(1+\theta)$. Because of that, in the presence of transaction costs the no-arbitrage condition has to be modified as follows

$$\frac{(1+\theta)}{(1-\theta)} S_{1,0} < F < \frac{(1-\theta)}{(1+\theta)} S_{1,1}.$$

Let us price a call option with strike K sandwiched between $S_{1,0}$ and $S_{1,1}$. To be concrete, we assume that this call is cash settled, so that, if it ends in-the-money, the seller has to pay the buyer $S_{1,1} - K$ dollars. We calculate the ask price first. At time $t = 0$ the seller creates a replicating portfolio by investing Δ^0 and Δ^1 in dollars and euros, respectively. Due to transaction costs the amount of money needed to construct this portfolio, which coincides with the value of a call, is

$$\Delta^0 + (1+\theta) \Delta^1 S_0 = C_0^a.$$

Discounted assets and obligations in different states of the market are matched as follows

$$\Delta^0 + \frac{(1-\theta) \Delta^1 (1+r^1) S_{1,0}}{(1+r^0)} = 0,$$

$$\Delta^0 + \frac{(1-\theta) \Delta^1 (1+r^1) S_{1,1}}{(1+r^0)} = \frac{S_{1,1} - K^{01}}{(1+r^0)}.$$

Accordingly,

$$\Delta^0 = -\frac{S_{1,0}\,(S_{1,1} - K)}{(1 + r^0)\,(S_{1,1} - S_{1,0})},$$

$$\Delta^1 = \frac{(S_{1,1} - K)}{(1 - \theta)\,(1 + r^1)\,(S_{1,1} - S_{1,0})},$$

$$C_0^a = \frac{((1 + \theta)\,F/\,(1 - \theta) - S_{1,0})\,(S_{1,1} - K)}{(1 + r^0)\,(S_{1,1} - S_{1,0})}.$$

In order to find the bid price, we have to price a call from the buyer's prospective. It is clear that all we need to do is to replace θ by $-\theta$, so that

$$C_0^b = \frac{((1 - \theta)\,F/\,(1 + \theta) - S_{1,0})\,(S_{1,1} - K)}{(1 + r^0)\,(S_{1,1} - S_{1,0})}.$$

It is interesting to note that the average of the bid-ask prices C^b, C^a is higher than the price of the corresponding call without transaction costs,

$$\frac{C_0^b + C_0^a}{2} > C_0,$$

where C_0 is given by equation (5.11).

So far, the real-world probability measure P has not appeared in our analysis. The reason is, that we were interested solely in the relative pricing of financial instruments which was accomplished via perfect replication, so that the actual price movements occurred simultaneously and the corresponding risks were eliminated entirely. We now turn our attention to the portfolio allocation problem in which the real-world probabilities of different states of the world play a role which is on a par with their risk-neutral probabilities. The formulation of the problem is as follows. A domestic investor who puts his money in the nonrisky MMA, or, equivalently, buys a bond, receives the rate of return on his investment equal to r^0. His relative rate of return is zero. At the same time, it is tempting to use investments into the foreign currency in order to boost the rate of return. We know that if the market ends up in the 1 state, the relative rate of return on dollars invested in euros is positive, $\hat\varrho_1^{01} > 0$; if the market ends up in the state 0, it is negative, $\hat\varrho_0^{01} < 0$. Thus, for an investor having the initial endowment of Π_0 dollars, the task is to split

the money between the nonrisky investment in dollars and the risky investment in euros, thus creating an investment portfolio allowing him to achieve
his investment objectives.

We already know that the risk-neutral expectation of rate of return on
investment in euros is zero, while its real-world expectation is, in general, positive, $\hat{R}^{01} > 0$, because investors expect to receive the so-called risk premium
for holding foreign currency. Let us assume that the risk premium is positive,
and consider a representative investor with a positive endowment Π_0. At time
$t = 0$, he creates a portfolio Π by choosing a trading strategy in such a way
that the initial value of the portfolio is equal to the endowment,

$$\Pi_0 = \Upsilon^0 + \Upsilon^1 S_0,$$

where Υ^0, Υ^1 are the amounts invested in dollars and euros, respectively. In
general, these amounts can be both positive (investing) and negative (borrowing). At time $t = 1$ the discounted value of this portfolio $\hat{\Pi}_1$ and the
corresponding rate of return $\hat{\varrho}_\Pi$ are random,

$$\hat{\Pi}_1 = \left(\Upsilon^0 + \Upsilon^1 \left(1 + \hat{\varrho}_0^{01} \right) S_0, \Upsilon^0 + \Upsilon^1 \left(1 + \hat{\varrho}_1^{01} \right) S_0 \right),$$

$$\hat{\varrho}_\Pi = \left(\frac{\Upsilon^1 \hat{\varrho}_0^{01} S_0}{\Pi_0}, \frac{\Upsilon^1 \hat{\varrho}_1^{01} S_0}{\Pi_0} \right).$$

The risk-neutral expectation of $\hat{\varrho}_\Pi$ is zero, its real-world expectation $\hat{R}_\Pi$ has
the form

$$\hat{R}_\Pi = \frac{\Upsilon^1 \hat{R}^{01} S_0}{\Pi_0}.$$

Thus, by choosing $\Upsilon^1 S_0 > \Pi_0$, $\Upsilon^0 < 0$ (i.e., by leveraging the portfolio)
the investor can achieve arbitrarily high expected rate of return. For given
expected rate of return ρ the composition of the corresponding portfolio is

$$\Upsilon^0 = \frac{\left(\hat{R}^{01} - \rho \right) \Pi_0}{\hat{R}^{01}}, \quad \Upsilon^1 = \frac{\rho \Pi_0}{\hat{R}^{01} S_0}.$$

All portfolios with $\rho > \hat{R}^{01}$ are leveraged.

Expected rates of return above zero cannot be achieved without assuming
some risks. To quantify these risks we use the variance of returns as a measure

of riskiness. The variance $\mathbb{V}_P\{\hat{\varrho}_\Pi\}$ has the form

$$\mathbb{V}_P\{\hat{\varrho}_\Pi\} = \left(p_0\left(\hat{\varrho}_0^{01}\right)^2 + p_1\left(\hat{\varrho}_1^{01}\right)^2 - \left(\hat{R}^{01}\right)^2\right)\left(\frac{\Upsilon^1 S_0}{\Pi_0}\right)^2 = \frac{\mathbb{V}_P\{\hat{\varrho}^{01}\}\rho^2}{\left(\hat{R}^{01}\right)^2}.$$

It grows quadratically with ρ. Thus, in order to achieve high returns investors should be able to tolerate their high volatility which can result in losses and even bankruptcy. (Who can forget the final days of LTCM.)

5.3 Binomial markets without nonrisky investments

So far, our analysis was strongly geared toward studying the random behavior of the FXR since we assumed that investments in MMAs produce deterministic returns. If we want to study the dynamics of debt instruments and their interplay with FXR, we have to assume that both returns on investments in MMAs and the FXR are uncertain. This assumption deserves some explanation. When the money is used to purchase a bond which is kept till maturity, it grows at a known rate of return with certainty. However, if the money is invested into a money-market account and the single period we are interested is long enough, its rate of return becomes uncertain because of the rollover effects. In addition, in some circumstances the default effects have to be taken into account as well. Since we want to construct a sufficiently flexible model, we have to allow for such a possibility.

As before, we consider a binomial two-country market which describes the behavior of the dollar and euro MMAs and the corresponding FXR, but now we assume that in the end of the period not only FXR S_1, but also returns earned by investments in MMAs, r^0, r^1, are uncertain. We assume that

$$\max\left\{r_0^0, r_1^0\right\} > 0, \quad \max\left\{r_0^1, r_1^1\right\} > 0,$$

where r_k^l are possible rates of return on investments in the corresponding currencies, so that investing money in MMAs does make sense (at least in some cases). At this stage a distinction between investments in dollars and euros becomes somewhat blurred. We assume that the following conditions are satisfied,

$$\min\left\{\hat{\varrho}_0^{01}, \hat{\varrho}_1^{01}\right\} < 0 < \max\left\{\hat{\varrho}_0^{01}, \hat{\varrho}_1^{01}\right\},$$

where $\hat{\varrho}^{01}$ is the relative rate of return on investments in euros for the domestic investor,

$$\hat{\varrho}_k^{01} = \frac{\left(1 + r_k^1\right) S_{1,k}}{\left(1 + r_k^0\right) S_0} - 1.$$

Similar conditions are satisfied for the foreign country. These conditions show that in the worst case scenario investors putting their money into dollars fare better than the ones investing in euros, while in the best case scenario the opposite is true. We want to find fair prices for the same derivative instruments as before, namely, for bonds, forwards, calls and puts, and to solve the portfolio selection problem.

It is clear that we have to start with finding the domestic risk-neutral probability measure Q^0. In order to do so we have to solve the same equations as before (due to the fact that we discount all returns), namely equations (5.2). The solution has the form (5.3) even though the actual meaning of the relative rates of return is more complicated than earlier. The foreign risk-neutral measure Q^1 is given by expression (5.4) and the corresponding Radon-Nikodym derivative N^{10} has the form (5.5). As before, we have

$$\mathbb{E}_{Q^0} \left\{ \frac{\left(1 + r^1\right) S_1}{\left(1 + r^0\right)} \right\} = S_0,$$

$$\mathbb{E}_{Q^0} \left\{ \hat{A}_1 \right\} = S_0,$$

i.e., the FXR at $t = 0$ is the risk-neutral expectation of the modified FXR at $t = 1$. The foreign risk-neutral measure is defined by analogy.

Example 5.3. *We consider a two-country market without nonrisky investments over a period of one year. The states of this market are described by the following table*

	p	r^0	r^1	S_0^{01}	S_1^{01}
ω_0	0.6	0.04	0.02	0.9	0.8
ω_1	0.4	0.08	0.06	0.9	1.0

We start with finding $\hat{\varrho}^{01}, q^0, q^1, N^{10}$. *An elementary calculation yields*

	$\hat{\varrho}^{01}$	q^0	q^1	N^{10}
ω_0	-0.128	0.414	0.361	0.872
ω_1	0.091	0.586	0.639	1.091

Now we show how to price the domestic bond in the market without non-risky investments. In this case the hedging strategy of the previous section does not work. The seller of a bond cannot hedge himself by putting the proceeds of the sale solely in the domestic MMA since returns on such an investment are uncertain, while his obligations are certain. Instead, the seller has to invest into both dollars and euros. Let Δ^0 and Δ^1 be the amounts invested in the dollar and euro MMAs at $t = 0$. Then, at $t = 0$ we have

$$B^0 = \Delta^0 + \Delta^1 S_0.$$

At time $t = 1$ the seller has to deliver one dollar regardless of the state of the market, so that he has to satisfy the following conditions

$$\Delta^0 + \Delta^1 \frac{\left(1 + r_0^1\right) S_{1,0}}{\left(1 + r_0^0\right)} = \frac{1}{\left(1 + r_0^0\right)},$$

$$\Delta^0 + \Delta^1 \frac{\left(1 + r_1^1\right) S_{1,1}}{\left(1 + r_1^0\right)} = \frac{1}{\left(1 + r_1^0\right)}.$$

Accordingly, the seller has to choose Δ^0, Δ^1, B^0, as follows

$$\Delta^0 = \frac{\left(1 + r_1^1\right) S_{1,1} - \left(1 + r_0^1\right) S_{1,0}}{\left(1 + r_0^0\right)\left(1 + r_1^1\right) S_{1,1} - \left(1 + r_1^0\right)\left(1 + r_0^1\right) S_{1,0}},$$

$$\Delta^1 = -\frac{\left(r_1^0 - r_0^0\right)}{\left(1 + r_0^0\right)\left(1 + r_1^1\right) S_{1,1} - \left(1 + r_1^0\right)\left(1 + r_0^1\right) S_{1,0}}.$$

$$B^0 = \frac{\left(1 + r_1^1\right) S_{1,1} - \left(1 + r_0^1\right) S_{1,0} - \left(r_1^0 - r_0^0\right) S_0}{\left(1 + r_0^0\right)\left(1 + r_1^1\right) S_{1,1} - \left(1 + r_1^0\right)\left(1 + r_0^1\right) S_{1,0}},$$

The absolute rate of return on a bond is defined as

$$\varrho^0 = \frac{1}{B^0} - 1.$$

In view of our assumptions concerning the ordering of returns at maturity, $\tilde{r}^0$ is sandwiched between r_0^0 and r_1^0,

$$\min\left\{r_0^0, r_1^0\right\} < \varrho^0 < \max\left\{r_0^0, r_1^0\right\},$$

as expected. Its relative rate of return is random,

$$\hat{\varrho}_k^0 = \frac{1}{\left(1 + r_k^0\right) B^0} - 1.$$

We come to the following surprising conclusion: in order to hedge the domestic bond, a prudent seller has to diversify as much as possible and to invest in all available classes of primary instruments including the euro MMA.

By using the risk-neutral probabilities, we can represent the price of the bond in the form

$$B^0 = \mathbb{E}_{Q^0} \left\{ \frac{1}{1 + r^0} \right\},$$

and similarly for the foreign bond.

Now we are in a position to value other derivative instruments. We start with a forward contract. As before, the seller of a forward contract has to buy the foreign bond with face value of one at $t = 0$ in order to cover his obligation at $t = 1$. Since a forward contract is costless, in order to buy euros he has to have $B^1 S_0$ dollars which he generates by selling at $t = 0$ a bond with the face value of $B^1 S_0 / B^0$. At maturity the seller receives F dollars in exchange for one euro he holds. This amount should be sufficient in order to cover seller's obligations regardless of the state of the market. At the same time, the buyer will not pay more than is necessary to cover these obligations. Accordingly, the mutually agreeable forward price and the corresponding hedges are

$$\Delta^0 = -B^1 S_0, \quad \Delta^1 = B^1, \quad F = \frac{B^1 S_0}{B^0}.$$

We can represent F as

$$F = \frac{\mathbb{E}_{Q^0} \left\{ S_1 / \left(1 + r^0\right) \right\}}{\mathbb{E}_{Q^0} \left\{ 1 / \left(1 + r^0\right) \right\}}. \tag{5.15}$$

Relation (5.15) expresses the interest parity theorem in the random interest rate environment.

The forward FXR can be written as the expected FXR at maturity in the so-called forward measure,

$$F = \mathbb{E}_{Q^0_{frwrd}} \left\{ S_1 \right\}.$$

We define the forward measure in an obvious way, namely,

$$\mathbb{E}_{Q^0_{frwrd}} \left\{ X \right\} = \frac{\mathbb{E}_{Q^0} \left\{ X / \left(1 + r^0\right) \right\}}{\mathbb{E}_{Q^0} \left\{ 1 / \left(1 + r^0\right) \right\}},$$

where X is a random variable. At this stage the reader might wonder if there exists an instrument whose price f is given by the expectation of the FXR S_1 with respect to the risk-neutral measure,

$$f = \mathbb{E}_{Q^0}\{S_1\}.$$

Such an instrument does exist and is known as the futures contract. However, for the single-period model the distinction between forward and futures contracts is irrelevant, and we have to wait until we introduce multi-period markets in order to appreciate its true meaning. Here we just note that

$$
\begin{aligned}
F &= \frac{\mathrm{cov}_{Q^0}\{S_1, 1/\left(1+r^0\right)\} + \mathbb{E}_{Q^0}\{S_1\}\,\mathbb{E}_{Q^0}\{1/\left(1+r^0\right)\}}{\mathbb{E}_{Q^0}\{1/\left(1+r^0\right)\}} \\
&= \frac{\mathrm{cov}_{Q^0}\{S_1, 1/\left(1+r^0\right)\}}{\mathbb{E}_{Q^0}\{1/\left(1+r^0\right)\}} + f.
\end{aligned}
$$

Depending on the sign of $\mathrm{cov}_{Q^0}\{S_1, 1/\left(1+r^0\right)\}$ the forward FXR can be both higher and lower that the futures FXR.

By now the pricing and hedging of calls and puts should be straightforward. The seller of a call creates a replicating portfolio by investing Δ^0, Δ^1 in dollars and euros, respectively. The initial balance is as follows

$$\Delta^0 + \Delta^1 S_0 = C_0.$$

Depending on the state of the market at $t = 1$ the seller has to satisfy one of the two conditions, either

$$\Delta^0 + \Delta^1 \frac{\left(1+r_0^1\right)S_{1,0}}{\left(1+r_0^0\right)} = 0,$$

or

$$\Delta^0 + \Delta^1 \frac{\left(1+r_1^1\right)S_{1,1}}{\left(1+r_1^0\right)} = \frac{(S_{1,1}-K)}{\left(1+r_1^0\right)}.$$

Accordingly,

$$\Delta^0 = -\frac{\left(1+r_0^1\right)S_{1,0}\left(S_{1,1}-K\right)}{\left(1+r_0^0\right)\left(1+r_1^1\right)S_{1,1} - \left(1+r_1^0\right)\left(1+r_0^1\right)S_{1,0}},$$

$$\Delta^1 = \frac{\left(1+r_0^0\right)\left(S_{1,1}-K\right)}{\left(1+r_0^0\right)\left(1+r_1^1\right)S_{1,1} - \left(1+r_1^0\right)\left(1+r_0^1\right)S_{1,0}}$$

$$C_0 = \frac{\left(\left(1 + r_0^0\right) S_0 - \left(1 + r_0^1\right) S_{1,0}\right) \left(S_{1,1} - K\right)}{\left(1 + r_0^0\right) \left(1 + r_1^1\right) S_{1,1} - \left(1 + r_1^0\right) \left(1 + r_0^1\right) S_{1,0}}.$$

As might be expected, the price of a call is the expectation of its discounted payoff at maturity,

$$C_0 = \mathbb{E}_{Q^0} \left\{ \frac{C_1}{(1 + r^0)} \right\}.$$

The price of the put can be written as

$$P_0 = \mathbb{E}_{Q^0} \left\{ \frac{P_1}{(1 + r^0)} \right\}.$$

Put-call parity relation has the same form as before, namely

$$C_0 - P_0 = B^0 \left(F - K\right).$$

The portfolio selection problem can be solved in the same fashion as before.

Example 5.4. *Now we show how to price and hedge all the relevant contingent claims in the market introduced above. We consider the domestic bond, forward contract, and call and put with strike $K = 0.85$ and obtain*

	B^0	F	C^0	P^0
V_0	0.941	0.915	0.081	0.020
Δ^0	1.103	−0.861	−0.554	0.240
Δ^1	−0.181	0.957	0.705	−0.244

The most interesting difference between Examples 5.4 and 5.2 is that hedging of the risky domestic bond requires investing in the foreign MMA.

5.4 General single-period markets

Above we analyzed the binomial two-country market in great detail and with relatively little effort. However, it is important to understand that this success is mostly a consequence of a very simple nature of our model. We now consider the general case of a single-period market with one country which is called domestic and distinguished by the superscript 0, and N foreign countries which are called foreign and distinguished by superscripts n. Below we assume that Greek superscripts μ, ν run from 0 to N while Latin superscripts m, n run from 1 to N. At time $t = 0$ (in the beginning of the period) one has to pay

S_0^{0n} units of the domestic currency (dollars) in order to acquire one unit of the nth currency. We formally put $S_0^{00} = 1$ and introduce the $(N+1)$-component augmented vector $\mathbf{Z}_0$ of the initial FXRs,

$$\mathbf{Z}_0 = \left(1, S_0^{01}, ..., S_0^{0N}\right)^T,$$

where the superscript T denotes the transpose. Here and below we use the notation $\mathbf{X}$ and $\mathbf{X}'$ for $(N+1)$ and N-component vectors, respectively. It is sufficient to know $\mathbf{Z}$ in order to find all cross rates, i.e. the price of one unit of the nth currency in terms of the mth currency. The corresponding rate has the form

$$S^{mn} = \frac{S^{0n}}{S^{0m}}.$$

At time $t = 1$ (in the end of the period) the return on one unit of currency invested into its own MMA is (in general) uncertain, and the FXRs are uncertain as well. To quantify the uncertainty, we assume that in the end of the period our market can be in one of the K states which we denote by either $\{0, 1, ..., K-1\}$, or $\omega_0, ..., \omega_{K-1}$, and assign to them some (real-world) probabilities $p_0, ..., p_{K-1}$, $p_k > 0$, $p_0 + ... + p_{K-1} = 1$, which define a probability measure P. The value of the νth MMA in the kth state is denoted by

$$A_{1,k}^{\nu} = 1 + r_k^{\nu},$$

where $r_k^{\nu} > -1$ is the rate of return, the nth FXR is denoted by $S_{1,k}^{0n} > 0$. For simplicity and in order to comply with notation of Chapter 3, we do not use the bold face to distinguish K-component vectors. At $t = 1$ the dollar value of one unit of currency n invested in the corresponding MMA is given by

$$A_k^{0n} = (1 + r_k^n) S_{1,k}^{0n}.$$

Its discounted value is

$$\hat{A}_{1,k}^{0n} = \frac{A_{1,k}^{0n}}{A_{1,k}^0} = \frac{(1 + r_k^n) S_{1,k}^{0n}}{(1 + r_k^0)}.$$

The corresponding relative rate of return has the form

$$\hat{\varrho}_k^{0n} = \frac{(1 + r_k^n) S_{1,k}^{0n}}{(1 + r_k^0) S_0^{0n}} - 1.$$

We represent this information succinctly via the augmented matrix $\mathcal{Z}_1$ and its transpose $\mathcal{Z}_1^T$,

$$
\mathcal{Z}_1 = \begin{pmatrix} 1 & \cdots & 1 \\ \hat{A}_{1,0}^{01} & \cdots & \hat{A}_{1,K-1}^{01} \\ \cdots & \cdots & \cdots \\ \hat{A}_{1,0}^{0N} & \cdots & \hat{A}_{1,K}^{0N} \end{pmatrix},
$$

$$
\mathcal{Z}_1^T = \begin{pmatrix} 1 & \hat{A}_{1,0}^{01} & \cdots & \hat{A}_{1,0}^{0N} \\ \cdots & \cdots & \cdots & \cdots \\ 1 & \hat{A}_{1,K-1}^{01} & \cdots & \hat{A}_{1,K-1}^{0N} \end{pmatrix}.
$$

For our immediate purposes the market is solely characterized by the initial vector $\mathbf{Z}_0$ of spot FXRs, the final matrix $\mathcal{Z}$ of MMAs values, and the probability measure P. The main objective of the single-period pricing theory is to find relations between the vector $\mathbf{Z}_0$ and the matrix $\mathcal{Z}_1$ which guarantee that the market in question is economically reasonable. Once these relations are found, we can price contingent claims and solve the asset allocation problem.

5.5 Economic constraints

Our idealized market is a playground for representative domestic investors which are characterized by their trading strategies $\Upsilon = (\Upsilon^0, \Upsilon^1, ..., \Upsilon^N)^T$. Such a trading strategy shows how much is invested in dollars and foreign currencies at time $t = 0$. The dollar value of this strategy at time $t = 0$ is given by

$$
\Pi_0 = \Upsilon^0 + \Upsilon^1 S_0^{01} + ... + \Upsilon^N S_0^{0N} = \Upsilon \cdot \mathbf{Z}_0,
$$

where the dot stands for the standard scalar product of two vectors. It is clear that the discounted value of a trading strategy at time $t = 1$ is a random variable of the form

$$
\hat{\Pi}_1 = \mathcal{Z}^T \Upsilon,
$$

$$
\hat{\Pi}_1 = \left(\hat{\Pi}_{1,0}, ..., \hat{\Pi}_{1,K-1} \right),
$$

where

$$
\hat{\Pi}_{1,k} = \Upsilon^0 + \Upsilon^1 \hat{A}_{1,k}^{01} + ... + \Upsilon^N \hat{A}_{1,k}^{0N}.
$$

We need to find the relations between $\mathbf{Z}_0$ and $\mathcal{Z}$ which guarantee that the market is financially reasonable. To do so, we need to remind the reader some elementary facts from linear algebra including the theorem of the alternative and two theorems of the separating hyperplane.

Consider a $p \times q$ matrix $\mathcal{X}$ and its transpose $\mathcal{X}^T$ which is a $q \times p$ matrix. These matrices define mappings from $\mathbb{R}^q$ to $\mathbb{R}^p$ and from $\mathbb{R}^p$ to $\mathbb{R}^q$, respectively. We introduce the four fundamental subspaces associated with the matrices $\mathcal{X}$, $\mathcal{X}^T$, and define their ranks. These subspaces are known as the range of $\mathcal{X}$, denoted by $\mathcal{R}(\mathcal{X})$; the nullspace of $\mathcal{X}$, denoted by $\mathcal{N}(\mathcal{X})$; the range of $\mathcal{X}^T$, denoted by $\mathcal{R}(\mathcal{X}^T)$; and the nullspace of $\mathcal{X}^T$, denoted by $\mathcal{N}(\mathcal{X}^T)$. The range $\mathcal{R}(\mathcal{X})$ is a subspace of $\mathbb{R}^p$ consisting of all the vectors of the form $\mathbf{Y} = \mathcal{X}\mathbf{X}$, where $\mathbf{X}$ is an arbitrary vector from $\mathbb{R}^q$; the nullspace $\mathcal{N}(\mathcal{X})$ is a subspace of $\mathbb{R}^q$ consisting of all the vectors $\mathbf{X}$, such that $\mathcal{X}\mathbf{X} = 0$; $\mathcal{R}(\mathcal{X}^T)$ and $\mathcal{N}(\mathcal{X}^T)$ are defined in a similar fashion, they are subspaces of $\mathbb{R}^q$ and $\mathbb{R}^p$, respectively. The rank of the matrix $\mathcal{X}$ which is denoted by $rnk(\mathcal{X})$ is defined as the dimension of its range $\mathcal{R}(\mathcal{X})$, so that $\dim(\mathcal{R}(\mathcal{X})) = rnk(\mathcal{X})$. It can be shown that the rank of $\mathcal{X}^T$ coincides with the rank of $\mathcal{X}$, and $\dim(\mathcal{R}(\mathcal{X}^T)) = rnk(\mathcal{X}^T) = rnk(\mathcal{X})$. It is clear that $rnk(\mathcal{X}) \le \min(p, q)$. Besides, $\dim(\mathcal{N}(\mathcal{X})) = q - rnk(\mathcal{X})$, $\dim(\mathcal{N}(\mathcal{X}^T)) = p - rnk(\mathcal{X})$.

Now we are ready to formulate the theorem of the alternative.

Theorem of the alternative (TA). *The subspaces $\mathcal{N}(\mathcal{X}^T)$ and $\mathcal{R}(\mathcal{X})$ are mutually orthogonal. Accordingly, either $\mathcal{N}(\mathcal{X}^T) \ne 0$ and $rnk(\mathcal{X}) < p$, or $\mathcal{R}(\mathcal{X}) = \mathbb{R}^p$ and $rnk(\mathcal{X}) = p$. In other words either the equation $\mathcal{X}^T\mathbf{Y}_1 = 0$ has a nontrivial solution $\mathbf{Y}_1 \in \mathbb{R}^p$, or else the equation $\mathcal{X}\mathbf{X} = \mathbf{Y}_2$ has a solution for any $\mathbf{Y}_2 \in \mathbb{R}^p$. Thus, either $\mathcal{X}\mathbf{X} = \mathbf{Y}_2$ has a solution, or else there is a $\mathbf{Y}_1$ such that $\mathcal{X}^T\mathbf{Y}_1 = 0$ and $\mathbf{Y}_1 \cdot \mathbf{Y}_2 \ne 0$.*

We also need two theorems of the separating hyperplane.

First theorem of the separating hyperplane (FTSH). *Either $\mathcal{X}\mathbf{X} = \mathbf{Y}_1$ has a nonnegative solution $\mathbf{X} \ge 0$, or else there is a vector $\mathbf{Y}_2$ such that $\mathcal{X}^T\mathbf{Y}_2 \ge 0$, and $\mathbf{Y}_1 \cdot \mathbf{Y}_2 < 0$.*

Second theorem of the separating hyperplane (STSH). *Either $\mathcal{X}\mathbf{X} = \mathbf{Y}_1$ has a positive solution $\mathbf{X} > 0$, or else there is a vector $\mathbf{Y}_2$ such that $\mathcal{X}^T\mathbf{Y}_2 \ge 0$ and $\mathbf{Y}_1 \cdot \mathbf{Y}_2 \le 0$.*

If $p \ne q$ we cannot define the inverse of a matrix $\mathcal{X}$. However, if $\mathcal{X}$ has the maximum possible rank, $rnk(\mathcal{X}) = \min(p, q)$, we can define the so-called right inverse $\mathcal{Y}$ of $\mathcal{X}$ as follows

$$\mathcal{Y} = \mathcal{X}^T(\mathcal{X}\mathcal{X}^T)^{-1}.$$

The right inverse has the property

$$\mathcal{X}\mathcal{Y} = \mathcal{I},$$

where $\mathcal{I}$ is the identity matrix in $\mathbb{R}^p$. The right inverse of $\mathcal{X}^T$ is defined in a similar fashion. Below we use right inverse matrices in order to find perfect hedges for attainable contingent claims.

Now we are ready to return to the discussion of our idealized market. For our purposes we can formulate *TA* as follows: either $\mathcal{Z}_1 a = \mathbf{Z}_0$ has a solution, or else there is a trading strategy Υ such that $\mathcal{Z}_1^T \Upsilon = 0$, and $\Upsilon \cdot \mathbf{Z}_0 \neq 0$. By using the *TA*, we can establish the first nontrivial relation between the initial FXRs $\mathbf{Z}_0$ and the final FXRs $\mathcal{Z}_1$. To do so, we consider two different trading strategies $\Upsilon^{(i)}$, $i = 1, 2$. Assume that at time $t = 1$ these strategies have the same discounted value, $\hat{\Pi}_1^{(1)} = \hat{\Pi}_1^{(2)}$, where $\hat{\Pi}_1^{(i)} = \mathcal{Z}_1^T \Upsilon^{(i)}$. Then we have to require that these strategies have the same value at time $t = 0$, $\Pi_0^{(1)} = \Pi_0^{(2)}$, where $\Pi_0^{(i)} = \Upsilon^{(i)} \cdot \mathbf{Z}_0$, so that the initial values of two trading strategies coincide provided that their discounted final values coincide, i.e., the *law of one price (LOP)* is satisfied. It is clear that a logically consistent pricing in the market where this law is violated is impossible. Due to the linearity of our market we can reformulate the *LOP* as follows: The initial value of a trading strategy is zero provided that its (discounted) final value is zero. The reader can prove as an exercise that these two formulations are equivalent.

We now reformulate the *LOP* as a linear algebra statement. The *LOP* is satisfied if and only if $\mathbf{Z}_0$ is orthogonal to the nullspace of $\mathcal{Z}_1^T$. Indeed, any trading strategy Υ with zero final value belongs to $\mathcal{N}(\mathcal{Z}_1^T)$. Its initial value is equal to $\Upsilon \cdot \mathbf{Z}_0$. This value is equal to zero if and only if $\mathbf{Z}_0$ and Υ are orthogonal. The *TA* allows us to conclude that subspace of vectors orthogonal to the nullspace $\mathcal{N}(\mathcal{Z}_1^T)$ coincides with the range $\mathcal{R}(\mathcal{Z}_1)$. Accordingly the *LOP* holds if and only if $\mathbf{Z}_0$ belongs to the range $\mathcal{R}(\mathcal{Z}_1)$, $\mathbf{Z}_0 \in \mathcal{R}(\mathcal{Z}_1)$, or, in other words, $\mathbf{Z}_0 = \mathcal{Z}_1 a$, where a is a certain vector in $\mathbb{R}^K$. The zeroth component of this relation shows that

$$1 = a_0 + ... + a_{K-1}.$$

However, in general, we cannot conclude that a defines a probability measure because some of a_k can be negative. The nth component of the relation between the initial and final FXRs yields

$$
\begin{aligned}
S_0^{0n} &= a_0 \frac{(1 + r_0^n) S_{1,0}^{0n}}{(1 + r_0^0)} + ... + a_{K-1} \frac{(1 + r_{K-1}^n) S_{1,K-1}^{0n}}{(1 + r_{K-1}^0)} \\
&= a_0 \hat{A}_{1,0}^{0n} + ... + a_{K-1} \hat{A}_{1,K-1}^{0n},
\end{aligned}
$$

so that today's FXR is the weighted average of the future relative FXRs and the weights are the same for all currencies traded in the market. To summarize, we can formulate the following statement:

$$LOP \iff \mathbf{Z}_0 = \mathcal{Z}_1 a. \tag{5.16}$$

The *LOP* is a very crude necessary condition for the market to behave sensibly. We need to find more sophisticated conditions which will ensure the practical applicability of our model. These conditions have to do with the ability to partially order trading strategies and say which one is better than the other. We compare trading strategies $\Upsilon^{(i)}$, with the same initial value Π_0. We say that the first strategy strongly dominates the second if $\hat{\Pi}_1^{(1)} > \hat{\Pi}_1^{(2)}$, where the latter inequality means that in every state of the market the first strategy has a larger discounted value than the second one, or, in other words, that the vector $\hat{\Pi}_1^{(1)} - \hat{\Pi}_1^{(2)}$ belongs to the strictly positive octant $\mathbb{R}_{++}^K$. We say that $\Upsilon^{(1)}$ weakly dominates $\Upsilon^{(2)}$ if $\hat{\Pi}_1^{(1)} \geq \hat{\Pi}_1^{(2)}$, i.e., in every state of the market the first strategy is at least as valuable as the second one and in some states the first strategy is more valuable than the second one, or, in other words, that the vector $\hat{\Pi}_1^{(1)} - \hat{\Pi}_1^{(2)}$ belongs to the nonnegative octant $\mathbb{R}_+^K$. As before, we can consider strategies Υ with zero initial value and say that such strategies are strongly (weakly) dominant if their final value is positive (nonnegative). It is clear that in a reasonable market strongly dominant strategies cannot exist because they allow an investor to obtain a positive final gain with zero initial investment. Accordingly, they will be infinitely attractive to investors who would buy infinite quantities of the underlying currencies thus destroying the pricing mechanism. Weakly dominant strategies cannot exist as well since they are only marginally less valuable than strongly dominant ones and would attract too much interest to be sustainable.

As we will see shortly, the absence of strongly dominant strategies implies the *LOP* but not *vice versa*, while the absence of weakly dominant strategies implies the absence of strongly dominant ones but not *vice versa*. The absence of weakly dominant strategies is also known as the no-arbitrage condition.

It is very convenient to reformulate the *no strongly dominant strategies condition (NSDSC)* as a linear algebra statement. To this end we apply the *FTSH* and conclude that either $\mathcal{Z}_1 b = \mathbf{Z}_0$ has a nonnegative solution $b \geq 0$, or else there is a trading strategy Υ such that $\mathcal{Z}_1^T \Upsilon \geq 0$, and $\Upsilon \cdot \mathbf{Z}_0 < 0$.

Now, the absence of strongly dominant strategies implies that every trading strategy Υ with nonnegative final value $\mathcal{Z}_1^T \Upsilon \geq 0$, has nonnegative initial value $\Upsilon \cdot \mathbf{Z}_0 \geq 0$. Indeed, if there is a strategy $\Upsilon = (\Upsilon^0, \Upsilon^1, ..., \Upsilon^N)$ which violates this requirement, then there is a strongly dominant trading strategy

$$\widetilde{\Upsilon} = (\Upsilon^0 - \Upsilon \cdot \mathbf{Z}_0, \Upsilon^1, ..., \Upsilon^N),$$

such that $\mathcal{Z}_1^T \widetilde{\Upsilon} > 0$, $\Upsilon \cdot \mathbf{Z}_0 = 0$. Accordingly, the *FTSH* shows that in the absence of strongly dominant strategies $\mathbf{Z}_0 = \mathcal{Z}_1 b$, where $b \geq 0$. The zeroth component of this relation yields

$$1 = b_0 + ... + b_{K-1},$$

so that b defines a probability measure. The nth component yields

$$
\begin{aligned}
S_0^{0n} &= b_0 \frac{(1 + r_0^n) S_{1,0}^{0n}}{(1 + r_0^0)} + ... + b_{K-1} \frac{(1 + r_{K-1}^n) S_{1,K-1}^{0n}}{(1 + r_{K-1}^0)} \\
&= b_0 \hat{A}_{1,0}^{0n} + ... + b_{K-1} \hat{A}_{1,K-1}^{0n},
\end{aligned}
$$

so that today's FXR is the expectation of the future modified FXR. Economies which satisfy *NSDSC* have just one drawback from a logical standpoint, namely, certain states, although subjectively possible (the corresponding $p_k > 0$) are objectively impossible ($b_k = 0$) and have to be excluded from consideration. To summarize,

$$NSDSC \Longleftrightarrow \mathbf{Z}_0 = \mathcal{Z}_1 b, \quad b \geq 0. \tag{5.17}$$

Finally, we discuss the *no weakly dominant strategies condition (NWDSC)* which we also call the *no arbitrage condition (NAC)* . Once again, we want to reformulate it as a linear algebra statement. To this end we use the *STSH* which we formulate as follows: either $\mathcal{Z}_1 q = \mathbf{Z}_0$ has a positive solution $q > 0$, or else there is a trading strategy Υ such that $\mathcal{Z}_1^T \Upsilon \geq 0$ and $\Upsilon \cdot \mathbf{Z}_0 \leq 0$. To start with, we need to show that in the absence of weakly dominant strategies the inequalities $\mathcal{Z}_1^T \Upsilon \geq 0$ and $\Upsilon \cdot \mathbf{Z}_0 \leq 0$ cannot be satisfied simultaneously. Indeed, if they are true for a certain trading strategy Υ, then the initial value of this strategy is nonpositive, while its final value is nonnegative, so that the modified strategy $\widetilde{\Upsilon}$ is weakly dominant. By virtue of *STSH*, we can conclude that the equation $\mathcal{Z}_1 q = \mathbf{Z}_0$ has a positive solution $q > 0$, which defines a domestic probability measure Q^0,

$$q_0 + ... q_{K-1} = 1,$$

and

$$
\begin{aligned}
S_0^{0n} &= q_0 \frac{(1 + r_0^n) S_{1,0}^{0n}}{(1 + r_0^0)} + ... + q_{K-1} \frac{(1 + r_{K-1}^n) S_{1,K-1}^{0n}}{(1 + r_{K-1}^0)} \\
&= q_0 \hat{A}_{1,0}^{0n} + ... + q_{K-1} \hat{A}_{1,K-1}^{0n},
\end{aligned}
$$

or, symbolically,

$$S_0^{0n} = \mathbb{E}_{Q^0}\left\{\frac{(1+r^n)\,S_1^{0n}}{(1+r^0)}\right\} = \mathbb{E}_{Q^0}\left\{\hat{A}_1^{0n}\right\}.$$

This measure is called a risk-neutral measure. It plays the key role in pricing theory. For markets which satisfy *NAC* spot FXRs are just expectations of the relative future FXRs which allows one to develop pricing theory for more complicated financial instruments in such markets.

In geometric terms, $\mathbf{Z}_0$ belongs to the convex hull span by the column-vectors forming $\mathcal{Z}_1$.

We emphasize that, in general, risk-neutral measure is not unique. If there are two different risk-neutral measures $q^{(1)}, q^{(2)}$, then their difference $q^{(1)} - q^{(2)} \in \mathcal{N}(\mathcal{Z}_1)$. Thus, multiple pricing measures exist if and only if $rnk(\mathcal{Z}_1) < K$. To summarize,

$$NWDSC \equiv NAC \Longleftrightarrow \mathbf{Z}_0 = \mathcal{Z}_1 q, \quad q > 0. \tag{5.18}$$

We call markets complete if there is only one risk-neutral pricing measure and incomplete otherwise. It is clear that for incomplete markets there are infinitely many risk-neutral measures.

Comparison of conditions (5.16), (5.17), (5.18) clearly shows that the following logical implications are true

$$NAC \Longrightarrow NSDSC \Longrightarrow LOP.$$

Example 5.5. *(The binomial two-country market.) In order to illustrate the ideas developed above we revisit the binomial two-country market studied in Section 5.3. The matrix of relative FXRs Z_1, and its transpose Z_1^T have the form*

$$\mathcal{Z}_1 = \begin{pmatrix} 1 & 1 \\ \hat{A}_{1,0}^{01} & \hat{A}_{1,1}^{01} \end{pmatrix}, \quad \mathcal{Z}_1^T = \begin{pmatrix} 1 & \hat{A}_{1,0}^{01} \\ 1 & \hat{A}_{1,1}^{01} \end{pmatrix}.$$

Our objective is to classify the market depending on the choice of the vector $\mathbf{Z}_0 = (1, S_0^{01})^T$ and the matrix $\mathcal{Z}_1$. We assume that $\hat{A}_{1,0}^{01} < \hat{A}_{1,1}^{01}$, or, equivalently, $S_{1,0}^{01} < S_{1,1}^{01}$, so that our market is nondegenerate. The equation $\mathbf{Z}_0 = \mathcal{Z}_1 a$ is uniquely solvable for any $\mathbf{Z}_0$, so that any positive S_0^{01} can be represented as

$$S_0^{01} = a_0 \hat{A}_{1,0}^{01} + a_1 \hat{A}_{1,1}^{01},$$
$$1 = a_0 + a_1.$$

Thus, any nondegenerate market obeys the LOP. The NSDSC is satisfied provided that

$$\hat{A}_{1,0}^{01} \leq S_0^{01} \leq \hat{A}_{1,1}^{01},$$

or, equivalently, if

$$S_{1,0}^{01} \leq F^{01} \leq S_{1,1}^{01}.$$

The NAC is true provided that these inequalities are strict. For the initial FXR S_0^{01} sandwiched between the final rates $\hat{A}_{1,0}^{01}, \hat{A}_{1,1}^{01}$, the corresponding unique risk-neutral probability density q has the form

$$q = \left(\frac{\hat{A}_{1,1}^{01} - S_0^{01}}{\hat{A}_{1,1}^{01} - \hat{A}_{1,0}^{01}}, \frac{S_0^{01} - \hat{A}_{1,0}^{01}}{\hat{A}_{1,1}^{01} - \hat{A}_{1,0}^{01}} \right)^T.$$

Example 5.6. *(The trinomial two-country market.) In this example we consider the trinomial two-country market which can end up in three different states. We can represent the corresponding matrices $\mathcal{Z}_1$, $\mathcal{Z}_1^T$ as*

$$\mathcal{Z}_1 = \begin{pmatrix} 1 & 1 & 1 \\ \hat{A}_{1,0}^{01} & \hat{A}_{1,1}^{01} & \hat{A}_{1,2}^{01} \end{pmatrix}, \quad \mathcal{Z}_1^T = \begin{pmatrix} 1 & \hat{A}_{1,0}^{01} \\ 1 & \hat{A}_{1,1}^{01} \\ 1 & \hat{A}_{1,2}^{01} \end{pmatrix},$$

where we assume that $\hat{A}_{1,0}^{01} < \hat{A}_{1,2}^{01}$, so that our market is nondegenerate. As before, we want to classify the market depending on the choice of the initial FXR vector $\mathbf{Z} = (1, S_0^{01})^T$. It is clear that any positive S_0^{01} can be written as

$$S_0^{01} = a_0 \hat{A}_{1,0}^{01} + a_1 \hat{A}_{1,1}^{01} + a_2 \hat{A}_{1,2}^{01},$$
$$1 = a_0 + a_1 + a_2,$$

so that the LOP is satisfied regardless of the choice of S_0^{01}. However, in general, we cannot guarantee that there are no strongly dominant strategies. The NSDSC is satisfied provided that

$$\hat{A}_{1,0}^{01} \leq S_0^{01} \leq \hat{A}_{1,2}^{01},$$

or, equivalently, if

$$S_{1,0}^{01} \leq F^{01} \leq S_{1,2}^{01}.$$

The NAC is satisfied when these inequalities are strict. If S_0^{01} is chosen in such a way that there is no arbitrage, then we can find the corresponding risk-neutral probability measures by solving the following system of equations

$$\hat{\varrho} \cdot q = 0, \quad E \cdot q = 1, \tag{5.19}$$

where

$$\hat{\varrho} = (\hat{\varrho}_0^{01}, \hat{\varrho}_1^{01}, \hat{\varrho}_2^{01})^T, \quad q = (q_0, q_1, q_2)^T, \quad E = (1,1,1)^T.$$

It is easy to check that the solution of equations (5.19) can be written in the vector form as follows

$$q = \frac{\hat{\varrho} \cdot \hat{\varrho} E - \hat{\varrho} \cdot E \hat{\varrho}}{\hat{\varrho} \cdot \hat{\varrho} E \cdot E - (\hat{\varrho} \cdot E)^2} + \gamma \hat{\varrho} \times E,$$

where $\times$ denotes the cross product of two vectors, while γ is a constant chosen in such a way that $q \gg 0$. It is obvious that all trinomial two-country markets are incomplete.

5.6   Pricing of contingent claims

From now on, we consider only no-arbitrage markets and assume that there is at least one domestic risk-neutral measure Q^0 such the initial FXRs $\mathbf{Z}_0$ can be expressed in terms of the discounted final FXRs $\mathcal{Z}_1$ by virtue of the relation $\mathbf{Z}_0 = \mathbb{E}_{Q^0}\{\mathcal{Z}_1\}$. A contingent claim is a contract between a buyer and a seller which they enter at time $t = 0$ obligating the seller to pay the buyer an amount $V_{1,k}$ at time $t = 1$ provided that the market is in final state k. On occasion the contract imposes mutual obligations on the buyer and the seller which means that some $V_{1,k}$ are negative. Since the amount of payoff is not known at time $t = 0$, a contingent claim can be considered as a random variable

$$V_1 = (V_{1,0}, ..., V_{1,K-1}),$$

or as a discounted random variable

$$\hat{V}_1 = \frac{V_1}{(1 + r^0)} = \left(\frac{V_{1,0}}{1 + r_0^0}, ..., \frac{V_{1,K-1}}{1 + r_{K-1}^0} \right).$$

Consistent pricing of contingent claims is one of the most important objectives of financial engineering which we study throughout this book. In this section we discuss the simplest aspects of the pricing problem in the context of the idealized no-arbitrage market model constructed in the previous section.

We call a contingent claim attainable (or marketable) if there is a trading strategy Δ such that $\hat{V}_1 = \mathcal{Z}_1^T \Delta$, otherwise we call a contingent claim unattainable. The corresponding trading strategy is called a replicating strategy for the contingent claim under consideration. In the language of linear algebra, attainable claims belong to the range $\mathcal{R}(\mathcal{Z}_1^T)$, while unattainable claims belong to its complement. The market is complete if and only if all contingent claims are attainable. The theorem of the alternative shows that $\mathcal{R}(\mathcal{Z}_1^T) = \mathbb{R}^K$ if and only if $\mathcal{N}(\mathcal{Z}_1) = 0$, or, equivalently, if the rank of the matrix $\mathcal{Z}_1$ is equal to K which is possible only when $K \leq N + 1$. It is clear that for complete no-arbitrage markets there is a unique risk-neutral pricing measure and vice versa.

It is easy to price attainable claims (in both complete and incomplete markets). The price V_0 of a contingent claim $\hat{V}_1 = \mathcal{Z}_1^T \Delta$ is given by

$$
\begin{aligned}
V_0 &= \Delta \cdot \mathbf{Z}_0 = \Delta \cdot \mathcal{Z}_1 q = \mathbb{E}_{Q^0} \left\{ \mathcal{Z}_1^T \Delta \right\} \qquad (5.20) \\
&= \mathbb{E}_{Q^0} \left\{ \hat{V}_1 \right\} = \mathbb{E}_{Q^0} \left\{ \frac{V_1}{1 + r^0} \right\}.
\end{aligned}
$$

In words, the initial price of an attainable claim is equal to its expected future value discounted at the risk-free rate. By virtue of the *LOP* this price is the same regardless of the choice of a replicating strategy. A rational investor is indifferent to being either a seller or a buyer of an attainable claim provided that it is priced according to formula (5.20). The remarkable fact is that attainable contingent claims can be priced by virtue of the risk-neutral measure without knowing the corresponding replicating strategy. [2] However, knowing such a strategy is useful because it allows the seller of a contract to be perfectly hedged, i.e., to be able to fulfil his obligations at maturity of the contract regardless of the final state of the market. In order to do so, the seller of a contingent contract has to construct a replicating portfolio which will produce as much cash at maturity as is needed to satisfy the buyer's claims regardless of the state of the market. (In general, replication requires either borrowing in dollars and investing the proceeds in foreign currencies or selling foreign currencies short and investing the proceeds in dollars.)

At this stage, the reader might start to think that attainable contingent claims are nothing more than the corresponding replicating strategies, so that

---

[2] Occasionally, an investor is said to be risk neutral if he is indifferent between receiving either an uncertain cash flow at maturity or the discounted expected value of this cash flow today.

there is no need to buy them at all. To a certain extend this is true, but in more realistic markets, where transaction costs and other frictions cannot be neglected, buying a contingent claim can be much more convenient than replicating it synthetically, so that buyers are prepared to pay a premium on top of the risk-neutral price for claims that suit their needs.

To hedge himself, the seller of an attainable claim needs to know at least one replicating strategy. In a complete market such a strategy can be found by virtue of the right inverse of the matrix $\mathcal{Z}_1^T$, which we denote by $\mathcal{Y}$. This matrix, which is well defined because the market is complete and $\mathcal{Z}_1$ has the maximum possible rank, has the form

$$\mathcal{Y} = \mathcal{Z}_1 \left(\mathcal{Z}_1^T \mathcal{Z}_1 \right)^{-1},$$

We can easily show that

$$\Delta = \mathcal{Y} \hat{V}_1,$$

is a replicating strategy. In general, other replicating strategies can exist as well.

In an incomplete market the right inverse matrix $\mathcal{Y}$ does not exist. However, we can study the matrix $\mathcal{Z}_1^T \mathcal{Z}_1$ on the subspace of attainable claims and denote the corresponding restricted matrix by $\widetilde{\mathcal{Z}_1^T \mathcal{Z}_1}$. The restricted matrix is invertible on the subspace of attainable claims, so that we can define the restricted right inverse

$$\widetilde{\mathcal{Y}} = \mathcal{Z}_1 (\widetilde{\mathcal{Z}_1^T \mathcal{Z}_1})^{-1},$$

and choose a replicating strategy of the form

$$\Delta = \widetilde{\mathcal{Y}} \hat{V}_1. \tag{5.21}$$

At the same time, for nonattainable claims (which exist only in incomplete markets) there are no replicating strategies, so that they cannot be priced uniquely. Instead, prices of unattainable claims can be sandwiched between the lowest price, denoted by $V_0^{(+)}$ at which a risk-averse investor is willing to sell such a claim, and the largest price $V_0^{(-)}$ at which he is ready to buy it,

$$V_0^{(-)} \leq V_0 \leq V_0^{(+)}.$$

All prices outside the interval $[V_0^{(-)}, V_0^{(+)}]$ are economically unreasonable and can be arbitraged, while prices within this interval are acceptable from our elementary economic standpoint. We emphasize that for attainable claims $V_0^{(-)} = V_0^{(+)}$.

In order to find $V_0^{(\pm)}$ we need to solve the following linear programming problems,

$$P^{(+)} = \left\{ \mathbb{E}_{Q^0} \left\{ \mathcal{Z}_1^T \Delta \right\} \to \min \quad \text{subject to} \quad \mathcal{Z}_1^T \Delta - \hat{V}_1 > 0 \right\}. \qquad (5.22)$$

$$P^{(-)} = \left\{ \mathbb{E}_{Q^0} \left\{ \mathcal{Z}_1^T \Delta \right\} \to \max \quad \text{subject to} \quad \mathcal{Z}_1^T \Delta - \hat{V}_1 < 0 \right\}. \qquad (5.23)$$

It is clear that if a nonattainable claim is sold for $V_0^{(0)}$ the seller can super-replicate it by using the minimizing strategy Δ, so that at maturity the seller can fulfil his obligations to the buyer and even make a profit in some cases. Similarly, if a claim is bought for $V_-(0)$ the buyer can finance it by using the opposite of the maximizing strategy and be sure that he will receive at maturity enough cash to cover his obligations and even more in some cases. Problems (5.22), (5.23) are standard linear programming problems. These problems are always solvable since there are deterministic claims (which can be replicated by investing solely into the domestic MMA) which are better (worse) than any given claim. Solutions of problems (5.22), (5.23) can be found by virtue of the standard simplex method of linear programming.

As before, we consider four basic contingent claims. To start with, we evaluate the domestic bond with the face value of one, i.e., the claim with payoff

$$V_1 = E = (1, ..., 1),$$

which obligates the seller to deliver one dollar to the buyer regardless of the final state of the market. The buyer of such a claim locks the rate of return on his investment regardless of the market behavior. Assuming that such a claim is attainable (which might not be the case in general), we can represent its price which we denote by B^0 as

$$B^0 = \frac{q_0}{1 + r_0^0} + ... + \frac{q_{K-1}}{1 + r_{K-1}^0} = \mathbb{E}_{Q^0} \left\{ \frac{1}{1 + r^0} \right\}.$$

The rate of return on the bond is

$$\varrho^0 = \frac{1}{B^0} - 1,$$

it is sandwiched between the lowest and the highest possible rates of return on the domestic MMA,

$$\min \left\{r_0^0, ..., r_{K-1}^0\right\} \le \varrho^0 \le \max \left\{r_0^0, ..., r_{K-1}^0\right\}.$$

When the rate of return on the money invested in the domestic MMA is certain, $r_0^0 = ... = r_{K-1}^0 = r^0$, the bond is always attainable, its price is given by $B^0 = 1/(1 + r^0)$, and the rate of return is equal to r^0. In this simple case, the seller of the bond has to sell it for B^0 and invest the proceeds into the domestic MMA. In general, the seller has to invest in the domestic and foreign MMAs in order to achieve a perfect hedge. The bond is attainable if and only if the vector

$$\hat{V}_1 = \hat{E} = \left(\frac{1}{1 + r_0^0}, ..., \frac{1}{1 + r_{K-1}^0} \right)$$

belongs to the range $\mathcal{R}(\mathcal{Z}_1^T)$, or, equivalently, is orthogonal to the nullspace $\mathcal{N}(\mathcal{Z}_1)$. If the latter condition is violated, the bond cannot be priced uniquely. Instead, a logically consistent price band

$$B^{0(-)} \le B^0 \le B^{0(+)},$$

where $B^{0(\pm)}$ are the solutions of linear programs (5.22), (5.23), can be established.

It is left to the reader as an exercise to check that the price of the foreign bond, if it is attainable, can be written as

$$B^n = \mathbb{E}_{Q^0} \left\{ \frac{1 + \hat{\varrho}^{0n}}{1 + r^n} \right\}.$$

Next, we consider a forward contract with strike K^{0n} on the nth foreign currency. Such a contract is a contingent claim with the payoff

$$FO\left(1, S_1^{0n}\right) = \left(S_{1,0}^{0n} - K^{0n}, ..., S_{1,K-1}^{0n} - K^{0n}\right),$$

its discounted value is

$$\begin{aligned}
\widehat{FO}\left(1, S_1^{0n}\right) &= \left(\frac{S_{1,0}^{0n}}{1 + r_0^0} - \frac{K^{0n}}{1 + r_0^0}, ..., \frac{S_{1,K-1}^{0n}}{1 + r_{K-1}^0} - \frac{K^{0n}}{1 + r_{K-1}^0} \right) \\
&= \left(\frac{\hat{A}_{1,0}^{0n}}{1 + r_0^n} - \frac{K^{0n}}{1 + r_0^0}, ..., \frac{\hat{A}_{1,K-1}^{0n}}{1 + r_{K-1}^n} - \frac{K^{0n}}{1 + r_{K-1}^0} \right).
\end{aligned}$$

Assuming that a forward contract is attainable (or, equivalently, that the domestic and foreign bonds are attainable) we can represent the initial value of such a contract for any K^{0n} by

$$
\begin{aligned}
FO_0 &= q_0^0 \left(\frac{\hat{A}_{1,0}^{0n}}{1+r_0^n} - \frac{K^{0n}}{1+r_0^0} \right) + \ldots + q_{K-1}^0 \left(\frac{\hat{A}_{1,K-1}^{0n}}{1+r_{K-1}^n} - \frac{K^{0n}}{1+r_{K-1}^0} \right) \\
&= \mathbb{E}_{Q^0} \left\{ \frac{1+\hat{\varrho}^{0n}}{1+r^n} \right\} S_0^{0n} - \mathbb{E}_{Q^0} \left\{ \frac{1}{1+r^0} \right\} K^{0n} \\
&= B^n S_0^{0n} - B^0 K^{0n}.
\end{aligned}
$$

This value is equal to zero provided that $K^{0n} = F^{0n}$, where

$$
F^{0n} = \frac{B^n S_0^{0n}}{B^0},
$$

is the fair forward FXR for the attainable forward contract. As before, we can represent F^{0n} as the expected value of S_1^{0n} with respect to the forward measure,

$$
F^{0n} = \frac{\mathbb{E}_{Q^0} \left\{ S_1^{0n} / \left(1+r^0\right) \right\}}{\mathbb{E}_{Q^0} \left\{ 1 / \left(1+r^0\right) \right\}} = \mathbb{E}_{Q_{frwrd}^0} \left\{ S_1^{0n} \right\}.
$$

If a forward contract is not attainable, the forward FXR can be sandwiched between $F^{0n(-)}$ and $F^{0n(+)}$,

$$
F^{0n(-)} \le F^{0n} \le F^{0n(+)},
$$

where

$$
F^{0n(\pm)} = \frac{B^{n(\pm)} S_0^{0n}}{B^{0(\mp)}}.
$$

When the rates of return on the money invested in the domestic and foreign MMAs are deterministic, F^{0n} is given by the interest rate parity theorem,

$$
F^{0n} = \frac{\left(1+r^0\right)}{\left(1+r^n\right)} S_0^{0n}.
$$

The replicating strategy for the seller of a fair contract consists in borrowing $S_0^{0n}/\left(1+r^n\right)$ dollars and immediately spending them on purchasing one foreign bond.

We now consider calls and puts. We price calls first. At maturity a call on the nth currency with strike K^{0n} pays

$$C_1^{0n} = \left((S_{1,0}^{0n} - K^{0n})_+, ..., (S_{1,K-1}^{0n} - K^{0n})_+ \right).$$

Assuming that this call is attainable, we represent its initial risk-neutral price as

$$C_0^{0n} = \sum_{k=0}^{K-1} q_k^0 \frac{(S_{1,k}^{0n} - K^{0n})_+}{1 + r_k^0} = \sum_{k=k'}^{K-1} q_k^0 \frac{(S_{1,k}^{0n} - K^{0n})}{1 + r_k^0},$$

where k' is the smallest k such that $S_{1,k}^{0n} > K^{0n}$. A hedging strategy for a makretable call is given by the general expression (5.21). If a call is not attainable, we can find the lower and upper limits for its price via the linear programming method.

For the put with strike K^{0n} the final payout is given by

$$P_1^{0n} = \left((K^{0n} - S_{1,0}^{0n})_+, ..., (K^{0n} - S_{1,K-1}^{0n})_+ \right),$$

If the put is attainable, its initial price has the form

$$P_0^{0n} = \sum_{k=0}^{K-1} q_k^0 \frac{(K^{0n} - S_{1,k}^{0n})_+}{1 + r_k^0} = \sum_{k=0}^{k''} q_k^0 \frac{(S_{1,k}^{0n} - K^{0n})}{1 + r_k^0},$$

where k'' is the largest k such that $S_{1,k}^{0n} < K^{0n}$.

It is clear that the difference

$$C_1^{0n} - P_1^{0n} = S_1^{0n} - K^{0n},$$

coincides with the payoff of a forward contract with strike K^{0n}. Assuming for simplicity that interest rates are nonrandom, we can conclude that a call and a put with the same strike are attainable or nonattainable simultaneously, and satisfy put-call parity relation

$$C_0^{0n} - P_0^{0n} = B^n S_0^{0n} - B^0 K^{0n} = B^0 \left(F^{0n} - K^{0n} \right).$$

For the market with several foreign currencies we can construct more complicated contingent claims. For example, we can study the so-called exchange (or Margrabe) option between the mth and n^{th} currencies with the final payoff of the form

$$C_1^{0mn} = \left(\left(S_{1,0}^{0n} - K^{mn} S_{1,0}^{0m} \right)_+, ..., \left(S_{1,K-1}^{0n} - K^{mn} S_{1,K-1}^{0m} \right)_+ \right).$$

Provided that such an option is attainable, its price can be written as

$$
\begin{aligned}
C_0^{0mn} &= \sum_{k=0}^{K-1} q_k^0 \frac{\left(S_{1,k}^{0n} - K^{mn} S_{1,k}^{0m}\right)_+}{1 + r_k^0} \\
&= \sum_{k=0}^{K-1} \left(\hat{A}_{1,k}^{0m} q_k^0\right) \frac{\left(S_{1,k}^{mn} - K^{mn}\right)_+}{1 + r_k^m} \\
&= S_0^{0m} \sum_{k=0}^{K-1} \left(\frac{\hat{A}_{1,k}^{0m}}{S_0^{0m}} q_k^0\right) \frac{\left(S_{1,k}^{mn} - K^{mn}\right)_+}{1 + r_k^m} \\
&= S_0^{0m} \sum_{k=0}^{K-1} q_k^m \frac{\left(S_{1,k}^{mn} - K^{mn}\right)_+}{1 + r_k^m} \\
&= S_0^{0m} C_0^{mn}.
\end{aligned}
$$

Here we use the fact (which we leave to the reader to check) that

$$
Q^m = (q_0^m, ..., q_{K-1}^m) = \left(\frac{\hat{A}_{1,0}^{0m}}{S_0^{0m}} q_0^0, ..., \frac{\hat{A}_{1,K-1}^{0m}}{S_0^{0m}} q_{K-1}^0\right).
$$

It is clear that the price of the exchange option is given by the dollar price of the ordinary call option allowing the buyer to exchange one unit of the nth currency for K^{mn} units of the mth currency. The situation becomes more complex for the so-called exchange options with nonzero strike with the payoff of the form

$$
C_1^{0mn} = \left(\left(S_{1,0}^{0n} - K^{mn} S_{1,0}^{0m} - K^{0n}\right)_+, ..., \left(S_{1,K-1}^{0n} - K^{mn} S_{1,K-1}^{0m} - K^{0n}\right)_+\right),
$$

where $K^{0n} \neq 0$. Their price can still be written as

$$
C_0^{0mn} = \sum_{k=0}^{K-1} q_k^0 \frac{\left(S_{1,k}^{0n} - K^{mn} S_{1,k}^{0m} - K^{0n}\right)_+}{1 + r_k^0},
$$

however, further reductions are not possible.

We have showed above in great detail how to price representative contracts for binomial two-country markets. As an exercise, the reader is encouraged to use the formalism developed in this section in order to repeat the corresponding calculations for trinomial two- and three-country markets.

5.7   Elementary portfolio theory

In this section we develop elementary portfolio theory. We measure the performance of various portfolios relative to the performance of the domestic MMA, so that the relative rate of return on a dollar invested in this MMA is zero.

So far we have been using the domestic risk-neutral probability measure Q^0 and did not say anything about the real-world measure P. Here we study the relation between the two measures. To start with, we introduce the state price density vector, which is the Radon-Nikodym derivative of Q^0 with respect to P,

$$N^0 = \left(\frac{q_0^0}{p_0}, ..., \frac{q_{K-1}^0}{p_{K-1}} \right) = \left(n_0^0, ..., n_{K-1}^0 \right) \gg 0,$$

which we can use in order to switch from the real-world to the risk-neutral measure according to the rule

$$\mathbb{E}_{Q^0} \{ X \} = \mathbb{E}_P \{ N^0 X \},$$

where X is an arbitrary random variable (contingent claim). In particular, by choosing $X = 1$ we get the useful identity

$$\mathbb{E}_P \{ N^0 \} = 1.$$

For the nth currency the rate of return is, by definition, the random variable $\hat{\varrho}^{0n}$. Its expectation with respect to Q^0 is zero. Its expectation with respect to P is denoted by R^{0n}. By using the state price density vector, we can find a useful representation for R^{0n}, namely,

$$\hat{R}^{0n} = \mathbb{E}_P \{ \hat{\varrho}^{0n} \} = \mathbb{E}_P \{ N^0 \} \mathbb{E}_P \{ \hat{\varrho}^{0n} \} - \mathbb{E}_P \{ N^0 \hat{\varrho}^{0n} \} = -\text{cov}_P \{ N^0, \hat{\varrho}^{0n} \}.$$

In general, the real-world rate of return is positive, $\hat{R}^{0n} > 0$, because investors expect to receive the risk premium for holding foreign currencies, accordingly, the corresponding covariance is negative.

Next, we defined the relative rate of return on a portfolio of currencies. Consider a portfolio Π corresponding to a certain trading strategy $\Upsilon = \left(\Upsilon^0, ..., \Upsilon^N \right)$ which shows the amounts invested in different currencies. Assuming that the initial value of this portfolio is positive, $\Pi_0 > 0$, we can define the relative rate of return on this portfolio by analogy with the rate of return on a currency, namely,

$$
\hat{\varrho}_\Pi = \left(\frac{\Pi_{1,0}}{\left(1 + r_0^0\right) \Pi_0} - 1, ..., \frac{\Pi_{1,K-1}}{\left(1 + r_{K-1}^0\right) \Pi_0} - 1 \right)
$$

$$
= \left(\sum_{n=1}^{N} \frac{\Upsilon^n S_0^{0n} \hat{\varrho}_0^{0n}}{\Pi_0}, ..., \sum_{n=1}^{N} \frac{\Upsilon^n S_0^{0n} \hat{\varrho}_{K-1}^{0n}}{\Pi_0} \right).
$$

The risk-neutral expectation of $\hat{\varrho}_\Pi$ is zero, its real-world expectation, which is denoted by R_Π, has the form

$$
\hat{R}_\Pi = \sum_{n=1}^{N} \frac{\Upsilon^n S_0^{0n} \hat{R}^{0n}}{\Pi_0}.
$$

It is easy to show that

$$
\hat{R}_\Pi = -\mathrm{cov}_P \left\{ N^0, \hat{\varrho}_\Pi \right\}.
$$

Suppose that there is at least one currency such that $\hat{R}^{0n} \neq 0$ (which is true in most cases). Then for any $\rho > 0$ there is a portfolio $\Pi^{(\rho)}$ such that $\hat{R}_{\Pi^{(\rho)}} = \rho$. For example, such a portfolio can be created by the trading strategy

$$
\Upsilon = \left(\frac{\left(\hat{R}^{0n} - \rho\right) \Pi_0}{\hat{R}^{0n}}, 0, ..., \frac{\rho \Pi_0}{\hat{R}^{0n} S_0^{0n}}, ..., 0 \right),
$$

which involves investments into dollars and just one foreign currency. It is clear that creating a portfolio with large ρ requires massive borrowing of dollars, so that all such portfolios are highly leveraged.

The average rate of return is just one characteristics of a portfolio (albeit a very important one) . As we have just seen, there are portfolios with arbitrary high expected rates of return. However, such portfolios might not be desirable from an investor's prospective because their returns, although very high, are also rather uncertain, or, in other words, have very high volatility. One criterion for choosing an "optimal" portfolio with given expected rate of return was introduced by Markowitz who proposed to consider portfolios with the smallest possible variance. Formally, for the set of portfolios Π with fixed initial value Π_0 and a given rate of return ρ one needs to solve the following optimization problem:

$$
\begin{cases}
\mathbb{V}_P\{\hat{\varrho}_\Pi\} \to \min, \\
\mathbb{E}_P\{\hat{\varrho}_\Pi\} = \rho, \\
\Pi\left(0\right) = \Pi_0.
\end{cases}
$$

Since

$$\mathbb{V}_P\{\hat{\varrho}_\Pi\} = \mathbb{E}_P\left\{(\hat{\varrho}_\Pi)^2\right\} - (\mathbb{E}_P\{\hat{\varrho}_\Pi\})^2,$$

we can reformulate the above problem as

$$\begin{cases} \frac{1}{2}\mathbb{E}_P\left\{(\hat{\varrho}_\Pi)^2\right\} \to \min, \\ \mathbb{E}_P\{\hat{\varrho}_\Pi\} = \rho, \\ \Pi(0) = \Pi_0, \end{cases}$$

where the factor of $1/2$ is introduced for the sake of convenience. By using the definition of the relative rate of return, we obtain the following final form of the Markowitz optimization problem

$$\begin{cases} \frac{1}{2}\mathbb{E}_P\left\{\left(\frac{\Pi_1}{(1+r^0)\Pi_0}\right)^2\right\} \to \min, \\ \mathbb{E}_P\left\{\frac{\Pi_1}{(1+r^0)\Pi_0}\right\} = 1+\rho, \\ \mathbb{E}_P\left\{N^0\frac{\Pi_1}{(1+r^0)\Pi_0}\right\} = 1. \end{cases}$$

This problem can be solved via the method of Lagrange multipliers. Proceeding in the usual manner, we obtain the following optimality condition

$$\frac{\Pi_1}{(1+r^0)\,\Pi_0} = \lambda E + \mu N^0,$$

where $E = (1,...,1)$, and λ, μ are Lagrange multipliers. Substituting this expression into the corresponding constraints, we get the following system of linear equations for λ, μ,

$$\lambda + \mu = 1 + \rho,$$
$$\lambda + \mu \mathbb{E}_{Q^0}\{N^0\} = 1,$$

so that

$$\lambda = \frac{(1+\rho)\,\mathbb{E}_{Q^0}\{N^0\} - 1}{\mathbb{E}_{Q^0}\{N^0\} - 1}, \quad \mu = -\frac{\rho}{\mathbb{E}_{Q^0}\{N^0\} - 1}.$$

Provided that $P \neq Q^0$ the Cauchy-Schwartz inequality yields

$$\begin{aligned} \mathbb{E}_{Q^0}\{N^0\} &= \mathbb{E}_P\left\{(N^0)^2\right\} = \mathbb{E}_P\left\{(N^0)^2\right\}\mathbb{E}_P\{1^2\} \\ &> (\mathbb{E}_P\{N^0\})^2 = 1, \end{aligned}$$

accordingly, we can conclude that $\lambda > 0$, $\mu < 0$. We denote the optimal portfolio by $\Pi^{(\rho)}$. We see that the discounted final value of the optimal portfolio is an affine function of the state price density vector. In order to find the actual composition of the optimal portfolio we have to solve the following linear system

$$\mathcal{Z}_1^T \Upsilon = \lambda E + \mu N^0,$$
$$\Upsilon \cdot \mathbf{Z}_0 = \Pi_0.$$

The rate of return on the optimal portfolio is an affine function of N^0, too,

$$\hat{\varrho}_{\Pi^{(\rho)}} = \lambda' + \mu' N^0, \quad \lambda' = \lambda - 1, \quad \mu' = \mu. \tag{5.24}$$

Since all optimal portfolios are affine functions of the state price density vector, they can be represented as affine functions of an optimal portfolio with arbitrarily chosen $\tilde{\rho}$. In other words, the following mutual fund principle holds: an optimal portfolio corresponding to any $\rho > 0$ can by created by investing into the optimal portfolio corresponding to $\tilde{\rho}$ (which can be called a mutual fund) and the domestic MMA. In other words, the optimal investment choice is essentially two-dimensional.

By using some elementary properties of the covariance, for any portfolio Π we can rewrite relation (5.24) in the form

$$\hat{R}_\Pi = -\frac{1}{\mu'} \mathrm{cov}_P(\hat{\varrho}_{\Pi^{(\rho)}}, \hat{\varrho}_{\Pi,}). \tag{5.25}$$

In particular,

$$\hat{R}_{\Pi^{(\rho)}} = -\frac{1}{\mu'} \mathrm{cov}_P(\hat{\varrho}_{\Pi^{(\rho)}}, \hat{\varrho}_{\Pi^{(\rho)}}) = -\frac{1}{\mu'} \mathrm{var}_P(\hat{\varrho}_{\Pi^{(\rho)}}).$$

Accordingly, we can rewrite relation (5.25) as

$$\hat{R}_\Pi = \frac{\mathrm{cov}_P(\hat{\varrho}_{\Pi^{(\rho)}}, \hat{\varrho}_{\Pi,})}{\mathrm{var}_P(\hat{\varrho}_{\Pi^{(\rho)}})} \hat{R}_{\Pi^{(\rho)}}.$$

This relation is the essence of the celebrated Capital Asset Pricing Model (CAPM). The corresponding ratio is called the beta of the portfolio Π and is denoted by β_Π,

$$\beta_\Pi = \frac{\mathrm{cov}_P(\hat{\varrho}_{\Pi^{(\rho)}}, \hat{\varrho}_{\Pi,})}{\mathrm{var}_P(\hat{\varrho}_{\Pi^{(\rho)}})},$$

it can be represented in the equivalent form

$$\beta_\Pi = \sqrt{\frac{\operatorname{var}_P(\hat{\varrho}_\Pi)}{\operatorname{var}_P(\hat{\varrho}_{\Pi^{(\rho)}})}} \operatorname{corr}_P(\hat{\varrho}_{\Pi^{(\rho)}}, \hat{\varrho}_{\Pi},),$$

which clearly shows that portfolios with higher expected returns have higher variance as well.

5.8   The optimal investment problem

In this section we study the single-period market from the viewpoint of an individual investor. Such an investor is characterized by the initial endowment $\Pi_0 > 0$ and the concave utility function $\mathcal{U}$ depending on the discounted final value of his portfolio. The objective of a rational investor is to choose a trading strategy which maximizes the expected utility function subject to constraints imposed by the initial endowment. Formally, an investor needs to solve the following optimization problem: find a trading strategy $\Upsilon = (\Upsilon^0, ..., \Upsilon^N)$ such that

$$\begin{cases} \sum_{k=0}^{K-1} p_k \mathcal{U}\left(\Upsilon^0 + \sum_{n=1}^{N} \Upsilon^n \hat{A}_{1,k}^{0n}\right) \to \max, \\ \Upsilon^0 + \sum_{n=1}^{N} \Upsilon^n S_0^{0n} = \Pi_0. \end{cases}$$

An adequate choice of the utility function is very important. Popular choices discussed in the literature are

$$\begin{aligned} \mathcal{U}(x) &= \alpha (x + \beta)^\gamma, \quad 0 < \gamma < 1, \\ \mathcal{U}(x) &= \alpha \ln (\beta x + \gamma), \\ \mathcal{U}(x) &= \alpha e^{\beta x}, \quad \alpha, \beta < 0. \end{aligned}$$

In general, it is difficult to solve the optimization problem; however, if the market is complete, its solution is straightforward. Indeed, we can study the optimization problem in two stages. First, we find the optimal discounted final portfolio value

$$\hat{\Pi} = (\hat{\Pi}_0, ..., \hat{\Pi}_{K-1}),$$

which solves the following maximization problem

$$\begin{cases} \mathbb{E}_P\left\{\mathcal{U}\left(\hat{\Pi}\right)\right\} = \sum_{k=0}^{K-1} p_k \mathcal{U}\left(\hat{\Pi}_k\right) \to \max, \\ \mathbb{E}_{Q^0}\left\{\hat{\Pi}\right\} = \Pi_0. \end{cases}$$

Provided that the optimal solution is found, we can find the corresponding trading strategy in a straightforward fashion. Accordingly, we can concentrate on solving the optimization problem. As before, we use the method of Lagrange multipliers and represent the optimality condition for $\hat{\Pi}$ in the form

$$\mathcal{U}'(\hat{\Pi}_k) = \mu \frac{q_k^0}{p_k} = \mu n_k^0, \tag{5.26}$$

where $\mathcal{U}'$ is the derivative of the utility function with respect to its argument which is known as the marginal utility function, n_k^0 are components of the state price density vector, and μ is the Lagrange multiplier. Since the utility function is concave, the marginal utility function is monotonically decreasing, and the kth equation (5.26) has at most one solution. Assuming that all of these equations are solvable, we can represent $\hat{\Pi}_k$ as

$$\hat{\Pi}_k = \mathcal{W}(\mu n_k^0),$$

where $\mathcal{W}$ the inverse marginal utility function. Substituting this expression into the initial endowment constraint we obtain a nonlinear equation for μ,

$$\sum_{k=0}^{K-1} q_k^0 \mathcal{W}(\mu n_k^0) = \Pi_0.$$

Once this equation is solved with respect to μ, we can determine $\hat{\Pi}$ and than, by using the price matrix right inverse, find the corresponding trading strategy.

Consider for example, the exponential utility function $\mathcal{U}(x) = -e^{-x}$. The optimality condition for such a function has the form

$$e^{-\hat{\Pi}_k} = \mu n_k^0,$$

so that

$$\hat{\Pi}_k = -\ln(\mu n_k^0),$$

where μ is the root of the equation

$$-\sum_{k=0}^{K-1} q_k^0 \ln(\mu n_k^0) = \Pi_0.$$

This equation has a unique solution

$$\mu = e^{-\Pi_0} \prod_{k=0}^{K-1} \left(n_k^0\right)^{1-q_k^0}.$$

Accordingly,

$$\hat{\Pi}_k = \Pi_0 + \sum_{k'=0}^{K-1} q_{k'}^0 \ln(n_{k'}^0) - \ln(n_k^0).$$

We leave it as an exercise for the reader to verify that the optimization problem for the quadratic utility function is equivalent to the mean-variance optimization problem studied in the previous section.

5.9   Elements of equilibrium theory

So far, we considered idealized markets with known initial FXR for all foreign currencies and known distributions of the final FXRs. We rationalized the choice of the initial FXRs by noting that in arbitrage-free markets they are expectations with respect to a risk-neutral (rather than the real-world) measure of the relative final FXRs. However, we have not found any guiding principle allowing us to choose the most "natural" risk-neutral probability measure, or, equivalently, the initial FXRs. Such a principle can be formulated in the framework of equilibrium pricing theory. Below we briefly outline one of the simplest nontrivial versions of such a theory.

We consider I domestic investors participating in the complete arbitrage-free $(N+1)$-country market which can be in K final states; the ith investor is characterized by the utility function $\mathcal{U}^{(i)}$ and the initial endowment $\Pi_0^{(i)}$. Assuming that the final relative FXRs in all K possible states of the market and their objective probabilities are known, we want to find "rational" initial FXRs for all foreign currencies. In other words, we want to find a unique "rational" risk-neutral measure Q^0. It is clear that for a particular choice of Q^0 every investor has to solve an optimization problem of the kind studied in the previous section; as a result the investor comes up with an optimal investment strategy $\Upsilon^{(i)} = (\Upsilon^{0(i)}, \Upsilon^{1(i)}, ..., \Upsilon^{N(i)})$. To restrict possible choices of Q^0 we have to impose some additional constraints, known as the market clearing constrains, on the total supply of foreign currencies available for sale at the initial time. (We assume that the supply of domestic currency is unlimited.) These constraints have the form

$$\sum_{i=1}^{I} \Upsilon^{n(i)} = \Xi^n, \quad n = 1, ..., N,$$

where $\Xi^n > 0$ is the total supply of the nth currency available for domestic investors. Since our market is complete, we know that $K \leq N + 1$. We have to determine a probability measure Q^0 which is characterized by the density q^0 with $K - 1$ independent components. Accordingly, we can expect the equilibrium problem to have a finite number of solutions if and only if $K = N + 1$. Assuming that this condition is satisfied, we can solve the equilibrium pricing problem in two stages. First, we choose a certain Q^0, compute the corresponding initial FXRs

$$S_0^{0n} = E_{Q^0}\left\{\hat{A}_1^{0n}\right\},$$

for all countries, and find the optimal trading strategies

$$\Upsilon^{(i)} = \Upsilon^{(i)}(Q^0),$$

for all investors. Second, we substitute these trading strategies into the market clearing conditions and vary Q^0 until these conditions are met. We emphasize that this approach to the equilibrium pricing problem can fail for several reasons, but in many cases it does produce a unique risk-neutral probability distribution Q^0 and the initial FXRs S_0^{0n}.

5.10 References and further reading

There are several good books covering single period markets including Dothan (1990), Duffie (1996), Fama and Miller (1972), Hull (2000), Markowitz (1990), and Pliska (1997). The latter book, which elucidates a lot of ideas discussed in this chapter, is particularly recommended. The relevant facts from linear algebra are standard and can be found in many sources, for instance, in the nice text by Strang (1988).

Chapter 6

Multi-Period markets

6.1 Introduction

In the previous chapter we considered single-period market models which are too simple and reflect only the most generic features of the real markets. Perhaps, the most severe drawback of these models is that they do not address the important issue of how the information is revealed to investors and how they react on it.

In the present chapter we generalize our previous results by introducing the so-called multi-period models. To this end, we extend the concept of the space of elementary events, endow it with an appropriate information structure, and objective and risk-neutral probability measures. In addition, we define predictable self-financing strategies (*PSFS*) which are compatible with the information structure and do not require additional investments to be carried out.

Multi-period economic models reflect market realities better than single-period ones. However, as a result, they are more complicated and require more elaborated mathematical techniques for their adequate description. In such models we monitor the dynamics of MMAs and FXRs not only at the initial and final times but at intermediate times as well. The corresponding moments of observation are $t = 0, 1, ..., T$. This allows market participants to make trading decisions and change their trading strategies as time progresses and the information about the true state of the market is revealed to them. It is clear that we should only consider strategies which are based on the information available to investors at the time when these strategies are chosen.

Besides, these strategies should preserve the amount of money available to investors at intermediate times. In principle, investors can receive or withdraw funds at these times, but the most natural assumption is that no additional funds are provided and all the trading strategies are self-financing. It is also clear that the number of financially relevant contingent claims in multi-period markets by far exceeds their number is single-period markets. For example, American and path-dependent options can only be introduced in the multi-period setting. The only simplification is that we do not need to assume that interest rates are stochastic in the corresponding single-period submarkets.

This chapter is organized as follows. In Section 2 we introduce stationary binomial multi-period two country markets and describe in detail their most important features including how the information is revealed to investors as time progresses and how it affects the choice of trading strategies. In Section 3 we extend our model and study the nonstationary markets which can be both nonrecombining and recombining. In Section 4 we introduce the general multi-nomial multi-country markets. We define *PSFSs*, no-arbitrage markets, and risk-neutral probability measures for the general markets in Section 5. We show how to price contingent claims in multi-period no-arbitrage markets in Section 6. The multi-period mean-variance portfolio selection problem is studied in Section 7. In Section 8 we consider the optimal investment problem. References are given in Section 9.

6.2   Stationary binomial markets

In the present section we analyze the simplest (and the most important) case of multi-period binomial two-country markets whose evolution is described by recombining trees. Once again, for concreteness we call the domestic and foreign currencies the dollar and the euro, respectively. The FXR is denoted by S^{01}, or, whenever possible, simply by S.

The "stochastic engine" for such markets is the random walk which we studied in some detail in Chapter 3. In order to construct a market, we have to define a mapping from the triangular lattice shown in Figure 3.1 onto the space of relevant economic variables. We also need to identify acceptable trading and hedging strategies. The first task is simple. All single-period markets are identical, they are characterized by the domestic and foreign interest rates r^0, r^1 and proportional changes of the FXR $S_k^{final}/S^{initial}$ which occur with real-world probabilities p_k, $k = 0, 1$. At $t = 0$ the FXR is S_0. We need to describe the evolution of S_t for $1 \leq t \leq T$. Without loss of generality we can choose parameters in such a way that $\hat{\varrho}_1^{01} = -\hat{\varrho}_0^{01} = \sigma$, so that the single-period risk-neutral probabilities of successes and failures are equal to each other, $q_{0,1} = 1/2$. It is easy to translate trajectories of the random walk into scenarios of the market evolution. Consider a certain trajectory ω corresponding to a sequence $\{x_1, ..., x_T\}$, or, equivalently, to a sequence $\{y_1, ..., y_T\}$, where $y_t = \sum x_{t'}$. Such a trajectory corresponds to the following evolution scenario for the dollar and euro MMAs, FXR, and the dollar value of the euro MMA:

$$A_{0,t}^0 = \left(1 + r^0\right)^t,$$

$$A_{0,t}^1 = \left(1 + r^1\right)^t,$$

$$S_t = \frac{\left(1 + r^0\right)^t}{\left(1 + r^1\right)^t} \prod_{t'=1}^t \left(1 + x_{t'}\sigma\right) S_0, \tag{6.1}$$

$$A_{0,t}^{01} = \left(1 + r^1\right)^t S_t = \left(1 + r^0\right)^t \prod_{t'=1}^t \left(1 + x_{t'}\sigma\right) S_0,$$

The real-world and risk-neutral probabilities of this scenario are

$$p = p_0^{\chi_0(\omega)} p_1^{\chi_1(\omega)}, \qquad q = \frac{1}{2^T},$$

the corresponding probability measures are P and Q. The total number of different scenarios is 2^T.

As in the single-period case, domestic investors are interested in relative values of the domestic and foreign MMAs which are given by

$$\hat{A}_{0,t}^0 = \frac{A_{0,t}^0}{A_{0,t}^0} = 1,$$

$$\hat{A}_{0,t}^{01} = \frac{A_{0,t}^{01}}{A_{0,t}^0} = \prod_{t'=1}^t \left(1 + x_{t'}\sigma\right) S_0^{01}.$$

These definitions show that the relative rate of return on a dollar invested domestically is zero, while the relative rate of return on a dollar invested in euros at time t and converted back at time $t+1$ has the form

$$\hat{\varrho}_{t+1}^{01} = x_t\sigma.$$

It can be both positive and negative.

Relation (6.1) defines the following mapping from the (t, y) plane on the (t, S) plane:

$$(t, y) \to (t, S) = \left(t, \mathcal{P}^t \mathcal{Q}^y S_0\right),$$

where

$$\mathcal{P} = \frac{\left(1 + r^0\right) \sqrt{1 - \sigma^2}}{\left(1 + r^1\right)}, \quad \mathcal{Q} = \sqrt{\frac{1 + \sigma}{1 - \sigma}}.$$

When $r^0 \sim r^1 \sim \sigma^2 \ll \sigma \ll 1$, we can approximate $\mathcal{P}, \mathcal{Q}$, as follows

$$\mathcal{P} \approx 1 + r^0 - r^1 - \frac{\sigma^2}{2}, \quad \mathcal{Q} \approx 1 + \sigma + \frac{\sigma^2}{2}.$$

Possible values of S_t at time $t, 0 < t \leq T$, are

$$S_t = \mathcal{P}^t \mathcal{Q}^y S_0,$$

where $y \in \Xi_t = [-t, -t + 2, ..., t - 2, t]$, their real-world and risk-neutral probabilities are

$$P\left(S_t = \mathcal{P}^t \mathcal{Q}^y S_0\right) = C^t_{(t-y)/2} p_0^{(t-y)/2} p_1^{(t+y)/2},$$

$$Q\left(S_t = \mathcal{P}^t \mathcal{Q}^y S_0\right) = \frac{C^t_{(t-y)/2}}{2^t}.$$

By using the properties of the binomial distribution we obtain

$$\mathbb{E}_Q \left\{ \frac{\left(1 + r^1\right)^t S_t}{\left(1 + r^0\right)^t} \right\} = \sum_{y \in \Xi_{-t,t}} \frac{C^t_{(t-y)/2} (1 - \sigma)^{(t-y)/2} (1 + \sigma)^{(t+y)/2} S_0}{2^t}$$

$$= \left(\frac{1 + \sigma}{2} + \frac{1 - \sigma}{2}\right)^t S_0 = S_0,$$

or, equivalently,

$$\mathbb{E}_Q \left\{ \hat{A}^{01}_{0,t} \right\} = S_0.$$

Thus, the expected relative value of the FXR does not change in time. More generally, we can verify that $\hat{A}^{01}_t$ is a martingale, i.e.,

$$\mathbb{E}_Q \left\{ \hat{A}^{01}_{0,t'} \,\Big|\, \mathfrak{F}_t \right\} = \hat{A}^{01}_{0,t},$$

or, equivalently,

$$\mathbb{E}_Q \left\{ \frac{(1+r^1)^{t'} S_{t'}}{(1+r^0)^{t'}} \middle| \mathfrak{F}_t \right\} = \frac{(1+r^1)^t S_t}{(1+r^0)^t},$$

$$\mathbb{E}_Q \left\{ \frac{(1+r^1)^{t'-t} S_{t'}}{(1+r^0)^{t'-t}} \middle| \mathfrak{F}_t \right\} = S_t,$$

where $t < t'$.

Example 6.1. *Consider a three-period market constructed of single-period submarkets with the following properties*

	p	r^0	r^1	σ
ω_0	0.6	0.06	0.04	0.2
ω_1	0.4	0.06	0.04	0.2

Assuming that $S_0 = 0.9$, we can describe the three-period market by the extended table of the form

	p	q	S_0	S_1	S_2	S_3
ω_0	0.216	0.125	0.900	0.734	0.598	0.488
ω_1	0.144	0.125	0.900	1.101	0.898	0.732
ω_2	0.144	0.125	0.900	0.734	0.898	0.732
ω_3	0.096	0.125	0.900	1.101	1.346	1.098
ω_4	0.144	0.125	0.900	0.734	0.598	0.732
ω_5	0.096	0.125	0.900	1.101	0.898	1.098
ω_6	0.096	0.125	0.900	0.734	0.898	1.098
ω_7	0.064	0.125	0.900	1.101	1.346	1.647

(6.2)

This market can be represented graphically by a tree shown in Figure 6.1. The corresponding information structure is shown in Figure 6.2 which describes a sequence of partitions which becomes more refined as time progresses. Since the tree is recombining, we cannot distinguish different scenarios solely by their terminal values and have to know their entire history.

Every investor is characterized by a trading strategy showing how much he invests in dollars and euros in different states of the market corresponding to different elementary events ω_l. For domestic investors these strategies can be described by a sequence of two-dimensional vectors

$$\Upsilon_t(\omega_l) = (\Upsilon_t^0(\omega_l), \Upsilon_t^1(\omega_l)) = (\Upsilon_{t,l}^0, \Upsilon_{t,l}^1),$$

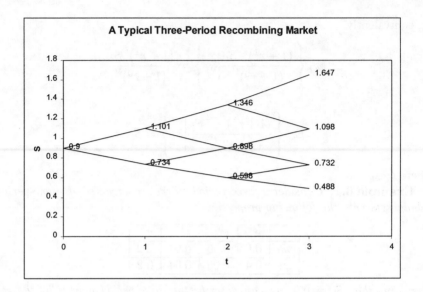

Figure 6.1: The three-period recombining market described by table (6.2).

showing the amounts invested in dollars and euros which they hold on the time interval $[t, t+1)$ provided that the market is in the state ω_l. The corresponding strategies can also be described in terms of two-dimensional vectors

$$\widehat{\Upsilon}_{t,l} = (\widehat{\Upsilon}^0_{t,l}, \widehat{\Upsilon}^1_{t,l}),$$

where

$$\widehat{\Upsilon}^\nu_{t,l} = \frac{\Upsilon^\nu_{t,l}}{A^\nu_{0,t}}, \qquad \nu = 0, 1,$$

showing the time $t = 0$ values of the amounts invested in dollars and euros at time t. At times t and $t + 1$ the discounted values of the portfolio $\widehat{\Pi}$ corresponding to a certain investment strategy have the form

$$\widehat{\Pi}^{(+)}_{t,l} = \frac{\Upsilon^0_{t,l}}{(1 + r^0)^t} + \frac{\Upsilon^1_{t,l} S_{t,l}}{(1 + r^0)^t} = \widehat{\Upsilon}^0_{t,l} + \widehat{\Upsilon}^1_{t,l} \hat{A}^{01}_{0,t,l},$$

$$\widehat{\Pi}^{(-)}_{t+1,l} = \frac{(1 + r^0)\, \Upsilon^0_{t,l}}{(1 + r^0)^{t+1}} + \frac{(1 + r^1)\, \Upsilon^1_{t,l} S_{t+1,l}}{(1 + r^0)^{t+1}} = \widehat{\Upsilon}^0_{t,l} + \widehat{\Upsilon}^1_{t,l} \hat{A}^{01}_{0,t+1,l},$$

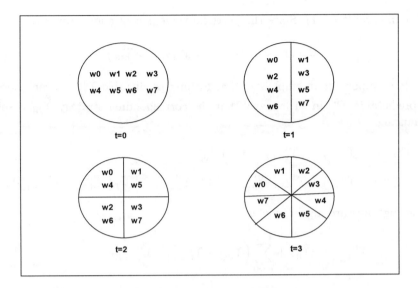

Figure 6.2: The information structure corresponding to the recombining tree shown in Figure 6.1. Scenarios which cannot be distinguished at time t are shown together.

respectively.

It is clear that meaningful investment strategies have to satisfy certain constraints. First, they have to agree with the filtration $\mathfrak{F}_t$, so that $\Upsilon_{t,l} = \Upsilon_{t,l'}$, $\widehat{\Upsilon}_{t,l} = \widehat{\Upsilon}_{t,l'}$, provided that ω_l and $\omega_{l'}$ belong to the same element of the partition $\mathfrak{G}_t$, or, in other words, if the corresponding scenarios are indistinguishable at time t. We call the corresponding strategies predictable. Next, we restrict ourselves to self-financing strategies. A self-financing strategy does not require an influx of new funds from the investor in order to be carried out. In mathematical terms, it means that the portfolio value is a continuous function of time, so that the following relation is satisfied

$$\widehat{\Pi}_{t,l}^{(-)} = \widehat{\Pi}_{t,l}^{(+)},$$

for $t = 1, ..., T - 1$. In economic terms, this relation shows that investors can use only funds accumulated at time t when they choose their strategy for the time interval $[t, t+1)$. Since the portfolio value is continuous, we have

$$\hat{\Pi}_{t+1,l} - \hat{\Pi}_{t,l} = \hat{\Upsilon}_{t,l}^1 \left(\hat{A}_{0,t+1,l}^{01} - \hat{A}_{0,t,l}^{01} \right).$$

It is important to emphasize that for any predictable $\hat{\Upsilon}_{t,l}^1$ we can choose a predictable $\hat{\Upsilon}_{t,l}^0$ in such a way that the corresponding strategy $\hat{\Upsilon}_{t,l}$ is self-financing:

$$
\begin{aligned}
\hat{\Upsilon}_{t,l}^0 &= \hat{\Upsilon}_{t-1,l}^0 + \left(\hat{\Upsilon}_{t-1,l}^1 - \hat{\Upsilon}_{t,l}^1 \right) \hat{A}_{0,t,l}^{01} \\
&= \hat{\Upsilon}_{t-1,l}^0 + \hat{\Upsilon}_{t-1,l}^1 \hat{A}_{0,t-1,l}^{01} - \hat{\Upsilon}_{t,l}^1 \hat{A}_{0,t,l}^{01} + \hat{\Upsilon}_{t-1,l}^1 \left(\hat{A}_{0,t,l}^{01} - \hat{A}_{0,t-1,l}^{01} \right).
\end{aligned}
$$

A straightforward algebra yields

$$
\begin{aligned}
\hat{\Upsilon}_{t,l}^0 &= \hat{\Upsilon}_{0,l}^0 + \sum_{t'=0}^{t-1} \left(\hat{\Upsilon}_{t',l}^1 - \hat{\Upsilon}_{t'+1,l}^1 \right) \hat{A}_{0,t'+1,l}^{01} \\
&= \Pi_0 - \hat{\Upsilon}_{t,l}^1 \hat{A}_{0,t,l}^{01} + \sum_{t'=0}^{t-1} \hat{\Upsilon}_{t',l}^1 \left(\hat{A}_{0,t'+1,l}^{01} - \hat{A}_{0,t',l}^{01} \right).
\end{aligned}
$$

It is clear that the corresponding $\hat{\Upsilon}^0$ is predictable.

Now our model is sufficiently rich to allow us to formulate and solve the valuation problem for derivative securities. While in the previous chapter we only dealt with forward contracts and European calls and puts, in the multi-period case we can study all the derivatives which we introduced in Chapter 1, for example, American calls and puts, lookbacks, etc.

The simplest financial instruments which appear in our model are dollar and euro denominated zero coupon bonds with face value of one. We can represent the price of domestic and foreign bonds sold at $t = 0$ and maturing at $t = T$ as follows

$$B_{0,T}^0 = \frac{1}{(1 + r^0)^T}, \qquad B_{0,T}^1 = \frac{1}{(1 + r^1)^T}.$$

More generally, the time t price of a bond maturing at t', $t < t'$, has the form

$$B_{t,t'}^0 = \frac{1}{(1 + r^0)^{(t'-t)}}, \qquad B_{t,t'}^1 = \frac{1}{(1 + r^1)^{(t'-t)}}.$$

More complicated instruments which we are already familiar with are forward contracts, and European calls and puts. These derivatives involve a single payment at maturity (at time T) and have the following payoffs:

$$FO(T, S_T) = S_T - K,$$

$$C(T, S_T) = (S_T - K)_+ ,$$

$$P(T, S_T) = (K - S_T)_+.$$

For a forward contract we have to choose the strike in such a way that the present value of the contract is zero (we denote the corresponding strike by $F_{0,T}$), for calls and puts the strike is supposed to be given.

In order to find the forward rate we can use the same logic as in Section 4.2 (with trivial modifications). At inception, the seller of the contract has to borrow $S_0 / (1 + r^1)^T$ dollars and to convert them into euros in order to buy one bond. At maturity he delivers one euro to the buyer of the contract in exchange for $(1 + r^0)^T S_0 / (1 + r^1)^T$ dollars which he pays back to the lender. Accordingly,

$$F_{0,T} = \frac{(1 + r^0)^T S_0}{(1 + r^1)^T} = \frac{B_{0,T}^1 S_0}{B_{0,T}^0}.$$

We can represent $F_{0,T}$ in the form

$$F_{0,T} = \mathbb{E}_Q \{S_T\}.$$

We emphasize that in order to price a forward contract we designed an appropriate replicating (or hedging) strategy. This strategy clearly has to be predictable and self-financing. In the case in question the strategy turns out to be static (buy and hold), for other derivative instruments it has to be dynamic.

Consider now a call option. In order to price a call we have to design an appropriate replicating strategy. We know how the corresponding strategy looks like for the single-period model. To extend it to the multi-period model we use the so-called backward induction which works as follows. For $t = T$ the call value is just its intrinsic value. Let us assume that the value of the FXR at $t = T - 1$ is

$$S_{T-1,y} = \mathcal{P}^{T-1} \mathcal{Q}^y S_0, \quad y \in \Xi_{-T+1,T-1}.$$

In order to find $C(T - 1, S_{T-1,y})$ we need to solve the single-period binomial pricing problem. We can use the results of the previous chapter and find the value of a call and an appropriate replicating strategy. If we repeat this exercise for all possible values of S_{T-1} (there are T of them) we can reduce our problem from the original T period problem to the new $T-1$ period problem (with a somewhat more complicated payoff). We continue this process until we end up at the root of our tree, i.e., at the point $(S_0, 0)$, where we know the price of a call and the corresponding hedge. We emphasize that the replicating strategy we construct is automatically predictable (in fact, it is Markovian) and self-financing. Thus, we can write the call price as

$$C_0 \equiv C(0, S_0) = \mathbb{E}_Q \left\{ \frac{C_T}{(1+r^0)^T} \right\}. \tag{6.3}$$

We come to the same conclusion as in the single-period case, namely, that the price of a derivative instrument is the risk-neutral expectation of its discounted payoff. In general, the following martingale property for the discounted call price holds

$$\mathbb{E}_Q \left\{ \frac{C_{t'}}{(1+r^0)^{t'}} \bigg| \mathfrak{F}_t \right\} = \frac{C_t}{(1+r^0)^t},$$

or, equivalently,

$$\mathbb{E}_Q \left\{ \frac{C_{t'}}{(1+r^0)^{t'-t}} \bigg| \mathfrak{F}_t \right\} = C_t,$$

where $C_t \equiv C(t, S_t)$. The most important special case of the above relation gives us a connection between C_t and

$$C_{t+1,k}(t+1) = C\left(t+1, \frac{(1+r^0)(1+(2k-1)\sigma)S_t}{(1+r^1)}\right), \quad k = 0, 1,$$

which can be written as

$$C_t = \frac{1}{2}\frac{C_{t+1,0}}{(1+r^0)} + \frac{1}{2}\frac{C_{t+1,1}}{(1+r^0)}. \tag{6.4}$$

We can use this relation in order to find the corresponding replicating portfolio. At $t=0$ this formula yields

$$C_0 = \frac{1}{2}\frac{C_{1,0}}{(1+r^0)} + \frac{1}{2}\frac{C_{1,1}}{(1+r^0)}.$$

In order to create a replicating portfolio at $t = 0$ the seller has to choose his positions in dollars Δ^0 and euros Δ^1 in such a way that

$$\Delta^0 + \Delta^1 (1 - \sigma) S_0 = \frac{C_{1,0}}{(1 + r^0)},$$

$$\Delta^0 + \Delta^1 (1 + \sigma) S_0 = \frac{C_{1,1}}{(1 + r^0)}.$$

Accordingly,

$$
\begin{aligned}
\Delta^0 &= -\frac{((1 - \sigma) C_{1,1} - (1 + \sigma) C_{1,0})}{2\sigma (1 + r^0)} \\
&= -\frac{(C_{1,1} - C_{1,0})}{2\sigma (1 + r^0)} + \frac{(C_{1,1} + C_{1,0})}{2 (1 + r^0)},
\end{aligned}
$$

$$\Delta^1 = \frac{(C_{1,1} - C_{1,0})}{2\sigma S_0 (1 + r^0)} = \frac{(C_{1,1} - C_{1,0})}{(1 + r^1)(S_{1,1} - S_{1,0})}.$$

This replication strategy requires to borrow dollars, or, equivalently, to sell dollar denominated bonds ($\Delta^0 < 0$) and to buy euros, or euro denominated bonds ($\Delta^1 > 0$). This replication strategy can be executed for later times with obvious modifications. The value of C_0 given by

$$C_0 = \Delta^0 + \Delta^1 S_0,$$

agrees with the value given by equation (6.3).

Example 6.2. *We can use the above formulas in order to price and hedge a European call with strike $K = 0.85$ in our three-period model. The corresponding results are summarized in the following table*

	C_0	Δ_0^1	C_1	Δ_1^1	C_2	Δ_2^1	C_3	
ω_0	0.162	0.609	0.055	0.376	0.000	0.000	0.000	
ω_1	0.162	0.609	0.288	0.805	0.117	0.651	0.000	
ω_2	0.162	0.609	0.055	0.376	0.117	0.651	0.000	
ω_3	0.162	0.609	0.288	0.805	0.493	0.962	0.248	(6.5)
ω_4	0.162	0.609	0.055	0.376	0.000	0.000	0.000	
ω_5	0.162	0.609	0.288	0.805	0.117	0.651	0.248	
ω_6	0.162	0.609	0.055	0.376	0.117	0.651	0.248	
ω_7	0.162	0.609	0.288	0.805	0.493	0.962	0.797	

The Taylor series expansion of the r.h.s. of equation (6.4) yields the Black-Scholes equation for $\tilde{C}(t, S_t)$ which interpolates the function C between the vertices of the tree, namely,

$$\tilde{C}_t + \frac{1}{2}\sigma^2 S^2 \tilde{C}_{SS} + \left(r^0 - r^1\right) S \tilde{C}_S - r^0 \tilde{C} = 0.$$

The final condition is

$$C(T, S) = (S - K)_+ .$$

Equation (6.4) is valid for all European contingent claims. It shows how to evaluate a European option (in the case in question a call) via the so-called backward induction (which is intuitively very appealing). However, this is not the only way one can price European options. The complementary method of forward induction is equally useful. In order to appreciate this method we need to define the so-called Arrow-Debreu securities (ADS) whose prices at the point t, S we denote by $\texttt{AD}(t, S, t', S')$. Such a security pays the buyer one dollar provided that the FXR at time t' is S', and zero otherwise. It is clear that $\texttt{AD}(t, S, t', S')$ is nothing more than the discounted t.p.d.f. $p(t, S, t', S')$,

$$\texttt{AD}(t, S, t', S') = \frac{p(t, S, t', S')}{(1 + r^0)^{(t'-t)}}.$$

As any other claim, we can price ADs via the backward induction. Once the prices $\texttt{AD}(0, S_0, T, S_T)$ for the terminal maturity T and all possible S_T are found, we can represent the price of any other European option with the same maturity, for example, a call option with strike K, in the form

$$\begin{aligned}
C(0, S_0, T, K) &= \sum_{S_T} (S_T - K)_+ \texttt{AD}(0, S_0, T, S_T) \\
&= \sum_{y \in \Xi_{-T,T}} \left(\mathcal{P}^T \mathcal{Q}^y S_0 - K^{01}\right)_+ \texttt{AD}\left(0, S_0, T, \mathcal{P}^T \mathcal{Q}^y S_0\right).
\end{aligned}$$

If the only way to price ADs were via the backward induction, they would be of theoretical rather than practical interest. Fortunately, they can also be priced in an alternative fashion. In order to do so, we need to consider the entire set of such securities maturing between $t' = 0$ and $t' = T$. It is clear that

$$\texttt{AD}(0, S_0, 0, S_0) = 1.$$

Let us assume that we know how to price all ADs with maturities between 0 and t'. In order to price

$$\text{AD}\left(0, S_0, t'+1, S_{t'+1} = \mathcal{P}^{t'+1}\mathcal{Q}^y S_0\right), \qquad y \in \Xi_{-(t'+1),(t'+1)},$$

we notice that $S_{t'+1} = \mathcal{P}^{t'+1}\mathcal{Q}^y S_0$ can be reached from just two nodes, namely, $S_{t'}^{(\pm)} = \mathcal{P}^{t'}\mathcal{Q}^{y\pm1} S_0$ (see Figure 6.1). We have

$$\text{AD}\left(t', S_{t'}, t'+1, S_{t'+1}\right) = \begin{cases} \dfrac{1}{2\left(1+r^0\right)}, & \text{if} \quad S_{t'} = \mathcal{P}^{t'}\mathcal{Q}^{y\pm1} S_0 \\ 0, & \text{otherwise} \end{cases}.$$

Accordingly,

$$\text{AD}\left(0, S_0, t'+1, S_{t'+1}\right) = \frac{1}{2}\frac{\text{AD}\left(0, S_0, t', S_{t'+1}/\mathcal{PQ}\right)}{\left(1+r^0\right)} + \frac{1}{2}\frac{\text{AD}\left(0, S_0, t', \mathcal{Q}S_{t'+1}/\mathcal{P}\right)}{\left(1+r^0\right)}.$$

This equation allows us to express values of ADSs at time $t'+1$ in terms of their values at time t' via the forward induction process. For the limiting values

$$S_{t'+1}^{(\pm)} = \left(\mathcal{PQ}^{\pm1}\right)^{t'+1} S_0,$$

this equation has to be modified as follows

$$\text{AD}\left(0, S_0, t'+1, S_{t'+1}^{(\pm)}\right) = \frac{1}{2}\frac{\text{AD}\left(0, S_0, t', S_{t'}^{(\pm)}\right)}{\left(1+r^0\right)}. \tag{6.6}$$

When we need to price a single call option with a given maturity T the backward induction is the method of choice. However, as we will see below, for the purposes of calibration it is necessary to price many options with different strikes and maturities. In this case the forward induction method is the only practical possibility.

By using the fact that the distribution of the terminal FXR is known, we can represent the price of a call in the form

$$C_0 \equiv C\left(0, S_0, T, K\right) = \sum_{y \in \Xi_{-T,T}} \frac{C_{(T-y)/2}^T \left(\mathcal{P}^T \mathcal{Q}^y S_0 - K\right)_+}{2^T \left(1+r^0\right)^T}.$$

We define y^* as the smallest $y \in \Xi_{-T,T}$, such that

$$y^* > \frac{\ln\left(K/\mathcal{P}^T S_0\right)}{\ln\left(\mathcal{Q}\right)},$$

and represent C_0 in the form

$$C_0 = \sum_{y \in \Xi_{y^*,T}} \frac{C_{(T-y)/2}^T \left(\mathcal{P}^T \mathcal{Q}^y S_0 - K\right)}{2^T \left(1 + r^0\right)^T}$$

$$= \frac{S_0}{\left(1 + r^1\right)^T} \sum_{y \in \Xi_{y^*,T}} \frac{C_{(T-y)/2}^T \left(1 - \sigma\right)^{(T-y)/2} \left(1 + \sigma\right)^{(T+y)/2}}{2^T}$$

$$- \frac{K}{\left(1 + r^0\right)^T} \sum_{y \in \Xi_{y^*,T}} \frac{C_{(T-y)/2}^T}{2^T}.$$

It is clear that the corresponding sums represent the probabilities of a random walk ending above y^*, or, equivalently, of the FXR ending above K; however, the first sum corresponds to a random walk with probabilities $p_k = \left(1 + (2k - 1)\sigma\right)/2$, while the second sum corresponds a symmetric random walk with probabilities $q_k = 1/2$.

The price of a put option can be found by the same token as before. Without going into details, we simply present the answer

$$P_0 = \frac{K}{\left(1 + r^0\right)^T} \sum_{y \in \Xi_{-T,y^*}} \frac{C_{(T-y)/2}^T}{2^T \left(1 + r^0\right)^T}$$

$$- \frac{S_0}{\left(1 + r^1\right)^T} \sum_{y \in \Xi_{-T,y^*}} \frac{C_{(T-y)/2}^T \left(1 - \sigma\right)^{(T-y)/2} \left(1 + \sigma\right)^{(T+y)/2}}{2^T}.$$

Put-call parity has the form

$$C_0 - P_0 = \frac{S_0}{\left(1 + r^1\right)^T} - \frac{K}{\left(1 + r^0\right)^T} = \frac{1}{\left(1 + r^0\right)^T} \left(F - K\right).$$

For

$$r^0 \sim r^1 \sim \sigma^2 \sim 1/T \ll \sigma \sim 1/\sqrt{T} \ll 1,$$

we can approximate y^* as follows:

$$y^* \approx \frac{\ln\left(K/S_0\right) - \left(r^0 - r^1 - \sigma^2/2\right)T}{\sigma} = -d_- \sqrt{T} = \sigma T - d_+ \sqrt{T},$$

where we use the notation

$$d_{\pm} = \frac{\ln(S_0/K) + \left(r^0 - r^1 \pm \sigma^2/2\right)T}{\sigma\sqrt{T}} \sim 1.$$

By using the integral De Moivre-Laplace theorem we approximate C_0 as follows

$$
\begin{aligned}
C_0 &\approx \frac{S_0}{(1+r^1)^T} \int_{-d_+}^{\infty} \frac{e^{-z^2/2}}{\sqrt{2\pi}} dz - \frac{K}{(1+r^0)^T} \int_{-d_-}^{\infty} \frac{e^{-z^2/2}}{\sqrt{2\pi}} dz \\
&= \frac{S_0}{(1+r^1)^T} N(d_+) - \frac{K}{(1+r^0)^T} N(d_-),
\end{aligned}
$$

and, similarly,

$$
\begin{aligned}
P_0 &\approx \frac{K}{(1+r^0)^T} \int_{-\infty}^{-d_-} \frac{e^{-z^2/2}}{\sqrt{2\pi_0}} dz - \frac{S_0}{(1+r^1)^T} \int_{-\infty}^{-d_+} \frac{e^{-z^2/2}}{\sqrt{2\pi}} dz \\
&= \frac{K}{(1+r^0)^T} N(-d_-) - \frac{S_0}{(1+r^1)^T} N(-d_+).
\end{aligned}
$$

These are the celebrated Black-Scholes formulas for the call and put prices (with discretely compounded discounting).

We see that pricing of forwards, and European calls and puts (and their linear combinations which can be used by investors having specific payoff requirements) is relatively simple. Now we consider several more complicated financial instruments which can be studied only in the multi-period framework. To start with, we describe the futures contract. At inception of the contract the buyer and seller agree that at its maturity they will exchange dollars into euros at the rate of $f_{0,T}$. The futures and forward contracts are similar in nature since both impose obligations on the buyer and seller alike. However, in contrast to forward contracts when the exchange of currencies takes place only at maturity, for futures contracts at each intermediate time $t, 0 < t < T$ the buyer (seller) has to deposit into the so-called margin account the amount $f_{t,T} - f_{0,T}$ when this amount is negative (positive), where $f_{t,T}$ is the futures FXR at time T as seen at time t. (It is clear that $F_{t,t} = f_{t,t} = S_t$ for any t.) This arrangement is known as marking-to-market, it allows to standardize the contact, and to reduce the risk of default of the parties involved. The futures FXR is chosen is such a way that entering into the contract is costless at time $t = 0$. It turns out that in our simplified market with constant (or, more generally, deterministic) interest rates the futures rate $f_{0,T}$ is equal to the forward rate $F_{0,T}$. In order to prove this fact, we follow the idea of Cox,

Ingersoll, and Ross and compare two investment strategies. The first strategy is as follows. At $t = 0$ the investor sells e^{r^0} futures contracts. At $t = 1$ he buys back the old contracts and sells e^{2r^0} new ones. At $t = 2$ he buys back contracts which were sold at $t = 1$ and sells e^{3r^0} new contracts, and so on until $t = T - 1$. At each time t he invests into or borrows from the domestic MMA. The discounted P&L of this strategy is

$$
\begin{aligned}
P\&L &= e^{-r^0}e^{r^0}\left(f_{0,T} - f_{1,T}\right) + e^{-2r^0}e^{2r^0}\left(f_{1,T} - f_{2,T}\right) + \ldots \\
&\quad + e^{-(T-1)r^0}e^{r^0(T-1)}\left(f_{T-1,T} - f_{T,T}\right) \\
&= f_{0,T} - f_{T,T} \\
&= f_{0,T} - S_T.
\end{aligned}
$$

The second strategy is to buy $e^{r^0 T}$ forward contracts. The corresponding discounted P&L is

$$
P\&L = e^{-r^0 T}e^{r^0 T}\left(S_T - F_{0,T}\right) = S_T - F_{0,T}.
$$

The combination of the two strategies produces the deterministic P&L of the form

$$
P\&L = f_{0,T} - F_{0,T}.
$$

Since the combined strategy is initially costless its P&L has to be equal to zero (since it is deterministic), so that

$$
f_{0,T} = F_{0,T}.
$$

Next, we study American calls (puts can be analyzed in a similar way). The buyer of such a call has an additional optionality compared to the buyer of a European call since he can choose any time (between inception and maturity) in order to exercise the option.[1] Accordingly, the price of an American call cannot be less than its intrinsic price, i.e.,

$$
C'_t \equiv C'(t, S_t) \geq (S_t - K)_+.
$$

Whenever a call is exercised, the buyer gets the corresponding intrinsic value. (This is true for Europeans calls, too, however, their intrinsic value is only relevant at maturity.) In is clear that the exercise time is a random variable

---

[1] It is worth noting that in practice American calls are often exercised suboptimally for a variety of reasons.

on the space of all possible market evolution scenarios, or, equivalently, on the space of all random walks starting at zero at $t = 0$ and ending at $t = T$. It has to be a stopping time since the buyer has to decide whether or not to exercise the option at time t based solely on the information which is available at this time. Thus, we can represent the price of an American call at inception as follows

$$C_0' = \sup_{\tau \in \mathfrak{T}} \left\{ \sum_\omega \frac{\left(S_{\tau(\omega)}(\omega) - K \right)_+}{2^T (1 + r^0)^{\tau(\omega)}} \right\},$$

where $\mathfrak{T}$ is the class of all stopping times. Since $\tau(\omega) = T$ is a stopping time, it is obvious that

$$C_0' \geq C_0.$$

The additional optionality results in the fact that the discounted price of an American call is no longer a martingale. Instead it is a supermartingale, i.e.,

$$\mathbb{E}_Q \left\{ \frac{C_{t'}'}{(1 + r^0)^{t'}} \Big| \mathfrak{F}_t \right\} \leq \frac{C_t'}{(1 + r^0)^t},$$

or, equivalently,

$$\mathbb{E}_Q \left\{ \frac{C_{t'}'}{(1 + r^0)^{t'-t}} \Big| \mathfrak{F}_t \right\} \leq C_t'.$$

In order to find the price of an American call explicitly, we can use backward induction. At $t = T - 1$, we have

$$C'(T - 1, S_{T-1})$$

$$= \max \left\{ \frac{\sum_{k=0,1} \left(\frac{(1+r^0)(1+(2k-1)\sigma)S_{T-1}}{(1+r^1)} - K \right)_+}{2(1 + r^0)}, (S_{T-1} - K)_+ \right\}$$

This formula allows us to find the price for all relevant values of S_{T-1}. Once this is done, we can price options at $t = T - 2$, via the formula

$$C'(T - 2, S_{T-2})$$

$$= \max \left\{ \frac{\sum_{k=0,1} C'\left(T - 1, \frac{(1+r^0)(1+(2k-1)\sigma)S_{T-2}}{(1+r^1)} \right)}{2(1 + r^0)}, (S_{T-2} - K)_+ \right\}$$

and so on until we reach $t = 0$ and find $C'(0, S_0)$. Delta hedging of American calls is similar in nature to delta hedging of European calls.

Example 6.3. *We can use the above formulas in order to price and hedge the American call with strike $K = 0.85$ in our three-period model. The corresponding results are summarized in the following table*

	C'_0	Δ'^1_0	C'_1	Δ'^1_1	C'_2	Δ'^1_2	C'_3
ω_0	0.162	0.614	0.055	0.376	0.000	0.000	0.000
ω_1	0.162	0.614	0.289	0.813	0.117	0.651	0.000
ω_2	0.162	0.614	0.055	0.376	0.117	0.651	0.000
ω_3	0.162	0.614	0.289	0.813	**0.496**	**1.000**	0.248
ω_4	0.162	0.614	0.055	0.376	0.000	0.000	0.000
ω_5	0.162	0.614	0.289	0.813	0.117	0.651	0.248
ω_6	0.162	0.614	0.055	0.376	0.117	0.651	0.248
ω_7	0.162	0.614	0.289	0.813	**0.496**	**1.000**	0.797

We see that the price of the American call is always greater than its intrinsic value which can be found from Table (6.2), and the price of the corresponding European call which is given in Table (6.5). The early exercise prices are shown in boldface.

It was mentioned earlier that in many cases path-independent options either do not provide an adequate protection for investors because they cannot streamline many cash flows or are too expensive to buy. In such cases investors have to use path dependent options with payoffs depending on the whole trajectory of FXR rather than on its terminal value alone. We already know that by their very nature these options are rather numerous. We restrict ourselves to a few representative examples, namely, to barrier, lookback and Asian options.

Recall the definitions of the corresponding derivatives. Let

$$M_{0,T} = \max_{0 \leq t \leq T} S_t, \quad m_{0,T} = \min_{0 \leq t \leq T} S_t, \quad A_{0,T} = \frac{1}{T+1} \sum_{t=0}^{T} S_t,$$

be the maximum, minimum and average values of the FXR between $t = 0$ and $t = T$. A typical knockout barrier option expires worthless if the FXR hits a certain level L, otherwise its payoff is identical to the payoff of the corresponding European option. For instance, the payoff of the down-and-out call has the form

$$V^{(DOC)}(T, S_T, m_{0,T}) = (S_T - K)_+ \, \theta \, (m_{0,T} - A),$$

where $A \leq K$ is the lower knockout level, and $\theta\left(x\right)$ is the Heaviside function. The payoff of the up-and-out call has the form

$$V^{(UOC)}\left(T, S_T, M_{0,T}\right) = \left(S_T - K\right)_+ \theta\left(B - M_{0,T}\right),$$

where $B \geq K$ is the upper knockout level. Knockin barrier options complement the corresponding knockout barrier option. For example, for the down-and-in call we have

$$V^{(DIC)}\left(T, S_T, m_{0,T}\right) = \left(S_T - K\right)_+ \theta\left(A - m_{0,T}\right),$$

etc. It is obvious that any European option can be decomposed into the corresponding knockout and knockin options, for instance,

$$C\left(T, S_T\right) = V^{(DOC)}\left(T, S_T, m_{0,T}\right) + V^{(DIC)}\left(T, S_T, m_{0,T}\right).$$

Barrier calls can be considerably cheaper than a European call. They are attractive to investors who believe that barriers will not be breached and to investors who do not need protection provided by a call option in case when barriers are breached.

The payoff of the floating strike lookback call has the form

$$V^{(LBC)}\left(T, S_T, m_{0,T}\right) = \left(S_T - m_{0,T}\right)_+.$$

The owner of the floating strike lookback call has the right to buy the foreign currency at the best possible price observed between 0 and T.

The payoff of the fixed strike lookback call is

$$V^{\left(\widehat{LBC}\right)}\left(T, S_T, M_{0,T}\right) = \left(M_{0,T} - K\right)_+.$$

The owner of the fixed strike lookback call has the right to buy the foreign currency at the rate K at any time between 0 and T.

Finally the payoff of the Asian call is

$$V^{(AsC)}\left(T, S_T, A_{0,T}\right) = \left(A_{0,T} - K\right)_+.$$

The owner of the Asian call has the right to buy the foreign currency at the average price observed between 0 and T.

In order to evaluate different barrier and lookback options explicitly, we need to find the distribution of the maximum FXR $M_{0,T}$ and the joint distribution of S_T and $M_{0,T}$. (Distributions involving $m_{0,T}$ can be studied by analogy.) Finding the distribution of $M_{0,T}$ is a classical problem of probability theory which can be solved by virtue of the reflection principle. For simplicity we assume that $\mathcal{P} = 1$, so that the mapping $(t, y) \to (t, S_t)$ has the form

$$(t, y) \to (t, \mathcal{Q}^y S_0).$$

It is clear that the random variable $M_{0,T}$ can assume $T + 1$ values $\mathcal{Q}^v$, where v is a nonnegative integer such that $0 \leq v \leq T$, and that

$$M_{0,T} = \mathcal{Q}^{Y_{0,T}} S_0,$$

where

$$Y_{0,T} = \max_{0 \leq t \leq T} y_t,$$

is the maximum of the corresponding "shadow" symmetric random walk. For the moment we concentrate on analyzing the behavior of $Y_{0,T}$. We consider a certain scenario $\omega = \{y_0 = 0, y_1, ..., y_T\}$, and introduce the first passage time τ_v for a given level v,

$$\tau_v = \begin{cases} \min_{0 \leq t \leq T}\{t : y_t = v\}, & \text{if } Y_{0,T} \geq v \\ \infty, & \text{if } Y_{0,T} < v \end{cases}.$$

It is clear that for a given scenario the conditions $Y_{0,T} \geq v$ and $\tau_v < \infty$ are satisfied or violated simultaneously, so that

$$Q\{Y_{0,T} \geq v\} = Q\{\tau_v < \infty\}.$$

The event $\tau_v < \infty$ can be decomposed into three mutually excluding events: (A) $y_T = v$, i.e., the random walk terminates at the level v; (B) $y_T > v$, i.e., the random walk ends above the level v (so that for some earlier t this level is hit for sure); (C) $y_T < v$ but $y_t = v$ for some $t < T$, i.e., at maturity the random walk is below v but at some point prior to maturity it hits the level v. These possibilities are shown in Figure 6.3.

It is very easy to find the probabilities of events A and B. We have

$$Q\{\text{event A}\} = \kappa_{T,v} \frac{C^T_{(T-v)/2}}{2^T},$$

$$Q\{\text{event B}\} = \sum_{v' \in \Xi_{v+1+\kappa_{T,v},T}} \frac{C^T_{(T-v')/2}}{2^T},$$

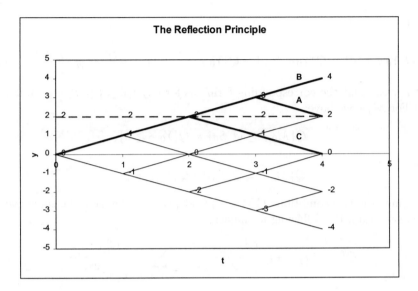

Figure 6.3: This figure illustrates three mutually exclusive possibilities for the event $\tau_2 < \infty$. Three representative scenarios A, B, and C are shown. Scenario B is a shadow of scenario C.

where

$$\kappa_{\alpha,\beta} = \begin{cases} 0, & \text{if } \alpha - \beta \text{ is odd} \\ 1, & \text{if } \alpha - \beta \text{ is even} \end{cases}.$$

At the same time, finding the probability of event C is less straightforward and this is where the reflection principle comes to the rescue. Inspection of Figure 6.3 shows that for every scenario satisfying condition C there exists a shadow scenario satisfying condition B and *vice versa*. Thus, the total number of paths satisfying condition C is equal to the number of paths satisfying condition B. Since in our risk-neutralized world the underlying random walk is symmetric, all paths are equally probable and

$$Q\{\text{event } C\} = Q\{\text{event } B\}.$$

Accordingly,

$$Q\{Y_{0,T} \geq v\} = \kappa_{T,v} \frac{C^T_{(T-v)/2}}{2^T} + \sum_{v' \in \Xi_{v+1+\kappa_{T,v},T}} \frac{C^T_{(T-v')/2}}{2^{T-1}},$$

and

$$Q\{Y_{0,T} = v\} = Q\{Y_{0,T} \geq v\} - Q\{Y_{0,T} \geq v+1\} = \frac{C^T_{(T-v+1-\kappa_{T,v})/2}}{2^T}. \quad (6.7)$$

It is clear that the corresponding formulas for any $t, 0 \leq t \leq T$, are similar.
For $M_{0,T}$ we have:

$$Q\{M_{0,T} \geq \mathcal{Q}^v S_0\} = Q\{Y_{0,T} \geq v\},$$

$$Q\{M_{0,T} = \mathcal{Q}^v S_0\} = Q\{Y_{0,T} = v\}.$$

Since the two conditions $\{Y_{0,t} \geq v\}$ and $\{\tau_v \leq t\}$ describe the same event, we also obtain the following formulas:

$$Q\{\tau_v \leq t\} = \kappa_{t,v} \frac{C^t_{(t-v)/2}}{2^t} + \sum_{v' \in \Xi_{v+1+\kappa_{t,v},t}} \frac{C^t_{(t-v')/2}}{2^t},$$

$$Q\{\tau_v = t\} = Q\{\tau_v \leq t\} - Q\{\tau_v \leq t-1\}. \quad (6.8)$$

Next, we find the joint probability $Q\{y_T = v, Y_{0,T} \geq v'\}$, $v \leq v'$, or, equivalently, the joint probability $Q\{y_T = v, \tau_{v'} \leq T\}$. By using the conditional probability concept we can write

$$Q\{y_T = v, \tau_{v'} \leq T\} = \sum_{0 \leq t' \leq T} Q\{y_T = v | \tau_{v'} = t'\} Q\{\tau_{v'} = t'\}.$$

We know the unconditional probability $Q\{\tau_{v'} = t'\}$ which is given by equation (6.8). We can find the conditional probability $Q\{y_T = v | \tau_{v'} = t'\}$ by noting that it is equal to the unconditional probability of the event that a random walk starting at the point v' at time t' reaches the point v at time T. Accordingly,

$$Q\{y_T = v | \tau_{v'} = t'\} = \kappa_{T-t',v-v'} \frac{C^{T-t'}_{(T-t'-v+v')/2}}{2^{T-t'}},$$

and

$$Q\{y_T = v, \tau_{v'} \leq T\} = \sum_{t' \in \Xi_{1-\kappa_{T,v-v'},T-1+\kappa_{T,v-v'}}} \frac{C^{T-t'}_{(T-t'-v+v')/2}}{2^{T-t'}} Q\{\tau_{v'} = t'\}.$$

It is clear that the probability of reaching the point v at time T without crossing the level v' at some intermediate time is

$$Q\{y_T = v, \tau_{v'} = \infty\} = Q\{y_T = v\} - Q\{y_T = v, \tau_{v'} \le T\}. \qquad (6.9)$$

By using equations (6.7), (6.9) we can price barrier and lookback options. Consider, for instance, an up-and-out call with strike K and barrier level $B > 0$, $B > K$. The risk-neutral valuation principle yields

$$
\begin{aligned}
V^{(UOC)}(0, S_0, M_{0,0}) &= \frac{1}{(1+r^0)^T} \mathbb{E}_Q \left\{ (S_T - K)_+ \, \theta \, (B - M_{0,T}) \right\} \\
&= \frac{1}{(1+r^0)^T} \sum_{\mu \le v < \nu} (Q^v S_0 - K) \, Q\{y_T = v, \tau_\nu = \infty\},
\end{aligned}
$$

where μ and ν are the smallest integers such that $K \le Q^\mu S_0$ and $B \le Q^\nu S_0$, respectively, and $M_{0,0} = S_0$. The value of a lookback call with fixed strike K^{01} can be written as

$$
\begin{aligned}
V^{(LBC)}(0, S_0, M_{0,0}) &= \frac{1}{(1+r^0)^T} \mathbb{E}_Q \left\{ (M_{0,T} - K)_+ \right\} \\
&= \frac{1}{(1+r^0)^T} \sum_{\mu \le v \le T} (Q^v S_0 - K) \, Q\{Y_{0,T} = v\},
\end{aligned}
$$

where μ has the same meaning as before.

It is more difficult to value an Asian call since a simple probability distribution for the average FXR $A_{0,T}$ does not exist. We can use the risk-neutral valuation principle and write the value of a call as

$$
\begin{aligned}
V^{(AsC)}(0, S_0, A_{0,0}) &= \frac{1}{(1+r^0)^T} \mathbb{E}_Q \left\{ (A_{0,T} - K)_+ \right\} \\
&= \frac{1}{(1+r^0)^T \, 2^T} \sum_{\omega_l} \left(\frac{1}{T+1} \sum_{0 \le t \le T} Q^{y_t(\omega_l)} S_0 - K \right)_+,
\end{aligned}
$$

where $A_{0,0} = S_0$ and ω_l are different scenarios of market evolution. Since there are 2^T scenarios in total this formula is very difficult to use in practice. In a due course we develop much better methods for the valuation of Asian calls and puts.

With minor modifications the above formulas can be used in order to price the corresponding options at intermediate times t, $0 < t < T$. Once this is done, the necessary hedges can be found via the backward induction method.

Example 6.4. *To illustrate the above ideas, we price and hedge a floating strike lookback call in our three-period model. The corresponding prices and hedges are*

	$V_0^{(LBC)}$	Δ_0^1	$V_1^{(LBC)}$	Δ_1^1	$V_2^{(LBC)}$	Δ_2^1	$V_3^{(LBC)}$
ω_0	0.172	0.377	0.111	0.349	0.063	0.526	0.000
ω_1	0.172	0.377	0.255	0.752	0.094	0.526	0.000
ω_2	0.172	0.377	0.111	0.349	0.172	0.956	0.000
ω_3	0.172	0.377	0.255	0.752	0.445	0.962	0.198
ω_4	0.172	0.377	0.111	0.349	0.063	0.526	0.133
ω_5	0.172	0.377	0.255	0.752	0.094	0.526	0.200
ω_6	0.172	0.377	0.111	0.349	0.172	0.956	0.364
ω_7	0.172	0.377	0.255	0.752	0.445	0.962	0.747

We see that a lookback call is expensive because it provides a much better pro-tection against possible appreciation of the foreign currency than a European call, say.

6.3   Non-stationary binomial markets

6.3.1   Introduction

So far, we considered a stationary problem and mapped recombining binomial lattices representing movements of the particle which generates randomness in our market model onto recombining binomial lattices representing the dynamics of FXR. However, in general, we cannot guarantee that the market is stationary. There are many reasons for considering nonstationary markets, the most obvious of which is that the economic conditions keep changing and this change cannot be adequately captured by stationary models. From the standpoint of derivative pricing the most undesirable feature of stationary models is that they cannot be calibrated to the market, and, consequently, are arbitrageable. Below we consider two methods for constructing nonstationary models. The first method uses time-dependent interest rates and volatilities (the term structure of relevant parameters) in order to construct a nonrecombining lattice which describes the evolution of FXR. In this model, the value of FXR at time t depends on the entire trajectory $\{y_0, y_1, ..., y_t\}$, rather than simply on y_t. The second method chooses interest rates and volatilities which depend not only on time but also on the state of the market at that time in such a way that the resulting lattice is recombining. Accordingly, the corresponding

FXRs depend solely on y_t (albeit in a complicated fashion). In principle, one can also capture the term structure effects by allowing time periods of unequal length.

6.3.2 The nonrecombining case

Perhaps, the simplest way of developing nonstationary models is to use the same construction of the multi-period market as before but to assume that the underlying single-period markets explicitly depend on time. In other words, the shadow particle movements which are represented by a certain trajectory $\omega = \{x_1, ..., x_T\}$ are mapped into the relevant financial variables according to the rule:

$$A_{0,t}^0 = \prod_{t'=1}^{t} \left(1 + r_{t'}^0\right),$$

$$S_t = \prod_{t'=1}^{t} \frac{\left(1 + r_{t'}^0\right)\left(1 + x_{t'}\sigma_{t'}\right)}{\left(1 + r_{t'}^1\right)} S_0,$$

$$A_{0,t}^{01} = \prod_{t'=1}^{t} \left(1 + r_{t'}^0\right)\left(1 + x_{t'}\sigma_{t'}\right) S_0,$$

$$\hat{A}_{0,t}^0 = 1,$$

$$\hat{A}_{0,t}^{01} = \prod_{t'=1}^{t} \left(1 + x_{t'}\sigma_{t'}\right) S_0,$$

Here r_t^0, r_t^1 are time-dependent deterministic interest rates prevailing for the period $[t-1, t)$, σ_t is the volatility of the dollar value of the euro MMA over the same period, and S_0^{01} is the initial FXR. The single-period objective probabilities $p_{t,k}$ are time-dependent as well. By construction, the corresponding risk-neutral probabilities are constant, $q_{t,k} = 1/2$.

By assumption, all of our single-period submarkets are non-arbitrageable and complete, and the corresponding risk-neutral probability measures are symmetric. It is natural to expect that the market at large is non-arbitrageable and complete (more on this in the next section). Accordingly, the multi-period market has a unique risk-neutral probability measure such that all scenarios ω_l have equal probability, $Q(\omega_l) = 1/2^T$. We emphasize that finding the risk-neutral measure for a non-recombining tree is as easy as for a recombining one (in fact, the visualization of different scenarios is even more straightforward), however, practical solution of the pricing and hedging problems for derivatives is significantly more difficult for non-recombining trees than for recombining ones, so that such trees have to be avoided whenever possible. Consider, for example a European call. We can write its price in the familiar form, namely,

$$C_0 = \frac{1}{2^T} \frac{\sum_{l=0}^{2^T-1} \left(S_T(\omega_l) - K^{01} \right)_+}{\prod_{t'=1}^{T} (1 + r_{t'}^0)}.$$

However, in contrast to the recombining case, this sum contains the number of terms which is exponential in T and there is no simple asymptotic expression for the price similar to the one given by the De Moivre-Laplace theorem.

Example 6.5. *At this stage it is useful to consider a representative three-period market. Let us assume that this market is constructed by combining three different single-period markets with deterministic interest rates and volatilities given by the table*

	r^0	r^1	σ
1	0.05	0.03	0.15
2	0.06	0.04	0.20
3	0.05	0.04	0.18

and that $S_0 = 0.9$. The states of the three-period market are described by the following table

	S_0	r_1^0	r_1^1	S_1	r_2^0	r_2^1	S_2	r_3^0	r_3^1	S_3
ω_0	0.9	0.05	0.03	0.780	0.06	0.04	0.636	0.05	0.04	0.526
ω_1	0.9	0.05	0.03	1.055	0.06	0.04	0.860	0.05	0.04	0.712
ω_2	0.9	0.05	0.03	0.780	0.06	0.04	0.954	0.05	0.04	0.790
ω_3	0.9	0.05	0.03	1.055	0.06	0.04	1.290	0.05	0.04	1.068
ω_4	0.9	0.05	0.03	0.780	0.06	0.04	0.636	0.05	0.04	0.758
ω_5	0.9	0.05	0.03	1.055	0.06	0.04	0.860	0.05	0.04	1.025
ω_6	0.9	0.05	0.03	0.780	0.06	0.04	0.954	0.05	0.04	1.136
ω_7	0.9	0.05	0.03	1.055	0.06	0.04	1.290	0.05	0.04	1.537

$$(6.10)$$

The tree describing possible states of the market is shown in Figure 6.4. This tree, which is obviously nonrecombining, is more complicated than the recombining tree shown in Figure 6.1. In particular, the terminal FXR can have

$8 = 2^3$ *distinct values* $S_3(\omega_l)$, $l = 0, ..., 7$, *rather that* $4 = 3 + 1$ *values it can have in the recombining case. Possible scenarios of the market evolution directly correspond to the branches of the tree; the corresponding information structure is shown in Figure 6.2. Since the tree is nonrecombining, we can distinguish different scenarios solely by their terminal values. It is clear that the risk-neutral probability of each market evolution scenario is* $1/8$. *We can use the risk-neutral valuation principle in order to price all relevant contingent claims. For instance, for a call with strike* $K = 0.85$, *the corresponding prices and hedges are*

	C_0	Δ_0^1	C_1	Δ_1^1	C_2	Δ_2^1	C_3
ω_0	0.146	0.629	0.064	0.412	0.000	0.000	0.000
ω_1	0.146	0.629	0.243	0.778	0.083	0.538	0.000
ω_2	0.146	0.629	0.064	0.412	0.136	0.794	0.000
ω_3	0.146	0.629	0.243	0.778	0.431	0.962	0.218
ω_4	0.146	0.629	0.064	0.412	0.000	0.000	0.000
ω_5	0.146	0.629	0.243	0.778	0.083	0.538	0.175
ω_6	0.146	0.629	0.064	0.412	0.136	0.794	0.286
ω_7	0.146	0.629	0.243	0.778	0.431	0.962	0.687

6.3.3 The recombining case

The above construction is conceptually very simple, but, unfortunately, produces a complicated nonrecombining lattice. Now we choose a different approach. Namely, we construct lattices for S_t which recombine and do not allow arbitrage. For simplicity we assume that the interest rates are deterministic functions of time, $r^0 = r_t^0, r^1 = r_t^1$, while FXRs are functions of t, y. In order to avoid arbitrage, we require that for all (t, y)

$$S_{t+1,y-1} < F_{t,t+1,y} < S_{t+1,y+1}, \qquad (6.11)$$

where $0 \leq t < T$, $y \in \Xi_{-t,t}$, and

$$F_{t,t+1,y} = \frac{(1 + r_{t+1}^0) S_{t,y}}{(1 + r_{t+1}^1)},$$

is the one-period forward, so that all single-period markets are arbitrage-free.

Inequalities (6.11) allow for a lot of freedom in constructing a recombining lattice. It is natural to use this freedom in order to calibrate the model to

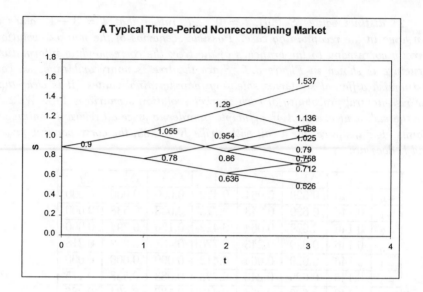

Figure 6.4: The three-period nonrecombining market described by table (6.10).

given market prices of vanilla calls and puts. Our objective is to construct the lattice for $0 \leq t \leq T$, which is consistent with known call prices given by a certain function

$$\eta(t, K) = C(0, S_0, t, K).$$

These prices reflect the observable market smile. The corresponding put prices can be computed via put-call parity. (Often market prices are given in a table form, so that prices corresponding to calls with intermediate strikes have to be found via interpolation.) We proceed by induction. The spot FXR is known. In order to find $S_{1, \pm 1}$ we have to solve the single-period calibration problem. As in Section 4.2, we use the ATMF call (or put) price $\eta(1, F_{0,1})$ as an input. We are free to choose the center of our lattice at $t = 1$. We assume that it is centered on the corresponding forward,

$$\sqrt{S_{1,-1} S_{1,1}} = F_{0,1}.$$

We use equations (5.12) to find $S_{1, \pm 1}$ and equations (6.6) to compute the prices AD of the corresponding Arrow-Debreu claims. We now assume that the lattice is constructed for $0 \leq t' \leq t$, and that all ADs with $t' \leq t$ are known. To advance the lattice one step further, we have to choose $t + 2$ FXRs $S_{t+1,y}$, $y \in \Xi_{-t-1,t+1}$, in such a way that they satisfy inequalities (6.11) and solve the calibration problem. It is natural to calibrate the model to call (or put) options maturing at time $t + 1$ with strikes $K = K_{t+1,y}$, where $y \in \Xi_{-t,t}$, which are sandwiched between $S_{t+1,y-1}$ and $S_{t+1,y+1}$. There are $t + 1$ calls in all, so that one parameter of the model is left underdetermined. We can use this freedom in order to specify the location of the center of the lattice at time $t + 1$.

We can write

$$\eta_{t+1,y} \equiv \eta\left(t + 1, K_{t+1,y}\right),$$

as

$$\eta_{t+1,y} = \sum_{y' \in \Xi_{y+1,t+1}} \left(S_{t+1,y'} - K_{t+1,y}\right) \mathrm{AD}_{t+1,y'},$$

where

$$\mathrm{AD}_{t+1,y} = \mathrm{AD}\left(0, S_0, t + 1, S_{t+1,y}\right).$$

Let $q_{-1,t,y}$ and $q_{1,t,y}$ be the risk-neutral probabilities of down and up moves in the single-period submarket with the vertex at $S_{t,y}$. By using the relations

$$q_{-1,t,y} + q_{1,t,y} = 1,$$

$$q_{-1,t,y} S_{t+1,y-1} + q_{1,t,y} S_{t+1,y+1} = F_{t,t+1,y},$$

$$\mathrm{AD}_{t+1,y} = q_{1,t,y-1} \frac{\mathrm{AD}_{t,y-1}}{\left(1 + r_{t+1}^0\right)} + q_{-1,t,y+1} \frac{\mathrm{AD}_{t,y+1}}{\left(1 + r_{t+1}^0\right)}, \quad y \in \Xi_{-t+1,t-1},$$

$$\mathrm{AD}_{t+1,\pm(t+1)} = q_{\pm 1,t,\pm t} \frac{\mathrm{AD}_{t,\pm t}}{\left(1 + r_{t+1}^0\right)},$$

we represent

$$\check{\eta}_{t+1,y} = \left(1 + r_{t+1}^0\right) \eta_{t+1,y},$$

in the form

$$\check{\eta}_{t+1,y} = (S_{t+1,y+1} - K_{t+1,y})\, q_{1,t,y} \mathrm{AD}_{t,y}$$
$$+ \sum_{y' \in \Xi_{y+2,t}} (q_{-1,t,y'} S_{t+1,y'-1} + q_{1,t,y'} S_{t+1,y'+1} - K_{t+1,y})\, \mathrm{AD}_{t,y'}$$

$$= (S_{t+1,y+1} - K_{t+1,y}) \frac{(F_{t,t+1,y} - S_{t+1,y-1})}{(S_{t+1,y+1} - S_{t+1,y-1})} \mathrm{AD}_{t,y}$$
$$+ \sum_{y' \in \Xi_{y+2,t}} (F_{t,t+1,y'} - K_{t+1,y})\, \mathrm{AD}_{t,y'}.$$

This relation allows us to express $S_{t+1,y+1}$ in terms of $S_{t+1,y-1}$ as follows

$$S_{t+1,y+1} = \frac{\left(\check{\eta}_{t+1,y} S_{t+1,y-1} - (K_{t+1,y} - S_{t+1,y-1}) F_{t,t+1,y} \mathrm{AD}_{t,y} - \varpi \right)}{\left(\check{\eta}_{t+1,y} - (K_{t+1,y} - S_{t+1,y-1}) \mathrm{AD}_{t,y} - \varpi \right)},$$

where

$$\varpi = \sum_{y' \in \Xi_{y,t}} (F_{t,t+1,y'} - K_{t+1,y})\, \mathrm{AD}_{t,y'}.$$

Thus, we can compute $S_{t+1,y}$ recurrently, starting with $S_{t+1,-(t+1)}$ which is assumed to be chosen. Once all $S_{t+1,y}$ are found, we can use the freedom in choosing $S_{t+1,-(t+1)}$ in order to center our lattice in such a way that for odd and even t we have

$$S_{t+1,0} = F_{0,t+1},$$

$$\sqrt{S_{t+1,-1} S_{t+1,+1}} = F_{0,t+1},$$

respectively. It goes without saying that the above calibration procedure can fail for many reasons, for instance because the no-arbitrage conditions are violated, so that it should be considered as a theoretical, rather that practical tool.

Once the lattice describing the possible values of $S_{t,y}$ for $0 \le t \le T$ is constructed, we can use it in order to find prices of other options such as American, barrier, lookback and Asian calls and puts, which are consistent with given prices of European options.

Example 6.6. *We calibrate a three-period recombining market with the spot FXR $S_0 = 0.9$ and constant interest rates $r^0 = 0.06$, $r^1 = 0.04$, to* *market prices of calls given by the following table*

$t \backslash \varkappa$	0.50	0.75	1.00	1.25	1.50
1	*	*	0.10	*	*
2	*	0.06	*	0.20	*
3	0.10	*	0.20	*	0.30

Here $\varkappa$ is the moneyness of the corresponding call which is defined as follows: $\varkappa = F_{0,t}/K$. Thus, calls with $\varkappa > 1$, $\varkappa = 1$, and $\varkappa < 1$ are ITMF, ATMF, and OTMF, respectively. We have $F_{0,1,0} = 0.917$. In order to find $S_{1,\pm 1}$ we use equations (5.12) and obtain

$$S_{1,-1} = 0.727, \qquad S_{1,1} = 1.157.$$

We use equations (6.6) and obtain $AD_{1,-1} = 0.526$, $AD_{1,1} = 0.417$. We continue by induction as explained above and construct the following tables which describe the corresponding FXRs and ADs:

$t \backslash y$	-3	-2	-1	0	1	2	3
0	*	*	*	0.900	*	*	*
1	*	*	0.727	*	1.157	*	*
2	*	0.647	*	0.935	*	1.764	*
3	0.160	*	0.750	*	1.211	*	2.220

$t \backslash y$	-3	-2	-1	0	1	2	3
0	*	*	*	1.000	*	*	*
1	*	*	0.526	*	0.417	*	*
2	*	0.335	*	0.439	*	0.116	*
3	0.048	*	0.500	*	0.228	*	0.064

The risk-neutral valuation principle allows us to find prices of various options in our market. For instance, the price of the American ATMF call is given by the table

$t \backslash y$	-3	-2	-1	0	1	2	3
0	*	*	*	0.141	*	*	*
1	*	*	0.033	*	0.297	*	*
2	*	0.000	*	0.107	*	**0.811**	*
3	0.000	*	0.000	*	0.258	*	1.267

The early exercise price is shown in boldface.

6.4   General multi-period markets

In this section we describe the general multi-period market. As before, we
assume that our market consists of $N + 1$ countries and use superscripts to
distinguish different countries. We reserve the superscript zero for the country
which we call domestic. As before, the domestic currency is called dollars.
We denote the domestic and foreign interest rates by r^0 and r^n, respectively.
These interest rates can depend on time, and, in principle, be stochastic. The
corresponding FXRs are denoted by S^{0n}. Cross-currency interest rates can be
determined as follows $S^{mn} = S^{0n}/S^{0m}$. We observe the dynamics of MMAs
and FXRs at discrete moments of time $t = 0, ..., t = T$. Initial values of FXRs
S_0^{0n} are known.

The key quantities which domestic investors are interested in are relative
dollar values of foreign MMAs (relative value of the dollar MMA is one).
A particular trajectory (or scenario) of the market evolution is described by
two sequences of $(N + 1)$-component vectors in $\mathbb{R}^{N+1}$, namely, $(\mathbf{r}_1, ..., \mathbf{r}_T)$, and
$(\mathbf{S}_0, ..., \mathbf{S}_T)$, where

$$\mathbf{r}_t = \left(r_t^0, r_t^1, ..., r_t^N\right),$$

is the vector of interest rates prevailing for the time interval $[t - 1, t)$, and

$$\mathbf{S}_t = \left(1, S_t^{01}, ..., S_t^{0N}\right),$$

is the vector of FXRs at time t. The corresponding vector of discounted MMA
values $\hat{\mathbf{A}}$ has the form

$$\hat{\mathbf{A}}_t = \left(1, \frac{\prod_{1 \leq t' \leq t}\left(1 + r_{t'}^1\right) S_t^{01}}{\prod_{1 \leq t' \leq t}\left(1 + r_{t'}^0\right)}, ..., \frac{\prod_{1 \leq t' \leq t}\left(1 + r_{t'}^N\right) S_t^{0N}}{\prod_{1 \leq t' \leq t}\left(1 + r_{t'}^0\right)}\right).$$

There are $L = K^T$ possible scenarios in total, their real-world probabilities are
denoted by $p_0, ..., p_{L-1}$. We assume that all p_l are positive, or, in other words,
that our description of the market evolution is as parsimonious as possible and
none of the scenarios (however improbable) is impossible.

We use the K-nomial Bernoulli process as the stochastic engine for our
market and introduce the information structure in the space of elementary
events which is compatible with this engine. An investment strategy can be
characterized by a sequence of $(N + 1)$-component vectors

$$\Upsilon_{t,l} = (\Upsilon_{t,l}^0, \Upsilon_{t,l}^1, ..., \Upsilon_{t,l}^N),$$

showing the amounts invested in (or borrowed from) the corresponding MMAs for the time period $[t, t+1)$ provided that the market follows the scenario ω_l. Alternatively, we can use the time $t = 0$ values of these investments, and characterize a strategy via the vector

$$\hat{\Upsilon}_{t,l} = (\hat{\Upsilon}_{t,l}^0, \hat{\Upsilon}_{t,l}^1, ..., \hat{\Upsilon}_{t,l}^N),$$

where

$$\hat{\Upsilon}_{t,l}^\nu = \frac{\Upsilon_{t,l}^\nu}{\prod_{1 \leq t' \leq t} \left(1 + r_{t',l}^\nu\right)},$$

$\nu = 0, 1, ..., N$. At times t and $t + 1$ the discounted values of the portfolio corresponding to a certain investment strategy are given by the expressions

$$\hat{\Pi}_{t,l}^{(+)} = \frac{\Upsilon_{t,l} \cdot \mathbf{S}_{t,l}}{\prod_{1 \leq t' \leq t} \left(1 + r_{t,l}^0\right)} = \hat{\Upsilon}_{t,l} \cdot \hat{\mathbf{A}}_{t,l},$$

$$\hat{\Pi}_{t+1,l}^{(-)} = \frac{(1 + \mathbf{r}_{t,l})\, \Upsilon_{t,l} \cdot \mathbf{S}_{t+1,l}}{\prod_{1 \leq t' \leq t+1} \left(1 + r_{t',l}^0\right)} = \hat{\Upsilon}_{t,l} \cdot \hat{\mathbf{A}}_{t+1,l}.$$

Here the superscripts $\pm$ are used in order to emphasize that the corresponding values are computed after the strategy is chosen at time t but before it is changed at time $t + 1$. As in the binomial case considered earlier, legitimate strategies have to be predictable and self-financing, so that they coincide for all the scenarios belonging to the same element of the partition $\mathfrak{G}_t$, and

$$\hat{\Pi}_{t,l}^{(-)} = \hat{\Pi}_{t,l}^{(+)},$$

for all scenarios ω_l. It is important to emphasize that if a predictable N-component vector $\Upsilon'_{t,l}$ describing the values of foreign investments at time t is given, we can always construct a *PSFS* $\Upsilon_{t,l} = \left(\Upsilon_{t,l}^0, \Upsilon'_{t,l}\right)$ by choosing $\Upsilon_{t,l}^0$ in the same fashion as in the two-country case.

Once the class of *PSFS* is defined, we can extend to the multi-period setting the important economical concepts introduced for single-period markets. Namely, we can define markets which satisfy the *law of one price* (*LOP*), markets which satisfy the *no dominant strategies condition* (*NDSC*), and markets with *no arbitrage condition* (*NAC*). For example, *LOP* is satisfied if for any two *PSFS* $\Upsilon^{(1)}, \Upsilon^{(2)}$ such that $\hat{\Pi}_{T,l}^{(1)} = \hat{\Pi}_{T,l}^{(2)}$ for all l, we have $\Pi_0^{(1)} = \Pi_0^{(2)}$.

There are no dominant strategies in the market if for all *PSFS* strategies such that $\hat{\Pi}_{T,l} > 0$ we have $\Pi_0 > 0$. Finally, the market does not allow arbitrage if for every *PSFS* such that $\hat{\Pi}_{T,l} \geqslant 0$ for all l and $\hat{\Pi}_{T,l} > 0$ for some l, we have $\Pi_0 > 0$.

As in the single-period case, the no-arbitrage properties of the market are closely related to the existence of risk-neutral measures equivalent to the objective measure. Namely, there is no arbitrage in a certain market if and only if there is at least one positive measure Q on the space of elementary events Ω such that for any $t, 0 \leq t \leq T$, we have

$$\mathbb{E}_Q \left\{ \hat{A}_{0,t}^{0n} \right\} = S_0^{0n}.$$

In other words, the market has to be compatible with the risk-neutral pricing, so that the nth FXR today coincides with the expectation of the relative FXR in the future.

It is very easy to prove that the existence of a risk-neutral measure is sufficient for the absence of arbitrage. Indeed, if such a measure exists, we can represent the present value of a portfolio corresponding to an arbitrary *PSFS* strategy Υ as its discounted future value, i.e.,

$$\Pi_0 = \mathbb{E}_Q \left\{ \frac{\Pi_T}{\prod_{t=1}^{T} \left(1 + r_t^0\right)} \right\}.$$

Thus, the present value of any portfolio such that $\hat{\Pi}_{T,l} \geqslant 0$ for all l, and $\hat{\Pi}_{T,l} > 0$ for some l, has to be strictly positive and arbitrage is not possible.

It is considerably more difficult to show that the existence of a risk-neutral measure is necessary for the absence of arbitrage. In order to do so, we first establish the following fact which is of independent interest. In the multi-period no-arbitrage market all single-period submarkets have to be no-arbitrage as well. Suppose that the multi-period market does not allow arbitrage, but a single-period market starting at time t' at a certain vertex corresponding to an equivalence class $\mathfrak{g}_{t'}$ belonging to the partition $\mathfrak{G}_{t'}$ can be arbitraged, and denote by $\boldsymbol{v}$ the corresponding arbitrage strategy, such that

$$\boldsymbol{v} \cdot \mathbf{S}_{t,l} = 0, \qquad \text{for all} \quad \omega_l \in \mathfrak{g}_{t'},$$
$$\boldsymbol{v} \cdot \mathbf{S}_{t+1,l} \geq 0, \qquad \text{for all} \quad \omega_l \in \mathfrak{g}_{t'},$$
$$\boldsymbol{v} \cdot \mathbf{S}_{t+1,l} > 0, \qquad \text{for some} \quad \omega_l \in \mathfrak{g}_{t'}.$$

The global arbitrage strategy can be chosen as follows

$$
\Upsilon_t = \begin{cases}
0, & 0 \leq t < t' \\
0, & t = t' \text{ and } \omega_l \notin \mathfrak{g}_{t'} \\
\boldsymbol{v}, & t = t' \text{ and } \omega_l \in \mathfrak{g}_{t'} \\
\left(\left(1 + r^0\right)^{t-t'-1} \widetilde{\Upsilon}_l \cdot \mathbf{S}_{t'+1,l}, 0, ..., 0 \right), & t > t'
\end{cases} ,
$$

where

$$
\widetilde{\Upsilon}_l = \begin{cases}
0, & \text{if} \quad \omega_l \notin \mathfrak{g}_{t'} \\
\boldsymbol{v}, & \text{if} \quad \omega_l \in \mathfrak{g}_{t'}
\end{cases} .
$$

In words, an investor does nothing until time t' when he decides if the market is in an arbitrageable state; if the market is in such a state, he uses a single-period arbitrage strategy, and immediately converts the proceeds into the bank account where he keeps them until maturity, otherwise he does nothing. The reader can easily check that this multi-period strategy describes an arbitrage.

Since none of the single-period submarkets allows arbitrage, all of them can be characterized by virtue of at least one risk-neutral measure. At time t these measures correspond to the elements of the partition $\mathfrak{G}_t$. In case when some of the single-period markets are incomplete, we choose one of many possible risk-neutral measures. We denote the measure corresponding to $\mathfrak{g}_{t,l}$ by $Q_{t,l} = (q_{t,l,0}, q_{t,l,1})$. Consider now a certain scenario ω_l and a sequence of partition elements $\mathfrak{g}_{0,l}, ..., \mathfrak{g}_{T,l}$ which contain all the scenarios equivalent to ω_l at time t,

$$
\mathfrak{g}_{0,l} = \Omega \supset \mathfrak{g}_{1,l} ... \supset \mathfrak{g}_{T,l} = \omega_l.
$$

We define the risk-neutral probability of this scenario as follows

$$
q_l = q(\omega_l) = \prod_{0 \leq t \leq T-1} q_{t,l,\omega_l}(t).
$$

In other words, we construct this risk-neutral probability as a product of the single-period risk-neutral probabilities. With this definition in mind, we can easily verify that FXR for the nth currency S_0^{0n} is the expectation of $\hat{A}_{0,t}^{0n}$ at any future time t. Moreover, we can prove a more general result and show that $\hat{A}_{0,t}^{0n}$ is a martingale, with respect to the risk-neutral measure Q, so that

$$
\mathbb{E}_Q \left\{ \hat{A}_{0,t'}^{0n} \,\Big|\, \mathfrak{F}_t \right\} = \hat{A}_{0,t}^{0n},
$$

or, equivalently,

$$
\mathbb{E}_Q \left\{ \frac{\prod_{t''=1}^{t'} \left(1 + r_{t''}^n\right) S_{t'}^{0n}}{\prod_{t''=1}^{t'} \left(1 + r_{t''}^0\right)} \,\bigg|\, \mathfrak{F}_t \right\} = \frac{\prod_{t''=1}^{t} \left(1 + r_{t''}^n\right) S_t^{0n}}{\prod_{t''=1}^{t} \left(1 + r_{t''}^0\right)},
$$

$$\mathbb{E}_Q \left\{ \frac{\prod_{t''=t+1}^{t'} (1 + r_{t''}^n) S_{t'}^{0n}}{\prod_{t''=t+1}^{t'} (1 + r_{t''}^0)} \middle| \mathfrak{F}_t \right\} = S_t^{0n}.$$

We emphasize that, in general, $\hat{A}_{0,t}^{0n}$ is not a martingale with respect to the objective measure P. We can use this martingale property in order to find a risk-neutral probability measure on the space of elementary events.

Example 6.7. *Consider the three-period recombining "arithmetic" binomial market with deterministic interest rates whose states are described by the following table*

	S_0	r_1^0	r_1^1	S_1	r_2^0	r_2^1	S_2	r_3^0	r_3^1	S_3
ω_0	0.9	0.05	0.03	0.8	0.06	0.04	0.7	0.05	0.04	0.6
ω_1	0.9	0.05	0.03	1.0	0.06	0.04	0.9	0.05	0.04	0.8
ω_2	0.9	0.05	0.03	0.8	0.06	0.04	0.9	0.05	0.04	0.8
ω_3	0.9	0.05	0.03	1.0	0.06	0.04	1.1	0.05	0.04	1.0
ω_4	0.9	0.05	0.03	0.8	0.06	0.04	0.7	0.05	0.04	0.8
ω_5	0.9	0.05	0.03	1.0	0.06	0.04	0.9	0.05	0.04	1.0
ω_6	0.9	0.05	0.03	0.8	0.06	0.04	0.9	0.05	0.04	1.0
ω_7	0.9	0.05	0.03	1.0	0.06	0.04	1.1	0.05	0.04	1.2

The objective is to find risk-neutral probabilities $q_i, i = 0, ..., 7$, of different scenarios. This can be done by two different methods. The first method uses risk-neutral probabilities of single-period sub-markets in order to construct the corresponding q_i. The corresponding single-period probabilities of down moves have the form

$t \backslash y$	-2	-1	0	1	2
0	*	*	0.413	*	*
1	*	0.423	*	0.404	*
2	0.466	*	0.457	*	0.447

Consider, for example, ω_0. If the market follows this scenario, the FXR has the following values 0.9, 0.8, 0.7, 0.6, with probabilities 0.413, 0.423, 0.466. Accordingly, the risk-neutral probability of ω_0 is

$$q_0 = 0.413 * 0.423 * 0.466 = 0.081.$$

By the same token we fill the rest of the table,

	ω_0	ω_1	ω_3	ω_4	ω_5	ω_6	ω_7	ω_8
q	0.081	0.108	0.109	0.157	0.093	0.129	0.129	0.194

The second (laborious yet instructive) method of finding risk-neutral probabilities of different evolutionary scenarios assigns probabilities to different scenarios is such a way that the discounted dollar value of the foreign MMA is a martingale. We leave it to the reader as an exercise to calculate risk-neutral probabilities by the second method.

6.5 Contingent claims and their valuation and hedging

Now we are in a position to introduce derivative securities in the general multi-period setting and describe their pricing. As usual, derivative securities are defined in terms of primary securities, i.e., MMAs and FXRs which constitute the multi-period market. We distinguish European derivatives which can be executed only at maturity, i.e., at time T and American derivatives which can be executed at any time t, $0 \le t \le T$. For a single FXR we can introduce the following European derivatives: forward and futures contracts, calls, puts, as well as their various linear combinations, such as straddles, strangles, and risk-reversals. In addition, we can consider path-dependent derivatives which depend on the entire history of the FXR evolution. We can also consider similar American derivatives on a single FXR. Besides, we can consider derivatives which involve several FXRs at once, for example, cross-currency calls and puts, as well as options on indices and baskets of different currencies. All this mind-boggling variety of options can be valued by using the risk-neutral valuation principle. Of course, as in the single period case pricing of a given derivative without its hedging (or replication) makes little sense and finding the right hedging *PSFS* can be very demanding. However, the backward induction makes this problem feasible. The pricing is unique if the market is complete. If it is incomplete, for some derivatives a unique price cannot be found, however, the lowest price at which such derivatives can be sold and the highest price at which they can be bought by a risk-averse investor can still be found.

For simplicity we consider complete markets. For a generic European derivative with the payoff of the form

$$\text{payoff} = V\left(\mathbf{S}_T\right).$$

the value at inception is

$$V_0 = \mathbb{E}_Q \left\{ \frac{V\left(\mathbf{S}_T\right)}{\prod_{t=1}^{T}\left(1 + r_t^0\right)} \right\} = \mathbb{E}_Q \left\{ \hat{V}\left(\mathbf{S}_T\right) \right\}.$$

The corresponding replicating strategy is determined by backward induction. Let $\mathbf{S}_{1,k}$, $k = 0, ..., K - 1$, where K is the number of different outcomes for a single Bernoulli trial, be possible FXRs at $t = 1$. We can represent the conditional values of the derivative in question in the form

$$V(1, \mathbf{S}_{1,k}) = \mathbb{E}_Q \left\{ \frac{V(\mathbf{S}_T)}{\prod_{t=2}^{T} (1 + r_t^0)} \middle| \mathfrak{F}_1 \right\}. \tag{6.12}$$

It is clear that to solve the hedging problem for $t = 0$ it is sufficient to find the hedge for the single period European option with payoff given by equation (6.12). Accordingly, we can use results of the previous chapter in order to construct the corresponding single-period hedge.

6.6 Portfolio theory

In this section we discuss multi-period aspects of portfolio theory. For simplicity we assume that our market is complete so that every European claim with maturity T can be replicated via a *PSFS*. Consider an investor with a positive initial endowment $\Pi_0 > 0$ who wants to solve the optimal mean-variance investment problem, i.e., to find a *PSFS* which generates the discounted terminal wealth with given expected value $(1 + \rho)^T \Pi_0$, where ρ is the desired rate of return per period, and the lowest possible variance. This investor needs to choose a *PSFS* $\Upsilon_{t,l} = \left(\Upsilon_{t,l}^0, \Upsilon_{t,l}^1, ..., \Upsilon_{t,l}^N \right)$, in such a way that the initial wealth is equal to Π_0,

$$\Pi_0 = \Upsilon_0 \cdot \mathbf{S}_0, \tag{6.13}$$

while the discounted terminal wealth

$$\hat{\Pi}_{T,l} = \frac{\Upsilon_{T,l} \cdot \mathbf{S}_{T,l}}{\prod_{1 \leq t' \leq T} \left(1 + r_{t',l}^0 \right)},$$

solves the optimization problem

$$\begin{cases} \frac{1}{2} \mathbb{E}_P \left\{ \hat{\Pi}_{T,l}^2 \right\} = \sum_{0 \leq l \leq L-1} p_l \left(\frac{\Upsilon_{T,l} \cdot \mathbf{S}_{T,l}}{\prod_{1 \leq t' \leq T} \left(1 + r_{t',l}^0 \right)} \right)^2 \to \min, \\ \mathbb{E}_P \left\{ \hat{\Pi}_{T,l} \right\} = \sum_{0 \leq l \leq L-1} p_l \frac{\Upsilon_{T,l} \cdot \mathbf{S}_{T,l}}{\prod_{1 \leq t' \leq T} \left(1 + r_{t',l}^0 \right)} = (1 + \rho)^T \Pi_0. \end{cases}$$

To simplify the constraint optimization we use the state price density vector

$$N_l \equiv N(\omega_l) = \frac{q_l}{p_l},$$

and rewrite the initial endowment constraint (6.13) in the form

$$\mathbb{E}_P\left\{N_l\hat{\Pi}_{T,l}\right\} = \sum_{0 \le l \le L-1} p_l n_l \frac{\Upsilon_{T,l} \cdot \mathbf{S}_{T,l}}{\prod_{1 \le t' \le T}\left(1 + r_{t',l}^0\right)} = \Pi_0.$$

Since our market is complete, we can solve the mean-variance investment problem in three steps. First, we identify the set of attainable claims for a given endowment Π_0, i.e., claims which can be replicated via *PSFSs*. The risk-neutral valuation principle shows that a claim $\Pi = (\Pi_0, ..., \Pi_{L-1})$ is attainable if and only if

$$\mathbb{E}_Q\left\{\hat{\Pi}_l\right\} = \mathbb{E}_P\left\{N_l\hat{\Pi}_l\right\} = \sum_{0 \le l \le L-1} p_l n_l \hat{\Pi}_l = \Pi_0. \qquad (6.14)$$

Second, we choose the attainable contingent claim $\hat{\Pi}$ which solves the constraint optimization problem

$$\begin{cases} \frac{1}{2}\mathbb{E}_P\left\{\hat{\Pi}_l^2\right\} = \sum_{0 \le l \le L-1} p_l \hat{\Pi}_l^2 \to \min, \\ \mathbb{E}_P\left\{\hat{\Pi}_l\right\} = \sum_{0 \le l \le L-1} p_l \hat{\Pi}_l = (1+\rho)^T \Pi_0. \end{cases} \qquad (6.15)$$

Finally, we replicate the optimal attainable claim.

The replication part can be done via the backward induction method used on several occasions before and we do not discuss it here. The constraint optimization step can be solved via the standard Lagrange multipliers method which produces the following optimality condition

$$\frac{\hat{\Pi}_l}{\Pi_0} = \lambda + \mu n_l, \quad l = 1, ..., L,$$

where λ, μ are Lagrange multipliers, or, in vector form

$$\frac{\hat{\Pi}}{\Pi_0} = \lambda E + \mu N,$$

where $E = (1, ..., 1)$. Substituting this expression in equations (6.14), (6.15), we obtain

$$\lambda + \mu = (1+\rho)^T,$$
$$\lambda + \mu\mathbb{E}_Q\{N\} = 1,$$

$$\lambda = \frac{(1+\rho)^T \, \mathbb{E}_Q \{N\} - 1}{\mathbb{E}_Q \{N\} - 1}, \qquad \mu = -\frac{(1+\rho)^T - 1}{\mathbb{E}_Q \{N\} - 1}.$$

We can repeat the calculation performed in Section 5.7 and show that $\mathbb{E}_Q \{N\} > 1$ (provided that $P \neq Q$). Accordingly, $\lambda > 0, \mu < 0$. Once we know $\hat{\Pi}_l$ for every ω_l, we can use the backward induction in order to find the corresponding replicating strategy $\Upsilon_{t,l}$.

It is clear that for complete markets the multi-period mean-variance investment problem boils down to solving the single-period investment problem for the time interval $[0, T]$ and using the backward induction to find an appropriate replicating strategy. In the incomplete case the problem is more complicated and we do not discuss it here. The main difficulty in the latter case lies in describing the set of attainable claims.

6.7   The optimal investment problem

In this section we discuss multi-period aspects of the optimal investment problem. As in the previous section, we assume that our market is complete. Consider an investor characterized by the terminal utility function $\mathcal{U}$ and the initial endowment Π_0. This investor needs to choose a predictable self-financing strategy $\Upsilon_{t,l}$ in such a way that the initial wealth is equal to Π_0, while the discounted terminal wealth $\hat{\Pi}_{T,l}$ maximizes the expected utility

$$\mathbb{E}_P \left\{ \mathcal{U}\left(\hat{\Pi}_T\right) \right\} = \sum_{0 \leq l \leq L-1} p_l \mathcal{U}\left(\frac{\Upsilon_{T,l} \cdot \mathbf{S}_{T,l}}{\prod_{1 \leq t' \leq T} \left(1 + r^0_{t',l}\right)} \right) \to \max.$$

As before the investor can solve the optimal investment problem in three steps. First, he should identify the set of attainable claims for a given endowment Π_0, i.e., such claims that

$$\mathbb{E}_Q \left\{ \hat{\Pi} \right\} = \sum_{0 \leq l \leq L-1} q_l \hat{\Pi}_l = \Pi_0.$$

Second, the investor has to choose the attainable contingent claim $\hat{\Pi}$ which maximizes the expected utility of the discounted wealth,

$$\mathbb{E}_P \left\{ \mathcal{U}\left(\hat{\Pi}\right) \right\} = \sum_{0 \leq l \leq L-1} p_l \mathcal{U}\left(\hat{\Pi}_l \right) \to \max.$$

Finally, he has to replicate the optimal attainable claim.

The replication part is standard. As before, the constraint optimization part can be solved via the Lagrange multipliers method. To facilitate its application, we rewrite the initial endowment constraint in the form

$$\mathbb{E}_P\left\{N\hat{\Pi}\right\} = \sum_{0\leq l\leq L-1} p_l n_l \hat{\Pi}_l = \Pi_0.$$

The corresponding optimality condition yields

$$\mathcal{U}'\left(\hat{\Pi}_l\right) = \mu n_l.$$

Assuming that $\mathcal{U}$ is concave, so that $\mathcal{U}'$ is monotonically decreasing, we can invert the above equation and write

$$\hat{\Pi}_l = \mathcal{W}\left(\mu n_l\right).$$

Finally, substituting this relation in the initial endowment constraint we obtain the following scalar condition for the Lagrange multiplier μ,

$$\sum_{0\leq l\leq L-1} q_l \mathcal{W}\left(\mu n_l\right) = \Pi_0.$$

By solving this equation we can find μ and then determine $\hat{\Pi}$ and construct the corresponding replicating strategy. We see that the multi-period optimization problem in a complete market can be solved by analogy with the single-period case provided that the space of elementary events is extended appropriately.

Consider an investor with the exponential utility function $U(x) = -e^{-x}$, and a positive endowment Π_0, and solve the corresponding optimization problem for the stationary T-period binomial market constructed in Section 2. Since the corresponding lattice is recombining and attainable contingent claims which we are interested in depend only on the final value of FXR at time T, we can partition the space of elementary events in accordance with the number of up and down moves $\chi_{0,1}(\omega_l)$. This partition contains $T+1$ events $\mathfrak{g}_0, ..., \mathfrak{g}_m, ..., \mathfrak{g}_T$, where the subscript m shows the number of up moves for all the scenarios belonging to $\mathfrak{g}_m$, $m = \chi_1(\omega_l)$, $\omega_l \in \mathfrak{g}_m$. The real-world and risk-neutral probabilities of $\mathfrak{g}_m$ are

$$P\left(\mathfrak{g}_m\right) = C_m^T p_0^{T-m} p_1^m, \quad Q\left(\mathfrak{g}_m\right) = \frac{C_m^T}{2^T}.$$

Accordingly, the state price density vector N has the form

$$N = (n_0, ..., n_m, ..., n_T), \qquad n_m = \frac{1}{(2p_0)^{T-m} (2p_1)^m}.$$

The optimality condition yields

$$e^{-\hat{\Pi}_m} = \frac{\mu}{(2p_0)^{T-m} (2p_1)^m},$$

so that

$$\hat{\Pi}_m = -\ln \left(\frac{\mu}{(2p_0)^{T-m} (2p_1)^m} \right).$$

The Lagrange multiplier μ is determined by the constraint

$$-\sum_{m=0}^{T} \frac{C_m^T}{2^T} \ln \left(\frac{\mu}{(2p_0)^{T-m} (2p_1)^m} \right) = \Pi_0,$$

which yields

$$\ln \mu = -\Pi_0 - \sum_{m=0}^{T} \frac{C_m^T}{2^T} \ln \left(\frac{1}{(2p_0)^{T-m} (2p_1)^m} \right).$$

Finally,

$$\hat{\Pi}_m = \Pi_0 + \sum_{m'=0}^{T} \frac{C_{m'}^T}{2^T} \ln \left(\frac{1}{(2p_0)^{T-m'} (2p_1)^{m'}} \right) - \ln \left(\frac{1}{(2p_0)^{T-m} (2p_1)^m} \right).$$

Since we know the optimal contingent claim $\hat{\Pi}$ at time T, we can construct the corresponding hedging *PSFS* via the standard backward induction.

6.8   References and further reading

Multi-period markets have been studied by numerous researchers. The following sources on the topics covered in this chapter are particularly useful: Cox *et al.* (1981), Cox and Rubinstein (1985), Derman and Kani (1994), Dothan (1990), Duffie (1996), Harrison and Kreps (1979), Huang and Litzenberger (1988), Hull (2000), Ingersoll (1987), Jamshidian (1991), Jarrow and Rudd (1983), Pliska (1997). As before, the author especially recommends the latter book.

Part IV

Continuous-time models

Part IV

Continuous-time models

Chapter 7

Stochastic dynamics of forex

7.1 Introduction

In this chapter we introduce several models describing the continuous time dynamics of fixed income instruments and FXRs in two- and multi-country economies. In the subsequent chapters we show how to use these models to price options and develop optimal investment strategies in currencies.

We start with two-country markets with deterministic investments in MMAs and bonds. For brevity, the domestic and foreign currencies are called dollar and euro, respectively. The standard assumption is that prices of dollar and euro denominated fixed income instruments in their respective currencies grow exponentially while FXR and hence dollar prices of euro denominated instruments (as well as euro prices of dollar denominated instruments) follow the geometric Brownian motion. Domestic returns on investment in foreign fixed income instruments follow the arithmetic Brownian motion and can be both positive and negative. At first, we consider the objective dynamics of FXR and dollar prices of foreign MMAs and bonds. Once this dynamics is understood, we introduce the concept of the market price of risk and show how to risk-neutralize the real-world dynamics. We extend our results by incorporating nonlinear local diffusions, jumps, stochastic volatility, etc. Then we study a more realistic case of two-country markets without deterministic fixed income investments. For such markets the distinction between domestic and foreign investments becomes blurred. We choose the simplest approach to modeling stochastic prices of fixed income instruments and describe them in terms of instantaneous interest rates. Then we study both objective and risk-free dynamics of FXRs and show how to model domestic prices of foreign fixed income instruments.

Finally, we consider multi-country markets with deterministic bond prices. We model the evolution of the FXRs and the domestic prices of foreign MMAs and bonds as multidimensional geometric Brownian motions. Returns on investments in foreign fixed income instruments follow the arithmetic Brownian motion. As before, we study the real-world evolution first, and risk-neutralize it afterward. We express the volatility of a particular FXR in terms of the market prices of risk in the corresponding countries by using the fact that cross-currency FXRs are quotients of reference FXRs. This observation serves as a useful illustration of the fact that volatility is a relative concept.

The chapter is organized as follows. In Sections 2 - 4 we assume that the FXR follows the geometric Brownian motion. In Section 2 we study two-country markets with non-risky fixed income investments, in Section 3 we extend our analysis to the case of two-country markets with risky fixed income instruments, finally in Section 4 we consider multi-currency markets. In Sections 5 - 8 we consider more general models describing the FXR evolution. Specifically, we study the nonlinear diffusion model in Section 5, the jump diffusion model in Section 6, the stochastic volatility model in Section 7, and their combinations in Section 8.

7.2   Two-country markets with deterministic investments

We start with the simplest case of a two-country economy and assume that in both countries investments in fixed income instruments are deterministic. We use the superscripts 0 and 1 in order to distinguish the corresponding countries, their currencies are called dollars and euros, respectively. For local fixed income investors the only relevant characteristics of their local economies are the continuously compounded interest rates r^μ, where $\mu = 0, 1$.

The dynamics of fixed income instrument prices in their respective currencies is easy to describe. Local investors can put their money in the MMA or invest it in (zero coupon) bonds. At time t the values of MMAs opened at time 0 and bonds maturing at time T in their respective currencies are denoted by $A_{0,t}^{\mu}$, $B_{t,T}^{\mu}$. They are governed by the ODEs of the form

$$\frac{dA_{0,t}^{\mu}}{A_{0,t}^{\mu}} = r^{\mu}dt, \quad A_{0,0}^{\mu} = 1,$$

$$\frac{dB_{t,T}^{\mu}}{B_{t,T}^{\mu}} = r^{\mu}dt, \quad B_{T,T}^{\mu} = 1.$$

Thus, A^{μ} evolves forward, while B^{μ} evolves backward in time. This distinction is of little consequence when the corresponding prices are deterministic. However, when they are stochastic, it becomes quite relevant. Assuming that interest rates are constant, we solve the above equations and get

$$A_{0,t}^{\mu} = e^{r^{\mu}t},$$

$$B_{t,T}^{\mu} = e^{-r^{\mu}(T-t)}.$$

We can use MMA for discounting values of all instruments to time 0, and zero coupon bonds for growing their values to time T. The discounted and grown values of fixed income instruments $\hat{A}$, $\hat{B}$ and $\check{A}$, $\check{B}$, which are time-independent, have the form

$$\hat{A}_{0,t}^{\mu} = \frac{A_{0,t}^{\mu}}{A_{0,t}^{\mu}} = 1,$$

$$\hat{B}_{0,t,T}^{\mu} = \frac{B_{t,T}^{\mu}}{A_{0,t}^{\mu}} = e^{-r^{\mu}T} = B_{0,T},$$

$$\check{A}_{0,t,T}^{\mu} = \frac{A_{0,t}^{\mu}}{B_{t,T}^{\mu}} = e^{r^{\mu}T} = A_{0,T},$$

$$\check{B}_{t,T}^{\mu} = \frac{B_{t,T}^{\mu}}{B_{t,T}^{\mu}} = 1,$$

respectively.

For finding the dollar price of euro denominated fixed income instruments we need to know the FXR S_t^{01}, i.e., the dollar price of one euro. As a first approximation, we assume that S_t^{01} follows the geometric Brownian motion with drift,

$$\frac{dS_t^{01}}{S_t^{01}} = b^{01}dt + \sigma^{01}dW_t, \qquad S_0^{01} \text{ is given.}$$

Here b^{01} is the real-world drift of the FXR, σ^{01} is its volatility, and W_t is the standard Wiener process modeling the real-world stochasticity. We introduce the domestic market price of risk λ^0 and represent the drift coefficient in the form

$$b^{01} = r^{01} + \sigma^{01}\lambda^0.$$

Here

$$r^{\mu\nu} = r^\mu - r^\nu.$$

Usually $\sigma^{01}\lambda^0$ positive. The interest rate differential describes the natural growth rate of FXR while the correction describes the premium which domestic investors demand for holding risky asset (foreign currency). By rewriting the above formula in the form

$$\lambda^0 = \frac{b^{01} - r^{01}}{\sigma^{01}},$$

we see that the market price of risk is a measure of excessive return per unit of risk. The above construction becomes more transparent if one considers the dynamics of dollar prices of euro denominated fixed income instruments. The corresponding prices are $A^{01} = S^{01}A^1$, $B^{01} = S^{01}B^1$. By Ito's lemma we have

$$\frac{dA_{0,t}^{01}}{A_{0,t}^{01}} = \left(r^0 + \sigma^{01}\lambda^0\right)dt + \sigma^{01}dW_t, \qquad A_{0,0}^{01} = S_0^{01},$$

$$\frac{dB_{t,T}^{01}}{B_{t,T}^{01}} = \left(r^0 + \sigma^{01}\lambda^0\right)dt + \sigma^{01}dW_t, \qquad B_{T,T}^{01} = S_T^{01}.$$

In general, the growth rate of A^{01}, B^{01} exceeds the deterministic growth rate of A^0, B^0 in order to compensate investors for uncertainties associated with foreign instruments. The evolution of the discounted and grown prices $\hat{A}^{01} = A^{01}/A^0$, $\hat{B}^{01} = B^{01}/A^0$, $\check{A}^{01} = A^{01}/B^0$, $\check{B}^{01} = B^{01}/B^0$ is described by

$$\frac{d\hat{A}_{0,t}^{01}}{\hat{A}_{0,t}^{01}} = \frac{d\hat{B}_{0,t,T}^{01}}{\hat{B}_{0,t,T}^{01}} = \frac{d\check{A}_{0,t,T}^{01}}{\check{A}_{0,t}^{01}} = \frac{d\check{B}_{t,T}^{01}}{\check{B}_{t,T}^{01}} = \sigma^{01}\left(\lambda^0 dt + dW_t\right).$$

The equations describing the market evolution from the viewpoint of euro investors are

$$\frac{dS_t^{10}}{S_t^{10}} = b^{10}dt + \sigma^{10}dW_t = \left(r^{10} + \sigma^{10}\lambda^1\right)dt + \sigma^{10}dW_t, \qquad (7.1)$$

$$\frac{dA_{0,t}^{10}}{A_{0,t}^{10}} = \frac{dB_{t,T}^{10}}{B_{t,T}^{10}} = \left(r^1 + \sigma^{10}\lambda^1\right)dt + \sigma^{10}dW_t,$$

$$\frac{d\hat{A}_{0,t}^{10}}{\hat{A}_{0,t}^{10}} = \frac{d\hat{B}_{0,t,T}^{10}}{\hat{B}_{0,t,T}^{10}} = \frac{d\check{A}_{0,t,T}^{10}}{\check{A}_{0,t}^{10}} = \frac{d\check{B}_{t,T}^{10}}{\check{B}_{t,T}^{10}} = \sigma^{10}\left(\lambda^1 dt + dW_t\right).$$

We can find relations between volatilities and market prices of risk by using the obvious fact that

$$S_t^{10} = \frac{1}{S_t^{01}}.$$

A simple algebra yields

$$\begin{aligned}\frac{dS_t^{10}}{S_t^{10}} &= \left(-b^{01} + \left(\sigma^{01}\right)^2\right)dt - \sigma^{01}dW_t \qquad (7.2)\\ &= \left(-r^{01} - \sigma^{01}\lambda^0 + \left(\sigma^{01}\right)^2\right)dt - \sigma^{01}dW_t.\end{aligned}$$

Comparison of equations (7.1) and (7.2) shows that

$$\sigma^{10} = -\sigma^{01},$$

$$r^{10} + \sigma^{10}\lambda^1 = -r^{01} - \sigma^{01}\lambda^0 + \left(\sigma^{01}\right)^2,$$

so that

$$\sigma^{01} = \lambda^0 - \lambda^1,$$

$$\sigma^{10} = \lambda^1 - \lambda^0.$$

Thus, the volatility of FXR can be expressed in terms of dollar and euro market prices of risk.

We can write the equations for FXRs, MMAs, and bonds as follows:

$$\frac{dS_t^{\mu\nu}}{S_t^{\mu\nu}} = \left(r^{\mu\nu} + (\lambda^\mu - \lambda^\nu)\lambda^\mu\right)dt + (\lambda^\mu - \lambda^\nu)\,dW_t, \qquad (7.3)$$

$$\frac{dA_{0,t}^{\mu\nu}}{A_{0,t}^{\mu\nu}} = \frac{dB_{t,T}^{\mu\nu}}{B_{t,T}^{\mu\nu}} = \left(r^\mu + (\lambda^\mu - \lambda^\nu)\lambda^\mu\right)dt + (\lambda^\mu - \lambda^\nu)\,dW_t, \qquad (7.4)$$

$$\frac{d\hat{A}_{0,t}^{\mu\nu}}{\hat{A}_{0,t}^{\mu\nu}} = \frac{d\hat{B}_{0,t,T}^{\mu\nu}}{\hat{B}_{0,t,T}^{\mu\nu}} = \frac{d\check{A}_{0,t,T}^{\mu\nu}}{\check{A}_{0,t}^{10}} = \frac{d\check{B}_{t,T}^{\mu\nu}}{\check{B}_{t,T}^{10}} = (\lambda^\mu - \lambda^\nu)\left(\lambda^\mu dt + dW_t\right), \qquad (7.5)$$

where $\mu, \nu = 0, 1$, and we put

$$S^{\mu\mu} = 1, \quad A^{\mu\mu} = A^\mu, \quad B^{\mu\mu} = B^\mu.$$

These equations are easy to solve via formula (4.50). For instance,

$$S_t^{\mu\nu} = \Phi^{\mu\nu}(t)\,e^{r^{\mu\nu}t}S_0^{\mu\nu},$$

where

$$\Phi^{\mu\nu}(t) = \exp\left\{\frac{1}{2}\left((\lambda^\mu)^2 - (\lambda^\nu)^2\right)t + (\lambda^\mu - \lambda^\nu)W_t\right\},$$

etc. It is easy to see that

$$\mathbb{E}_P\left\{\Phi^{\mu\nu}(t)\right\} = \lambda^\mu(\lambda^\mu - \lambda^\nu).$$

By using Cameron-Martin-Girsanov's theorem, we can risk-neutralize the dynamics of FXRs and bond prices. To this end, we do the standard change of measure, introduce the new Wiener processes with respect to this measure according to the rule

$$W_t^\mu = W_t + \lambda^\mu t,$$

and rewrite equations (7.3) - (7.5) as

$$\frac{dS_t^{\mu\nu}}{S_t^{\mu\nu}} = r^{\mu\nu}dt + (\lambda^\mu - \lambda^\nu)\,dW_t^\mu,$$

$$\frac{dA_{0,t}^{\mu\nu}}{A_{0,t}^{\mu\nu}} = \frac{dB_{t,T}^{\mu\nu}}{B_{t,T}^{\mu\nu}} = r^{\mu}dt + (\lambda^{\mu} - \lambda^{\nu})\, dW_t^{\mu},$$

$$\frac{d\hat{A}_{0,t}^{\mu\nu}}{\hat{A}_{0,t}^{\mu\nu}} = \frac{d\hat{B}_{0,t,T}^{\mu\nu}}{\hat{B}_{0,t,T}^{\mu\nu}} = \frac{d\check{A}_{0,t,T}^{\mu\nu}}{\check{A}_{0,t}^{10}} = \frac{d\check{B}_{t,T}^{\mu\nu}}{\check{B}_{t,T}^{10}} = (\lambda^{\mu} - \lambda^{\nu})\, dW_t^{\mu}.$$

We emphasize that the original Wiener process was common for both countries, while the processes W^{μ} are country specific. Thus, in the risk-neutral world, the drift of every quantity is determined solely by its dimension. In other words, for domestic bonds which are measured in dollars the growth rate is r^0, for FXR which is measured in dollars/euros the growth rate is r^{01}, etc. The corresponding solution for $S_t^{\mu\nu}$, say, has the form

$$S_t^{\mu\nu} = \tilde{\Phi}^{\mu\nu}(t)\, e^{r^{\mu\nu}t} S_0^{\mu\nu}$$

where

$$\tilde{\Phi}^{\mu\nu}(t) = \exp\left\{ -\frac{1}{2} (\lambda^{\mu} - \lambda^{\nu})^2 t + (\lambda^{\mu} - \lambda^{\nu}) W_t^{\mu} \right\}.$$

It is clear that

$$\mathbb{E}_Q\left\{ \tilde{\Phi}^{\mu\nu}(t) \right\} = 1.$$

The corresponding t.p.d.f. has the standard lognormal form.

The r.h.s. of equations (7.3) - (7.5) which describe the real-world dynamics of FXRs and fixed income instrument prices are clearly different for dollar and euro investors. We can introduce the so-called "natural numeraires" (also known as Long portfolios) in such a way that the dynamics of bond prices relative to these numeraires depends only on the currency in which bonds are denominated. The natural numeraires evolve as follows

$$\frac{d\Xi_{0,t}^{\mu}}{\Xi_{0,t}^{\mu}} = \left(r^{\mu} + (\lambda^{\mu})^2 \right) dt + \lambda^{\mu}dW_t, \quad \Xi_{0,0}^{\mu} = 1.$$

To put it differently, the volatility of natural numeraires is equal to the market price of risk. It can be shown in the framework of the mean-variance portfolio theory that Long portfolios have optimal risk-return characteristics. Straightforward application of Ito's lemma yields

$$
\frac{d\tilde{A}_{0,t}^{\mu\nu}}{\tilde{A}_{0,t}^{\mu\nu}} = \frac{d\tilde{B}_{0,t,T}^{\mu\nu}}{\tilde{B}_{0,t,T}^{\mu\nu}}
$$
$$
= \left(r^\mu + (\lambda^\mu - \lambda^\nu)\lambda^\mu - r^\mu - (\lambda^\mu)^2 + (\lambda^\mu)^2 - (\lambda^\mu - \lambda^\nu)\lambda^\mu \right) dt
$$
$$
+ (\lambda^\mu - \lambda^\nu - \lambda^\mu)\, dW_t
$$
$$
= -\lambda^\nu dW_t,
$$

where $\tilde{A}^{\mu\nu} = A^{\mu\nu}/\Xi^\mu$, $\tilde{B}^{\mu\nu} = B^{\mu\nu}/\Xi^\mu$. Thus, we can create a market in which the governing equations for the evolution of the relative fixed income instrument prices coincide for dollar and euro investors. Of course, such a simplification comes at a price since in this market prices of all instruments (and not just of foreign ones) are stochastic. On the other hand, these prices are martingales, so that their conditional expectations are constant,

$$
\mathbb{E}_P \left\{ \left(\begin{array}{c} \tilde{A}_{0,t'}^{\mu\nu} \\ \tilde{B}_{0,t',T}^{\mu\nu} \end{array} \right) \middle| \mathfrak{F}_t \right\} = \left(\begin{array}{c} \tilde{A}_{0,t}^{\mu\nu} \\ \tilde{B}_{0,t,T}^{\mu\nu} \end{array} \right),
$$

where $t' > t$.

In the more general case when the interest rates are deterministic functions of time, $r^\mu = r_t^\mu$, $\mu = 0,1$, the deterministic fixed income instrument prices can be written as

$$
A_{0,t}^\mu = e^{\int_0^t r_{t'}^\mu dt'}, \qquad B_{t,T}^\mu = e^{-\int_t^T r_{t'}^\mu dt'},
$$

$$
\hat{A}_{0,t}^\mu = 1, \qquad \hat{B}_{0,t,T}^\mu = B_{0,T}^\mu,
$$

$$
\check{A}_{0,t,T}^\mu = A_{0,T}^\mu, \qquad \check{B}_{t,T}^\mu = 1.
$$

The corresponding market prices of risk are time-dependent, too, $\lambda^\mu = \lambda_t^\mu$,

$$
W_t^\mu = W_t + \int_0^t \lambda_{t'}^\mu dt',
$$

etc.

The above notation is cumbersome due to the presence of the superscripts which are used to distinguish different countries. When it does not cause confusion, we suppress these superscripts for the sake of brevity. For instance, we write S_t rather than $S_t^{\mu\nu}$, etc.

7.3 Two-country markets without deterministic investments

In the previous sections we assumed that prices of fixed income instruments are deterministic while FXR is stochastic. This is a strong assumption which is violated in many situations. We now discuss what happens when both prices of fixed income instrument and FXRs are stochastic. To start with, we need to develop a framework for describing the dynamics of fixed income instruments. There are several approaches to describing the bond price dynamics. Bond prices can be: (A) modeled directly; (B) expressed in terms of instantaneous interest rates; (C) expressed in terms of forward interest rates. We concentrate on the second approach which is conceptually straightforward and can be viewed as a direct extension of the approach used in the deterministic case.

Every country is characterized by the instantaneous interest rate r_t^μ, $\mu = 0, 1$, which characterizes the rate of return on short term investments in its MMA. This rate follows a stochastic process. It is important to choose the SDE for r_t^μ in such a way that, in agreement with the market data, r_t^μ is mean-reverting. It is also desirable to make sure that r_t^μ stays positive. Many models have been proposed in the literature, for instance,

$$dr_t^\mu = \varkappa^\mu \left(\varrho^\mu - r_t^\mu \right) dt + \varsigma^\mu d\Omega_t^\mu, \quad r_0^\mu \text{ is given.} \tag{7.6}$$

$$dr_t^\mu = \varkappa^\mu \left(\varrho^\mu - r_t^\mu \right) dt + \varsigma^\mu \sqrt{r_t^\mu} d\Omega_t^\mu, \quad r_0^\mu \text{ is given.}$$

$$\frac{dr_t^\mu}{r_t^\mu} = \varkappa^\mu \left(\varrho^\mu - \ln r_t^\mu \right) dt + \varsigma^\mu d\Omega_t^\mu, \quad r_0^\mu \text{ is given.}$$

which are due to Vasicek, Cox, Ingersoll and Ross, and Black and Karasinski, respectively. The general SDE for r_t^μ can be written in the form

$$dr_t^\mu = f^\mu \left(t, r_t^\mu \right) dt + g^\mu \left(t, r_t^\mu \right) d\Omega_t^\mu, \quad r_0^\mu \text{ is given.} \tag{7.7}$$

It is assumed that the standard Wiener processes Ω_t^0, Ω_t^1 are independent. (The latter assumption can be dropped if necessary.)

For every country we have to describe the evolution of MMA A^μ and zero coupon bond B^μ which is compatible with SDE (7.7). It was mentioned above that the values of A^μ, B^μ are governed by the forward and backward pricing equations, respectively. The evolution of A^μ is governed by the forward SDE of the form

$$dA_{0,t}^\mu = r_t^\mu dt, \quad A_{0,0}^\mu = 1,$$

which has to be solved together with (7.7). The corresponding solution is

$$A_{0,t}^{\mu} = \exp\left\{\int_0^t r_{t'}^{\mu} dt'\right\}.$$

It is clear that $A_{0,t}^{\mu}$ is not a function of r_t^{μ} alone and depends on the entire history of its evolution until time t. At the same time, the value of $B_{t,T}^{\mu}$ reflects the expectations of the changes in interest rates, so that

$$B_{t,T}^{\mu} = \mathbb{E}\left\{\exp\left\{-\int_t^T r_{t'}^{\mu} dt'\right\} | \mathfrak{F}_t\right\}.$$

The Feynman-Kac formula shows that $B_{t,T}^{\mu}$ is a function of t, r^{μ} which solves the following backward parabolic equation

$$B_t^{\mu} + \frac{1}{2}\left(g\left(t,r\right)\right)^2 B_{rr}^{\mu} + f\left(t,r\right) B_r^{\mu} - r B^{\mu} = 0,$$

$$B^{\mu}\left(T,r\right) = 1.$$

Here r is considered as a dummy variable representing r_t^{μ}, and $B^{\mu} = B^{\mu}\left(t,r\right)$. Thus, by solving the pricing problem, we can express B^{μ} in terms of r^{μ} and *vice versa*.

We leave it to the reader to check (by using Ito's lemma and equation (7.7)) that the SDEs for the bond price $B_{t,T}^{\mu}$ and the discounted bond price $\hat{B}_{0,t,T}^{\mu} = B_{t,T}^{\mu}/A_{0,t}^{\mu}$ can be written as:

$$dB_{t,T}^{\mu} = r_t^{\mu} B_{t,T}^{\mu} dt + g\left(t,r_t^{\mu}\right)\frac{\partial B^{\mu}\left(t,r_t^{\mu}\right)}{\partial r}d\Omega_t^{\mu}, \qquad B_{0,T}^{\mu} \text{ is given,}$$

$$d\hat{B}_{0,t,T}^{\mu} = g\left(t,r_t^{\mu}\right)\frac{\partial B^{\mu}\left(t,r_t^{\mu}\right)}{\partial r}d\Omega_t^{\mu}, \qquad \hat{B}_{0,T}^{\mu} \text{ is given.}$$

or, symbolically,

$$\frac{dB_{t,T}^{\mu}}{B_{t,T}^{\mu}} = r_t^{\mu} dt + \Sigma^{\mu}\left(t, B_{t,T}^{\mu}\right) d\Omega_t^{\mu}, \qquad B_{0,T}^{\mu} \text{ is given,}$$

$$\frac{d\hat{B}_{0,t,T}^{\mu}}{\hat{B}_{0,t,T}^{\mu}} = \Sigma^{\mu}\left(t, B_{t,T}^{\mu}\right) d\Omega_t^{\mu},$$

where

$$\Sigma^\mu\left(t, B^\mu_{t,T}\right) = \frac{g\left(t, r^\mu_t\right) \partial B^\mu\left(t, r^\mu_t\right)/\partial r}{B^\mu\left(t, r^\mu_t\right)}.$$

For the sake of completeness, we show how to write the governing SDE for B^μ in the Vasicek framework. (We emphasize that equation (7.6) does not prevent r^μ from becoming negative but we disregard this issue for simplicity.) The Vasicek pricing problem has the form

$$B^\mu_t + \frac{1}{2}\left(\varsigma^\mu\right)^2 B^\mu_{rr} + \varkappa^\mu\left(\varrho^\mu - r\right) B^\mu_r - r B^\mu = 0,$$

$$B^\mu\left(T, r\right) = 1.$$

Its solution can be represented via the so-called affine ansatz:

$$B^\mu\left(t, r\right) = e^{\alpha^\mu(t) - \beta^\mu(t) r}.$$

Differentiation of the above formula yields:

$$B^\mu_t = \left(\dot{\alpha}^\mu - \dot{\beta}^\mu r\right) B^\mu, \quad B^\mu_r = -\beta^\mu B^\mu, \quad B^\mu_{rr} = \left(\beta^\mu\right)^2 B^\mu.$$

Here the overdot denotes the time derivative. Substituting these expressions into the pricing equation and the final conditions and collecting terms proportional to r^1 and r^0, we obtain the following system of ODEs for α^μ, β^μ:

$$\dot{\beta}^\mu - \varkappa^\mu \beta^\mu + 1 = 0, \quad \beta^\mu\left(T\right) = 0,$$

$$\dot{\alpha}^\mu + \frac{1}{2}\left(\varsigma^\mu \beta^\mu\right)^2 - \varkappa^\mu \varrho^\mu \beta^\mu = 0, \quad \alpha^\mu\left(T\right) = 0.$$

The equation for β^μ is a linear inhomogeneous equation which can solved by the standard technique; the equation for α^μ can be solved by simple integration:

$$\beta^\mu = \frac{1 - e^{-\varkappa(T-t)}}{\varkappa},$$

$$\alpha^\mu = -\left(\varrho^\mu - \frac{1}{2}\left(\frac{\varsigma^\mu}{\varkappa^\mu}\right)^2\right)\left(T - t\right) + \left(\varrho^\mu - \left(\frac{\varsigma^\mu}{\varkappa^\mu}\right)^2\right)\frac{\left(1 - e^{-\varkappa(T-t)}\right)}{\varkappa}$$
$$+ \frac{1}{2}\left(\frac{\varsigma^\mu}{\varkappa^\mu}\right)^2 \frac{\left(1 - e^{-2\varkappa(T-t)}\right)}{2\varkappa}.$$

It is clear that

$$r^\mu = \frac{\alpha^\mu - \ln B^\mu}{\beta^\mu},$$

$$\Sigma^\mu\left(t, B^\mu\right) = -\varsigma^\mu \beta^\mu,$$

$$\frac{dB^\mu}{B^\mu} = \frac{\alpha^\mu - \ln B^\mu}{\beta^\mu} dt - \varsigma^\mu \beta^\mu d\Omega_t^\mu.$$

Thus, the bond price in Vasicek model follows the Black-Karasinski process. Equations for B^μ are rather cumbersome, accordingly, whenever possible, we use equations for r^μ instead.

Once the behavior of domestic and foreign bond prices in their respective currencies is analyzed, we can introduce FXR into the picture and determine the cross-currency bond prices. We assume that $S_t^{\mu\nu}$ follows the geometric Brownian motion with one source of uncertainty:

$$\frac{dS_t^{\mu\nu}}{S_t^{\mu\nu}} = r^{\mu\nu} dt + \left(\lambda^\mu - \lambda^\nu\right)\left(dW_t + \lambda^\mu dt\right),$$

where W_t is the standard Wiener process which is correlated with both Ω_t^1, Ω_t^2,

$$dW_t \cdot d\Omega_t^\mu = \rho^\mu dt.$$

We can represent W_t in the form

$$W_t = \rho^1 \Omega_t^1 + \rho^2 \Omega_t^2 + \sqrt{1 - \left(\rho^1\right)^2 - \left(\rho^2\right)^2}\,\tilde{W}_t,$$

where $\tilde{W}_t$ is the standard Wiener process independent of the processes Ω_t^1, Ω_t^2.

After some algebra we obtain the following SDE for the μ-price of the ν-bond:

$$\frac{dB_{t,T}^{\mu\nu}}{B_{t,T}^{\mu\nu}} = \left(r^\mu + \rho^\nu\left(\lambda^\mu - \lambda^\nu\right)\Sigma^\nu\right) dt + \left(\lambda^\mu - \lambda^\nu\right)\left(dW_t + \lambda^\mu dt\right) + \Sigma^\nu d\Omega^\nu.$$

The discounted price $\hat{B}^{\mu\nu}$ is governed by the SDE

$$\frac{d\hat{B}_{0,t,T}^{\mu\nu}}{\hat{B}_{0,t,T}^{\mu\nu}} = \rho^\nu\left(\lambda^\mu - \lambda^\nu\right)\Sigma^\nu dt + \left(\lambda^\mu - \lambda^\nu\right)\left(dW_t + \lambda^\mu dt\right) + \Sigma^\nu d\Omega^\nu.$$

The risk-neutralized versions of the above equations have the form

$$\frac{dS_t^{\mu\nu}}{S_t^{\mu\nu}} = r^{\mu\nu}dt + (\lambda^\mu - \lambda^\nu)\,dW_t^\mu,$$

$$\frac{dB_{t,T}^{\mu\nu}}{B_{t,T}^{\mu\nu}} = (r^\mu + \rho^\nu\,(\lambda^\mu - \lambda^\nu)\,\Sigma^\nu)\,dt + (\lambda^\mu - \lambda^\nu)\,dW_t^\mu + \Sigma^\nu d\Omega^\nu,$$

$$\frac{d\hat{B}_{0,t,T}^{\mu\nu}}{\hat{B}_{0,t,T}^{\mu\nu}} = \rho^\nu\,(\lambda^\mu - \lambda^\nu)\,\Sigma^\nu dt + (\lambda^\mu - \lambda^\nu)\,dW_t^\mu + \Sigma^\nu d\Omega^\nu,$$

where

$$W_t^\mu = \lambda^\mu t + W_t.$$

7.4 Multi-country markets

We now construct the multi-country analogue of the two-country market considered above. Due to the judicious choice of notation, very little needs to be added in order to do so. We assume that there are $N + 1$ countries in our market. One country is called domestic and is distinguished by the superscript 0, all others are called foreign and distinguished by the superscripts n, $n = 1, ..., N$. (Below Latin superscripts run from 1 to N, while Greek superscripts run from 0 to N.) As before, we assume that the domestic currency is the dollar. Prices of the dollar denominated MMAs and bonds are denoted by A^0, B^0. The FXRs between the dollar and foreign currencies (i.e., the number of dollars per one unit of foreign currency) are denoted by S^{0n}, prices of foreign MMAs and bonds in their respective currencies by A^n, B^n, while their prices in dollars by $A^{0n} = S^{0n}A^n$, $B^{0n} = S^{0n}B^n$, the corresponding discounted prices are $\hat{A}^{0n} = A^{0n}/A^0$, $\hat{B}^{0n} = B^{0n}/B^0$. The prices A^μ, B^μ are governed by the ODEs of the form

$$\frac{dA^\mu}{A^\mu} = \frac{dB^\mu}{B^\mu} = r^\mu dt.$$

At the most basic level, we have to satisfy just a few simple constraints in order to get a viable model of the FXRs dynamics. First, this model has to ensure that FXRs are positive. Second, it has to respect the so-called cross-currency rule which defines the FXR S^{mn} between the mth and n^{th} currencies as a quotient of the FXRs S^{0m} and S^{0n},

$$S^{mn} = \frac{S^{0n}}{S^{0m}}.$$

It turns out that the cross-currency rule results in the same connection between the volatility of FXRs and the market prices of risk for different currencies as was found in the two-country case.

We assume that there are K independent stochastic engines in our market, introduce the market prices of risk $\boldsymbol{\lambda}^\mu$ for different currencies ($\boldsymbol{\lambda}^\mu$ are K component vectors) and write the system of SDEs governing the evolution of FXRs as follows

$$\frac{dS^{0n}}{S^{0n}} = \left(r^0 - r^n + \left(\boldsymbol{\lambda}^0 - \boldsymbol{\lambda}^n\right) \cdot \boldsymbol{\lambda}^0\right) dt + \left(\boldsymbol{\lambda}^0 - \boldsymbol{\lambda}^n\right) \cdot d\mathbf{W}_t,$$

where $\mathbf{W}_t = \left(W_t^1, ..., W_t^K\right)$. In general, the dynamics of $S^{\mu\nu}$ is governed by

$$\frac{dS^{\mu\nu}}{S^{\mu\nu}} = \left(r^{\mu\nu} + \left(\boldsymbol{\lambda}^\mu - \boldsymbol{\lambda}^\nu\right) \cdot \boldsymbol{\lambda}^\mu\right) dt + \left(\boldsymbol{\lambda}^\mu - \boldsymbol{\lambda}^\nu\right) \cdot d\mathbf{W}_t.$$

It is easy to show that this equation is compatible with the cross-currency rule. Indeed, Ito's differentiation of the quotient yields

$$
\begin{aligned}
\frac{dS^{\mu\nu}}{S^{\mu\nu}} &= \frac{d\left(S^{0\nu}/S^{0\mu}\right)}{S^{0\nu}/S^{0\mu}} \\
&= [r^0 - r^\nu + \left(\boldsymbol{\lambda}^0 - \boldsymbol{\lambda}^\nu\right) \cdot \boldsymbol{\lambda}^0 - r^0 + r^\mu - \left(\boldsymbol{\lambda}^0 - \boldsymbol{\lambda}^\mu\right) \cdot \boldsymbol{\lambda}^0 \\
&= + \left(\boldsymbol{\lambda}^0 - \boldsymbol{\lambda}^\mu\right) \cdot \left(\boldsymbol{\lambda}^0 - \boldsymbol{\lambda}^\mu\right) - \left(\boldsymbol{\lambda}^0 - \boldsymbol{\lambda}^\mu\right) \cdot \left(\boldsymbol{\lambda}^0 - \boldsymbol{\lambda}^\nu\right)] dt \\
&+ \left(\boldsymbol{\lambda}^0 - \boldsymbol{\lambda}^\nu - \boldsymbol{\lambda}^0 + \boldsymbol{\lambda}^\mu\right) \cdot d\mathbf{W}_t \\
&= \left(r^{\mu\nu} + \left(\boldsymbol{\lambda}^\mu - \boldsymbol{\lambda}^\nu\right) \cdot \boldsymbol{\lambda}^\mu\right) dt + \left(\boldsymbol{\lambda}^\mu - \boldsymbol{\lambda}^\nu\right) \cdot d\mathbf{W}_t.
\end{aligned}
\tag{7.8}
$$

The evolution of MMAs and bond prices is governed by similar SDEs

$$\frac{dA^{\mu\nu}}{A^{\mu\nu}} = \frac{dB^{\mu\nu}}{B^{\mu\nu}} = \left(r^\mu + \left(\boldsymbol{\lambda}^\mu - \boldsymbol{\lambda}^\nu\right) \cdot \boldsymbol{\lambda}^\mu\right) dt + \left(\boldsymbol{\lambda}^\mu - \boldsymbol{\lambda}^\nu\right) \cdot d\mathbf{W}_t. \tag{7.9}$$

The corresponding discounted and projected equations are

$$\frac{d\hat{A}^{\mu\nu}}{\hat{A}^{\mu\nu}} = \frac{d\hat{B}^{\mu\nu}}{\hat{B}^{\mu\nu}} = \frac{d\check{A}^{\mu\nu}}{\check{A}^{\mu\nu}} = \frac{d\check{B}^{\mu\nu}}{\check{B}^{\mu\nu}} = \left(\boldsymbol{\lambda}^\mu - \boldsymbol{\lambda}^\nu\right) \cdot \left(\boldsymbol{\lambda}^\mu dt + d\mathbf{W}_t\right). \tag{7.10}$$

The market model is complete provided that $K = N$. It is overdetermined when $N > K$, and underdetermined (incomplete) if $K > N$. Equations (7.8) - (7.10) are easy to solve. For instance, equation (7.8) yields

$$S_t^{\mu\nu} = \Phi^{\mu\nu}\left(t\right) e^{r^{\mu\nu}t} S_0^{\mu\nu},$$

where

$$\Phi^{\mu\nu}(t) = \exp\left\{\frac{1}{2}\left(|\lambda^{\mu}|^2 - |\lambda^{\nu}|^2\right)t + (\lambda^{\mu} - \lambda^{\nu}) \cdot \mathbf{W}_t\right\}.$$

To describe the risk-neutralized dynamics we have to replace $\Phi^{\mu\nu}(t)$ by

$$\tilde{\Phi}^{\mu\nu}(t) = \exp\left\{\frac{1}{2}|\lambda^{\mu} - \lambda^{\nu}|^2 t + (\lambda^{\mu} - \lambda^{\nu}) \cdot \mathbf{W}_t\right\},$$

in the above formula.

As before, for every currency we can introduce a "natural numeraire" Ξ^{μ} with dynamics governed by

$$\frac{d\Xi^{\mu}}{\Xi^{\mu}} = \left(r^{\mu} + |\lambda^{\mu}|^2\right)dt + \lambda^{\mu} \cdot d\mathbf{W}_t,$$

such that the prices of all MMAs and bonds relative to this numeraire are martingales.

In our model volatilities of FXRs are expressed in terms of market prices of risk as follows

$$\sigma^{\mu\nu} = \lambda^{\mu} - \lambda^{\nu}.$$

This relation can be explained geometrically if we interpret volatilities and market prices of risk as vectors in the Euclidean space $\mathbb{R}^K$. Assuming that there are three countries in our market with their respective currencies called the dollar, euro, and yen, we can illustrate the above relation graphically, see Figure 7.1. This figure shows that by shifting all market prices of risk by the same constant vector, we do not change volatilities of FXRs and bond prices. This fact nicely illustrates the relative nature of volatility. In addition, this Figure shows that the scalar volatility $\sigma^{\mu\nu}$ of $S^{\mu\nu}$ is given by the length of the vector $\sigma^{\mu\nu}$,

$$\sigma^{\mu\nu} = |\sigma^{\mu\nu}| = \sqrt{\sum_{k=0}^{K-1}\left(\sigma^{\mu\nu,k}\right)^2},$$

while the correlation between two FXRs $S^{\mu\nu}$ and $S^{\mu'\nu'}$ is given by the cosine of the angle between the vectors $\sigma^{\mu\nu}$ and $\sigma^{\mu'\nu'}$,

$$\rho^{\mu\nu,\mu'\nu'} = \frac{\sigma^{\mu\nu} \cdot \sigma^{\mu'\nu'}}{|\sigma^{\mu\nu}||\sigma^{\mu'\nu'}|} = \frac{\sum_{k=0}^{K-1}\sigma^{\mu\nu,k}\sigma^{\mu'\nu',k}}{\sigma^{\mu\nu}\sigma^{\mu'\nu'}}.$$

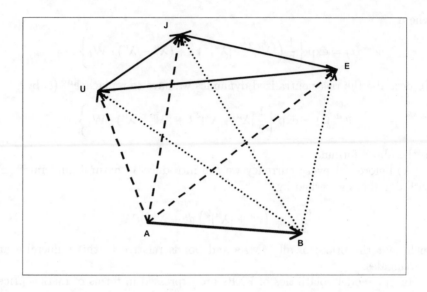

Figure 7.1: This figure illustrates the fact that volatility is relative in nature. Market prices of risk for USD (U), Euro (E), and JPY (J) are represented either by vectors AU, AE, AJ or BU, BE, BJ. The difference is due to the shift AB. In both cases volatilities of the currency pairs USD/Euro, USD/JPY and Euro/JPY are represented by vectors UE, UJ, EJ. The cosine of the angle JUE is equal to the correlation between USD/JPY and USD/Euro currency pairs.

7.5   The nonlinear diffusion model

In this section we consider the simplest extension of the standard geometric Brownian motion model for FXR. Namely, we assume that S_t^{01} follows a more general process of the form

$$\frac{dS_t^{01}}{S_t^{01}} = b^{01} dt + \sigma^{01}\left(t, \frac{S_t^{01}}{\bar{S}^{01}}\right) dW_t, \quad S_0^{01} \text{ is given.}$$

where $\bar{S}^{01}$ is an appropriately chosen reference FXR, while $\sigma^{01}(t, s)$ is a known function of its arguments which represents the lognormal volatility of FXR. The choice of $\bar{S}^{01}$ is, by its very nature, somewhat arbitrary. A reasonable possibility is to choose the FXR for a particular date in the past. For the geometric Brownian motion this function reduces to the form

$$\sigma(t, s) = \sigma(t).$$

The reason for generalizing the geometric Brownian motion model is simple - very often this model is not supported by the real market data. Even though the above generalization is conceptually the simplest, it is not necessarily the most relevant for pricing options on FXR. A number of alternatives are considered below.

There are several popular choices of the volatility function considered in the literature. For example, the so-called constant elasticity of variance model which assumes that

$$\sigma(t, s) = \sigma(t) s^{-\beta},$$

with the power β sandwiched between -1 and 1, $-1 \leq \beta \leq 1$, is very popular. This model includes as special cases the geometric ($\beta = 0$) and arithmetic ($\beta = 1$) Brownian motions. The process for FXR can be reduced to the Bessel process and analyzed in great detail. The classical assumption used in the equity context is that the power β is sandwiched between 0 and 1 (which simplifies the mathematics considerably). The reason why it has to be extended in the forex context is explained below.

Another popular choice is the hyperbolic volatility model which assumes that

$$\sigma(t, s) = \sigma_2(t) s + \sigma_1(t) + \frac{\sigma_0(t)}{s},$$

This model also includes the geometric and arithmetic Brownian motions as special cases. When σ_i are time-independent the process for FXR is reducible to the arithmetic Brownian motion (see Section 10.5).

In the forex context it is very important to understand what happens when the domestic and foreign countries are switched, or, in other words, when the market is analyzed from the viewpoint of euro investors.

The SDE for $S_t^{10} = 1/S_t^{01}$ can be derived via Ito's lemma:

$$\frac{dS_t^{10}}{S_t^{10}} = \left(-b^{01} + \left(\sigma^{01}\left(t, \frac{1}{S_t^{10} \overline{S}^{01}} \right) \right)^2 \right) dt - \sigma^{01}\left(t, \frac{1}{S_t^{10} \overline{S}^{01}} \right) dW_t.$$

It is shown below that drift in this equation can be altered by an appropriate change of measure, so that the governing equation for S_t^{10} can be written in the form

$$\frac{dS_t^{10}}{S_t^{10}} = b^{10}dt + \sigma^{10}\left(t, \frac{S_t^{10}}{\bar{S}^{10}}\right)dW_t, \quad S_0^{10} \text{ is given,}$$

where

$$\bar{S}^{10} = 1/\bar{S}^{01}, \quad b^{10} = -b^{01}, \quad \sigma^{10}(t,s) = -\sigma^{01}\left(t, \frac{1}{s}\right). \tag{7.11}$$

For the CEV model equation (7.11) yields

$$\sigma^{10}(t,s) = -\sigma(t)s^\beta,$$

hence the need to consider powers β belonging to the interval $[-1, 1]$ which is invariant with respect to the transformation $\beta \to -\beta$ corresponding to the switch between the domestic and foreign countries.

For the hyperbolic volatility model we have

$$\sigma^{10}(t,s) = -\left(\sigma_0(t)s + \sigma_1(t) + \frac{\sigma_2(t)}{s}\right),$$

so that the functional form of the volatility surface is invariant with respect to the switch between the domestic and foreign countries.

7.6 The jump diffusion model

For many currency pairs the market data suggests that the evolution of FXR has jumps. To account for such a possibility we model the dynamics of FXR as a jump diffusion process driven by the standard Wiener process W_t and the Poisson process N_t with intensity $\lambda > 0$. The Wiener and Poisson processes are supposed to be independent. Logarithmic jump sizes are described as a sequence of i.i.d. (independent identically distributed) random numbers J, the corresponding probability density is denoted by $f(J)$.

Thus, the evolution of FXR with jumps is described by the following SDE

$$\frac{dS_t^{01}}{S_t^{01}} = b^{01}dt + \sigma^{01}dW_t + \left(e^{J^{01}} - 1\right)dN_t, \quad S_0^{01} \text{ is given,} \tag{7.12}$$

which generalizes the geometric Brownian motion model. The meaning of this equation is simple: between t and $t + dt$ FXR changes as follows

$$S_t^{01} \to S_{t+dt}^{01}$$
$$= \begin{cases} \left(1 + b^{01}dt + \sigma^{01}dW_t\right)S_t^{01}, & \text{if no jumps occurred} \\ \left(e^{J^{01}} + b^{01}dt + \sigma^{01}dW_t\right)S_t^{01}, & \text{if one jump occurred} \end{cases}.$$

The probability of more than one jump occurring between t and $t + \delta t$ is negligible.

The reader can easily check as an exercise that the instantaneous expected rate of return on investment in euros (kept as cash) which is denoted by α^{01} is given by

$$\alpha^{01} = \mathbb{E}\left\{\frac{dS_t^{01}}{S_t^{01}}\right\} = \left(b^{01} + \lambda\kappa^{01}\right) dt,$$

where

$$\kappa^{01} = \mathbb{E}\left\{e^{J^{01}} - 1\right\} = \int_{-\infty}^{\infty} \left(e^J - 1\right) f(J)dJ.$$

Thus, the governing SDE can be rewritten in a more intuitive form, namely,

$$\frac{dS_t^{01}}{S_t^{01}} = \left(\alpha^{01} - \lambda\kappa^{01}\right) dt + \sigma^{01} dW_t + \left(e^{J^{01}} - 1\right) dN_t.$$

To describe the risk-neutral evolution of the FXR we have to put $\alpha^{01} = r^{01}$.

We leave it to the reader as an exercise to verify that the jump-diffusion model is invariant with respect to the switch between the domestic and foreign countries.

7.7 The stochastic volatility model

The stochastic volatility model extends the geometric Brownian motion model by introducing one more source of stochasticity into the picture. In the opinion of the present author, this extension is particularly useful in the forex context. The stochastic volatility model assumes that both FXR S_t^{01} and its variance $v_t^{01} = \left(\sigma_t^{01}\right)^2$ are stochastic processes. The standard assumption is that

$$\frac{dS_t^{01}}{S_t^{01}} = b^{01}dt + \sqrt{v_t^{01}}dW_t, \qquad S_0^{\mu\nu} \text{ is given}, \tag{7.13}$$

so that for given variance v_t^{01} FXR follows the geometric Brownian motion. The dollar return on investment in euros ,

$$X_t^{01} = \ln\left(\frac{S_t^{01}}{S_0^{01}}\right),$$

evolves according to the SDE of the form

$$dX_t^{01} = \left(b^{01} - \frac{1}{2} \left(v_t^{01} \right)^2 \right) dt + \sqrt{v_t^{01}} dW_t, \qquad X_0^{01} = 0.$$

Several different choices of stochastic processes for v_t^{01} have been considered in the literature. Among the most popular choices are:

$$\frac{dv_t^{01}}{v_t^{01}} = \alpha^{01} dt + \gamma^{01} d\Omega_t, \quad v_0^{01} \text{ is given,} \tag{7.14}$$

$$dv_t^{01} = \kappa^{01} \left(\theta^{01} - v_t^{01} \right) dt + \gamma^{01} d\Omega_t, \quad v_0^{01} \text{ is given,} \tag{7.15}$$

$$dv_t^{01} = \kappa^{01} \left(\theta^{01} - v_t^{01} \right) dt + \varepsilon^{01} \sqrt{v_t^{01}} d\Omega_t, \quad v_0^{01} \text{ is given,} \tag{7.16}$$

which were proposed by Hull and White, Stein and Stein, and Heston, respectively. Here Ω_t is a standard Wiener processes such that, $corr(dW_t, d\Omega_t) = \rho$. Equations (7.14), (7.15), (7.16) assume that v_t^{01} follows the standard geometric Brownian motion, the mean-reverting Ornstein-Uhlenbeck process, and the mean-reverting Feller (square-root) process, respectively.

The first process ensures that the variance always stays positive, but it does not capture the important mean-reversion property of variance which tends to oscillate within a band. The second process captures the mean-reversion property but it does not preclude the variance from becoming negative (which is clearly very undesirable). At the same time, the third process does have both properties and is analytically tractable. Accordingly, we choose equation (7.16) as our governing equation for $v_t^{\mu\nu}$ and assume that it follows the mean-reverting square-root process with constant reversion level θ^{01}, reversion rate κ^{01} and volatility of variance ε^{01}. Dimensions of these quantities are

$$\left[\theta^{01} \right] = \left[\kappa^{01} \right] = \left[\varepsilon^{01} \right] = T^{-1}.$$

It is easy to extend the model by making these parameters time-dependent. When $\varepsilon^{01} = 0$ equation (7.16) is just a deterministic equation describing the relaxation of v_t^{01} to its mean level.

The equation for the volatility $\sigma_t^{01} = \sqrt{v_t^{01}}$ is found via Ito's lemma. We leave it to the reader as an exercise to check that the equation for the volatility σ_t^{01} has the form

$$d\sigma_t^{01} = \frac{\kappa^{01}}{2} \left[\frac{\theta^{01} - \left(\varepsilon^{01} \right)^2 / 4\kappa^{01}}{\sigma_t^{01}} - \sigma_t^{01} \right] dt + \frac{\varepsilon^{01}}{2} d\Omega_t, \quad \sigma_0^{01} \text{ is given.}$$

Thus, the volatility of volatility is half the volatility of variance. Since the diffusion does not vanish when $\sigma_t^{01} \to 0$ the drift has a singularity at $\sigma_t^{01} = 0$ to preclude σ_t^{01} from becoming negative.

Thus, the coupled system of SDEs describing the real-world evolution of S_t^{01}, v_t^{01} has the form (7.13), (7.16). Their risk neutral evolution is governed by the following SDEs

$$\frac{dS_t^{01}}{S_t^{01}} = r^{01} dt + \sqrt{v_t^{01}} dW_t^0, \qquad S_0^{01} \text{ is given,}$$

$$dv_t^{01} = \left(\kappa^{01} \left(\theta^{01} - v_t^{01} \right) - \varpi^{01} \varepsilon^{01} \sqrt{v_t^{01}} \right) dt + \varepsilon^{01} \sqrt{v_t^{01}} d\Omega_t^0, \quad v_0^{01} \text{ is given,}$$

where ϖ^{01} is the market price of risk associated with the stochastic process for variance. Even though the exact form of the market price of risk cannot be chosen unambiguously, there are compelling reasons (on which we don't dwell) which suggest that $\varpi^{01} \sim \sqrt{v^{01}}$. This assumption is also very convenient technically, because it allows one to write the risk-neutralized equation for v_t^{01} in the form (7.16),

$$dv_t^{01} = \tilde{\kappa}^{01} \left(\tilde{\theta}^{01} - v_t^{01} \right) dt + \varepsilon^{01} \sqrt{v_t^{01}} d\Omega_t, \qquad v_0^{01} \text{ is given,}$$

with an adjusted reversion level $\tilde{\theta}^{01}$. (Below we omit tildes for the sake of brevity.)

An important nondimensional characteristics of the process v_t is

$$\vartheta = \frac{2\kappa\theta}{\varepsilon^2} - 1.$$

According to Feller's classification of the boundary points given in Section 4.4 the process v_t can never reach infinity; it cannot (can) reach zero when $\vartheta > 0$ ($\vartheta < 0$); in both cases it remains nonnegative. The t.p.d.f. for the square-root diffusion between two dates $t, t', t' > t$, has the form

$$q(\tau, v, v') = \overline{M} e^{-\overline{M}(\bar{v}+v')} \left(\frac{v'}{\bar{v}} \right)^{\vartheta/2} I_{|\vartheta|} \left[2\overline{M} \sqrt{\bar{v}v'} \right],$$

where

$$\tau = t' - t, \qquad \bar{v} = e^{-\kappa\tau} v, \qquad \overline{M} = \frac{2\kappa}{\varepsilon^2 (1 - e^{-\kappa\tau})},$$

and $I_{|\vartheta|}$ is the modified Bessel function of order $|\vartheta|$. The derivation of this formula is given in Section 13.11. In the limit $\tau \to \infty$ q approaches the steady-state density

$$q_\infty \left(v'\right) = \frac{2\kappa}{\Gamma\left(\vartheta+1\right)\varepsilon^2} \left(\frac{2\kappa v'}{\varepsilon^2}\right)^\vartheta e^{-2\kappa v'/\varepsilon^2},$$

where Γ is the Gamma (factorial) function.

One of the main advantages of using the stochastic volatility model in the forex context is that its functional form is invariant with respect to switching between the domestic and foreign countries. The reader is encouraged to derive the equations for S_t^{10}, v_t^{10}.

7.8   The general forex evolution model

For some currency pairs both jumps and stochastic volatility have to be taken into consideration in order to obtain an adequate description of the FXR behavior. This is obviously true when the dollar values of the emerging market currencies such as Thai baht or Mexican peso are considered. More surprisingly, it is also true for the Japanese yen and some other major currencies. Besides, when long-dated options on forex are considered, we have to account for the stochastic nature of the domestic and foreign interest rates.

The general evolutionary model combines all the above features. The corresponding risk-neutralized SDEs for $S_t^{01}, v_t^{01}, r^0, r^1$ are

$$\frac{dS_t^{01}}{S_t^{01}} = \left(r^0 - r^1 - \zeta\kappa^{01}\right)dt + \sqrt{v_t^{01}}dW_t + \left(e^{J^{01}} - 1\right)dN_t, \quad S_0^{\mu\nu} \text{ is given,}$$

$$dv_t^{01} = \kappa^{01}\left(\theta^{01} - v_t^{01}\right)dt + \epsilon^{01}\sqrt{v_t^{01}}d\Omega_t, \quad v_0^{01} \text{ is given,}$$

$$dr_t^0 = \varkappa^0\left(\varrho^0 - r_t^0\right)dt + \varsigma^0 d\Omega_t^0, \quad r_0^0 \text{ is given,}$$

$$dr_t^1 = \varkappa^1\left(\varrho^1 - r_t^1\right)dt + \varsigma^1 d\Omega_t^1, \quad r_0^1 \text{ is given.}$$

This model is switch invariant since all of its parts are. Below we do not attempt to price options and construct optimal portfolios in the general framework because it is technically very demanding (but not impossible). Instead, we use special models of the FXR evolution which are adequate for the particular problems we need to solve.

7.9   References and further reading

The original sources used in this chapter are as follows: Black and Karasinski (1991), Cox *et al.* (1985), Feller (1952), Heston (1993), Hull and White (1987, 1988), Long (1990), Stein and Stein (1991), Uhlenbeck and Ornstein (1930), Vasicek (1977). A useful discussion of some of the topics covered in this chapter is given by Hughston (1997).

Chapter 8

European options: the group-theoretical approach

8.1 Introduction

In this chapter we show how to price and hedge European options on forex. We start with two-country markets. Assuming that in both countries bond prices are deterministic, while the FXR follows the standard geometric Brownian motion with constant volatility, we derive the homogeneous Black-Scholes equation for pricing contingent claims. This equation, which is a one-factor backward parabolic equation, is universal in nature. It can be derived from the natural requirement that the prices of all contingent claims (which coincide with the prices of self-financing replicating portfolios) are homogeneous functions of degree one of the prices of the underlying securities, i.e., domestic and foreign bonds. This derivation is a nice application of the general group-theoretical approach to studying problems of financial engineering. The Black-Scholes equation is supplemented by the claim specific final condition at maturity. We define the so-called Greeks, i.e., the first and second derivatives of the option price with respect to the spot FXR rate (which are called Delta and Gamma, respectively) and its first derivative with respect to time (which is called Theta) and discuss their role in hedging and risk managing of options. We also define the so-called Vega which is the derivative of the price with respect to volatility. It is a natural measure of sensitivity of the price to small changes in volatility. We solve the pricing problem by reducing it to the initial value problem for the standard heat equation. For forward contracts, calls and puts we evaluate the corresponding pricing formula explicitly by completing the squares. We also show how to solve the pricing problem via the Fourier and Laplace methods. In addition, we establish the familiar put-call parity and symmetry relations. Then we consider options with general payoffs which can be used to execute different strategies and show how to decompose them into vanilla instruments and price accordingly.

Next, we drop the assumption that bond prices are deterministic and derive the corresponding generalized Black-Scholes pricing equation which is a two-factor backward parabolic equation. We show how to use homogeneity in order to reduce it to the one-factor form. This allows us to price general contingent claims, and, in particular, to find closed form expressions for forwards, calls and puts.

Once standard two-country markets are analyzed, we consider $(N + 1)$-country markets with deterministic bond prices and FXRs following the geometric Brownian motion. We derive the N-factor homogeneous Black-Scholes equation. We express prices of multi-factor options as N-dimensional integrals and show how these options can be hedged. We illustrate the general theory by analyzing a few important multi-factor options including the outperformance, basket and index options, as well as options on the maximum and minimum on several currencies.

The chapter is organized as follows. In Section 2 we study the pricing problem for derivatives in two-country markets with deterministic investments. In Section 3 we demonstrate how to solve the pricing problem for the simplest (plain vanilla) options, namely, forwards, calls and puts. In Section 4 we consider options with general payoffs. Section 5 is devoted to the dynamic asset allocation problem. In Section 6 we discuss the homogeneous Black-Scholes problem for two-country markets without deterministic investments. In Section 7 we discuss the derivative pricing problem for multi-country markets. In Section 8 we show how to price several representative multi-factor options, such as outperformance, best of several FXRs, basket, and index options. We give references in Section 9.

8.2 The two-country homogeneous problem, I

8.2.1 Formulation of the problem

In this section we derive the pricing equation for European contingent claims in the two-country market. We assume that these claims mature at time T. As we know, dollar investors can put their money in domestic (dollar denominated) and foreign (euro denominated) bonds. For now we assume that domestic bond prices are deterministic, while dollar prices of euro bonds are stochastic. The real-world dynamics of these prices are governed by the SDEs of the form

$$\frac{dB^0_{t,T}}{B^0_{t,T}} = r^0 dt, \quad B^0_{0,T} \text{ is given,}$$

$$\frac{dB^{01}_{t,T}}{B^{01}_{t,T}} = b^{01} dt + \sigma^{01} dW_t, \quad B^0_{0,T} \text{ is given.}$$

To be concrete we consider bonds with unit face values. By definition,

$$B^{01}_{t,T} = S^{01}_t B^1_{t,T}.$$

The final payoff of a European contingent claim depends on the prices of the domestic and foreign bonds with face values K^0 and K^1, respectively. Often their face values are normalized in such a way that $K^1 = 1$, while $K^0 = K^{01}$, where K^{01} is called the strike rate. At time t the values of the domestic and foreign bonds are $K^0 B^0_{t,T}$ and $K^1 B^1_{t,T}$. To simplify the notation, we denote σ^{01}, $K^0 B^0$, $K^1 B^{01}$ by σ, Z^0, Z^1, respectively.

Consider a contingent claim with the general payoff of the form

$$\text{payoff} = v\left(Z^0_{T,T}, Z^1_{T,T}\right) = v\left(K^0, K^1 S^{01}_T\right),$$

where v is a homogeneous function of Z^0, Z^1 of degree one, so that

$$v\left(\theta Z^0, \theta Z^1\right) = \theta v\left(Z^0, Z^1\right).$$

This homogeneity reflects an obvious requirement that prices of derivative instruments are scaled in the same way as prices of the primary instruments, so that if the unit of currency is changed from dollars to cents, say, all prices increase by a factor of a hundred. The price of the claim at time t, which depends on the prices of Z^0 and Z^1 at this time, is denoted by $V\left(t, Z^0, Z^1\right)$. It is clear that V has to be a homogeneous function of Z^0, Z^1 of degree one, too, i.e.,

$$V\left(t, \theta Z^0, \theta Z^1\right) = \theta V\left(t, Z^0, Z^1\right). \tag{8.1}$$

In order to price contingent claims in a way which does not allow arbitrage, we have to be able to reproduce them via predictable, self-financing, replicating trading strategies. A trading strategy is a rule which shows how much is invested in primary instruments Z^0, Z^1. The corresponding amounts are denoted by Υ^0, Υ^1. In principle, the value of the vector $\Upsilon_t = \left(\Upsilon_t^0, \Upsilon_t^1 \right)$ at time t depends on the entire trajectory of the price vector $\mathbf{Z}_{t'} = \left(Z_{t'}^0, Z_{t'}^1 \right)$ for $0 \leq t' \leq T$.

A strategy is predictable if Υ_t depends (possibly in a rather complicated fashion) on the values of $\mathbf{Z}_{t'}$ for $0 \leq t' \leq t$. Thus, the choice of Υ_t depends only on the information about the market dynamics available at time t. It is obvious that for our purposes only predictable strategies are of interest.

The dollar value of a trading strategy is given by

$$\Pi_t = \Upsilon_t^0 Z_t^0 + \Upsilon_t^1 Z_t^1 = \Upsilon_t \cdot \mathbf{Z}_t.$$

It is called self-financing if the change of its value occurs solely due to the change of the value of the underlying instruments, i.e.,

$$d\Pi_t = \Upsilon_t \cdot d\mathbf{Z}_t.$$

Such a strategy does not require an influx of funds to be carried through time.

A trading strategy replicates a contingent claim V at maturity if

$$V_T = \Pi_T.$$

In order to preclude the possibility of arbitrage the values of V and Π have to be the same for all t,

$$V_t = \Pi_t, \quad 0 \leq t \leq T.$$

We now show how to use homogeneity in order to construct a predictable, self-financing, replicating trading strategy for a given claim. Homogeneity has a lot of consequences of which the so-called Euler identity is the most important one. This identity has the form

$$Z^0 V_{Z^0} + Z^1 V_{Z^1} = V,$$

or, symbolically,

$$Z^\mu \partial_{Z^\mu} V = V, \tag{8.2}$$

where $\mu = 0, 1$, and the usual summation convention over repeated indices is used. In order to derive this identity, we differentiate equation (8.1) with respect to θ using the chain rule and put $\theta = 1$:

$$\left. \frac{dV\left(t, \theta Z^0, \theta Z^1\right)}{d\theta} \right|_{\theta=1} = Z^0 V_{Z^0}\left(t, \theta Z^0, \theta Z^1\right)|_{\theta=1} + Z^1 V_{Z^1}\left(t, \theta Z^0, \theta Z^1\right)|_{\theta=1}$$

$$= V\left(t, Z^0, Z^1\right).$$

Differentiating identity (8.2) we get

$$\partial_{Z^\nu}\left(Z^\mu\partial_{Z^\mu}V\right) = Z^\mu\partial_{Z^\mu}\left(\partial_{Z^\nu}V\right) + \partial_{Z^\nu}V = \partial_{Z^\nu}V,$$

so that

$$Z^\mu\partial_{Z^\mu}\left(\partial_{Z^\nu}V\right) = 0. \tag{8.3}$$

It is obvious that for any contingent claim we can define the trading strategy $\Upsilon_t = (V_{Z^0}, V_{Z^1})$ by investing V_{Z^0} in domestic bonds and V_{Z^1} in foreign bonds. By construction this strategy is predictable. Identity (8.2) shows that the corresponding portfolio replicates V. In order to use this fact for pricing, we have to find conditions under which this portfolio is self-financing. Ito's lemma yields

$$dV = V_{Z^0}dZ^0 + V_{Z^1}dZ^1 + \left(V_t + \frac{1}{2}\sigma^2\left(Z^1\right)^2 V_{Z^1Z^1}\right)dt.$$

Thus, when V satisfies the equation

$$V_t + \frac{1}{2}\sigma^2\left(Z^1\right)^2 V_{Z^1Z^1} = 0, \tag{8.4}$$

we have

$$dV = V_{Z^0}dZ^0 + V_{Z^1}dZ^1,$$

so that the strategy (V_{Z^0}, V_{Z^1}) is self-financing. Equation (8.4), which is a backward parabolic equation is remarkably simple. In particular, it is completely independent on the domestic and foreign interest rates. It is supplied with the final conditions of the form

$$V\left(T, Z^0, Z^1\right) = v\left(Z^0, Z^1\right),$$

and the boundary conditions as appropriate. The variable Z^0 enters into the pricing problem only through the final conditions. (This simplification is due to the fact that Z^0 is a deterministic function of time). We call equation (8.4) the homogeneous Black-Scholes equation.

The SDE corresponding to PDE (8.4) describes the geometric Brownian motion without drift;

$$\frac{dZ^1_t}{Z^1_t} = \sigma dW_t.$$

to the fact that Z^0 is a deterministic function of time). We call equation (8.4) the homogeneous Black-Scholes equation.

The SDE corresponding to PDE (8.4) describes the geometric Brownian motion without drift;

$$\frac{dZ_t^1}{Z_t^1} = \sigma dW_t.$$

According to the general formula, its solution can be written as

$$Z_T^1 = e^{-\sigma^2(T-t)/2 + \sigma W_{T-t}} Z_t^1.$$

We refer to the difference

$$\tilde{V}\left(\chi, Z^0, Z^1\right) = V\left(\chi, Z^0, Z^1\right) - v\left(Z^0, Z^1\right),$$

as the time value of the option. The pricing problem for $\tilde{V}$ can be written as

$$\tilde{V}_t + \frac{1}{2}\sigma^2 \left(Z^1\right)^2 \tilde{V}_{Z^1 Z^1} = -\frac{1}{2}\sigma^2 \left(Z^1\right)^2 v_{Z^1 Z^1}\left(Z^0, Z^1\right).$$

Duhamel's principle shows that $\tilde{V} \geq 0$ provided that $v_{Z^1 Z^1} \geq 0$, i.e., the payoff is convex. We emphasize that this conclusion is true for forward prices and can be violated for spot prices (see Section 9.3 below).

We can introduce the homogeneous differential operator $\mathcal{D} = Z^1 \partial_{Z^1}$, and rewrite the pricing equation as follows

$$V_t + \frac{1}{2}\sigma^2 \left(\mathcal{D}^2 - \mathcal{D}\right) V = 0.$$

This equation has constant coefficients with respect to $\mathcal{D}$.

We can go further and introduce the nondimensional time $\vartheta = \sigma^2 t$, the time to maturity $\tau = T - t$, and the nondimensional time to maturity $\chi = \sigma^2(T-t) = \sigma^2 \tau$. The corresponding pricing equations are

$$V_\vartheta + \frac{1}{2}\left(Z^1\right)^2 V_{Z^1 Z^1} = 0, \tag{8.5}$$

$$V_\tau - \frac{1}{2}\sigma^2 \left(Z^1\right)^2 V_{Z^1 Z^1} = 0, \tag{8.6}$$

$$V_\chi - \frac{1}{2}\left(Z^1\right)^2 V_{Z^1 Z^1} = 0, \tag{8.7}$$

respectively. Equation (8.5) is supplied with the terminal data at $\hat{T} = \sigma^2 T$, equations (8.6), (8.7) are supplied with the initial data at $\tau = 0$ and $\chi = 0$, respectively.

8.2.2 Reductions of the pricing problem

The pricing problem is degenerate since the price depends on two spatial variables Z^0, Z^1 while the differentiation is performed only with respect to Z^1. There are two complementary ways of reducing the number of spatial variables by one and, at the same time, making the pricing problem nondimensional.

In order to perform the reduction of the first kind, we represent the price in the form

$$V\left(\chi, Z^0, Z^1\right) = Z^0 \Phi\left(\chi, \xi\right),$$ (8.8)

where $\xi = Z^1/Z^0$. Since Z^0 is a parameter, we immediately get

$$\Phi_\chi - \frac{1}{2}\xi^2 \Phi_{\xi\xi} = 0,$$ (8.9)

$$\Phi\left(0, \xi\right) = \phi\left(\xi\right),$$ (8.10)

where

$$\phi\left(\xi\right) = \frac{v\left(Z^0, Z^1\right)}{Z^0} = v\left(1, \xi\right).$$

The associated SDE is

$$\frac{d\xi_\vartheta}{\xi_\vartheta} = dW_\vartheta.$$ (8.11)

Alternatively, we can perform the reduction of the second kind and represent V as

$$V\left(\chi, Z^0, Z^1\right) = Z^1 \Psi\left(\chi, \eta\right),$$

where $\eta = Z^0/Z^1$. Straightforward (but instructive) algebra which is left to the reader as an exercise yields the following one-factor pricing problem for Ψ :

$$\Psi_\chi - \frac{1}{2}\eta^2 \Psi_{\eta\eta} = 0,$$ (8.12)

$$\Psi\left(0, \eta\right) = \psi\left(\eta\right),$$ (8.13)

where

$$\psi\left(\eta\right) = \frac{v\left(Z^0, Z^1\right)}{Z^1} = v\left(\eta, 1\right).$$

The associated SDE has the form

$$\frac{d\eta_\vartheta}{\eta_\vartheta} = dW_\vartheta.$$

In this chapter we concentrate on pricing problem (8.9), (8.10). However, in subsequent chapters we consider pricing problem (8.12), (8.13) as well.

Let us show now how to reduce problem (8.9), (8.10) to the initial value problem for the standard heat equation. We introduce the logarithmic spatial variable

$$X = \ln \xi,$$

and obtain the pricing problem of the form

$$\Phi_\chi - \frac{1}{2}\Phi_{XX} + \frac{1}{2}\Phi_X = 0, \tag{8.14}$$

$$\Phi(0, X) = \phi(e^X).$$

The SDE corresponding to PDE (8.14) describes the arithmetic Brownian motion with negative drift:

$$dX_\vartheta = -\frac{1}{2}d\vartheta + dW_\vartheta.$$

Next, we change the dependent variable according to

$$U(\chi, X) = e^{\chi/8 - X/2}\Phi(\chi, X),$$

and obtain the following pricing problem for U:

$$U_\chi - \frac{1}{2}U_{XX} = 0, \tag{8.15}$$

$$U(0, X) = u(X) = e^{-X/2}\phi(e^X).$$

Thus, the pricing problem is reduced to the initial value problem for the heat equation. The SDE corresponding to PDE (8.15) describes the standard arithmetic Brownian motion without drift

$$dX_\vartheta^1 = dW_\vartheta.$$

This problem can be solved via the Feynman-Kac formula:

$$
\begin{aligned}
U\left(\chi, X\right) &= \int_{-\infty}^{\infty} \frac{e^{-\left(X'-X\right)^2/2\chi}}{\sqrt{2\pi\chi}} u\left(X'\right) dX' \\
&= \int_{-\infty}^{\infty} \frac{e^{-\left(X'-X\right)^2/2\chi}}{\sqrt{2\pi\chi}} e^{-X'/2} \phi\left(e^{X'}\right) dX' \\
&= e^{\chi/8 - X/2} \int_{-\infty}^{\infty} \frac{e^{-\left(X'-X+\chi/2\right)^2/2\chi}}{\sqrt{2\pi\chi}} \phi\left(e^{X'}\right) dX' \\
&= e^{\chi/8 - X/2} \int_{-\infty}^{\infty} \frac{e^{-Y^2/2}}{\sqrt{2\pi}} \phi\left(e^{X - \chi/2 + \sqrt{\chi} Y}\right) dY.
\end{aligned}
$$

Written in terms of χ, ξ the value of the contingent claim is:

$$
\Phi\left(\chi, \xi\right) = \int_{-\infty}^{\infty} \frac{e^{-Y^2/2}}{\sqrt{2\pi}} \phi\left(e^{-\chi/2 + \sqrt{\chi} Y} \xi\right) dY. \tag{8.16}
$$

In order to interpret formula (8.16) in probabilistic terms we use equation (8.11) and conclude that the value of a contingent claim at time t is the expectation of its value at time T.

We can obtain formula (8.16) via a complementary approach. Indeed, Feynman-Kac formula shows that we can represent $\Phi\left(\chi, \xi\right)$ in the form

$$
\Phi\left(\chi, \xi\right) = \int_{0}^{\infty} p\left(\chi, \xi, \xi'\right) \phi\left(\xi'\right) d\xi', \tag{8.17}
$$

where $p\left(\chi, \xi, \xi'\right)$ is the lognormal transition probability density associated with the process (8.11),

$$
p\left(\chi, \xi, \xi'\right) = \frac{e^{-d_{-}^2\left(\chi, \xi/\xi'\right)/2}}{\sqrt{2\pi\chi}\xi'},
$$

where

$$
d_{\pm}\left(\chi, \zeta\right) = \frac{\ln\zeta}{\sqrt{\chi}} \pm \frac{\sqrt{\chi}}{2}. \tag{8.18}
$$

We leave it to the reader to check that formulas (8.16), (8.17) are equivalent.

We emphasize that the price implicitly depends on σ since χ does.

In the original variables the value of the option is given by

$$V\left(t, Z^0, Z^1\right) = \int_{-\infty}^{\infty} \frac{e^{-Y^2/2}}{\sqrt{2\pi}} v\left(Z^0, e^{-\sigma^2(T-t)/2 + \sigma\sqrt{T-t}Y} Z^1\right) dY$$

$$= \int_0^{\infty} \frac{e^{-\left(\ln\left(Z^1/Z^{1'}\right)/\sigma\sqrt{T-t} - \sigma\sqrt{T-t}/2\right)^2/2}}{\sqrt{2\pi\sigma^2(T-t)}} v\left(Z^0, Z^{1'}\right) \frac{dZ^{1'}}{Z^{1'}}.$$

8.2.3 Continuous hedging and the Greeks

In view of the previous discussion it is clear that pricing a derivative product has to be done in conjunction with devising a strategy for its hedging. Assuming that σ is given, all we need to know for the purposes of dynamic hedging of a given instrument whose price is $\Phi(\chi, \xi)$ are the so-called Delta Δ, Gamma Γ, and Theta Θ. In the traders' parlance, these quantities are called the Greeks. The nondimensional Greeks are defined by the following expressions

$$\Delta(\chi, \xi) = \Phi_\xi(\chi, \xi), \qquad \Gamma(\chi, \xi) = \Phi_{\xi\xi}(\chi, \xi), \qquad \Theta(\chi, \xi) = -\Phi_\chi(\chi, \xi).$$

It is clear that Δ, Θ measure the price sensitivity to spot and time changes, respectively, while Γ measures the Δ sensitivity to spot changes. Gamma shows how the Delta amount changes with infinitesimal changes of FXR. Finally, Theta characterizes the time change in the price. The pricing equation can be rewritten as a relation between the Greeks,

$$\Theta + \frac{1}{2}\xi^2\Gamma = 0.$$

Due to homogeneity, we can represent the amounts invested in domestic and foreign bonds in terms of the price and Delta:

$$\Upsilon^0 = \Phi - \xi\Delta, \qquad \Upsilon^1 = \Delta.$$

If $\Gamma > 0$, or, in other words, if the instrument is convex (both calls and puts are convex instruments since convexity of the payoff at maturity is preserved throughout the life of the option), then Δ increases (decreases) when ξ increases (decreases). Thus, in order to hedge a convex instrument, the option seller has to buy (sell) foreign currency when FXR increases (decreases). In other words, the seller loses money (by buying high and selling low, the reverse of the usual money-making strategy) in order to hedge himself. This is precisely the reason why the seller has to charge an upfront premium for the instrument. This remark should make it clear to the reader that hedging of instruments which are locally nonconvex can generate a profit. Because of that, the existence of inflection points for the payoff functions has important financial consequences. (In this respect mathematical finance is somewhat similar to hydrodynamic stability theory.)

The P&L (profit & loss) of a perfectly hedged instrument is equal to zero,

$$P\&L = \Phi(\hat{T}, \xi_0) - \Phi(0, \xi_{\hat{T}}) + \int_0^{\hat{T}} \Delta\left(\hat{T} - \vartheta', \xi_{\vartheta'}\right) d\xi_{\vartheta'} = 0,$$

regardless of the actual realized path for ξ_ϑ. We can say that the option price Φ, its Delta Δ, and the FXR ξ_χ play the role of energy, temperature, and entropy in thermodynamics.

As long as we assume that the volatility σ is given, we can execute a successful hedging strategy without computing derivatives of Φ with respect to σ. However, in the real world we seldom have the exact estimate of σ. Moreover, as we will see later, in many cases it is natural to assume that σ is a stochastic variable on a par with ξ. Because of that, the derivatives of Φ with respect to σ are of great interest. Accordingly, for a given option we define the so-called Vega, dVega/dVol, and dVega/dSpot which we denote by $\mathcal{V}, \mathcal{VV}, \mathcal{VS}$, and define as follows:

$$\mathcal{V}(\chi, \xi) = \frac{2\chi\Phi_\chi(\chi, \xi)}{\sigma} = \frac{\chi\xi^2\Phi_{\xi\xi}(\chi, \xi)}{\sigma},$$

$$\mathcal{VV}(\chi, \xi) = \frac{4\chi^2\Phi_{\chi\chi}(\chi, \xi) + 2\chi\Phi_\chi(\chi, \xi)}{\sigma^2},$$

$$\mathcal{VS}(\chi, \xi) = \frac{2\chi\Phi_{\chi\xi}(\chi, \xi)}{\sigma}.$$

To the best of author's knowledge Vega is not a standard Greek character, which is why it difficult to choose an adequate notation for Vega. Moreover, the terminology is not completely settled upon. Occasionally, one can see such colorful names for dVega/dVol as Vomma. Vega measures the price sensitivity with respect to the volatility changes.

8.3 Forwards, calls and puts

8.3.1 Definitions

The simplest (plain vanilla) contingent claims are forward contracts, calls and puts. Their payoffs are

$$FO\left(T, Z^0, Z^1\right) = Z^1 - Z^0,$$

$$C\left(T, Z^0, Z^1\right) = \left(Z^1 - Z^0\right)_+,$$

$$P\left(T, Z^0, Z^1\right) = \left(Z^0 - Z^1\right)_+,$$

or, equivalently,

$$\Phi^{(FO)}\left(0, \xi\right) = \xi - 1,$$

$$\Phi^{(C)}\left(0, \xi\right) = \left(\xi - 1\right)_+,$$

$$\Phi^{(P)}\left(0, \xi\right) = \left(1 - \xi\right)_+.$$

The relevant boundary conditions are

$$\Phi^{(FO)}\left(\chi, 0\right) = -1, \quad \Phi^{(FO)}\left(\chi, \xi \to \infty\right) \to \xi - 1,$$

$$\Phi^{(C)}\left(\chi, 0\right) = 0, \quad \Phi^{(C)}\left(\chi, \xi \to \infty\right) \to \xi - 1,$$

$$\Phi^{(P)}\left(\chi, 0\right) = 1, \quad \Phi^{(P)}\left(\chi, \xi \to \infty\right) \to 0.$$

8.3.2 Pricing via the Feynman-Kac formula

We can use formula (8.16) in order to price a number of contingent claims. We start with pricing of a forward contract. Straightforward calculation which is left to the reader yields

$$\Phi^{(FO)}\left(\chi, \xi\right) = \xi - 1. \tag{8.19}$$

This formula can be derived without any calculation at all by noticing that $\xi - 1$ solves the pricing equation and satisfies the initial and boundary conditions. The corresponding Greeks are

$$\Delta^{(FO)} = 1, \quad \Gamma^{(FO)} = 0, \quad \Theta^{(FO)} = 0,$$
$$\mathcal{V}^{(FO)} = 0, \quad \mathcal{V}\mathcal{V}^{(FO)} = 0, \quad \mathcal{V}\mathcal{S}^{(FO)} = 0.$$

Next, we show how to price a European call. Its price $\Phi^{(C)}(\chi, \xi)$ can be found via formula (8.16):

$$\Phi^{(C)}(\chi, \xi) = \int_{-\infty}^{\infty} \frac{e^{-Y^2/2}}{\sqrt{2\pi}} \left(e^{-\chi/2 + \sqrt{\chi}Y} \xi - 1 \right)_+ dY \qquad (8.20)$$

$$= \xi \int_{-d_-}^{\infty} \frac{e^{-Y^2/2 - \chi/2 + \sqrt{\chi}Y}}{\sqrt{2\pi}} dY - \int_{-d_-}^{\infty} \frac{e^{-Y^2/2}}{\sqrt{2\pi}} dY$$

$$= \xi \int_{-d_+}^{\infty} \frac{e^{-Y^2/2}}{\sqrt{2\pi}} dY - \int_{-d_-}^{\infty} \frac{e^{-Y^2/2}}{\sqrt{2\pi}} dY$$

$$= \xi \mathfrak{N}(d_+(\chi, \xi)) - \mathfrak{N}(d_-(\chi, \xi)),$$

where $d_\pm$ are defined by formula (8.18). The corresponding Greeks are

$$\Delta^{(C)}(\chi, \xi) = \mathfrak{N}(d_+(\chi, \xi)), \qquad (8.21)$$

$$\Gamma^{(C)}(\chi, \xi) = \frac{\mathfrak{n}(d_+(\chi, \xi))}{\sqrt{\chi}\xi}, \qquad (8.22)$$

$$\Theta^{(C)}(\chi, \xi) = \frac{\xi \mathfrak{n}(d_+(\chi, \xi))}{2\sqrt{\chi}},$$

$$\mathcal{V}^{(C)}(\chi, \xi) = \frac{\sqrt{\chi}\xi \mathfrak{n}(d_+(\chi, \xi))}{\sigma},$$

$$\mathcal{V}\mathcal{V}^{(C)}(\chi, \xi) = \frac{\sqrt{\chi}\xi d_+(\chi, \xi) d_-(\chi, \xi) \mathfrak{n}(d_+(\chi, \xi))}{\sigma^2},$$

$$\mathcal{V}\mathcal{S}^{(C)}(\chi, \xi) = -\frac{d_-(\chi, \xi) \mathfrak{n}(d_+(\chi, \xi))}{\sigma}.$$

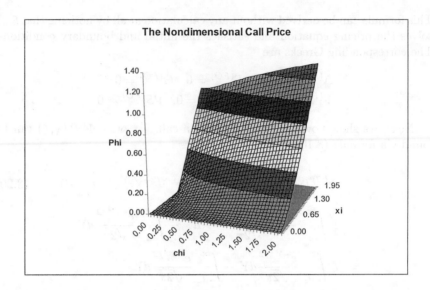

Figure 8.1: The nondimensional call price $\Phi^{(C)}(\chi,\xi)$ as a function of χ,ξ.

The call price and some of the Greeks are shown in Figures 8.1 - 8.4.

The price of the put $\Phi^{(P)}(\chi,\xi)$ can be found via formula (8.16) as well. Omitting the corresponding calculation for the sake of brevity, we simply present the answer

$$\Phi^{(P)}(\chi,\xi) = \mathfrak{N}(-d_-(\chi,\xi)) - \xi\mathfrak{N}(-d_+(\chi,\xi)). \qquad (8.23)$$

We leave it to the reader as an exercise to evaluate the corresponding Greeks.

The call and put prices can be rewritten in a manifestly symmetric form,

$$\Phi^{\pm}(\chi,\xi) = \pm\xi\mathfrak{N}(\pm d_+(\chi,\xi)) \mp \mathfrak{N}(\pm d_-(\chi,\xi)),$$

where the $+$ and $-$ superscripts distinguish calls and puts, respectively.

Next, we establish put-call parity. Subtracting equation (8.23) from equation (8.20) we get the relation

$$\Phi^{(C)}(\chi,\xi) - \Phi^{(P)}(\chi,\xi) = \xi - 1,$$

which expresses put-call parity. Of course, the above equation can be obtained directly. Indeed, at $\chi = 0$ we have

$$\Phi^{(C)}(0,\xi) - \Phi^{(P)}(0,\xi) = \xi - 1.$$

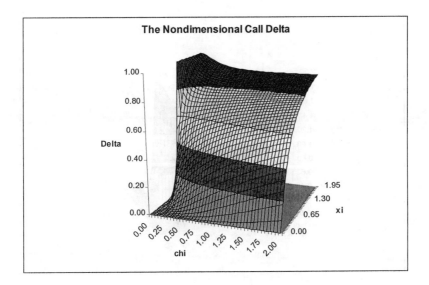

Figure 8.2: The nondimensional call Delta $\Delta^{(C)}(\chi, \xi)$ as a function of χ, ξ.

Since both $\Phi^{(C)}(\chi, \xi) - \Phi^{(P)}(\chi, \xi)$, and $\xi - 1$ solve the same pricing equation, they coincide at any χ as long as they coincide at $\chi = 0$.

Finally, we use the fact that equation (8.9) is invariant with respect to the Kelvin transform

$$\xi \rightarrow \frac{1}{\xi}, \quad \Phi(\chi, \xi) \rightarrow \frac{\Phi(\chi, \xi)}{\xi}.$$

to establish put-call symmetry. It is clear that at maturity

$$\Phi^{(C)}(0, \xi) = \xi \Phi^{(P)}\left(0, \frac{1}{\xi}\right).$$

Since both sides of this formula satisfy the pricing equation, the above relation is valid for all χ:

$$\Phi^{(C)}(\chi, \xi) = \xi \Phi^{(P)}\left(\chi, \frac{1}{\xi}\right).$$

Financially, this relation means that the right to buy euros at a below market rate is equivalent to the right to sell dollars at an above market rate.

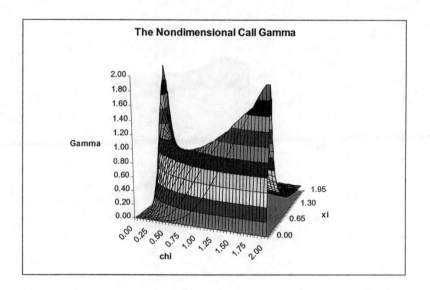

Figure 8.3: The nondimensional call Gamma $\Gamma^{(C)}(\chi, \xi)$ as a function of χ, ξ. The spike at $\chi = 0$, $\xi = 1$ is due to the nondifferentiability of the initial data.

When we discussed the discrete version of the pricing formula for calls in Section 5.2 we pointed out that it has at least two probabilistic interpretations. A similar observation is true in the continuous case. From the probabilistic standpoint the second term in the Black-Scholes formula is the risk-neutral (for domestic investors) probability that the FXR ξ ends up above 1 at maturity (i.e., that the call is exercised) times the normalized amount the buyer has to pay the seller in this case. Usually, the first term is interpreted as the expected value of ξ conditional on the fact that at maturity it is above the unit strike. However, an alternative (and frequently more convenient) interpretation is possible. Namely, we can say that this term is the risk-neutral (for foreign investors) probability that the reciprocal rate $1/\xi$ ends below the unit strike times the normalized amount the seller has to pay the buyer in this case.

We can use the probabilistic pricing formula (8.17) in order to separate the

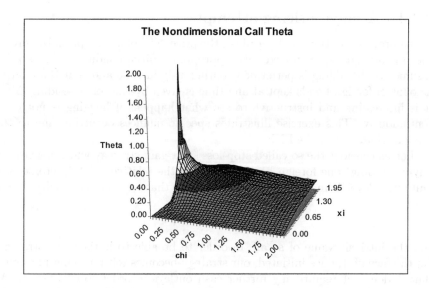

Figure 8.4: The nondimensional call Theta $\Theta^{(C)}(\chi,\xi)$ as a function of χ,ξ. The spike at $\chi=0,\xi=1$ is due to the nondifferentiability of the initial data.

intrinsic and time value of a call. We have

$$
\begin{aligned}
\Phi^{(C)}(\chi,\xi) &= \int_0^\infty p(\chi,\xi,\xi')(\xi'-1)_+\,d\xi' \\
&= \int_0^\infty \left(\delta(\xi-\xi') + \int_0^\chi p_\chi(\chi,\xi,\xi')\,d\chi \right)(\xi'-1)_+\,d\xi' \\
&= (\xi-1)_+ + \frac{1}{2}\int_0^\infty \int_0^\chi (\xi'^2 p(\chi,\xi,\xi'))_{\xi'\xi'} (\xi'-1)_+\,d\chi d\xi' \\
&= (\xi-1)_+ + \frac{1}{2}\int_0^\chi \int_0^\infty \xi'^2 p(\chi,\xi,\xi')\,\delta(\xi'-1)\,d\xi' d\chi \\
&= (\xi-1)_+ + \frac{1}{2}\int_0^\chi p(\chi,\xi,1)\,d\chi.
\end{aligned}
$$

Thus, in the nondimensional framework we can represent the time value of a call in the following form:

$$
\tilde\Phi^{(C)}(\chi,\xi) = \frac{1}{2}\int_0^\chi p(\chi,\xi,1)\,d\chi.
$$

8.3.3   A naive pricing attempt

In the previous section we determined the price $\Phi^{(C)}$ of a call option by solving the pricing equation supplied with appropriate initial conditions. This price assumes that hedging is performed continuously in time and that the relative amount of foreign bonds kept at any time is given by the corresponding $\Delta^{(C)}$. It is interesting and instructive to see what happens if hedging is not done continuously. This exercise illustrates specific nuances occurring due to the random character of the FXR.

Let us consider the so-called stop-loss start-gain strategy which consists in buying (selling) one foreign bond every time the relative FXR ξ_ϑ crosses the unit strike level from below (above). It is clear that we need to initially charge

$$\Phi^{(C)} = (\xi_\vartheta - 1)_+ \,,$$

i.e., the intrinsic value of a call, in order to be able to initiate our strategy. On the face of it, once initiated, our strategy becomes self-financing in a sense that it does not require any further cash outlays in order to exercise it. At maturity two possibilities can occur: (A) $\xi_{\hat{T}} > 1$, (B) $\xi_{\hat{T}} \leq 1$. In case (A) we will physically have a unit of foreign currency which we bought at the unit relative rate and can deliver to the buyer at the spot rate $\xi_{\hat{T}}$ without any loss (recall that we are dealing with relative quantities, so that the time value of money is automatically taken care of), in case (B) we will not hold any foreign currency, but, at the same time, we will not have an obligation to deliver it, either. We can write our P&L in the form

$$P\&L = (\xi_0 - 1)_+ - (\xi_{\hat{T}} - 1)_+ + \int_0^{\hat{T}} 1_{\{\xi_{\vartheta'} > 1\}} d\xi_{\vartheta'} \,,$$

where $1_{\{\xi_{\vartheta'} > 1\}}$ is the indicator function which is equal to one when $\xi_\vartheta > 1$ and zero otherwise. The first term on the r.h.s. represents the profit at inception, the second one the loss at maturity, and the third one the loss (or gain) due to hedging. It seems plausible that the $P\&L = 0$. However, this is not the case, as is easy to verify by modelling the corresponding FXR dynamics numerically via the Monte Carlo method. Why does it happen? The informal answer is, of course, that the perfect execution of our strategy is not feasible because of the random nature of ξ_ϑ which forces the hedger to buy the foreign currency at the rate which is slightly higher that 1 and sell it at the rate which is slightly lower than 1. While for a nonrandom variable this discrepancy would be negligible, for the random one it has to be taken into account. The corresponding P&L can be explained in terms of Levy's local time showing how often the FXR ξ_ϑ

hits the strike level 1. The Meyer-Tanaka formula (4.43) yields

$$P\&L = (\xi_0 - 1)_+ - (\xi_{\hat{T}} - 1)_+ + \int_0^{\hat{T}} 1_{\{\xi_{\vartheta'} > 1\}} d\xi_{\vartheta'} - \frac{1}{2}\lambda_{0,\hat{T}}(\xi_0, 1), \quad (8.24)$$

where $\lambda_{0,\hat{T}}(\xi_0, 1)$ is the local time at 1 for the random process ξ_ϑ. We see that in order to achieve zero P&L we need to charge more that the intrinsic value for a call option, and that the excess amount to be added to the intrinsic value is equal to one half of the local time. Since the local time is random we have not achieved our goal of pricing a call and devising the hedging strategy for it which produces zero P&L regardless of the behavior of the underlying. In fact, formula (8.24) suggests that the time value of a call option is precisely the expected value of $-P\&L$ generated by the above strategy.

8.3.4 Pricing via the Fourier transform method

Because of its importance, it is useful to discuss different approaches to solving the option pricing problem for a call option. In this subsection we show how to solve this problem via the Fourier transform method.[1] Application of the Fourier transform is a little difficult because the initial data grows too fast at positive infinity. We treat this difficulty at the heuristic level. The pricing problem for a call has the form

$$U_X^{(C)} - \frac{1}{2}U_{XX}^{(C)} = 0, \quad (8.25)$$

$$U^{(C)}(0, X) = \left(e^{X/2} - e^{-X/2}\right)_+.$$

The Fourier transform of $U^{(C)}$ in X has the form

$$\Xi^{(C)}(\chi, k) = \int_{-\infty}^{\infty} U^{(C)}(\chi, X) e^{ikX} dX.$$

Here k is a real-valued parameter, $-\infty < k < \infty$. The inverse Fourier transform is defined by

$$U^{(C)}(\chi, X) = \frac{1}{2\pi} \int_{-\infty}^{\infty} \Xi^{(C)}(\chi, k) e^{-ikX} dk.$$

---

[1] Stricly speaking, we should be using the so-called Mellin transform method applied to equation (8.9). However, to simplify the exposition, we choose to apply the Fourier transform method to equation (8.25).

The transformed pricing problem can be written as

$$\Xi_\chi^{(C)} + \frac{1}{2}k^2 \Xi^{(C)} = 0, \tag{8.26}$$

$$\Xi^{(C)}(0,k) = \int_0^\infty \left(e^{X/2} - e^{-X/2}\right) e^{ikX} dX. \tag{8.27}$$

In order to evaluate this integral we use the following general formula (its derivation, which is conceptually difficult, is beyond the scope of the book):

$$\int_0^\infty e^{(ik+\kappa)X} dX = -\frac{1}{(ik+\kappa)} + \begin{cases} 0, & \kappa < 0 \\ \pi\delta(k), & \kappa = 0 \\ 2\pi\delta(k - i\kappa), & \kappa > 0 \end{cases}. \tag{8.28}$$

Straightforward application of the above formula yields

$$\Xi^{(C)}(0,k) = \left(-\frac{1}{(ik+1/2)} + 2\pi\delta(k - i/2) + \frac{1}{(ik-1/2)}\right).$$

The solution of problem (8.26), (8.27) can be represented in the form

$$\Xi^{(C)}(\chi,k) = e^{-k^2\chi/2}\left(-\frac{1}{(ik+1/2)} + 2\pi\delta(k - i/2) + \frac{1}{(ik-1/2)}\right).$$

Accordingly,

$$\begin{aligned}
U^{(C)}(\chi, X) & \\
= -\frac{1}{2\pi} &\int_{-\infty}^\infty \frac{e^{-k^2\chi/2 - ikX}}{(ik+1/2)} dk + e^{\chi/8+X/2} + \frac{1}{2\pi}\int_{-\infty}^\infty \frac{e^{-k^2\chi/2 - ikX}}{(ik-1/2)} dk \\
= -\mathcal{I}^{(1)} &+ e^{\chi/8+X/2} + \mathcal{I}^{(2)}.
\end{aligned}$$

We start with the integral $\mathcal{I}^{(1)}$. Since its direct evaluation is involved, we take a step backwards, rewrite $\mathcal{I}^{(1)}$ as a double integral, change the order of integration and get

$$
\begin{aligned}
\mathcal{I}^{(1)} &= \frac{1}{2\pi} \int_{-\infty}^{\infty} \int_{\infty}^{0} e^{-k^2\chi/2+(ik+1/2)\varpi-ikX} \, d\varpi dk \\
&= \frac{1}{2\pi} \int_{\infty}^{0} \int_{-\infty}^{\infty} e^{-k^2\chi/2+(ik+1/2)\varpi-ikX} \, dk d\varpi \\
&= \frac{1}{2\pi} \int_{\infty}^{0} \left(\int_{-\infty}^{\infty} e^{-\left(k\sqrt{\chi}-i(\varpi-X)/\sqrt{\chi}\right)^2/2} dk \right) e^{-(\varpi-X)^2/2\chi+\varpi/2} d\varpi \\
&= e^{\chi/8+X/2} \int_{\infty}^{0} \frac{e^{-\left((\varpi-X)/\sqrt{\chi}-\sqrt{\chi}/2\right)^2/2}}{\sqrt{2\pi\chi}} \, d\varpi \\
&= e^{\chi/8+X/2} \mathfrak{N}\left(-\frac{X}{\sqrt{\chi}} - \frac{\sqrt{\chi}}{2} \right).
\end{aligned}
$$

By the same token,

$$
\mathcal{I}^{(2)} = -e^{\chi/8-X/2} \mathfrak{N}\left(\frac{X}{\sqrt{\chi}} - \frac{\sqrt{\chi}}{2} \right).
$$

Finally, we obtain the pricing formula

$$
\begin{aligned}
U^{(C)}(\chi, X) &= e^{\chi/8+X/2} \mathfrak{N}\left(\frac{X}{\sqrt{\chi}} + \frac{\sqrt{\chi}}{2} \right) - e^{\chi/8-X/2} \mathfrak{N}\left(\frac{X}{\sqrt{\chi}} - \frac{\sqrt{\chi}}{2} \right) \\
&= M\left(\chi, X, \frac{1}{2} \right) - M\left(\chi, X, -\frac{1}{2} \right),
\end{aligned}
$$

where

$$
M(\chi, X, \hat{\gamma}) = e^{\hat{\gamma}^2\chi/2+\hat{\gamma}X} \mathfrak{N}\left(\frac{X}{\sqrt{\chi}} + \hat{\gamma}\sqrt{\chi} \right). \tag{8.29}
$$

The above formula is equivalent to formula (8.20), as might be expected.

8.3.5 Pricing via the Laplace transform method

In this subsection we solve the pricing problem for a call option via the standard Laplace transform. The Laplace transform of $\Phi^{(C)}$ is defined by

$$
\Xi^{(C)}(\lambda, \xi) = \int_{0}^{\infty} e^{-\lambda\chi} \Phi^{(C)}(\chi, \xi) \, d\chi.
$$

The Laplace transformed pricing problem can be represented in the form

$$\lambda \Xi^{(C)} - \frac{1}{2}\xi^2 \Xi^{(C)}{}_{\xi\xi} = (\xi - 1)_+ .$$

We can solve the above equation separately for $\xi < 1$ and $\xi > 1$ and match the solutions at $\xi = 1$. For $\xi < 1$ we represent solutions vanishing at zero in the form

$$\Xi^{(C)}(\lambda, \xi) = p_+ \xi^{\alpha_+},$$

where

$$\alpha_\pm = \frac{1}{2} \pm \sqrt{\frac{1}{4} + 2\lambda}.$$

and p_+ is an undetermined (yet) coefficient. For $\xi > 1$ we represent solutions approaching $\xi - 1$ at positive infinity as

$$\Xi^{(C)}(\lambda, \xi) = \frac{\xi - 1}{\lambda} + p_- \xi^{\alpha_-} .$$

In order to find $p_\pm$ we use the matching condition and require the continuity of $\Xi^{(C)}$ and $\Xi^{(C)}_\xi$ at $\xi = 1$. These conditions yield

$$p_+ = p_-, \quad \alpha_+ p_+ = \frac{1}{\lambda} + \alpha_- p_- .$$

A simple algebra shows that

$$p_\pm = \frac{1}{\lambda\sqrt{1 + 8\lambda}} .$$

Thus,

$$\Xi^{(C)}(\lambda, \xi) = \begin{cases} \xi^{\alpha_+}/\lambda\sqrt{1 + 8\lambda}, & \xi < 1 \\ (\xi - 1)/\lambda + \xi^{\alpha_-}/\lambda\sqrt{1 + 8\lambda}, & \xi > 1 \end{cases} .$$

To be specific, we assume that $\xi < 1$. A simple calculation yields

$$\Xi^{(C)}(\lambda, \xi) = 2 \left(\frac{\xi^{1/2 + \sqrt{1/4 + 2\lambda}}}{\sqrt{1/4 + 2\lambda} - 1/2} + \frac{\xi^{1/2 + \sqrt{1/4 + 2\lambda}}}{\sqrt{1/4 + 2\lambda} + 1/2} - \frac{2\xi^{1/2 + \sqrt{1/4 + 2\lambda}}}{\sqrt{1/4 + 2\lambda}} \right) .$$

To find the inverse Laplace transform of $\Xi^{(C)}$ we use the Laplace transform tables and obtain

$$\Phi^{(C)}(\chi,\xi)$$

$$= e^{-\chi/8}\xi^{1/2}\left(\frac{1}{\sqrt{\pi\chi/2}}e^{-\ln^2(\xi)/2\chi} + \frac{1}{2}e^{\chi/8+\ln(\xi)/2}\mathrm{erfc}\left(-\frac{\ln\xi}{\sqrt{2\chi}}-\sqrt{\frac{\chi}{8}}\right)\right.$$

$$+\frac{1}{\sqrt{\pi\chi/2}}e^{-\ln^2(\xi)/2\chi} - \frac{1}{2}e^{\chi/8-\ln(\xi)/2}\mathrm{erfc}\left(-\frac{\ln\xi}{\sqrt{2\chi}}+\sqrt{\frac{\chi}{8}}\right)$$

$$\left.-\frac{2}{\sqrt{\pi\chi/2}}e^{-\ln^2(\xi)/2\chi}\right)$$

$$= \frac{1}{2}\xi\,\mathrm{erfc}\left(-\frac{\ln\xi}{\sqrt{2\chi}}-\sqrt{\frac{\chi}{8}}\right) - \frac{1}{2}\mathrm{erfc}\left(-\frac{\ln\xi}{\sqrt{2\chi}}+\sqrt{\frac{\chi}{8}}\right)$$

$$= \xi\mathfrak{N}\left(\frac{\ln\xi}{\sqrt{\chi}}+\frac{\sqrt{\chi}}{2}\right) - \mathfrak{N}\left(\frac{\ln\xi}{\sqrt{\chi}}-\frac{\sqrt{\chi}}{2}\right),$$

as before. For $\xi > 1$ we obtain an identical expression.

8.3.6 The limiting behavior of calls and puts

In this section we analyze the asymptotic behavior of the call price and the corresponding Greeks as a function of its nondimensional arguments χ and ξ. The limits we are interested in are as follows:

$$\xi \to 0, \ \ \xi \to \infty, \ \ \chi \to 0, \ \ \chi \to \infty.$$

The price of a call option at maturity is sandwiched between $\xi - 1$ and ξ,

$$\xi - 1 \le (\xi - 1)_+ < \xi.$$

Since $\xi - 1$ and ξ both solve the pricing equation, similar inequalities are valid for all χ:

$$\xi - 1 \le \Phi^{(C)}(\chi,\xi) < \xi.$$

Asymptotic analysis confirms these qualitative estimates and allows one to obtain more precise results. Straightforward manipulation of formulas (8.20) - (8.22) yields

$$\Phi^{(C)}(\chi,\xi \to 0) \to 0, \ \ \Delta^{(C)}(\chi,\xi \to 0) \to 0, \ \ \Gamma^{(C)}(\chi,\xi \to 0) \to 0; \quad (8.30)$$

$$\Phi^{(C)}\left(\chi,\xi\to\infty\right)\to\xi-1,\quad \Delta^{(C)}\left(\chi,\xi\to\infty\right)\to1,\quad \Gamma^{(C)}\left(\chi,\xi\to\infty\right)\to0;$$
$$(8.31)$$

$$\Phi^{(C)}\left(\chi\to\infty,\xi\right)\to\xi,\quad \Delta^{(C)}\left(\chi\to\infty,\xi\right)\to1,\quad \Gamma^{(C)}\left(\chi\to\infty,\xi\right)\to0.\quad(8.32)$$

In these formulas the rate of convergence is exponential. Formulas (8.30) show that deep out-of-the-money call options have no value; formulas (8.31) show that for deep in-the-money call options optionality is irrelevant, so that they are very similar in nature to forward contracts; formulas (8.32) suggest that buying a call option with a very long maturity is equivalent to owning the foreign currency outright.

The asymptotic behavior of the price and the Greeks is more complex when $\chi\to0$. When $\xi\neq1$ we have

$$\Phi^{(C)}\left(\chi\to0,\xi\right)\to(\xi-1)_{+}\,,\quad \Delta^{(C)}\left(\chi\to0,\xi\right)\to\theta\left(\xi\right),\quad \Gamma^{(C)}\left(\chi\to0,\xi\right)\to0,$$

where, as usual, $\theta\left(\xi\right)$ is the Heaviside function. As before, the rate of convergence is exponential. Thus, for ITMF and OTMF options with very short maturities there is no true optionality. The behavior of ATMF calls is different. Putting $\xi=1$ and Taylor expanding formulas (8.20) - (8.22), we obtain

$$\Phi^{(C)}\left(\chi\to0,1\right)=\mathfrak{N}\left(\frac{\sqrt{\chi}}{2}\right)-\mathfrak{N}\left(-\frac{\sqrt{\chi}}{2}\right)$$

$$\to\quad \mathfrak{N}\left(0\right)+\frac{1}{2}\mathfrak{N}'\left(0\right)\sqrt{\chi}+\frac{1}{8}\mathfrak{N}''\left(0\right)\chi+\frac{1}{48}\mathfrak{N}'''\left(0\right)\chi\sqrt{\chi}$$

$$-\mathfrak{N}\left(0\right)+\frac{1}{2}\mathfrak{N}'\left(0\right)\sqrt{\chi}-\frac{1}{8}\mathfrak{N}''\left(0\right)\chi+\frac{1}{48}\mathfrak{N}'''\left(0\right)\chi\sqrt{\chi}$$

$$=\quad \frac{\sqrt{\chi}}{\sqrt{2\pi}}\left(1-\frac{\chi}{24}\right),$$

$$\Delta^{(C)}\left(\chi\to0,1\right)\to\frac{1}{2}+\frac{\sqrt{\chi}}{2\sqrt{2\pi}}-\frac{\chi\sqrt{\chi}}{48\sqrt{2\pi}},$$

$$\Gamma^{(C)}\left(\chi\to0,1\right)\to\frac{1-\chi/8}{\sqrt{2\pi\chi}}.$$

Thus, ATMF calls with short maturity have small price, finite Delta and huge positive Gamma, which makes their hedging rather difficult.

We can express the above observations in a more compact form by noticing that for $\chi \to 0$ the time value of a call

$$\tilde{\Phi}^{(C)}(\chi, \xi) = \Phi^{(C)}(\chi, \xi) - (\xi - 1)_+ ,$$

behaves as

$$\tilde{\Phi}^{(C)}(\chi \to 0, \xi) \to \frac{1}{2} \chi \delta (\xi - 1),$$

where δ is the Dirac delta.

8.4 Contingent claims with arbitrary payoffs

8.4.1 Introduction

Above we spent a lot of effort in order to evaluate calls and puts. Now we show how to apply this knowledge in order to price options with more general payoffs.

8.4.2 The decomposition formula

It is easy to show that a proper combination of forward contracts and European calls and puts can represent a European option with an arbitrary (homogeneous) payoff

$$\text{payoff} = v(\xi).$$

(Different choices of $v(\xi)$ may appeal to different investors with specific market views. Details are discussed later.) Indeed, since two portfolios whose prices coincide at maturity must have the same price at any time t, all we need to do is to represent $v(\xi)$ as a linear combination of 1, ξ, $(\xi - K)_+$, $(K - \xi)_+$, for different values of K, or, in words, as a combination of the domestic and foreign bonds, and calls and puts with different strikes. There are infinitely many ways of expanding a given function in such a combination. Let κ be an arbitrary break point. We claim that

$$
\begin{aligned}
v(\xi) \;=\;& v(\kappa) + (\xi - \kappa) v'(\kappa) \qquad\qquad (8.33)\\
& + \int_0^\kappa v''(K)(K - \xi)_+ \, dK + \int_\kappa^\infty v''(K)(\xi - K)_+ \, dK,
\end{aligned}
$$

where the prime denotes the derivative of v with respect to its argument. Integration by parts allows to transform the r.h.s. of this relation for fixed ξ as follows (to be concrete we assume that $\xi > \kappa$, so that the first integral vanishes while the second one assumes the form $\int_{\kappa}^{\xi} v''(K)(\xi - K)\,dK$):

$$
\begin{aligned}
r.h.s. \;&=\; v(\kappa) + (\xi - \kappa)\,v'(\kappa) + \int_{\kappa}^{\xi} v''(K)(\xi - K)\,dK \\
&=\; v(\kappa) + (\xi - \kappa)\,v'(\kappa) - (\xi - \kappa)\,v'(\kappa) + \int_{\kappa}^{\xi} v'(K)\,dK \\
&=\; v(\kappa) + v(\xi) - v(\kappa) \\
&=\; v(\xi).
\end{aligned}
$$

By using equation (8.33) we can obtain the following decomposition formula for the price of a deal with an arbitrary payoff:

$$
\begin{aligned}
v(\chi, \xi) \;=\;& v(\kappa) + (\xi - \kappa)\,v'(\kappa) + \int_{0}^{\kappa} v''(K)\,\Phi^{(P)}\left(\chi, \frac{\xi}{K}\right) K\,dK \quad (8.34) \\
&+ \int_{\kappa}^{\infty} v''(K)\,\Phi^{(C)}\left(\chi, \frac{\xi}{K}\right) K\,dK.
\end{aligned}
$$

We leave it to the reader to rewrite the above expression in terms of t, Z^0, Z^1.

8.4.3   Call and put bets

Call and put bets have the following payoffs:

$$
V^{(CB)}\left(T, Z^0, Z^1\right) = \theta\left(Z^1 - Z^0\right),
$$

$$
V^{(PB)}\left(T, Z^0, Z^1\right) = \theta\left(Z^0 - Z^1\right),
$$

or, equivalently,

$$
\Phi^{(CB)}(0, \xi) = \theta(\xi - 1),
$$

$$
\Phi^{(PB)}(0, \xi) = \theta(\xi - 1).
$$

Their financial meaning is simple: the seller of a call (put) bet pays the buyer a dollar if the terminal FXR is above (below) the strike level.

It is easy to price call and put bets via the decomposition formula. Consider, for example, a call bet and choose $\kappa = 0$ in the decomposition formula. We have

$$
\begin{aligned}
\Phi^{(CB)}(\chi,\xi) &= \int_0^\infty \left(\theta\left(K-1\right)\right)'' \Phi^{(C)}\left(\chi,\frac{\xi}{K}\right) K dK \\
&= \int_0^\infty \delta'\left(K-1\right) \Phi^{(C)}\left(\chi,\frac{\xi}{K}\right) K dK \\
&= -\int_0^\infty \delta\left(K-1\right) \left(\Phi^{(C)}\left(\chi,\frac{\xi}{K}\right) K\right)' dK \\
&= -\left(\Phi^{(C)}\left(\chi,\frac{\xi}{K}\right) K\right)' \bigg|_{K=1} \\
&= \xi\Delta^{(C)}(\chi,\xi) - \Phi^{(C)}(\chi,\xi) \\
&= \mathfrak{N}\left(d_-(\chi,\xi)\right).
\end{aligned}
$$

Similarly,

$$
\Phi^{(PB)}(\chi,\xi) = \mathfrak{N}\left(-d_-(\chi,\xi)\right).
$$

We leave it to the reader to verify the formulas by solving the corresponding pricing problems directly.

8.4.4 Log contracts and modified log contracts

Formula (8.34) becomes particularly simple for log contracts (LC) which are intimately connected with the variance and volatility swaps as explained in Chapter 13. The payoff of such contracts is simply

$$
\Phi^{(LC)}(0,\xi) = \ln(\xi).
$$

We emphasize that LC are closer in spirit to forward contracts than to calls and puts since their payoff can be both positive and negative. Formula (8.34) with $\kappa = 1$ yields

$$
\begin{aligned}
\Phi^{(LC)}(\chi,\xi) &= (\xi-1) - \int_0^1 \Phi^{(P)}\left(\chi,\frac{\xi}{K}\right) \frac{dK}{K} \\
&\quad - \int_1^\infty \Phi^{(C)}\left(\chi,\frac{\xi}{K}\right) \frac{dK}{K}.
\end{aligned}
\tag{8.35}
$$

We leave it to the reader as an exercise to check that the solution of pricing problem (8.9), (8.10) has the form

$$
\Phi^{(LC)}(\chi,\xi) = \ln\xi - \frac{1}{2}\chi.
\tag{8.36}
$$

Comparison of expressions (8.35), (8.36) yields the following useful expression for the deannualized volatility:

$$
\frac{1}{2}\chi = \ln\xi - (\xi - 1) + \int_0^1 \Phi^{(P)}\left(\chi, \frac{\xi}{K}\right)\frac{dK}{K}
$$
$$
+ \int_1^\infty \Phi^{(C)}\left(\chi, \frac{\xi}{K}\right)\frac{dK}{K}.
$$

We use this expression later in our analysis of variance swaps.

In addition to (or instead of) ordinary LC it is often useful to consider the so-called modified log contracts (MLC) whose payoff has the form

$$
\Phi^{(MLC)}(0, \xi) = \ln\left(\frac{\kappa}{\xi}\right) + \frac{\xi}{\kappa} - 1,
$$

where $\kappa > 0$ is an arbitrary strike. It is clear that

$$
\Phi^{(MLC)}(0, \kappa) = 0, \quad \Phi_\xi^{(MLC)}(0, \kappa) = 0,
$$
$$
\Phi^{(MLC)}(0, \xi) \geq 0, \quad \Phi_{\xi\xi}^{(MLC)}(0, \xi) > 0,
$$

so that the MLC is an option (an asset for the holder) similar to a call option, as opposite to the standard LC which, as was mentioned earlier, can be both an asset and a liability. The decomposition formula yields

$$
\Phi^{(MLC)}(\chi, \xi) = \int_0^\kappa \Phi^{(P)}\left(\chi, \frac{\xi}{K}\right)\frac{dK}{K} + \int_\kappa^\infty \Phi^{(C)}\left(\chi, \frac{\xi}{K}\right)\frac{dK}{K}.
$$

8.5   Dynamic asset allocation

Merton pioneered the analysis of the optimal consumption, asset allocation and bequest problem in continuous time. He solved this problem for investors having hyperbolic absolute risk averse utility functions. In the present section we solve the bequest problem for mean-variance investors in its relative form.

We assume that the only venues available for investment are domestic and foreign bonds. The relative value of domestic bonds which is denoted by $Y_t^0 = Z_t^0/Z_t^0$ is constant. The relative value of foreign bonds which is denoted by $Y_t^1 = Z_t^1/Z_t^0$ is random. The governing equations are

$$
\frac{dY_t^0}{Y_t^0} = 0, \quad Y_0^0 = 1,
$$

$$\frac{dY_t^1}{Y_t^1} = \mu dt + \sigma dW_t, \quad Y_0^1 \text{ is given.}$$

Here we assume that $\mu \neq 0$. We emphasize that μ is the relative real-world drift rather than the risk-neutral drift (which is equal to zero). Let $\Upsilon_t = \left(\Upsilon_t^0, \Upsilon_t^1\right)$ be a predictable self-financing trading strategy, Π_t the corresponding wealth:

$$\Pi_t = \Upsilon_t^0 + \Upsilon_t^1 Y_t^1,$$

and ϖ_t^1 the fraction of wealth invested in foreign bonds,

$$\varpi_t^1 = \frac{\Upsilon_t^1 Y_t^1}{\Pi_t},$$

the fraction of wealth invested in domestic bonds is simply $\varpi_t^0 = 1 - \varpi_t^1$. Since our strategy is self-financing we have

$$d\Pi_t = \Upsilon_t^1 dY_t^1 = \Upsilon_t^1 Y_t^1 (\mu dt + \sigma dW_t), \quad \Pi_0 \text{ is given,}$$

or, equivalently, and more conveniently,

$$d\Pi_t = \varpi_t^1 \Pi_t (\mu dt + \sigma dW_t), \quad \Pi_0 \text{ is given.}$$

We are interested in finding strategies ϖ_t^1 which keep the expected wealth (the first moment) at time T fixed (and greater than the initial wealth Π_0), and minimize the variance (or, equivalently, the second moment) of wealth at maturity. Explicitly,

$$\begin{cases} \mathbb{M}^{(2)} = \mathbb{E}_0\{\Pi_T^2\} \rightarrow \min, \\ \mathbb{M}^{(1)} = \mathbb{E}_0\{\Pi_T\} = \pi > \Pi_0. \end{cases} \tag{8.37}$$

As usual, we solve this problem by using Lagrange multiplies. In other words, we minimize the functional $\mathbb{M}^{(2)} - \lambda \mathbb{M}^{(1)}$ and satisfy the constraint *a posteriori*. We introduce the function $J(t, Y^1, \Pi)$ according to

$$J(t, Y^1, \Pi) = \min_{\varpi^1} \mathbb{E}_0 \left\{ \Pi_T^2 - \lambda \Pi_T \right\}.$$

It is well known that this function solves the so-called Hamilton-Jacobi-Bellman (HJB) final value problem:

$$\min_{\varpi^1} \left\{ \begin{array}{l} J_t + \frac{1}{2}\sigma^2 \left(\left(Y^1\right)^2 J_{Y^1 Y^1} + 2\varpi^1 Y^1 \Pi J_{Y^1 \Pi} + \left(\varpi^1\right)^2 \Pi^2 J_{\Pi\Pi} \right) \\ + \mu Y^1 J_{Y^1} + \varpi^1 \mu \Pi J_\Pi \end{array} \right\} = 0,$$

$$J(T, Y^1, \Pi) = \Pi^2 - \lambda\Pi.$$

Equivalently,

$$\max_{\varpi^1} \left\{ \begin{array}{l} J_\chi - \frac{1}{2}\left(\left(Y^1\right)^2 J_{Y^1 Y^1} + 2\varpi^1 Y^1 \Pi J_{Y^1 \Pi} + \left(\varpi^1\right)^2 \Pi^2 J_{\Pi\Pi} \right) \\ -\hat{\mu} Y^1 J_{Y^1} - \varpi^1 \hat{\mu}\, \Pi J_\Pi \end{array} \right\} = 0,$$

$$J(0, Y^1, \Pi) = \Pi^2 - \lambda\Pi,$$

where, as usual, $\chi = \sigma^2\,(T - t)$ and $\hat{\mu} = \mu/\sigma^2$.

In general, it is very difficult to solve the above problem because it is nonlinear. However, since the initial data is independent of Y^1, so is the solution, which greatly simplifies the situation. [2] We assume that $J = J(\chi, \Pi)$ and rewrite the HJB equation as

$$\max_{\varpi} \left\{ J_\chi - \frac{1}{2}\left(\varpi^1\right)^2 \Pi^2 J_{\Pi\Pi} - \varpi^1 \hat{\mu}\, \Pi J_\Pi \right\} = 0,$$

$$J(0, \Pi) = \Pi^2 - \lambda\Pi.$$

In addition, we assume that J is convex, $J_{\Pi\Pi} > 0$, (this inequality is verified later,) so that the minimization problem with respect to ϖ^1 has a finite solution of the form

$$\varpi^1 = -\frac{\hat{\mu}\, J_\Pi}{\Pi J_{\Pi\Pi}}.$$

We substitute this expression back into the HJB equation and get a closed problem for J, namely,

$$J_\chi + \frac{\hat{\mu}^2 J_\Pi^2}{2 J_{\Pi\Pi}} = 0, \tag{8.38}$$

$$J(0, \Pi) = \Pi^2 - \lambda\Pi. \tag{8.39}$$

---

[2] Later, we will deal with a similar HJB equation in our analysis of passport options. For reasons which will become apparent in a due course, the corresponding solution is considerably more complex.

This problem can be solved by virtue of a simple ansatz

$$J(\chi, \Pi) = \alpha(\chi)\Pi^2 + \beta(\chi)\Pi + \gamma(\chi). \tag{8.40}$$

We substitute expression (8.40) in equation (8.38) and obtain a system of ODEs for α, β, γ,

$$\dot{\alpha} + \hat{\mu}^2\alpha = 0, \quad \alpha(0) = 1,$$

$$\dot{\beta} + \hat{\mu}^2\beta = 0, \quad \beta(0) = -\lambda,$$

$$\dot{\gamma} + \frac{\hat{\mu}^2\beta^2}{4\alpha} = 0, \quad \gamma(0) = 0,$$

where the overdot denotes the derivative with respect to χ. A simple algebra yields

$$\alpha = e^{-\hat{\mu}^2\chi}, \quad \beta = -\lambda e^{-\hat{\mu}^2\chi}, \quad \gamma = \frac{\lambda^2}{4}\left(e^{-\hat{\mu}^2\chi} - 1\right),$$

so that

$$J(\chi, \Pi) = e^{-\hat{\mu}^2\chi}\left(\Pi - \frac{\lambda}{2}\right)^2 - \frac{\lambda^2}{4}. \tag{8.41}$$

This formula shows that $J_{\Pi\Pi} > 0$ as advertised. We have

$$\varpi^1 = \hat{\mu}\left(\frac{\lambda}{2\Pi} - 1\right).$$

An alternative way to solve problem (8.38), (8.39) is via the Legendre transform which we now briefly describe. The Legendre transform is a simultaneous change of the independent and dependent variables of the form

$$(\chi, \Pi) \to (\chi, p), \qquad J(\chi, \Pi) \to K(\chi, p),$$

where

$$p = J_\Pi(\chi, \Pi), \quad K(\chi, p) = \Pi J_\Pi(\chi, \Pi) - J(\chi, \Pi). \tag{8.42}$$

The inverse Legendre transform is reciprocal in nature:

$$\Pi = K_p(\chi, p), \quad J(\chi, \Pi) = pK_p(\chi, p) - K(\chi, p).$$

A simple application of the chain rule yields

$$\partial_\chi = \partial_\chi + K_{\chi p}\partial_\Pi, \quad \partial_p = K_{pp}\partial_\Pi,$$

$$\partial_\chi = \partial_\chi - \frac{K_{\chi p}}{K_{pp}}\partial_p, \quad \partial_\Pi = \frac{1}{K_{pp}}\partial_p,$$

so that

$$J_\chi(\chi, \Pi) = -K_\chi(\chi, p), \quad J_{\Pi\Pi}(\chi, \Pi) = \frac{1}{K_{pp}(\chi, p)}.$$

Substituting these formulas in equation (8.38) we obtain the following Black-Scholes type equation

$$K_\chi - \frac{1}{2}\hat{\mu}^2 p^2 K_{pp}(\chi, p) = 0. \tag{8.43}$$

We find the corresponding initial data by explicitly performing transformations (8.42):

$$p = 2\Pi - \lambda, \quad K(0, p) = \Pi^2 = \frac{1}{4}(p + \lambda)^2. \tag{8.44}$$

Thus, the Legendre transform completely linearizes the original nonlinear problem. We leave it to the reader as a very useful exercise to solve the linearized problem (8.43), (8.44) and to use the inverse Legendre transform to recover formula (8.41).

In order to determine λ we have to satisfy constraint (8.37), or equivalently, to find λ such that the solution of the problem

$$I_\chi^{(1)} - \frac{1}{2}\hat{\mu}^2(\frac{\lambda}{2} - \Pi)^2 I_{\Pi\Pi}^{(1)} - \hat{\mu}^2(\frac{\lambda}{2} - \Pi)I_\Pi^{(1)} = 0,$$

$$I^{(1)}(0, \Pi) = \Pi,$$

satisfies the condition

$$I^{(1)}(\hat{T}, \Pi_0) = \pi.$$

(Recall that $\hat{T} = \sigma^2 T$.) It is easy to solve the above problem by the same token as before. Its solution has the form

$$I^{(1)}(\chi, \Pi) = e^{-\hat{\mu}^2\chi}\left(\Pi - \frac{\lambda}{2}\right) + \frac{\lambda}{2}.$$

The constraint is satisfied provided that

$$\lambda = 2\frac{e^{\hat{\mu}^2 \hat{T}} \pi - \Pi_0}{e^{\hat{\mu}^2 \hat{T}} - 1} = 2\left(\Pi_0 + \frac{e^{\hat{\mu}^2 \hat{T}} P}{e^{\hat{\mu}^2 \hat{T}} - 1}\right) = 2(\Pi_0 + Q),$$

where

$$P = \pi - \Pi_0, \qquad Q = \frac{e^{\hat{\mu}^2 \hat{T}} P}{e^{\hat{\mu}^2 \hat{T}} - 1}.$$

We notice that P is the expected profit.

In order to compute the corresponding variance we solve the problem for the second moment

$$I_\chi^{(2)} - \frac{1}{2}\hat{\mu}^2(\frac{\lambda}{2} - \Pi)^2 I_{\Pi\Pi}^{(2)} - \hat{\mu}^2(\frac{\lambda}{2} - \Pi)I_\Pi^{(2)} = 0,$$

$$I^{(2)}(0, \Pi) = \Pi^2.$$

Its solution has the form

$$I^{(2)}(\chi, \Pi) = e^{-\hat{\mu}^2 \chi}\left(\Pi^2 - \frac{\lambda^2}{4}\right) + \frac{\lambda^2}{4}.$$

Accordingly, the variance has the form

$$\begin{aligned}
V &= I^{(2)}(\hat{T}, \Pi_0) - \left[I^{(1)}(\hat{T}, \Pi_0)\right]^2 \\
&= e^{-\hat{\mu}^2 \hat{T}}\left(\Pi_0^2 - \frac{\lambda^2}{4}\right) + \frac{\lambda^2}{4} - \pi^2 \\
&= \frac{P^2}{e^{\hat{\mu}^2 \hat{T}} - 1}.
\end{aligned}$$

The dynamic Sharpe ratio is

$$SR_{dyn} = \sqrt{e^{\hat{\mu}^2 \hat{T}} - 1} = \sqrt{e^{\mu^2 T/\sigma^2} - 1}.$$

Since we can express the fraction of the wealth which has to be invested in stock in terms of the wealth itself, we can easily describe the dynamics of the optimized portfolio. Indeed, the governing SDE for Π_t can be written as

$$\begin{aligned}
d\Pi_t &= \hat{\mu}\left(\frac{\lambda}{2} - \Pi_t\right)(\mu dt + \sigma dW_t) \\
&= \hat{\mu}(\Pi_0 + Q - \Pi_t)(\mu dt + \sigma dW_t),
\end{aligned}$$

Accordingly, $\Pi_0 + Q - \Pi_t$ is a lognormal variable and we can solve the above equation to get

$$\Pi_t = \Pi_0 + Q - Q e^{-\left(3\mu^2 t/2\sigma^2 + \mu W_t/\sigma\right)}.$$

Thus, Π_t is bounded above by $\Pi_0 + Q$ but, unfortunately, it is unbounded below. The p.d.f. for Π_T has the shifted lognormal form

$$\rho(X) = \frac{\exp\left\{ -\frac{1}{2\hat{\mu}^2 \hat{T}} \left[\frac{3\hat{\mu}^2 \hat{T}}{2} + \ln\left(\frac{\Pi_0 + Q - X}{Q} \right) \right]^2 \right\}}{\hat{\mu}\sqrt{2\pi \hat{T}}\,(\Pi_0 + Q - X)}.$$

It is easy now to find the optimal amounts which need to be invested in domestic and foreign bonds:

$$\Pi_t^0 = (1 + \hat{\mu})\,\Pi_t - \hat{\mu}\,(\Pi_0 + Q),$$

$$\Pi_t^1 = \hat{\mu}\,(\Pi_0 + Q - \Pi_t).$$

For the benefit of the reader who prefers to describe the investment strategy in terms of Υ rather than ϖ (as is customary in the Black-Scholes framework), we give the corresponding expression for Υ^1. Since

$$\Upsilon_t^1 = \frac{\hat{\mu}\,(\Pi_0 + Q - \Pi_t)}{Y_t^1},$$

we can write the self-financing condition in the form

$$d\Pi_t = \frac{\hat{\mu}\,(\Pi_0 + Q - \Pi_t)}{Y_t^1} dY_t^1.$$

This is a first-order separable ODE which can be solved explicitly (for now t is treated as a parameter):

$$\frac{d\Pi_t}{(\Pi_0 + Q - \Pi_t)} = \frac{\hat{\mu}\,dY_t^1}{Y_t^1}.$$

The corresponding solution is

$$\Pi_0 + Q - \Pi_t = \kappa_t \left(\frac{Y_0^1}{Y_t^1} \right)^{\hat{\mu}},$$

where κ_t is an arbitrary function of time, so that

$$\Upsilon_t^1 = \frac{\hat{\mu}\kappa_t}{Y_0^1} \left(\frac{Y_0^1}{Y_t^1}\right)^{\hat{\mu}+1}.$$

In order to determine the form of the yet unknown function κ_t we use the explicit expressions for the lognormal variables $\Pi_0 + Q - \Pi_t$ and Y_t^1. We have

$$
\begin{aligned}
\kappa_t &= (\Pi_0 + Q - \Pi_t)\left(\frac{Y_0^1}{Y_t^1}\right)^{\hat{\mu}} \\
&= Q\exp\left[-\left(\frac{3\mu^2 t}{2\sigma^2} + \frac{\mu W_t}{\sigma}\right)\right]\exp\left[\left(\frac{\mu^2}{\sigma^2} - \frac{\mu}{2}\right)t + \frac{\mu W_t}{\sigma}\right] \\
&= Q\exp\left[-\frac{1}{2}\left(\frac{\mu^2}{\sigma^2} + \mu\right)t\right].
\end{aligned}
$$

Finally, we obtain

$$\Upsilon_t^1 = \frac{\hat{\mu}Q}{Y_0^1}\exp\left[-\frac{1}{2}\left(\frac{\mu^2}{\sigma^2} + \mu\right)t\right]\left(\frac{Y_0^1}{Y_t^1}\right)^{\hat{\mu}+1}.$$

It is interesting to compare the dynamic asset allocation strategy with the static buy-and-hold asset allocation strategy. Assuming that $\Upsilon_t^0 = v^0$ and $\Upsilon_t^1 = v^1$ we obtain

$$\Pi_t = v^0 + v^1 Y_t^1,$$

$$\varpi_t^1 = \frac{v^1 Y_t^1}{v^0 + v^1 Y_t^1} = \frac{\Pi_t - v^0}{\Pi_t} = 1 - \frac{v^0}{\Pi_t}.$$

The terminal wealth has the shifted lognormal p.d.f.,

$$\Pi_T = v^0 + (\Pi_0 - v^0)e^{(\hat{\mu}-1/2)\hat{T}+W_{\hat{T}}}.$$

The expected wealth, expected profit and its variance have the form

$$\pi = v^0 + (\Pi_0 - v^0)e^{\hat{\mu}\hat{T}},$$

$$P = \pi - \Pi_0 = (\Pi_0 - v^0)\left(e^{\hat{\mu}\hat{T}} - 1\right),$$

$$\mathbb{V} = (\Pi_0 - v^0)^2 e^{2\hat{\mu}\hat{T}} \left(e^{\hat{T}} - 1\right).$$

In sharp contrast to the dynamic allocation strategy, the static allocation strategy results in the distribution of wealth which has limited downside and unlimited upside. At the same time, the static Sharpe ratio is

$$\mathsf{SR}_{stat} = \frac{\left|1 - e^{-\hat{\mu}\hat{T}}\right|}{\sqrt{e^{\hat{T}} - 1}}.$$

We leave it to the reader to verify that the static Sharpe ratio is smaller than the corresponding dynamic one.

The p.d.f.'s corresponding to the dynamic and static asset allocation strategies described in this section are shown in Figure 8.5.

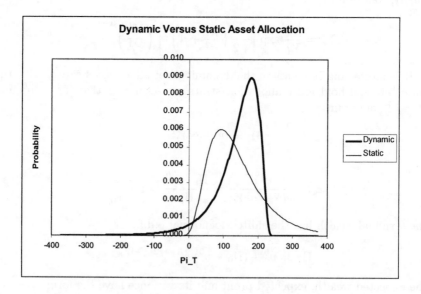

Figure 8.5: The p.d.f.'s corresponding to the dynamic and static asset allocation strategies. The relevant parameters are $\mu = 0.05$, $\sigma = 0.2$, $T = 5$, $\Pi_0 = 100$, $\pi = 140$.

8.6 The two-country homogeneous problem, II

In this section we show how to price European call options in two-country markets without deterministic investments. We use the same notation as before and write the system of SDEs describing the evolution of dollar prices of dollar and euro denominated bonds in the form

$$\frac{dZ_t^0}{Z_t^0} = b^0 dt + \boldsymbol{\sigma}^0 \cdot d\mathbf{W}_t = b^0 dt + \sigma^{0,0} dW_t^0,$$

$$\frac{dZ_t^1}{Z_t^1} = b^1 dt + \boldsymbol{\sigma}^1 \cdot d\mathbf{W}_t = b^1 dt + \sigma^{1,0} dW_t^0 + \sigma^{1,1} dW_t^1,$$

where b^0, b^1 and $\boldsymbol{\sigma}^0 = \left(\sigma^{0,0}, 0\right)$, $\boldsymbol{\sigma}^1 = \left(\sigma^{1,0}, \sigma^{1,1}\right)$ are the scalar drifts and two-component vector volatilities, while $\mathbf{W}_t = \left(W_t^0, W_t^1\right)$ is the standard two-component Wiener process. We assume that time-dependent volatilities are chosen in such a way that pull-to-par property is satisfied.

As before, we use homogeneity in order to derive the governing equation for the price of a contingent claim. This equation has the form

$$V_t + \frac{1}{2}\sigma^{\mu} \cdot \sigma^{\nu} Z^{\mu} Z^{\nu} V_{Z^{\mu}Z^{\nu}} = 0.$$

Explicitly we can write the above equation as follows:

$$V_t + \frac{1}{2}\left(\sigma^0 Z^0\right)^2 V_{Z^0 Z^0} + \rho\sigma^0\sigma^1 Z^0 Z^1 V_{Z^0 Z^1} + \frac{1}{2}\left(\sigma^1 Z^1\right)^2 V_{Z^1 Z^1} = 0, \quad (8.45)$$

where

$$\sigma^0 = \sigma^{0,0}, \quad \sigma^1 = \sqrt{\left(\sigma^{1,0}\right)^2 + \left(\sigma^{1,1}\right)^2},$$

are the scalar volatilities of bond prices, and

$$\rho = \frac{\sigma^{1,0}}{\sqrt{\left(\sigma^{1,0}\right)^2 + \left(\sigma^{1,1}\right)^2}},$$

is the corresponding correlation. This equation is supplied with the final condition

$$V\left(T, Z^0, Z^1\right) = v\left(Z^0, Z^1\right).$$

Identities (8.3) yield

$$\left(Z^0\right)^2 V_{Z^0 Z^0} = \left(Z^1\right)^2 V_{Z^1 Z^1} = -Z^0 Z^1 V_{Z^0 Z^1}.$$

Accordingly, equation (8.45) can be rewritten as

$$V_t + \frac{1}{2}\Sigma^2 \left(Z^1\right)^2 V_{Z^1 Z^1} = 0, \tag{8.46}$$

where

$$\Sigma^2 = \left|\sigma^0 - \sigma^1\right|^2 = \left(\sigma^{0,0} - \sigma^{1,0}\right)^2 + \left(\sigma^{1,1}\right)^2 = \left(\sigma^0\right)^2 - 2\rho\sigma^0\sigma^1 + \left(\sigma^1\right)^2.$$

We can establish a more general result. Let $\boldsymbol{\delta} = \left(\delta^0, \delta^1\right)$ be an arbitrary vector. Then

$$
\begin{aligned}
&\left(\sigma^\mu - \boldsymbol{\delta}\right) \cdot \left(\sigma^\nu - \boldsymbol{\delta}\right) Z^\mu Z^\nu \partial_{Z^\mu} \partial_{Z^\nu} V \\
=\ & \sigma^\mu \cdot \sigma^\nu Z^\mu Z^\nu \partial_{Z^\mu} \partial_{Z^\nu} V - \boldsymbol{\delta} \cdot \sigma^\nu Z^\mu Z^\nu \partial_{Z^\mu} \partial_{Z^\nu} V \\
& - \sigma^\mu \cdot \boldsymbol{\delta} Z^\mu Z^\nu \partial_{Z^\mu} \partial_{Z^\nu} V + \boldsymbol{\delta} \cdot \boldsymbol{\delta} Z^\mu Z^\nu \partial_{Z^\mu} \partial_{Z^\nu} V \\
=\ & \sigma^\mu \cdot \sigma^\nu Z^\mu Z^\nu \partial_{Z^\mu} \partial_{Z^\nu} V,
\end{aligned}
$$

since all the terms on the right except for the first one vanish due to identities (8.3). For instance,

$$\boldsymbol{\delta} \cdot \sigma^\nu Z^\mu Z^\nu \partial_{Z^\mu} \partial_{Z^\nu} V = \boldsymbol{\delta} \cdot \sigma^\nu Z^\mu \left(\left(Z^\nu \partial_{Z^\nu}\right) \partial_{Z^\mu} V\right) = 0.$$

Thus, the pricing equation is invariant with respect to shifts $\sigma^\mu \to \sigma^\mu - \boldsymbol{\delta}$ and can be written as

$$V_t + \frac{1}{2}\left(\sigma^\mu - \boldsymbol{\delta}\right) \cdot \left(\sigma^\nu - \boldsymbol{\delta}\right) Z^\mu Z^\nu V_{Z^\mu Z^\nu} = 0. \tag{8.47}$$

By choosing $\boldsymbol{\delta} = \sigma^0$ we can write it in the form (8.46). Equation (8.47) shows that volatility is a relative concept and depends on the units we choose to measure a particular quantity, or, in other words, which quantity is used as a numeraire. To illustrate this point, we return back to the market with deterministic bond prices. If we use the domestic bond as a numeraire than its price is deterministic (it is equal to one) while the price of the foreign bond is stochastic. However, if we use the foreign bond as a numeraire, then its price becomes deterministic while the price of the domestic bond becomes stochastic.

As before, we can represent $V\left(t, Z^0, Z^1\right)$ in the form (8.8). Substituting this expression into equation (8.46) we get after some algebra the following equation for Φ:

$$\Phi_t + \frac{1}{2}\Sigma^2\xi^2\Phi_{\xi\xi} = 0.$$

The time change

$$T - t \to \chi = \int_t^T \left(\left(\sigma_{t'}^0\right)^2 - 2\rho_{t'}\sigma_{t'}^0\sigma_{t'}^1 + \left(\sigma_{t'}^1\right)^2\right) dt',$$

transforms this equation into the standard equation (8.9). Thus, in order to price options in two-country markets without deterministic investments we can use the standard formulas, provided that we interpret the corresponding variables appropriately.

8.7 The multi-country homogeneous problem

8.7.1 Introduction

In $(N + 1)$-country markets with deterministic prices of bonds in their respective currencies domestic investors with investment horizon T can invest into one deterministic instrument (domestic bond maturing at time T) and N stochastic instruments (foreign bonds maturing at time T). Let $Z^0, Z^1, ..., Z^N$ be dollar prices of bonds with face values $K^0, K^1, ..., K^N$ maturing at time T,

$$Z_t^\nu = e^{-r^\nu(T-t)}K^\nu S_t^{0\nu}.$$

We know that their dynamics is governed by the system of SDEs of the form

$$\frac{dZ^\nu}{Z^\nu} = r^0 dt + \boldsymbol{\sigma}^{0\nu} \cdot \left(\boldsymbol{\lambda}^0 dt + d\mathbf{W}_t\right),$$

where $\mathbf{W}_t$ is the N-component Wiener process which is the stochastic engine for the market in question, $\boldsymbol{\lambda}^\nu$ is the market price of risk in the νth country, and $\boldsymbol{\sigma}^{0\nu} = \boldsymbol{\lambda}^\nu - \boldsymbol{\lambda}^0$ is the volatility of the νth FXR. It is clear that $\boldsymbol{\sigma}^{00} = 0$, so that the dynamics of Z^0 is deterministic.

In this section we show how to derive and solve the pricing equation in the multi-country setting.

8.7.2   The homogeneous pricing problem

The derivation of the $(N + 1)$-country homogeneous Black-Scholes equation is the same as in the two-country case. This equation is the N-dimensional backward parabolic equation for the price $V\left(t, Z^0, ..., Z^N\right)$ of the form

$$V_t + \frac{1}{2} \sum_{m,n} a^{mn} Z^m Z^n V_{Z^m Z^n} = 0. \tag{8.48}$$

Here

$$a^{mn} = \sigma^{0m} \cdot \sigma^{0n},$$

are the elements of the diffusion matrix $\mathcal{A} = (a^{mn})$. Below we assume that this matrix is nondegenerate, i.e., that $\det \mathcal{A} \neq 0$. This equation is supplied with the final condition

$$V\left(T, Z^0, Z^1, ..., Z^N\right) = v\left(Z^0, Z^1, ..., Z^N\right),$$

which determines the nature of the derivative security we are pricing. We emphasize that the dependence on Z^0 is parametric in nature since it enters only into the final condition. The corresponding replicating strategy is described by the vector

$$\Upsilon_t = \nabla_{\mathbf{Z}_t} V\left(t, \mathbf{Z}_t\right) = (V_{Z^0}, V_{Z^1}, ..., V_{Z^N}),$$

where ∇ denotes the gradient.

We can also write equation (8.48) in terms of the time to maturity $\tau = T - t$:

$$V_\tau - \frac{1}{2} \sum_{m,n} a^{mn} Z^m Z^n V_{Z^m Z^n} = 0.$$

It is not possible to introduce unambiguously the nondimensional time to maturity. Further, we use homogeneity to nondimensionalize the problem:

$$V\left(\tau, Z^0, ..., Z^N\right) = Z^0 \, \Phi\left(\tau, \xi^1, ..., \xi^N\right), \tag{8.49}$$

where $\xi^n = Z^n / Z^0$. The corresponding pricing problem has the form

$$\Phi_\tau - \frac{1}{2} \sum_{m,n} a^{mn} \xi^m \xi^n \Phi_{\xi^m \xi^n} = 0, \tag{8.50}$$

$$\Phi\left(0,\xi^1,...,\xi^N\right) = \phi\left(\xi^1,...,\xi^N\right) = v\left(1,\xi^1,...,\xi^N\right).$$

The system of SDE's corresponding to PDE (8.50) has the form

$$\frac{d\xi_t^n}{\xi_t^n} = \sigma^{0n}\cdot d\mathbf{W}_t = \sum_{k=1}^N \sigma^{nk}dW_t^k. \tag{8.51}$$

We emphasize that any Z^n can be used for nondimensionalizing the problem. We leave it to the reader as a very useful exercise to derive the pricing problem arising when Z^0 is replaced by Z^1 (say) in equation (8.49).

8.7.3 Reductions

In order to reduce the pricing equation (8.50) to the simplest possible form (which happens to be the multi-dimensional heat equation) we transform both independent and dependent variables. First, we introduce the logarithmic variables $X^n = \ln\xi^n$ and rewrite the pricing problem as follows

$$\Phi_\tau - \frac{1}{2}\sum_{m,n} a^{mn}\Phi_{X^m X^n} + \frac{1}{2}\sum_m a^{mm}\Phi_{X^m} = 0,$$

$$\Phi\left(0,X^1,...,X^N\right) = \phi\left(X^1,...,X^N\right) = \phi\left(e^{X^1},...,e^{X^N}\right),$$

where $\Phi = \Phi\left(\tau,X^1,...,X^N\right)$. Second, we represent the dependent variable as

$$U = e^{-\alpha\tau-\beta\cdot\mathbf{X}}\Phi,$$

where α is a scalar and β is a vector which are to be determined, and get

$$U_\tau - \frac{1}{2}\sum_{m,n} a^{mn}U_{X^m X^n} + \sum_m \left(\frac{1}{2}a^{mm} - \sum_n a^{mn}\beta^n\right)U_{X^m}$$

$$+ \quad \left(\alpha - \frac{1}{2}\sum_{m,n} a^{mn}\beta^m\beta^n + \frac{1}{2}\sum_m a^{mm}\beta^m\right)U = 0.$$

Thus, by choosing

$$\beta = -A^{-1}\gamma, \qquad \alpha = -\frac{1}{2}A^{-1}\gamma\cdot\gamma,$$

where

$$\gamma = -\frac{1}{2} diag\,(\mathcal{A})$$

we reduce equation (8.50) to the desired form of the heat equation (with anisotropic heat conductivity), namely,

$$U_\tau - \frac{1}{2} \sum_{m,n} a^{mn} U_{X^m X^n} = 0. \qquad (8.52)$$

The corresponding initial condition is

$$U\,(0, \mathbf{X}) = u\,(\mathbf{X}) = e^{-\beta \cdot \mathbf{X}} \phi\,(\mathbf{X}).$$

The SDE corresponding to PDE (8.52) is simply

$$d\mathbf{X}_t = \boldsymbol{\sigma} \cdot d\mathbf{W}_t,$$

where $\boldsymbol{\sigma} = (\boldsymbol{\sigma}^\nu)$ is the matrix of foreign bond volatilities.

8.7.4   Probabilistic pricing and hedging

We know that the p.d.f. corresponding to equation (8.51) has the form

$$p\,(\tau, \mathbf{X}, \mathbf{X}') = \frac{e^{-\mathcal{A}^{-1}(\mathbf{X}' - \mathbf{X}) \cdot (\mathbf{X}' - \mathbf{X})/2\tau}}{\sqrt{(2\pi\tau)^N \det \mathcal{A}}}.$$

Accordingly, we can represent $\Phi\,(\tau, \mathbf{X})$ as follows

$$
\begin{aligned}
&\Upsilon\,(\tau, \mathbf{X}) \\
&= \int \cdots \int \frac{e^{-\mathcal{A}^{-1}(\mathbf{X}' - \mathbf{X}) \cdot (\mathbf{X}' - \mathbf{X})/2\tau}}{\sqrt{(2\pi\tau)^N \det \mathcal{A}}} \upsilon\,(\mathbf{X}')\, d\mathbf{X}' \\
&= e^{-\alpha\tau - \beta \cdot \mathbf{X}} \int \cdots \int \frac{e^{-\mathcal{A}^{-1}(\mathbf{X}' - \mathbf{X} - \tau\gamma) \cdot (\mathbf{X}' - \mathbf{X} - \tau\gamma)/2\tau}}{\sqrt{(2\pi\tau)^N \det \mathcal{A}}} \phi\,(\mathbf{X}')\, d\mathbf{X}' \\
&= e^{-\alpha\tau - \beta \cdot \mathbf{X}} \int \cdots \int \frac{e^{-\mathcal{A}^{-1}\mathbf{X}'' \cdot \mathbf{X}''/2\tau}}{\sqrt{(2\pi\tau)^N \det \mathcal{A}}} \phi\,(\mathbf{X} + \tau\gamma + \mathbf{X}'')\, d\mathbf{X}''.
\end{aligned}
$$

Since the matrix $\mathcal{A}$ is symmetric and positive definite we can write it as

$$\mathcal{A} = \mathcal{O}^*\mathcal{D}\mathcal{O},$$

where $\mathcal{O}$ and $\mathcal{D}$ are orthogonal and diagonal matrices, respectively, and $\mathcal{O}^*$ is the transpose of $\mathcal{O}$. Introducing the new independent variable $\mathbf{Y}$ such that

$$\mathbf{Y} = \left(\sqrt{\tau\mathcal{D}}\right)^{-1}\mathcal{O}\mathbf{X}'',$$

we represent $\Upsilon(\tau, \mathbf{X})$ in the form

$$\Upsilon(\tau, \mathbf{X}) = e^{-\alpha\tau - \beta\cdot\mathbf{X}} \int \cdots \int \frac{e^{-\frac{1}{2}\mathbf{Y}\cdot\mathbf{Y}}}{(2\pi)^{N/2}} \phi\left(\mathbf{X} + \tau\gamma + \sqrt{\tau\mathcal{D}}\mathcal{O}^*\mathbf{Y}\right) d\mathbf{Y}.$$

Here we use the facts that

$$\mathcal{A}^{-1}\mathbf{X}'' \cdot \mathbf{X}'' = \tau\mathbf{Y}\cdot\mathbf{Y},$$

$$d\mathbf{X}'' = \sqrt{\tau^N \det \mathcal{A}}\, d\mathbf{Y}.$$

Returning back to the original variables we obtain

$$\Phi(\tau, \xi) = \int \cdots \int \frac{e^{-\mathcal{A}^{-1}\left(\ln(\xi'/\xi) - \tau\gamma\right)\cdot\left(\ln(\xi'/\xi) - \tau\gamma\right)/2\tau}}{\sqrt{(2\pi\tau)^N \det \mathcal{A}}}\phi(\xi')\frac{d\xi'}{\xi'}. \qquad (8.53)$$

Thus, all we need to do in order to price a multi-currency European option is to compute an appropriate N-dimensional integral (8.53). Unfortunately, in most cases its explicit analytical evaluation is difficult or impossible. For moderate values of $N \sim 1 - 10$ numerical evaluation of the corresponding integrals is not difficult. However, for higher values of N, it is less straightforward. The standard Monte Carlo method and its modifications based on N-dimensional quasi-random sequences are conventional tools used for handling the integrals in question.

8.8 Some representative multi-factor options

8.8.1 Introduction

By their very nature, multi-factor options are numerous and hard to classify. In this section we demonstrate how to price a few representative options which are of particular practical interest.

8.8.2   Outperformance options

We analyze one of the simplest and most popular multi-factor options, namely, the so-called outperformance option. In its simplest form this option gives the buyer the right to exchange K^m units of the mth currency for K^n units of the nth currency at maturity T. The payoff of this option has the form

$$\text{payoff} = (Z^n - Z^m)_+ \,,$$

or, equivalently,

$$\text{payoff} = (\xi^n - \xi^m)_+ \,.$$

It is clear that in order to price this option we can restrict ourselves to the submarket consisting of just three countries - the domestic country, and the mth and n^{th} foreign countries. The corresponding diffusion matrix has the form

$$\mathcal{A} = \begin{pmatrix} \left(\sigma^{0m}\right)^2 & \rho^{0mn}\sigma^{0m}\sigma^{0n} \\ \rho^{0mn}\sigma^{0m}\sigma^{0n} & \left(\sigma^{0n}\right)^2 \end{pmatrix},$$

where

$$\sigma^{0m} = \left|\boldsymbol{\sigma}^{0m}\right|, \qquad \sigma^{0n} = \left|\boldsymbol{\sigma}^{0n}\right|, \qquad \rho^{0mn} = \boldsymbol{\sigma}^{0m} \cdot \boldsymbol{\sigma}^{0n} / \sigma^{0m}\sigma^{0n}.$$

Accordingly, the two-dimensional pricing problem can be written as

$$\Phi_\tau^{(OP)} - \tfrac{1}{2}\left(\sigma^{0m}\right)^2 (\xi^m)^2 \, \Phi_{\xi^m\xi^m}^{(OP)} - \rho^{0mn}\sigma^{0m}\sigma^{0n}\xi^m\xi^n\Phi_{\xi^m\xi^n}^{(OP)}$$
$$- \tfrac{1}{2}\left(\sigma^{0n}\right)^2 (\xi^n)^2 \, \Phi_{\xi^n\xi^n}^{(OP)} = 0,$$

$$\Phi^{(OP)}\left(0, \xi^m, \xi^n\right) = (\xi^n - \xi^m)_+ \,.$$

Due to the fact that both the pricing equation and the initial data are homogeneous of degree one with respect to scaling transformations, we can reduce the two-dimensional pricing problem to the one-dimensional form by representing $\Phi^{(OP)}$ as

$$\Phi^{(OP)}\left(\tau, \xi^m, \xi^n\right) = \xi^m\Xi^{(OP)}\left(\tau, \xi^{mn}\right),$$

where

$$\xi^{mn} = Z^n / Z^m = \xi^n / \xi^m.$$

Straightforward calculation yields the pricing equation for $\Xi^{(OP)}\left(\tau, \xi^{mn}\right)$:

$$\Xi_{\tau}^{(OP)} - \frac{1}{2}\left(\sigma^{mn}\right)^2\left(\xi^{mn}\right)^2 \Xi_{\xi^{mn}\xi^{mn}}^{(OP)} = 0,$$

where

$$\sigma^{mn} = \sqrt{\left(\sigma^{0m}\right)^2 - 2\rho^{0mn}\sigma^{0m}\sigma^{0n} + \left(\sigma^{0n}\right)^2},$$

is the volatility of the FXR ξ^{mn}. The corresponding initial condition is

$$\Xi^{(OP)}\left(0, \xi^{mn}\right) = \left(\xi^{mn} - 1\right)_+ .$$

Thus, for dollar investors the value of the outperformance option is

$$\Phi^{(OP)}\left(\tau, \xi^m, \xi^n\right) = \xi^m \Phi^{(C)}\left(\chi^{mn}, \xi^{mn}\right), \tag{8.54}$$

where

$$\chi^{mn} = \left(\sigma^{mn}\right)^2 \tau,$$

i.e., the mth currency value of the standard call option allowing the mth country investors to buy K^n units of the nth currency for K^m units of the mth currency, which is converted into dollars at the spot FXR. We leave it to the reader to verify that the option value given by integral (8.53) is the same as (8.54). The price of a typical outperformance option is shown in Figure 8.6.

We emphasize that the above reduction is possible only due to the fact that the terminal payoff is a homogeneous function of its arguments. For the more general outperformance options with the payoff of the form

$$\text{payoff} = \left(Z^n - Z^m - Z^0\right)_+,$$

or, equivalently,

$$\text{payoff} = \left(\xi^n - \xi^m - 1\right)_+,$$

which gives the buyer the right to exchange K^n units of the nth currency for K^m units of the mth currency and K^0 dollars, the pricing problem cannot be reduced to the one-factor problem. The simplest solution of the pricing problem is given by integral (8.53).

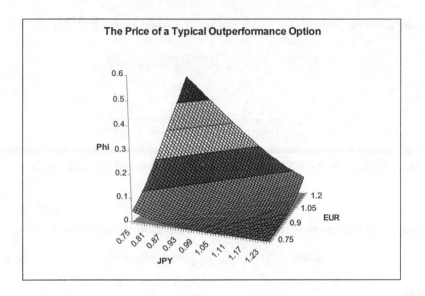

Figure 8.6: The price $\Phi\left(\tau, \xi^{01}, \xi^{02}\right)$ of a typical outperformance option as a function of ξ^{01}, ξ^{02}. The option gives the buyer the right to exchange 100 JPY for 1 Euro. Here ξ^{01}, ξ^{02} are the dollar prices of a 100 JPY and 1 Euro, respectively. The relevant parameters are $\tau = 1.00$, $\sigma^{01} = 0.15$, $\sigma^{02} = 0.10$, $\rho = 0.3$.

8.8.3   Options on the maximum or minimum of several FXRs

A typical call option on the maximum of several FXRs, also known as an option on the best of several FXRs, gives the buyer the right to receive the known amount of the foreign currency of his choice in exchange for the known amount of dollars. Let $K^v \geq 0$ be the corresponding amounts in appropriate currencies (some of them can be equal to zero). The option in question has the following payoff

$$\text{payoff} = \left(\max_{1 \leq n \leq N} \{Z_T^n\} - Z_T^0 \right)_+ .$$

The general expression for the price is given by integral (8.53). It is relatively difficult to evaluate this integral explicitly. However, by using the probabilistic interpretation of the call price given in Section 8.3, we can price the corresponding option directly. We consider the situation from the standpoint of the option seller. If the option is exercised, he has to deliver K^n units of the nth currency (for an appropriate n) and receives in exchange K^0 dollars. The probability of exercise conditional on the information available at time t is

$$\text{Prob}\left\{\max_{1\leq n\leq N}\{Z_T^n\} > Z_T^0 | Z_t^0, ..., Z_T^N\right\}$$

$$= 1 - \text{Prob}\left\{Z_T^1 < Z_T^0, ..., Z_T^N < Z_T^0 | Z_t^0, ..., Z_T^N\right\}$$

$$= 1 - \mathfrak{N}_N\left(-d_-\left(\chi^{01}, \frac{Z^1}{Z^0}\right), ..., -d_-\left(\chi^{0N}, \frac{Z^N}{Z^0}\right), \rho^{012}, \rho^{013}, ...\right).$$

Here, as always, $\mathfrak{N}_N$ is the standard N-dimensional cumulative normal distribution,

$$\mathfrak{N}_N\left(\mathbf{X}, \boldsymbol{\rho}\right) = \int_{-\infty}^{X^1} ... \int_{-\infty}^{X^N} \frac{e^{-\mathcal{A}^{-1}\mathbf{X}'\cdot\mathbf{X}'/2}}{\sqrt{(2\pi)^N \det \mathcal{A}}} d\mathbf{X}',$$

$$\mathcal{A} = \begin{pmatrix} 1 & \rho^{012} & \rho^{013} & ... \\ \rho^{012} & 1 & \rho^{023} & ... \\ \rho^{013} & \rho^{023} & 1 & ... \\ ... & ... & ... & ... \end{pmatrix}.$$

The probability that the nth currency is delivered is

$$\text{Prob}\left\{Z_T^0 < Z_T^n, ..., Z_T^N < Z_T^n | Z_t^0, ..., Z_T^N\right\}$$

$$= \mathfrak{N}_N\left(-d_-\left(\chi^{n0}, \frac{Z^0}{Z^n}\right), ..., -d_-\left(\chi^{nN}, \frac{Z^N}{Z^n}\right), \rho^{n12}, \rho^{n13}, ...\right)$$

$$= \mathfrak{N}_N\left(d_+\left(\chi^{n0}, \frac{Z^n}{Z^0}\right), ..., d_+\left(\chi^{nN}, \frac{Z^n}{Z^0}\right), \rho^{n12}, \rho^{n13}, ...\right).$$

Since payments of the mth and n^{th} currencies are mutually exclusive (apart from the case when $Z_T^m = Z_T^n$ which happens with probability zero), we can represent the price of a call option on the maximum as follows

$$V^{(MAX)}\left(\tau, Z^0, Z^1, ..., Z^N\right)$$

$$= \sum_{n=1}^{N} Z^n \mathfrak{N}_N\left(d_+\left(\chi^{n0}, \frac{Z^n}{Z^0}\right), ..., d_+\left(\chi^{nN}, \frac{Z^n}{Z^N}\right), \rho^{n12}, \rho^{n13}, ...\right)$$

$$- Z^0\left(1 - \mathfrak{N}_N\left(-d_-\left(\chi^{01}, \frac{Z^1}{Z^0}\right), ..., -d_-\left(\chi^{0N}, \frac{Z^N}{Z^0}\right), \rho^{012}, \rho^{013}, ...\right)\right).$$

Due to homogeneity, the corresponding Δ's are given by

$$\Delta_n = \frac{\partial C_{\max}}{\partial Z^n}$$

$$= \mathfrak{N}_N \left(d_+ \left(\chi^{n0}, \frac{Z^n}{Z^0} \right), ..., d_+ \left(\chi^{nN}, \frac{Z^n}{Z^N} \right), \rho^{n12}, \rho^{n13}, ... \right).$$

Needless to say that for $N = 1$ this formula reduces to the standard Black-Scholes form.

For $N = 2$ the corresponding expression assumes the form

$$V^{(MAX)} \left(\tau, Z^0, Z^1, Z^2 \right)$$

$$= Z^1 \mathfrak{N}_2 \left(d_+ \left(\chi^{10}, \frac{Z^1}{Z^0} \right), d_+ \left(\chi^{12}, \frac{Z^1}{Z^2} \right), \rho^{112} \right)$$

$$+ Z^2 \mathfrak{N}_2 \left(d_+ \left(\chi^{20}, \frac{Z^2}{Z^0} \right), d_+ \left(\chi^{21}, \frac{Z^2}{Z^1} \right), \rho^{212} \right)$$

$$- Z^0 \left(1 - \mathfrak{N}_2 \left(-d_- \left(\chi^{01}, \frac{Z^1}{Z^0} \right), -d_- \left(\chi^{02}, \frac{Z^2}{Z^0} \right), \rho^{012} \right) \right).$$

It is useful to note that when $K^0 = 0$, (so that $Z^0 = 0$) i.e., when the buyer receives foreign currency of his choice without paying anything in return, so that there is no true optionality in the problem, the price $V^{(MAX)}$ can be expressed in terms of $V^{(OP)}$. Indeed, in this case the payoff can be written as

$$\text{payoff} = \max \left\{ Z_T^1, Z_T^2 \right\} = \left(Z_T^2 - Z_T^1 \right)_+ + Z_T^1.$$

Accordingly,

$$V^{(MAX)} \left(\tau, 0, Z^1, Z^2 \right) = V^{(OP)} \left(\tau, Z^1, Z^2 \right) + Z^1.$$

We leave it to the reader as a useful exercise to derive this relation directly by manipulating the pricing problem.

8.8.4 Basket options

Basket options are very popular multi-factor options. These options give the buyer the right to exchange K^0 dollars for a basket consisting of N different currencies, whose amounts are denoted by K^n. In principle, certain K^n can be negative, so that the buyer might need to deliver some of the currencies as part of the transaction. In this case we put $Z^n = |K^n| B^n$. The corresponding payoff is

$$\text{payoff} = \left(\sum_{n=1}^{N} \varpi_n Z_T^n - Z_T^0 \right)_+ ,$$

or, equivalently,

$$\text{payoff} = \left(\sum_{n=1}^{N} \varpi_n \xi_T^n - 1 \right)_+ .$$

Here $\varpi_n = \text{sign}(K^n)$. The general formula (8.53) can be used in order to value a basket option, but it is relatively inefficient, so that indirect methods for pricing baskets have to be developed. One interesting possibility is to introduce a new random variable

$$\varsigma_t = \sum_{n=1}^{N} \varpi_n \xi_t^n ,$$

and consider the basket option as a one-factor call option on ς_t with the corresponding payoff

$$\text{payoff} = (\varsigma_T - 1)_+ .$$

Needless to say that the standard call pricing formula is not applicable in this case because ς_t is not a driftless lognormal variable. However, the distribution of ς_T can be approximated by a lognormal distribution (or other suitable distribution), which opens the possibility for using the standard techniques described above. Let $p_{\varsigma_T}(x)$ be the exact distribution of ς_T conditional on information available at time t. Then the value of a basket option can be written in the form

$$\Phi^{(BSKT)}(\tau, \boldsymbol{\xi}) = \int_1^{\infty} (x - 1) p_{\varsigma_T}(x) \, dx.$$

Since a linear combination of lognormal variables is not lognormal, it is relatively difficult to give a precise quantitative description of the p.d.f. $p_{\varsigma_T}(x)$. However, it is not difficult to find its first three moments and choose a shifted lognormal p.d.f. having the same moments. By solving SDEs (8.51) we get

$$\xi_T^n = \exp \left\{ -\frac{(\sigma^{0n})^2 \tau}{2} + \sum_{k=1}^{N} \sigma^{0nk} \sqrt{\tau} \vartheta^k \right\} \xi_t^n ,$$

where ϑ^k are i.i.d. standard normal variables. In order to compute the relevant moments of ς_T we need to evaluate the following expectations:

$$\eta^n = \mathbb{E}\{\xi_T^n|\boldsymbol{\xi}_t\}, \ \eta^{mn} = \mathbb{E}\{\xi_T^m\xi_T^n|\boldsymbol{\xi}_t\}, \ \eta^{lmn} = \mathbb{E}\left\{\xi_T^l\xi_T^m\xi_T^n\Big|\boldsymbol{\xi}_t\right\}.$$

A straightforward algebra which is based on completing the squares (we leave it to the reader as a very instructive exercise) yields the following formulas:

$$\eta^n = \xi_t^n, \ \eta^{mn} = \Xi^{mn}\xi_t^m\xi_t^n, \ \eta^{lmn} = \Xi^{lm}\Xi^{mn}\Xi^{nl}\xi_t^l\xi_t^m\xi_t^n,$$

where

$$\Xi^{mn} = e^{\rho^{mn}\hat{\sigma}^m\hat{\sigma}^n\tau}.$$

By using these formulas we obtain the following expressions for the non-central moments of ς_T :

$$\mu_1 \equiv \mathbb{M}_1(\varsigma_T) = \sum_{n=1}^{N} \varpi_n\xi_t^n,$$

$$\mu_2 \equiv \mathbb{M}_2(\varsigma_T) = \sum_{m,n=1}^{N} \varpi_m\varpi_n\Xi^{mn}\xi_t^m\xi_t^n,$$

$$\mu_3 \equiv \mathbb{M}_3(\varsigma_T) = \sum_{l,m,n=1}^{N} \varpi_l\varpi_m\varpi_n\Xi^{lm}\Xi^{mn}\Xi^{nl}\xi_t^l\xi_t^m\xi_t^n.$$

We now construct an auxiliary shifted lognormal variable of the form

$$\varrho = Ae^{-\Sigma^2\tau/2+\Sigma\sqrt{\tau}\vartheta} + C,$$

where ϑ is the standard normal variable, while A, C, Σ are fixed parameters which are chosen in such a way that the first three moments of ϱ and ς_T coincide. The moments of ϱ are

$$\mathbb{M}_1(\varrho) = A + C,$$

$$\mathbb{M}_2(\varrho) = A^2B + 2AC + C^2,$$

$$\mathbb{M}_3\left(\varrho\right) = A^3 B^3 + A^2 BC + 3AC^2 + C^3,$$

where

$$B = e^{\Sigma^2 (T-t)}.$$

In order to find A, C, Σ we need to solve the system of nonlinear algebraic equations

$$\begin{cases} A + C = \mu_1 \\ A^2 B + 2AC + C^2 = \mu_2 \\ A^3 B^3 + A^2 BC + 3AC^2 + C^3 = \mu_3 \end{cases}.$$

We rewrite it in terms of central moments:

$$\begin{cases} A + C = \mu_1 \\ A^2 (B - 1) = \mu_2 - \mu_1^2 \\ A^3 (B - 1)^2 (B + 2) = \mu_3 - 3\mu_1\mu_2 + 2\mu_1^3 \end{cases}.$$

Simple manipulations yield

$$\gamma_3 \equiv (B - 1)(B + 2)^2 = \frac{\left(\mu_3 - 3\mu_1\mu_2 + 2\mu_1^3\right)^2}{\left(\mu_2 - \mu_1^2\right)^3},$$

$$A = \frac{\left(\mu_3 - 3\mu_1\mu_2 + 2\mu_1^3\right)}{\left(\mu_2 - \mu_1^2\right)(B - 1)(B + 2)},$$

$$C = \mu_1 - A.$$

Here γ_3 is the skewness of ϱ. Thus, the nontrivial part is to find B. The latter task can be accomplished by solving the corresponding cubic equation numerically.[3] It is clear that we need to take the root of this equation such that $B > 1$. Such root is unique. Once B (and hence $\Sigma = \sqrt{\ln B / \tau}$) is determined, A and C are found without a difficulty. Since some of the coefficients ϖ_n can be negative, the reader should not be surprised if A turns out to be negative. The "three-moment" approximation for the basket price is

$$\Phi^{(BSKT)}\left(\tau, \xi\right) = \begin{cases} (1 - C)\,\Phi^{(C)}\left(\Sigma^2 \tau, \frac{A}{1-C}\right), & A > 0, \quad C < 1, \\ A + C - 1, & A > 0, \quad C \geq 1, \\ 0, & A < 0, \quad C < 1, \\ (C - 1)\,\Phi^{(P)}\left(\Sigma^2 \tau, \frac{A}{C-1}\right), & A < 0, \quad C \geq 1. \end{cases} \quad (8.55)$$

---

[3] The reader interested in mathematical details can use Cardano's formula for this purpose.

8.8.5   Index options

In contrast to basket options whose payoff depends on the arithmetic average of several currencies, the payoff of index options depends on their geometric average:

$$\text{payoff} = \left(\frac{Z_T^0}{\prod_{n=1}^{N} (Z_T^n)^{w_n}} - 1 \right)_+ ,$$

or, equivalently,

$$\text{payoff} = \left(\prod_{n=1}^{N} (\xi_T^n)^{-w_n} - 1 \right)_+ .$$

Here w_n are weights assigned to different currencies. These weights are positive and sum up to one,

$$0 < w_n < 1, \qquad \sum_{n=1}^{N} w_n = 1.$$

A naive way of pricing a European index option is via integral (8.53). However, a much better way is based on reducing such an option to a one-factor option of the auxiliary random variable

$$\varsigma_T = \prod_{n=1}^{N} (\xi_T^n)^{-w_n} .$$

The corresponding payoff is

$$\text{payoff} = (\varsigma_T - 1)_+ .$$

In contrast to the case of basket options, the variable ς_T is in fact lognormal which allows us to use the standard Black-Scholes valuation formula (after the volatility of ς_T is found) without any difficulty. Equations (8.51) yield

$$\xi_T^n = \exp \left\{ -\frac{\left(\sigma^{0n}\right)^2 \tau}{2} + \sum_{k=1}^{N} \sigma^{0nk} \sqrt{\tau} \vartheta^k \right\} \xi_t^n ,$$

$$\varsigma_T = \exp\left\{ \frac{\left(\sum_{n=1}^{N} w_n \left(\sigma^{0n}\right)^2\right)\tau}{2} - \sum_{k=1}^{N}\left(\sum_{n=1}^{N} w_n \sigma^{0nk}\sqrt{\tau}\right)\vartheta^k \right\}\varsigma_t$$

$$= \exp\left\{ \frac{\left(\tilde{\Sigma}^2 + \Sigma^2\right)\tau}{2} \right\}\exp\left\{ -\frac{\Sigma^2\tau}{2} + \Sigma\sqrt{\tau}\vartheta \right\}\varsigma_t,$$

where ϑ is the standard normal variable and

$$\Sigma = \sum_{m,n=1}^{N} w_m w_n \rho^{0mn}\sigma^{0m}\sigma^{0n}, \quad \tilde{\Sigma}^2 = \sum_{n=1}^{N} w_n \left(\sigma^{0n}\right)^2.$$

Accordingly,

$$\Phi^{(INDX)}(\tau,\boldsymbol{\xi}) = \Phi^{(C)}\left(\Sigma^2\tau, e^{(\tilde{\Sigma}^2+\Sigma^2)\tau/2}\varsigma\right). \tag{8.56}$$

We emphasize that, in contrast with formula (8.55), formula (8.56) is exact.

8.8.6 The multi-factor decomposition formula

It is shown in Section 8.4 how to decompose a European option with an arbitrary payoff in terms of standard calls and puts. In order to find an analogue of formula (8.34) valid for multi-factor options we need to choose a sufficiently rich set of "standard options" which are reasonably liquid in the market. Basket options form such a set. For the sake of brevity we study the two-factor case only.

Consider a two-factor option with the general payoff

$$\text{payoff} = v(S_1, S_2).$$

For convenience we assume that $v = 0$ for negative S_1, S_2. As a set of standard options we choose basket options with payoffs of the form

$$\text{payoff} = (pS_1 + S_2 - q)_+,$$

where p, q are given constants, $-\infty < p, q < \infty$. We write the decomposition formula in the form

$$v(S_1, S_2) = \int_{-\infty}^{\infty}\int_{-\infty}^{\infty} w_{qq}(p, q)(pS_1 + S_2 - q)_+ \, dp dq.$$

After integration by parts we obtain

$$v\left(S_1, S_2\right) = \int_{-\infty}^{\infty} \int_{-\infty}^{\infty} w\left(p, q\right) \delta\left(pS_1 + S_2 - q\right) dp dq.$$

Hence

$$v\left(S_1, S_2\right) = \mathcal{R}\left[w\left(p, q\right)\right]\left(S_1, S_2\right),$$

where $\mathcal{R}\left[w\right]$ is the Radon transform of w. The inversion formula for the Radon transform yields

$$w\left(p, q\right) = \frac{d}{dq}\left\{\frac{1}{2\pi} \int_{-\infty}^{\infty} \mathcal{H}_2\left[v\right]\left(S_1, q - pS_2\right) dS_1\right\},$$

where

$$\mathcal{H}_2\left[v\right]\left(S_1, y\right) = \frac{1}{2\pi} \int_{-\infty}^{\infty} \frac{v\left(S_1, S_2\right)}{S_2 - y} dS_2,$$

is the Hilbert transform of v with respect to the second argument.

We illustrate the usage of the decomposition formula by applying it to the standard basket option with the payoff of the form

$$\text{payoff} = \left(PS_1 + S_2 - Q\right)_+.$$

A simple calculation which is left to the reader as an exercise yields

$$w\left(p, q\right) = \delta\left(p - P\right) \delta\left(q - Q\right),$$

where $\delta\left(.\right)$ is the Dirac delta function, so that a given basket option is decomposed in terms of itself (as might be expected).

8.9   References and further reading

The original sources for this chapter are as follows: Bredeen and Litzenberger (1978), Carr and Madan (1998), Grabbe (1983), Green and Jarrow (1987), Harrison and Pliska (1981), Hoogland and Neumann (2000), Inglis and Pugachevsky (1998), Johnson (1987), Kocic (1997), Lipton (2000), Margrabe (1978), Merton (1971), Nachman (1988), Neuberger (1996), Reiner (1997), Stulz (1982). Further details can be found in the following books: Barenblatt (1996) (scaling and self-similarities), Dixit and Pindyck (1994) (investment), Fleming and Rishel (1975), Korn and Korn (2001) (stochastic optimal control), Kholodnyi and Press (1998) (symmetries), Merton (1990) (scaling, investment, etc.). The handbook by Abramowitz and Stegun (1972) contains a lot of useful formulas including a helpful table of Laplace transforms.

Chapter 9

European options, the classical approach

9.1 Introduction

For markets with deterministic bond prices we show how to reduce the homogeneous pricing equation to the standard Black-Scholes form. Because of the paramount importance of the Black-Scholes equation for option pricing, we present its conventional derivation. Specifically, we show how to construct the riskless portfolio consisting of a given contingent claim and dynamically changing amount of foreign currency and use this construction in order to derive the one-factor pricing equation for the corresponding contingent claim. This equation is the discounted backward Kolmogoroff equation corresponding to the risk-neutral dynamics of FXR. Its solution can be found via the Feynman-Kac formula, which in the context of option pricing is known as the discounted risk-neutral expectation formula.

In this chapter we discuss the classical Black-Scholes-Garman-Kohlhagen problem of finding prices and hedges for European derivatives as functions of spot FXRs. Since all the hard work is already done above, we can solve the corresponding problem via the method of projections. This method allows one to derive the classical pricing equation and find its solutions by using the homogeneous pricing equation as a starting point.

The chapter is organized as follows. In Section 2 we derive the classical pricing problem for two-country markets with deterministic investments via two complementary methods: (A) the projection method, (B) the original

293

Black-Scholes-Merton method. In Section 3 we show how to solve the classical
pricing problem for simple options. In Section 4 we discuss the classical pricing
problem for two-country markets without deterministic investments. In Section 5 we study the classical pricing problem for multi-country markets with
deterministic investments. References are given in Section 6.

9.2 The classical two-country pricing problem, I

9.2.1 The projection method

The classical Black-Scholes-Garman-Kohlhagen equation governs the price of
a contingent claim considered as a function of the calendar time t and the spot
FXR S_t^{01} in two-country markets with deterministic investments. (To simplify
the notation below we denote S_t^{01} by S_t and σ^{01} by σ.) In order to derive this
equation we start with the homogeneous Black-Scholes equation. Since prices
of dollar and euro denominated bonds are deterministic, we can represent the
spot price V of a contingent claim considered as a function of t and S as

$$
\begin{aligned}
V\left(t, S\right) &= V\left(t, Z^0, Z^1\right) = Z^0 \Phi\left(\chi, \xi\right) \\
&= K^0 e^{-r^0(T-t)} \Phi\left(\sigma^2\left(T-t\right), \frac{K^1 e^{-r^1(T-t)} S}{K^0 e^{-r^0(T-t)}}\right).
\end{aligned}
$$

The chain rule yields

$$
\begin{aligned}
V_t &= r^0 V - \sigma^2 K^0 e^{-r^0(T-t)} \Phi_\chi - r^{01} K^1 e^{-r^1(T-t)} S \Phi_\xi \\
&= r^0 V - \sigma^2 K^0 e^{-r^0(T-t)} \Phi_\chi - r^{01} K^0 e^{-r^0(T-t)} \xi \Phi_\xi,
\end{aligned}
$$

$$
S V_S\left(t, S\right) = K^1 e^{-r^1(T-t)} S \Phi_\xi = K^0 e^{-r^0(T-t)} \xi \Phi_\xi,
$$

$$
S^2 V_{SS}\left(t, S\right) = \frac{\left(K^1 e^{-r^1(T-t)} S\right)^2}{K^0 e^{-r^0(T-t)}} \Phi_{\xi\xi} = K^0 e^{-r^0(T-t)} \xi^2 \Phi_{\xi\xi}.
$$

Substituting these expressions in equation (8.9) we obtain after some straightforward algebra the pricing equation for contingent claims written in terms of
t, S:

$$
V_t\left(t, S\right) + \frac{1}{2} \sigma^2 S^2 V_{SS}\left(t, S\right) + r^{01} S V_S\left(t, S\right) - r^0 V\left(t, S\right) = 0, \tag{9.1}
$$

or, equivalently,

$$V_t + \frac{1}{2}\sigma^2 \mathcal{D}^2 V + \left(r^{01} - \frac{1}{2}\sigma^2\right)\mathcal{D}V - r^0 V = 0.$$

where $\mathcal{D} = S\partial_S$. The terminal condition for equation (9.1) is

$$V(T,S) = v(S) = K^0\phi\left(\frac{K^1 S}{K^0}\right) = K^0\phi\left(\frac{S}{K}\right),$$

where $K = K^0/K^1$.

Equation (9.1), which is due to Black-Scholes and Merton is the single most important equation of financial engineering. As is often the case in natural sciences, this equation is a consequence of a deep conservation law (in this case, of homogeneity of option prices with respect to scaling transformations).

The dimensional (dollar) price of a European option is a function of seven dimensional variables, namely, the time to maturity $\tau = T - t$, spot S, strikes K^0, K^1, volatility σ, and domestic and foreign interest rates r^0, r^1:

$$V = V(\tau, S, K^0, K^1, \sigma, r^0, r^1).$$

These variables have units of time, DC/FC, DC, FC, $1/\sqrt{\text{time}}$, 1/time, 1/time, respectively. Below we often put $K^1 = 1$ for normalization purposes. (The reader, however, should keep in mind that the correct dimension of V is DC, rather than DC/FC as is tempting to assume.)

The time-value of an option is defined by

$$\tilde{V}(t, S) = V(t, S) - v(S),$$

Since European options can be exercised only at maturity, there is no reason for $\tilde{V}$ to stay positive even if the payoff of the option in question is convex. (This is not the case for American options which are studied in Chapter 11.)

The most interesting feature of the Black-Scholes equation is that it is completely independent of the drift of the underlying FXR and involves only the domestic and foreign interest rates. (Recall that similar equations involving actual rather than risk-neutral drift were derived by Sprenkle, Boness, and Samuelson several years prior to the publication of the Black-Scholes formula.) Thus, for the purposes of derivative valuation the actual dynamics of the FXR can be replaced by its risk-free dynamics governed by the SDE of the form

$$\frac{dS_t}{S_t} = r^{01}dt + \sigma dW_t, \qquad S_0 \text{ is given.} \qquad (9.2)$$

Equation (9.1) is the backward Kolmogoroff equation with killing corresponding to SDE (9.2).

In terms of the forward FXR $F_{t,T} = e^{r^{01}(T-t)}S_t$ SDE (9.2) can be rewritten as follows

$$\frac{dF_{t,T}}{F_{t,T}} = \sigma dW_t, \qquad F_{0,T} \text{ is given.} \tag{9.3}$$

The Black-Scholes equation for the forward price of a contingent claim written in terms of the forward FXR,

$$\check{V}(t, F_{t,T}) = e^{r^0(T-t)}V(t, S_t),$$

assumes a particularly simple form, namely,

$$\check{V}_t(t, F) + \frac{1}{2}\sigma^2 F^2 \check{V}_{FF}(t, F) = 0. \tag{9.4}$$

Not surprisingly, equations (9.4) and (8.4) are identical. Equation (9.4) is the backward Kolmogoroff equations associated with SDE (9.3). The corresponding terminal condition is

$$V(T, F) = v(F). \tag{9.5}$$

9.2.2 The classical method

The derivation of the Black-Scholes pricing equation given in the previous subsection is technically appealing but not intuitive. Here we rederive this equation via the original methodology of Black and Scholes. Their main idea is that the pricing has to be done in conjunction with hedging which has to be done continuously throughout the life of the option. We consider the situation from the standpoint of the option seller. Assuming that the price of a contingent claim $V(t, S)$ is a continuous function of its arguments, at any given time we buy Δ units of the foreign currency, where

$$\Delta(t, S) = V_S(t, S),$$

and form a portfolio $\Pi(t, S)$ of the form

$$\Pi(t, S) = -V(t, S) + \Delta(t, S)S.$$

By forming this portfolio, we attempt to insulate ourselves from the movements of the underlying FXR. To compute the change in the value of Π we think of think of Δ as a constant for the purpose of differentiation (here the predictable nature of our hedging strategy becomes important), and assume that the foreign currency is used to buy foreign bonds maturing at time T. Ito's lemma yields

$$
\begin{aligned}
d\Pi &= -(V_t dt + V_S dS + \frac{1}{2}\sigma^2 S^2 V_{SS} dt) + \Delta(dS + r^1 S dt) \\
&= -(V_t dt + \frac{1}{2}\sigma^2 S^2 V_{SS} dt) + \Delta r^1 S dt.
\end{aligned}
$$

Accordingly, $d\Pi$ is a nonrandom variable (i.e., it is insulated from the random movements of the underlying), so that it should grow at the domestic risk-free rate, i.e.,

$$
d\Pi - r^0 \Pi dt = 0,
$$

or, explicitly, after dividing by $(-dt)$,

$$
V_t(t,S) + \frac{1}{2}\sigma^2 S^2 V_{SS}(t,S) + r^{01} S V_S(t,S) - r^0 V(t,S) = 0.
$$

This is the Black-Scholes pricing equation (9.1).

9.2.3 The impact of the actual drift

We emphasize the fact that although the Black-Scholes pricing problem is explicitly independent of the actual drift of the FXR, the evolution of the contingent claim price does depend on this drift implicitly since the evolution of the FXR does. Indeed, we can apply Ito's lemma and use the Black-Scholes pricing equation to obtain

$$
\begin{aligned}
dV(t,S_t) &= \left(V_t(t,S_t) + \frac{1}{2}\sigma^2 S_t^2 V_{SS}(t,S_t) \right) dt + V_S(t,S_t) dS_t \qquad (9.6) \\
&= \left(V_t(t,S_t) + \mu S_t V_S(t,S_t) + \frac{1}{2}\sigma^2 S_t^2 V_{SS}(t,S_t) \right) dt + \sigma S_t V_S(t,S_t) dW_t \\
&= \left((\mu - r^{01}) S_t V_S(t,S_t) + r^0 V(t,S_t) \right) dt + \sigma S_t V_S(t,S_t) dW_t.
\end{aligned}
$$

Here we assume that the actual dynamics of S_t is governed by the SDE of the form

$$
\frac{dS_t}{S_t} = \mu dt + \sigma dW_t, \qquad S_0 \text{ is given.}
$$

It is clear that μ cannot be removed from equation (9.6).

9.3   Solution of the classical pricing problem

9.3.1   Nondimensionalization

As always, it is very useful to nondimensionalize the pricing problem. There are two ways for reducing the pricing problem to the nondimensional form. We can use either K or S as a unit of FXR, σ^{-2} as a unit of time, and represent the price V in two equivalent forms

$$V = K^0 \Phi \left(\chi, \xi, \hat{r}^0, \hat{r}^1 \right)$$

$$V = K^1 S \Psi \left(\chi, \eta, \hat{r}^0, \hat{r}^1 \right), \tag{9.7}$$

where $\chi = \sigma^2 \tau$, $\xi = S/K$ and $\eta = K/S$ are the nondimensional time to maturity, moneyness and inverse moneyness, respectively; $\hat{r}^0 = r^0/\sigma^2$, $\hat{r}^1 = r^1/\sigma^2$ are the nondimensional interest rates. Thus, in accordance with the well-known Π-theorem, the "nontrivial" information contained in the price is a function of four variables, namely, χ, ξ (or χ, η) and $\hat{r}^0$, $\hat{r}^1$. This observation allows one to reduce the computational effort to a very large degree. The pricing problem for $\Phi(\chi, \xi)$ on the semi-axis $0 \leq \xi < \infty$ is:

$$\Phi_\chi - \frac{1}{2}\xi^2 \Phi_{\xi\xi} - \hat{r}^{01}\xi \Phi_\xi + \hat{r}^0 \Phi = 0, \tag{9.8}$$

$$\Phi(0, \xi) = \phi(\xi). \tag{9.9}$$

The pricing problem for $\Psi(\chi, \eta)$ on the semi-axis $0 \leq \eta < \infty$ is:

$$\Psi_\chi - \frac{1}{2}\eta^2 \Psi_{\eta\eta} - \hat{r}^{10}\eta \Psi_\eta + \hat{r}^1 \Psi = 0, \tag{9.10}$$

$$\Psi(0, \eta) = \psi(\eta). \tag{9.11}$$

We emphasize that in the Ψ representation the roles of r^0 and r^1 are switched.

9.3.2   Reductions

As before, the most efficient method for solving problem (9.8), (9.9) is based on its reduction to the initial value problem for the heat equation on the whole axis. The corresponding reductions are

$$\chi \;\; \to \;\; \chi, \; \xi \to X = \ln(\xi), \tag{9.12}$$

$$\Phi(\chi, \xi) \;\; \to \;\; U(\chi, X) = e^{\left(\hat{r}^0 + \hat{\gamma}_-^2/2\right)x + \hat{\gamma}_- X} \Phi(\chi, \xi),$$

where

$$\hat{\gamma}_\pm = \pm 1/2 + \hat{r}^{01}$$

As a result we get the standard heat equation on the whole axis

$$U_X - \frac{1}{2}U_{XX} = 0,$$

supplied with the initial condition of the form

$$U(0, X) = e_+^{\hat{\gamma}_- X} \phi\left(e^X\right).$$

The corresponding reductions for problem (9.10), (9.11) are similar in nature.

9.3.3 The pricing and hedging formulas for forwards, calls and puts

We already know how to express the prices of vanilla options in terms of $Z^0, \xi = Z^1/Z^0$. Because of their extraordinary practical importance we show how to express these prices in spot terms now.

In order to price a particular security, we have to supply the Black-Scholes pricing equation with the terminal condition at maturity and the boundary conditions for $S \to 0$ and $S \to \infty$. For forward contracts, calls and puts these conditions are

$$FO(T, S, T, K) = S - K,$$

$$FO(t, 0, T, K) = -e^{-r^0(T-t)}K, \qquad FO(t, S \to \infty, T, K) \sim e^{-r^1(T-t)}S,$$

$$C(T, S, T, K) = (S - K)_+,$$

$$C(t, 0, T, K) = 0, \qquad C(t, S \to \infty, T, K) \sim e^{-r^1(T-t)}S,$$

$$P(T, S, T, K) = (K - S)_+,$$

$$P(t, 0, T, K) = e^{-r^0(T-t)}K, \qquad P(t, S \to \infty, T, K) = 0,$$

respectively.[1]

We can use formulas (8.19), (8.20), (8.23) in order to find FO, C, P. Elementary substitutions yield

$$FO\,(t, S, T, K) = e^{-r^1(T-t)} S - e^{-r^0(T-t)} K = e^{-r^0(T-t)} \left(F - K \right).$$

Usually the strike is chosen in such a way that

$$FO\,(0, S, T, K) = 0.$$

Therefore, the corresponding strike K has the form

$$K = F_{0,T}^{01} = e^{r^{01} T} S_0^{01}.$$

It is given by the familiar interest rate parity theorem.

For calls and puts we get

$$
\begin{aligned}
& C(t, S, T, K) \hspace{5cm} (9.13) \\
&= e^{-r^1(T-t)} S \mathfrak{N} \left(\frac{\ln\left(S/K\right) + r^{01}\left(T-t\right)}{\sigma\sqrt{T-t}} + \frac{1}{2}\sigma\sqrt{T-t} \right) \\
&\quad - e^{-r^0(T-t)} K \mathfrak{N} \left(\frac{\ln\left(S/K\right) + r^{01}\left(T-t\right)}{\sigma\sqrt{T-t}} - \frac{1}{2}\sigma\sqrt{T-t} \right) \\
&= e^{-r^0(T-t)} F \mathfrak{N} \left(\frac{\ln\left(F/K\right)}{\sigma\sqrt{T-t}} + \frac{1}{2}\sigma\sqrt{T-t} \right) \\
&\quad - e^{-r^0(T-t)} K \mathfrak{N} \left(\frac{\ln\left(F/K\right)}{\sigma\sqrt{T-t}} - \frac{1}{2}\sigma\sqrt{T-t} \right) \\
&= e^{-r^1(T-t)} S \mathfrak{N}\left(d_+\right) - e^{-r^0(T-t)} K \mathfrak{N}\left(d_-\right)
\end{aligned}
$$

---

[1] We deliberately use the notation which is similar to our notation for the t.p.d.'s. We will see in a due course that there is a close relation between prices of vanilla options and transition probabilities for FXRs.

$$P(t,S,T,K) \tag{9.14}$$

$$
\begin{aligned}
=\ & e^{-r^0(T-t)} K \mathfrak{N} \left(-\frac{\ln(S/K) + r^{01}(T-t)}{\sigma\sqrt{T-t}} + \frac{1}{2}\sigma\sqrt{T-t} \right) \\
& -e^{-r^1(T-t)} S \mathfrak{N} \left(-\frac{\ln(S/K) + r^{01}(T-t)}{\sigma\sqrt{T-t}} - \frac{1}{2}\sigma\sqrt{T-t} \right) \\
=\ & e^{-r^0(T-t)} K \mathfrak{N} \left(-\frac{\ln(F/K)}{\sigma\sqrt{T-t}} + \frac{1}{2}\sigma\sqrt{T-t} \right) \\
& -e^{-r^0(T-t)} F \mathfrak{N} \left(-\frac{\ln(F/K)}{\sigma\sqrt{T-t}} - \frac{1}{2}\sigma\sqrt{T-t} \right) \\
=\ & e^{-r^0(T-t)} K \mathfrak{N}(-d_-) - e^{-r^1(T-t)} S \mathfrak{N}(-d_+),
\end{aligned}
$$

where

$$
\begin{aligned}
d_{\pm} &= \frac{\ln(S/K) + r^{01}(T-t)}{\sigma\sqrt{T-t}} \pm \frac{1}{2}\sigma\sqrt{T-t} \\
&= \frac{\ln(F/K)}{\sigma\sqrt{T-t}} \pm \frac{1}{2}\sigma\sqrt{T-t}.
\end{aligned}
$$

The corresponding prices are shown in Figures 9.1, 9.2.

The reader is encouraged to check that formulas (9.13), (9.14) allow the following probabilistic interpretation:

$$
\begin{aligned}
C(t,S,T,K) &= e^{-r^0(T-t)} \int_0^\infty (S'-K)_+ \, p(t,S,T,S') \, dS' \\
&= e^{-r^0(T-t)} \int_K^\infty (S'-K) \, p(t,S,T,S') \, dS',
\end{aligned}
$$

$$
\begin{aligned}
P(t,S,T,K) &= e^{-r^0(T-t)} \int_0^\infty (K-S')_+ \, p(t,S,T,S') \, dS' \\
&= e^{-r^0(T-t)} \int_0^K (K-S') \, p(t,S,T,S') \, dS',
\end{aligned}
$$

where $p(t,S,T,S')$ is the transitional probability density for the lognormal process with drift,

$$
p(t,S,T,S') = \frac{\exp\left\{-d_-^2/2\right\}}{\sqrt{2\pi\sigma^2(T-t)}S'}.
$$

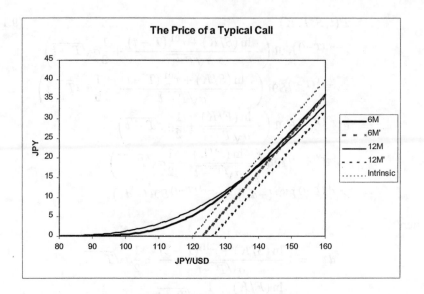

Figure 9.1: The price of representative calls with 6 and 12 months to maturity as a function of the spot FXR. The relevant parameters are $K = 120$, $\sigma = 20\%$, $r^0 = 0.5\%$, $r^1 = 5.5\%$.

Put-call parity and put-call symmetry can be verified directly:

$$C(t, S, T, K) - P(t, S, T, K) = e^{-r^1(T-t)}S - e^{-r^0(T-t)}K, \qquad (9.15)$$

$$
\begin{aligned}
C\left(t, S, T, K, \sigma, r^0, r^1\right) &= SKP\left(t, \frac{1}{S}, T, \frac{1}{K}, \sigma, r^1, r^0\right) \\
&= P\left(t, K, T, S, \sigma, r^1, r^0\right).
\end{aligned}
$$

Below we mostly concentrate on pricing and hedging calls. Once this problem is solved we can deal with puts via put-call parity and put-call symmetry.

For a call the computation of the Greeks is straightforward:

$$\Delta^{(C)} = e^{-r^1(T-t)}\mathfrak{N}\left(d_+\right), \qquad (9.16)$$

$$\Gamma^{(C)} = \frac{e^{-r^1(T-t)}\mathfrak{n}\left(d_+\right)}{\sigma\sqrt{T-t}S} = \frac{e^{-r^0(T-t)}K\mathfrak{n}\left(d_-\right)}{\sigma\sqrt{T-t}S^2},$$

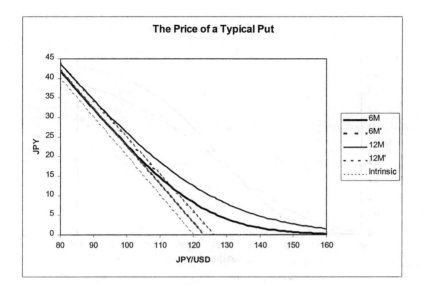

Figure 9.2: The price of representative puts with 6 and 12 months to maturity as a function of the spot FXR. The relevant parameters are the same as in Figure 9.1

$$
\begin{aligned}
\Theta^{(C)} &= -\frac{\sigma e^{-r^1(T-t)} Sn\left(d_+\right)}{2\sqrt{T-t}} + r^1 e^{-r^1(T-t)} S\mathfrak{N}\left(d_+\right) - r^0 e^{-r^0(T-t)} K\mathfrak{N}\left(d_-\right) \\
&= -\frac{\sigma^{-r^0(T-t)} Kn\left(d_-\right)}{2\sqrt{T-t}} + r^1 e^{-r^1(T-t)} S\mathfrak{N}\left(d_+\right) - r^0 e^{-r^0(T-t)} K\mathfrak{N}\left(d_-\right),
\end{aligned}
$$

$$
\mathcal{V}^{(C)} = \sqrt{T-t}\, e^{-r^1(T-t)} Sn\left(d_+\right) = \sqrt{T-t}\, e^{-r^0(T-t)} Kn\left(d_-\right), \qquad (9.17)
$$

etc. We show the corresponding Greeks in Figures 9.3-9.6.

We leave it to the reader to compute the Greeks for the put.

The change of the call and put prices with respect to a positive change in the value of a particular argument, all other arguments being kept fixed, is as

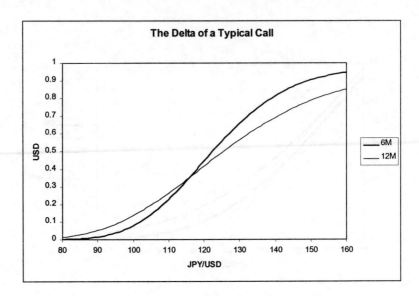

Figure 9.3: The Delta of representative calls with 6 and 12 months to maturity. The relevant parameters are the same as in Figure 9.1.

follows:

$$\begin{aligned}
\delta\tau : \quad & \delta C \gtreqless 0, \quad \delta P \gtreqless 0, \\
\delta S : \quad & \delta C > 0, \quad \delta P < 0, \\
\delta K : \quad & \delta C < 0, \quad \delta P > 0, \\
\delta\sigma : \quad & \delta C > 0, \quad \delta P > 0, \\
\delta r^0 : \quad & \delta C > 0, \quad \delta P < 0, \\
\delta r^1 : \quad & \delta C < 0, \quad \delta P > 0.
\end{aligned}$$

It is clear that Δ, Θ measure the price sensitivity to spot and time changes, respectively, while Γ measures the Δ sensitivity to spot changes. To hedge an instrument dynamically, we have to own Delta units of the foreign currency. The pricing equation can be rewritten as a relation between the price and the Greeks,

$$\Theta + \frac{1}{2}\sigma^2 S^2 \Gamma + r^{01} S\Delta - r^0 V = 0.$$

Depending on the relation between the forward and strike rates F and K, $F < K$, $F = K$, $F > K$, we can distinguish out-of-the-money (OTMF)

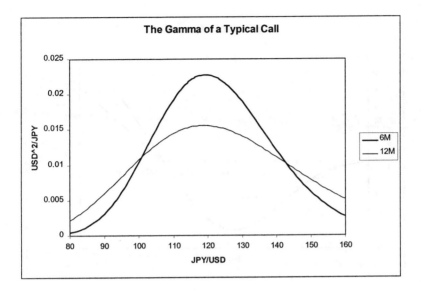

Figure 9.4: The Gamma of representative calls with 6 and 12 months to maturity. The relevant parameters are the same as in Figure 9.1.

calls (in-the-money (ITMF) puts), at-the-money (ATMF) calls and puts whose prices coincide by virtue of equation (9.15), and in-the-money calls (out-of-the-money puts). It is clear that at maturity the price of ATMF and OTMF options is zero, while the price of ITMF options is $|S - K|$. The essence of optionality becomes particularly clear for ATMF options. Assuming that

$$\sigma\sqrt{T - t} \ll 1,$$

we can approximate this price as

$$
\begin{aligned}
C(t, S, T, F) &= P(t, S, T, F) \\
&\approx \frac{\sigma\sqrt{T - t}\, e^{-r^1(T-t)} S}{\sqrt{2\pi}} \left(1 - \frac{\sigma^2\,(T - t)}{24}\right) \\
&\approx \frac{\sigma\sqrt{T - t}\, e^{-r^0(T-t)} F}{\sqrt{2\pi}} \left(1 - \frac{\sigma^2\,(T - t)}{24}\right).
\end{aligned}
$$

This formula gives the time value of an option compared to its intrinsic value (which is equal zero). It plays a very important role in practice as a "quick and dirty" indicator of an option price.

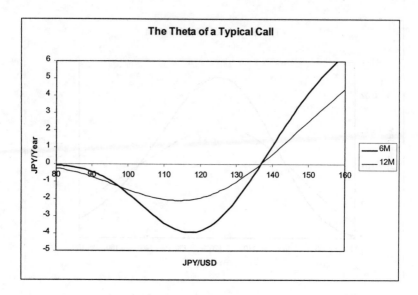

Figure 9.5: The Theta of representative calls with 6 and 12 months to maturity. The relevant parameters are the same as in Figure 9.1.

Very often in the forex market calls and puts are quoted by their Deltas rather then strikes. By inverting equation (9.16) we can find the relation between K and $\Delta^{(C)}$ for a call:

$$K = S \exp\left\{-\mathfrak{N}^{-1}\left(e^{r^1(T-t)}\Delta^{(C)}\right)\sigma\sqrt{T-t} + \left(r^{01} + \frac{\sigma^2}{2}\right)(T-t)\right\}.$$

A similar relation is valid for the put.

9.3.4 European options with exotic payoffs

We already know that by combining calls, puts, and forwards investors can create contingent claims which better reflect their market views and suit their particular needs.

For instance, a bull spread is a difference of a call with maturity T and strike K and a call with the same maturity and a larger strike $K' = K + \delta K$,

$$V^{(BLLSPRD)}(t, S, T, K, \delta K) = C(t, S, T, K) - C(t, S, T, K + \delta K).$$

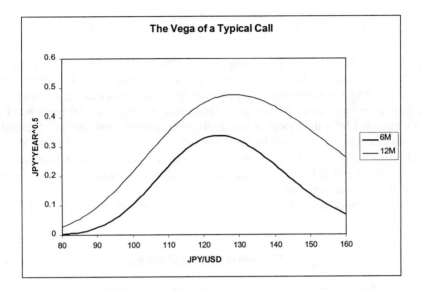

Figure 9.6: The Vega of representative calls with 6 and 12 months to maturity. The relevant parameters are the same as in Figure 9.1. Expression (9.17) is divided by 100 in order to account to the fact that σ is measured in percent.

It is clear that an investor buying the bull spread expects the FXR to go up. An investor having the opposite view can sell the bull spread, or, equivalently, sell a call with strike K and buy a call with strike K'. Such an investor receives some premium at inception, at the same time assuming some obligations at maturity. This position is also known as the bear spread.

Linear combinations of calls and puts which are particularly popular in the forex markets are straddles, strangles and risk reversals. Their payoffs at maturity are given by

$$V^{(STRDDL)}(T, S, T, K, \delta K) = (S - K)_+ + (K - S)_+,$$

$$V^{(STRNGL)}(T, S, T, K, \delta K) = \left(S - K - \frac{1}{2}\delta K\right)_+ + (K - \frac{1}{2}\delta K - S)_+,$$

$$V^{(RR)}\left(T, S, T, K, \delta K\right) = \left(S - K - \frac{1}{2}\delta K\right)_+ - (K - \frac{1}{2}\delta K - S)_+.$$

Similarly to vanilla options, strangles and risk reversals are often quoted by their Deltas, rather than strikes, for instance, a ten-delta risk reversal, etc. Strangles combine the protection provided by a put and a call, and, because of that, can be expensive. At the same time, risk reversals can be considered as calls financed by selling puts, accordingly, they are relatively cheap. Strangles are convex instruments, while risk reversals are not. Due to the lax of convexity, the valuation of risk reversals becomes rather involved when some of the standard Black-Scholes assumptions are dropped, while straddles can be studied with relative ease.

Prices of representative strangles and risk reversals are shown in Figures 9.7, 9.8.

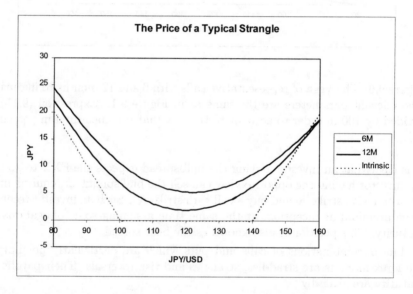

Figure 9.7: The price of representative strangles with 6 and 12 months to maturity. The relevant parameters are the same as in Figure 9.1. The corresponding strikes are $K_1 = 100$, $K_2 = 140$. The price is a convex function of the spot.

Two more options which are of great theoretical value are calendar spreads and butterflies. The calendar spread is the scaled difference of two calls with

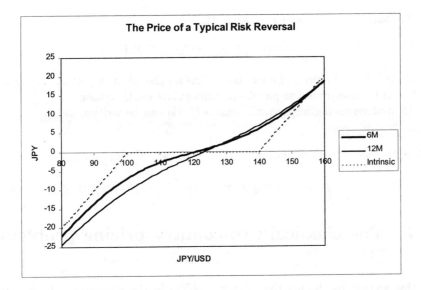

Figure 9.8: The price of representative risk reversals with 6 and 12 months to maturity. The relevant parameters are the same as in Figure 9.7. The price is not a convex function of the spot.

the same strikes and maturities T and $T' = T + \delta T$:

$$V^{(CSPRD)}(t, S, T, \delta T, K) = \frac{C(t, S, T + \delta T, K) - C(t, S, T, K)}{\delta T}.$$

The butterfly is the scaled second difference of three calls with the same maturities and strikes of the form $K - \delta K, K, K + \delta K$:

$$
V^{(BUT)}(t, S, T, K, \delta K)
$$
$$
= \frac{C(t, S, T, K - \delta K) - 2C(t, S, T, K) + C(t, S, T, K + \delta K)}{(\delta K)^2}.
$$

In the limit we have

$$V^{(CSPRD)}(t, S, T, \delta T \to 0, K) \to C_T(t, S, T, K),$$

$$V^{(BUT)}(t, S, T, K, \delta K \to 0) \to C_{KK}(t, S, T, K).$$

We leave it to the reader to verify that

$$-V^{(CB)}(t, S, T, K) = C_K(t, S, T, K),$$

where $V^{(CB)}$ is the price of a call bet. Thus all the relevant partial derivatives of C can be interpreted as payoffs of appropriate exotic options.

In spot terms decomposition formula (8.34) can be written as

$$
\begin{aligned}
V(t, S) &= e^{-r^0(T-t)}v(\kappa) + \left(e^{-r^1(T-t)}S - e^{-r^0(T-t)}\kappa\right)v'(\kappa) \\
&+ \int_0^\kappa v''(K)P(t, S, T, K)\,dK + \int_\kappa^\infty v''(K)C(t, S, T, K)\,dK.
\end{aligned}
$$

9.4   The classical two-country pricing problem, II

In this section we discuss the pricing problem in the stochastic interest rate environment. This problem is easy to formulate but difficult to solve. We consider a typical two-country market and assume that in both countries interest rates follow the Ornstein-Uhlenbeck-Vasicek processes:

$$dr_t^\nu = \kappa^\nu(\varrho^\nu - r_t^\nu)\,dt + \varsigma^\nu d\Omega_t^\nu, \quad \nu = 0, 1,$$

where the standard Wiener processes Ω_t^0 and Ω_t^1 are uncorrelated. (It is easy to drop the latter assumption.) The risk-neutral evolution of FXR is governed by

$$\frac{dS_t}{S_t} = \left(r_t^0 - r_t^1\right)dt + \sigma dW_t,$$

where $d\Omega_t^\nu dW_t = \rho^\nu dt$. In the stochastic interest rate environment the pricing problem for a derivative security assumes the form

$$V_t + \frac{1}{2}\sigma^2 S^2 V_{SS} + \frac{1}{2}\left(\varsigma^0\right)^2 V_{r^0 r^0} + \frac{1}{2}\left(\varsigma^1\right)^2 V_{r^1 r^1} \qquad (9.18)$$
$$+ \quad \rho^0 \sigma \varsigma^0 S V_{Sr^0} + \rho^1 \sigma \varsigma^1 S V_{Sr^1} + \left(r^0 - r^1\right) S V_S$$
$$+ \quad \kappa^0\left(\varrho^0 - r^0\right)V_{r^0} + \left(\kappa^1\left(\varrho^1 - r^1\right) - \rho^1 \sigma \varsigma^1\right)V_{r^1} - r^0 V = 0,$$

$$V\left(T, S, r^0, r^1\right) = v(S). \qquad (9.19)$$

We emphasize that the drift in the r^1 direction is modified by the so-called quanto correction. The reason why this correction is introduced will become apparent shortly.

The pricing equation is a three-dimensional parabolic equation which is much more difficult to solve than the classical one-dimensional Black-Scholes equation (9.1). However, when we are interested in pricing forwards the picture is less gloomy. The terminal condition for a forward contract is

$$FO\left(T, S, r^0, r^1\right) = S - K.$$

For $t < T$ we can use the ansatz

$$FO\left(t, S, r^0, r^1\right) = P\left(t, r^1\right) S - Q\left(t, r^0\right) K. \tag{9.20}$$

Substituting this expression into equations (9.18), (9.19) and collecting terms proportional to S, K we obtain

$$P_t + \frac{1}{2}\left(\varsigma^1\right)^2 P_{r^1 r^1} + \kappa^1\left(\varrho^1 - r^1\right) P_{r^1} - r^1 P = 0,$$

$$Q_t + \frac{1}{2}\left(\varsigma^0\right)^2 Q_{r^0 r^0} + \kappa^0\left(\varrho^0 - r^0\right) Q_{r^0} - r^0 Q = 0,$$

$$P\left(T, r^0, r^1\right) = Q\left(T, r^0, r^1\right) = 1.$$

It is clear that

$$Q\left(t, r^0\right) = B^0\left(t, r^0\right),$$

where B^0 is the domestic bond price, while

$$P\left(t, r^0, r^1\right) = B^1\left(t, r^1\right),$$

where B^1 is the foreign bond price. We emphasize that without the quanto correction $P \neq B^1$. The forward price is defined as the value of K which makes a forward contract initially costless. Formula (9.20) yields

$$F_{t,T} = \frac{B^1\left(t, r^1\right)}{B^0\left(t, r^0\right)} S_t,$$

which is the familiar interest rate parity result.

We can also evaluate futures prices $f_{t,T}$ which are different from forward prices because interest rates are stochastic. The corresponding pricing problem is

$$FU_t + \frac{1}{2}\sigma^2 S^2 FU_{SS} + \frac{1}{2}\left(\varsigma^0\right)^2 FU_{r^0r^0} + \frac{1}{2}\left(\varsigma^1\right)^2 FU_{r^1r^1}$$
$$+ \quad \rho^0\sigma\varsigma^0 SFU_{Sr^0} + \rho^1\sigma\varsigma^1 SFU_{Sr^1} + \left(r^0 - r^1\right)SFU_S$$
$$+ \quad \kappa^0\left(\varrho^0 - r^0\right)FU_{r^0} + \left(\kappa^1\left(\varrho^1 - r^1\right) - \rho^1\sigma\varsigma^1\right)FU_{r^1} = 0,$$

$$FU\left(T, S, r^0, r^1\right) = S - K,$$

where the strike $K = f_{t,T}$ is chosen in such a way that at time t the value of the contract is zero. Here the discounting term $-r^0 FU$ is omitted because of the continuous marking to market. Ansatz (9.20) has to be modified:

$$FU\left(t, S, r^0, r^1\right) = P\left(t, r^0, r^1\right)S - K,$$

where P solves the problem

$$P_t + \frac{1}{2}\left(\varsigma^0\right)^2 P_{r^0r^0} + \frac{1}{2}\left(\varsigma^1\right)^2 P_{r^1r^1} + \left(\kappa^0\left(\varrho^0 - r^0\right) + \rho^0\sigma\varsigma^0\right)P_{r^0}$$
$$+ \quad \kappa^1\left(\varrho^1 - r^1\right)P_{r^1} + \left(r^0 - r^1\right)P = 0,$$

$$P\left(T, r^0, r^1\right) = 1.$$

We can separate variables in the latter problem and write P as

$$P\left(t, r^0, r^1\right) = C\left(t, r^0\right)B^1\left(t, r^1\right),$$

where

$$C_t + \frac{1}{2}\left(\varsigma^0\right)^2 C_{r^0r^0} + \left(\kappa^0\varrho^0 + \rho^0\sigma\varsigma^0 - \kappa^0 r^0\right)C_{r^0} + r^0 C = 0,$$

$$C\left(T, r^0\right) = 1.$$

We leave it to the reader to solve this problem by analogy with the bond valuation problem considered in Section 7.3. The corresponding futures price is

$$f_{t,T} = C\left(t, r^0\right)B^1\left(t, r^1\right)S_t.$$

In general,

$$C\left(t, r^0\right) \neq \frac{1}{B^0\left(t, r^0\right)},$$

so that forward and futures prices are indeed different. Of course, when $\varsigma^0 = 0$, i.e., the domestic rate is deterministic,

$$C\left(t, r^0\right) = \frac{1}{B^0\left(t, r^0\right)},$$

so that forward and futures prices are equal (verification is left to the reader as an exercise).

In order to price derivatives efficiently, we have to transform the pricing equation. First, we change the dependent variable:

$$V \to \check{V} = \frac{V}{B^0\left(t, r^0\right)}.$$

As a result, the pricing equation becomes

$$\check{V}_t + \frac{1}{2}\sigma^2 S^2 \check{V}_{SS} + \frac{1}{2}\left(\varsigma^0\right)^2 \check{V}_{r^0 r^0} + \frac{1}{2}\left(\varsigma^1\right)^2 \check{V}_{r^1 r^1} \tag{9.21}$$
$$+ \quad \rho^0 \sigma \varsigma^0 S\, \check{V}_{Sr^0} + \rho^1 \sigma \varsigma^1 S\, \check{V}_{Sr^1}$$
$$+ \quad \left(\rho^0 \sigma \varsigma^0 \beta^0 + r^0 - r^1\right) S\, \check{V}_S + \left(\kappa^0 \varrho^0 + \left(\varsigma^0\right)^2 \beta^0 - \kappa^0 r^0\right) \check{V}_{r^0}$$
$$+ \quad \left(\kappa^1 \varrho^1 - \rho^1 \sigma \varsigma^1 - \kappa^1 r^1\right) \check{V}_{r^1} = 0,$$

$$\check{V}\left(T, S, r^0, r^1\right) = v\left(S\right). \tag{9.22}$$

Second, we change the independent variables:

$$t \to t, \quad S \to F = \frac{B^1\left(t, r^1\right) S}{B^0\left(t, r^0\right)}, \quad r^0 \to r^0, \quad r^1 \to r^1.$$

The chain rule yields the following relations between partial derivatives in the old (l.h.s) and new (r.h.s) coordinates

$$\partial_t = \partial_t + \left(\dot{\alpha}^1 - \dot{\beta}^1 r^1 - \dot{\alpha}^0 + \dot{\beta}^0 r^0\right) F \partial_F, \quad S \partial_S = F \partial_F,$$
$$\partial_{r^0} = \partial_{r^0} + \beta^0 F \partial_F, \quad \partial_{r^1} = \partial_{r^1} - \beta^1 F \partial_F.$$

We use these relations in order to rewrite problem (9.21), (9.22) in the form (very tedious details are left to the reader to verify):

$$\check{V}_t + \frac{1}{2}\Sigma^2 F^2 \check{V}_{FF} + \frac{1}{2}\left(\varsigma^0\right)^2 \check{V}_{r^0 r^0} + \frac{1}{2}\left(\varsigma^1\right)^2 \check{V}_{r^1 r^1}$$

$$+ \quad \left(\rho^0 \sigma \varsigma^0 + \left(\varsigma^0\right)^2 \beta^0\right) F \check{V}_{F r^0} + \left(\rho^1 \sigma \varsigma^1 - \left(\varsigma^1\right)^2 \beta^1\right) F \check{V}_{F r^1}$$

$$+ \quad \left(\kappa^0 \varrho^0 - \left(\varsigma^0\right)^2 \beta^0 - \kappa^0 r^0\right) \check{V}_{r^0} + \left(\kappa^1 \varrho^1 - \rho^1 \sigma \varsigma^1 - \kappa^1 r^1\right) \check{V}_{r^1} = 0,$$

$$\check{V}\left(T, F, r^0, r^1\right) = v\left(F\right).$$

Here

$$\Sigma^2 = \left(\sigma^2 + \left(\varsigma^0 \beta^0\right)^2 + \left(\varsigma^1 \beta^1\right)^2 + 2\rho^0 \sigma \varsigma^0 \beta^0 - 2\rho^1 \sigma \varsigma^1 \beta^1\right).$$

Now the beauty of the above transformation becomes clear: since the final solution is independent of r^0, r^1 so is the solution! Accordingly, $\check{V}\left(t, F, r^0, r^1\right) = \check{V}\left(t, F\right)$ solves the classical Black-Scholes problem with time dependent volatility:

$$\check{V}_t + \frac{1}{2}\Sigma^2 F^2 \check{V}_{FF} = 0, \tag{9.23}$$

$$\check{V}\left(T, F\right) = v\left(F\right). \tag{9.24}$$

The final change of time

$$t \to \chi = \int_t^T \Sigma^2\left(t'\right) dt',$$

transforms equations (9.23), (9.24), into equations (9.4), (9.5). For instance, for a call we get

$$\check{V}^{(C)}\left(t, F\right) = K\Phi^{(C)}\left(\chi, \frac{F}{K}\right),$$

or, equivalently,

$$V^{(C)}\left(t, S, r^0, r^1\right) = B^0\left(t, r^0\right) K\Phi^{(C)}\left(\int_t^T \Sigma^2\left(t'\right) dt', \frac{B^1\left(t, r^1\right) S}{B^0\left(t, r^0\right) K}\right).$$

9.5 The multi-country classical pricing problem

9.5.1 Introduction

The classical multi-country Black-Scholes problem can easily be derived and its solutions be obtained by the method of projections. In this section we briefly demonstrate how this is done.

9.5.2 Derivation

In order to derive the classical Black-Scholes problem based on its homogeneous form we represent V in the form

$$
\begin{aligned}
V\left(t, S^{01}, ..., S^{0N}\right) &= V\left(t, Z^0, Z^1, ..., Z^N\right) \\
&= Z^0 \Phi\left(t, \xi^1, ..., \xi^N\right) \\
&= Z^0 \Phi\left(t, \frac{K^1 e^{-r^1(T-t)} S^{01}}{K^0 e^{-r^0(T-t)}}, ..., \frac{e^{-r^N(T-t)} S^{0N}}{K^0 e^{-r^0(T-t)}}\right).
\end{aligned}
$$

The chain rule yields the pricing equation for $V_t\left(t, S^{01}, ..., S^{0N}\right)$:

$$
V_t + \frac{1}{2} \sum_{m,n} a^{mn} S^{0m} S^{0n} V_{S^{0m} S^{0n}} + \sum_n r^{0n} S^{0n} V_{S^{0n}} - r^0 V = 0.
$$

The corresponding final condition is

$$
V\left(T, S^{01}, ..., S^{0N}\right) = v\left(S^{01}, ..., S^{0N}\right) = K^0 \phi\left(\frac{K^1 S^{01}}{K^0}, ..., \frac{K^N S^{0N}}{K^0}\right).
$$

There are many financially relevant choices of the final condition. Depending on nature of the particular contingent claim of interest, the function v can depend on just a few FXRs (exchange options) or on all of them (basket and index options).

9.5.3 Reductions

In order to reduce the pricing equation to the multi-dimensional heat equation we apply the following transformations

$$
t \to \tau = T - t, \quad K^n S^{0n}/K^0 \to X^n = \ln\left(K^n S^{0n}/K^0\right), \quad (9.25)
$$

$$
V(t, \mathbf{S}) \to U(\tau, \mathbf{X}) = e^{-\alpha \tau - \boldsymbol{\beta} \cdot \mathbf{X}} V(t, \mathbf{S})/K^0,
$$

where

$$\beta = -\mathcal{A}^{-1}\gamma, \quad \alpha = -r^0 - \frac{1}{2}\mathcal{A}^{-1}\gamma \cdot \gamma,$$

$$\gamma = \left(\gamma^1, ..., \gamma^N\right) = \left(r^{01} - \frac{1}{2}a^{11}, ..., r^{0N} - \frac{1}{2}a^{NN}\right).$$

As a result, we obtain the heat equation with anisotropic heat conductivity for U, namely,

$$U_\tau - \frac{1}{2}\sum_{m,n}a^{mn}U_{X^m X^n} = 0.$$

The corresponding initial condition is

$$U(0, \mathbf{X}) = u(\mathbf{X}) = \frac{e^{-\beta \cdot \mathbf{X}}v(\mathbf{S})}{K^0}.$$

To illustrate the above formulas we put $N = 2$ (the three-country economy) and write the two-factor Black-Scholes problem as

$$V_t + \frac{1}{2}\left(\sigma^{01}\right)^2\left(S^{01}\right)^2 V_{S^{01}S^{01}} + \rho^{012}\sigma^{01}\sigma^{02}S^{01}S^{02}V_{S^{01}S^{02}}$$

$$+ \quad \frac{1}{2}\left(\sigma^{02}\right)^2\left(S^{02}\right)^2 V_{S^{02}S^{02}} + r^{01}S^{01}V_{S^{01}} + r^{02}S^{02}V_{S^{02}} - r^0V = 0,$$

$$V\left(T, S^1, S^2\right) = v\left(S^1, S^2\right).$$

Transformations (9.25) assume the form

$$t \quad \to \quad \tau = T - t, \quad S^{01} \to X^1 = \ln\left(K^1 S^{01}/K^0\right), \tag{9.26}$$

$$S^{02} \quad \to \quad X^2 = \ln\left(K^2 S^{02}/K^0\right), \quad V \to U = e^{-\alpha\tau - \beta^1 X^1 - \beta^2 X^2}V,$$

where

$$\alpha = -r^0 - \frac{\left(\sigma^{01}\right)^2\left(\hat{\gamma}_-^{01}\right)^2 - 2\rho^{012}\sigma^{01}\sigma^{02}\hat{\gamma}_-^{01}\hat{\gamma}_-^{02} + \left(\sigma^{02}\right)^2\left(\hat{\gamma}_-^{02}\right)^2}{2\left(\bar{\rho}^{012}\right)^2},$$

$$\beta^1 = \frac{\sigma^{01}\hat{\gamma}_-^{01} - \rho^{012}\sigma^{02}\hat{\gamma}_-^{02}}{\left(\bar{\rho}^{012}\right)^2\sigma^{01}}, \quad \beta^2 = \frac{-\rho^{012}\sigma^{01}\hat{\gamma}_-^{01} + \sigma^{02}\hat{\gamma}_-^{02}}{\left(\bar{\rho}^{012}\right)^2\sigma^{02}}, \tag{9.27}$$

$$\hat{\gamma}_-^{01} = -\frac{1}{2} + \frac{r^{01}}{\left(\sigma^{01}\right)^2}, \quad \hat{\gamma}_-^{02} = -\frac{1}{2} + \frac{r^{02}}{\left(\sigma^{02}\right)^2}, \quad \bar{\rho}^{012} = \sqrt{1 - \left(\rho^{012}\right)^2}.$$

The corresponding pricing problem is

$$U_\tau - \frac{1}{2}\left(\sigma^{01}\right)^2 U_{X^1 X^1} - \rho^{012}\sigma^{01}\sigma^{02}U_{X^1 X^2} - \frac{1}{2}\left(\sigma^{02}\right)^2 U_{X^2 X^2} = 0,$$

$$U\left(0, X^1, X^2\right) = e^{-\beta^1 X^1 - \beta^2 X^2} v\left(K^0 e^{X^1}/K^1, K^0 e^{X^2}/K^2\right)/K^0.$$

9.5.4 Pricing and hedging of multi-factor options

After reducing the pricing problem to the initial value problem for the standard heat equation, we can find option prices and the corresponding Delta hedges via a simple integration. We leave it to the reader as an exercise to rewrite the relevant formulas derived in Section 8.8 in spot terms.

9.6 References and further reading

The key original references are as follows: Black and Scholes (1973), Bredeen and Litzenberger (1978), Gazizov and Ibragimov (1998), Grabbe (1983), Green and Jarrow (1987), Merton (1973), Nachman (1988), Rabinovitch (1989), Reiner (1998), Schmidt (1997), Vasicek (1977). Additional information can be found in the books quoted in Chapter 1. As always, many relevant mathematical formulas are given by Abramowitz and Stegun (1972).

Chapter 10

Deviations from the Black-Scholes paradigm I: nonconstant volatility

10.1 Introduction

In the previous chapter we gave a detailed discussion of the classical Black-Scholes theory. Now we discuss various deviations from the Black-Scholes paradigm and their implications for pricing and hedging. It is necessary to consider such deviations because market prices of European options on forex with different strikes and maturities cannot be reproduced via the standard Black-Scholes formula with a single volatility. Instead, to price a given option we need to use the so-called implied volatility which explicitly depends on the option strike and maturity. In other words, for matching the market data, we have to take into account smiles and skews of the implied volatility (i.e., the fact that the implied volatility surface is not flat).

There are many ways in which the Black-Scholes framework can be extended. First, we can introduce the term structure (explicit time dependence) for the interest rates and volatilities of FXRs. It is easy to show that in this case simple transformations reduce the pricing problem in the presence of term structure to the classical constant parameter problem, so that all the options which can be priced explicitly in the classical framework can also be priced in the presence of term structure. Next, we can assume that at maturity the

319

FXR has a distribution which deviates from the lognormal distribution and price options with the corresponding maturity as discounted expectations of their payoffs. Alternatively, we can solve a more complicated inverse problem and find the distribution of the FXR at maturity which is consistent with given option prices. If prices of calls and puts with all possible strikes are available, this can be done via the so-called Breeden and Litzenberger formula. However, in practice, when only few prices are known, the distribution of FXR has to be determined via the entropy maximization which we describe in some detail.

More generally, we can introduce the concept of the local volatility which governs the stochastic dynamics of FXR and deduce the shape of the local volatility surface from the information encapsulated in the prices of European options with different strikes and maturities. Once the local volatility surface is determined, we can price exotic options in a way which is consistent with our pricing of European options. Whether or not the stochastic dynamics of FXR can be found for a given set of data is market specific; for forex markets the answer is negative more often than positive. Nonetheless, for the sake of completeness, we derive the Dupire formula for the local volatility which provides a conceptual solution to the above problem. Even if the corresponding pricing equation is known, it cannot be solved explicitly in the general case. However, for some special choices of the local volatility surface we can solve the pricing problem by reducing it to the problem with known solution. In particular, we show how such a reduction works for the so-called Constant Elasticity of Variance (CEV) model. We also use the reduction method for studying options on banded FXRs (i.e., FXRs which are kept within certain bounds due to the government intervention).

Analysis of market data suggests that jumps play an important role in the dynamics of FXRs and have to be incorporated into the option pricing formulas. We discuss Merton's theory which addresses this issue and illustrate it with a few representative examples.

At present the experts unanimously agree that stochastic volatility plays an outstanding role in the forex context. We discuss in detail various approaches which can be used in order to price options on FXRs with stochastic volatility, including analytical, perturbative and numerical ones. In Chapter 14 we give a brief account of the so-called uncertain volatility approach which is aimed at deriving some bounds for option prices which are consistent with the assumption that volatility is sandwiched within certain bounds.

The chapter is organized as follows. In Section 2 we define volatility term structures and smiles and study them in some detail. In particular, we define implied and local volatility surfaces and show how to construct the local volatility corresponding to a given implied volatility. Section 3 is devoted to pricing formulas based on implied t.p.d.f.'s. We describe the so-called sticky-strike and sticky-delta models, which are popular among practitioners, in Section 4. We study the general local volatility model via the method of reductions in Section 5. We develop an asymptotic approach to pricing short-dated options in the general local volatility framework in Section 6. We present a detailed discussion of the CEV model in Section 7. We show how to price options in the jump-diffusion framework in Section 8. We study the general stochastic volatility model (which is, arguably, the most adequate model for studying options on forex) in Section 9. We analyze an important special case of the general model (the case of small volatility of volatility) in Section 10. In Section 11 we briefly discuss multi-factor problems. Finally, in Section 12 we give the relevant references.

10.2   Volatility term structures and smiles

10.2.1   Introduction

In order to apply the Black-Scholes formulas for calls and puts we need to know the volatility of the FXR. In principle, the same volatility has to be used across different strikes and maturities. We should be able to find the corresponding volatility from the historic data. However, analysis of option price data in forex markets suggests that there is no unique volatility which can be used in order to produce market prices for the whole set of tradable options.

10.2.2   The implied volatility

In order to describe the market data in quantitative terms, we consider a call option, say, with maturity T and strike K, assume that its price C is given, and introduce the so-called implied volatility σ_I in such a way that

$$C = C^{BS}\left(0, S, T, K, \sigma_I, r^0, r^1\right),$$

where C^{BS} is the Black-Scholes call price. It is clear that, in general, σ_I depends on T, K:

$$\sigma_I = \sigma_I\left(T, K\right).$$

The Black-Scholes paradigm is valid only when σ_I is constant,

$$\sigma_I = \sigma^*.$$

Typical implied volatilities for dollar calls / yen puts are shown in Figure 10.1. This figure suggests that some of the underlying Black-Scholes assumptions are violated.[1]

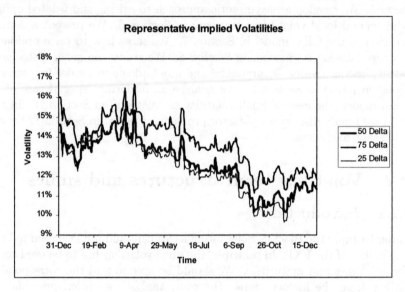

Figure 10.1: The implied volatilities for 50, 75 and 25 Delta dollar calls / yen puts with 6 months to maturity over a representative period of one year.

Depending on the properties of the implied volatility surface, we can distinguish several possibilities. We say that a given market is characterized by the volatility term structure if σ_I depends only on time to maturity,

$$\sigma_I = \sigma_I\left(T\right).$$

There is a smile or skew in the market if σ_I is a function of strike and

$$\sigma_I\left(T,K\right) > \sigma_I\left(T,F\right) \quad \text{when} \quad K \neq F,$$

$$\sigma_I\left(T,K\right) \left\{ \begin{array}{c} > \\ < \end{array} \right\} \sigma_I\left(T,F\right) \quad \text{when} \quad K \left\{ \begin{array}{c} < \\ > \end{array} \right\} F,$$

---

[1] We emphasize that, regardless of these violations, the forward FXR is defined by the interest rate parity theorem.

respectively.

We can find rational bounds on the implied volatility. We know simple no-arbitrage conditions for calls and puts which have to be satisfied regardless of the actual model which we use to describe the market, namely:

$$\frac{\partial C}{\partial K} \leq 0, \qquad \frac{\partial P}{\partial K} \geq 0, \tag{10.1}$$

$$\frac{\partial^2 C}{\partial K^2} \geq 0, \qquad \frac{\partial^2 P}{\partial K^2} \geq 0. \tag{10.2}$$

It is easy to translate these inequalities into conditions on the behavior of the implied volatility as a function of $X = \ln(S/K)$. Consider, for example, the first inequality (10.1). We have

$$\frac{\partial C}{\partial K} = \frac{\partial C^{BS}}{\partial K} - \frac{\partial C^{BS}}{\partial \sigma} \frac{\partial \sigma}{\partial X} \frac{1}{K}.$$

By using expressions (9.16), (9.17) we obtain:

$$\frac{\partial \sigma}{\partial X} \geq -\frac{\mathfrak{N}(d_-)}{\sqrt{T - \mathfrak{tn}(d_-)}}.$$

Similarly, the second inequality (10.1) yields

$$\frac{\partial \sigma}{\partial X} \leq \frac{\mathfrak{N}(-d_+)}{\sqrt{T - \mathfrak{tn}(d_+)}}.$$

We leave it to the reader as a useful exercise to translate inequalities (10.2) into conditions on σ_I and, in particular, to show that σ_I cannot grow faster than $\sqrt{|X|}$ when $|X| \to \infty$.

10.2.3 The local volatility

There are several approaches to explaining why option prices deviate from their theoretical Black-Scholes values, or, equivalently, why σ_I is not constant. The simplest is to assume that the FXR follows a one-dimensional stochastic process other than the geometric Brownian motion with constant parameters, so that

$$\frac{dS_t}{S_t} = r^{01} dt + \sigma_L(t, S) dW_t, \tag{10.3}$$

were $\sigma_L(t, S)$ is called the local volatility of the FXR. Strictly speaking, σ_L depends on the nondimensional ratio $S/\bar{S}$, where $\bar{S}$ is a typical FXR, rather than S *per se*, but we ignore this fact for now. Since our main objective is to price options on S, we assume, without loss of generality, that the drift of S in equation (10.3) is risk-neutral. The Black-Scholes pricing equation for a call (and all other contingent claims) can be derived via the usual hedging arguments. This equation has the form

$$C_t + \frac{1}{2}\sigma_L^2(t, S) S^2 C_{SS} + r^{01} S C_S - r^0 C = 0.$$

The terminal condition is

$$C(T, S) = (S - K)_+.$$

In the Black-Scholes framework the call price is a function of σ,

$$C(t, S, T, K) = C_{BS}(t, S, T, K; \sigma).$$

In the local volatility framework the price is a functional of $\sigma_L(t, S)$,

$$C(t, S, T, K) = C(t, S, T, K; \{\sigma_L(t, S)\}).$$

Accordingly, in the Black-Scholes framework the price sensitivity to small changes of σ is measured by

$$\mathcal{V} = \partial C/\partial\sigma,$$

while in the local volatility framework its sensitivity to changes of σ_L is measured by the so-called Vega functional which is the functional derivative of C with respect to σ_L:

$$\mathcal{V} = \delta C/\delta\sigma_L(t, S).$$

To put it differently, instead of a single number, the sensitivity measure is a function.

It is not difficult to establish the following useful relation between σ_L and σ_I. Consider a call with maturity T, strike K, and implied volatility $\sigma_I(T, K)$. By definition,

$$C(0, S_0, T, K; \{\sigma_L(t, S)\}) = C^{BS}(0, S_0, T, K, \sigma_I(T, K)),$$

where S_0 is the spot FXR today. We introduce the difference

$$\tilde{C}(t, S, T, K) = C(t, S, T, K; \{\sigma_L(t, S)\}) - C^{BS}(t, S, T, K, \sigma_I(T, K)),$$

and obtain the following problem for $\tilde{C}$:

$$\tilde{C}_t + \frac{1}{2}\sigma_L^2(t,S) S^2 \tilde{C}_{SS} + r^{01} S \tilde{C}_S - r^0 \tilde{C} \tag{10.4}$$

$$= -\frac{1}{2}\left(\sigma_L^2(t,S) - \sigma_I^2(T,K)\right) S^2 C_{SS}^{BS},$$

$$\tilde{C}(T,S,T,K) = 0. \tag{10.5}$$

Besides,

$$\tilde{C}(0,S_0,T,K) = 0. \tag{10.6}$$

The inhomogeneous problem (10.4), (10.5) can be solved via Duhamel's principle. Let us assume for the sake of the argument that the difference $\sigma_L^2(t,S) - \sigma_I^2(T,K)$ is positive,

$$\sigma_L^2(t,S) > \sigma_I^2(T,K) \quad \text{for} \quad 0 < S < \infty, 0 \le t \le T.$$

In this case the r.h.s. of equation (10.4) is negative since, as we know, the Gamma of a call is positive. Then, Duhamel's principle shows that $\tilde{C}(t,S,T,K)$ is positive. In view of equation (10.6) it is impossible. Similarly, we arrive at a contradiction if we assume that the difference $\sigma_L^2(t,S) - \sigma_I^2(T,K)$ is negative. Thus, we conclude that

$$\inf_{t,S} \sigma_L(t,S) \le \sigma_I(T,K) \le \sup_{t,S} \sigma_L(t,S),$$

or, more generally,

$$\inf_{t,S} \sigma_L(t,S) \le \inf_{t,S} \sigma_I(t,S) \le \sup_{t,S} \sigma_I(t,S) \le \sup_{t,S} \sigma_L(t,S).$$

These inequalities clearly show that the implied smile is always less pronounced that the corresponding local smile.

10.2.4 The inverse problem

In order to choose $\sigma_L(t,S)$ such that it reproduces the market data, we have to solve an inverse (or calibration) problem and devise a mechanism for mapping σ_I onto σ_L. As is often the case, this inverse problem is ill-posed and rather difficult to solve. We start with the simplest interesting case and consider the term structure of volatility $\sigma_I = \sigma_I(T)$. In order to do so, we assume that the local volatility depends only on time, $\sigma = \sigma_L(t)$. The pricing equation written in forward terms assumes the form

$$\check{C}_t + \frac{1}{2}\sigma_L^2(t)F^2\check{C}_{FF} = 0.$$

By introducing the nondimensional time to maturity

$$\chi = \int_t^T \sigma_L^2(t')\,dt',$$

we can rewrite it as

$$\check{C}_\chi - \frac{1}{2}F^2\check{C}_{FF} = 0.$$

Accordingly, the corresponding solution is

$$\check{C} = \check{C}^{BS}\left(0, F, T, K, \sqrt{\frac{1}{T}\int_0^T \sigma_L^2(t')\,dt'}\right).$$

On the other hand, by definition, we have

$$\check{C} = \check{C}^{BS}(0, S, T, K, \sigma_I(T)).$$

Thus,

$$\sqrt{\frac{1}{T}\int_0^T \sigma_L^2(t')\,dt'} = \sigma_I(T), \tag{10.7}$$

$$\sigma_L(T) = \sqrt{(T\sigma_I^2(T))_T}, \quad 0 < T < \infty.$$

Formula (10.7) captures some important features of the general mapping of σ_I onto σ_L and encapsulates the difficulties of the local volatility approach. First, it involves differentiation of a given function $\sigma_I(T)$ representing the market data with respect to its argument, and, because of that, is ill-posed. Second, even if $\sigma_I(T)$ is sufficiently smooth, it cannot be chosen arbitrarily since the product $T\sigma_I^2(T)$ has to be a nondecreasing function of T (otherwise the square root in (10.7) cannot be extracted).

Consider now the more general case when σ_I depends on both K and T. Once again, we use forward variables. By definition, the forward price of a call has the form

$$\check{C} = \check{C}^{BS}(0, F_{0,T}, T, K, \sigma_I(T, K)).$$

In terms of the transition probability density $p(t, F_{t,T}, T, S_T)$ we can represent it as follows

$$\check{C} = \int_K^\infty (S' - K) p(0, F_{0,T}, T, S') \, dS'. \tag{10.8}$$

Differentiating equation (10.8) with respect to K twice, we obtain

$$\check{C}_K = -\int_K^\infty p(0, F_{0,T}, T, S') \, dS',$$

$$\check{C}_{KK} = p(0, F_{0,T}, T, K). \tag{10.9}$$

On the other hand, we know that as a function of the second pair of its arguments p satisfies the Fokker-Planck forward equation, which, in the case in question, can be written as follows:

$$p_T - \frac{1}{2} \left(\sigma_L^2 (T, K) K^2 p\right)_{KK} = 0.$$

Using equation (10.9) we obtain

$$\check{C}_{TKK} - \frac{1}{2} \left(\sigma_L^2 (T, K) K^2 \check{C}_{KK}\right)_{KK} = 0.$$

Thus,

$$\check{C}_T - \frac{1}{2}\sigma_L^2 (T, K) K^2 \check{C}_{KK} = A(T) + B(T) K,$$

where $A(T), B(T)$ are arbitrary functions of time. Since for large values of K the l.h.s. tends to zero, so should its r.h.s. Accordingly,

$$A(T) = B(T) = 0,$$

and

$$\check{C}_T - \frac{1}{2}\sigma_L^2 (T, K) K^2 \check{C}_{KK} = 0. \tag{10.10}$$

In principle, $\check{C}_T$ and $\check{C}_{KK}$ can be determined from the market data. In practice, of course, this procedure is ill-posed since it requires differentiation of functions which are not necessarily smooth. Assuming that differentiation is legitimate, we obtain the following expression for σ_L^2:

$$\sigma_L^2 (T, K) = \frac{2\check{C}_T}{K^2 \check{C}_{KK}}, \tag{10.11}$$

or, explicitly,

$$\sigma_L^2\left(T,K\right) = \frac{2\sigma_{I,T} + \sigma_I/T}{K^2\left(\sigma_{I,KK} + \left(1/K\sqrt{T} + d_+\sigma_{I,K}\right)^2/\sigma_I - d_+\sqrt{T}\sigma_{I,K}^2\right)}.$$

(10.12)

We leave it to the reader to derive the above formula by using the chain rule several times in a row. Equation (10.11) is often called the Dupire formula.

Once the local volatility surface is constructed, call prices are determined from the pricing equation

$$\check{C}_t + \frac{1}{2}\sigma_L^2\left(t,F\right)F^2\check{C}_{FF} = 0,$$

and the usual terminal conditions.

If we assume that $r^0 = r^1 = 0$, then we can rewrite equation (10.11) in the form

$$\sigma_L^2\left(T,K\right) = \frac{2V^{(CSPRD)}\left(0,S,T,K\right)}{K^2V^{(BUT)}\left(0,S,T,K\right)},$$

where $V^{(CSPRD)}$ and $V^{(BUT)}$ are the prices of the corresponding calendar spread and butterfly. Thus, we can think of the local variance as the relative price of the calendar spread expressed in terms of the corresponding butterfly. In fact, relation (10.11) can be derived solely from dimensional considerations.

We note in passing that equation (10.10) is useful when one needs to price many options with different strikes and maturities on the same FXR. Indeed, this equation assumes that the current spot rate and calendar time are fixed parameters, while strikes and maturities are independent variables. Accordingly, it covers the entirety of vanilla options at once.

We can also express the local variance in terms of spot prices and theirs derivatives. The derivation is straightforward and is left as an exercise. The answer is

$$\sigma_L^2\left(T,K\right) = \frac{2\left(C_T + r^{01}KC_K + r^1C\right)}{K^2C_{KK}},$$

or, explicitly,

$$\sigma_L^2\left(T,K\right) = \frac{2\sigma_{I,T} + \sigma_I/T + 2r^{01}K\sigma_{I,K}}{K^2\left(\sigma_{I,KK} + \left(1/K\sqrt{T} + d_+\sigma_{I,K}\right)^2/\sigma_I - d_+\sqrt{T}\sigma_{I,K}^2\right)}.$$

(10.13)

Practical experience of the author suggests that formulas (10.12), (10.13) are too complicated to be successfully used in practice. Their sheer complexity suggests that the idea of choosing the local volatility surface in order to match the market data needs to be altered. Besides, due to the explicit dependence of σ_L on the derivatives of σ_I with respect to T and K, the local volatility surface is very sensitive to the choice of interpolation scheme used for constructing continuous implied volatility surface from the discrete market data. This makes the local volatility surface very unstable.

10.2.5 How to deal with the smile

There are several practical approaches to dealing with the market smile. We list them in the increasing order of sophistication. One can: (A) choose a functional form of the t.p.d.f. for the FXR, and use this form to price European options as discounted risk-neutral expectations of their payoffs; (B) choose a particular hypothesis describing the evolution of the initial implied volatility in time and price European options accordingly; (C) use the assumption that the local volatility depends only on the spot FXR and try to choose this volatility in a way which is compatible with option prices for a single maturity; (D) specify a sufficiently flexible functional form for the local volatility in the hope that the resulting option prices match the market data better than the Black-Scholes formulas with constant (or time-dependent) volatility; (E) assume that trajectories of the FXR have jumps, price European options appropriately, adjust model parameters and verify if the market data are better matched with jumps than without them; (F) assume that the volatility is stochastic, price European options and adjust parameters of the model until the market data is matched. If need be, the stochastic volatility model can be enriched by incorporating the static smile. The first approach is the simplest, however, it has the least scope and is difficult to use for pricing anything beyond simple European options. Although, in the opinion of the present author, the last approach is the most adequate for the purposes of forex modeling, below we briefly discuss all of them.

10.3 Pricing via implied t.p.d.f.'s

10.3.1 Implied t.p.d.f.'s and entropy maximization

In order to price European calls with fixed maturity T and varying strike K we assume that the probability density function for the future FXR S_T conditional on known spot rate S_0 is $p(0, S_0, T, S_T)$ and represent C as

$$C(0, S, T, K) = e^{-r^0 T} \int_K^\infty (S' - K) p(0, S, T, S') \, dS'. \tag{10.14}$$

Formula (10.14) allows us to express the terminal probability density in terms of prices of the corresponding calls. Unfortunately, since the corresponding expression involves derivatives of the market data, the procedure is ill-posed. Its drawbacks become particularly clear if we only know prices of calls with discrete strikes $K_1, ..., K_N$ (as is always the case in practice). In this case prices of calls with intermediate strikes are determined via interpolation which (naturally) introduces a lot of irregularities into the whole procedure. A good way to suppress these irregularities is to use some sort of regularization technique, for instance, the method of entropy maximization which we briefly describe now.

The problem requires the evaluation of the "best" probability distribution $p(S_T)$ (to simplify the notation we suppress the first argument) which satisfies the following constraints:

$$p(S) \geq 0, \quad \int_0^\infty p(S) \, dS = 1, \quad \int_0^\infty p(S) C_n(S) \, dS = \pi_n, \tag{10.15}$$

where

$$C_n(S) = e^{-r^0 T} (S - K_n)_+,$$

and π_n represent the discounted terminal values of call options and their prices, respectively. The meaning of the first two constraints (10.15) is self-explanatory while the remaining constraints (10.15) represent the market data. We use the well-known Principle of Maximum Entropy (PME) and say that the "best" probability distribution is the one which maximizes the entropy functional

$$\Phi(p) = - \int_0^\infty p(S) \ln(p(S)) \, dS,$$

because such a distribution reflects only the information encapsulated in constraints (10.15) and no other.

The maximization problem

$$\Phi(p) \to \max \quad \text{subject to constraints,}$$

can be solved via the Lagrange multipliers method. Instead of Φ we maximize the functional Ψ of the form

$$\Psi = -\int_0^\infty p(S) \ln(p(S)) \, dS$$

$$+ (1 + \lambda_0) \int_0^\infty p(S) \, dS + \sum_{n=1}^N \lambda_n \int_0^\infty p(S) C_n(S) \, dS,$$

where $\lambda_0, ..., \lambda_n, ...$ are the corresponding Lagrangian multipliers. The variation $p(S) \to p(S) + \delta p(S)$ results in the leading order variation of Ψ of the form

$$\delta\Psi = \int_0^\infty [-\ln(p(S)) - 1 + (1 + \lambda_0) + \lambda_n C_n(S)] \, \delta p(S) \, dS$$

$$= \int_0^\infty [-\ln(p(S)) + \lambda_0 + \lambda_n C_n(S)] \, \delta p(S) \, dS.$$

Since the variation $\delta p(S)$ can be chosen arbitrarily, the condition which guarantees that the variation $\delta\Psi$ vanishes is

$$-\ln(p(S)) + \lambda_0 + \lambda_n C_n(S) = 0.$$

Accordingly,

$$p(S) = \frac{\exp\left\{\sum_{n=1}^N \lambda_n C_n(S)\right\}}{\int_0^\infty \exp\left\{\sum_{n=1}^N \lambda_n C_n(S)\right\} dS}.$$

This formula shows that the positivity and normalization constraints are satisfied automatically. In order to match the market data we have to choose the multipliers $\lambda_1, ..., \lambda_N$ in such a way that

$$\frac{\int_0^\infty \exp\left\{\sum_{n=1}^N \lambda_n C_n(S)\right\} C_m(S) \, dS}{\int_0^\infty \exp\left\{\sum_{n=1}^N \lambda_n C_n(S)\right\} dS} = \pi_m, \quad m = 1, ..., N.$$

This is a system of N nonlinear equations for N unknowns which has to be solved numerically. Both the standard Newton-Raphson method and its numerous modifications can be used for this purpose.

Above we have not used any information about the distribution $p(S)$ other than the information provided by the market data. However, in some cases we can have such an information. For instance, we can assume that $p(S)$ is "close" to some known probability distribution $q(S)$ such as the lognormal distribution, say. In order to incorporate this information into the picture, we can use the Principle of Minimum Cross-Entropy (PMCE) which states that the "best" probability density $p(S)$ minimizes the so-called Kullback's cross-entropy functional

$$\Phi(p, q) = \int_0^\infty p(S) \ln\left(\frac{p(S)}{q(S)}\right) dS.$$

We emphasize that the sign in front of the integral is changed which guarantees that Φ is non-negative. (The latter statement is left to the reader to check as a useful exercise.) Thus, we have to solve the minimization problem

$$\Phi(p, q) \to \min \quad \text{subject to constraints.}$$

Its solution can be found in the same way as before. This solution has the form

$$p(S) = \frac{\exp\left\{\sum_{n=1}^N \lambda_n C_n(S)\right\} q(S)}{\int_0^\infty \exp\left\{\sum_{n=1}^N \lambda_n C_n(S)\right\} q(S) \, dS},$$

where λ_n solve the equations

$$\frac{\int_0^\infty \exp\left\{\sum_{n=1}^N \lambda_n C_n(S)\right\} q(S) C_m(S) \, dS}{\int_0^\infty \exp\left\{\sum_{n=1}^N \lambda_n C_n(S)\right\} q(S) \, dS} = \pi_m, \quad m = 1, ..., N.$$

10.3.2   Possible functional forms of t.p.d.f.'s

If we want to price European calls as discounted values of their terminal payoffs and obtain the standard Black-Scholes formula as a result all we need to do is to assume that the terminal FXR is a lognormal random variable of the form

$$S_T = e^{r^{01}(T-t)} S_t e^{-\sigma_{LN}^2(T-t)/2 + \sigma_{LN}\sqrt{T-t}\xi}, \tag{10.16}$$

where ξ is the standard normal variable, and σ_{LN} is the lognormal volatility of S_T. This choice is advantageous because it guarantees that S_T is positive. Besides, it is consistent with the interest rate parity theorem. The corresponding call option price $C_{LN}(t, S, T, K)$ is given by the familiar Black-Scholes formula.

However, since the Black-Scholes formula does not match the market data exactly, the lognormality assumption has to be relaxed. The simplest possibility is to assume that S_T is distributed normally,

$$S_T = e^{r^{01}(T-t)} S_t + \sigma_N \sqrt{T-t}\xi, \tag{10.17}$$

where σ_N is the so-called normal volatility of S_T, its dimension is $DC/FC\sqrt{time}$. This choice is compatible with the interest rate parity, but is does not prevent S_T from becoming negative. The corresponding call option prices, which are easy to find, have the form

$$C_N(t, S, T, K) = \left(e^{-r^1(T-t)} S - e^{-r^0(T-t)} K \right) \mathfrak{N} \left(\frac{e^{r^{01}(T-t)} S - K}{\sigma_N \sqrt{T-t}} \right)$$

$$+ e^{-r^0(T-t)} \sigma_N \sqrt{T-t}\, \mathfrak{n} \left(\frac{e^{r^{01}(T-t)} S - K}{\sigma_N \sqrt{T-t}} \right).$$

In forward terms this formula can be written as

$$\check{C}_N(t, F, T, K) = (F - K) \mathfrak{N} \left(\frac{F-K}{\sigma_N \sqrt{T-t}} \right) + \sigma_N \sqrt{T-t}\, \mathfrak{n} \left(\frac{F-K}{\sigma_N \sqrt{T-t}} \right). \tag{10.18}$$

In its original form formula (10.18) is due to Bachelier. Samuelson criticized assumption (10.17) and the corresponding formula (10.18) on several grounds. In particular, he pointed out that S_T can become negative. Accordingly, Samuelson advocated using assumption (10.16). His constructive criticism caused a sharp increase in research aimed at option pricing consistent with the basic economic assumptions. The outcome of this research was the Black-Scholes formula. It should be noted, however, that it is possible to address Samuelson's concerns by simply introducing an absorbing barrier at $S = 0$. We will return to this point below. The implied Black-Scholes volatility corresponding to the Bachelier model in shown in Figure 10.2.

We can mix several lognormal distributions and assume that

$$S_T = e^{r^{01}(T-t)} S_t \sum_{0 \leq i \leq I} p_i e^{-\sigma_{LN,i}^2 (T-t)/2 + \sigma_{LN,i} \sqrt{T-t}\xi},$$

where p_i, $0 < p_i < 1$, $\sum p_i = 1$, are given probabilities of a particular volatility scenario. The corresponding pricing formula for a call with strike K and

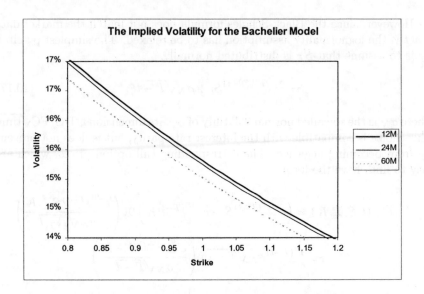

Figure 10.2: The "Bachelier" implied volatility $\sigma_I(T, K)$ as a function of K for three representative maturities, $T = 12, 24, 60$ months. The relevant parameters are $S_0 = 0.95$, $\sigma = 15\%$, $r^0 = 5.5\%$, $r^1 = 4.5\%$. The Bachelier model demonstrates a persistent skew.

maturity T depends on $\sigma_{LN,i}$, p_i. It can be derived as follows. Let $\xi^*(t, T, K)$ be the solution of the equation

$$e^{r^{01}(T-t)} S_t \sum_{0 \le i \le I} p_i e^{-\sigma_{LN,i}^2(T-t)/2 + \sigma_{LN,i}\sqrt{T-t}\xi^*} = K.$$

Although this equation does not have a simple explicit solution, it can easily be solved numerically. We can represent C^{MXD} as follows:

$$
\begin{aligned}
C^{MXD}(t, S, T, K) &= e^{-r^1(T-t)} S_t \sum_{0 \le i \le I} p_i \left(e^{-\sigma_{LN,i}^2(T-t)/2 + \sigma_{LN,i}\sqrt{T-t}\xi} \right.\\
&\quad \left. -e^{-\sigma_{LN,i}^2(T-t)/2 + \sigma_{LN,i}\sqrt{T-t}\xi^*} \right)_+\\
&= e^{-r^1(T-t)} S_t \sum_{0 \le i \le I} p_i C_{BS} \left(t, 1, T, e^{r^{01}(T-t) - \sigma_{LN,i}^2(T-t)/2 + \sigma_{LN,i}\sqrt{T-t}\xi^*} \right).
\end{aligned}
$$

The implied volatility corresponding to a typical mixed lognormal model is shown in Figure 10.3.

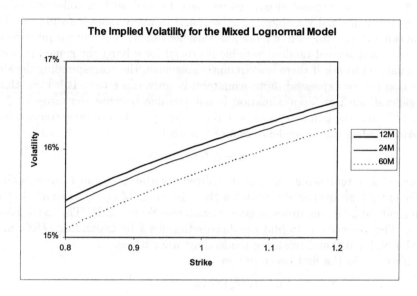

Figure 10.3: The "mixed lognormal" implied volatility $\sigma_I(T, K)$ as a function of K for three representative maturities, $T = 12, 24, 60$ months. The relevant parameters are $S_0 = 0.95$, $\sigma_{LN,0} = 30\%$, $\sigma_{LN,1} = 10\%$, $p_0 = 0.3$, $p_1 = 0.7$, $r^0 = 5.5\%$, $r^1 = 4.5\%$. The expected volatility $\bar{\sigma}_{LN} = p_0\sigma_{LN,0} + p_1\sigma_{LN,1} = 16\%$.

In need occurs, we can consider the general mixed lognormal/normal representation and choose S_T in the form

$$S_T = e^{r^{01}(T-t)}S_t \sum_i p_i e^{-\sigma_{LN,i}^2(T-t)/2 + \sigma_{LN,i}\sqrt{T-t}\xi} + \sigma_N \sqrt{T-t}\xi.$$

10.3.3   The chi-square pricing formula, I

In the previous subsection we discussed a few possible *ad hoc* choices for the distribution of S_T. In this subsection we develop a general technique for finding an approximate distribution function for a random variable

$$\theta = G(\xi),$$

functionally depending on a standard normal variable ξ, and pricing options on θ. (In more general situations we have to deal with a collection of M independent normal variables $\xi_m, m = 1, M$.) In many cases knowing the distribution density function of a random variable which is a nonlinear function of the standard normal random variable is crucial for solving the smile problem. It is natural to ask if there are circumstances when the corresponding density function can be expressed (approximately) in universal terms. It is clear that, in general, such an approximation is not possible because the range of ξ is too wide and the behavior of G over the entire range has to be accounted for. However, when the dependence of θ of ξ is weak,

$$\theta = G\left(\varepsilon\xi\right),$$

where $\varepsilon \ll 1$ represents small deannualized volatility, we can assume with a sufficiently high degree of confidence that the range of $\varepsilon\xi$ is so small that G can replaced by its quadratic approximation (see Section 2.3). This is the basic idea. The objective is to find the distribution for θ by expanding $G\left(X\right)$ in a Taylor series at 0 and retaining the leading order terms.

If we retain the first two terms we get

$$\theta = G\left(\varepsilon\xi\right) \approx G_0 + \varepsilon G_1 \xi,$$

where $G_0 = G\left(0\right)$, $G_1 = G_X\left(0\right)$. It is clear that in this approximation θ is a normal variable,

$$\theta = \mathfrak{N}\left(G_0, \varepsilon^2 G_1^2\right).$$

This approximation is crude but useful as a first cut. By retaining the first three terms in the Taylor expansion we get

$$
\begin{aligned}
\theta &= G_0 + \varepsilon G_1 \xi + \frac{1}{2}\varepsilon^2 G_2 \xi^2 \\
&= G_0 - \frac{G_1^2}{2G_2} + \frac{1}{2}\left(\varepsilon\sqrt{G_2}\xi + \frac{G_1}{\sqrt{G_2}}\right)^2 \\
&= G_0 - \frac{G_1^2}{2G_2} + \frac{\varepsilon^2 G_2}{2}\left[\mathfrak{N}\left(\frac{G_1}{\varepsilon G_2}, 1\right)\right]^2,
\end{aligned}
$$

where $G_2 = G_{XX}\left(0\right)$. Thus, the random variable θ is an affine function of a noncentral chi-square distribution with one degree of freedom whose p.d.f. of the form

$$
f_\theta\left(x\right) = \begin{cases}
\dfrac{e^{-\left(\sqrt{2(x-\alpha)}-\beta\right)^2/2\varepsilon^2\gamma} + e^{-\left(\sqrt{2(x-\alpha)}+\beta\right)^2/2\varepsilon^2\gamma}}{\sqrt{4\pi\varepsilon^2\gamma(x-\alpha)}}, & x > \alpha \\
f_\theta\left(x\right) = 0, & x \leq \alpha
\end{cases}, \qquad (10.19)
$$

where

$$\alpha = G_0 - \frac{G_1^2}{2G_2}, \quad \beta = \frac{G_1}{\sqrt{G_2}}, \quad \gamma = G_2.$$

We see that noncentral chi-square distributions appear naturally as approximations of general distributions.

If we assume that θ represents the terminal FXR S_T, we can use approximate formula (10.19) in order to price the corresponding call option with strike K. Assuming that $K > \alpha$ we can write the forward risk-neutral price of a call in the form

$$
\begin{aligned}
\check{C} &= \frac{1}{2} \int_{X^*}^{\infty} \left(X^2 - X^{*2} \right) \frac{e^{-(X-\beta)^2/2\varepsilon^2\gamma}}{\sqrt{2\pi\varepsilon^2\gamma}} dX + \frac{1}{2} \int_{-\infty}^{-X^*} \left(X^2 - X^{*2} \right) \frac{e^{-(X-\beta)^2/2\varepsilon^2\gamma}}{\sqrt{2\pi\varepsilon^2\gamma}} dX \\
&= \frac{1}{2} \int_{X^*-\beta}^{\infty} \left(Y^2 + 2\beta Y + \beta^2 - X^{*2} \right) \frac{e^{-Y^2/2\varepsilon^2\gamma}}{\sqrt{2\pi\varepsilon^2\gamma}} dY \\
&\quad + \frac{1}{2} \int_{X^*+\beta}^{\infty} \left(Y^2 - 2\beta Y + \beta^2 - X^{*2} \right) \frac{e^{-Y^2/2\varepsilon^2\gamma}}{\sqrt{2\pi\varepsilon^2\gamma}} dY \\
&= \frac{1}{2} \left(\varepsilon^2\gamma + \beta^2 - X^{*2} \right) \left(\mathfrak{N}\left(\frac{\beta - X^*}{\varepsilon\sqrt{\gamma}} \right) + \mathfrak{N}\left(-\frac{\beta + X^*}{\varepsilon\sqrt{\gamma}} \right) \right) \\
&\quad + \frac{1}{2}\varepsilon\sqrt{\gamma}\left(\beta + X^* \right) \mathfrak{n}\left(\frac{\beta - X^*}{\varepsilon\sqrt{\gamma}} \right) - \frac{1}{2}\varepsilon\sqrt{\gamma}\left(\beta - X^* \right) \mathfrak{n}\left(\frac{\beta + X^*}{\varepsilon\sqrt{\gamma}} \right),
\end{aligned}
$$

where $X^* = \sqrt{2\left(K - \alpha \right)}$.

Example 10.1. *Assume that θ a lognormal variable,*

$$\theta = A e^{\varepsilon\xi}, \quad \varepsilon \ll 1,$$

or, in other words, the classical Black-Scholes case with small volatility. We have $G_0 = G_1 = G_2 = A$, $\alpha = A/2$, $\beta = \sqrt{A}$, $\gamma = A$. The first and second order p.d.f.'s have the form

$$f_{\theta,1}(x) = \frac{e^{-(x/A-1)^2/2\varepsilon^2}}{\sqrt{2\pi}\varepsilon A},$$

$$f_{\theta,2}(x) = \begin{cases} \dfrac{e^{-(\sqrt{2x/A-1}-1)^2/2\varepsilon^2} + e^{-(\sqrt{2x/A-1}+1)^2/2\varepsilon^2}}{\sqrt{2\pi}(2x/A-1)\varepsilon A}, & x > A/2 \\ 0, & x < A/2 \end{cases}.$$

These distributions have to be compared with the exact lognormal distribution of the form

$$f_\theta(x) = \begin{cases} \dfrac{e^{-\ln^2(x/A)/2\epsilon^2}}{\sqrt{2\pi}\epsilon x}, & x > 0 \\ 0, & x < 0 \end{cases}.$$

The results of this comparison for $A = 1$, $\varepsilon = 0.25$ are shown in Figure 10.4.

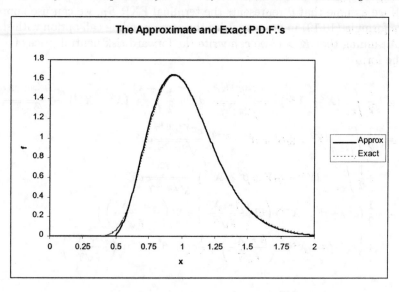

Figure 10.4: The comparison of the approximate and exact p.d.f.'s.

10.3.4   The Edgeworth-type pricing formulas

We can attempt to explain the smile by using the Edgeworth expansions which were introduced in Section 2.4 where we discussed the central limit theorem. This discussion suggests that it is natural to generalize the standard lognormal formula (10.16) and to represent S_T in the form

$$S_T = \frac{e^{\hat{r}^{01}\chi + \sqrt{\chi}\vartheta}}{\mathbb{E}\left\{e^{\sqrt{\chi}\vartheta}\right\}} S_t,$$

where $\chi = \sigma^2(T - t)$ is the nondimensional time to maturity, and ϑ is a random variable whose p.d.f. has the form

$$f_\vartheta(x) = \left(1 - \left(\frac{\gamma_3}{6\sqrt{\chi}} + \frac{\gamma_3^2}{72\chi}\right)\frac{d^3}{dx^3} + \frac{\gamma_4}{24\chi}\frac{d^4}{dx^4}\right)\mathfrak{n}(x)$$

$$= \left(1 - \frac{\varrho_3}{6}\frac{d^3}{dx^3} + \frac{\varrho_4}{24}\frac{d^4}{dx^4}\right)\mathfrak{n}(x),$$

Here γ_3, γ_4 are skewness and kurtosis of short-term returns on forex investments, while

$$\varrho_3 = \gamma_3/\sqrt{\chi} + \gamma_3^2/12\chi, \qquad \varrho_4 = \gamma_4/\chi.$$

By using integration by parts we obtain

$$\mathbb{E}\left\{e^{\sqrt{\chi}\varrho}\right\} = \int_{-\infty}^{\infty} e^{\sqrt{\chi}x}\left(1 - \frac{\varrho_3}{6}\frac{d^3}{dx^3} + \frac{\varrho_4}{24}\frac{d^4}{dx^4}\right)\mathfrak{n}(x)\,dx$$

$$= \int_{-\infty}^{\infty}\left(1 + \frac{\varrho_3}{6}\frac{d^3}{dx^3} + \frac{\varrho_4}{24}\frac{d^4}{dx^4}\right)e^{\sqrt{\chi}x}\mathfrak{n}(x)\,dx$$

$$= \left(1 + \frac{\varrho_3\chi^{3/2}}{6} + \frac{\varrho_4\chi^2}{24}\right)\int_{-\infty}^{\infty} e^{\sqrt{\chi}x}\mathfrak{n}(x)\,dx$$

$$= \left(1 + \frac{\varrho_3\chi^{3/2}}{6} + \frac{\varrho_4\chi^2}{24}\right)e^{\chi/2}.$$

We introduce the adjusted forward

$$\tilde{F}_{t,T} = \frac{e^{\hat{r}^{01}\chi}}{\left(1 + \varrho_3\chi^{3/2}/6 + \varrho_4\chi^2/24\right)}S_t,$$

and represent S_T in the form

$$S_T = e^{-\chi/2 + \sqrt{\chi}\varrho}\tilde{F}_{t,T}.$$

The price of a call option with strike K can be written as

$$\check{C}(t,S) = K\Phi(\chi,\xi),$$

where $\xi = \tilde{F}_{t,T}/K$ is the corresponding moneyness. The risk-neutral valuation formula yields

$$\Phi(\chi,\xi) = \int_{-\infty}^{\infty}\left(\xi e^{-\chi/2 + \sqrt{\chi}x} - 1\right)_+\left(1 - \frac{\varrho_3}{6}\frac{d^3}{dx^3} + \frac{\varrho_4}{24}\frac{d^4}{dx^4}\right)\mathfrak{n}(x)\,dx$$

$$= \int_{-\infty}^{\infty}\left(1 + \frac{\varrho_3}{6}\frac{d^3}{dx^3} + \frac{\varrho_4}{24}\frac{d^4}{dx^4}\right)\left(\left(\xi e^{-\chi/2 + \sqrt{\chi}x} - 1\right)_+\right)\mathfrak{n}(x)\,dx$$

$$= \Phi^{BS}(\chi,\xi) + \frac{\varrho_3}{6}\Phi_3(\chi,\xi) + \frac{\varrho_4}{24}\Phi_4(\chi,\xi),$$

where $\Phi^{BS}(\chi, \xi)$ is the standard Black-Scholes price, and

$$\Phi_3(\chi, \xi) = \int_{-\infty}^{\infty} \frac{d^3}{dx^3} \left(\left(\xi e^{-\chi/2 + \sqrt{\chi}x} - 1 \right)_+ \right) \mathfrak{n}(x) \, dx,$$

$$\Phi_4(\chi, \xi) = \int_{-\infty}^{\infty} \frac{d^4}{dx^4} \left(\left(\xi e^{-\chi/2 + \sqrt{\chi}x} - 1 \right)_+ \right) \mathfrak{n}(x) \, dx.$$

A simple algebra yields

$$\frac{d}{dx} \left(\left(\xi e^{-\chi/2 + \sqrt{\chi}x} - 1 \right)_+ \right) = \xi \sqrt{\chi} e^{-\chi/2 + \sqrt{\chi}x} \theta(x - x^*),$$

$$\frac{d^2}{dx^2} \left(\left(\xi e^{-\chi/2 + \sqrt{\chi}x} - 1 \right)_+ \right) = \xi \chi e^{-\chi/2 + \sqrt{\chi}x} \theta(x - x^*) + \sqrt{\chi}\delta(x - x^*),$$

$$\frac{d^3}{dx^3} \left(\left(\xi e^{-\chi/2 + \sqrt{\chi}x} - 1 \right)_+ \right) = \xi \chi \sqrt{\chi} e^{-\chi/2 + \sqrt{\chi}x} \theta(x - x^*)$$
$$+ \chi\delta(x - x^*) + \sqrt{\chi}\delta'(x - x^*),$$

$$\frac{d^4}{dx^4} \left(\left(\xi e^{-\chi/2 + \sqrt{\chi}x} - 1 \right)_+ \right) = \xi \chi^2 e^{-\chi/2 + \sqrt{\chi}x} \theta(x - x^*) + \chi\sqrt{\chi}\delta(x - x^*)$$
$$+ \chi\delta'(x - x^*) + \sqrt{\chi}\delta''(x - x^*),$$

where $x^* = -d_-(\chi, \xi)$. Accordingly,

$$\Phi_3(\chi, \xi) = \xi \chi \sqrt{\chi} \mathfrak{N}(d_+(\chi, \xi)) + (\sqrt{\chi} - d_-(\chi, \xi)) \sqrt{\chi} \mathfrak{n}(d_-(\chi, \xi)),$$

$$\Phi_4(\chi, \xi) = \xi \chi^2 \mathfrak{N}(d_+(\chi, \xi))$$
$$+ (\chi - \sqrt{\chi}d_-(\chi, \xi) + d_-^2(\chi, \xi) - 1) \sqrt{\chi} \mathfrak{n}(d_-(\chi, \xi)).$$

By construction, for long-dated options the Edgeworth-type volatility smiles flatten.

10.4   The sticky-strike and the sticky-delta models

By its very nature, the implied volatility concept allows one to describe only the snapshot picture of the market as it is seen today, and, without further assumptions cannot be used in order to describe its future states.[2]   Indeed, when we say that

$$\check{C}^{MKT}\left(0,F,T,K\right)=\check{C}^{BS}\left(0,F,T,K,\sigma_I\left(0,T,K\right)\right),$$

we simply reflect market realities without making any attempt to explain them. This situation is undesirable (to say the least) from the hedger's prospective. There are several plausible hypothesis which can be made in order to make the implied volatility model descriptive. We briefly discuss just two possibilities.

The sticky-strike hypothesis is the simplest possible: the implied volatility corresponding to a given strike K does not change in time. Accordingly, in the sticky-strike model the time t price of a call option with strike K has the form:

$$\check{C}^{MKT}\left(t,F,T,K\right)=\check{C}^{BS}\left(t,F,T,K,\sigma_I\left(0,T,K\right)\right).$$

By using this formula the hedger can compute the Delta in the usual way and construct the familiar risk-free portfolio:

$$\check{\Delta}^{MKT}\left(t,F,T,K\right)=\check{\Delta}^{BS}\left(t,F,T,K,\sigma_I\left(0,T,K\right)\right).$$

The model has many (some would say too many) deficiencies which stem from its simplicity (being its main strength) and can hardy be recommended for practical purposes.

The sticky-delta hypothesis is in the spirit of our scale-invariant treatment of the homogeneous Black-Scholes equation: the implied volatility is a function of the moneyness. In the sticky-delta model the time t price of a call option with strike K has the form:

$$\check{C}^{MKT}\left(t,F,T,K\right)=\check{C}^{BS}\left(t,F,T,K,\sigma_I\left(t,T,\xi\right)\right)\equiv K\Xi\left(t,T,\xi\right),\quad(10.20)$$

where $\xi=F/K$ is the moneyness. The name stems from the fact that volatilities are associated with moneyness and hence Deltas of call options rather than

---

[2] This situation should be contrasted with the classical Black-Scholes model which allows one to find option prices at any time t, $0\le t\le T$, as functions of the spot FXR S_t.

with their strikes. The corresponding Delta is a combination of the Black-Scholes Delta and Vega terms:

$$\check{\Delta}\left(t,F,T,K\right) = \check{\Delta}^{BS}\left(t,F,T,K,\sigma_I\left(t,T,\frac{F}{K}\right)\right)$$
$$+ \check{\mathcal{V}}^{BS}\left(t,F,T,K,\sigma_I\left(t,T,\frac{F}{K}\right)\right)\frac{\sigma_{I,\xi}\left(t,T,F/K\right)}{K}.$$

At first glance it seems that formula (10.20) does not have predictive powers since only $\sigma_I\left(0,T,\xi\right)$ is given by the market data. However, by skillfully applying the no-arbitrage condition we can actually determine $\sigma_I\left(t,T,\xi\right)$ and hence conditional future prices. A simple integration by parts (combined with the fact that for $\xi = 0$ both $\Xi\left(t,T,0\right)$ and $\Xi_\xi\left(t,T,0\right)$ have to vanish) shows that, regardless of the actual form of Ξ we have

$$K\Xi\left(t,T,\frac{F_{t,T}}{K}\right) = \int_0^\infty \left(F_{t,T} - \xi'K\right)_+ \Xi_{\xi\xi}\left(t,T,\xi'\right) d\xi'. \tag{10.21}$$

For $t = 0$ this formula reads

$$K\Xi\left(0,T,\frac{F_{0,T}}{K}\right) = \int_0^\infty K\xi'\Xi\left(0,t,\frac{F_{0,t}}{\xi'K}\right) \Xi_{\xi\xi}\left(t,T,\xi'\right) d\xi'. \tag{10.22}$$

This is the key formula which relates the spot price of a call maturing at time T with spot prices of calls maturing at some intermediate time t and prices of the so-called forward starting calls whose inception time is t and maturity time T.

Formula (10.21) shows that the t.p.d.f. for the process $F_{t,T}$ can be written as

$$\begin{aligned}
p\left(t,F,t',F'\right) &= \left.\frac{\partial^2}{\partial K^2}\left(K\Xi\left(t,t',\frac{F}{K}\right)\right)\right|_{K=F'} \\
&= \left.\frac{\xi^2\Xi_{\xi\xi}\left(t,t',\xi\right)}{F'}\right|_{\xi=F/F'} \\
&= \frac{q\left(t,T,F/F'\right)}{F'}.
\end{aligned}$$

We apply the operator $K\partial_{KK}$ to relation (10.22), put $K = F'$ and after some algebra obtain

$$q\left(0,T,\frac{F}{F'}\right) = \int_0^\infty q\left(0,t,\frac{F}{\xi'F'}\right) q\left(t,T,\xi'\right) \frac{d\xi'}{\xi'}. \tag{10.23}$$

This relation is the Chapman-Kolmogoroff equation (4.4) in disguise. In logarithmic variables $X = \ln(F/F')$, $Y = \ln \xi'$, equation (10.23) assumes the form of the integral equation in convolutions:

$$q(0,T,X) = \int_{-\infty}^{\infty} q(0,t,X-Y) q(t,T,Y) \, dY. \tag{10.24}$$

We emphasize that $q(t,T,X)$ are nonnegative and satisfy the normalization condition

$$\int_{-\infty}^{\infty} q(t,T,X) \, dX = 1,$$

so that they can be considered as p.d.f.'s. Equation (10.24) decomposes the p.d.f. for a process which starts as 0 at time 0 and ends at X at time T into the convolution of the p.d.f. for a process which starts as 0 at time 0 and ends at $X - Y$ at time t and the p.d.f. for a process which starts as $X - Y$ at time t and ends at X at time T.

We apply the Fourier transform to equation (10.24) and get

$$\varpi(0,T,\varsigma) = \varpi(0,t,\varsigma)\,\varpi(t,T,\varsigma).$$

Thus, the set of spot characteristic functions $\varpi(0,t,\varsigma)$, $0 \leq t \leq T$, defines all forward characteristic functions:

$$\varpi(t,T,\varsigma) = \frac{\varpi(0,T,\varsigma)}{\varpi(0,t,\varsigma)}. \tag{10.25}$$

This is precisely what we want from a model which has predictive powers and can be used for hedging of vanilla options, and ultimately, for dealing with exotic options. There is a snag, however, since, in general, we cannot guarantee that $\varpi(t,T,\varsigma)$ defined by equation (10.25) is a characteristic function for a p.d.f.! According to the celebrated Bochner-Khinchine theorem, $\varpi(0,t,\varsigma)$ has to satisfy the positivity and normalization conditions of the form

$$\sum_{m,n=1}^{N} \varpi(0,t,\varsigma_m - \varsigma_n)\, \varrho_m \bar{\varrho}_n \geq 0, \tag{10.26}$$

$$\varpi(0,t,0) = 1. \tag{10.27}$$

Inequality (10.26) holds for any collection of points ς_m and any complex numbers ϱ_m. Whether or not these conditions are satisfied depends on a particular market snapshot.

In the simplest case of the Gaussian p.d.f.'s defined by a given volatility term structure, we have

$$q\left(0,t,X\right) = \frac{e^{-X^2/2\chi(t)}}{\sqrt{2\pi\chi\left(t\right)}},$$

$$\varpi\left(0,t,\varsigma\right) = e^{-\chi(t)\varsigma^2/2},$$

with

$$\chi\left(t\right) = t\sigma_I^2\left(t\right) = \int_0^t \sigma_L\left(t'\right)dt'.$$

Accordingly,

$$\varpi\left(t,T,\varsigma\right) = \exp\left\{-\left(T\sigma_I^2\left(T\right) - t\sigma_I^2\left(t\right)\right)\varsigma^2/2\right\} \quad (10.28)$$
$$= \exp\left\{-\left(\int_t^T \sigma_L\left(t'\right)dt'\right)\varsigma^2/2\right\}.$$

Thus, conditions (10.26), (10.27) reduce to the simple requirement of monotonicity of $t\sigma_I^2\left(t\right)$ which insures that forward volatilities are positive.

In addition to Gaussian p.d.f.'s (10.28) the so-called Levy p.d.f.'s with characteristic functions of the form

$$\varpi\left(0,t,\varsigma\right) = \exp\left\{\int_0^t\left[i\alpha\left(t'\right)\varsigma - \frac{\beta\left(t'\right)\varsigma^2}{2} + \int_{|x|\leq1}\left(e^{i\varsigma x} - 1 - \varsigma x\right)d\Pi\left(t',x\right)\right.\right.$$
$$\left.\left. + \int_{|x|>1}\left(e^{i\varsigma x} - 1\right)d\Pi\left(t',x\right)\right]dt'\right\},$$

where $d\Pi\left(t,x\right)$ is an appropriate measure, are attractive candidates for p.d.f.'s compatible with the sticky-delta model. However, their detailed discussion is outside the scope of this book.

10.5   The general local volatility model

10.5.1   Introduction

As we saw earlier the standard lognormality assumption for the distribution of FXRs is seldom (if ever) in agreement with the markets. Because of that, it is useful to study processes for the evolution of FXRs which are different from the geometric Brownian motion. In principle, the variety of such processes is enormous. However, more often than not the corresponding pricing problem cannot be solved explicitly which makes it important to identify processes for which an explicit solution is feasible.

The most efficient method for pricing derivatives in the non-Black-Scholes framework is to transform the pricing problem into the Black-Scholes problem, or, even better, to the initial value problem for the standard heat equation. If this is not possible, we can use the Bessel equation (say) as a benchmark. In this section we describe some general transformations which can be used to this end and derive a sufficient condition which guarantees that these transformations fulfil their purpose. We also give a couple of representative examples demonstrating the efficiency of our approach.

10.5.2 Possible functional forms of local volatility

In view of the relation (7.11) we cannot choose the functional form for σ^{01} arbitrarily if we want σ^{10} to have the same functional form. An interesting and sufficiently general choice is

$$\sigma(t, s) = \sqrt{\theta_2(t) s^2 + \theta_1(t) s + \theta_0(t) + \theta_{-1}(t) s^{-1} + \theta_{-2}(t) s^{-2}},$$

which generalizes the hyperbolic volatility model[3]

$$\sigma(t, s) = \theta_1(t) s + \theta_0(t) + \theta_{-1}(t) s^{-1}.$$

Assuming that θ_n are time-independent, we want to find conditions on θ which guarantee that the equation

$$C_t + \frac{1}{2}\sigma^2 \left(\frac{S}{\bar{S}}\right) S^2 C_{SS} + r^{01} S C_S - r^0 C = 0,$$

is reducible to the standard heat equation. We use the solvability condition of Section 4.10. Assuming that $P(t) = 1, Q(t) = 0$, we get

$$\Omega = -\frac{\theta_2 s + \frac{3}{4}\theta_2 + \left(\frac{1}{2}\theta_0 - r^{01}\right) s^{-1} + \frac{1}{4}\theta_{-1} s^{-2}}{\theta_2 s^2 + \theta_1 s + \theta_0 + \theta_{-1} s^{-1} + \theta_0 s^{-2}},$$

$$\frac{1}{2}\sigma^2 \left(\Omega_s - \Omega^2\right) + r^{01} s \Omega = \frac{\delta_2 s^2 + \delta_1 s + \delta_0 + \delta_{-1} s^{-1} + \delta_{-2} s^{-2}}{\theta_2 s^2 + \theta_1 s + \theta_0 + \theta_{-1} s^{-1} + \theta_0 s^{-2}}, \quad (10.29)$$

---

[3]More generally, we can consider σ to be a function of a symmetric Laurent series, i.e., $\sigma = f\left(\sum_{-N}^{N} \theta_n s^n\right)$.

where

$$\delta_2 = \frac{1}{32}\left(3\theta_1^2 - 8\theta_2\theta_0 - 48r^{01}\theta_2\right),$$

$$\delta_1 = \frac{1}{8}\left(\theta_1\theta_0 - 8r^{01}\theta_1 + 6\theta_2\theta_{-1}\right),$$

$$\delta_0 = \frac{1}{16}\left(2\theta_0^2 - 24\theta_2\theta_{-2} - 3\theta_1\theta_{-1} - 8r^{01}\left(\theta_0 - r^{01}\right)\right),$$

$$\delta_{-1} = \frac{1}{8}\left(\theta_0\theta_{-1} - 6\theta_1\theta_{-2}\right),$$

$$\delta_{-2} = \frac{1}{32}\left(3\theta_{-1}^2 - 8\left(\theta_0 - 2r^{01}\right)\theta_{-2}\right).$$

The solvability condition is satisfied if the r.h.s. of equation (10.29) is constant, or, in other words, if

$$\frac{\delta_2}{\theta_2} = ... = \frac{\delta_{-2}}{\theta_{-2}}. \tag{10.30}$$

We leave it to the reader as a (very involved) exercise to find the general solution of system (10.30) and restrict ourselves to presenting a few special solutions some of which are known and some are new. For $r^{01} = 0$ we can solve the above equations by choosing θ_n as follows

$$\theta_2 = \sigma_0^2/\left(B - A\right)^2,$$
$$\theta_1 = -2\theta_2\left(A + B\right),$$
$$\theta_0 = \theta_2\left(\left(A + B\right)^2 + 2AB\right),$$
$$\theta_{-1} = -2\theta_2 AB\left(A + B\right),$$
$$\theta_{-2} = \theta_2 A^2 B^2,$$

which corresponds to the choice

$$\sigma\left(s\right) = \frac{\sigma_0\left(s - A\right)\left(B - s\right)}{\left(B - A\right)s},$$

i.e., to the hyperbolic volatility model. Its limiting cases are $\sigma\left(s\right) = \sigma$ and $\sigma\left(s\right) = \sigma s^{-1}$ corresponding to the lognormal and normal volatility models.

We already know that analytical pricing is possible in the limiting cases. The fact that it is possible in the general case comes as a pleasant surprise.

The fact that the hyperbolic volatility model is the only reducible time-independent model in the case when $r^{01} = 0$ can be established as follows. The time-independent pricing equation which can be written as

$$V_t + \frac{1}{2}\sigma^2 \left(\frac{S}{\bar{S}}\right) S^2 V_{SS} = 0.$$

We follow the general recipe given in Section 4.10, restrict ourselves to time-independent transformations, and put $P(t) = 1$, $Q(t) = 0$. Then

$$\theta = t, \quad X = \Psi(s) = \int \frac{ds}{\sigma(s)s}, \quad \Omega = -\frac{1}{2}\left(\frac{\sigma_s}{\sigma} + \frac{1}{s}\right),$$

and the reducibility condition yields

$$s\sigma_{sss}(s) + 3\sigma_{ss} = (s\sigma(s))_{sss} = 0.$$

Thus, the most general time-independent normal volatility which can be treated via the transformations described above is quadratic in s. We can extend the domain of applicability of the problem and include the case $r^{01} \neq 0$ by allowing the coefficients A, B to grow at their natural rate, i.e., by choosing them in the form $A_t = e^{r^{01}t}A_0$, $B_t = e^{r^{01}t}B_0$ (see below).

When $r^{01} \geq 0$ we can put

$$\theta_2 = \theta_1 = \theta_{-1} = 0, \quad \theta_0 = 2r^{01}, \quad \theta_{-2} \geq 0 \text{ is arbitrary,}$$

so that

$$\sigma(s) = \sqrt{2r^{01} + \theta_{-2}s^{-2}}.$$

The corresponding model is called the displaced diffusion model. Its sister model which seems to be new is obtained by switching from foreign to domestic country. The corresponding $\sigma(s)$ is

$$\sigma(s) = \sqrt{\theta_2 s^2 - 2r^{10}}.$$

(Recall that by assumption $r^{10} \leq 0$, so that the square root is well-defined for all s.) Two new models are variations of the previous ones:

$$\sigma(s) = \begin{cases} \sqrt{2r^{01}/3 + \theta_{-2}s^{-2}}, & r^{01} \geq 0 \\ \sqrt{\theta_2 s^2 - 2r^{10}/3}, & r^{10} \leq 0 \end{cases}.$$

10.5.3   The hyperbolic volatility model

In fact, the above observation can be used in order to price options on FXRs which are kept within a certain band due to the government intervention. Let us assume that at $t = 0$ the lower and upper limits A_0, B_0 are chosen,

$$A_0 < S_0 < B_0.$$

Due to the interest rate parity theorem these limits have to evolve in time as follows

$$A_t = e^{r^{01}t}A_0, \quad B_t = e^{r^{01}t}B_0.$$

We want to model the dynamics of the spot FXR in such a way that S_t cannot reach the points A_t, B_t. We can achieve this goal by assuming that the corresponding volatility is a hyperbolic function of s vanishing at A_t, B_t :

$$\sigma(t,s) = \frac{\sigma_0(s - e^{r^{01}t}A_0)(e^{r^{01}t}B_0 - s)}{e^{r^{01}t}(B_0 - A_0)s}.$$

The risk-neutralized dynamics of FXR is governed by the SDE of the form

$$\frac{dS_t}{S_t} = r^{01}dt + \sigma\left(t, \frac{S_t}{\bar{S}}\right)dW_t.$$

When written in terms of the forward FXR this equation assumes the form

$$\frac{dF_{t,T}}{F_{t,T}} = \sigma\left(\frac{F_{t,T}}{\bar{S}}\right)dW_t,$$

where

$$\sigma(f) = \frac{\sigma_0(f - A_T)(B_T - f)}{(B_T - A_T)f}.$$

The corresponding pricing problem for $\check{C}$ has time-independent coefficients:

$$\check{C}_t + \frac{1}{2}\sigma^2\left(\frac{F}{\bar{S}}\right)F^2\check{C}_{FF} = 0,$$

$$\check{C}(T, F) = (F - K)_+,$$

where $A_T < K < B_T$. Since the normal volatility is a quadratic function of its argument, the pricing problem satisfies the reducibility condition. The actual transformation is done as follows:

$$t \quad \rightarrow \quad \chi = \sigma_0^2 \, (T - t), \quad F \rightarrow X = \ln \left(\frac{F - A_T}{B_T - F} \right),$$

$$\check{C}(t, F) \quad \rightarrow \quad U(\chi, X) = e^{X/8} \left(e^{X/2} + e^{-X/2} \right) \check{C}(t, F).$$

The pricing problem for U has the form

$$U_\tau - \frac{1}{2} U_{XX} = 0,$$

$$U(0, X) = \left((B_T - K) \, e^{X/2} - (K - A_T) \, e^{-X/2} \right)_+ .$$

This problem is similar to the pricing problem for the standard call and can be solved by the same means. The corresponding solution has the form

$$U(\chi, X) = e^{X/8} \left((B_T - K) \, e^{X/2} \mathfrak{N}(\tilde{d}_+) - (K - A_T) \, e^{-X/2} \mathfrak{N}(\tilde{d}_-) \right).$$

Restoring the original variables we obtain the price of a call

$$\check{C}(t, F) = \frac{(B_T - K)(F - A_T)}{(B_T - A_T)} \mathfrak{N}(\tilde{d}_+) - \frac{(K - A_T)(B_T - F)}{(B_T - A_T)} \mathfrak{N}(\tilde{d}_-).$$

Here

$$\tilde{d}_\pm = \frac{X + \ln \left((B_T - K)/(K - A_T) \right)}{\sqrt{\chi}} \pm \frac{\sqrt{\chi}}{2}$$

$$= \frac{\ln \left((B_T - K)(F - A_T)/(B_T - F)(K - A_T) \right)}{\sigma_0 \sqrt{T - t}} \pm \frac{\sigma_0 \sqrt{T - t}}{2}.$$

The price of a put can be found via call-put parity.

We show the forward call price $\check{C}$ as a function of the forward FXR F in Figure 10.5. For comparison, we also show the standard Black-Scholes forward call price. We choose the equivalent lognormal volatility $\hat{\sigma}$ according to the rule

$$\hat{\sigma} = \frac{(B_T - A_T)}{3(B_T + A_T)} \sigma_0, \tag{10.31}$$

which ensures that the "average" volatilities are the same in both models.

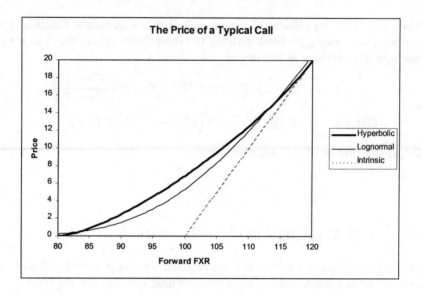

Figure 10.5: The price of a typical call as a function of the forward FXR for $A_T = 80$, $B_T = 120$, $K = 100$, $\sigma_0 = 2$, $\tau = 1$ in the hyperbolic volatility model. The equivalent Black-Scholes price with σ given by equation (10.31), and the intrinsic price are shown for comparison.

10.5.4   The displaced diffusion model

Above we accounted for the presence of the risk-neutral drift by writing the evolution problem in forward terms. In this subsection we use a different tactic. We consider the evolution problem

$$\frac{dS_t}{S_t} = r^{01}dt + \sigma\left(\frac{S_t}{\overline{S}}\right)dW_t, \quad S_0 \text{ is given,}$$

with $r^{01} > 0$, and choose a time-independent $\sigma(s)$ in such a way that the corresponding Ω vanishes, $\Omega = 0$, so that the reducibility condition is trivially satisfied. Then

$$-\frac{\sigma_s(s)}{2\sigma(s)} - \frac{1}{2s} + \frac{r^{01}}{s\sigma^2(s)} = 0,$$

so that

$$\sigma(s) = \sqrt{2r^{01} + \sigma_0^2 s^{-2}} = \sqrt{2r^{01}}\sqrt{1 + \tilde{\sigma}_0^2 s^{-2}},$$

where $\tilde{\sigma}_0^2 = \sigma_0^2/2r^{01}$. Since the point $S = 0$ is regular, we need to impose the Dirichlet condition in order to guarantee that S_t stays nonnegative. In terms of τ, S the pricing problem for the forward call price can be written as

$$\check{C}_\tau - \frac{1}{2}\left(2r^{01} + \sigma_0^2\left(\frac{S}{\bar{S}}\right)^{-2}\right)S^2\check{C}_{SS} - r^{01}S\check{C}_S = 0,$$

$$\check{C}(0, S) = (S - K)_+,$$

$$\check{C}(\tau, 0) = 0.$$

In the limiting case $\sigma_0 = 0$, S_t follows the geometric Brownian motion while $\ln\left(S_t/\bar{S}\right)$ follows the arithmetic Brownian motion with zero drift. In general, the volatility does not approach zero when the FXR does, hence the name of the model.

Following the general recipe, we introduce a new dependent variable

$$X = \frac{1}{\sqrt{2r^{01}}}\ln\left(\frac{s + \sqrt{s^2 + \tilde{\sigma}_0^2}}{\tilde{\sigma}_0}\right), \qquad (10.32)$$

where $s = S/\bar{S}$. This variable is non-negative, $0 \le X < \infty$, its dimension is $\sqrt{\text{time}}$. We verify that

$$X_s = \frac{1}{\sqrt{2r^{01}}\left(s^2 + \tilde{\sigma}_0^2\right)^{1/2}},$$

$$X_{ss} = -\frac{s}{\sqrt{2r^{01}}\left(s^2 + \tilde{\sigma}_0^2\right)^{3/2}},$$

and use Ito's lemma to show that X_t is a Wiener process:

$$dX_t = dW_t,$$

killed at zero. The inversion of formula (10.32) yields:

$$s = \frac{\tilde{\sigma}_0}{2} \left(e^{\sqrt{2r^{01}}X} - e^{-\sqrt{2r^{01}}X} \right) = \tilde{\sigma}_0 \sinh\left(\sqrt{2r^{01}}X \right).$$

In terms of τ, X the pricing problem for $\check{C}$ can be written as

$$\check{C}_\tau - \frac{1}{2}\check{C}_{XX} = 0,$$

$$\check{C}(0, X) = \frac{\tilde{\sigma}_0}{2} \left(e^{\sqrt{2r^{01}}X} - e^{-\sqrt{2r^{01}}X} - 2\tilde{K} \right)_+,$$

$$\check{C}(\tau, 0) = 0,$$

where $\tilde{K} = K/\tilde{\sigma}_0$. Since, by assumption, the process X is killed at zero, we can write $\check{C}$ in the form

$$\check{C}(\tau, X) = \int_{X^*}^{\infty} \frac{e^{-(X-X')^2/2\tau} - e^{-(X+X')^2/2\tau}}{\sqrt{2\pi\tau}}$$
$$\times \left(e^{\sqrt{2r^{01}}X'} - e^{-\sqrt{2r^{01}}X'} - 2\tilde{K} \right) dX',$$

where $X^* = \text{arcsinh}\left(\tilde{K} \right)$. Thus, in order to find $\check{C}(\tau, X)$ we need to compute six Gaussian integrals. We leave simple details to the (patient) reader and present the final expression for $C(\tau, S) = e^{-r^{01}\tau}\check{C}(\tau, S)$:

$$C(\tau, S) \tag{10.33}$$
$$= \frac{1}{2}e^{-r^1\tau} \left(S + \sqrt{S^2 + \tilde{\sigma}_0^2 \bar{S}^2} \right) \left(\mathfrak{N}\left(\tilde{d}_{+,+} \right) + \mathfrak{N}\left(\tilde{d}_{-,-} \right) \right)$$
$$- \frac{1}{2}e^{-r^1\tau} \left(-S + \sqrt{S^2 + \tilde{\sigma}_0^2 \bar{S}^2} \right) \left(\mathfrak{N}\left(\tilde{d}_{+,-} \right) + \mathfrak{N}\left(\tilde{d}_{-,+} \right) \right)$$
$$- e^{-r^0\tau} K \left[\mathfrak{N}\left(\frac{\tilde{d}_{+,+} + \tilde{d}_{+,-}}{2} \right) - \mathfrak{N}\left(\frac{\tilde{d}_{-,+} + \tilde{d}_{-,-}}{2} \right) \right],$$

where

$$\tilde{d}_{\pm,\pm} = \frac{\ln\left(\frac{\pm S + \sqrt{S^2 + \tilde{\sigma}_0^2 \bar{S}^2}}{K + \sqrt{K^2 + \tilde{\sigma}_0^2 \bar{S}^2}} \right)}{\sqrt{2r^{01}\tau}} \pm \sqrt{2r^{01}\tau}.$$

We plot the corresponding implied volatility for several representative cases in Figure 10.6.

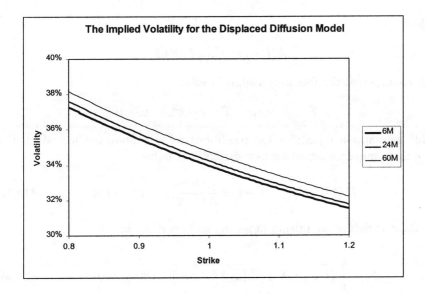

Figure 10.6: The "displaced diffusion" implied volatility $\sigma_I(T, K)$ as a function of K for three representative maturities, $T = 6, 24, 60$ months. The relevant parameters are $S_0 = 0.95$, $\bar{S} = 1.00$, $\sigma_0 = 30\%$, $r^0 = 5.5\%$, $r^1 = 4.5\%$.

10.6 Asymptotic treatment of the local volatility model

In this section we discuss the behavior of short-dated options which are approximately ATMF (otherwise the problem is uninteresting) in the local volatility framework. We assume that the underlying process for forward prices follows a scalar SDE with a given local volatility,

$$\frac{dF_{t,T}}{F_{t,T}} = \sigma\left(t, \frac{F_{t,T}}{\bar{F}}\right) dW_t.$$

The pricing equation has a familiar form

$$\check{C}_t + \frac{1}{2} A(t, F) \check{C}_{FF} = 0,$$

$$\check{C}(T, F) = (F - K)_+.$$

where

$$A(t, F) = \sigma^2 \left(t, F/\bar{F} \right) F^2.$$

We assume that the following scaling is valid:

$$F - K \sim \varepsilon, \qquad T - t \sim \varepsilon^2, \qquad \varepsilon \to 0.$$

This assumption quantifies the conditions we are interested in. With this scaling in mind we introduce new variables as follows

$$F = K(1 + \varepsilon X), \qquad T - t = \frac{\varepsilon^2 K^2 \chi}{A(T, K)}, \qquad C = \varepsilon K \Phi. \tag{10.34}$$

In these variables the pricing problem can be written as

$$\Phi_\chi - \frac{1}{2} \left(1 + \varepsilon a_1 X + \varepsilon^2 \left(a_2 X^2 + c_2 \chi \right) ... \right) \Phi_{XX} = 0, \tag{10.35}$$

$$\Phi(0, X) = X_+, \tag{10.36}$$

where

$$a_1 = \frac{K A_K(T, K)}{A(T, K)} = 2 + \frac{2 K \sigma_K(T, K)}{\sigma(T, K)} = 2 + 2\alpha_1,$$

$$
\begin{aligned}
a_2 &= \frac{K^2 A_{KK}(T, K)}{2 A(T, K)} \\
&= 1 + \frac{4 K \sigma_K(T, K)}{\sigma(T, K)} + \frac{K^2 \sigma_K^2(T, K)}{\sigma^2(T, K)} + \frac{K^2 \sigma_{KK}(T, K)}{\sigma(T, K)} \\
&= 1 + 4\alpha_1 + \alpha_1^2 + \alpha_2,
\end{aligned}
$$

$$c_2 = -\frac{K^2 A_T(T, K)}{A^2(T, K)} = -\frac{2 \sigma_T(T, K)}{\sigma^3(T, K)}.$$

The solution of this problem for $\varepsilon = 0$ is

$$\Phi^{(0)}(\chi, X) = X \mathfrak{N} \left(\frac{X}{\sqrt{\chi}} \right) + \sqrt{\chi} \mathfrak{n} \left(\frac{X}{\sqrt{\chi}} \right) \equiv \Xi(\chi, X),$$

where $\Xi(\chi, X)$ is the classical Bachelier solution. A straightforward calculation yields

$$\Xi_\chi = \frac{1}{2}H,$$

$$\Xi_{\chi X} = -\frac{1}{2}\frac{X}{\chi}H,$$

$$\Xi_{XX} = \frac{1}{2}\frac{(X^2 - \chi)}{2\chi^2}H,$$

$$\Xi_{\chi X X} = -\frac{1}{2}\frac{X(X^2 - 3\chi)}{2\chi^3}H,$$

where

$$H(\chi, X) = \frac{e^{-X^2/2\chi}}{\sqrt{2\pi\chi}},$$

is the standard heat kernel.

We want to find the solution of (10.35), (10.36) for $\varepsilon \to 0$. We use the power series expansion

$$\Phi^{(\varepsilon)}(\chi, X) = \Xi(\chi, X) + \varepsilon \Phi^{(1)}(\chi, X) + \varepsilon^2 \Phi^{(2)}(\chi, X). \tag{10.37}$$

Substituting this expression into equation (10.35), using the fact that Ξ solves the unperturbed equation, and collecting terms proportional to $\varepsilon, \varepsilon^2$ we obtain

$$\Phi^{(1)}_\chi - \frac{1}{2}\Phi^{(1)}_{XX} = a_1 X \Xi_X, \tag{10.38}$$

$$\Phi^{(2)}_\chi - \frac{1}{2}\Phi^{(2)}_{XX} = a_1 X \Phi^{(1)}_X + \left((a_2 - a_1^2)X^2 + c_2\chi\right)\Xi_X. \tag{10.39}$$

It is inconvenient to deal with expansion (10.37) directly. The idea is to write $\Phi^{(\varepsilon)}$ in terms of the "implied time to maturity" instead:

$$\Phi^{(\varepsilon)}(\chi, X) = \Xi\left(\left(1 + \varepsilon b_1 X + \varepsilon^2\left(b_2 X^2 + d_2\chi\right)\right)\chi, X\right).$$

To put it another way, we use the near-identity transform in order to express $\Phi^{(\varepsilon)}$ in terms of Ξ.[4] A simple calculation yields:

$$\Phi^{(\varepsilon)} = \Xi + \varepsilon b_1 \chi X \Xi_\chi + \varepsilon^2\left(\left(b_2 X^2 + d_2\chi\right)\chi\Xi_\chi + \frac{1}{2}b_1^2\chi^2 X^2\Xi_{\chi\chi}\right) + ...,$$

---

[4] Transforms of this kind are extremely useful in many situations occurring in applied mathematics and physics. In particular, they play an outstanding role in perturbation theory.

so that

$$\Phi^{(1)} = b_1 \chi X \Xi_\chi, \tag{10.40}$$

$$\Phi^{(2)} = \left(b_2 X^2 + d_2 \chi\right) \chi \Xi_\chi + \frac{1}{2} b_1^2 \chi^2 X^2 \Xi_{\chi\chi}.$$

We substitute (10.40) in equation (10.38) and obtain the following equation for b_1:

$$b_1 \left(X \Xi_\chi - \chi \Xi_\chi X\right) = a_1 X \Xi_\chi,$$

$$b_1 = \frac{1}{2} a_1.$$

Accordingly,

$$\Phi^{(1)} = \frac{1}{2} a_1 \chi X \Xi_\chi,$$

$$\Phi^{(2)} = \left(b_2 X^2 + d_2 \chi\right) \chi \Xi_\chi + \frac{1}{8} a_1^2 \chi^2 X^2 \Xi_{\chi\chi}.$$

Substituting these expressions in equation (10.39) we get the equations for b_2, d_2:

$$\left(b_2 X^2 + 2 d_2 \chi\right) \Xi_\chi - 2 b_2 \chi X \Xi_{\chi X} - b_2 \chi \Xi_\chi$$

$$= -\frac{1}{4} a_1^2 \chi X^2 \Xi_{\chi\chi} + \frac{1}{4} a_1^2 \chi^2 X \Xi_{\chi\chi X} + \frac{1}{8} a_1^2 \chi^2 \Xi_{\chi\chi}$$

$$+ \frac{1}{2} a_1^2 \chi X^2 \Xi_{\chi\chi} + \frac{1}{2} a_1^2 X^2 \Xi_\chi + \left(\left(a_2 - a_1^2\right) X^2 + c_2 \chi\right) \Xi_\chi,$$

or, after simplifications,

$$b_2 X^2 \Xi_\chi + (2 d_2 - b_2) \chi \Xi_\chi - 2 b_2 X \chi \Xi_{\chi X}$$

$$= \left(a_2 - \frac{1}{2} a_1^2\right) X^2 \Xi_\chi + c_2 \chi \Xi_\chi + \frac{1}{4} a_1^2 \chi X^2 \Xi_{\chi\chi}$$

$$+ \frac{1}{4} a_1^2 \chi^2 X \Xi_{\chi\chi X} + \frac{1}{8} a_1^2 \chi^2 \Xi_{\chi\chi}.$$

Equivalently,

$$3 b_2 X^2 + (2 d_2 - b_2) \chi = \left(a_2 - \frac{3}{16} a_1^2\right) X^2 + \left(c_2 - \frac{1}{16} a_1^2\right) \chi.$$

Thus,

$$b_2 = -\frac{1}{16}a_1^2 + \frac{1}{3}a_2,$$

$$d_2 = \frac{1}{2}c_2 - \frac{1}{16}a_1^2 + \frac{1}{6}a_2,$$

$$\Phi^{(2)} = \left(\frac{1}{16}a_1^2 X^4 + \left(-\frac{1}{8}a_1^2 + \frac{1}{3}a_2 \right) \chi X^2 \right.$$
$$\left. + \left(\frac{1}{2}c_2 - \frac{1}{16}a_1^2 + \frac{1}{6}a_2 \right) \chi^2 \right) \Xi_\chi.$$

The corresponding implied time to maturity is

$$\chi_I = \left(1 + \frac{1}{2}a_1 \varepsilon X + \left(-\frac{1}{16}a_1^2 + \frac{1}{3}a_2 \right) \varepsilon^2 X^2 \right.$$
$$\left. + \left(\frac{1}{2}c_2 - \frac{1}{16}a_1^2 + \frac{1}{6}a_2 \right) \varepsilon^2 \chi \right) \chi.$$

Consider now the classical Black-Scholes pricing problem with $A(K) = \left(\sigma^{BS} \right)^2 K^2$. We use overbars to distinguish new variables and write

$$F = K(1 + \varepsilon X), \qquad T - t = \frac{\varepsilon^2 \bar{\chi}}{\left(\sigma^{BS} \right)^2}, \qquad C = \varepsilon K \Phi. \qquad (10.41)$$

$$\bar{a}_1 = 2, \qquad \bar{a}_2 = 1, \qquad c_2 = 0.$$

The corresponding implied time to maturity is

$$\bar{\chi}_I = \left(1 + \varepsilon X + \frac{1}{12}\varepsilon^2 X^2 - \frac{1}{12}\varepsilon^2 \bar{\chi} \right) \bar{\chi}.$$

We express $\bar{\chi}$ in terms of $\bar{\chi}_I$:

$$\bar{\chi} = \left(1 - \varepsilon X + \frac{11}{12}\varepsilon^2 X^2 + \frac{1}{12}\varepsilon^2 \bar{\chi}_I \right) \bar{\chi}_I,$$

assume that $\chi_I = \bar{\chi}_I$, and obtain the following relation between χ and $\bar{\chi}$:

$$\bar{\chi} = \left(1 + \alpha_1 \varepsilon X + \frac{1}{12} \left(-2\alpha_1 + \alpha_1^2 + 4\alpha_2 \right) \varepsilon^2 X^2 \right.$$
$$\left. + \frac{1}{12} \left(6c_2 + 2\alpha_1 - \alpha_1^2 + 2\alpha_2 \right) \varepsilon^2 \chi \right) \chi.$$

We substitute expressions (10.34), (10.41) in the above relation and obtain

$$
\left(\sigma^{BS}\right)^2 = \left(1 + \alpha_1 \left(\frac{F-K}{K}\right) + \frac{1}{12}\left(-2\alpha_1 + \alpha_1^2 + 4\alpha_2\right)\left(\frac{F-K}{K}\right)^2 \right.
$$
$$
\left. + \frac{1}{12}\left(6c_2 + 2\alpha_1 - \alpha_1^2 + 2\alpha_2\right)\sigma_L^2\left(T-t\right)\right)\sigma_L^2,
$$

$$
\sigma^{BS} \tag{10.42}
$$
$$
= \left(1 + \frac{\alpha_1}{2}\left(\frac{F-K}{K}\right) + \frac{1}{12}\left(-\alpha_1 - \alpha_1^2 + 2\alpha_2\right)\left(\frac{F-K}{K}\right)^2 \right.
$$
$$
\left. + \frac{1}{24}\left(6c_2 + 2\alpha_1 - \alpha_1^2 + 2\alpha_2\right)\sigma_L^2\left(T-t\right)\right)\sigma_L
$$
$$
= \left(1 + \frac{1}{24}\left(-2\alpha_1 - 2\alpha_1^2 + \alpha_2\right)\left(\frac{F-K}{K}\right)^2 \right.
$$
$$
\left. + \frac{1}{24}\left(2\alpha_1 - \alpha_1^2 + 2\alpha_2\right)\sigma_L^2\left(T-t\right)\right)
$$
$$
\times \left(1 + \frac{\alpha_1}{2}\left(\frac{F-K}{K}\right) + \frac{\alpha_2}{8}\left(\frac{F-K}{K}\right)^2 + \frac{c_2}{4}\sigma_L^2\left(T-t\right)\right)\sigma_L
$$
$$
= \left(1 + \frac{1}{24}\left(-2\tilde{\alpha}_1 - 2\tilde{\alpha}_1^2 + \tilde{\alpha}_2\right)\left(\frac{F-K}{K}\right)^2 \right.
$$
$$
\left. + \frac{1}{24}\left(2\tilde{\alpha}_1 - \tilde{\alpha}_1^2 + 2\tilde{\alpha}_2\right)\tilde{\sigma}_L^2\left(T-t\right)\right)\tilde{\sigma}_L.
$$

Here, without loss of accuracy, we assume that the volatility $\tilde{\sigma}_L$ and its derivatives $\tilde{\alpha}_1, \tilde{\alpha}_2$ are evaluated at the same midpoint,

$$
\tilde{\sigma}_L = \sigma_L\left(\frac{t+T}{2}, \frac{F+K}{2}\right). \tag{10.43}
$$

Relation (10.43) can be used as a tool for approximately solving the calibration problem. Indeed, if we consider it as a relation between the implied volatility $\sigma^{BS}(T, K)$ (which is assumed to be given) and the local volatility $\sigma_L(t, F)$ we can invert it and express σ_L in terms of σ^{BS}. We emphasize that, in sharp contrast with the Dupire procedure described in Section 10.2 which requires differentiation of the implied volatility surface, this one requires its integration and, as a result, is potentially much more stable. The leading order relation between σ^{BS} and σ_L has a remarkably simple form. If t^*, F^* denote the current time and forward FXR, then

$$\sigma_L(t, F) = \sigma^{BS}(2t - t^*, 2F - F^*). \tag{10.44}$$

This expression for σ_L can be used as a starting point for a more elaborate inversion procedure. Among other things it shows that the following equality holds (approximately)

$$\sigma_L(t^*, F^*) = \sigma^{BS}(t^*, F^*).$$

We note in passing that formula (10.44) can be used to explain the old rule of thumb which states that the slope of the local volatility is twice the slope of the implied volatility.

10.7   The CEV model

10.7.1   Introduction

In this section we show how to use the above considerations in order to study the so-called constant elasticity of variance (CEV) model. Recall that this model is based on the assumption that the volatility depends on the FXR according to a power law:

$$\sigma(t, s) = \sigma(t) s^{-\beta}.$$

The model tries to account for both the term structure and smile effects. The corresponding SDE for S_t has the form

$$\frac{dS_t}{S_t} = r^{01} dt + \sigma_t \left(\frac{S_t}{\overline{S}}\right)^{-\beta} dW_t, \quad S_0 \text{ is given}. \tag{10.45}$$

Since

$$\frac{d\ln\left(\sigma^2(t, s)\right)}{d\ln s} = -\beta,$$

we say that -2β is the elasticity of the lognormal variance.

The classical lognormal case corresponds to $\beta = 0$, while the normal case corresponds to $\beta = 1$. Below we assume that $-1 \leq \beta \leq 1$, so that functional form of SDE (10.45) remains invariant with respect to the switch between the domestic and foreign markets (cf. equation (7.11)). We derive the pricing formulas for the case $0 < \beta \leq 1$ first, and use put-call symmetry to cover the case $-1 \leq \beta < 0$. For $\beta = 0$ we can use the standard Black-Scholes formula. The pricing problem for a European call can be written as

$$C_t + \frac{1}{2}\sigma^2(t)\left(\frac{S}{\bar{S}}\right)^{-2\beta} S^2 C_{SS} + r^{01} S C_S - r^0 C = 0,$$

$$C(T, S) = (S - K)_+.$$

In order to solve the above problem we use a multi-step strategy. First, we reduce the pricing problem to the simplest possible form. Then we find the Green's function for the modified pricing equation. Finally, we use the Green's function in order to price calls and puts (although the latter can be priced via put-call parity which holds for the problem under consideration).

10.7.2   Reductions of the pricing problem

As usual, the most efficient way of solving a complicated parabolic equation is via an appropriate reduction of this equation to a simpler form. We start with removing the interest rate terms by rewriting the pricing problem in forward terms

$$C(t, S) = e^{-r^0(T-t)} \check{C}\left(t, e^{r^{01}(T-t)}S\right) = e^{-r^0(T-t)} \check{C}(t, F).$$

The pricing problem for $\check{C}(t, F)$ has the form

$$\check{C}_t + \frac{1}{2}\sigma^2(t) e^{2\beta r^{01}\tau}\left(\frac{F}{\bar{S}}\right)^{-2\beta} F^2 \check{C}_{FF} = 0,$$

$$\check{C}(T, F) = (F - K)_+.$$

Next, we introduce the scaled nondimensional time to maturity as follows

$$\chi = \int_t^T \sigma^2(t') e^{2\beta r^{01} t'} dt'.$$

When σ is time-independent, the above formula reduces to

$$\chi = \frac{\sigma^2\left(e^{2\beta r^{01}(T-t)} - 1\right)}{2\beta r^{01}}.$$

In terms of χ, F the pricing problem can be written as

$$\check{C}_\chi - \frac{1}{2}\left(\frac{F}{\bar{S}}\right)^{-2\beta} F^2 \check{C}_{FF} = 0,$$

$$\check{C}(0, F) = (F - K)_+.$$

Now the difficult part begins. We follow the standard recipe, change the independent variable according to the rule

$$F \to X = \frac{1}{\beta}\left(\frac{F}{\bar{S}}\right)^\beta, \tag{10.46}$$

and after some algebra obtain the following pricing equation for $U(\chi, X) = \check{C}(t, F)/\bar{S}$,

$$U_\chi - \frac{1}{2}U_{XX} - \frac{(1 - 1/\beta)}{2X}U_X = 0. \tag{10.47}$$

We emphasize that for now we assume that β is positive, so that transformation (10.46) keeps the positive semi-axis invariant. The corresponding initial condition is

$$U(0, X) = \left((\beta X)^{1/\beta} - \kappa\right)_+, \tag{10.48}$$

where $\kappa = K/\bar{S}$. In order to formulate the correct boundary conditions it is necessary to classify the boundary points $X = 0$ and $X = \infty$. It is easy to see that for positive β the speed measure density $\mathsf{m}_\beta(X)$ and scale function $\mathsf{s}_\beta(X)$ have the form

$$\mathsf{m}_\beta(X) = 2\beta X^{1 - 1/\beta}, \qquad \mathsf{s}_\beta(X) = X^{1/\beta},$$

respectively. Thus, according to Feller's classification of the boundaries, the boundary point $X = \infty$ is natural. The boundary point $X = 0$ is non-singular when $1/2 < \beta \le 1$, and exit-no-entrance when $0 < \beta \le 1/2$. Accordingly, we need to formulate a boundary condition at zero for equation (10.47) when $1/2 < \beta \le 1$, and can use a regularity condition when $\beta \le 1/2$. We impose the Dirichlet (killing) condition

$$U(\chi, 0) = 0,$$

and notice that for $\beta \le 1/2$ this condition is satisfied automatically.

10.7.3   Evaluation of the t.p.d.f.

In order to solve problem (10.47), (10.48) we first find the t.p.d.f. $p(\tau, X, X')$ which satisfies the pricing equation supplied with the Dirichlet (or regularity) boundary condition at $X = 0$, regularity condition at $X = \infty$, and the initial condition

$$p(0, X, X') = \delta(X - X').$$

To find the t.p.d.f. we use the Laplace transform in time

$$\pi(s, X, X') = \int_0^\infty e^{-s\chi} p(\chi, X, X') \, d\chi,$$

and obtain the following ordinary differential equation for the transformed t.p.d.f.:

$$\frac{1}{2}\pi_{XX} + \frac{(1 - 1/\beta)}{2X}\pi_X - s\pi = -\delta(X - X'), \qquad (10.49)$$

which can be recognized as the inhomogeneous Lommel equation. It is well known (and is not difficult to check) that the homogeneous Lommel equation has two linearly independent solutions of the form

$$\pi_1 = X^{1/2\beta} I_{1/2\beta}(\sqrt{2s}X), \qquad \pi_2 = X^{1/2\beta} K_{1/2\beta}(\sqrt{2s}X),$$

where $I_{1/2\beta}$, $K_{1/2\beta}$, are the modified Bessel functions of the first and second kind of order $1/2\beta$. Using the boundary and regularity conditions, we can write the solution of equation (10.49) in the form

$$\pi(s, X, X') = CX^{1/2\beta} I_{1/2\beta}(\sqrt{2s}X_<) K_{1/2\beta}(\sqrt{2s}X_>),$$

where

$$X_< = \min\{X, X'\}, \qquad X_> = \max\{X, X'\}.$$

In order to find the prefactor C we use the jump condition at $X = X'$, which states that the first derivative, π_X, has to have a negative jump of size two in order to balance the δ function on the r.h.s. To calculate this jump we apply the well-known formula for the Wronskian of two modified Bessel functions

$$w\left(I_{1/2\beta}(\xi), K_{1/2\beta}(\xi)\right) = -\frac{1}{\xi},$$

and obtain

$$\pi(s, X, X') = 2X' (X/X')^{1/2\beta} I_{1/2\beta}(\sqrt{2s}X_<)K_{1/2\beta}(\sqrt{2s}X_>).$$

We emphasize that for $1/2 < \beta \leq 1$ other t.p.d.f.'s can be constructed (they satisfy different boundary condition at zero). It is obvious that π is not a symmetric function of X, X'. However, according to the general theory, the t.p.d.f. with respect to the speed measure, which is defined by

$$\tilde{\pi}(s, X, X') = \frac{\pi(s, X, X')}{m_\beta(X')} = \frac{(XX')^{1/2\beta}}{\beta} I_{1/2\beta}(\sqrt{2s}X_<)K_{1/2\beta}(\sqrt{2s}X_>),$$

is a symmetric function of its arguments.

At this stage we use the well-known MacDonald's formula which says

$$\int_0^\infty \frac{1}{\chi} \exp\left(-s\chi - \frac{X^2 + X'^2}{2\chi}\right) I_\nu\left(\frac{XX'}{\chi}\right) d\chi = 2I_\nu(\sqrt{2s}X_<)K_\nu(\sqrt{2s}X_>),$$

$$(10.50)$$

and find the inverse Laplace transform of $\pi(s, X, X')$, and hence $p(\tau, X, X')$, explicitly:

$$p(\chi, X, X') = \frac{X' (X/X')^{2\beta}}{\chi} \exp\left(-\frac{X^2 + X'^2}{2\chi}\right) I_{1/2\beta}\left(\frac{XX'}{\chi}\right).$$

Again, with respect to the speed measure, the t.p.d.f. is symmetric,

$$\tilde{p}(\chi, X, X') = \frac{p(\chi, X, X')}{m_\beta(X')} = \frac{(XX')^{1/2\beta}}{2\beta\chi} \exp\left(-\frac{X^2 + X'^2}{2\chi}\right) I_{1/2\beta}\left(\frac{XX'}{\chi}\right).$$

$$(10.51)$$

Formula (10.51) is very attractive but it involves the modified Bessel function of order $1/2\beta$ and for this reason is somewhat difficult to use. In order to obviate the need to compute it directly, we use the Fourier representation for modified Bessel functions and rewrite $p(\chi, X, X')$ as

$$p(\chi, X, X') = 2X' (X/X')^{1/\beta} q(\chi, X, X'),$$

where

$$q(\chi, X, X')$$
$$= \int_{-\infty}^\infty (1 + 4\pi i k\chi)^{-(1/2\beta+1)} \exp\left(-\frac{2\pi i k X^2}{1 + 4\pi i k\chi} + 2\pi i k X'^2\right) dk$$
$$= \frac{(X/X')^{-1/2\beta}}{2\chi} \exp\left(-\frac{X^2 + X'^2}{2\chi}\right) I_{1/2\beta}\left(\frac{XX'}{\chi}\right).$$

The auxiliary function q can be found via the fast Fourier transform (FFT).

10.7.4   Derivative pricing

Once we know an explicit expression for the t.p.d.f., we can price a call via a simple integration:

$$
U(\chi, X) = \int_{X^*}^{\infty} \left((\beta X')^{1/\beta} - \kappa \right) p(\chi, X, X') dX'
$$

$$
= \int_{X^*}^{\infty} \left((\beta^2 X X')^{1/2\beta} - \kappa \left(\frac{X}{X'} \right)^{1/2\beta} \right) \frac{X'}{\chi} \exp \left(-\frac{X^2 + X'^2}{2\chi} \right)
$$

$$
\times I_{1/2\beta} \left(\frac{X X'}{\chi} \right) dX',
$$

where $X^* = \left(K/\bar{S} \right)^{\beta} / \beta$. The value of a call option can also be written as

$$
C(t, S) = \frac{e^{-r^0(T-t)} \sqrt{e^{r^{01}(T-t)} S}}{\beta \chi(t, T) \bar{S}^{2\beta}} \int_{K}^{\infty} (Z - K) Z^{2\beta - 3/2}
$$

$$
\times \exp \left(-\frac{\left(e^{2\beta r^{01}(T-t)} S^{2\beta} + Z^{2\beta} \right)}{2\beta^2 \chi(t, T) \bar{S}^{2\beta}} \right) I_{1/2\beta} \left(\frac{e^{\beta r^{01}(T-t)} S^{\beta} Z^{\beta}}{\beta^2 \chi(t, T) \bar{S}^{2\beta}} \right) dZ.
$$

It is convenient to rewrite the above formula in the form which directly generalizes the standard Black-Scholes formula:

$$
C(t, S) = e^{-r^1(T-t)} S \int_{L}^{\infty} \left(\frac{Y}{Y'} \right)^{1/4\beta} e^{-Y-Y'} I_{1/2\beta} \left(2\sqrt{YY'} \right) dY'
$$

$$
- e^{-r^0(T-t)} K \int_{L}^{\infty} \left(\frac{Y'}{Y} \right)^{1/4\beta} e^{-Y-Y'} I_{1/2\beta} \left(2\sqrt{YY'} \right) dY',
$$

where

$$
Y = \frac{F^{2\beta}}{2\beta^2 \chi \bar{S}^{2\beta}}, \qquad Y' = \frac{Z^{2\beta}}{2\beta^2 \chi \bar{S}^{2\beta}}, \qquad L = \frac{K^{2\beta}}{2\beta^2 \chi \bar{S}^{2\beta}}. \tag{10.52}
$$

The integrands can be recognized as noncentral chi-square density functions of the form $p(2Y', 2 + 1/\beta, 2Y)$ and $p(2Y, 2 + 1/\beta, 2Y')$.[5] In these expressions

---

[5] See the earlier discussion it Section 10.3 where we dealt with the simplest noncentral chi-square distribution with one degree of freedom.

the arguments are the value of the random variable, number of degrees of freedom, and noncentral parameter, respectively. Accordingly, the first integral is $Q(2L, 2 + 1/\beta, 2Y)$, where Q is the corresponding complementary distribution function. The second integral is more difficult to interpret because the integration is carried with respect to the noncentral parameter rather than the value of the random variable. However, cleverly using properties of modified Bessel functions it can be shown that this integral is given by $1 - Q(2Y, 1/\beta, 2L)$. Accordingly, the CEV price of a call is given by

$$C(t, S) = e^{-r^1(T-t)} SQ(2L, 2 + 1/\beta, 2Y) \qquad (10.53)$$
$$-e^{-r^0(T-t)} K(1 - Q(2Y, 1/\beta, 2L))$$

The price of the put can be found via the usual put-call parity:

$$P(t, S) = e^{-r^0(T-t)} KQ(2Y, 1/\beta, 2L)$$
$$-e^{-r^1(T-t)} S(1 - Q(2L, 2 + 1/\beta, 2Y)).$$

We show the implied volatility for calls evaluated in the CEV framework in Figure 10.7.

By expanding the modified Bessel function I_ν in a power series we can obtain an alternative expression for the price of a call option in the CEV. We represent this expression in the original Cox's form (with slight modifications):

$$C(t, S) = e^{-r^1(T-t)} S \sum_{n=1}^{\infty} g(n, Y) G\left(n + \frac{1}{2\beta}, L\right) \qquad (10.54)$$
$$-e^{-r^0(T-t)} K\left(1 - \sum_{n=1}^{\infty} g(n, L) G\left(n + \frac{1}{2\beta} - 1, Y\right)\right),$$

and in the ingenious form proposed by Schroder which is computationally advantageous compared with (10.54):

$$C(t, S) = e^{-r^1(T-t)} S\left(1 - \sum_{n=1}^{\infty} g\left(n + 1 + \frac{1}{2\beta}, L\right) \sum_{m=1}^{n} g(m, Y)\right)$$
$$-e^{-r^0(T-t)} K \sum_{n=1}^{\infty} g\left(n + \frac{1}{2\beta}, Y\right) \sum_{m=1}^{n} g(m, L).$$

Here $G(m, x)$ is the complementary Gamma distribution and $g(m, x)$ is its density:

$$G(m, x) = \int_x^{\infty} g(m, x') \, dx',$$

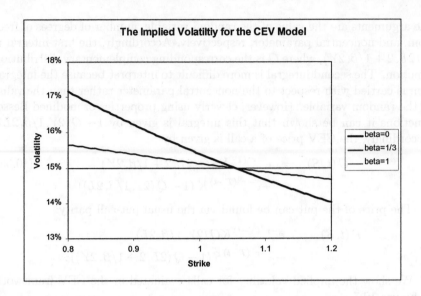

Figure 10.7: The "CEV" implied volatility $\sigma_I(T, K)$ as a function of K for $T = 12$ months, and three representative values of β, $\beta = 0, 1/3, 1$. The relevant parameters are $S_0 = 0.95$, $\bar{S} = 1.00$, $\sigma_0 = 15\%$, $r^0 = r^1 = 5\%$.

$$g(m, x) = \frac{e^{-x} x^{m-1}}{\Gamma(m)}.$$

For special values of β such that the corresponding ν has the form $\nu = n + 1/2$, the corresponding Bessel function I_ν can be expressed in elementary functions. In these cases the price of a call can be found explicitly. For example, when $\beta = 1$, i.e., in the case of normal volatility, $\nu = 1/2$ and we can use the well-known formula

$$I_{1/2}(z) = \sqrt{\frac{2}{\pi z}} \sinh(z),$$

and write

$$\check{C}(\chi, F) \tag{10.55}$$

$$= \int_K^\infty (Z - K) \frac{e^{-(F-Z)^2/2\chi\bar{S}^2} - e^{-(F+Z)^2/2\chi\bar{S}^2}}{\sqrt{2\pi\chi}\bar{S}} dZ$$

$$= (F - K)\,\mathfrak{N}\left(\frac{F - K}{\sqrt{\chi}\bar{S}}\right) + \sqrt{\chi}\bar{S}\mathfrak{n}\left(\frac{F - K}{\sqrt{\chi}\bar{S}}\right)$$

$$+ (F + K)\,\mathfrak{N}\left(-\frac{F + K}{\sqrt{\chi}\bar{S}}\right) - \sqrt{\chi}\bar{S}\mathfrak{n}\left(\frac{F + K}{\sqrt{\chi}\bar{S}}\right),$$

which is a familiar expression for the price of a call on the arithmetic Brownian motion killed at zero.

Similarly we can study other special cases, such as $\beta = 1/3$. We leave it as an exercise for the reader to check that for $\beta = 1/3$ the price of a call can be written as

$$\check{C}(\chi, F) \tag{10.56}$$

$$= (F - K)\,\mathfrak{N}\left(3\frac{\left(F^{1/3} - K^{1/3}\right)}{\sqrt{\chi}\bar{S}^{1/3}}\right) + (F + K)\,\mathfrak{N}\left(-3\frac{\left(F^{1/3} + K^{1/3}\right)}{\sqrt{\chi}\bar{S}^{1/3}}\right)$$

$$+ \frac{\chi\sqrt{\chi}\bar{S}}{27}\left(9\frac{\left(F^{2/3} + (FK)^{1/3} + K^{2/3}\right)}{\chi\bar{S}^{2/3}} - 1\right)\mathfrak{n}\left(3\frac{\left(F^{1/3} - K^{1/3}\right)}{\sqrt{\chi}\bar{S}^{1/3}}\right)$$

$$- \frac{\chi\sqrt{\chi}\bar{S}}{27}\left(9\frac{\left(F^{2/3} - (FK)^{1/3} + K^{2/3}\right)}{\chi\bar{S}^{2/3}} - 1\right)\mathfrak{n}\left(3\frac{\left(F^{1/3} + K^{1/3}\right)}{\sqrt{\chi}\bar{S}^{1/3}}\right).$$

It is also important to analyze the limiting case $\beta \to 0$. First, we need the asymptotic expression for the corresponding Bessel function. We write this expression in the form

$$I_{1/2\beta}\left(\frac{a}{\beta^2}\right) \sim \frac{\beta e^{a/\beta^2 - 1/8a}}{\sqrt{2\pi a}}.$$

By using this asymptotic formula, we obtain

$$\check{C}(\chi, F) \tag{10.57}$$

$$\sim \int_K^\infty (Z - K) \frac{\exp\left(-(F^\beta - Z^\beta)^2/2\beta^2\chi\bar{S}^{2\beta} - \chi/8\right)}{\sqrt{2\pi\chi}} F^{1/2} Z^{-3/2} dZ$$

$$\sim F\,\mathfrak{N}\left(\frac{\ln(F/K)}{\sqrt{\chi}} + \frac{\sqrt{\chi}}{2}\right) - K\,\mathfrak{N}\left(\frac{\ln(F/K)}{\sqrt{\chi}} - \frac{\sqrt{\chi}}{2}\right),$$

which is the familiar Black-Scholes formula.

Formulas (10.55), (10.56), (10.57) can be used in order to interpolate the value of call prices between 0 and 1. For instance, we can use Newton's interpolation formula on the interval $[0, 1]$ and write

$$\check{C}^{(\beta)} = \check{C}^{(0)} + 3\beta \left(\check{C}^{(1/3)} - \check{C}^{(0)} \right)$$

$$+ \frac{3}{2}\beta \left(\beta - \frac{1}{3} \right) \left(\check{C}^{(1)} - 3\check{C}^{(1/3)} + 2\check{C}^{(0)} \right).$$

This formula is surprisingly accurate.

We can use put-call parity and put-call symmetry in order to extend our results to the case $-1 \leq \beta < 0$. Indeed, when we switch domestic and foreign countries β switches to $-\beta$. Assuming that $\beta < 0$ we write

$$C^{(\beta)} \left(t, S, K, \sigma, r^0, r^1 \right) = SKP^{(-\beta)} \left(t, \frac{1}{S}, \frac{1}{K}, \sigma, r^1, r^0 \right)$$

$$= SK \left(\frac{e^{-r^1(T-t)}}{K} Q\left(2Y, -1/\beta, 2L\right) - \frac{e^{-r^0(T-t)}}{S} \left(1 - Q\left(2L, 2 - 1/\beta, 2Y\right)\right) \right)$$

$$= e^{-r^1(T-t)} SQ\left(2Y, -1/\beta, 2L\right) - e^{-r^0(T-t)} K \left(1 - Q\left(2L, 2 - 1/\beta, 2Y\right)\right),$$

where, as before, Y, L are given by expressions (10.52).

10.7.5   ATMF approximation

For ATMF calls we have $K = (\beta X)^{1/\beta} \bar{S}$, so that the general valuation formula reduces to

$$U\left(\chi, X\right) = \int_X^\infty \frac{1}{\chi} X^{1/2\beta} \xi^{-1/2\beta+1} e^{-\left(X^2+\xi^2\right)/2\chi} I_{1/2\beta} \left(\frac{X\xi}{\chi} \right)$$

$$\times \left((\beta\xi)^{1/\beta} - (\beta X)^{1/\beta} \right) d\xi.$$

We want to evaluate the above expression in the limit $\chi \to 0$. To this end we use the familiar formula

$$I_{1/2\beta} \left(\frac{X\xi}{\chi} \right) \sim \frac{e^{X\xi/\chi}\sqrt{\chi}}{\sqrt{2\pi X\xi}} \left\{ 1 - \frac{\left(1 - \beta^2\right)\chi}{8\beta^2 X\xi} + \dots \right\},$$

and get

$$U(\chi, X) = \int_X^\infty \frac{e^{-(\xi-X)^2/2\chi}}{\sqrt{2\pi\chi}} X^{1/2\beta-1/2}\xi^{-1/2\beta+1/2}$$
$$\times \left\{ 1 - \frac{(1-\beta^2)\chi}{8\beta^2 X\xi} + ... \right\} \left((\beta\xi)^{1/\beta} - (\beta X)^{1/\beta} \right) d\xi.$$

Symbolically

$$U(\chi, X) = \int_X^\infty \frac{e^{-(\xi-X)^2/2\chi}}{\sqrt{2\pi\chi}} \left(f(X, \xi) - \chi g(X, \xi) \right) d\xi,$$

where

$$f(X, \xi) = X^{1/2\beta-1/2}\xi^{-1/2\beta+1/2} \left((\beta\xi)^{1/\beta} - (\beta X)^{1/\beta} \right),$$

$$g(X, \xi) = \frac{(1-\beta^2)}{8\beta^2} X^{1/2\beta-3/2}\xi^{-1/2\beta-1/2} \left((\beta\xi)^{1/\beta} - (\beta X)^{1/\beta} \right).$$

We expand f, g at $\xi = X$ and write

$$f(X, \xi) = f_\xi(X, \xi)|_{\xi=X} (\xi - X) + \frac{1}{2} f_{\xi\xi}(X, \xi)|_{\xi=X} (\xi - X)^2$$
$$+ \frac{1}{6} f_{\xi\xi\xi}(X, \xi)|_{\xi=X} (\xi - X)^3 ...$$
$$= (\beta X)^{1/\beta-1} (\xi - X) + 0 + \frac{(1-\beta^2)}{24} (\beta X)^{1/\beta-3} (\xi - X)^3 + ...,$$

$$g(X, \xi) = g_\xi(X, \xi)|_{\xi=X} (\xi - X) + ... = \frac{(1-\beta^2)}{8} (\beta X)^{1/\beta-3} (\xi - X).$$

Accordingly,

$$
\begin{aligned}
U\left(\chi, X\right) &\approx \int_X^\infty \frac{e^{-(\xi-X)^2/2\chi}}{\sqrt{2\pi\chi}}\left(\xi - X\right) d\xi \\
&\quad \times \left\{ (\beta X)^{1/\beta - 1} - \frac{\left(1 - \beta^2\right)}{8}(\beta X)^{1/\beta - 3}\chi \right\} \\
&\quad + \int_X^\infty \frac{e^{-(\xi-X)^2/2\chi}}{\sqrt{2\pi\chi}}\left(\xi - X\right)^3 d\xi \frac{\left(1 - \beta^2\right)}{24}(\beta X)^{1/\beta - 3} \\
&= \frac{(\beta X)^{1/\beta - 1}\sqrt{\chi}}{\sqrt{2\pi}}\left\{ 1 - \frac{\left(1 - \beta^2\right)}{8}(\beta X)^{-2}\chi + \frac{\left(1 - \beta^2\right)}{12}(\beta X)^{-2}\chi \right\} \\
&= \frac{(\beta X)^{1/\beta - 1}\sqrt{\chi}}{\sqrt{2\pi}}\left\{ 1 - \frac{\left(1 - \beta^2\right)}{24}(\beta X)^{-2}\chi \right\}.
\end{aligned}
$$

Equivalently,

$$
\check{C}\left(\chi, F\right) = \frac{\sqrt{\chi} F^{1-\beta}\bar{S}^\beta}{\sqrt{2\pi}}\left\{ 1 - \frac{\left(1 - \beta^2\right)}{24}\chi \bar{S}^{2\beta}F^{-2\beta} \right\}.
$$

This formula is similar to the familiar Black-Scholes approximation (although the limit $\beta \to 0$ is singular)

$$
\check{C}\left(\chi, F\right) = \frac{\sqrt{\chi} F}{\sqrt{2\pi}}\left\{ 1 - \frac{1}{24}\chi \right\}. \tag{10.58}
$$

In order to illustrate the above formula and to show that it is correct we consider a special case and put $\beta = 1/3$. In this case the ATMF solution can be found explicitly:

$$
\begin{aligned}
\check{C}(\chi, F) &= 2F\mathfrak{N}\left(-6\frac{F^{1/3}}{\sqrt{\chi}\bar{S}^{1/3}}\right) + \frac{1}{27}\frac{\chi\sqrt{\chi}\bar{S}}{\sqrt{2\pi}}\left(27\frac{F^{2/3}}{\chi\bar{S}^{2/3}} - 1\right) \\
&\quad - \frac{1}{27}\chi\sqrt{\chi}\bar{S}\left(9\frac{F^{2/3}}{\chi\bar{S}^{2/3}} - 1\right)\mathfrak{n}\left(6\frac{F^{1/3}}{\sqrt{\chi}\bar{S}^{1/3}}\right).
\end{aligned}
$$

When $\chi \to 0$ we obtain (with exponential accuracy):

$$
\check{C}(\chi, F) = \frac{\sqrt{\chi} F^{2/3}\bar{S}^{1/3}}{\sqrt{2\pi}}\left(1 - \frac{1}{27}\chi\bar{S}^{2/3}F^{-2/3}\right).
$$

It is clear that

$$\frac{1 - (1/3)^2}{24} = \frac{1}{27},$$

in agreement with the general formula.

We can also use general formula (10.42) in order to study short-dated approximately ATMF calls in the CEV framework. A straightforward calculation yields

$$\alpha_1 = -\beta, \qquad \alpha_2 = \beta(\beta + 1),$$

so that

$$
\begin{aligned}
\sigma^{BS} &= \left(1 + \frac{1}{24}(3\beta - \beta^2)\frac{(F-K)^2}{K^2} \right. \\
&\quad \left. + \frac{1}{24}\beta^2\sigma^2 \left(\frac{2\bar{S}}{F+K}\right)^{2\beta}(T-t)\right)\sigma\left(\frac{2\bar{S}}{F+K}\right)^{\beta}.
\end{aligned}
$$

10.8 The jump diffusion model

10.8.1 Introduction

In this section we discuss the pricing problem for the FXR following the jump-diffusion process whose dynamics is governed by equation (7.12).

10.8.2 The pricing problem

For the purposes of option pricing we have to choose the value of α in equation (7.12). By using the familiar Delta-hedging strategy, we can assume that without jumps $\alpha = r^{01}$. We emphasize that Delta-hedging is not sufficient for creating a riskless portfolio since it does not account for jumps. However, for simplicity, we disregard this issue, assume that risks related to jumps can be diversified, and put $\alpha = r^{01}$. We emphasize that there are more subtle ways of addressing the above problem but they result in a similar conclusion. With the above choice of α we can write the pricing problem in the form

$$V_t(t,S) + \frac{1}{2}\sigma^2 S^2 V_{SS}(t,S) + \left(r^{01} - \lambda\kappa\right)SV_S(t,S) - r^0 V(t,S)$$

$$+ \quad \lambda \int_{-\infty}^{\infty}\left[V\left(t,e^J S\right) - V(t,S)\right]df(J) = 0,$$

supplied with the standard final condition

$$V(T, S) = v(S).$$

As always, the solution of the pricing problem can be written as

$$V(t, S_t) = e^{-r^0(T-t)} \int_0^\infty p(t, S_t, T, S_T) v(S_T) dS_T, \qquad (10.59)$$

where p is the t.p.d.f. corresponding to SDE (7.12).

10.8.3   Evaluation of the t.p.d.f.

Formula (10.59) suggests that we can initially concentrate on studying the t.p.d.f. Because of the multiplicative character of jumps we can find the distribution of the terminal value S_T conditional on the spot value S_t and the number of jumps N which occur between t and T. Assuming for the sake of brevity that all the parameters are time independent, we obtain

$$S_{T;N} = e^{(r^{01} - \lambda\kappa - \sigma^2/2)(T-t) + \sigma\sqrt{T-t}\xi + J_N} S_t, \qquad (10.60)$$

where ξ is the standard normal variable, and $J_N = \sum_{n=1}^N j_n$ is the cumulative jump magnitude. The distribution of J_N which we denote by F_N can be expressed in terms of the distribution F of a single jump size by computing the corresponding convolutions. The determination of F_N can be done efficiently via the product rule for characteristic functions. Indeed, the characteristic function Φ_N of J_N can be expressed in terms of the characteristic function Φ of J as follows

$$\Phi_N(\varsigma) = [\Phi(\varsigma)]^N.$$

Accordingly,

$$f_N(x) = \frac{1}{2\pi} \int_{-\infty}^\infty e^{-i\varsigma x} [\Phi(\varsigma)]^N d\varsigma.$$

A formal calculation yields the following important result

$$\mathbb{E}\left\{e^{J_N}\right\} = \Phi_N(-i) = [\Phi(-i)]^N = \left[\mathbb{E}\{e^J\}\right]^N = (\kappa + 1)^N,$$

where $\kappa = \mathbb{E}\{e^J - 1\}$.

For some important distributions F the corresponding F_N can be found explicitly. For example, if J is a normal variable with parameters μ, ν,

$$J \sim \mathfrak{N}\left(\mu, \nu^2\right),$$

then J_N is the normal distribution with parameters $N\mu, N\nu^2$,

$$J_N \sim \mathfrak{N}\left(N\mu, N\nu^2\right).$$

The corresponding κ is

$$\kappa = e^{\mu + \nu^2/2} - 1.$$

If J has a one-sided exponential distribution with parameter μ, whose p.d.f. has the form

$$f(x) = \left\{ \begin{array}{ll} \mu e^{-\mu x}, & x \geq 0 \\ 0, & x < 0 \end{array} \right.,$$

then J_N has a Gamma distribution with parameters (N, μ), whose p.d.f. is given by

$$f_N(x) = \left\{ \begin{array}{ll} \mu^N x^{N-1} e^{-\mu x}/(N-1)!, & x \geq 0 \\ 0, & x < 0 \end{array} \right..$$

10.8.4 Risk-neutral pricing

We know the distribution of both ξ and J_N in formula (10.60). Hence we also know the conditional distribution of S_T. We can capitalize on this knowledge in order to price options on the FXR with jumps via formula (10.59).

First of all, we find the forward FXR. Since we know in advance that this price is totally independent of the actual dynamics of the FXR, this exercise is useful for checking our logic. We assume that exactly N jumps occur between the valuation and maturity dates. Then, as usual, we have

$$F_{t,T;N} = \mathbb{E}_t\{S_{T;N}|S_t\} = e^{(r^{01} - \lambda\kappa)(T-t)}\mathbb{E}\{e^{J_N}\}S_t = e^{-\lambda\kappa(T-t)}\left(\kappa + 1\right)^N F_{t,T;0},$$

where λ is the intensity of the driving Poisson process. The averaging with Poisson weights yields

$$\begin{aligned} F_{t,T} &= e^{-\lambda(1+\kappa)(T-t)} \left(\sum_{n=0}^{\infty} \frac{(\lambda\tau(\kappa+1))^n}{n!} \right) F_{t,T;0} \\ &= F_{t,T;0} = e^{r^{01}(T-t)} S_t, \end{aligned}$$

as might be expected.

The pricing of a call proceeds along similar lines. We can rewrite the expression for S_T in the form

$$S_{T;N} = e^{\left(r^{01} - \sigma^2/2\right)(T-t) + \sigma\sqrt{T-t}\xi} \zeta_{t;N},$$

where

$$\zeta_{t;N} = e^{-\lambda\kappa\tau + J_N} S_t.$$

It is clear that $\zeta_{t;N}$ can be thought of as a modified (random) spot price. Accordingly, we can represent a call price via Merton's formula

$$C_{JD}(t, S, T, K; \sigma, r^0, r^1) = \sum_{n=0}^{\infty} \frac{e^{-\lambda(T-t)} \left(\lambda\left(T-t\right)\right)^n}{n!}$$

$$\times \mathbb{E}\{C_{BS}(t, e^{-\lambda\kappa(T-t)+J_N} S, T, K; \sigma, r^0, r^1)\}$$

$$= \sum_{n=0}^{\infty} \frac{e^{-\lambda(T-t)} \left(\lambda\left(T-t\right)\right)^n}{n!}$$

$$\times \int_{-\infty}^{\infty} C_{BS}(t, e^{-\lambda\kappa(T-t)+x} S, T, K; \sigma, r^0, r^1) f_N\left(x\right) dx.$$

In general, this formula is relatively difficult to handle, even though most of the time only the first few terms of the sum have to be computed. However, for certain special distributions the corresponding terms can be found analytically. For instance, if $J \sim \mathfrak{N}\left(\mu, \nu^2\right)$, then, as we know, $J_N \sim \mathfrak{N}\left(N\mu, N\nu^2\right)$, so that we can represent S_T in the form

$$S_{T,N} = e^{\left(r^{01} - \lambda\kappa + N\mu/(T-t) - \sigma^2/2\right)(T-t) + \sqrt{\sigma^2(T-t)+N\nu^2}\xi} S_t$$

$$= e^{\left(r_N^0 - r^1 - \sigma_N^2/2\right)(T-t) + \sigma_N\sqrt{(T-t)}\xi} S_t,$$

and represent the corresponding price in the form

$$C_{JD}(t, S, T, K; \sigma, r^0, r^1) = \sum_{n=0}^{\infty} \frac{e^{-\tilde{\lambda}(T-t)} \left(\tilde{\lambda}\left(T-t\right)\right)^n}{n!} \tag{10.61}$$

$$\times C_{BS}(t, S, T, K; \sigma_n, r_n^0, r^1)\},$$

where

$$\tilde{\lambda} = \lambda e^{\mu+\nu^2/2}, \quad \sigma_n^2 = \sigma^2 + \frac{n\nu^2}{T-t}, \quad r_n^0 = r + \lambda - \tilde{\lambda} + \frac{n\left(\mu + \nu^2/2\right)}{T-t}.$$

We show the implied volatility for calls evaluated in the jump diffusion framework in Figure 10.8.

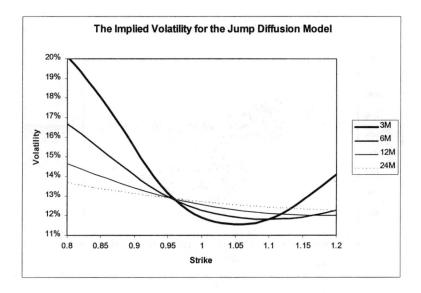

Figure 10.8: The "jump diffusion" implied volatility $\sigma_I(T, K)$ as a function of K for four representative maturities, $T = 3, 6, 12, 24$ months. The relevant parameters are $S_0 = 0.95$, $\sigma = 10\%$, $r^0 = r^1 = 5\%$, $\lambda = 0.5$, $\mu = 0.05$, $\nu = 0.10$. When $T \to \infty$ the smile obviously flattens.

10.9 The stochastic volatility model

10.9.1 Introduction

Even a cursory analysis of the actual market data suggests that the variability of the implied volatility of European options on forex cannot be explained within the local volatility or jump diffusion environment. In Figure 10.9 we show the dependence of the implied volatility of ATMF dollar calls / yen puts with six months to maturity as a function of the spot FXR. This Figure clearly illustrates the random nature of this dependence. In order to account for this randomness, we assume that the local volatility of the FXR is stochastic. In this section we study the valuation of contingent claims in the stochastic volatility framework.

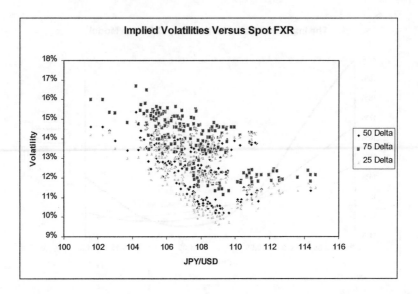

Figure 10.9: The implied volatility of dollar calls / yen puts with six months to maturity as a function of the spot FXR for a representative one year period.

10.9.2   Basic equations

To start with, we formulate the pricing problem for a call in the Heston stochastic volatility framework. Due to the fact that the volatility process is cannot be hedged, we have to write the pricing problem as follows

$$C_\tau - \frac{1}{2}vS^2C_{SS} - \varepsilon\rho vSC_{Sv} - \frac{1}{2}\varepsilon^2 vC_{vv}$$
$$- \quad r^{01}SC_S - \left[\kappa(\theta - v) - \lambda\varepsilon\sqrt{v}\right]C_v + r^0 C = 0,$$

$$C(0, S, v) = (S - K)_+ , \tag{10.62}$$

where λ is the market price of the volatility risk. We emphasize that the payoff function is independent of v. In general, because the local volatility is not a trading asset we cannot put $\lambda = 0$. There is little guidance in choosing the proper form for λ (although some rational choices based on the utility function theory are possible), in order to avoid unnecessary complications, we assume that

$$\lambda \sim \sqrt{v}.$$

With this choice of the market price of risk the pricing equation can be rewritten as

$$C_\tau - \frac{1}{2}vS^2C_{SS} - \varepsilon\rho vSC_{Sv} - \frac{1}{2}\varepsilon^2 vC_{vv} \qquad (10.63)$$
$$- \quad r^{01}SC_S - \bar{\kappa}(\bar{\theta} - v)C_v + r^0 C = 0,$$

where $\bar{\kappa}$ and $\bar{\theta}$ are modified mean-reversion rate and level, respectively. Below we omit bars for brevity. As usual, the final value problem (10.63), (10.62) has to be supplied with appropriate boundary conditions. The boundary conditions in the S direction which are imposed for $S = 0, \infty$ coincide with their deterministic counterparts and have the form

$$C(\tau, 0, v) = 0, \quad C(\tau, S \to \infty, v) \to e^{-r^1\tau}S. \qquad (10.64)$$

It is easy to write the boundary conditions in the v direction but it is difficult to deal with them or to implement them numerically. When $v \to 0$ some terms in equation (10.63) disappear and some assume simpler forms, so that the natural boundary condition at $v = 0$ can be written as

$$C_\tau(\tau, S, 0) - r^{01}SC_S(\tau, S, 0) - \kappa\theta C_v(\tau, S, 0) + r^0 C(\tau, S, 0) = 0.$$

For $v \to \infty$ terms proportional to v have to disappear which means that C has to be a linear function of S independent of v. Substituting such a function into equation (10.63) and using the second boundary condition (10.64), we conclude that

$$C(\tau, S, v \to \infty) \to e^{-r^1\tau}S.$$

We emphasize that the practical implementation of these conditions is difficult since they have to be formulated for some finite values $v = v_L$ and $v = v_U$ approximating $v = 0$ and $v = \infty$, respectively. However, v is a dimensional quantity so that statements like $v \ll 1$, and $v \gg 1$ make no sense per se. Financially it means that no volatility is small if one waits for a sufficiently long time, and, similarly, no volatility is large if the time to expiry is small. Besides, the condition $v = 0$ is not preserved by the dynamics of v_t.

As usual, the pricing problem written in forward terms is easier to deal with. The pricing problem for $\check{C}(\tau, F, v)$ has the form

$$\check{C}_\tau - \frac{1}{2}vF^2\check{C}_{FF} - \varepsilon\rho vF\check{C}_{Fv} - \frac{1}{2}\varepsilon^2 v\check{C}_{vv} - \kappa(\theta - v)\check{C}_v = 0,$$

$$\check{C}\left(0, F, v\right) = \left(F - K\right)_{+},$$

$$\check{C}\left(\tau, 0, v\right) = 0, \quad \check{C}\left(\tau, F \to \infty, v\right) \to F,$$

$$\check{C}_{\tau}\left(\tau, F, 0\right) - \kappa\theta\check{C}_{v}\left(\tau, F, 0\right) = 0, \quad \check{C}\left(\tau, F, v \to \infty\right) \to F.$$

We nondimensionalize the problem in the usual way and represent $\check{C}$ as follows

$$\check{C}\left(\tau, F, v\right) = K\Phi\left(\tau, \xi, v\right),$$

where $\xi = F/K$. In order to reduce the problem to the simplest possible form we apply the usual transformations[6]:

$$\tau \to \tau, \quad \xi \to X = \ln\xi, \quad \Phi\left(\tau, \xi, v\right) \to U\left(\tau, X, v\right) = e^{-X/2}\Phi\left(\tau, \xi, v\right),$$

and obtain the following pricing problem:

$$U_{\tau} - \frac{1}{2}vU_{XX} - \varepsilon\rho vU_{Xv} - \frac{1}{2}\varepsilon^{2}vU_{vv} - \hat{\kappa}\left(\hat{\theta} - v\right)U_{v} + \frac{1}{8}vU = 0, \quad (10.65)$$

$$U\left(0, X, v\right) = \left(e^{X/2} - e^{-X/2}\right)_{+},$$

where $\hat{\kappa} = \left(\kappa - \varepsilon\rho/2\right)$, $\hat{\theta} = \kappa\theta/\hat{\kappa}$. (It is useful to note that $\kappa\theta = \hat{\kappa}\hat{\theta}$.) The boundary conditions are changed appropriately. Equation (10.65) is the Kolmogoroff equation with killing for the following system of SDEs

$$dX = \sqrt{v}dW_{t}, \quad (10.66)$$
$$dv = \hat{\kappa}\left(\hat{\theta} - v\right)dt + \varepsilon\sqrt{v}d\Omega_{t},$$

with the corresponding killing rate equal to $v/8$.

In principle, it is not difficult to go further and eliminate the killing term altogether. Let $\Xi\left(\tau, v\right)$ be the solution of the problem

$$\Xi_{\tau} - \frac{1}{2}\varepsilon^{2}v\Xi_{vv} - \hat{\kappa}\left(\hat{\theta} - v\right)\Xi_{v} + \frac{1}{8}v\Xi = 0,$$

---

[6] This transformation is a "partial" version of the transformation applicable in the case of constant volatility.

$$\Xi\left(0,v\right)=1.$$

This problem is similar in nature to the stochastic bond pricing problem considered in Section 7.3. We leave it to the reader to check that Ξ can be presented in the affine form

$$\Xi\left(\tau,v\right)=e^{2(\alpha(\tau)-\beta(\tau)v)/\varepsilon^{2}},$$

and to determine the functions α,β. Once Ξ is found, we can introduce the new dependent variable $\tilde{U}=U/\Xi$ and derive the following pricing problem for $\tilde{U}$:

$$\tilde{U}_{\tau}-\frac{1}{2}v\tilde{U}_{XX}-\varepsilon\rho v\tilde{U}_{Xv}-\frac{1}{2}\varepsilon^{2}v\tilde{U}_{vv}-\tilde{\kappa}\left(\tilde{\theta}-v\right)\tilde{U}_{v}=0, \qquad (10.67)$$

$$\tilde{U}\left(0,X,v\right)=\left(e^{X/2}-e^{-X/2}\right)_{+}, \qquad (10.68)$$

where $\tilde{\kappa}=\hat{\kappa}+2\beta$, $\tilde{\theta}=\kappa\theta/\tilde{\kappa}$. Although we do not follow this route below (because the coefficients of equation (10.67) are time-dependent which makes its analysis a little involved), problem (10.67), (10.68) does have a considerable appeal.

10.9.3 Evaluation of the t.p.d.f.

For the purposes of pricing of options on the FXR with stochastic volatility it is necessary to find the t.p.d.f. (Green's function) $p\left(t,X,v,t',X',v'\right)$ for the vector process governed by SDEs (10.66) and killed at the rate of $v/8$. Since the coefficients of the corresponding SDEs and the killing rate are independent of t,X, the density p depends on the differences $\tau=t'-t$, $Y=X'-X$, rather than the arguments themselves,

$$p\left(t,X,v,t',X',v'\right)=p\left(\tau,Y,v,v'\right).$$

We know that p as a function of t',X',v' is governed by the forward Fokker-Planck equation, while as a function of t,X,v it is governed by the backward Kolmogoroff equation. These equations can be written as follows

$$p_{\tau}-\frac{1}{2}\frac{\partial^{2}}{\partial Y^{2}}\left(v'p\right)_{YY}-\left(\varepsilon\rho v'p\right)_{Yv'}-\frac{1}{2}\left(\varepsilon^{2}v'p\right)_{v'v'}$$

$$+\quad\left(\hat{\kappa}(\hat{\theta}-v')p\right)_{v'}+\frac{1}{8}v'p=0,$$

$$p_\tau - \frac{1}{2}vp_{YY} + \varepsilon\rho vp_{Yv} - \frac{1}{2}\varepsilon^2 vp_{vv} - \hat{\kappa}(\hat{\theta} - v)p_v + \frac{1}{8}vp = 0. \qquad (10.69)$$

The corresponding initial conditions are the same in both cases, namely,

$$p(\tau \to 0, Y, v,v') \to \delta(Y)\delta(v' - v).$$

A complete solution of the above problems is rather complex. It is given in Section 13.11 where we study the general path-dependent options. Fortunately, due to the fact that the payoff of a European option is independent of v' significant simplifications are possible. Indeed, rather than finding $p(\tau, Y, v,v')$ we can restrict ourselves to finding its integral over v' which is denoted by $q(\tau, Y, v)$,

$$q(\tau, Y, v) = \int_0^\infty p(\tau, Y, v, v')\, dv'.$$

It is clear that q solves the Kolmogoroff equation (10.69) supplied with the initial condition

$$q(0, Y, v) = \delta(Y).$$

Due to the fact that its coefficients are linear functions of v, we can write q in the affine form:

$$q(\tau, Y, v) = \frac{1}{2\pi}\int_{-\infty}^\infty e^{ikY + 2(\text{A}(\tau,k) - \text{B}(\tau,k)v)/\epsilon^2}\, dk, \qquad (10.70)$$

where the functions $\text{A}(\tau, k)$, $\text{B}(\tau, k)$ have to be determined. Equation (10.70) suggests that solutions of the stochastic pricing equation might behave irregularly when $\epsilon \to 0$, i.e., in the deterministic limit. However, it can be checked that both $\text{A} \to 0$ and $\text{B} \to 0$ when $\epsilon \to 0$, so that this transition is smooth. Substituting expression (10.70) into the governing equation we obtain the following system of ODEs and initial conditions for A, B:

$$\frac{d}{d\tau}\text{B} + \text{B}^2 + (ik\varepsilon\rho + \hat{\kappa})\text{B} - \frac{1}{4}\varepsilon^2(k^2 + \frac{1}{4}) = 0, \quad \text{B}(0, k) = 0, \qquad (10.71)$$

$$\frac{d}{d\tau}\text{A} + \kappa\theta\text{B} = 0, \quad \text{A}(0, k) = 0. \qquad (10.72)$$

We recognize that equation (10.71) is a Riccati equation and use the standard substitution

$$\text{B} = \text{C}_\tau/\text{C},$$

in order to linearize it. In terms of C the corresponding A can be written as

$$A = -\kappa\theta\ln C.$$

The linear second-order ODE and appropriate initial conditions for C have the form:

$$\frac{d^2}{d\tau^2}C + (ik\varepsilon\rho + \hat{\kappa})\frac{d}{d\tau}C - \frac{1}{4}\varepsilon^2(k^2 + \frac{1}{4})C = 0, \tag{10.73}$$

$$C(0, k) = 1, \quad \frac{d}{d\tau}C(0, k) = 0. \tag{10.74}$$

The general solution of equation (10.73) can be written in the form

$$C = c_+ e^{\Lambda_+ \tau} + c_- e^{\Lambda_- \tau},$$

where $\Lambda_\pm$ are roots of the quadratic equation

$$\Lambda^2 + (ik\varepsilon\rho + \hat{\kappa})\Lambda - \frac{1}{4}\varepsilon^2(k^2 + \frac{1}{4}) = 0,$$

$$\Lambda_\pm(k) = \mu(k) \pm \zeta(k),$$

$$\mu(k) = -\frac{1}{2}(ik\varepsilon\rho + \hat{\kappa}), \tag{10.75}$$

$$\zeta(k) = \frac{1}{2}\sqrt{k^2\varepsilon^2\bar{\rho}^2 + 2ik\varepsilon\rho\hat{\kappa} + \hat{\kappa}^2 + \frac{\varepsilon^2}{4}}. \tag{10.76}$$

where $\bar{\rho}^2 = 1 - \rho^2$, and $c_\pm$ are arbitrary constants. The solution of the initial value problem (10.73), (10.74) can be written as

$$C(\tau, k) = \frac{e^{(\mu+\zeta)\tau}\left(-\mu + \zeta + (\mu + \zeta)e^{-2\zeta\tau}\right)}{2\zeta}.$$

We emphasize the fact that all the formulas we have to deal with are defined in the complex plane. Accordingly, we have to be careful when we define such functions as $\sqrt{Z}$ and $\log(Z)$, where Z is a complex number. We consider the branches of the square root and the logarithm defined in the complex plane with a branch cut along the negative semi-axis, such that $\sqrt{1} = 1$ and $\ln(1) = 0$.

We emphasize that these functions are discontinuous along the negative semi-axis where we have a branch cut; however, the discontinuity of the square root is irrelevant for our purposes, while the discontinuity of the logarithm can be accounted for. We have,

$$B(\tau, k) = \frac{\varepsilon^2 (k^2 + 1/4)(1 - e^{-2\zeta\tau})}{4\left(-\mu + \zeta + (\mu + \zeta)e^{-2\zeta\tau}\right)},$$

$$A(\tau, k) = -\kappa\theta\left(\mu + \zeta\right)\tau - \kappa\theta \ln\left(\frac{-\mu + \zeta + (\mu + \zeta)e^{-2\zeta\tau}}{2\zeta}\right).$$

These formulas show (after some effort) that A, B, C, are all even functions of ζ, so that, as promised, the sign of ζ does not affect their values. At the same time, with the choice of the branch of the logarithm we made (or any other choice for that matter), we cannot guarantee that $A(\tau, k)$ is a continuous function of τ (as it should be). It is not a purely theoretical concern since this function can indeed become discontinuous. To rectify this problem, we have to add to (or subtract from) the imaginary part of the logarithm 2π every time the curve in the complex plane defined by the equation

$$\tau \to Z_R + iZ_I,$$

where Z_R, Z_I are the real and imaginary parts of

$$Z = \frac{-\mu + \zeta + (\mu + \zeta)e^{-2\zeta\tau}}{2\zeta}, \tag{10.77}$$

intersects with the negative semi-axis in the Z-plane. This is a very difficult rule to implement since it has to be applied for all real k. Fortunately, there is a way out. Namely, it is easy to verify that for $k = 0$ and arbitrary τ the argument of the logarithm is positive, so that its imaginary part is zero. Starting at $k = 0$ we can define the logarithm to be a continuous function of k. This way we will make it a continuous function of τ as well. Thus, we can consider the curve defined by the equation

$$k \to Z_R + iZ_I,$$

where Z_R, Z_I are given by equation (10.77), and count the number of times (with signs) this curve intersects with the negative semi-axis in the Z-plane and add or subtract $2\pi i$ every time it does so. We introduce the following function

$N(\tau, k)$ with integer values which counts the number of the corresponding intersections,

$$N(\tau, k) = \begin{cases} -\sum_{0 < k_j < k} \text{sign}[dZ_I(\tau, k_j)/dk], & \text{when} \quad k > 0 \\ \sum_{0 < k_j < k} \text{sign}[dZ_I(\tau, k_j)/dk], & \text{when} \quad k < 0 \end{cases},$$

where k_j are roots of the function $Z_I(\tau, k)$ such that $Z_R(\tau, k) < 0$, and define $A(\tau, k)$ as

$$A(\tau, k) = -\kappa\theta (\mu + \zeta) \tau - \kappa\theta \left[\ln\left(\frac{-\mu + \zeta + (\mu + \zeta)e^{-2\zeta\tau}}{2\zeta} \right) + 2\pi i N \right].$$

This rule makes $A(\tau, k)$ a continuous function of its arguments.

Thus, we can represent $q(\tau, Y, v)$ in the form

$$q(\tau, Y, v) = \frac{1}{2\pi} \int_{-\infty}^{\infty} Z(\tau, k, Y, v)dk, \tag{10.78}$$

where

$$\begin{aligned} Z(\tau, k, Y, v) &= \exp\left\{ \frac{\hat{\kappa}\kappa\theta}{\varepsilon^2}\tau + ik\left(Y + \frac{\rho\kappa\theta}{\varepsilon}\tau\right) - \frac{2\kappa\theta}{\epsilon^2}\left[\zeta\tau \right.\right. \\ &\quad + \ln\left(\frac{-\mu + \zeta + (\mu + \zeta)e^{-2\zeta\tau}}{2\zeta} \right) + 2\pi i N\right] \\ &\quad \left.\left. - \frac{v(k^2 + 1/4)\left(1 - e^{-2\zeta\tau}\right)}{2\left(-\mu + \zeta + (\mu + \zeta)e^{-2\zeta\tau}\right)} \right\} \right. \\ &= Z_R(\tau, k, Y, v) + iZ_I(\tau, k, Y, v). \end{aligned}$$

To be sure that this formula makes sense we need to verify that the integrand is a rapidly decaying function of k. For $k \to \infty$ we have

$$\mu \to \frac{i}{2}k\epsilon\rho, \qquad \zeta \to \frac{1}{2}|k|\,\epsilon\bar{\rho},$$

so that the real part of the exponent β inside the integral in equation (10.78) can be evaluated as

$$\Re\beta \to -\frac{\bar{\rho}\kappa\theta\tau\,|k|}{\epsilon} - \frac{v\bar{\rho}\,|k|}{\epsilon} = -\frac{\bar{\rho}(\kappa\theta\tau + v)\,|k|}{\epsilon}. \tag{10.79}$$

It is clear that $\Re\beta \to -\infty$ so that the integrand is a sufficiently rapidly decaying function and integral (10.78) does make sense. It is interesting to note that the rate of decay is linear in k while for the standard heat equation it is quadratic in k. However, the rate of decay increases when $\epsilon \to 0$ so that there is no contradiction.

Equation (10.79) is important not only from a theoretical viewpoint, but from a practical viewpoint as well, since it allows us to replace the infinite limit of integration by finite limits $\pm k_{\max}$ such that

$$k_{\max} \gg \max\left\{ \frac{\epsilon}{\bar{\rho}(\kappa\theta\tau + v)}, \frac{\kappa}{\epsilon\rho} \right\},$$

provided that $\rho, \bar{\rho} \neq 0$.

10.9.4   The pricing formula

Now we are in a position to price call options (semi-)explicitly. By using Green's function we can represent $U(\tau, X, v)$ as follows:

$$
\begin{aligned}
U(\tau, X, v) &= \int_0^\infty q(\tau, X' - X, v)\left(e^{X'/2} - e^{-X'/2}\right) dX' \\
&= \frac{1}{2\pi} \int_0^\infty \int_{-\infty}^\infty Z(\tau, k, X' - X, v)\left(e^{X'/2} - e^{-X'/2}\right) dk dX'.
\end{aligned}
$$

Interchanging the order of integration reduces to the evaluation of the integral

$$\iota(k) = \int_0^\infty e^{ikX'}\left(e^{X'/2} - e^{-X'/2}\right) dX'.$$

By using formulas (8.28) we obtain

$$\iota(k) = -\frac{1}{ik + 1/2} + 2\pi\delta(k - i/2) + \frac{1}{ik - 1/2}.$$

Accordingly,

$$
\begin{aligned}
&U(\tau, X, v) \\
&= \frac{1}{2\pi} \int_{-\infty}^\infty Z(\tau, k, -X, v)\left(-\frac{1}{ik + 1/2} + 2\pi\delta(k - i/2) + \frac{1}{ik - 1/2}\right) dk \\
&= Z(\tau, i/2, -X, v) - \frac{1}{2\pi} \int_{-\infty}^\infty \frac{Z(\tau, k, -X, v)}{k^2 + 1/4} dk.
\end{aligned}
$$

Noting that the reflection $k \to -k$ is equivalent to the complex conjugation, we get

$$U(\tau, X, v) = e^{X/2} - \frac{1}{\pi} \int_0^\infty \frac{Z_R(\tau, k, -X, v)}{k^2 + 1/4} dk.$$

Returning back to the original nondimensional variables, we obtain the following expression for $\Phi(\tau, \xi, v)$,

$$\Phi(\tau, \xi, v) = \xi - \frac{\sqrt{\xi}}{\pi} \int_0^\infty \frac{Z_R(\tau, k, -\ln\xi, v)}{k^2 + 1/4} dk. \qquad (10.80)$$

This formula can easily be coded and used to obtain the expression for $\Phi(\tau, \xi, v)$ numerically.

Implied volatilities of calls in the stochastic volatility framework are shown in Figure 10.10.

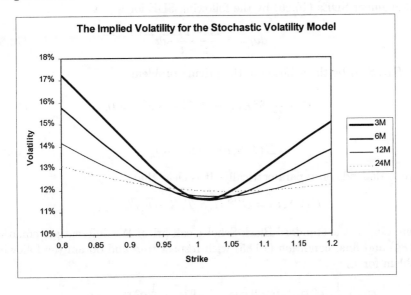

Figure 10.10: The "stochastic volatility" implied volatility $\sigma_I(T, K)$ as a function of K for four representative maturities, $T = 3, 6, 12, 24$ months. The relevant parameters are $S_0 = 0.95$, $v = (12.5\%)^2$, $r^0 = r^1 = 5\%$, $\theta = (12.5\%)^2$, $\kappa = 4$, $\varepsilon = 0.50$, $\rho = 0.10$.

The put price can be found by analogy or via put-call parity which holds in the stochastic case as well.

10.9.5   The case of zero correlation

In the case of zero correlation we can study the pricing problem from a different angle. The price of a call option is governed by

$$C_t + \frac{1}{2}vS^2C_{SS} + \frac{1}{2}\varepsilon^2 vC_{vv} + r^{01}SC_S - r^0C = 0, \tag{10.81}$$

$$C(T, S, v) = (S - K)_+. \tag{10.82}$$

We introduce the average variance

$$\nu_{t,t'} = \frac{\int_t^{t'} v_{t''}dt''}{(t' - t)},$$

and augment SDEs (10.66) by the following SDE for ν:

$$d\nu_{t,t'} = \frac{v_{t'} - \nu_{t,t'}}{t' - t}dt'. \tag{10.83}$$

Let $E(t, S, \nu)$ be the solution of the pricing problem

$$E_t + \frac{1}{2}\nu S^2 E_{SS} + r^{01}SE_S - r^0E = 0, \tag{10.84}$$

$$E(T, S, \nu) = (S - K)_+. \tag{10.85}$$

Here E depends on ν parametrically. It is clear that

$$E(t, S, \nu) = C^{BS}\left(t, S, T, K, \sqrt{\nu}, r^0, r^1\right),$$

where C^{BS} is the standard Black-Scholes call price. We differentiate equation (10.84) and final condition (10.85) with respect to ν and obtain the following problem for E_ν:

$$E_{\nu t} + \frac{1}{2}\nu S^2 E_{\nu SS} + r^{01}SE_{\nu S} - r^0 E_\nu + \frac{1}{2}S^2 E_{SS} = 0,$$

$$E_\nu(T, S, \nu) = 0.$$

Straightforward calculation which is left to the reader as an exercise yields

$$E_\nu(t, S, v) = \frac{1}{2}(T - t)S^2 E_{SS}(t, S, v).$$

We can associate with SDEs (10.66), (10.83) the following backward-forward equation

$$H_t + \frac{1}{2}\varepsilon^2 v H_{vv} + \kappa \left(\theta - v \right) H_v - \left[\frac{(v - \nu)}{(T - t)} H \right]_\nu = 0,$$

$$H \left(T, v, \nu \right) = \delta \left(v - \nu \right).$$

It turns out that the solution of the pricing problem (10.81), (10.82) can be represented in the form

$$V \left(t, S, v \right) = \int_0^\infty E \left(t, S, \nu \right) H \left(t, v, \nu \right) d\nu. \qquad (10.86)$$

Indeed, by substituting the above integral in equation (10.81) we obtain

$$C_t + \frac{1}{2} v S^2 C_{SS} + \frac{1}{2} \varepsilon^2 v C_{vv} + r^{01} S C_S - r^0 C$$

$$= \int_0^\infty \left\{ \left[E_t + \frac{1}{2} v S^2 E_{SS} \right] H + E \left[H_t + \frac{1}{2} \varepsilon^2 v H_{vv} + \kappa \left(\theta - v \right) H_v \right] \right\} d\nu$$

$$= \int_0^\infty \left\{ \left[E_t + \frac{1}{2} v S^2 E_{SS} \right] H + E \left[\frac{(v - \nu)}{(T - t)} H \right]_\nu \right\} d\nu$$

$$= \int_0^\infty \left[E_t + \frac{1}{2} v S^2 E_{SS} - \frac{(v - \nu)}{(T - t)} E_\nu \right] H d\nu$$

$$= \int_0^\infty \left[E_t + \frac{1}{2} \nu S^2 E_{SS} \right] H d\nu = 0.$$

Representation (10.86) is very intuitively appealing because it shows that in the stochastic volatility environment the price of a call is the weighted average of the Black-Scholes prices corresponding to different average variances provided that Wiener processes governing the evolution of S and v are uncorrelated.

10.10 Small volatility of volatility

10.10.1 Introduction

In the previous section we analyzed the general pricing problem and found its solution via the Fourier transform method. However, the basic formulas for the Green's function and the call price cannot be expressed in elementary functions and have to be found via numerical integration. Although this integration is relatively straightforward, it is of interest to analyze cases when the corresponding formulas can be found analytically. In this section we consider the case of small volatility of volatility and find the Green's function and the call price via the theory of perturbations. Our approach is based on the series expansion method which is much more flexible than the Fourier transform method. Accordingly, we can consider more general laws governing the evolution of volatility.

10.10.2   Basic equations

We start with the general system of SDEs for forward FXR and its variance:

$$\frac{dF_{t,T}}{F_{t,T}} = \sqrt{v_t}dW_t,$$

$$dv_t = \kappa(\theta - v_t)dt + \varepsilon v_t^{\zeta}d\Omega_t,$$

where $0 \leq \zeta \leq 1$, and $corr(dW_1, dW_2) = \rho$. For simplicity we assume that all the parameters of the model are time-independent. (It is not difficult to extend our analysis in order to cover the time-dependent case.) This model includes all the popular models for the variance dynamics, such as the Heston ($\zeta = 1/2$), Stein and Stein ($\zeta = 0$), and lognormal or Hull-White ($\zeta = 1$) models which were mentioned earlier.

The pricing problem for $\check{C}(\tau, F, v)$ has the form

$$\check{C}_\tau - \frac{1}{2}vF^2\check{C}_{FF} - \varepsilon\rho v^{1/2+\zeta}F\check{C}_{Fv} - \frac{1}{2}\varepsilon^2 v^{2\zeta}\check{C}_{vv} - \kappa(\theta - v)\check{C}_v = 0,$$

$$\check{C}(0, F, v) = (F - K)_+.$$

It is our intention to solve this problem for $\varepsilon \to 0$. Since ε is a dimensional parameter, the usual inequality $\varepsilon \ll 1$ cannot be applied directly.

10.10.3   The martingale formulation

We want to introduce a new martingale variable ν instead of the variance v. We introduce

$$\nu = \alpha v + \beta, \qquad v = \frac{\nu - \beta}{\alpha},$$

where α, β are time-dependent functions, and write the governing equation for ν as

$$d\nu = \left[\left(\frac{\alpha'}{\alpha} - \kappa \right) \nu + \frac{\alpha\beta' - \alpha'\beta}{\alpha} + \kappa\theta\alpha + \kappa\beta \right] dt + \varepsilon\alpha^{1-\zeta} (\nu - \beta)^\zeta \, d\Omega_t,$$

where $' = d/dt$. By choosing α, β in such a way that

$$\alpha' - \kappa\alpha = 0, \quad \alpha(T) = 1,$$

$$\beta' + \kappa\theta\alpha = 0, \quad \beta(T) = 0,$$

we obtain ν which is a martingale variable governed by the SDE of the form

$$d\nu_t = \varepsilon\alpha^{1-\zeta} (\nu_t - \beta)^\zeta \, d\Omega_t.$$

The evolution of F is governed by the following SDE

$$\frac{dF_{t,T}}{F_{t,T}} = \alpha^{-1/2}(\nu_t - \beta)^{1/2} dW_t.$$

The pricing problem for $\check{C}(\tau, F, \nu)$ has the form

$$\check{C}_\tau - \frac{1}{2}\alpha^{-1}(\nu - \beta)F^2\check{C}_{FF} - \varepsilon\rho\alpha^{1/2-\zeta}(\nu - \beta)^{1/2+\zeta}F\check{C}_{F\nu}$$

$$- \frac{1}{2}\varepsilon^2\alpha^{2-2\zeta}(\nu - \beta)^{2\zeta}\check{C}_{\nu\nu} = 0,$$

$$\check{C}(0, F, \nu) = (F - K)_+.$$

10.10.4 Perturbative expansion

We represent the solution of the pricing problem as a series in powers of ε,

$$\check{C} = \check{C}^{(0)} + \varepsilon\check{C}^{(1)} + \varepsilon^2\check{C}^{(2)},$$

substitute this expansion into the pricing problem and balance powers of ε to obtain a triangular system of equations for $\check{C}^{(i)}$,

$$\mathcal{L}^{(0)}\check{C}^{(0)} = 0, \quad \check{C}^{(0)}(0) = (F - K)_+,$$

$$\mathcal{L}^{(0)}\check{C}^{(1)} + \mathcal{L}^{(1)}\check{C}^{(0)} = 0, \quad \check{C}^{(1)}(0) = 0,$$

$$\mathcal{L}^{(0)}\check{C}^{(2)} + \mathcal{L}^{(1)}\check{C}^{(1)} + \mathcal{L}^{(2)}\check{C}^{(0)} = 0, \quad \check{C}^{(2)}(0) = 0,$$

where $\mathcal{L}^{(i)}$ are differential operators of the form

$$\mathcal{L}^{(0)} = \partial_\tau - \frac{1}{2}\alpha^{-1}(\nu - \beta)\mathcal{D}(\mathcal{D} - 1),$$

$$\mathcal{L}^{(1)} = -\rho\alpha^{1/2-\zeta}(\nu - \beta)^{1/2+\zeta}\mathcal{D}\partial_\nu,$$

$$\mathcal{L}^{(2)} = -\frac{1}{2}\alpha^{2-2\zeta}(\nu - \beta)^{2\zeta}\partial_\nu^2,$$

and $\mathcal{D} = F\partial_F$. To proceed further we need the following commutation relations,

$$\left[\mathcal{D}, \mathcal{L}^{(0)}\right] \equiv \mathcal{D}\mathcal{L}^{(0)} - \mathcal{L}^{(0)}\mathcal{D} = 0,$$

$$\left[\partial_\nu, \mathcal{L}^{(0)}\right] \equiv \partial_\nu\mathcal{L}^{(0)} - \mathcal{L}^{(0)}\partial_\nu = -\frac{1}{2}\alpha^{-1}\mathcal{D}(\mathcal{D} - 1),$$

which can be verified directly. In effect, these relations say that if $\check{C}$ is a solution of $\mathcal{L}^{(0)}\check{C} = 0$, then so are all its derivatives with respect to $\ln F$, while its derivatives with respect to ν are "almost" solutions. We emphasize that the commutation relations exist only in the absence of the static smile.

The idea behind the method can be formulated as follows. Assume that $\check{C}^{(0)}$ is found. Then, its derivatives $\check{C}_\nu^{(0)}, \check{C}_{\nu\nu}^{(0)}$ as well as higher order terms $\check{C}^{(1)}, \check{C}^{(2)}$ and their derivatives can be expressed in terms of $\check{C}^{(0)}, \mathcal{D}\check{C}^{(0)}$, etc., in a relatively simple way which involves solution of ODEs rather than the original PDEs.

We start with $\check{C}_\nu^{(0)}$ and use the commutation relations to obtain the following equation

$$\mathcal{L}^{(0)}\check{C}_\nu^{(0)} - \frac{1}{2}\alpha^{-1}\mathcal{D}(\mathcal{D} - 1)\check{C}^{(0)} = 0.$$

We use the ansatz

$$\check{C}_\nu^{(0)} = h_1\mathcal{D}(\mathcal{D} - 1)\check{C}^{(0)},$$

and get the first ODE we are looking for

$$\dot{h}_1 - \frac{1}{2}\alpha^{-1} = 0, \qquad h_1(0) = 0.$$

Here and below the overdot stands for $d/d\tau$. To find a simple expression for $\check{C}^{(0)}_{\nu\nu}$ we use the commutation relations once more and obtain the equation of the form

$$\mathcal{L}^{(0)}\check{C}^{(0)}_{\nu\nu} - \alpha^{-1}\mathcal{D}(\mathcal{D}-1)\check{C}^{(0)}_{\nu} = 0,$$

or, equivalently,

$$\mathcal{L}^{(0)}\check{C}^{(0)}_{\nu\nu} - \alpha^{-1}h_1\mathcal{D}^2(\mathcal{D}-1)^2\check{C}^{(0)} = 0.$$

It is clear that by the same token as before we are able to write $\check{C}^{(0)}_{\nu\nu}$ as

$$\check{C}^{(0)}_{\nu\nu} = h_1^2\mathcal{D}^2(\mathcal{D}-1)^2\check{C}^{(0)}.$$

Now we are ready to find $\check{C}^{(1)}$. We use the explicit expression for $\check{C}^{(0)}_{\nu}$ and write the equation for $\check{C}^{(1)}$ as

$$\mathcal{L}^{(0)}\check{C}^{(1)} - \rho\alpha^{1/2-\varsigma}(\nu-\beta)^{1/2+\varsigma}h_1\mathcal{D}^2(\mathcal{D}-1)\check{C}^{(0)} = 0.$$

Accordingly, we can represent $\check{C}^{(1)}$ in the form

$$\check{C}^{(1)} = f_1^{(1)}\mathcal{D}^2(\mathcal{D}-1)\check{C}^{(0)},$$

where $f_1^{(1)}$ satisfies the following ODE,

$$\dot{f}_1^{(1)} - \rho\alpha^{1/2-\varsigma}(\nu-\beta)^{1/2+\varsigma}h_1 = 0, \qquad f_1^{(1)}(0) = 0.$$

To proceed further, we need to find $\check{C}^{(1)}_{\nu}$. The commutation relations yield

$$\mathcal{L}^{(0)}\check{C}^{(1)}_{\nu} - \frac{1}{2}\alpha^{-1}\mathcal{D}(\mathcal{D}-1)\check{C}^{(1)} - \rho\alpha^{1/2-\varsigma}(\nu-\beta)^{1/2+\varsigma}h_1\mathcal{D}^2(\mathcal{D}-1)\check{C}^{(0)}_{\nu}$$
$$-(1/2+\varsigma)\rho\alpha^{1/2-\varsigma}(\nu-\beta)^{-1/2+\varsigma}h_1\mathcal{D}^2(\mathcal{D}-1)\check{C}^{(0)} = 0,$$

or, explicitly,

$$\mathcal{L}^{(0)}\check{C}^{(1)}_{\nu} - \left[\rho\alpha^{1/2-\varsigma}(\nu-\beta)^{1/2+\varsigma}h_1^2 + \frac{1}{2}\alpha^{-1}f_1^{(1)}\right]\mathcal{D}^3(\mathcal{D}-1)^2\check{C}^{(0)}$$
$$-(1/2+\varsigma)\rho\alpha^{1/2-\varsigma}(\nu-\beta)^{-1/2+\varsigma}h_1\mathcal{D}^2(\mathcal{D}-1)\check{C}^{(0)} = 0.$$

We use our usual ansatz and write $\check{C}_\nu^{(1)}$ as

$$\check{C}_\nu^{(1)} = h_3 \mathcal{D}^3 (\mathcal{D}-1)^2 \check{C}^{(0)} + h_2 \mathcal{D}^2 (\mathcal{D}-1) \check{C}^{(0)}.$$

The ODEs for h_1, h_2 are

$$\dot{h}_2 - (1/2 + \zeta)\rho\alpha^{1/2-\zeta}(\nu-\beta)^{-1/2+\zeta}h_1 = 0, \quad h_2(0) = 0,$$

$$\dot{h}_3 - \rho\alpha^{1/2-\zeta}(\nu-\beta)^{1/2+\zeta}h_1^2 - \frac{1}{2}\alpha^{-1}f_1^{(1)} = 0, \quad h_3(0) = 0.$$

We now know all the functions we need in order to find the second-order perturbation $\check{C}^{(2)}$. The corresponding equation has the form

$$\mathcal{L}^{(0)}\check{C}^{(2)} - \rho\alpha^{1/2-\zeta}(\nu-\beta)^{1/2+\zeta}\mathcal{D}\check{C}_\nu^{(1)} - \frac{1}{2}\alpha^{2-2\zeta}(\nu-\beta)^{2\zeta}\check{C}_{\nu\nu}^{(0)} = 0.$$

By using the explicit expressions for $\check{C}_{\nu\nu}^{(0)}$ and $\check{C}_\nu^{(1)}$ we can rewrite this equation as follows

$$\mathcal{L}^{(0)}\check{C}^{(2)} - \rho\alpha^{1/2-\zeta}(\nu-\beta)^{1/2+\zeta}h_3\mathcal{D}^4(\mathcal{D}-1)^2\check{C}^{(0)}$$
$$-\rho\alpha^{1/2-\zeta}(\nu-\beta)^{1/2+\zeta}h_2\mathcal{D}^3(\mathcal{D}-1)\check{C}^{(0)}$$
$$-\frac{1}{2}\alpha^{2-2\zeta}(\nu-\beta)^{2\zeta}h_1^2\mathcal{D}^2(\mathcal{D}-1)^2\check{C}^{(0)} = 0.$$

Accordingly,

$$\check{C}^{(2)} = f_3^{(2)}\mathcal{D}^4(\mathcal{D}-1)^2\check{C}^{(0)} + f_2^{(2)}\mathcal{D}^3(\mathcal{D}-1)\check{C}^{(0)} + f_1^{(2)}\mathcal{D}^2(\mathcal{D}-1)^2\check{C}^{(0)},$$

where $f_i^{(2)}$ satisfy the following ODEs

$$\dot{f}_1^{(2)} - \frac{1}{2}\alpha^{2-2\zeta}(\nu-\beta)^{2\zeta}h_1^2 = 0, \quad f_3^{(2)}(0) = 0.$$

$$\dot{f}_2^{(2)} - \rho\alpha^{1/2-\zeta}(\nu-\beta)^{1/2+\zeta}h_2 = 0, \quad f_2^{(2)}(0) = 0,$$

$$\dot{f}_3^{(2)} - \rho\alpha^{1/2-\zeta}(\nu-\beta)^{1/2+\zeta}h_3 = 0, \quad f_1^{(2)}(0) = 0,$$

10.10.5 Summary of ODEs

For the sake of clarity, we summarize in this subsection all the ODEs which need to be solved in order to compute the solution of the perturbation problem. They are

$$\dot{\alpha} + \kappa\alpha = 0, \quad \alpha(0) = 1,$$

$$\dot{\beta} - \kappa\theta\alpha = 0, \quad \beta(0) = 0,$$

$$\dot{h}_1 - \frac{1}{2}\alpha^{-1} = 0, \quad h_1(0) = 0,$$

$$\dot{f}_1^{(1)} - \rho\alpha^{1/2-\zeta}(\nu - \beta)^{1/2+\zeta}h_1 = 0, \quad f_1^{(1)}(0) = 0,$$

$$\dot{h}_2 - (1/2 + \zeta)\rho\alpha^{1/2-\zeta}(\nu - \beta)^{-1/2+\zeta}h_1 = 0, \quad h_2(0) = 0,$$

$$\dot{h}_3 - \rho\alpha^{1/2-\zeta}(\nu - \beta)^{1/2+\zeta}h_1^2 - \frac{1}{2}\alpha^{-1}f_1^{(1)} = 0, \quad h_3(0) = 0,$$

$$\dot{f}_1^{(2)} - \frac{1}{2}\alpha^{2-2\zeta}(\nu - \beta)^{2\zeta}h_1^2 = 0, \quad f_1^{(2)}(0) = 0,$$

$$\dot{f}_2^{(2)} - \rho\alpha^{1/2-\zeta}(\nu - \beta)^{1/2+\zeta}h_2 = 0, \quad f_2^{(2)}(0) = 0,$$

$$\dot{f}_3^{(2)} - \rho\alpha^{1/2-\zeta}(\nu - \beta)^{1/2+\zeta}h_3 = 0, \quad f_3^{(2)}(0) = 0.$$

These ODEs are clearly integrable. However, this integration is somewhat tedious and generally is done numerically. Because of that, we want to simplify this set of ODEs. We leave it to the reader as a useful exercise to show that

$$f_3^{(2)} = \frac{1}{2}\left(f_1^{(1)}\right)^2.$$

Thus, the sixth equation of our set is not needed while the last one can be solved explicitly. We see that the total number of equations which we need to solve is seven. It is important to notice that the first three of these equations are independent of ζ and can be solved once and for all.

10.10.6   Solution of the leading order pricing problem

Our perturbative scheme uses the expression for the leading order price $\check{C}^{(0)}$ and its derivatives $\mathcal{D}\check{C}^{(0)}, \mathcal{D}^2\check{C}^{(0)}, ...$, as important building blocks of the general solution. In this section we show how to compute $\check{C}^{(0)}$. We determine $\check{C}^{(0)}$ from

$$\partial_\tau \check{C}^{(0)} - \frac{1}{2}\alpha^{-1}(\nu - \beta)\mathcal{D}(\mathcal{D} - 1)\check{C}^{(0)} = 0,$$

$$\check{C}^{(0)}(0, F, \nu) = (F - K)_+.$$

This is simply a Black-Scholes pricing problem with time-dependent coefficients. Its solution has the form

$$\check{C}^{(0)}(\tau, F, \nu) = \check{C}\left(\tau, F, K, \sigma_{t,T}^{(0)}\right),$$

where the leading-order volatility is determined from

$$\sigma_{t,T}^{(0)} = \sqrt{\frac{\int_t^T \alpha^{-1}(\nu - \beta)dt'}{T - t}} = \sqrt{(\nu - \theta)\frac{(e^{\kappa\tau} - 1)}{\kappa\tau} + \theta}. \qquad (10.87)$$

10.10.7   The square-root model

For the purposes of illustration, in this subsection we study the Heston model with constant coefficients. After some tedious algebra we obtain,

$$\alpha = e^{-\kappa\tau},$$

$$\beta = \theta\left(1 - e^{-\kappa\tau}\right),$$

$$h_1 = \frac{1}{2\kappa}\left(e^{\kappa\tau} - 1\right),$$

$$f_1^{(1)} = \frac{\rho\nu}{2\kappa^2}\left(e^{\kappa\tau} - 1 - \kappa\tau\right) - \frac{\rho\theta}{2\kappa^2}\left(e^{\kappa\tau} - e^{-\kappa\tau} - 2\kappa\tau\right) \equiv \rho g_1^{(1)},$$

$$h_2 = \frac{\rho}{2\kappa^2}\left(e^{\kappa\tau} - 1 - \kappa\tau\right),$$

$$f_1^{(2)} = \frac{\nu}{8\kappa^3}\left(e^{\kappa\tau} - e^{-\kappa\tau} - 2\kappa\tau\right) - \frac{\theta}{16\kappa^3}\left(2e^{\kappa\tau} + 3 - 6\kappa\tau - 6e^{-\kappa\tau} + e^{-2\kappa\tau}\right),$$

$$
\begin{aligned}
f_2^{(2)} &= \frac{\rho^2\nu}{4\kappa^3}\left(2e^{\kappa\tau} - 2 - 2\kappa\tau - (\kappa\tau)^2\right) \\
&\quad - \frac{\rho^2\theta}{4\kappa^3}\left(2e^{\kappa\tau} - 2(2 + \kappa\tau)e^{-\kappa\tau} + 2 - 4\kappa\tau - (\kappa\tau)^2\right) \\
&\equiv \rho^2 g_2^{(2)},
\end{aligned}
$$

$$f_3^{(2)} = \frac{1}{2}\left(f_1^{(1)}\right)^2 \equiv \frac{1}{2}\rho^2\left(g_1^{(1)}\right)^2.$$

The leading-order volatility $\sigma^{(0)}$ has the from (10.87). By using the following formula

$$\nu - \theta = (v - \theta)\, e^{-\kappa\tau},$$

and rewriting the corresponding expressions in terms of v, we obtain:

$$\sigma^{(0)} = \sqrt{(v - \theta)\frac{(1 - e^{-\kappa\tau})}{\kappa\tau} + \theta}.$$

In financial variables $\check{C}^{(0)}$ assumes the familiar form of the Black-Scholes price for a call on an underlying asset with deterministic time-dependent volatility:

$$\check{C}^{(0)}(\tau, F, v) = F\mathfrak{N}(d_+) - K\mathfrak{N}(d_-),$$

while $\check{C}^{(1)}$, $\check{C}^{(2)}$ have the form

$$\check{C}^{(1)}(\tau, F, v) = -\frac{\rho g_1^{(1)} d_-}{\gamma}K\mathfrak{n}(d_-),$$

$$
\begin{aligned}
\check{C}^{(2)}(\tau, F, v) &= \left[-\frac{f_1^{(2)}(1 - d_+ d_-)}{\gamma\sqrt{\gamma}} - \frac{\rho^2 g_2^{(2)}(1 - d_-^2)}{\gamma\sqrt{\gamma}} \right. \\
&\quad \left. + \frac{\rho^2 g_3^{(2)}(3 - 3d_+ d_- - 3d_-^2 + d_+ d_-^3)}{\gamma^2\sqrt{\gamma}} \right] K\mathfrak{n}(d_-).
\end{aligned}
$$

Here γ is the deannualized mean variance on the interval $(0, \tau)$,

$$\gamma = (v - \theta)\frac{(1 - e^{-\kappa \tau})}{\kappa} + \theta \tau.$$

and

$$d_{\pm} = d_{\pm}(\gamma, F/K) = \frac{\ln(F/K)}{\sqrt{\gamma}} \pm \frac{\sqrt{\gamma}}{2}.$$

The resulting approximate price of a call can be written as

$$\check{C}(\tau, F, v) = \check{C}^{(0)}(\tau, F, v) + \epsilon \check{C}^{(1)}(\tau, F, v) + \epsilon^2 \check{C}^{(2)}(\tau, F, v). \tag{10.88}$$

Extensive numerical comparison of formulas (10.80) and (10.88) shows that the latter approximates the former within one basis point of accuracy for most realistic values of parameters. This conclusion is of great importance since it allows us to build intuition concerning the impact of the stochastic volatility on the price of an option. When the movements of the stock price and its volatility are correlated the main correction is given by the term

$$-\frac{\epsilon \rho g_1^{(1)} d_-}{\gamma} K \mathfrak{n}(d_-).$$

It can be shown that the function $g_1^{(1)}$ is positive. Thus, the stochastic price correction is positive when ρd_- is negative, or, equivalently, when

$$\rho(\ln(F/K) - \gamma/2) < 0,$$

and negative otherwise. There is clearly only one change of sign in this case. When the movements of the FXR and its volatility are uncorrelated, the leading order price correction is given by

$$-\frac{\epsilon^2 f_1^{(2)}(1 - d_+ d_-)}{\gamma \sqrt{\gamma}} K \mathfrak{n}(d_-).$$

Once again, the function $f_1^{(2)}$ is positive, so that the price correction is positive when $(1 - d_+ d_-)$ is negative, or, equivalently, when

$$|\ln(F/K)| > \sqrt{\frac{\gamma^2}{4} + \gamma},$$

and negative otherwise. There are two sign changes in this case.

10.10.8 Computation of the implied volatility

In this subsection we show how to find the implied volatility of a call option (say) computed via perturbative expansions. To start with, we find convenient expressions for the call Vega and dVega/dVol. We do so by virtue of the commutation relations. Consider the classical forward Black-Scholes pricing equation

$$\mathcal{L}\check{C} \equiv \partial_\tau \check{C} - \frac{1}{2}\sigma^2 \mathcal{D}(\mathcal{D} - 1)\check{C} = 0.$$

It is obvious that

$$[\partial_\sigma, \mathcal{L}] = -\sigma \mathcal{D}(\mathcal{D} - 1),$$

so that we can write

$$\mathcal{L}\check{C}_\sigma - \sigma \mathcal{D}(\mathcal{D} - 1)\check{C} = 0.$$

Accordingly, $\check{C}_\sigma$ has the form

$$\check{C}_\sigma = g_1 \mathcal{D}(\mathcal{D} - 1)\check{C},$$

where

$$g_1 = \sigma\tau.$$

Similarly,

$$\mathcal{L}\check{C}_{\sigma\sigma} - 2\sigma \mathcal{D}(\mathcal{D} - 1)\check{C}_\sigma - \mathcal{D}(\mathcal{D} - 1)\check{C} = 0,$$

or, explicitly,

$$\mathcal{L}\check{C}_{\sigma\sigma} - 2\sigma g_1 \mathcal{D}^2(\mathcal{D} - 1)^2\check{C} - \mathcal{D}(\mathcal{D} - 1)\check{C} = 0.$$

Thus,

$$\check{C}_{\sigma\sigma} = g_3 \mathcal{D}^2(\mathcal{D} - 1)^2\check{C} + g_2 \mathcal{D}(\mathcal{D} - 1)\check{C},$$

where

$$g_2 = \tau, \qquad g_3 = \sigma^2\tau^2.$$

Now we are ready to find the perturbative expansion for the implied volatility σ_I which is determined by the relation

$$\check{C}^{(0)}(\tau, F, \nu) + \varepsilon\check{C}^{(1)}(\tau, F, \nu) + \varepsilon^2\check{C}^{(2)}(\tau, F, \nu) = C(\tau, F; \sigma_I).$$

We represent σ_I as a series in powers of ε:

$$\sigma_I = \sigma^{(0)} + \varepsilon\sigma^{(1)} + \varepsilon^2\sigma^{(2)},$$

where $\sigma^{(0)}$ is given by equation (10.87), while $\sigma^{(1)}$ and $\sigma^{(2)}$ are to be determined. Substituting this expression into the above equation, using the explicit expressions for $\check{C}^{(0)}, \check{C}^{(1)}, \check{C}^{(2)}$ and $\check{C}_\sigma, \check{C}_{\sigma\sigma}$, and balancing terms, we obtain the following equations

$$f_1^{(1)}\mathcal{D}^2(\mathcal{D}-1)\check{C}^{(0)} = \sigma^{(1)}g_1\mathcal{D}(\mathcal{D}-1)\check{C}^{(0)},$$

$$f_3^{(2)}\mathcal{D}^4(\mathcal{D}-1)^2\check{C}^{(0)} + f_2^{(2)}\mathcal{D}^3(\mathcal{D}-1)\check{C}^{(0)} + f_1^{(2)}\mathcal{D}^2(\mathcal{D}-1)^2\check{C}^{(0)}$$
$$= \sigma^{(2)}g_1\mathcal{D}(\mathcal{D}-1)\check{C}^{(0)} + \frac{1}{2}\left(\sigma^{(1)}\right)^2\left[g_3\mathcal{D}^2(\mathcal{D}-1)^2\check{C}^{(0)} + g_2\mathcal{D}(\mathcal{D}-1)\check{C}^{(0)}\right].$$

Accordingly,

$$\sigma^{(1)} = \frac{f_1^{(1)}\mathcal{D}^2(\mathcal{D}-1)\check{C}^{(0)}}{g_1\mathcal{D}(\mathcal{D}-1)\check{C}^{(0)}},$$

$$\sigma^{(2)} = \frac{f_3^{(2)}\mathcal{D}^4(\mathcal{D}-1)^2\check{C}^{(0)} + f_2^{(2)}\mathcal{D}^3(\mathcal{D}-1)\check{C}^{(0)} + f_1^{(2)}\mathcal{D}^2(\mathcal{D}-1)^2\check{C}^{(0)}}{g_1\mathcal{D}(\mathcal{D}-1)\check{C}^{(0)}}$$
$$- \frac{\left[f_1^{(1)}\mathcal{D}^2(\mathcal{D}-1)\check{C}^{(0)}\right]^2\left[g_3\mathcal{D}^2(\mathcal{D}-1)^2\check{C}^{(0)} + g_2\mathcal{D}(\mathcal{D}-1)\check{C}^{(0)}\right]}{\left[g_1\mathcal{D}(\mathcal{D}-1)\check{C}^{(0)}\right]^3}.$$

These formulas become particularly simple when $\rho \equiv 0$. In this case we have

$$\sigma^{(1)} = 0,$$

$$\sigma^{(2)} = \frac{f_1^{(2)}\mathcal{D}^2(\mathcal{D}-1)^2\check{C}^{(0)}}{g_1\mathcal{D}(\mathcal{D}-1)\check{C}^{(0)}}.$$

10.11   Multi-factor problems

10.11.1   Introduction

Extension of the Black-Scholes framework in the multi-country case is a challenging task. Even the definition of such quantities as implied volatilities and correlations is not unambiguous. At the same time, local volatilities and correlations can be introduced without any difficulty. The pricing problem for a typical multi-factor option can be written as follows

$$V_t + \frac{1}{2}\sum_{m,n} a^{mn}\left(t,\mathbf{S}\right) S^{0m} S^{0n} V_{S^{0m}S^{0n}} + \sum_{n} r^{0n} S^{0n} V_{S^{0n}} - r^0 V = 0,$$

$$V\left(T,\mathbf{S}\right) = v\left(\mathbf{S}\right),$$

where the spot-dependent matrix $a^{mn}\left(t,\mathbf{S}\right)$ represents the local volatility surface.

Of course, this problem is much easier to write than to solve. Very few exact results in this direction are known and the effort is almost exclusively aimed at numerics. A viable alternative is to study possible distributions of the vector random variable $\mathbf{S}_T$ conditional on its known value $\mathbf{S}_t$, or, even better, the distribution of the scalar random variable $F\left(\mathbf{S}_T\right)$ conditional on the known value $\mathbf{S}_t$. ($F\left(\mathbf{S}_T\right)$ is a particular combination of FXRs which is relevant for a given option such as the basket option, say.) In this section we discuss the latter approach in some detail.

10.11.2 The chi-square pricing formula, II

In this subsection we describe a simple theory which can explain some universal features common to a large variety of multi-factor financial products. This theory is based on the assumption that the relevant scalar financial variable θ such as the value of the basket of currencies, say, weakly depends on a set of independent standard normal variables. Since the corresponding dependence is weak, we can use the quadratic approximation to study θ. Once this approximation is adopted, it becomes a relatively simple technical matter to represent θ as a sum of *independent* chi-square variables and (possibly) a normal variable. Since the terms are independent, the distribution of the sum can be found by virtue of a highly efficient numerical procedure which is outlined below. As a result, we obtain the universal distribution function p_θ and can value European options on θ in a simple and unified way. In principle, we can explain the volatility smile in this fashion.

We develop a general technique for finding an approximate distribution function for a random variable θ functionally depending on a collection of m independent standard normal variables ξ_j, $j = 1, ..., m$. Our approach extends the approach we used in the scalar case. We assume that

$$\theta = G\left(\mathbf{X}\right),$$

where $X_1, ..., X_n$ is a collection of n correlated normal variables such that

$$X_i = \varepsilon B_{ij} \xi_j, \qquad i = 1, ..., n, \qquad j = 1, ..., m,$$

or, in the vector form

$$\mathbf{X} = \varepsilon \mathcal{B} \boldsymbol{\xi},$$

where $\mathcal{B}$ is an $n \times m$ matrix. We adopt the normalization constraint

$$\| \mathcal{B}^T \mathcal{B} \| = 1,$$

and think of ε as a single parameter characterizing the norm of the covariance matrix for $\mathbf{X}$. Our approach, which is approximate in nature, is based on the assumption that the deannualized volatility ε is small,

$$\varepsilon \ll 1.$$

It allows us to find the distribution for the random variable θ.

Since the deviations of the underlying random variables from their means are small we can assume that these variables are (relatively) close to their mean values, i.e., $\mathbf{X} \approx \mathbf{0}$, and comfortably expand $G(\mathbf{X})$ in the Taylor series in the vicinity of $\mathbf{0}$. In the linear approximation we represent θ in the form

$$\theta = G(\mathbf{X}) \approx G_0 + \varepsilon \mathbf{G}_1 \cdot \mathcal{B} \boldsymbol{\xi} = G_0 + \varepsilon \mathcal{B}^T \mathbf{G}_1 \cdot \boldsymbol{\xi},$$

where $G_0 = G(\mathbf{0})$, and $G_1 = \nabla G(\mathbf{0})$ are the value of G and its gradient at $\mathbf{0}$, respectively. Since a linear combination of normal variables is a normal variable itself, we can immediately write the first order approximation for θ and its distribution function $f_\theta(x)$,

$$\theta \approx \mathfrak{N}(G_0, \varepsilon^2 \| \mathcal{B}^T \mathbf{G}_1 \|^2),$$

$$f_\theta(x) = \frac{e^{-(x - G_0)^2 / 2\varepsilon^2 \| \mathcal{B}^T \mathbf{G}_1 \|^2}}{\sqrt{2\pi} \varepsilon \| \mathcal{B}^T \mathbf{G}_1 \|}.$$

Although this approximation is way too crude, it is often used for the valuation of value at risk and for other purposes.

Next, we retain constant, linear and quadratic terms, and represent Y in the form

$$\begin{aligned} \theta = G(\mathbf{X}) &\approx G_0 + \varepsilon \mathbf{G}_1 \cdot \mathcal{B} \boldsymbol{\xi} + \frac{1}{2} \varepsilon^2 \mathcal{G}_2 \mathcal{B} \boldsymbol{\xi} \cdot \mathcal{B} \boldsymbol{\xi} \\ &\approx G + \varepsilon \mathcal{B}^T \mathbf{G}_1 \cdot \boldsymbol{\xi} + \frac{1}{2} \varepsilon^2 \mathcal{B}^T \mathcal{G}_2 \mathcal{B} \boldsymbol{\xi} \cdot \boldsymbol{\xi}, \end{aligned}$$

where $G_2 = \nabla\nabla G(0)$ is the Hessian of G at 0. As usual, we can diagonalize the $m \times m$ symmetric matrix $\mathcal{B}^T G_2 \mathcal{B}$ and write it as

$$\mathcal{B}^T G_2 \mathcal{B} = \mathcal{O}^T \mathcal{D} \mathcal{O},$$

where $\mathcal{D}$ and $\mathcal{O}$ are diagonal and orthogonal matrices, respectively,

$$\mathcal{D} = \mathrm{diag}(D_1, \ldots, D_m), \quad D_1 \leq \cdots \leq D_m,$$

and

$$\mathcal{O}^T \mathcal{O} = \mathcal{I}.$$

We emphasize that some of D_i can be equal to zero. Introducing the rotated variables $\boldsymbol{\eta} = \mathcal{O}\boldsymbol{\xi}$, $\eta_j = O_{jk}\xi_k$, which are independent standard normal random variables by construction, and the standard normal random variable

$$\vartheta = \frac{\mathbf{E} \cdot \boldsymbol{\eta}}{\|\mathbf{E}\|},$$

where $\mathbf{E} = \mathcal{O}\mathcal{B}^T G_1$, we write $G(\mathbf{X})$ as

$$\theta = G(\mathbf{X}) \approx G_0 + \varepsilon \|\mathbf{E}\| \vartheta + \frac{1}{2}\varepsilon^2 \sum{}' D_j \eta_j^2,$$

where $\sum'$ is extended over j such that $D_j \neq 0$. Since ϑ is clearly correlated with the basis variables η_j,

$$\rho_j = \mathrm{corr}(\vartheta, \eta_j) = \frac{E_j}{\|\mathbf{E}\|}, \tag{10.89}$$

the above formula has to be simplified further. In order to do so, we introduce new independent normal random variables $\tilde{\eta}_j$, $\tilde{\vartheta}$, of the form

$$\tilde{\eta}_j = \eta_j + \frac{E_j}{\varepsilon D_j} \quad \text{when} \quad D_j \neq 0,$$

$$\tilde{\vartheta} = \frac{\sum'' E_j P_j}{\sqrt{\sum'' E_j^2}},$$

where $\sum''$ is extended over j such that $D_j = 0$. In the case when $D_j \neq 0$ for all j we assume $\tilde{\vartheta} = 0$. Provided that $\tilde{\vartheta} \neq 0$, it is a standard normal random variable which is independent of $\tilde{\eta}_j$ corresponding to $D_j \neq 0$, while $\tilde{\eta}_j$ are $\mathfrak{N}(E_j/\varepsilon D_j, 1)$ normal variables. In terms of $\tilde{\eta}_j$, $\tilde{\vartheta}$, $G(\mathbf{X})$ can be written as

$$\theta = G(\mathbf{X}) \approx G_0 - \frac{1}{2} \sum{}' \frac{E_j^2}{D_j} + \varepsilon \sqrt{\sum{}'' E_j^2} \, \tilde{\vartheta} + \frac{1}{2} \varepsilon^2 \sum{}' D_j \tilde{\eta}_j^2.$$

We introduce the normal variable

$$\varpi_0 = \mathfrak{N}(\alpha, \varepsilon^2 \beta^2),$$

where

$$\alpha = G_0 - \frac{1}{2} \sum{}' \frac{E_j^2}{D_j}, \qquad \beta = \sqrt{\sum{}'' E_j^2},$$

and the scaled noncentral chi-square variables

$$\varpi_j = \frac{\varepsilon^2 D_j}{2} \left[\mathfrak{N}\left(\frac{E_j}{\varepsilon D_j}, 1 \right) \right]^2,$$

and represent Y in the following final form

$$\theta = \varpi_0 + \sum{}' \varpi_j.$$

Our objective is to find the distribution density f_θ of θ. Since θ is a sum of *independent* random variables ϖ_j, its distribution density is a convolution of the distribution densities of the individual terms. We know that the corresponding density f_0 of ϖ_0 has the form

$$f_0(y) = \frac{e^{-(y-\alpha)^2/2\varepsilon^2\beta^2}}{\sqrt{2\pi}\varepsilon\beta},$$

while the densities f_j, $j > 0$, $D_j \neq 0$, can be written as (see equation (10.19)):

$$f_j(x) = \begin{cases} \dfrac{e^{-(\sqrt{2D_jx}-E_j)^2/2\varepsilon^2 D_j^2} + e^{-(\sqrt{2D_jx}+E_j)^2/2\varepsilon^2 D_j^2}}{2\varepsilon\sqrt{\pi D_j x}}, & D_j x > 0 \\ 0, & D_j x < 0 \end{cases}.$$

The resulting distribution density f_θ has the form

$$f_\theta(x) = \frac{e^{-(x-\alpha)^2/2\varepsilon^2\beta^2}}{\sqrt{2\pi}\varepsilon\beta} * (*' f_j(x)),$$

where the convolution $*'$ is extended over all j such that $D_j \neq 0$.

As usual, the fastest way to actually compute this convolution is to use the Fourier transform. Denoting the Fourier transforms of $f_\theta(x)$, $f_0(x)$, and $f_j(x)$ by $\Phi_\theta(\varsigma)$, $\Phi_0(\varsigma)$, and $\Phi_j(\varsigma)$, respectively, we obtain

$$\Phi_\theta(\varsigma) = \Phi_0(\varsigma) \prod{}' \Phi_j(\varsigma).$$

It can be shown that

$$\Phi_0(\varsigma) = \exp\left\{ i\alpha\varsigma - \frac{1}{2}\varepsilon^2\beta^2\varsigma^2 \right\},$$

$$\Phi_j(\varsigma) = \exp\left\{ \frac{1}{2}\left[\frac{iE_j^2\varsigma}{D_j(1 - i\varepsilon^2 D_j\varsigma)} - \log(1 - i\varepsilon^2 D_j\varsigma) \right] \right\}.$$

Accordingly,

$$\Phi_Y(\varsigma) = \exp\left\{ i\alpha\varsigma - \frac{1}{2}\varepsilon^2\beta^2\varsigma^2 \right.$$
$$\left. + \frac{1}{2}\sum{}' \left[\frac{iE_j^2\varsigma}{D_j(1 - i\varepsilon^2 D_j\varsigma)} - \log(1 - i\varepsilon^2 D_j\varsigma) \right] \right\}.$$

Numerically computing the inverse Fourier transform of $\Phi_Y(\varsigma)$ we can find the distribution density $f_\theta(x)$ we are interested in:

$$
\begin{aligned}
f_\theta(x) &= \frac{1}{2\pi} \int_{-\infty}^{\infty} \exp[-ix\varsigma]\Phi_Y(\varsigma)d\varsigma \\
&= \frac{1}{2\pi} \int_{-\infty}^{\infty} \exp\left\{ i(\alpha - x)\varsigma - \frac{1}{2}\varepsilon^2\beta^2\varsigma^2 \right. \\
&\quad \left. + \frac{1}{2}\sum{}' \left[\frac{iE_j^2\varsigma}{D_j(1 - i\varepsilon^2 D_j\varsigma)} - \log(1 - i\varepsilon^2 D_j\varsigma) \right] \right\} d\varsigma.
\end{aligned}
$$

In the scheme described above the values of α and β are determined by the structure of the problem. However, in some cases it might be beneficial to use them as adjustable parameters in order to guarantee that the mean and variance of θ fit the mean and variance of $G(\mathbf{X})$ exactly (provided that the latter quantities are known). Changing α results is the parallel shift of the density function as a whole, while changing β alters the structure of its wings. In general, the corresponding changes are relatively small.

Once $f_\theta(x)$ is found, we can price options on θ via the risk-neutral valuation principle. Alternatively, we can use the Fourier transform for option pricing.

10.12   References and further reading

There are numerous original papers dealing with the topics covered in this chapter. The following ones are particularly relevant for our presentation: Amin and Ng (1993), Andersen and Andreasen (1999), Andersen and Brotherton-Ratcliffe (1998), Ball (1993), Ball and Roma (1994), Balland and Hughston (2000), Bates (1996), Beckers (1980), Black (1988), Bouchouev and Isakov (1997), Bredeen and Litzenberger (1978), Britten-Jones and Neuberger (2000), Britten-Jones and Schaefer (1997), Buchen and Kelly (1996), Carr *et al.* (2000), Chesney and Scott (1989), Cox (1975), Cox and Ross (1976), Das and Sundaram (1999), Derman (1999), Derman and Kani (1994), Duan (1995), Dumas *et al.* (1998), Dupire (1994, 1996), Emanuel and MacBeth (1982), Frey and Sin (1999), Gatheral (2000), Goldenberg (1991), Hagan and Woodward (1998), Heston (1993), Hobson (1998), Hoffman *et al.* (1992), Hull and White (1987, 1988), Hyer and Lipton (1998), Hyer and Pugachevsky (1998), Ingersoll (1996), Inglis (1998), Johnson and Shanno (1987), Jamshidian (1989), Jarrow and Rudd (1982), Lipton (1997), Lipton and Pugachevsky (1997), Merton (1976), Rady (1997), Reiner (1998), Renault and Touzi (1996), Rubinstein (1983, 1994), Schroder (1989), Scott (1989), Stein and Stein (1991), Taylor (1994), Wiggins (1987), Xu and Taylor (1994), Zuhlsdorff (1999). An alternative treatment of the stochastic volatility problem can be found in the recent book by Lewis (2000). The relevant mathematical formulas are given by Abramowitz and Stegun (1972) and Erdelyi (1953).

Chapter 11

American Options

11.1 Introduction

In this chapter we study American options on forex which can be exercised at any time between their inception and maturity. Many of the traded options have this feature. The pricing of American options is more difficult than their European counterparts since the corresponding pricing problem is nonlinear due to the possibility of an early exercise. In particular, except for some special cases, explicit expressions for the prices of American calls and puts are not known because it is impossible to determine the location of the early exercise boundary explicitly. Efficient numerical valuation of American options attracted much attention over the last decade or so, and by now does not pose a serious problem in practice (at least for one-factor options).

To start with, we study American options in the classical two-country market framework. We introduce the early exercise constraint which states that the price of an American option cannot fall below its intrinsic value (simply because it would be rational in this case to exercise it immediately). The curve (or curves) separating the domains where the price of an option exceeds its intrinsic value (the no-exercise domain) and is equal to its intrinsic value (the exercise domain) is (are) called the early exercise boundary. It is the presence of this boundary which makes American options difficult to value. We define the early exercise premium, i.e., the price differential between an American option and its European counterpart which is a fair compensation for the additional optionality provided by the American option. We present the so-called high contact conditions which show that the value of an American option and its Delta (when applicable) have to be continuous across the early exercise boundary. We use the first principles in order to derive some rational bounds for the prices of American calls and puts, and to find the American analogue of put-call parity and symmetry relations. Subsequently, we mostly concentrate on pricing and hedging issues for American calls, and use put-call symmetry in order to price puts. We describe the risk-neutral valuation principle for American options. Then we present several complementary formulations of the pricing problem which we discuss in detail: (A) We introduce the inhomogeneous Black-Scholes problem for American options which replaces the homogeneous problem for European options. (B) We formulate the valuation problem as a linear complementarity problem. (C) We formulate the valuation problem as a linear program. The advantage of the formulations (B) and (C) compared to the formulation (A) is that these formulations do not require to know the location of the early exercise boundary, and, in fact, allow one to determine this location as a by-product of the general analysis. We show that switching from the domestic to the foreign country transforms the valuation problem for calls into the valuation problem for puts thus confirming formally put-call symmetry relation which was established on financial grounds.

We solve the inhomogeneous Black-Scholes problem via Duhamel's principle, find the integral representation for the early exercise premium and use this representation to derive an integral equation for the location of the early exercise boundary. It was mentioned already that, in general, it is impossible to price an American call in the closed form. For this reason, approximate and numerical methods for pricing American calls are particularly important and over the last thirty years or so a lot of research was directed towards developing such methods. Although it is rather easy to evaluate an individual option numerically, doing so efficiently for large portfolios of American options is a serious challenge. To give the reader a taste of what can be expected, we consider short-dated and very long-dated (perpetual) American calls. Recall that for all practically important cases the price of European perpetual calls is equal to zero. The only exception occurs when the foreign interest rate is zero, in which case the call price is equal to the spot FXR. We carefully analyze the corresponding pricing formulas with a special emphasis on the role of the free boundary. Then we discuss two approximate methods for pricing American calls. We start with a simple (but practically important) approximation and replace American calls by Bermudan calls which can be exercised only at some predetermined times between their inception and maturity. In principle, one can derive explicit formulas for pricing Bermudan calls, however, for many exercise dates these formulas are too complicated to be used in practice. We show how to use prices of Bermudan calls with just a few exercise dates in order to approximate prices of American calls and then improve the quality of approximation by using the extrapolation to the limit. We also describe the so-called quadratic approximation for pricing American calls which is related to our solution of the pricing problem for perpetual calls. Since approximate methods for pricing American calls are limited in scope, we discuss in some detail a number of numerical methods which can be used for this purpose. Specifically we consider numerical solutions based on Bermudan discretization, linear complementarity, linear program, integral equation, and Monte-Carlo technique. We briefly discuss pricing and hedging of American calls when the standard Black-Scholes assumptions on the dynamics of FXR are violated. Finally, we consider multi-factor American options and present some of the methods which can be used in order to price and hedge them.

It is possible to analyze American options using the group-theoretical approach, however, for the sake of brevity we present here only the classical treatment.

The chapter is organized as follows. In Section 2 we discuss general properties of American options. In Section 3 we establish the risk-neutral valuation principle. In Section 4 we present three complementary formulations of the valuation problem, namely, the inhomogeneous pricing equation, linear complementarity, and liner program formulation. In Section 5 we establish duality between American calls and puts. In Section 6 we study the inhomogeneous pricing problem via Duhamel's principle. In Section 7 we present the asymptotic analysis of the valuation problem, in Section 8 we discuss its approximate solution, while in Section 9 we discuss the numerical methods for solving the above problem. We devote Section 10 to the analysis of the impact of the violations of the basic Black-Scholes assumptions on the pricing of American options. In Section 11, we discuss multi-factor American options. Finally, in Section 12 we give the relevant references.

11.2   General considerations

11.2.1   The early exercise constraint

American options are determined by the terminal payoffs depending on the value of FXR at maturity T, however, as opposite to their European counterparts, they can be exercised at any time between 0 and T. Because of this additional optionality, their prices cannot fall below their intrinsic values. Thus, for American options the pricing problem is supplied with an additional constraint which shows that the option value cannot fall below its intrinsic value.

$$V'(t, S) \geq v(S).$$

The above condition makes the pricing problem nonlinear.

Under special market conditions there are European options for which the inequality

$$V(t, S) \geq v(S),$$

is satisfied automatically. If this is the case, then the valuation problem for the corresponding American options is simple, since the values of American and European options coincide:

$$V'(t, S) = V(t, S).$$

The reason is that is never beneficial to exercise the option early.

11.2.2   The early exercise premium

The difference

$$V''(t, S) = V'(t, S) - V(t, S) \geq 0,$$

is called the early exercise premium. It shows by how much the price of an American option exceeds the price of its European counterpart.

The high contact conditions

For every t the positive semi-axis $0 < S < \infty$ is divided into the exercise domain $\mathcal{D}_t^E$ and the no-exercise domain $\mathcal{D}_t^{NE}$. Inside the domain $\mathcal{D}_t^{NE}$ the value $V'(t, S)$ is governed by the familiar Black-Scholes equation

$$V_t'(t, S) + \frac{1}{2}\sigma^2 S^2 V_{SS}'(t, S) + r^{01} S V_S'(t, S) - r^0 V'(t, S) = 0.$$

When $S_t \in \mathcal{D}_t^{NE}$ the option has to be Delta-hedged in the usual fashion. Inside the domain $\mathcal{D}_t^E$ the value $V'(t, S)$ coincides with its intrinsic value, i.e.,

$$V'(t, S) = v(S).$$

The domains $\mathcal{D}_t^{NE}, \mathcal{D}_t^E$ are separated by the early exercise boundary $\mathcal{B}_t$. Its position is determined from the matching conditions. One matching condition is obvious: the value of the option has to be a continuous function of S, i.e.,

$$V'(t, \mathcal{B}_t) = v(\mathcal{B}_t). \tag{11.1}$$

The second condition is somewhat more involved: the option Delta has to be a continuous function of S, too, i.e.,

$$V_S'\left(t, \mathcal{B}_t\right) = v_S\left(\mathcal{B}_t\right). \tag{11.2}$$

Needless to say that the second condition is applicable only when $v(S)$ is sufficiently smooth at the point $\mathcal{B}_t$, so that the r.h.s. makes sense. Conditions (11.1), (11.2) are known as the high contact (Samuelson) conditions. While the first matching condition is self-explanatory, the second one requires some justification. We present the heuristic derivation of condition (11.2) based on the cost of hedging argument. Suppose that this condition is violated, so that the Δ-profile of an American option is discontinuous at the early exercise boundary, while its Γ-profile is singular there,

$$\Delta^E(t, \mathcal{B}_t) \equiv \lim v_S(t, S \in \mathcal{D}^E \to \mathcal{B}_t) = \delta_t^E,$$

$$\Delta^{NE}(t, \mathcal{B}_t) \equiv \lim V_S'(t, S \in \mathcal{D}^{NE} \to \mathcal{B}_t) = \delta_t^{NE},$$

where $\delta_t^E \neq \delta_t^{NE}$. The option seller has to have $\Delta\left(t, S_t\right)$ units of the foreign currency (provided that the option has not been exercised yet). When S_t crosses the early exercise boundary from below, he has δ^{NE} units of the foreign currency (while he needs to have δ^E units of the foreign currency). Thus, the usual Δ-hedging fails if $\delta^{NE} \neq \delta^E$. Accordingly, the seller has to price an American option is such a way that $\delta_t^E = \delta_t^{NE}$. Since the situation is reversible, the buyer and the seller should be able to agree on such a price.

By introducing the nondimensional time to maturity $\chi = \sigma^2\left(T - t\right)$ we can rewrite the pricing problem in the form

$$V_\chi'\left(\chi, S\right) - \frac{1}{2}S^2 V_{SS}'\left(\chi, S\right) - \hat{r}^{01} S V_S'\left(\chi, S\right) + \hat{r}^0 V\left(\chi, S\right) = 0, \quad S \in \mathcal{D}_\chi^{NE},$$

$$V\left(\chi, S\right) = v\left(S\right), \quad S \in \mathcal{D}_\chi^E,$$

$$V\left(0, S\right) = v\left(S\right).$$

Below, whenever possible, we use χ rather than t as the time variable.

11.2.3   Some representative examples

Consider an American call. We know that for the corresponding European call the inequality

$$C\left(\chi, S, K\right) \geq \left(S - K\right)_+,$$

is satisfied for $S = 0$ and violated for $S \to \infty$ (provided that $r^1 \neq 0$). Accordingly, the domains $\mathcal{D}_\chi^{NE}$ and $\mathcal{D}_\chi^E$ have the form

$$\mathcal{D}_\chi^{NE} = \left(0, \mathcal{B}_\chi^C\right), \quad \mathcal{D}_\chi^E = \left(\mathcal{B}_\chi^C, \infty\right),$$

where the early exercise boundary $\mathcal{B}_\chi^C$ is characterized by the relations

$$\mathcal{B}_\chi^C = \sup\left\{S : C'\left(\chi, S, K\right) > S - K\right\} = \inf\left\{S : C'\left(\chi, S, K\right) = S - K\right\},$$

Similarly, for an American put (provided that $r^0 \neq 0$) we have

$$\mathcal{D}_\chi^{NE} = \left(\mathcal{B}_\chi^P, \infty\right), \quad \mathcal{D}_\chi^E = \left(0, \mathcal{B}_\chi^P\right),$$

$$\mathcal{B}_\chi^P = \inf\left\{S : P'\left(\chi, S, K\right) > K - S\right\} = \sup\left\{S : P'\left(\chi, S, K\right) = K - S\right\}.$$

For a call bet with the payoff of the form

$$v\left(S\right) = \theta\left(S - K\right), \tag{11.3}$$

the boundary $\mathcal{B}_\chi^{CB}$ is time-independent and coincides with the strike level, $\mathcal{B}_\chi^{CB} = K$,

$$\mathcal{D}_\chi^{NE} = \left(0, K\right), \quad \mathcal{D}_\chi^E = \left(K, \infty\right), \quad \mathcal{B}_\chi^{CB} = K.$$

For the put bet with the payoff of the form

$$v\left(S\right) = \theta\left(K - S\right),$$

we have

$$\mathcal{D}_\chi^{NE} = \left(K, \infty\right), \quad \mathcal{D}_\chi^E = \left(0, K\right), \quad \mathcal{B}_\chi^{PB} = K.$$

In general, the boundary can contain more than one component. For instance, for a European covered call with the payoff of the form

$$v\left(S\right) = \max\left\{K, S\right\},$$

the price falls below its intrinsic value when $S \to 0$ and $S \to \infty$, so that the domain $\mathcal{D}_\chi^E$ consists of two intervals while the domain $\mathcal{D}_\chi^{NE}$ consist of one interval,

$$\mathcal{D}_\chi^{NE} = \left(\mathcal{B}_\chi, \bar{\mathcal{B}}_\chi\right), \qquad \mathcal{D}_\chi^E = \left(0, \mathcal{B}_\chi\right) \bigcup \left(\bar{\mathcal{B}}_\chi, \infty\right),$$

where the boundary components $\mathcal{B}_\chi, \bar{\mathcal{B}}_\chi$, are determined by

$$\mathcal{B}_\chi = \sup\left\{S : V'\left(\chi, S\right) = K\right\}, \qquad \bar{\mathcal{B}}_\chi = \inf\left\{S : V'\left(\chi, S\right) = S\right\}.$$

Of all the American options considered in this section we can easily price only call and put bets. The reason is that we know the location of the early exercise boundary explicitly, so that the valuation problem is linear.

To be concrete we consider a call bet with the payoff (11.3). We know that the early exercise boundary is flat, $\mathcal{B}_\chi^{(CB)} = K$. Moreover, only the continuity condition for the option value (but not for the value of its Delta) has to be satisfied, so that

$$V^{(CB)\prime}\left(\chi, K\right) = 1.$$

Thus, the value of an American call bet coincides with the value of a one-touch option which pays the buyer a dollar the first time FXR hits the level K from below. We discuss pricing and hedging of one-touch and other barrier options in the next chapter. Here we simply present the value of the corresponding call bet (see equation (12.16) with obvious changes):

$$V^{(CB)\prime}\left(\chi, S, K\right) = \left(\frac{K}{S}\right)^{\hat{\gamma}_- + \sqrt{\hat{\gamma}_-^2 + 2\hat{r}^0}} \mathfrak{N}\left(\frac{\ln\left(S/K\right)}{\sqrt{\chi}} - \sqrt{\hat{\gamma}_-^2 + 2\hat{r}^0}\sqrt{\chi}\right)$$
$$+ \left(\frac{K}{S}\right)^{\hat{\gamma}_- - \sqrt{\hat{\gamma}_-^2 + 2\hat{r}^0}} \mathfrak{N}\left(\frac{\ln\left(S/K\right)}{\sqrt{\chi}} + \sqrt{\hat{\gamma}_-^2 + 2\hat{r}^0}\sqrt{\chi}\right).$$

The prices of $V^{(CB)\prime}$ and $V^{(CB)}$ are shown in Figure 11.1.

11.2.4 Rational bounds

In this section we concentrate on general properties of American calls and puts whose prices are denoted by $C'\left(\chi, S, K\right), P'\left(\chi, S, K\right)$. Recall that for American

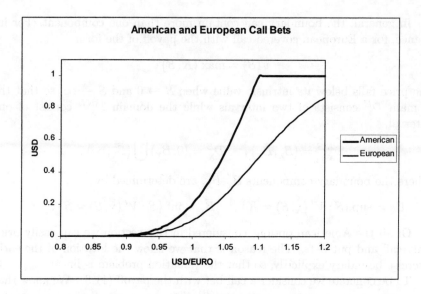

Figure 11.1: The prices $V^{(CB)'}(\tau, S)$ and $V^{(SB)}(\tau, S)$ as functions of S for $\tau = 3$ months. The relevant parameters are $K = 1.1$, $\sigma = 15\%$, $r^0 = 5.5\%$, $r^1 = 4.5\%$.

options we have established bounds (1.9), (1.10). These bounds are relatively crude. It is useful to find sharper bounds for C'. To do so we consider the so called American capped call with strike K, and cap level $B > K$. The corresponding payoff is

$$v(S) = \min\left((S - K)_+, B\right).$$

It is easy to understand that such a call can also be considered as an up-and-out call with the strike K, barrier B, and rebate $B - K$ paid when the barrier is hit. As before, we postpone the discussion of barrier options until the next chapter. Here we simply present the value of the corresponding call which we denote by $C(\chi, S, K, B)$:

$$C(\chi, S, K, B) = C(\chi, S, K) - C(\chi, S, B)$$
$$- \left(\frac{B}{S}\right)^{2\hat{\gamma}_-} \left[C\left(\tau, \frac{B^2}{S}, K\right) - C\left(\tau, \frac{B^2}{S}, B\right)\right]$$
$$- (B - K) \left[V^{(CB)}(\tau, S, B) - \left(\frac{B}{S}\right)^{2\hat{\gamma}_-} V^{(CB)}\left(\tau, \frac{B^2}{S}, B\right)\right]$$
$$+ (B - K) \left[\left(\frac{B}{S}\right)^{\hat{\gamma}_- + \sqrt{\hat{\gamma}_-^2 + 2\hat{r}^0}} \mathfrak{N}\left(\frac{\ln(S/B)}{\sqrt{\chi}} - \sqrt{\hat{\gamma}_-^2 + 2\hat{r}^0}\sqrt{\chi}\right)\right.$$
$$+ \left.\left(\frac{B}{S}\right)^{\hat{\gamma}_- - \sqrt{\hat{\gamma}_-^2 + 2\hat{r}^0}} \mathfrak{N}\left(\frac{\ln(S/B)}{\sqrt{\chi}} + \sqrt{\hat{\gamma}_-^2 + 2\hat{r}^0}\sqrt{\chi}\right)\right].$$

Here the first six terms represent the price of the up-and-out call given by equation (12.5), while the last two terms represent the value of the one-touch option which pays the rebate $B - K$ provided that S_χ hits the level B for some χ, $0 < \chi < \hat{T} = \sigma^2 T$ given by equation (12.16). Since the buyer can choose to exercise his American option the first time the FXR hits the level B, it is clear that

$$C(\chi, S, K, B) \leq C'(\chi, S, K).$$

To get as tight an estimate as possible we maximize the l.h.s. of this inequality and get

$$\bar{C}(\chi, S, K) \leq C'(\chi, S, K),$$

where

$$\bar{C}(\chi, S, K) = \max_B C(\chi, S, K, B).$$

Our current estimate improves estimate (1.9) since

$$C(\chi, S, K, B \to \infty) \to C(\chi, S, K),$$

and

$$C(\chi, S, K, B \to S) \to (S - K),$$

provided that $S > K$. Finding $\bar{B}$ such that $C(\chi, S, K, \bar{B}) = \bar{C}(\chi, S, K)$ can be done via standard methods of one-dimensional optimization, including such old favorites as the golden section and Brent's methods which do not use any derivative information, as well as methods which explicitly use the knowledge of the first derivative $C_B(\chi, S, K, B)$. Although $\bar{B}$ has to be found numerically, this task is straightforward. Analysis of a large number of options with representative parameters suggests that the approximation

$$C'(\chi, S, K) \approx \bar{C}(\chi, S, K),$$

is accurate within a couple per cent for realistic parameter values.

We leave it to the reader to obtain similar bounds for puts.

When $r^1 = 0$ ($r^0 = 0$) the values of European and American calls (puts) coincide since

$$C(\chi, S, K) \geq S - e^{-\hat{r}^0 \chi} K > S - K,$$

$$P(\chi, S, K) \geq K - e^{-\hat{r}^1 \chi} S > K - S,$$

i.e., European calls (puts) do not fall below their intrinsic values, otherwise American calls and puts are more expensive than their European counterparts.

We can generalize the above observation and prove the following statement. When $r^1 = 0$ the prices of American and European options with convex payoff $v(S)$ such that $v(0) = 0$ coincide. As before, the reason is that the European option price $V(\chi, S)$ is always greater than the intrinsic price. Indeed, the risk-neutral valuation principle combined with the Jensen inequality yields

$$
\begin{aligned}
V(\chi, S) &= e^{-\hat{r}^0 \chi} \mathbb{E}_Q \{v(S_T) | S_t = S\} \geq e^{-\hat{r}^0 \chi} v(\mathbb{E}_Q \{S_T | S_t = S\}) \\
&= e^{-\hat{r}^0 \chi} v\left(e^{\hat{r}^0 \chi} S\right) \geq v(S),
\end{aligned}
$$

where the last inequality follows from the definition of convexity and the fact that $v(0) = 0$,

$$v(S) \leq \left(1 - e^{-\hat{r}^0 \chi}\right) v(0) + e^{-\hat{r}^0 \chi} v\left(e^{\hat{r}^0 \chi} S\right) = e^{-\hat{r}^0 \chi} v\left(e^{\hat{r}^0 \chi} S\right).$$

Similarly, for $r^0 = 0$ the prices of American and European options with convex payoff $v(S)$ such that $v(\infty) = 0$ coincide.

11.2.5   Parity and symmetry

We cannot expect that *put-call parity* is preserved for American options since the early exercise feature destroys linearity. Instead, weaker inequalities can be proved, namely

$$e^{-\hat{r}^1 \chi} S - K \le C'(\chi, S, K) - P'(\chi, S, K) \le S - e^{-\hat{r}^0 \chi} K.$$

Their verification is left to the reader as a useful exercise. (Hint: construct appropriate portfolios.)

At the same time, the dual nature of the forex transactions suggests that *put-call symmetry* is preserved for American options since both the pricing equations and the constraints are invariant with respect to switching from the domestic to the foreign country (the Kelvin transform). (A formal calculation is given below.) Thus,

$$P'(\chi, S, K, \hat{r}^0, \hat{r}^1) = KSC'(\chi, 1/S, 1/K, \hat{r}^1, \hat{r}^0),$$

or, alternatively,

$$P'(\chi, S, K, \hat{r}^0, \hat{r}^1) = C'\left(\chi, K, S, \hat{r}^1, \hat{r}^0\right).$$

These relations allow us to concentrate on pricing calls and find prices of puts as a by-product.

11.3   The risk-neutral valuation

Recall that from the probabilistic prospective the price of a European option is just the discounted expected value of its payoff at maturity,

$$V(t, S) = e^{-r^0(T-t)} \int_0^\infty p(t, S, T, S_T) \, v(S_T) \, dS_T,$$

where $p(t, S, T, S_T)$ is the standard lognormal t.p.d.f. Because of the expanded optionality of American options, this simple formula is no longer valid. Instead, the value of the corresponding American option is given by the so-called Snell envelope of the discounted payoff, i.e.,

$$V'(t, S_t) = \sup_{\zeta \in \mathfrak{T}_{t,T}} \mathbb{E}_Q \left\{ e^{-r^0(\zeta-t)} v(S_\zeta) \, |\mathfrak{F}_t \right\},$$

where ζ is a stopping time, $\mathfrak{T}_{t,T}$ is the set of all possible stopping times sandwiched between t and T, and conditional expectation is taken with respect to the risk-neutral measure in the space of all possible evolution scenarios. Due to the Markovian property of the price evolution, we can represent it in the form

$$V'(t, S) = \sup_{\zeta \in \mathfrak{T}_{t,T}} \mathbb{E}_Q \left\{ e^{-r^0(\zeta - t)} v(S_\zeta) | S_t = S \right\}.$$

It is clear that the direct evaluation of the corresponding expectation is a difficult task involving integration in functional spaces, so that some additional insights are needed.

The early exercise time is the first time when the FXR crosses the early exercise boundary and leaves the domain $\mathcal{D}_t^{NE}$, so that

$$\zeta = \inf \left\{ \zeta' \in [t, T] : S_{\zeta'} = \mathcal{B}_{\zeta'} \right\}.$$

For calls and puts we can be more specific and say that the early exercise time is the first time the FXR crosses the early exercise boundary from below (above).

11.4 Alternative formulations of the valuation problem

11.4.1 Introduction

There are many complementary ways of formulating (and solving) the valuation problem. In this section we present the most popular and efficient ones.

11.4.2 The inhomogeneous Black-Scholes problem formulation

The value of an American call can be written as

$$C'(\chi, S, K) = \begin{cases} C(\chi, S, K) + C''(\chi, S, K), & 0 < S < \mathcal{B}_\chi^C \\ S - K, & \mathcal{B}_\chi^C < S < \infty \end{cases},$$

where $C''(\chi, S, K)$ is the early exercise premium, such that

$$C_\chi'' - \frac{1}{2} S^2 C_{SS}'' - \hat{r}^{01} S C_S'' + \hat{r}^0 C'' = 0,$$

for $0 < S < \mathcal{B}_\chi^C$, and

$$C''(\chi, 0, K) = 0.$$

In other words, below the early exercise boundary the value of an American call is the sum of the value of a European call and the early exercise premium, while above this boundary it is simply the intrinsic value of the option. In order to avoid arbitrage possibilities, the price $C'(\chi, S, K)$ has to satisfy the high-contact (or Samuelson) matching conditions of the form:

$$C'(\chi, \mathcal{B}^C_\chi, K) \equiv C\left(\chi, \mathcal{B}^C_\chi, K\right) + C''\left(\chi, \mathcal{B}^C_\chi, K\right) = \mathcal{B}^C_\chi - K, \tag{11.4}$$

$$C'_S(\chi, \mathcal{B}^C_\chi, K) \equiv C_S\left(\chi, \mathcal{B}^C_\chi, K\right) + C''_S\left(\chi, \mathcal{B}^C_\chi, K\right) = 1. \tag{11.5}$$

Conditions (11.4), (11.5) guarantee that $C'(\chi, S, K)$ is sufficiently smooth. This fact allows us to apply the Black-Scholes operator to the function $C'(\chi, S, K)$. Straightforward calculation shows that

$$C'_\chi - \frac{1}{2}S^2 C'_{SS} - \hat{r}^{01}SC'_S + \hat{r}^0 C' = \left(\hat{r}^1 S - \hat{r}^0 K\right)\theta\left(S - \mathcal{B}^C_\chi\right), \tag{11.6}$$

where θ is the Heaviside function. Thus, C' satisfies the inhomogeneous Black-Scholes equation supplied with the final condition

$$C'(0, S, K) = (S - K)_+, \tag{11.7}$$

and natural boundary conditions

$$C'(\chi, S \to 0, K) \to 0, \quad C'(\chi, S \to \infty, K) = S - K. \tag{11.8}$$

We emphasize that C' defined as the solution of problem (11.6) - (11.8) satisfies the matching conditions provided that the early exercise boundary is determined appropriately.

In order to solve the pricing problem we need to find the early exercise boundary explicitly. As we will show shortly, it is relatively easy to find the location of the free boundary when χ is either small or large, $\chi \ll 1$ or $\chi \gg 1$. For intermediate values of χ finding the boundary is more difficult. It is clear from the financial standpoint that $\mathcal{B}^C_\chi$ starts at or above the strike level K and moves to the right when χ increases. For $\chi > 0$ the function $\mathcal{B}^C_\chi$ is smooth. For a typical set of parameters the early exercise boundary is shown in Figure 11.2, while the prices of American calls are shown in Figure 11.3

The price of an American put in the no-exercise domain can be decomposed into the European put price and the early exercise premium, in the exercise domain it coincides with the intrinsic value:

$$P'(\chi, S, K) = \begin{cases} K - S, & 0 < S < \mathcal{B}^P_\chi \\ P(\chi, S, K) + P''(\chi, S, K), & \mathcal{B}^P_\chi < S < \infty \end{cases}.$$

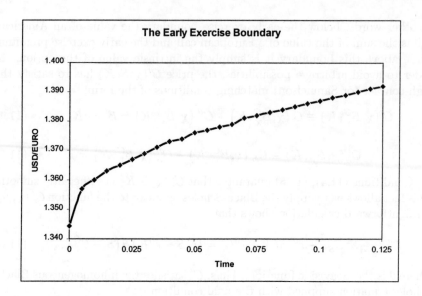

Figure 11.2: The early exercise boundary $\mathcal{B}$ as a function of the time to maturity. The relevant parameters are the same as in Figure 11.1. The boundary emanates from the point $r^0 K / r^1 = 1.344$.

The price $P'(\chi, S, K)$ solves the inhomogeneous Black-Scholes pricing problem

$$P'_\chi - \frac{1}{2} S^2 P'_{SS} - \hat{r}^{01} S P'_S + \hat{r}^0 P' = \left(\hat{r}^0 K - \hat{r}^1 S\right) \theta \left(\mathcal{B}^P_\chi - S\right),$$

$$P'(0, S, K) = (K - S)_+,$$

$$P'(\chi, 0, K) = K, \qquad P'(\chi, S \to \infty, K) \to 0.$$

As before, P' automatically satisfies the matching conditions at $S = \mathcal{B}^P_\chi$.

11.4.3   The linear complementarity formulation

It is also possible to write the American call pricing problem as the so-called Linear Complementarity Problem (LCP). In this section we discuss this possibility is some detail. The advantage of the LCP formulation is that it does not

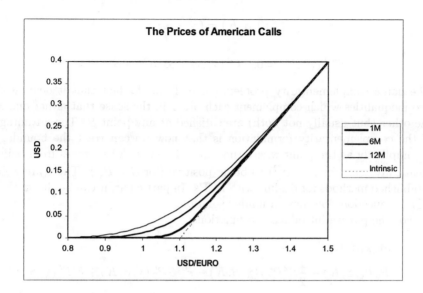

Figure 11.3: The prices of American calls for three maturities $T = 1, 6, 12$ months. The relevant parameters are the same as in Figure 11.1.

require finding the early exercise boundary beforehand and, in fact, produces it as a by-product of the solution procedure.

We consider a sufficiently smooth function $C'(\chi, S, K)$ and define two functions

$$
\begin{aligned}
&\mathcal{A}(\chi, S, K) \\
&= C'_\chi(\chi, S, K) - \frac{1}{2} S^2 C'_{SS}(\chi, S, K) - \hat{r}^{01} S C'_S(\chi, S, K) + r^0 C(\chi, S, K),
\end{aligned}
$$

and

$$
\mathcal{E}(\chi, S, K) = C'(\chi, S, K) - (S - K)_+.
$$

If $C'(\chi, S, K)$ solves the valuation problem, then, in view of our discussion in the previous section, we can conclude that the following relations are satisfied

$$
\begin{cases}
\mathcal{A}(\chi, S, K) \geq 0, \\
\mathcal{E}(\chi, S, K) \geq 0, \\
\mathcal{A}(\chi, S, K) \mathcal{E}(\chi, S, K) = 0,
\end{cases}
\tag{11.9}
$$

$$C'(0, S, K) = (S - K)_+,$$

$$C'(\chi, 0, K) = 0, \quad C'(\chi, S \to \infty, K) \to S - K.$$

The name complementarity problem comes from the fact that it deals with two inequalities which complement each other in the sense that either one or the other (but usually not both) are satisfied at any point S. The advantage of the complementarity formulation is that now we can treat the boundary $\mathcal{B}_\chi^C$ implicitly as the point where the value of $\mathcal{E}(\chi, S, K)$ switches from being identically zero (for $S > \mathcal{B}_\chi^C$) to being positive (for $S < \mathcal{B}_\chi^C$). There are well-established methods for dealing with LCPs. In particular, it can be shown that LCP in question does have a unique solution.

For the put we introduce two functions:

$$\mathcal{A}(\chi, S, K)$$
$$= P'_\chi(\chi, S, K) - \frac{1}{2}S^2 P'_{SS}(\chi, S, K) - \hat{r}^{01}SP'_S(\chi, S, K) + \hat{r}^0 P'(\chi, S, K),$$

and

$$\mathcal{E}(\chi, S, K) = P'(\chi, S, K) - (K - S)_+,$$

and write the corresponding LCP in the form

$$\begin{cases} \mathcal{A}(\chi, S, K) \geq 0, \\ \mathcal{E}(\chi, S, K) \geq 0, \\ \mathcal{A}(\chi, S, K)\,\mathcal{E}(\chi, S, K) = 0, \end{cases}$$

$$P'(0, S, K) = (K - S)_+,$$

$$P'(\chi, 0, K) = K, \quad P'(\chi, S \to \infty, K) \to 0.$$

11.4.4 The linear program formulation

The linear complementarity approach to the valuation of an American call has been known for a long time. In this section we discuss a more recent method which allows one to use alternative techniques for pricing American calls. The key observation is that $C'(\chi, S, K)$ is a solution of a linear program of the form

$$\inf_\Xi \int_0^\infty \Xi(\chi, S)\,dS,$$

where Ξ belongs to the constraint set of continuous, piecewise differentiable functions satisfying the nonnegativity conditions $\mathcal{A} \geq 0$, $\mathcal{E} \geq 0$. The reason is that the function $C'(\chi, S, K)$ is the coordinatewise least element of the constraint set and hence minimizes the corresponding integral. In other words, the minimization procedure guarantees that the complementarity condition $\mathcal{A}\mathcal{E} = 0$ is satisfied for the minimizer. Thus, we can use a variety of methods of linear programming (some of which are very efficient) in order to find C'.

A linear program for $P'(\chi, S, K)$ has a similar form.

11.5   Duality between puts and calls

By switching from the domestic country to the foreign country (or, equivalently, by applying the Kelvin transform), we represent P' in the form

$$P'\left(\chi, S^{01}, K^{01}, \hat{r}^0, \hat{r}^1\right) = K^{01} S^{01} \Phi\left(\chi, S^{10}\right).$$

As always $S^{10} = 1/S^{01}$ is the price of the domestic currency expressed in terms of the foreign currency, while $K^{10} = 1/K^{01}$ is the corresponding strike price. This transform turns the pricing problem for $P'(\chi, S^{01}, K)$ into the pricing problem for $\Phi(\chi, S^{10})$ of the form

$$\Phi_\chi - \frac{1}{2}\left(S^{10}\right)^2 \Phi_{S^{10}S^{10}} - \hat{r}^{10} S^{10} \Phi_{S^{10}} + \hat{r}^1 \Phi = \left(\hat{r}^0 S^{10} - \hat{r}^1 K^{01}\right) \theta\left(S^{10} - 1/\mathcal{B}_\chi^P\right),$$

$$\Phi\left(0, S^{10}\right) = \left(S^{10} - K^{10}\right)_+,$$

$$\Phi\left(0, S^{10} \to 0\right) \to 0, \quad \Phi\left(0, S^{10} \to \infty\right) = S^{10} - K^{10}.$$

It is obvious that $\Phi(\chi, S^{10})$ is the price of an American call evaluated from the standpoint of a foreign investor,

$$\Phi\left(\chi, S^{10}\right) = C'\left(\chi, S^{10}, K^{10}, \hat{r}^1, \hat{r}^0\right),$$

so that

$$P'\left(\chi, S^{01}, K^{01}, \hat{r}^0, \hat{r}^1\right) = K^{01} S^{01} C'\left(\chi, \frac{1}{S^{01}}, \frac{1}{K^{01}}, \hat{r}^1, \hat{r}^0\right), \qquad (11.10)$$

or, by homogeneity,

$$P'\left(\chi, S^{01}, K^{01}, \hat{r}^0, \hat{r}^1\right) = C'\left(\chi, K^{01}, S^{01}, \hat{r}^1, \hat{r}^0\right). \tag{11.11}$$

Thus, we formally derive put-call symmetry relations (11.10), (11.11) which were derived in Section 1.5 from purely financial considerations.

The early exercise boundaries $\mathcal{B}_\chi^C$ and $\mathcal{B}_\chi^P$ are dual:

$$\mathcal{B}_\chi^P\left(K^{01}, \hat{r}^0, \hat{r}^1\right) = \frac{1}{\mathcal{B}_\chi^C\left(1/K^{01}, \hat{r}^1, \hat{r}^0\right)} = \frac{\left(K^{01}\right)^2}{\mathcal{B}_\chi^C\left(K^{01}, \hat{r}^1, \hat{r}^0\right)}.$$

By virtue of duality, we can concentrate on pricing calls and leave it to the reader to price puts either by using put-call symmetry or directly.

11.6 Application of Duhamel's principle

11.6.1 The value of the early exercise premium

The inhomogeneous Black-Scholes problem can be solved via Duhamel's principle (see Section 4.4). Its solution C' can be written as the sum of the European call price C and the early exercise premium C'' which satisfies the inhomogeneous equation supplied with zero final condition and natural boundary conditions. Duhamel's principle yields

$$C''(\chi, S) = \int_0^\chi e^{-\hat{r}^0\chi'} \int_{\mathcal{B}_{\chi'}}^\infty p\left(\chi', S, S'\right)\left(\hat{r}^1 S' - \hat{r}^0 K\right) dS' d\chi',$$

where $p(\chi', S, S')$ is the familiar lognormal t.p.d.f. giving the distribution of S' at time χ' conditional on known value of S at time 0,

$$p(\chi', S, S') = \frac{\exp\left(-d_-^2\left(\chi', e^{\hat{r}^{01}\chi'} S/S'\right)/2\right)}{\sqrt{2\pi\chi'}S'}.$$

We compute the integral with respect to S' by the same token as for a European call, and obtain

$$\int_{\mathcal{B}_{\chi'}}^\infty p\left(\chi', S, S'\right)\left(\hat{r}^1 S' - \hat{r}^0 K\right) dS'$$

$$= \hat{r}^1 e^{\hat{r}^{01}\chi'} S \mathfrak{N}\left(d_+\left(\chi', \frac{e^{\hat{r}^{01}\chi'} S}{\mathcal{B}_{\chi'}}\right)\right) - \hat{r}^0 K \mathfrak{N}\left(d_-\left(\chi', \frac{e^{\hat{r}^{01}\chi'} S}{\mathcal{B}_{\chi'}}\right)\right).$$

Accordingly, for $S < \mathcal{B}_{\chi'}$ we can write

$$C''(\chi, S) = \hat{r}^1 S \int_0^\chi e^{-\hat{r}^1 \chi'} \mathfrak{N}\left(d_+\left(\chi', \frac{e^{\hat{r}^{01}\chi'} S}{\mathcal{B}_{\chi'}}\right)\right) d\chi' \quad (11.12)$$

$$-\hat{r}^0 K \int_0^\chi e^{-\hat{r}^0 \chi'} \mathfrak{N}\left(d_-\left(\chi', \frac{e^{\hat{r}^{01}\chi'} S}{\mathcal{B}_{\chi'}}\right)\right) d\chi',$$

$$C'(\chi, S) = C(\chi, S) + C''(\chi, S). \quad (11.13)$$

Expression (11.13) shows that the buyer of an American call will receive at least the payoff of a European call and, possibly, some extra cash if he exercises the option early. We emphasize that, in general, there is no guarantee that for a particular scenario of the FXR evolution an American option generates greater proceeds than the corresponding European one.

The above decomposition can be understood in terms of the stop-loss start-gain trading strategy. Assume that every time the FXR hits the early exercise boundary from below the call buyer liquidates his position in option and, in addition, borrows $\mathcal{B}_\chi$ dollars in order to buy one unit of foreign currency, every time the FXR hits the early exercise boundary from above, he buys the call option back. Recall that for European calls the stop-loss start-gain strategy is not self-financing because of the fact that the payoff is not continuously differentiable, however, for American calls the high contact condition guarantees that this strategy is self-financing.

We leave it to the reader to derive a similar decomposition formula for an American put.

For an American option with the general payoff $v(S)$ the decomposition formula reads:

$$V'(\chi, S) = V(\chi, S) + \int_0^\chi e^{-\hat{r}^0 \chi'} \left(\int_{\mathcal{D}_{\chi'}^{NE}} p(\chi', S, S') w(S') dS'\right) d\chi',$$

where

$$w(S) = -\left(\frac{1}{2} S^2 v_{SS}(S) + \hat{r}^{01} S v_S(S) - \hat{r}^0 v(S)\right).$$

11.6.2 The location of the early exercise boundary

We can use formulas (11.12), (11.13) in order to find the equation for the early exercise boundary. Substituting $S = \mathcal{B}_\chi$ into this formula and using the matching conditions, we obtain the following nonlinear integral equation of Volterra type for the location of the boundary

$$\mathcal{B}_\chi - K = C(\chi, \mathcal{B}_\chi, K) \tag{11.14}$$

$$+\hat{r}^1 \mathcal{B}_\chi \int_0^\chi e^{-\hat{r}^1 \chi'} \mathfrak{N}\left(d_+\left(\chi', \frac{e^{\hat{r}^{01}\chi'}\mathcal{B}_\chi}{\mathcal{B}_{\chi'}}\right)\right) d\chi'$$

$$-\hat{r}^0 K \int_0^\chi e^{-\hat{r}^0 \chi'} \mathfrak{N}\left(d_-\left(\chi', \frac{e^{\hat{r}^{01}\chi'}\mathcal{B}_\chi}{\mathcal{B}_{\chi'}}\right)\right) d\chi'.$$

Once the boundary is determined, the price of an American call can be found via a simple integration.

Equation (11.14) is a little difficult to deal with because the integrand involves the standard cumulative normal distribution which is a transcendental function and is relatively costly to evaluate repeatedly. A simple trick comes to the rescue. Equation (11.14) is valid for all $S > 0$, in particular, for $S > \mathcal{B}_\chi$. For $S > \mathcal{B}_\chi$ it has the form

$$S - K = C(\chi, S, K)$$

$$+\hat{r}^1 S \int_0^\chi e^{-\hat{r}^1 \chi'} \mathfrak{N}\left(d_+\left(\chi', \frac{e^{\hat{r}^{01}\chi'}S}{\mathcal{B}_{\chi'}}\right)\right) d\chi'$$

$$-\hat{r}^0 K \int_0^\chi e^{-\hat{r}^0 \chi'} \mathfrak{N}\left(d_-\left(\chi', \frac{e^{\hat{r}^{01}\chi'}S}{\mathcal{B}_{\chi'}}\right)\right) d\chi'.$$

Differentiating the above relation with respect to S twice and substituting $S = \mathcal{B}_\chi$, we obtain a simpler integral equation for $\mathcal{B}_\chi$ which involves only elementary functions:

$$0 = e^{-\hat{r}^1 \chi} \mathcal{B}_\chi \mathfrak{n}\left(d_+\left(\chi, \frac{e^{\hat{r}^{01}\chi}S}{K}\right)\right)$$

$$+\ \hat{r}^1 \sqrt{\chi} \mathcal{B}_\chi \int_0^\chi e^{-\hat{r}^1 \chi'} \mathfrak{n}\left(d_+\left(\chi', \frac{e^{\hat{r}^{01}\chi'}\mathcal{B}_\chi}{\mathcal{B}_{\chi'}}\right)\right) d_-\left(\chi', \frac{e^{\hat{r}^{01}\chi'}\mathcal{B}_\chi}{\mathcal{B}_{\chi'}}\right) \frac{d\chi'}{\chi'}$$

$$+\ \hat{r}^0 \sqrt{\chi} K \int_0^\chi e^{-\hat{r}^1 \chi'} \mathfrak{n}\left(d_-\left(\chi', \frac{e^{\hat{r}^{01}\chi'}\mathcal{B}_\chi}{\mathcal{B}_{\chi'}}\right)\right) d_+\left(\chi', \frac{e^{\hat{r}^{01}\chi'}\mathcal{B}_\chi}{\mathcal{B}_{\chi'}}\right) \frac{d\chi'}{\chi'}.$$

11.7 Asymptotic analysis of the pricing problem

11.7.1 Short-dated options

In this section we study American calls with short maturity (or, equivalently, close to expiry). To start with, we explain under what conditions the right of early exercise makes an American option more expensive than its European counterpart. The price of a European call $C(\chi, S, K)$ is given by the standard Black-Scholes formula. We assume that this option expires in the money. Assuming that (nondimensional) time to maturity of the option is short, $\chi \ll 1$, its price can be approximated as follows

$$
\begin{aligned}
C(\chi, S, K) &\approx e^{-\hat{r}^1 \chi} S - e^{-\hat{r}^0 \chi} K \\
&\approx (1 - \hat{r}^1 \chi) S - (1 - \hat{r}^0 \chi) K \\
&= S - K - (\hat{r}^1 S - \hat{r}^0 K) \chi.
\end{aligned}
$$

This formula shows that the European price falls below the intrinsic value for $S > \mathcal{B}_0 \equiv \mathcal{B}^{C*}$, where

$$
\mathcal{B}^{C*} = \max\left(\frac{\hat{r}^0}{\hat{r}^1}, 1\right) K. \tag{11.15}
$$

Thus, if $\hat{r}^1 > 0$ the early exercise is always beneficial for sufficiently deep in the money American options. It is clear that $\mathcal{B}^{C*}$ is the limiting value of the early exercise boundary $\mathcal{B}_\chi$, i.e., that

$$
\mathcal{B}_{\chi \to 0} \to \mathcal{B}^{C*}.
$$

This relation shows that the price of an American call coincides with the price of a European call when the foreign risk-free rate is zero (as is approximately the case for yen calls / dollar puts). In addition, it shows that when the foreign risk-free interest decreases or the domestic rate increases, the early exercise boundary moves to the right and the early exercise premium decreases.

An interesting complementary approach to studying the limiting location of the early exercise boundary is to study American calls on the FXR with zero volatility. If $\sigma = 0$ the value of a European call is simply

$$
C(\chi, S, K) = e^{-\hat{r}^0 \chi} \left(e^{\hat{r}^{01} \chi} S - K\right)_+,
$$

while the intrinsic value is $(S - K)_+$. Thus, the early exercise boundary can be found from the following equation

$$\left(e^{\hat{r}^{01}\chi}\mathcal{B}_\chi - K\right)_+ = e^{\hat{r}^0\chi}\left(\mathcal{B}_\chi - K\right)_+.$$

The corresponding solution is

$$\mathcal{B}_\chi = \begin{cases} \dfrac{1 - e^{-\hat{r}^0\chi}}{1 - e^{-\hat{r}^1\chi}}K, & \text{if} \quad \hat{r}^0 > \hat{r}^1 \\ K & \text{if} \quad \hat{r}^1 > \hat{r}^0 \end{cases},$$

so that equation (11.15) is satisfied.

In order to determine the location of the boundary and the early exercise premium for $0 < \chi \ll 1$, we make the following self-similar ansatz

$$\mathcal{B}_\chi = \mathcal{B}^{C*}\left(1 + \varsigma\chi^{1/2}\right), \tag{11.16}$$

$$C''(\chi, S) = K\chi^{3/2}w\left(\frac{S - \mathcal{B}^{C*}}{\chi^{1/2}\mathcal{B}^{C*}}\right) = K\chi^{3/2}w(\eta), \tag{11.17}$$

where

$$\eta = \frac{S - \mathcal{B}^{C*}}{\chi^{1/2}\mathcal{B}^{C*}}.$$

Substituting these expressions into the boundary value problem for C'', expanding them in powers of $\chi^{1/2}$, and retaining the leading order terms, we obtain the following *ordinary* differential equation for $w(\eta)$:

$$w_{\eta\eta}(\eta) + \eta w_\eta(\eta) - 3w(\eta) = 0.$$

This equation has to be supplied with appropriate boundary conditions at $\eta = -\infty$ and $\eta = \varsigma$. It is clear that

$$w(-\infty) = 0.$$

In order to find the boundary conditions at the free boundary which is determined by the equation $\eta = \varsigma$ we substitute expression (11.17) into matching conditions (11.4), (11.5) and obtain

$$w(\varsigma) = \varpi\varsigma, \qquad w_\eta(\varsigma) = \varpi,$$

where

$$\varpi = \max\left(\hat{r}^0, \hat{r}^1\right).$$

This boundary value problem is overdetermined (since three, rather than two, boundary conditions on w are imposed), and has a solution only for a specially chosen ς.

The corresponding ordinary differential equation can be recognized as the modified Hermite equation. Accordingly, one of its solutions, odd in η, can be chosen in the form of the modified Hermite polynomial of degree 3,

$$w_1(\eta) = \eta^3 + 3\eta,$$

which can easily be verified by substitution. The second solution, linearly independent of the first one and even in η, can be chosen in the form

$$w_2(\eta) = (\eta^3 + 3\eta)\left(\mathfrak{N}(\eta) - \frac{1}{2}\right) + (\eta^2 + 2)\mathfrak{n}(\eta).$$

The general solution $w(\eta)$ of the boundary value problem has the form

$$w(\eta) = A_1 w_1(\eta) + A_2 w_2(\eta).$$

The boundary conditions yield

$$A_1 - A_2/2 = 0,$$
$$A_2\left((\varsigma^3 + 3\varsigma)\mathfrak{N}(\varsigma) + (\varsigma^2 + 2)\mathfrak{n}(\varsigma)\right) = \varpi\varsigma,$$
$$3A_2\left((\varsigma^2 + 1)\mathfrak{N}(\varsigma) + \varsigma\mathfrak{n}(\varsigma)\right) = \varpi.$$

Eliminating A_1, A_2, we get the dispersion relation for ς,

$$\varsigma^3\mathfrak{N}(\varsigma) + (\varsigma^2 - 1)\mathfrak{n}(\varsigma) = 0.$$

It is easy to show graphically that this transcendental equation has a unique positive root. Applying the standard Newton-Raphson method we can show that this root has the form

$$\varsigma = 0.638833.$$

This is the "universal constant" of the American call pricing. (It is surprisingly close the Golden Mean

$$\frac{\sqrt{5} - 1}{2} = .61803,$$

which the ancient Greeks held so dear.) Since ς is positive, the boundary moves to the right as time to maturity increases (as might be expected). The boundary is a singular function of χ. Its derivative blows up when $\chi \to 0$.

It is possible (but relatively difficult) to derive a more accurate representation for the early exercise boundary, namely,

$$\mathcal{B}_\chi \sim \begin{cases} K e^{\sqrt{-\chi \ln(\kappa_1 \chi)}}, & \hat{r}^{01} < 0 \\ K e^{\sqrt{-2\chi \ln(\kappa_2 \chi)}}, & \hat{r}^{01} = 0 \\ \dfrac{\hat{r}^0}{\hat{r}^1} K e^{\varsigma \sqrt{\chi}}, & \hat{r}^{01} > 0 \end{cases},$$

where

$$\kappa_1 = 8\pi \left(\hat{r}^{01}\right)^2, \qquad \kappa_2 = \sqrt{8\pi}\hat{r}^0.$$

Once ς is found, A_1, A_2 can be determined as

$$A_1 = \frac{\varsigma^3 \varpi}{6n(\varsigma)}, \quad A_2 = \frac{\varsigma^3 \varpi}{3n(\varsigma)},$$

and the price of an American call can be written in the form

$$C'(\chi, S, K) = \begin{cases} C(\chi, S, K) + \frac{\varsigma^3 \varpi \chi^{3/2} \left((\eta^3 + 3\eta)\mathfrak{N}(\eta) + (\eta^2 + 2)\mathfrak{n}(\eta) \right)}{3n(\varsigma)} K, & S \in \mathcal{D}_\chi^{NE} \\ S - K, & S \in \mathcal{D}_\chi^E \end{cases}.$$

The procedure outlined above is by no means specific for the call valuation problem. It is used, for example, in order to solve simple versions of the Stephan problem describing the process of ice melting. In the context of the latter problem the ansatz similar to (11.17) has a much wider validity domain.

We can also determine the asymptotic behavior of the boundary by using the integral equation (11.14). Assuming for concreteness that $\hat{r}^1 < \hat{r}^0$, so that the boundary starts at some point $\mathcal{B}^{C*} > K$, we can show via balancing leading-order terms in powers of $\chi^{1/2}$ (we omit details for the sake of brevity) that locally the boundary has the form (11.16), i.e.,

$$\mathcal{B}_\chi \approx \mathcal{B}^{C*} \left(1 + \tilde{\varsigma}\chi^{1/2}\right),$$

where $\tilde{\varsigma}$ has to be determined. Retaining the leading-order terms in powers of $\chi^{1/2}$, we can rewrite the integral equation for $\chi \to 0$ as

$$\mathcal{B}_\chi - K = \mathcal{B}_\chi - K - \left(\hat{r}^1 \mathcal{B}_\chi - \hat{r}^0 K\right)\chi + \left(\hat{r}^1 \mathcal{B}_\chi - \hat{r}^0 K\right)\mathcal{I}_1$$
$$- \left(\hat{r}^1 \hat{\gamma}_+ \mathcal{B}^{C*} - \hat{r}^0 \hat{\gamma}_- K\right)\mathcal{I}_2.$$

After some algebra it can be written as

$$0 \approx -\chi^{3/2} + \chi^{1/2}\mathcal{I}_1 + \mathcal{I}_2,$$

where

$$\mathcal{I}_1 \approx \int_0^\chi \mathfrak{N}\left(\frac{\tilde{\varsigma}\left(\chi^{1/2} - \chi'^{1/2}\right)}{(\chi - \chi')^{1/2}}\right) d\chi' \backsim \chi,$$

$$\mathcal{I}_2 \approx \int_0^\chi \mathfrak{N}\left(\frac{\tilde{\varsigma}\left(\chi^{1/2} - \chi'^{1/2}\right)}{(\chi - \chi')^{1/2}}\right)(\chi - \chi')^{1/2} d\chi' \backsim \chi^{3/2}.$$

Introducing the new variable

$$\vartheta = \frac{\chi^{1/2} - \chi'^{1/2}}{(\chi - \chi')^{1/2}},$$

and integrating by parts, we rewrite the integrals $\mathcal{I}_1, \mathcal{I}_2$ as

$$\mathcal{I}_1 = \chi\left[\frac{1}{2} + \tilde{\varsigma}\int_0^1 \frac{(1 - \vartheta^2)^2}{(1 + \vartheta^2)^2}\mathfrak{n}(\tilde{\varsigma}\vartheta)d\vartheta\right],$$

$$\mathcal{I}_2 = \chi^{3/2}\int_0^1 \frac{16\vartheta^2(1 - \vartheta^2)}{(1 + \vartheta^2)^4}\mathfrak{n}(\tilde{\varsigma}\vartheta)d\vartheta,$$

and represent the equation for $\tilde{\varsigma}$ in the final form

$$-\frac{1}{2}\tilde{\varsigma} + \int_0^1 \left[\frac{\tilde{\varsigma}^2(1 - \vartheta^2)^2}{(1 + \vartheta^2)^2} + \frac{16\vartheta^2(1 - \vartheta^2)}{(1 + \vartheta^2)^4}\right]\mathfrak{n}(\tilde{\varsigma}\vartheta)d\vartheta = 0.$$

This equation can be solved by iterations, its solution has the form

$$\tilde{\varsigma} = 0.638833,$$

i.e., $\tilde{\varsigma} = \varsigma$. Once again we obtain the "universal constant" of the American call pricing.

We leave it to the reader as an exercise to analyze the short-dated pricing problem for an American put directly (rather than by using put-call symmetry) and to demonstrate that

$$\mathcal{B}^{P*} = \min\left(\frac{\hat{r}^0}{\hat{r}^1}, 1\right)K.$$

This relation shows that the price of an American put coincides with the price of a European put when the domestic risk-free rate is zero (for instance, for dollar puts / yen calls). In addition, it shows that when the domestic risk-free interest decreases or the foreign rate increases, the early exercise boundary moves to the left and the early exercise premium decreases.

11.7.2   Long-dated and perpetual options

It is not difficult to find the location $\mathcal{B}^{C**}$ of the early exercise boundary for perpetual American calls which do not expire until they are exercised, i.e., calls with $\chi \to \infty$. Indeed, the price of such calls is independent of χ, $C'(\chi, S, K) = C'(S, K)$; so that

$$\begin{cases} \frac{1}{2}S^2 C'_{SS} + \hat{r}^{01} S C'_S - \hat{r}^0 C' = 0, & 0 < S < \mathcal{B}^{C**} \\ C'(S, K) = S - K, & \mathcal{B}^{C**} < S < \infty \end{cases} . \qquad (11.18)$$

The boundary and continuity conditions for C' have the form

$$C'(0, K) = 0, \quad C'(\mathcal{B}^{C**}, K) = \mathcal{B}^{C**} - K, \quad C'_S(\mathcal{B}^{C**}, K) = 1,$$

where the first condition has the usual meaning, while the other two express the fact that the price and the Delta are continuous across the early exercise boundary. The boundary value problem for C' is overdetermined and can be made consistent via an appropriate choice of $\mathcal{B}^{C**}$. The first equation (11.18) is the so-called Euler equation, it is well known that its general solution can be written in the form

$$C'(S, K) = A_+ K \left(\frac{S}{K}\right)^{\alpha_+} + A_- K \left(\frac{S}{K}\right)^{\alpha_-}, \qquad (11.19)$$

where

$$\alpha_\pm = -\hat{\gamma}_- \pm \sqrt{\hat{\gamma}_-^2 + 2\hat{r}^0}.$$

Since C' vanishes at $S = 0$, we put $A_- = 0$. In order to find A_+ we use the continuity conditions and get the following system of nonlinear equations for $A_+, \mathcal{B}^{C**}$:

$$\begin{cases} A_+ K \left(\frac{\mathcal{B}^{C**}}{K}\right)^{\alpha_+} = \mathcal{B}^{C**} - K, \\ \alpha_+ A_+ \left(\frac{\mathcal{B}^{C**}}{K}\right)^{\alpha_+ - 1} = 1. \end{cases}$$

A simple algebra yields

$$\mathcal{B}^{C**} = \frac{\alpha_+}{\alpha_+ - 1}K, \quad A_+ = \frac{(\alpha_+ - 1)^{\alpha_+ - 1}}{\alpha_+^{\alpha_+}}. \tag{11.20}$$

Accordingly, the price of a perpetual American call can be written the form

$$C'(S,K) = \begin{cases} \frac{1}{\alpha_+}\left(\frac{\alpha_+ - 1}{\alpha_+}\right)^{\alpha_+ - 1}\left(\frac{S}{K}\right)^{\alpha_+} K, & 0 < S < \mathcal{B}^{C**} \\ S - K, & \mathcal{B}^{C**} < S < \infty \end{cases}, \tag{11.21}$$

see Figure 11.4.

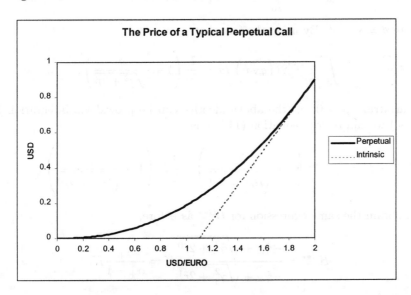

Figure 11.4: The price of a typical perpetual American call as a function of the spot FXR. The relevant parameters are the same as in Figure 11.1.

It is clear that for $\hat{r}^1 > 0$ the entire price of a perpetual American call can be considered as the early exercise premium because the price of the perpetual European call is equal to zero. On the other hand, if $r^1 = 0$, then $\alpha_+ = 1$, so that $\mathcal{B}^{C**} = \infty$, the prices of American and European calls coincide,

$$C'(S,K) = C(S,K) = S,$$

and the early exercise premium is equal to zero.

We can also use the integral equation in order to determine the location of the early exercise boundary for a perpetual American call. Indeed, when $\chi \to \infty$ the boundary becomes time-independent and the integral equation for $\mathcal{B}_\chi$ reduces to the algebraic equation for $\mathcal{B}^{C**}$. Taking into account that the price of a perpetual European call is equal to zero, we can write the equation for $\mathcal{B}^{C**}$ as

$$\mathcal{B}^{C**} - K = \hat{r}^1 \mathcal{B}^{C**} \int_0^\infty e^{-\hat{r}^1 \vartheta} \mathfrak{N}\left(\hat{\gamma}_+ \sqrt{\vartheta}\right) d\vartheta \qquad (11.22)$$

$$-\hat{r}^0 K \int_0^\infty e^{-\hat{r}^0 \vartheta} \mathfrak{N}\left(\hat{\gamma}_- \sqrt{\vartheta}\right) d\vartheta,$$

where $\vartheta = \chi - \chi'$. By using the fact that

$$\int_0^\infty e^{-p\vartheta} \mathfrak{N}\left(q\sqrt{\vartheta}\right) d\vartheta = \frac{1}{2p}\left(1 + \frac{q}{\sqrt{q^2 + 2p}}\right),$$

for arbitrary $p > 0$, q, (the above identity can be proved via integration by parts,) we can rewrite equation (11.22) as

$$\mathcal{B}^{C**} - K = \frac{1}{2}\mathcal{B}^{C**}\left(1 + \frac{\hat{\gamma}_+}{\sqrt{\hat{\gamma}_+^2 + 2\hat{r}^1}}\right) - \frac{1}{2}K\left(1 + \frac{\hat{\gamma}_-}{\sqrt{\hat{\gamma}_-^2 + 2\hat{r}^0}}\right),$$

and obtain the same expression for $\mathcal{B}^{C**}$ as before,

$$\mathcal{B}^{C**} = \frac{-\hat{\gamma}_- + \sqrt{\hat{\gamma}_-^2 + 2\hat{r}^0}}{-\hat{\gamma}_+ + \sqrt{\hat{\gamma}_+^2 + 2\hat{r}^1}}K = \frac{\alpha_+}{\alpha_+ - 1}K,$$

since

$$\hat{\gamma}_+^2 + 2\hat{r}^1 = \hat{\gamma}_-^2 + 2\hat{r}^0.$$

It is useful to evaluate the expected time to execution for a perpetual American call. This time coincides with the expected time it takes the process S_t to hit the level $\mathcal{B}^{C**}$. We denote this time measured in terms of σ^{-2} by $\hat{H}\left(S, \mathcal{B}^{C**}\right)$. The function $\hat{H}\left(S, \mathcal{B}^{C**}\right)$ solves the inhomogeneous ODE

$$\frac{1}{2}S^2 \hat{H}_{SS} + \hat{r}^{01} S \hat{H}_S = -1, \qquad (11.23)$$

supplied with the Dirichlet boundary condition at $S = \mathcal{B}^{C**}$,

$$\hat{H}\left(\mathcal{B}^{C**}, \mathcal{B}^{C**}\right) = 0,$$

and the regularity condition at $S = 0$. The general solution of equation (11.23) is

$$\hat{H}\left(S, \mathcal{B}^{C**}\right) = \frac{1}{\hat{\gamma}_-} \ln\left(\frac{\mathcal{B}^{C**}}{S}\right) + p + q \left(\frac{\mathcal{B}^{C**}}{S}\right)^{2\hat{\gamma}_-}.$$

To satisfy the boundary and regularity conditions we have to put $p = q = 0$. Thus,

$$\hat{H}\left(S, \mathcal{B}^{C**}\right) = \begin{cases} \ln\left(\mathcal{B}^{C**}/S\right)/\hat{\gamma}_-, & \text{if} \quad \hat{\gamma}_- > 0 \\ \infty, & \text{if} \quad \hat{\gamma}_- < 0 \end{cases}.$$

In order to illustrate the possibility of having a multi-component early exercise boundary we analyze the pricing problem for a covered American call in the perpetual setting. Figure 11.5 suggests that there are two exercise boundaries in the problem in question since it is beneficial to exercise the option both when S become either small or large. These boundaries (which are time independent in the perpetual setting) are denoted by $\mathcal{B}^{CC**}$ and $\bar{\mathcal{B}}^{CC**}$ respectively. Outside of the interval $\left[\mathcal{B}^{CC**}, \bar{\mathcal{B}}^{CC**}\right]$ the function $CC'(S, K)$ has the form

$$CC'(S, K) = \begin{cases} K, & S < \mathcal{B}^{CC**} \\ S, & S > \bar{\mathcal{B}}^{CC**} \end{cases}.$$

The matching conditions guaranteeing that $CC'(S)$ is sufficiently smooth are

$$\begin{cases} CC'\left(\mathcal{B}^{CC**}, K\right) = K, \\ CC'_S\left(\mathcal{B}^{CC**}, K\right) = 0, \\ CC'\left(\bar{\mathcal{B}}^{CC**}, K\right) = \bar{\mathcal{B}}^{CC**}, \\ CC'_S\left(\bar{\mathcal{B}}^{CC**}, K\right) = 1. \end{cases}$$

For $\mathcal{B}^{CC**} < S < \bar{\mathcal{B}}^{CC**}$ we represent $CC'(S, K)$ in the form

$$CC'(S, K) = KA_+ \left(\frac{S}{K}\right)^{\alpha_+} + KA_- \left(\frac{S}{K}\right)^{\alpha_-}. \tag{11.24}$$

By using the matching conditions we obtain the following system of nonlinear equations for $\mathcal{B}^{CC**}$, $\bar{\mathcal{B}}^{CC**}$, A_+, A_-:

$$
\begin{cases}
A_+ \left(\frac{\mathcal{B}^{CC**}}{K}\right)^{\alpha_+} + A_- \left(\frac{\mathcal{B}^{CC**}}{K}\right)^{\alpha_-} = 1, \\[2mm]
\alpha_+ A_+ \left(\frac{\mathcal{B}^{CC**}}{K}\right)^{\alpha_+ - 1} + \alpha_- A_- \left(\frac{\mathcal{B}^{CC**}}{K}\right)^{\alpha_- - 1} = 0, \\[2mm]
A_+ \left(\frac{\bar{\mathcal{B}}^{CC**}}{K}\right)^{\alpha_+} + A_- \left(\frac{\bar{\mathcal{B}}^{CC**}}{K^{21}}\right)^{\alpha_-} = \frac{\bar{\mathcal{B}}^{CC**}}{K}, \\[2mm]
\alpha_+ A_+ \left(\frac{\bar{\mathcal{B}}^{CC**}}{K}\right)^{\alpha_+ - 1} + \alpha_- A_- \left(\frac{\bar{\mathcal{B}}^{CC**}}{K}\right)^{\alpha_- - 1} = 1.
\end{cases}
$$

Its solution has the form

$$
\begin{aligned}
\mathcal{B}^{CC**} &= \left(\frac{1}{1-1/\alpha_+}\right)^{\frac{(\alpha_+ - 1)}{(\alpha_+ - \alpha_-)}} \left(\frac{1}{1-1/\alpha_-}\right)^{\frac{(1-\alpha_-)}{(\alpha_+ - \alpha_-)}} K, \\[2mm]
\bar{\mathcal{B}}^{CC**} &= \left(\frac{1}{1-1/\alpha_+}\right)^{\frac{\alpha_+}{(\alpha_+ - \alpha_-)}} \left(\frac{1}{1-1/\alpha_-}\right)^{-\frac{\alpha_-}{(\alpha_+ - \alpha_-)}} K, \\[2mm]
A_+ &= -\frac{\alpha_-}{\alpha_+ - \alpha_-} \left(\frac{1}{1-1/\alpha_+}\right)^{\frac{\alpha_+(1-\alpha_+)}{(\alpha_+ - \alpha_-)}} \left(\frac{1}{1-1/\alpha_-}\right)^{\frac{\alpha_+(\alpha_- - 1)}{(\alpha_+ - \alpha_-)}}, \\[2mm]
A_- &= \frac{\alpha_+}{\alpha_+ - \alpha_-} \left(\frac{1}{1-1/\alpha_+}\right)^{\frac{\alpha_-(1-\alpha_+)}{(\alpha_+ - \alpha_-)}} \left(\frac{1}{1-1/\alpha_-}\right)^{\frac{\alpha_-(\alpha_- - 1)}{(\alpha_+ - \alpha_-)}}.
\end{aligned}
\tag{11.25}
$$

The corresponding price of a covered perpetual call is shown in Figure 11.5.

11.8 Approximate solution of the valuation problem

11.8.1 Introduction

Since the closed form solution of the American valuation problem is not available, a lot of effort was devoted to developing approximate methods for solving this problem. Here we present two approximate methods which are of great historical interest.

11.8.2 Bermudan approximation and extrapolation to the limit

Bermudan calls can be exercised only at some predetermined (say, equidistant) times $t_n = nk$, $n = 0, ..., N$, $k = T/N$, between $t_0 = 0$ and T. We denote their prices by $\tilde{C}_N(t, S, T, K)$. It is clear that for $N = 1$ Bermudan and European calls have the same price,

$$
\tilde{C}_1(0, S, T, K) = C(0, S, T, K),
$$

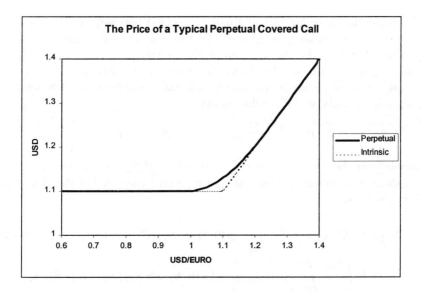

Figure 11.5: The price of a typical perpetual covered American call as a function of the spot FXR. The relevant parameters are the same as in Figure 11.1.

while in the limit $N \to \infty$ the price of a Bermudan call approaches the price of the corresponding American call,

$$\tilde{C}_N(0, S, T, K) \to C'(0, S, T, K).$$

Thus, Bermudan calls have characteristic features intermediate between European and American calls. This simple observation combined with the Richardson extrapolation forms the foundation of the Geske and Johnson method for the approximate evaluation of American calls.

For Bermudan options the early exercise constraint assumes the form

$$\tilde{V}_N(t_n, S) \geq v(S), \quad n = 0, ..., N.$$

In particular, for a Bermudan call

$$\tilde{C}_N(t_n, S, K, T) \geq (S - K)_+, \quad n = 0, ..., N.$$

It is much simpler (although not completely trivial) to evaluate a Bermudan call than its American counterpart, because the early exercise constraint has to be taken into account only at times t_n, so that between these times a call is European and as such is governed by the standard Black-Scholes pricing equation. Let $\mathcal{B}_{n,N}$ be the location of the exercise boundary at $t = t_n$. A simple argument based on the observation that it is advantageous to the buyer of a call to retain as much optionality as possible suggests that the sequence $\mathcal{B}_{1,N}, ..., \mathcal{B}_{n,N}, ...\mathcal{B}_{N,N} = K$, is decreasing,

$$\mathcal{B}_{1,N} \geq ... \geq \mathcal{B}_{n,N} \geq ... \geq \mathcal{B}_{N,N} = K.$$

Assuming for the moment that the exact values of $\mathcal{B}_n$ are known, we can use the risk-neutral valuation principle and represent the price of the Bermudan call in the form

$$\tilde{C}_N\left(0, S_0, T, K\right) = e^{-r^0 k} \int_{\mathcal{B}_{1,N}}^{\infty} p\left(0, S_0, k, S_1\right)\left(S_1 - K\right) dS_1 \tag{11.26}$$

$$+e^{-2r^0 k} \int_0^{\mathcal{B}_{1,N}} \int_{\mathcal{B}_{2,N}}^{\infty} p\left(0, S_0, k, S_1\right) p\left(k, S_1, 2k, S_2\right)\left(S_2 - K\right) dS_1 dS_2$$

$$+e^{-3r^0 k} \int_0^{\mathcal{B}_{1,N}} \int_0^{\mathcal{B}_{2,N}} \int_{\mathcal{B}_{3,N}}^{\infty} p\left(0, S_0, k, S_1\right) p\left(k, S_1, 2k, S_2\right) p\left(2k, S_2, 3k, S_3\right)$$

$$\times \left(S_3 - K\right) dS_1 dS_2 dS_3 + ...,$$

and similarly for $0 < t < T$. It is easy to understand the meaning of the corresponding integrals. The first integral is the discounted expected value of the payoff of the Bermudan call exercised at time t_1; the second one is the discounted expected value of a call exercised at time t_2 provided that it had not been exercised at time t_1, and so on.

We write equation (11.26) in terms of $\chi = \sigma^2 \left(T - t\right)$ as follows

$$\tilde{C}_N\left(\hat{T}, S_0, K\right) = e^{-\hat{r}^0 \hat{k}} \int_{\mathcal{B}_{1,N}}^{\infty} p\left(\hat{k}, S_0, S_1\right)\left(S_1 - K\right) dS_1 \tag{11.27}$$

$$+e^{-2\hat{r}^0 \hat{k}} \int_0^{\mathcal{B}_{1,N}} \int_{\mathcal{B}_{2,N}}^{\infty} p\left(\hat{k}, S, S_1\right) p\left(\hat{k}, S_1, S_2\right)\left(S_2 - K\right) dS_1 dS_2$$

$$+e^{-3\hat{r}^0 \hat{k}} \int_0^{\mathcal{B}_{1,N}} \int_0^{\mathcal{B}_{2,N}} \int_{\mathcal{B}_{3,N}}^{\infty} p\left(\hat{k}, S, S_1\right) p\left(\hat{k}, S_1, S_2\right) p\left(\hat{k}, S_2, S_3\right)$$

$$\times \left(S_3 - K\right) dS_1 dS_2 dS_3 + ... = \mathcal{I}_1 + \mathcal{I}_2 + \mathcal{I}_3 + ...,$$

By introducing the familiar logarithmic variables $X_n = \ln\left(S_n/S_0\right)$, $E_{n,N} =$

$\ln(\mathcal{B}_{n,N}/S_0)$, we represent the integrals $\mathcal{I}_n$ in the form

$$\mathcal{I}_1 = e^{-\hat{r}^0 \hat{k}} \int_{E_{1,N}}^{\infty} \frac{e^{-G^{(1)}/2}}{\left(2\pi \hat{k}\right)^{1/2}} \left(S_0 e^{X_1} - K\right) dX_1$$

$$= e^{-\hat{r}^1 \hat{k}} S \mathfrak{N}\left(d_+^{(1)}\right) - e^{-r^0 \hat{k}} K \mathfrak{N}\left(d_-^{(1)}\right),$$

$$\mathcal{I}_2 = e^{-2\hat{r}^0 \hat{k}} \int_{-\infty}^{E_{1,N}} \int_{E_{2,N}}^{\infty} \frac{e^{-G^{(2)}/2}}{2\pi \hat{k}} \left(S_0 e^{X_2} - K\right) dX_1 dX_2$$

$$= e^{-2\hat{r}^1 \hat{k}} S \mathfrak{N}_2\left(-d_+^{(1)}, d_+^{(2)}, -\frac{1}{\sqrt{2}}\right)$$

$$- e^{-2\hat{r}^0 \hat{k}} K \mathfrak{N}_2\left(-d_-^{(1)}, d_-^{(2)}, -\frac{1}{\sqrt{2}}\right),$$

$$\mathcal{I}_3 = e^{-3\hat{r}^0 \hat{k}} \int_{-\infty}^{E_{1,N}} \int_{-\infty}^{E_{2,N}} \int_{E_{3,N}}^{\infty} \frac{e^{-G^{(3)}/2}}{\left(2\pi \hat{k}\right)^{3/2}} \left(S_0 e^{X_3} - K\right) dX_1 dX_2 dX_3$$

$$= e^{-3\hat{r}^1 \hat{k}} S \mathfrak{N}_3\left(-d_+^{(1)}, -d_+^{(2)}, d_+^{(3)}, \frac{1}{\sqrt{2}}, -\frac{1}{\sqrt{3}}, -\frac{\sqrt{2}}{\sqrt{3}}\right)$$

$$- e^{-3\hat{r}^0 \hat{k}} K \mathfrak{N}_3\left(-d_-^{(1)}, -d_-^{(2)}, d_-^{(3)}, \frac{1}{\sqrt{2}}, -\frac{1}{\sqrt{3}}, -\frac{\sqrt{2}}{\sqrt{3}}\right),$$

where

$$d_\pm^{(n)} = d_\pm\left(n\hat{k}, e^{n\hat{r}^{01}\hat{k} - E_{n,N}}\right),$$

$$G^{(n)} = \frac{1}{\hat{k}}\left(\left(X_1 - \hat{\gamma}_- \hat{k}\right)^2 + \dots + \left(X_n - X_{n-1} - \gamma_- \hat{k}\right)^2\right).$$

and $\mathfrak{N}_n$ is the standard n-dimensional cumulative normal distribution, for example,

$$\mathfrak{N}_2(Y_1, Y_2, \rho_{12}) = \int_{-\infty}^{Y_1} \int_{-\infty}^{Y_2} \frac{\exp\left[-\frac{1}{2}C^{-1}\mathbf{Y} \cdot \mathbf{Y}\right]}{\sqrt{(2\pi)^2 \det C}} d\mathbf{Y},$$

$$C = \begin{pmatrix} 1 & \rho_{12} \\ \rho_{12} & 1 \end{pmatrix},$$

$$\mathfrak{N}_3(Y_1, Y_2, Y_3, \rho_{12}, \rho_{13}, \rho_{23}) = \int_{-\infty}^{Y_1} \int_{-\infty}^{Y_2} \int_{-\infty}^{Y_3} \frac{\exp\left[-\frac{1}{2}C^{-1}\mathbf{Y} \cdot \mathbf{Y}\right]}{\sqrt{(2\pi)^3 \det C}} d\mathbf{Y},$$

$$C_3 = \begin{pmatrix} 1 & \rho_{12} & \rho_{13} \\ \rho_{12} & 1 & \rho_{23} \\ \rho_{13} & \rho_{23} & 1 \end{pmatrix}.$$

In order to derive the above formulas we use the following identities

$$G^{(n)} = C_n \mathbf{Y}_- \cdot \mathbf{Y}_-, \quad G^{(n)} - 2X_n = C_n^{-1}\mathbf{Y}_+ \cdot \mathbf{Y}_+ - n\,\hat{r}^{01}\hat{k},$$

where we put

$$Y_{n,\pm} = \left(X_n - \hat{\gamma}_{\pm} n\hat{k}\right) / \sqrt{n\hat{k}},$$

$$C_1 = (1),$$

$$C_2 = \begin{pmatrix} 1 & 1/\sqrt{2} \\ 1/\sqrt{2} & 1 \end{pmatrix},$$

$$C_3 = \begin{pmatrix} 1 & 1/\sqrt{2} & 1/\sqrt{3} \\ 1/\sqrt{2} & 1 & \sqrt{2}/\sqrt{3} \\ 1/\sqrt{3} & \sqrt{2}/\sqrt{3} & 1 \end{pmatrix}.$$

It is clear that C_n are the correlation matrices for the standard Wiener process introduced in Section 4.5.

In order to use the Bermudan approximation, we have to obtain closed-form expressions for $\tilde{C}_1, \tilde{C}_2, \tilde{C}_3$. It is clear that $\tilde{C}_1$ is given by the standard Black-Scholes formula. In order to evaluate $\tilde{C}_2$, i.e., to price a Bermudan call which can be exercised twice, namely, half-time to maturity and at maturity (provided it was not exercised at half-time) we have to find $\mathcal{B}_{1,2}$. The early exercise boundary (to be precise just one point) can be found from the algebraic equation

$$C\left(0, \mathcal{B}_{1,2}, \hat{T}/2, K\right) = \mathcal{B}_{1,2} - K,$$

which can be solved via the Newton-Raphson method. Once this equation is solved, we can represent $\tilde{C}_2(0, S, T, K)$ via the first two terms of expansion (11.27) with $N = 2$. It is clear that from a financial viewpoint at time $t = 0$ we deal with a compounded option which matures at $T/2$ and pays the buyer the best of two calls expiring at $T/2$ and T, respectively.

We can evaluate $\tilde{C}_3(0, S, T, K)$ in a similar way. First, we find the location of the Bermudan exercise points $\mathcal{B}_{1,3}, \mathcal{B}_{2,3}$ by solving the following algebraic equations via the Newton-Raphson method,

$$C(0, \mathcal{B}_{2,3}, T/3, K) = \mathcal{B}_{1,3} - K,$$
$$\tilde{C}_2(0, \mathcal{B}_{2,3}, 2T/3, K) = \mathcal{B}_{2,3} - K.$$

Assuming that these points are found, we can represent $\tilde{C}_3(0, S, T, K)$ via the first three terms of expansion (11.27) with $N = 3$.

The simplest approximation for C' is given by

$$C'(0, S, T, K) \approx \tilde{C}_3(0, S, T, K).$$

A more sophisticated approximation, which is called the Richardson extrapolation, is based on the fact that two additional prices $\tilde{C}_1 = C$, and $\tilde{C}_2$ are known. Assuming that the price $\tilde{C}_N(0, S, T, K)$ can be expanded in a standard Taylor series in powers of $1/N$,

$$\tilde{C}_N(0, S, T, K) = C'(0, S, T, K) + \theta_1 \left(\frac{1}{N} \right) + \theta_2 \left(\frac{1}{N} \right)^2 + ...,$$

where $\theta_{1,2}$ are unknown coefficients, and dropping higher-order terms, we obtain the system of three equations for C', θ_1, θ_2,

$$
\begin{aligned}
\tilde{C}_1 &= C' + \theta_1 + \theta_2, \\
\tilde{C}_2 &= C' + \theta_1/2 + \theta_2/4, \\
\tilde{C}_3 &= C' + \theta_1/3 + \theta_2/9.
\end{aligned}
$$

Eliminating θ_1, θ_2, we express C' in terms of $\tilde{C}_N$, $N = 1, 2, 3$,

$$C'(0, S, T, K) = \frac{1}{2}\tilde{C}_1(0, S, T, K) - 4\tilde{C}_2(0, S, T, K) + \frac{9}{2}\tilde{C}_3(0, S, T, K).$$

This formula, which is due to Richardson, is one of the key formulas of numerical analysis. It is very general in nature and succinctly expresses the idea of extrapolation to the limit which allows one to obtain a more accurate estimate for C' than $\tilde{C}_3$. Notice that the coefficients $1/2, -4, 9/2$ sum up to 1 (as might be expected).

11.8.3 Quadratic approximation

By now we know two points belonging to the early exercise boundary, namely, its starting point $\mathcal{B}^{C*}$ corresponding to $\chi = 0$ and its terminal point $\mathcal{B}^{C**}$ corresponding to $\chi = \infty$. In addition, we know that this boundary changes very rapidly in the beginning and very slowly in the end. In essence, to solve the free-boundary problem we need to connect the starting and the ending point in a natural way and find the corresponding early exercise premium. Here we restrict ourselves to developing an approximate procedure for finding the boundary and the premium. This procedure is based on the so-called quadratic approximation which can be described as follows.

(A) We represent the early exercise premium in the form

$$C''(\chi, S, K) = h(\chi) E(\chi, S, K),$$

where $h(\chi)$ is a smooth function vanishing when $\chi = 0$ and approaching unity when $\chi \to \infty$. There are many possible choices. To be concrete, we choose

$$h(\chi) = 1 - e^{-\hat{r}^0 \chi}.$$

The pricing problem for E has the form

$$E_\chi - \frac{1}{2} S^2 E_{SS} - \hat{r}^{01} S E_S + \frac{\hat{r}^0}{h} E = 0,$$

$$E(\chi, 0, K) = 0,$$
$$h(\chi) E(\chi, \mathcal{B}_\chi, K) = \mathcal{B}_\chi - K - C(\chi, \mathcal{B}_\chi, K),$$
$$h(\chi) E_S(\chi, \mathcal{B}_\chi, K) = 1 - C_S(\chi, \mathcal{B}_\chi, K).$$

Here we use the obvious relation

$$\frac{dh}{d\chi} + \hat{r}^0 h - \hat{r}^0 = 0.$$

Representation (11.17) valid for small χ shows that the time derivative in the pricing equation can be dropped when $\chi \ll 1$, it can also be dropped for $\chi \gg 1$ since for large χ the corresponding solution changes very slowly. We assume that the time derivative can be dropped not only for small and large values of χ but for intermediate $\chi \sim 1$ as well (this is the key assumption of the quadratic approximation) and write the pricing equation as a second-order ordinary differential equation parametrically depending on χ, or equivalently, on h:

$$\frac{1}{2}S^2 E_{SS} + \hat{r}^{01} S E_S - \frac{\hat{r}^0}{h} E = 0, \tag{11.28}$$

In this equation and the corresponding boundary conditions h is considered as an external parameter changing from 0 to 1. It is clear that for $h = 1$ ($\chi = \infty$) the pricing equation coincides with perpetual pricing equation (11.18). We will see shortly that this equation is broadly compatible with representation (11.16), (11.17) when $h \to 0$ ($\chi \to 0$). For $0 < h < 1$ we deal with the intermediate case. Equation (11.28) is of the Euler type. It can be solved by the same token as equation (11.18). All solutions vanishing at zero have the form

$$E\left(\chi, S, K\right) = A_{h,+} K \left(\frac{S}{K}\right)^{\alpha_{h,+}},$$

where

$$\alpha_{h,\pm} = -\hat{\gamma}_- \pm \sqrt{\hat{\gamma}_-^2 + 2\hat{r}^0/h},$$

while $A_{h,+}$ and $\mathcal{B}_h^C$ can be found from the matching conditions

$$hA_{h,+} K \left(\frac{\mathcal{B}_h^C}{K}\right)^{\alpha_{h,+}} = \mathcal{B}_h^C - K - C\left(\chi, \mathcal{B}_h^C, K\right)$$

$$= \mathcal{B}_h^C - K - e^{-\hat{r}^1 \chi} \mathcal{B}_h^C \mathfrak{N}\left(d_+\left(\chi, \frac{e^{\hat{r}^{01} \chi} \mathcal{B}_h^C}{K}\right)\right)$$

$$+ e^{-\hat{r}^0 \chi} K \mathfrak{N}\left(d_-\left(\chi, \frac{e^{\hat{r}^{01} \chi} \mathcal{B}_h^C}{K}\right)\right),$$

$$h\alpha_{h,+} A_{h,+} \left(\frac{\mathcal{B}_h^C}{K}\right)^{\alpha_{h,+}-1} = 1 - C_S\left(\chi, \mathcal{B}_h^C, K\right)$$

$$= 1 - e^{-\hat{r}^1 \chi} \mathfrak{N}\left(d_+\left(\chi, \frac{e^{\hat{r}^{01} \chi} \mathcal{B}_h^C}{K}\right)\right),$$

where χ is thought of as a function of h,

$$\chi = -\frac{\ln\left(1 - h\right)}{\hat{r}^0}.$$

Eliminating $A_{h,+}$ we obtain the dispersion relation for $\mathcal{B}_h^C$:

$$\mathcal{B}_h^C = \frac{\alpha_{h,+} \left(1 - e^{-\hat{r}^0 \chi} \mathfrak{N}\left(d_-\left(\chi, e^{\hat{r}^{01} \chi} \mathcal{B}_h^C/K\right)\right)\right)}{(\alpha_{h,+} - 1)\left(1 - e^{-\hat{r}^1 \chi} \mathfrak{N}\left(d_+\left(\chi, e^{\hat{r}^{01} \chi} \mathcal{B}_h^C/K\right)\right)\right)} K,$$

which can easily be solved by the Newton-Raphson method. Once $\mathcal{B}_h^C$ is found the product $h A_{h,+}$ can be represented as

$$h A_{h,+} = \left(\frac{\alpha_{h,+} - 1}{1 - e^{-\hat{r}^0 \chi} \mathfrak{N}\left(d_-\left(\chi, e^{\hat{r}^{01} \chi} \mathcal{B}_h^C/K\right)\right)}\right)^{\alpha_{h,+} - 1}$$

$$\times \left(\frac{1 - e^{-\hat{r}^1 \chi} \mathfrak{N}\left(d_+\left(\chi, e^{\hat{r}^{01} \chi} \mathcal{B}_h^C/K\right)\right)}{\alpha_{h,+}}\right)^{\alpha_{h,+}}.$$

The dispersion relation clearly shows that $\mathcal{B}_h^C \to \mathcal{B}^{C**}$ when $h \to 1$ ($\chi \to \infty$). It is relatively easy to see that $\mathcal{B}_h^C \to \mathcal{B}^{C*}$ when $h \to 0$ ($\chi \to 0$). In order to study the asymptotic behavior of $\mathcal{B}_h^C$ for small h we represent the r.h.s. of the dispersion relation in the form

$$\mathcal{B}_h^C \approx \frac{\alpha_{h,+}}{(\alpha_{h,+} - 1)} \mathcal{B}^{C*},$$

expand $\alpha_{h,+}$ in powers of h, and get

$$\mathcal{B}_h^C \approx \frac{\sqrt{2\hat{r}^0} - \hat{\gamma}_- \sqrt{h}}{\sqrt{2\hat{r}^0} - \hat{\gamma}_+ \sqrt{h}} \mathcal{B}^{C*} \approx \left(1 - \frac{\hat{\gamma}_- - \hat{\gamma}_+}{\sqrt{2\hat{r}^0}} \sqrt{h}\right) \mathcal{B}^{C*} = \left(1 + \frac{\sqrt{h}}{\sqrt{2}}\right) \mathcal{B}^{C*}.$$

We see that for small h (or χ) the boundary is described by ansatz (11.16) with the "universal constant" $\tilde{\varsigma} = 1/\sqrt{2} = 0.707107$ which is relatively close to the exact value $\varsigma = 0.638833$. In general, the boundary obtained in the quadratic approximation framework is shifted to the right of the true boundary. The price of an American call can be written as

$$C'(\chi, S, K) = \begin{cases} C(\chi, S, K) + h A_{h,+} K (S/K)^{\alpha_{h,+}}, & S \in \mathcal{D}_h^{NE} \\ S - K, & S \in \mathcal{D}_h^{E} \end{cases} \quad (11.29)$$

11.9 Numerical solution of the pricing problem

11.9.1 Bermudan approximation

The simplest numerical approach to solving the pricing problem for an American call (say) is based on its approximation by a Bermudan call. As always, we discretize time t, and introduce the grid points

$$t_0 = 0, ..., t_n = nk, ..., t_N = T,$$

where $k = T/N$, or, equivalently,

$$\chi_0 = 0, ..., \chi_n = n\hat{k}, ..., \chi_N = \hat{T},$$

where $\hat{T} = \sigma^2 T$, $\hat{k} = \hat{T}/N$. We use the usual Crank-Nicolson scheme to move forward from χ_n to χ_{n+1} (or, equivalently, backward from t_{N-n} to t_{N-n-1}), thus constructing a mapping

$$\tilde{C}_n (S, K) \to \bar{C}_{n+1} (S, K),$$

and then apply the Bermudan exercise condition to find $\tilde{C}_{n+1} (S, K)$:

$$\tilde{C}_{n+1} (S, K) = \max \left\{ \bar{C}_{n+1} (S, K), (S - K)_+ \right\}.$$

Even though this approach ignores the high-contact conditions, it is surprisingly robust and produces very reasonable values for C'. If need be, it can be combined with the Richardson extrapolation in k.

11.9.2 Linear complementarity

We now consider the discretization of LCP (11.9). We represent the discretized LCP in the Crank-Nicolson form

$$\begin{cases} \mathcal{A}_n (S, K) \geq 0, \\ \mathcal{E}_n (S, K) \geq 0, \\ \mathcal{A}_n (S, K) \mathcal{E}_n (S, K) = 0. \end{cases}$$

Here

$$C_n' (S, K) \equiv C' (\chi_n, S, K),$$

$$\mathcal{A}_n (S, K) = C_{n+1}' (S, K) - C_n' (S, K)$$

$$- \frac{\hat{k}}{2} \left[\frac{1}{2} S^2 C_{n+1SS}' (S, K) + \hat{r}^{01} S C_{n+1S}' (S, K) - \hat{r}^0 C_{n+1} (S, K) \right.$$

$$\left. + \frac{1}{2} S^2 C_{nSS}' (S, K) + \hat{r}^{01} S C_{nS}' (S, K) - \hat{r}^0 C_n (S, K) \right],$$

$$\mathcal{E}_n\left(S, K\right) = C'_n\left(S, K\right) - \left(S - K\right)_+ \, .$$

We solve the discretized problem by induction. We put

$$C'_0\left(S, K\right) = \left(S - K\right)_+ \, .$$

Assuming that $C'_n\left(S, K\right)$ is known, we observe that $C'_{n+1}\left(S, K\right)$ solves the LCP which can be treated by the projected successive over-relaxation (PSOR) method, say. This popular method is well-described in the references, so that we do not discuss it here.

11.9.3   Integral equation

In order to solve integral equation (11.14) numerically we discretize the interval $[0, \hat{T}]$, denote $\mathcal{B}_{\chi_n}$ by $\mathcal{B}_n$, and use Simpson's integration rule in order to replace the integral equation by a system of nonlinear algebraic equations of the form

$$
\begin{aligned}
\mathcal{B}_n - K &= C(\chi_n, \mathcal{B}_n, K) \\
&+ \hat{k}\hat{r}^1 \mathcal{B}_n \left[\frac{1}{2}\mathfrak{N}\left(d_+ \left(\chi_n, \frac{e^{\hat{r}^{01}}\chi \mathcal{B}_n}{\mathcal{B}_0} \right) \right) + \frac{1}{4}e^{-\hat{r}^1\chi_n} \right. \\
&\left. + \sum_{m=1}^{n-1} e^{-\hat{r}^1\chi_m}\mathfrak{N}\left(d_+ \left(\chi_n, \frac{e^{\hat{r}^{01}}\chi \mathcal{B}_n}{\mathcal{B}_m} \right) \right) \right] \\
&- \hat{k}\hat{r}^0 K \left[\frac{1}{2}\mathfrak{N}\left(d_- \left(\chi_n, \frac{e^{\hat{r}^{01}}\chi \mathcal{B}_n}{\mathcal{B}_0} \right) \right) + \frac{1}{4}e^{-\hat{r}^0\chi_n} \right. \\
&\left. + \sum_{m=1}^{n-1} e^{-\hat{r}^0\chi_m}\mathfrak{N}\left(d_- \left(\chi_n, \frac{e^{\hat{r}^{01}}\chi \mathcal{B}_n}{\mathcal{B}_m} \right) \right) \right] \, .
\end{aligned}
$$

This equation can be solved inductively, starting with $\mathcal{B}_0 = \mathcal{B}^{C*}$, and $\mathcal{B}_1 = \mathcal{B}^{C*}\left(1 + \varsigma\hat{k}^{1/2}\right)$. Assuming that $\mathcal{B}_0, ..., \mathcal{B}_{n-1}$ are known, we can determine $\mathcal{B}_n$ from a *scalar* nonlinear algebraic equation (which can be solved via the Newton-Raphson method, say,) and continue until $\mathcal{B}_N$ is found. As soon as the early exercise boundary is found, an approximate price of the early exercise premium below this boundary can be found by discretizing formula (11.12).

11.9.4   Monte-Carlo valuation

For a long time it was thought that pricing American options via the Monte-Carlo method is impossible because the location of the early exercise boundary is not known in advance and cannot be determined for a particular path considered in isolation. However, eventually a number of methods capable of pricing American options were developed. Some of these methods are based on careful "bunching" of neighboring passes, others on linear interpolations. However, for one-factor (and two-factor) problems finite-difference methods are by far superior, so we do not discuss Monte-Carlo methods here and refer the interested reader to the literature cited in the end of this chapter.

11.10 American options in a non-Black-Scholes framework

Pricing of American options in a non-Black-Scholes framework is a challenging task. Very few analytical results in this direction are known and most of the work is done numerically. It is worth mentioning, however, that it is possible to find prices of perpetual American options in the CEV model, as well as for some carefully chosen jump-diffusion models. However, no analytical simplifications are possible for the stochastic volatility model. Additional information can be found in the references given in the end of this chapter.

11.11 Multi-factor American options

11.11.1 Formulation

So far, we dealt exclusively with one-factor American options. It is easy to formulate the multi-factor valuation problem but quite difficult to solve it. In the $N + 1$-country economy we can formulate the valuation problem for the price $V'(t, \mathbf{S})$ of an American option whose payoff is $v(\mathbf{S})$ in several equivalent ways. For example, we can introduce the no-exercise domain $\mathcal{D}_t^{NE}$ and the exercise domain $\mathcal{D}_t^E$ and write the valuation problem in these domains as

$$V_t' + \frac{1}{2} \sum_{m,n} a^{mn} S^{0m} S^{0n} V_{S^{0m}S^{0n}}' + \sum_n r^{0n} S^{0n} V_{S^{0n}}' - r^0 V' = 0, \quad \mathbf{S} \in \mathcal{D}_t^{NE},$$

$$V'(t, \mathbf{S}) = v(\mathbf{S}), \quad \mathbf{S} \in \mathcal{D}_t^E.$$

The high-contact matching conditions which have to be satisfied at the early exercise boundary $\mathcal{B}_t$ are

$$V'(t, \mathbf{S}) = v(\mathbf{S}), \quad \mathbf{S} \in \mathcal{B}_t,$$

$$\nabla_{\mathbf{S}} V'(t, \mathbf{S}) = \nabla_{\mathbf{S}} v(\mathbf{S}), \qquad \mathbf{S} \in \mathcal{B}_t,$$

where $\nabla_{\mathbf{S}}$ denotes the gradient of a function, provided that the corresponding gradients exist. These conditions have the same meaning as in the one-dimensional case. The final condition is

$$V'(T, \mathbf{S}) = v(\mathbf{S}).$$

It is assumed that $V'(t, \mathbf{S})$ satisfies the natural boundary conditions.

Instead of splitting the pricing equation in two, we can write it as a single inhomogeneous pricing equation of the form

$$V'_t + \frac{1}{2} \sum_{m,n} a^{mn} S^{0m} S^{0n} V'_{S^{0m} S^{0n}} + \sum_n r^{0n} S^{0n} V'_{S^{0n}} - r^0 V' = \chi^E(\mathbf{S})\, w,$$

where $\chi^E(\mathbf{S})$ is the characteristic function of the exercise domain $\mathcal{D}_t^E$,

$$\chi^E(\mathbf{S}) = \left\{ \begin{array}{ll} 1, & \mathbf{S} \in \mathcal{D}_t^E \\ 0, & \mathbf{S} \in \mathcal{D}_t^{NE} \end{array} \right.,$$

$$w = \frac{1}{2} \sum_{m,n} a^{mn} S^{0m} S^{0n} v_{S^{0m} S^{0n}} + \sum_n r^{0n} S^{0n} v_{S^{0n}} - r^0 v.$$

It is also possible to cast the pricing problem in the linear complementarity form and as a linear program.

11.11.2   Two representative examples

We now consider two representative examples. First, we study the simplest two-factor option, namely, an exchange call option allowing the buyer to exchange one foreign currency for another provided that such an exchange is beneficial. The payoff of such an option is

$$\text{payoff} = \left(S^{01} - K^{21} S^{02} \right)_+.$$

Its price is denoted by $C'\left(\tau, S^{01}, S^{02}\right)$, where $\tau = T - t$ is the dimensional time to maturity. In contrast to the one-dimensional case the nondimensional time to maturity cannot be introduced in advance.

The pricing problem for a European exchange option is discussed in detail in Section 8.8. In particular, it is shown there how to reduce the pricing problem to a one-factor form by virtue of homogeneity. Since the early exercise constraint preserves homogeneity, at time τ the early exercise boundary is a straight line passing through the origin of the (S^{01}, S^{02})-plane which is governed by the equation

$$S^{01} = \mathcal{B}_\tau^{21} S^{02}.$$

Accordingly, the inhomogeneous American pricing equation can be written in the form

$$C'_\tau - \frac{1}{2}\left(\sigma^{01}\right)^2 \left(S^{01}\right)^2 C'_{S^{01}S^{01}} - \rho^{21}\sigma^{01}\sigma^{02}S^{01}S^{02}C'_{S^{01}S^{02}}$$

$$- \frac{1}{2}\left(\sigma^{02}\right)^2 \left(S^{02}\right)^2 C'_{S^{02}S^{02}} - r^{01}S^{01}C'_{S^{01}} - r^{02}S^{02}C'_{S^{02}} + r^0 C'$$

$$= \left(r^1 S^{01} - r^2 K^{21} S^{02}\right) \theta \left(S^{01} - \mathcal{B}_\tau^{21} S^{02}\right).$$

This equation is supplied with the initial condition

$$C'\left(0, S^{01}, S^{02}\right) = \left(S^{01} - K^{21} S^{02}\right)_+,$$

the high contact conditions

$$C'\left(\tau, \mathcal{B}_\tau^{21} S^{02}, S^{02}\right) = \left(\mathcal{B}_\tau^{21} - K^{21}\right) S^{02},$$

$$C'_{S^{01}}\left(\tau, \mathcal{B}_\tau^{21} S^{02}, S^{02}\right) = 1, \quad C'_{S^{02}}\left(\tau, \mathcal{B}_\tau^{21} S^{02}, S^{02}\right) = -K^{21},$$

and natural boundary conditions.

In order to reduce the pricing problem to the one-factor form we represent C' as

$$C'\left(\tau, S^{01}, S^{02}\right) = S^{02}\Phi\left(\chi, \xi\right),$$

where

$$\chi = \left(\sigma^{21}\right)^2 \tau, \quad \xi = S^{01}/S^{02},$$

$$\sigma^{21} = \sqrt{\left(\sigma^{01}\right)^2 - 2\rho^{021}\sigma^{01}\sigma^{02} + \left(\sigma^{02}\right)^2}.$$

By the same token as in Section 8.8 and obtain the one-factor American pricing problem of the form

$$\Phi_\chi - \frac{1}{2}\xi^2\Phi_{\xi\xi} - \hat{r}^{21}\xi\Phi_\xi + \hat{r}^2\Phi = \left(\hat{r}^1\xi - \hat{r}^2 K^{21}\right)\theta\left(\xi - \mathcal{B}_\chi^{21}\right),$$

$$\Phi\left(0,\xi\right) = \left(\xi - K^{21}\right)_{+},$$

$$\Phi\left(\chi, \mathcal{B}_{\chi}^{21}\right) = \mathcal{B}_{\chi}^{21} - K^{21},$$

$$\Phi_{\xi}\left(\chi, \mathcal{B}_{\chi}^{21}\right) = 1,$$

plus the usual regularity conditions. Here

$$\hat{r}^{1} = \frac{r^{1}}{\left(\sigma^{21}\right)^{2}}, \quad \hat{r}^{2} = \frac{r^{2}}{\left(\sigma^{21}\right)^{2}}, \quad \hat{r}^{21} = \frac{r^{2} - r^{1}}{\left(\sigma^{21}\right)^{2}}.$$

Thus, all we need to do is to price the standard American cross-currency option with strike K^{21}. The corresponding "domestic" and "foreign" interest rates are $\hat{r}^{2}$ and $\hat{r}^{1}$, respectively. All the results obtained above are applicable in the case in question. In particular, we can easily price the perpetual American cross-currency option. The corresponding formulas have the form (11.21) with trivial changes.

We now show how to price an American option to receive the better of two currencies with the payoff of the form

$$\text{payoff} = \max\left(S^{01}, K^{21}S^{02}\right).$$

In order to price the corresponding European option we noticed that it can be considered as a position in one currency and an option to exchange one currency for the other one since

$$\max\left(S^{01}, K^{21}S^{02}\right) = K^{21}S^{02} + \left(S^{01} - K^{21}S^{02}\right)_{+},$$

and used linearity to price the option. As we know, the early exercise feature destroys linearity, so that we have to do some extra work in order to price an American option to receive the better of two currencies. Once again, homogeneity comes to the rescue. We represent the price $V'\left(\tau, S^{01}, S^{02}\right)$ in the form

$$V'\left(\tau, S^{01}, S^{02}\right) = S^{02}\Phi\left(\chi, \xi\right),$$

and write the problem for Φ as follows

$$\Phi_{\chi} - \frac{1}{2}\xi^{2}\Phi_{\xi\xi} - \hat{r}^{21}\xi\Phi_{\xi} + \hat{r}^{2}\Phi = \hat{r}^{1}\xi\theta\left(\xi - \bar{\mathcal{B}}_{\chi}^{21}\right) + \hat{r}^{2}K^{21}\theta\left(\mathcal{B}_{\chi}^{21} - \xi\right),$$

$$\Phi\left(0,\xi\right) = \max\left(\xi, K^{21}\right),$$

where $\mathcal{B}_\chi^{21}, \bar{\mathcal{B}}_\chi^{21}$ are the lower and upper early exercise boundaries. We emphasize that there are two exercise boundaries in the problem in question since it is beneficial to exercise the option when either S^{01} or S^{02} become large, or, equivalently, when $\xi \to \infty$ or $\xi \to 0$. Outside of the interval $\left(\mathcal{B}_\chi^{21}, \bar{\mathcal{B}}_\chi^{21}\right)$ the function $\Phi\left(\chi, \xi\right)$ has the form

$$\Phi\left(\chi, \xi\right) = \begin{cases} \xi, & \xi > \bar{\mathcal{B}}_\chi^{21} \\ K^{21}, & \xi < \mathcal{B}_\chi^{21} \end{cases}.$$

The high contact matching conditions are

$$\begin{aligned}
\Phi\left(\chi, \mathcal{B}_\chi^{21}\right) &= K^{21}, & \Phi\left(\chi, \bar{\mathcal{B}}_\chi^{21}\right) &= \bar{\mathcal{B}}_\chi^{21}, \\
\Phi_\xi\left(\chi, \mathcal{B}_\chi^{21}\right) &= 0, & \Phi_\xi\left(\chi, \bar{\mathcal{B}}_\chi^{21}\right) &= 1.
\end{aligned}$$

This problem can be solved by the same token as the pricing problem for a covered American call considered in Section 11.2. As before, the perpetual problem is particularly simple since all the relevant functions are time-independent. Its solution is given by appropriately modified formulas (11.24), (11.25).

11.12 References and further reading

The number of papers devoted to the valuation of American options is vast. In the opinion of the author, the following papers are particularly relevant for our presentation: Barles *et al.* (1995), Barone-Adesi and Elliot (1991), Barone-Adesi and Whaley (1987), Broadie and Glasserman (1997), Broadie and Detemple (1996), Carr (1998), Carr *et al.* (1992), Dempster and Hutton (1997), Gerber and Shiu (1996), Geske and Johnson (1984), Geske and Shastri (1985), Jacka (1991), Kim (1990), Kou (2000), Little *et al.* (2000), Longstaff and Schwartz (2000), Mane (1999), McKean (1965), Mordecki (1999), Myneni (1992), Tilley (1993), van Moerbecke (1976), Yu (1992). Additional information can be found in the following books: Baker (1977), Crank (1984, 1989), Lamberton and Lapeyere (1996), Rubinstein (1971), Wilmott *et al.* (1993), Wilmott *et al.* (1995).

Chapter 12

Path-dependent options I: barrier options

12.1 Introduction

Options which we considered in the previous two chapters are path-independent. In this chapter we start our discussion of path-dependent options. We continue this discussion in the next chapter. Specifically, we consider barrier options which have weak path-dependent features. Barrier options are cheaper alternatives for ordinary calls and puts. They payoffs depend not only on the terminal FXR but also on the FXR observed throughout the life of the deal. Out-style barrier options are deactivated (while in-style options are activated) if the FXR hits a certain predetermined level at some time between the inception of the option and its maturity. If this triggering event does not happen, the out-style barrier option has the same payoff as its no-barrier counterpart (while the in-style option pays nothing). Since a barrier option can become worthless prior to maturity, its price can be considerably cheaper that the price of a similar no-barrier option. There are many different barrier options such as knock-outs (with or without rebate), knock-ins, double barrier options, one-touch and double-no-touch bets, etc. Below we concentrate on a few representative cases, which, in our opinion, are particularly important in practice.

As always, we start with our standard constant-parameter two-country model. First, we consider the case when just one constant barrier is present and show how to extend the Black-Scholes formula in order to incorporate barrier features. This extension was proposed by Merton in the early days of modern option pricing theory. We derive Metron's formula via the method of images. Even though pricing of single-straight-barrier options is not difficult, their risk management is a demanding task which we discuss in some detail. Next, we study the case of a single curvilinear barrier which is technically more difficult. Curvilinear barriers as such seldom appear in practice but they do occur naturally in the context of pricing barrier options in the presence of term structure of volatilities and interest rates. We show how to solve the corresponding pricing problem via the method of heat potentials. After that, we turn our attention to the case of double-barrier options, and solve the pricing problem via the methods of images and Fourier series. We discuss various issues which arise when the standard BS assumptions are replaced by more realistic ones and derive some useful formulas applicable in the general case. Next, we study multi-factor multi-barrier options which play an important role in the modern forex markets. We discuss in detail a particular problem of pricing two-factor, two- and four-barrier options (which is technically difficult) and briefly comment on possible extensions of this problem.

In the bulk of the chapter we concentrate on continuously monitored barrier options. However, because of their practical importance, we also briefly discuss discretely monitored barrier options and present some useful formulas for their approximate pricing.

The chapter is organized as follows. In Section 2 we study single-factor, single-barrier options. Both straight and curvilinear barriers are considered. In Section 3 we show how to construct static hedges for single-barrier options. In Section 4 we discuss pricing and hedging of single-factor, double-barrier options. We discuss the impact of deviations from the Black-Scholes paradigm on prices of barrier options in Section 5 where several representative models are considered. We give a brief description of multi-currency options in Section 6. In Section 7 we study two-currency options with payoffs depending on one currency and barriers imposed on the other currency. In Section 8 we consider two-currency options with barriers imposed on both currencies. Finally, in Section 9 we give the relevant references.

12.2 Single-factor, single-barrier options

12.2.1 Introduction

In the present section we consider the simplest and the most important class of out-style barrier options, namely, single-barrier knock-out options without and with rebate. The corresponding knock-in options can be analyzed as complements of their knock-out counterparts. We formulate the corresponding pricing problem and solve it via the methods of images and heat potentials. The barrier, which is not necessarily straight, can be monitored either continuously or discretely.

Single-barrier knock-out and knock-in options, which are substantially cheaper than their non-barrier counterparts, appeal to many investors who have specific views on the evolution of the FXR and believe that it will not hit the barrier (or will hit it for sure) between the inception of the option and its maturity.

12.2.2 Pricing of single-barrier options via the method of images

We start with down-and-out calls (up-and-out puts can be treated in the same way). We choose a strike level K and a flat barrier level $A < K$ and assume that the down-and-out call pays zero if $S_t = A$ for some $t, 0 \leq t \leq T$, and $(S_T - K)_+$ otherwise. The price of such a call is denoted by $V^{(DOC)}(t, S, T, K, A)$ or simply $V(t, S)$.

It is clear that the pricing equation and the final condition for $V(t, S)$ are the same as in the no-barrier case:

$$V_t + \frac{1}{2}\sigma^2 S^2 V_{SS} + r^{01} S V_S - r^0 V = 0,$$

$$V(T, S) = (S - K)_+ .$$

The boundary conditions, however, are different, and can be written as

$$V(t, A) = 0, \quad V(t, S \to \infty) \to e^{-r^1(T-t)}S .$$

In the familiar nondimensional variables the pricing problem assumes the form

$$U_\chi - \frac{1}{2}U_{XX} = 0,$$

$$U(0, X) = \left(e^{\hat{\gamma}_+ X} - e^{\hat{\gamma}_- X}\right)_+ ,$$

$$U(\chi, a) = 0, \quad U(\chi, X \to \infty) \to e^{\hat{\gamma}_+^2 \chi/2 + \hat{\gamma}_+ X},$$

where $a = \ln(A/K) < 0$ is the nondimensional barrier level.

We solve the nondimensional pricing problem first. We use the classical method of images and represent the corresponding Green's function for the heat equation with zero boundary condition at $X = a$ (or, equivalently, the t.p.d.f. for the Wiener process killed at zero) as

$$G(\chi, X, X') = H(\chi, X - X') - H\left(\chi, X - (2a - X')\right), \qquad (12.1)$$

where

$$H(\chi, X) = \frac{e^{-X^2/2\chi}}{\sqrt{2\pi\chi}},$$

is the standard heat kernel on the whole axis.[1] By using formula (12.1) we write

$$U(\chi, X) = \int_0^\infty G(\chi, X, X') \left[e^{\hat{\gamma}_+ X'} - e^{\hat{\gamma}_- X'}\right] dX'$$

$$= M(\chi, X, \hat{\gamma}_+) - M(\chi, X, \hat{\gamma}_-) - M(\chi, 2a - X, \hat{\gamma}_+) + M(\chi, 2a - X, \hat{\gamma}_-),$$

where M is defined by equation (8.29).

The dimensional price of the down-and-out call can be written as

$$V^{(DOC)}(t, S, T, K, A) = C(t, S, T, K) - \left(\frac{A}{S}\right)^{2\hat{\gamma}_-} C\left(t, \frac{A^2}{S}, T, K\right). \qquad (12.2)$$

This price corresponds to a dynamic hedging strategy consisting of buying $\Delta = V_S^{(DOC)}$ units of foreign currency. We show the corresponding price in Figure 12.1.

In the symmetric case, $r^0 = r^1$, the forward FXR is independent of time and, we have $\hat{\gamma}_- = -1/2$, so that we can use put-call symmetry and rewrite equation (12.2) in the form

$$V^{(DOC)}(t, S, T, K) = C(t, S, T, K) - \left(\frac{K}{A}\right) P\left(t, S, T, \frac{A^2}{K}\right). \qquad (12.3)$$

Even though this formula is applicable only under special conditions, it is quite interesting because it illustrates the essence of the so-called static hedging, which consists of buying and selling plain vanilla options in order to replicate an exotic one. Conceptually such a strategy is very attractive because it allows one to price exotics in the model-independent fashion.

---

[1] It is clear that the nondimensional reflection $X \to 2a - X$ is equivalent to the dimensional Kelvin transform $S \to A^2/S$.

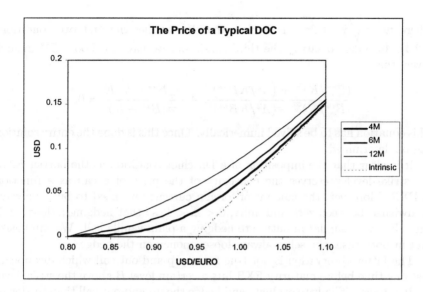

Figure 12.1: The price of a typical DOC as a function of the spot FXR for three representative maturities. The relevant parameters are $K = 0.95$, $\tau = 4M$, $6M$, $12M$, $\sigma = 15\%$, $r^0 = 5.5\%$, $r^1 = 4.5\%$. The lower barrier is at $A = 0.80$.

We illustrate early exercise features of an American down-and-out call in the perpetual setting. The time-independent pricing equation is the same as in the no-barrier case:

$$\begin{cases} \frac{1}{2}S^2V'_{SS} + \hat{r}^{01}SV'_S - \hat{r}^0 V' = 0, & A < S < B^{**} \\ V' = S - K, & B^{**} < S < \infty \end{cases} .$$

However, now it has to be considered on the semi-infinite interval $[A, \infty)$, so that it has to be supplied with the following conditions

$$V'(A) = 0, \quad V'(B^{**}) = B^{**} - K, \quad V'_S(B^{**}) = 1. \tag{12.4}$$

We use formula (11.19) and write the corresponding solution for $A \leq S \leq B^{**}$ in the form

$$V'^{(DOC)}(S)$$
$$= \frac{B^{**} - K}{(B^{**}/K)^{\varpi} - (A^2/KB^{**})^{\varpi}} \left(\frac{S}{B^{**}}\right)^{-\hat{\gamma}_-} \left[\left(\frac{S}{K}\right)^{\varpi} - \left(\frac{A^2}{KS}\right)^{\varpi}\right],$$

where $\varpi = \sqrt{\hat{\gamma}_-^2 + 2\hat{r}^0}$. It is clear that V' satisfies the first two conditions (12.4). In order to satisfy the third condition, we have to choose $\mathcal{B}^{**}$ in such a way that

$$\frac{(\mathcal{B}^{**}/K)^\varpi + (A^2/K\mathcal{B}^{**})^\varpi}{(\mathcal{B}^{**}/K)^\varpi - (A^2/K\mathcal{B}^{**})^\varpi} + \frac{\hat{\gamma}_+\mathcal{B}^{**} + \hat{\gamma}_-K}{\varpi(\mathcal{B}^{**} - K)} = 0.$$

This equation has to be solved numerically. Once this is done the entire solution can be determined.

It is clear that the imposition of a Dirichlet condition at the barrier *below* the strike level preserves the convexity of the price of a call as a function of FXR. Moreover, the amount of foreign currency we need to buy is always sandwiched between zero and unity, $0 < \Delta < 1$, so that hedging a down-and-out call is very similar in nature to hedging a plain vanilla call. We emphasize that in both cases the seller always looses money on the hedge.

The latter observation is not true for an up-and-out call which disappears if at any time before maturity FXR hits a certain level B above the strike level K. It is more difficult to evaluate and hedge the up-and-out call than its down-and-out counterpart because the payoff function is discontinuous at $S = B$. This discontinuity causes major mathematical problems and has important financial consequences. It is easy to show by the same token as before that in the nondimensional variables the price of an up-and-out call has the form

$$U(\chi, X)$$
$$= M^b(\chi, X, \hat{\gamma}_+) - M^b(\chi, X, \hat{\gamma}_-) - M^b(\chi, 2b - X, \hat{\gamma}_+) + M^b(\chi, 2b - X, \hat{\gamma}_-),$$

where $b = \ln(B/K) > 0$, and

$$M^b(\chi, X, \hat{\gamma}) = M(\chi, X, \hat{\gamma}) - \exp(\hat{\gamma}b)M(\chi, X - b, \hat{\gamma}).$$

In financial variables this price can be written as

$$V^{(UOC)}(t, S, T, K) = C(t, S, T, K) - C(t, S, T, B) \qquad (12.5)$$
$$- \left(\frac{B}{S}\right)^{2\hat{\gamma}_-} \left[C\left(t, \frac{B^2}{S}, T, K\right) - C\left(t, \frac{B^2}{S}, T, B\right)\right]$$
$$- (B - K)\left[V^{(CB)}(t, S, T, B) - \left(\frac{B}{S}\right)^{2\hat{\gamma}_-} V^{(CB)}\left(t, \frac{B^2}{S}, T, B\right)\right],$$

where $V^{(CB)}(t, S, T, K)$ stands for the price of a call bet which pays one unit of domestic currency if FXR at maturity is above K, and nothing otherwise. The price of an up-and-out call is shown in Figure 12.2.

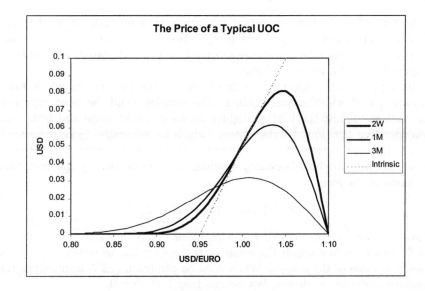

Figure 12.2: The price of a typical UOC as a function of the spot FXR for three representative maturities. The relevant parameters are the same as in Figure 12.1. The upper barrier is at $B = 1.10$.

In the symmetric case, $r^0 = r^1$, equation (12.5) simplifies to

$$V^{(UOC)}(t, S, T, K) = C(t, S, T, K) - \left(1 - \frac{K}{B}\right) C(t, S, T, B) \quad (12.6)$$

$$-\frac{K}{B} C\left(t, S, T, \frac{B^2}{K}\right) - 2(B - K)V^{(CB)}(t, S, T, B),$$

which shows that in this case an up-and-out call can be hedged statically. Again, when static hedging is possible, it has considerable advantages.

In general dynamical hedging of an up-and-out call represents a major problem because

$$\Delta(t \to T, S \to B) \to -\infty, \quad \Gamma(t \to T, S \to B) \to -\infty.$$

As a result the hedger of the short $V^{(UOC)}$ might be forced to sell an unlimited amount of the foreign currency to hedge his risk near the barrier, which is clearly impossible in practice. We emphasize that there is an *inflection point* in the vicinity of the barrier, so that Γ is negative there, and, hence, the seller of an option makes money on its hedge. However, if the barrier is broken from below, having a large short position which is accumulated as a results of hedging becomes a major problem.

It is practically important to develop a pricing mechanism which takes into account short-selling constraints. The simplest (and the most common) approach is to shift the barrier slightly outward and to price and hedge the corresponding fictitious barrier option (which is, naturally, more expensive) rather than the actual one. A somewhat more sophisticated alternative is to replace the Dirichlet boundary condition at the barrier by the boundary condition of the form

$$BV_S\left(t, B\right) + \Lambda V\left(t, B\right) = 0, \tag{12.7}$$

where Λ is the leverage coefficient. Condition (12.7) shows that the value of the foreign currency which the seller of the option has to sell is equal to Λ times the value of the option. When $\Lambda \to \infty$ condition (12.7) approaches the standard Dirichlet condition. We assume that $V\left(t, 0\right) = 0$.

In order to solve the modified pricing problem we use the trick of Sommerfeld and introduce the new variable

$$W\left(t, S\right) = SV_S\left(t, S\right) + \Lambda V\left(t, S\right). \tag{12.8}$$

It is easy to see that W solves the following pricing problem:

$$W_t + \frac{1}{2}\sigma^2 S^2 W_{SS} + r^{01} S W_S - r^0 W = 0,$$

$$W\left(t, 0\right) = 0, \quad W\left(t, B\right) = 0,$$

$$W\left(0, S\right) = \left(1 + \Lambda\right)\left(S - K\right)_+ + K\theta\left(S - K\right).$$

Thus, W is equal to the price of the portfolio consisting of $(1 + \Lambda)$ up-and-out calls and K up-and-out call bets. We know how to price an up-and-out call. The price of the corresponding up-and-out call bet is opposite to the value of the derivative of the call price with respect to its strike K. Accordingly, we can consider W as known. To find V for known W we solve ODE (12.8) supplied with the trivial initial condition at $S = 0$. A simple calculation yields:

$$V\left(t, S\right) = S^{-\Lambda} \int_0^S \left(S'\right)^\Lambda W\left(t, S^\Lambda\right) dS^\Lambda.$$

The interested readers can evaluate this integral analytically, more practically oriented readers can do so numerically. The actual price increase computed using the above approach is very close to the once computed by using an appropriate barrier shift.

The price of a barrier option also has to be adjusted in the (practically important) case of discrete sampling. Suppose that instead of monitoring a barrier (say, an upper barrier) continuously between the inception of the option and its maturity, the barrier condition is checked only at times $t_n = nT/N$, where $1 \leq n \leq N$. The payoff of the discretely monitored up-and-out call is zero if $\max_n \{S_{t_n}\} > B$ and $(S_T - K)_+$, otherwise. A simple analytical formula for pricing such calls does not exist. However, it is relatively easy to find a good approximation for their price by constructing an "equivalent" continuously monitored up-and-out call. It is clear that the corresponding continuous barrier level has to be shifted upward compared to the discretely monitored level. The exact upward shift is given by the formula

$$B \to B e^{\vartheta \sigma \sqrt{T/N}},$$

where

$$\vartheta = -\frac{\zeta(1/2)}{\sqrt{2\pi}} \approx 0.583,$$

and ζ is the Riemann zeta function. The prices of discretely and continuously monitored up-and-out calls are related by

$$V_N^{(UOC)}(B) = V^{(UOC)}\left(B e^{\vartheta \sigma \sqrt{T/N}}\right) + o\left(\frac{1}{\sqrt{N}}\right).$$

Similarly, for a discretely monitored down-and-out call the downward shift is given by

$$A \to A e^{-\vartheta \sigma \sqrt{T/N}},$$

and

$$V_N^{(DOC)}(A) = V^{(DOC)}\left(A e^{-\vartheta \sigma \sqrt{T/N}}\right) + o\left(\frac{1}{\sqrt{N}}\right).$$

Although pricing and hedging of a European up-and-out call is difficult, its American counterpart is relatively easy to handle, because the possibility of an early exercise makes the barrier features much less profound. Once again, for the purpose of illustration we consider a perpetual call. It is easy to show that the no-barrier expression (11.20) for $\mathcal{B}^{**}$ can be used when $\mathcal{B}^{**} < B$. If this inequality is violated, the solution can be written as

$$V'^{(UOC)}(S, K) = (B - K) \left(\frac{S}{B}\right)^{\alpha_+}.$$

This formula clearly shows that the price of an American up-and-out call does not vanish at the barrier (because it can be exercised there).

So far we considered the case of flat (time-independent) barriers. Now we consider the simplest time-dependent situation and assume that the dimensional down-and-out barrier (say) is an exponential function of time:

$$A(t) = A(T) e^{\alpha(T-t)}.$$

For the sake of variety we consider a single-no-touch (SNT) option which obligates the seller to pay the buyer a dollar provided that the FXR does not cross the level $A(t)$ from above between inception of the option and its maturity. The pricing problem has the form

$$V_t + \frac{1}{2}\sigma^2 S^2 V_{SS} + r^{01} S V_S - r^0 V = 0, \quad S > A(T) e^{\alpha(T-t)},$$

$$V(T, S) = 1,$$

$$V\left(t, A(T) e^{\alpha(T-t)}\right) = 0.$$

We use $A(T)$ to nondimensionalize the problem and represent the barrier as a linear function of χ:

$$a(\chi) = \hat{\alpha}\chi,$$

where $\hat{\alpha} = \alpha/\sigma^2$. The corresponding pricing problem has the form

$$U_\chi - \frac{1}{2}U_{XX} = 0,$$

$$U(0, X) = e^{\hat{\gamma}_- X},$$

$$U(\chi, \hat{\alpha}\chi) = 0, \quad U(\chi, X \to \infty) \to e^{\hat{\gamma}_-^2 \chi/2 + \hat{\gamma}_- X}.$$

We want to reduce it to a pricing problem with a flat barrier. To this end, we perform the Galilean transform:

$$\chi, X \to \chi, Y, \quad Y = X - \alpha\chi.$$

In χ, Y variables the pricing problem assumes the form

$$U_\chi - \frac{1}{2}U_{YY} - \hat{\alpha}U_Y = 0,$$

$$U(0, Y) = e^{\hat{\gamma}_- Y},$$

$$U(\chi, 0) = 0, \quad U(\chi, Y \to \infty) \to e^{(\hat{\gamma}_-^2/2 + \hat{\alpha}\hat{\gamma}_-)\chi + \hat{\gamma}_- Y},$$

Finally, we introduce the new dependent variable according to

$$W(\chi, Y) = e^{\hat{\alpha}^2\chi/2 + \hat{\alpha}Y}U(\chi, Y),$$

and obtain the standard flat-boundary pricing problem:

$$W_\chi - \frac{1}{2}W_{YY} = 0,$$

$$W(0, Y) = e^{(\hat{\gamma}_- + \hat{\alpha})Y},$$

$$W(\chi, 0) = 0, \quad W(\chi, Y \to \infty) \to e^{(\hat{\gamma}_- + \hat{\alpha})^2\chi/2 + (\hat{\gamma}_- + \hat{\alpha})Y}.$$

We leave it to the reader as a useful exercise to verify that

$$W(\chi, Y) = M(\chi, Y, \hat{\gamma}_- + \hat{\alpha}) - M(\chi, -Y, \hat{\gamma}_- + \hat{\alpha}).$$

Inverting the coordinate transforms we obtain

$$U(\chi, X) = M(\chi, X, \hat{\gamma}_-) - M(\chi, -X, \hat{\gamma}_- + 2\hat{\alpha}),$$

$$V^{(SNT)}(t, S) \tag{12.9}$$

$$= V^{(CB)}(t, S, T, A(T)) - \left(\frac{A(t)}{S}\right)^{2(\hat{\gamma}_- + \hat{\alpha})} V^{(CB)}\left(t, \frac{A^2(t)}{S}, T, A(T)\right).$$

Formula (12.9) shows that there the no-touch option can be decomposed into a sum of two European bet options and hedged statically provided that $\alpha = -r^{01}$, or, in other words, the barrier is flat when written in forward terms.

12.2.3   Pricing of single-barrier options via the method of heat potentials

Occasionally, we have to deal with barriers which are neither flat nor exponential. Curvilinear barriers *per se* appear in practice only infrequently, but, they do occur naturally when term structure effects are incorporated into the picture. Our objective is to derive a stable, accurate and fast algorithm for solving pricing problems with curvilinear barriers. In principle, we can use finite differences in order to solve such problems although the presence of the curvilinear boundary makes this undertaking less than straightforward. A viable alternative is provided by the method of heat potentials which we now describe. As we will see shortly, this method is also useful for pricing barrier options with rebate.

To be concrete we consider a one-touch option which pays a dollar provided that the FXR crosses the barrier level $A(t)$ from above (say) at some time t between the inception of the option and its maturity. The payment can be instantaneous or it can be delayed until maturity. The pricing problem for a one-touch option can be written as

$$V_t + \frac{1}{2}\sigma^2 S^2 V_{SS} + r^{01} S V_S - r^0 V = 0, \quad S > A(t),$$

$$V(T, S) = 0, \quad S > A(T)$$

$$V(t, A(t)) = 1, \quad V(t, S \to \infty) \to 0,$$

in case of immediate rebate, or

$$V(t, A(t)) = e^{-r^0(T-t)}, \quad V(t, S \to \infty) \to 0,$$

in case of postponed rebate.

We use $A(T)$ for nondimensionalization and write the pricing problem in the form:

$$U_X - \frac{1}{2}U_{XX} = 0, \tag{12.10}$$

$$U(0, X) = 0, \quad X \geq 0, \tag{12.11}$$

$$U(\chi, a(\chi)) = \left\{ \begin{array}{ll} \eta_{IR}(\chi), & \text{(immediate rebate)} \\ \eta_{PR}(\chi), & \text{(postponed rebate)} \end{array} \right\}, \tag{12.12}$$

$$U(\chi, X \to \infty) \to 0.$$

Here

$$a\left(\chi\right) = \ln\left(A\left(t\right)/A\left(T\right)\right),$$
$$\eta_{IR}\left(\chi\right) = e^{\left(\hat{r}^{0}+\hat{\gamma}_{-}^{2}/2\right)\chi+\hat{\gamma}_{-}a(\chi)},$$
$$\eta_{PR}\left(\chi\right) = e^{\hat{\gamma}_{-}^{2}/2\chi+\hat{\gamma}_{-}a(\chi)}.$$

The main idea is to represent U as a superposition of the so-called double layer potentials with (unknown) weights $\nu(\chi)$:

$$U(\chi, X) = \int_{0}^{\chi} \frac{\left(X - a\left(\chi'\right)\right)e^{-\left(X-a(\chi')\right)^{2}/2(\chi-\chi')}}{\sqrt{2\pi\left(\chi-\chi'\right)^{3}}}\nu(\chi')d\chi'. \qquad (12.13)$$

It is obvious that this integral defines a solution of the heat equation. In order to ensure that this solution satisfies the boundary conditions, the weights have to satisfy the following integral Volterra equation

$$\nu(\chi) + \int_{0}^{\chi} \frac{\left(a\left(\chi\right) - a\left(\chi'\right)\right)e^{-\left(a(\chi)-a(\chi')\right)^{2}/2(\chi-\chi')}}{\sqrt{2\pi\left(\chi-\chi'\right)^{3}}}\nu(\chi')d\chi' = \eta\left(\chi\right). \qquad (12.14)$$

Once equation (12.14) is solved and the corresponding ν is found, it is substituted into equation (12.13) and the expression for U is obtained. The corresponding integrals have to be dealt with care because they have singularities at $\chi = \chi'$ which need to be regularized.

First, we regularize the integral equation for ν. We represent the difference $a\left(\chi\right) - a\left(\chi\right)$ in the form

$$a\left(\chi\right) - a\left(\chi'\right) = (\chi - \chi')\vartheta(\chi, \chi'),$$

where $\vartheta(\chi, \chi')$ is a smooth function of its arguments, and rewrite the equation for ν as

$$\nu(\chi) + \int_{0}^{\chi} \frac{\vartheta\left(\chi, \chi'\right)e^{-\vartheta^{2}(\chi,\chi')(\chi-\chi')/2}}{\sqrt{2\pi\left(\chi-\chi'\right)}}\nu(\chi')d\chi' = \eta\left(\chi\right).$$

Our next step is aimed at massaging the inverse square-root singularity at $\chi = \chi'$. To this end, we rewrite the integral equation as

$$\Xi\left(\chi\right)\nu(\chi) + \int_{0}^{\chi} \frac{\vartheta\left(\chi, \chi'\right)e^{-\vartheta^{2}(\chi,\chi')(\chi-\chi')/2}}{\sqrt{2\pi\left(\chi-\chi'\right)}}\left[\nu(\chi') - \nu(\chi)\right]d\chi' = \eta\left(\chi\right),$$

where

$$\begin{aligned}
\Xi(\chi) &= 1 + \int_0^\chi \frac{\vartheta\left(\chi, \chi'\right) e^{-\vartheta^2\left(\chi, \chi'\right)\left(\chi - \chi'\right)/2}}{\sqrt{2\pi\left(\chi - \chi'\right)}} d\chi' \\
&= 1 + 2 \int_0^{\sqrt{\chi}} \frac{\vartheta(\chi, \chi - \zeta^2) e^{-\vartheta^2\left(\chi, \chi - \zeta^2\right)\zeta^2/2}}{\sqrt{2\pi}} d\zeta,
\end{aligned}$$

Now the integrand is nonsingular and can be treated via standard methods.

Second, we regularize integral representation (12.13) by introducing a cutoff time ϖ and writing $U(\chi, X)$ as

$$\begin{aligned}
U(\chi, X) &= \int_0^{\chi - \varpi} \frac{\left(X - a(\chi')\right) e^{-\left(X - a(\chi')\right)^2/2\left(\chi - \chi'\right)}}{\sqrt{2\pi\left(\chi - \chi'\right)^3}} \nu(\chi') d\chi' \\
&\quad + \int_{\chi - \varpi}^\chi \frac{\left(X - a(\chi')\right) e^{-\left(X - a(\chi')\right)^2/2\left(\chi - \chi'\right)}}{\sqrt{2\pi\left(\chi - \chi'\right)^3}} \nu(\chi') d\chi' \\
&= U_1(\chi, X) + U_2(\chi, X).
\end{aligned}$$

We compute the first integral numerically using the trapezoidal rule (say). We approximate the second one by replacing $a(\chi')$ by its tangent at $\chi' = \chi$,

$$a(\chi') \approx a(\chi) - \dot{a}(\chi)(\chi - \chi'),$$

where $\dot{a}(\chi) = da(\chi)/d\chi$, and $\nu(\chi')$ by its value at $\chi' = \chi$, $\nu(\chi') = \nu(\chi)$. As a result we obtain

$$\begin{aligned}
&U_2(\chi, X) \\
&\approx \nu(\chi) \int_{\chi - \varpi}^\chi \frac{\left(X - a(\chi) + \dot{a}(\chi)(\chi - \chi')\right) e^{-\left(X - a(\chi) + \dot{a}(\chi)(\chi - \chi')\right)^2/2\left(\chi - \chi'\right)}}{\sqrt{2\pi\left(\chi - \chi'\right)^3}} d\chi' \\
&= \nu(\chi)(X - a(\chi)) e^{-(X - a(\chi))\dot{a}(\chi)} \int_0^\varpi \frac{e^{-(X - a(\chi))^2/2\zeta - \dot{a}^2(\chi)\zeta/2}}{\sqrt{2\pi\zeta^3}} d\zeta \\
&\quad + \nu(\chi)\dot{a}(\chi) e^{-(X - a(\chi))\dot{a}(\chi)} \int_0^\varpi \frac{e^{-(X - a(\chi))^2/2\zeta - \dot{a}^2(\chi)\zeta/2}}{\sqrt{2\pi\zeta}} d\zeta.
\end{aligned}$$

In the first and second integrals we change the independent variable according to $\zeta = 1/u^2$ and $\zeta = u^2$, respectively, and after some relatively cumbersome algebra obtain

$$U_2(\chi, X)$$

$$\approx\ 2\nu\left(\chi\right)\left(X - a\left(\chi\right)\right)e^{-(X-a(\chi))\dot{a}(\chi)}\int_{1/\sqrt{\varpi}}^{\infty}\frac{e^{-(X-a(\chi))^2 u^2/2 - \dot{a}^2(\chi)/2u^2}}{\sqrt{2\pi}}du$$

$$+2\nu\left(\chi\right)\dot{a}\left(\chi\right)e^{-(X-a(\chi))\dot{a}(\chi)}\int_0^{\sqrt{\varpi}}\frac{e^{-(X-a(\chi))^2/2u^2 - \dot{a}^2(\chi)u^2/2}}{\sqrt{2\pi}}du$$

$$=\ 2\nu\left(\chi\right)e^{-\dot{a}^2(\chi)\varpi/2 - (X-a(\chi))\dot{a}(\chi)}M\left(\varpi, -\left(X - a\left(\chi\right)\right), \dot{a}\left(\chi\right)\right).$$

Example 12.1. *(Flat-boundary one-touch option). Consider a flat boundary one-touch option. It is clear that for such an option*

$$a\left(\chi\right) = 0, \qquad \eta\left(\chi\right) = e^{\lambda\chi},$$

where

$$\lambda = \begin{cases} \hat{r}^0 + \hat{\gamma}_-^2/2, & \text{(immediate rebate)} \\ \hat{\gamma}_-^2/2, & \text{(postponed rebate)} \end{cases}.$$

so that the pricing problem can be written as

$$U_\chi - \frac{1}{2}U_{XX} = 0,$$

$$U\left(0, X\right) = 0, \quad X \geq 0,$$

$$U\left(\chi, 0\right) = e^{\lambda\chi}, \quad U\left(\chi, X \to \infty\right) \to 0.$$

In the case in question the integral equations becomes trivial and yields

$$\nu\left(\chi\right) = \eta\left(\chi\right) = e^{\lambda\chi}.$$

The integral representation for the solution assumes the form

$$U\left(\chi, X\right) = \int_0^{\chi}\frac{Xe^{-X^2/2(\chi-\chi') + \lambda\chi'}}{\sqrt{2\pi(\chi - \chi')^3}}d\chi'.$$

This integral can be recognized as a convolution of two functions, namely,

$$\Phi_1\left(\chi, X\right) = \frac{Xe^{-X^2/2\chi}}{\sqrt{2\pi\chi^3}}, \quad \Phi_2\left(\chi\right) = e^{\lambda\chi}.$$

Accordingly, we can compute this integral via a combination of the direct and inverse Laplace transforms. The direct Laplace transform yields:

$$u(s,X) = \phi_1(s,X)\phi_2(s) = \frac{e^{-X\sqrt{2s}}}{s-\lambda}$$

$$= \frac{1}{2\sqrt{\lambda}}\left(\frac{e^{-X\sqrt{2s}}}{\sqrt{s}-\sqrt{\lambda}} - \frac{e^{-X\sqrt{2s}}}{\sqrt{s}+\sqrt{\lambda}}\right).$$

The inverse Laplace transform yields:

$$U(\chi,X) = \frac{1}{2\sqrt{\lambda}}\left(\sqrt{\lambda}e^{\lambda\chi-\sqrt{2\lambda}X}\operatorname{erfc}\left(\frac{X}{\sqrt{2\chi}} - \sqrt{\lambda\chi}\right)\right.$$

$$\left. +\sqrt{\lambda}e^{\lambda\chi+\sqrt{2\lambda}X}\operatorname{erfc}\left(\frac{X}{\sqrt{2\chi}} + \sqrt{\lambda\chi}\right)\right) \tag{12.15}$$

$$= e^{\lambda\chi-\sqrt{2\lambda}X}N\left(-\frac{X}{\sqrt{\chi}} + \sqrt{2\lambda\chi}\right) + e^{\lambda\chi+\sqrt{2\lambda}X}N\left(-\frac{X}{\sqrt{\chi}} - \sqrt{2\lambda\chi}\right).$$

Formula (12.15) can be used in order to check the accuracy of the general approximation. In financial variables this formula assumes the form

$$V(\chi,S) = \left(\frac{A}{S}\right)^{\hat{\gamma}_- + \sqrt{\hat{\gamma}_-^2 + 2\hat{r}^0}}\mathfrak{N}\left(\frac{\ln(A/S)}{\sqrt{\chi}} + \sqrt{\hat{\gamma}_-^2 + 2\hat{r}^0}\sqrt{\chi}\right) \tag{12.16}$$

$$+ \left(\frac{A}{S}\right)^{\hat{\gamma}_- - \sqrt{\hat{\gamma}_-^2 + 2\hat{r}^0}}\mathfrak{N}\left(\frac{\ln(A/S)}{\sqrt{\chi}} - \sqrt{\hat{\gamma}_-^2 + 2\hat{r}^0}\sqrt{\chi}\right),$$

(immediate rebate), and

$$V(\chi,S) = e^{-\hat{r}^0\chi}\left[\left(\frac{A}{S}\right)^{2\hat{\gamma}_-}\mathfrak{N}\left(\frac{\ln(A/S)}{\sqrt{\chi}} + \hat{\gamma}_-\sqrt{\chi}\right) + \mathfrak{N}\left(\frac{\ln(A/S)}{\sqrt{\chi}} - \hat{\gamma}_-\sqrt{\chi}\right)\right],$$

(postponed rebate).

Example 12.2. *(Exponential-boundary one-touch option). Consider now the one-touch option with an exponential boundary. The nondimensional boundary is straight,*

$$a(\chi) = \alpha\chi.$$

The pricing problem has the form (12.10) - (12.12). The integral equation for $\nu(\chi)$ assumes the form

$$\nu(\chi) + \alpha \int_0^\chi \frac{e^{-\alpha^2(\chi-\chi')/2}}{\sqrt{2\pi(\chi-\chi')}} \nu(\chi')d\chi' = e^{\mu\chi},$$

where

$$\mu = \lambda = \begin{cases} \hat{r}^0 + \hat{\gamma}_-^2/2 + \alpha\hat{\gamma}_-, & \text{(immediate rebate)} \\ \hat{\gamma}_-^2/2 + \alpha\hat{\gamma}_-, & \text{(postponed rebate)} \end{cases}$$

It is an equation in convolutions which can be solved via the Laplace transforms. The usual sequence of operations which are left to the reader as an exercise yields the following expression for the Laplace transformed density,

$$\nu(s) = \frac{\sqrt{s+\alpha^2/2}}{(s-\mu)\left(\sqrt{s+\alpha^2/2}+\alpha/\sqrt{2}\right)}.$$

Taking the inverse Laplace transform we obtain the following explicit expression for $\nu(\chi)$,

$$\nu(\chi) = e^{\mu\chi} + \frac{\alpha^2}{\mu}\left[e^{\mu x}\left(\frac{1}{2} - \sqrt{1+\frac{2\mu}{\alpha^2}}\,\mathfrak{N}\left(-\sqrt{(2\mu+\alpha^2)\chi}\right)\right)\right.$$
$$\left. - \left(\frac{1}{2} - \mathfrak{N}\left(-\sqrt{\alpha^2\chi}\right)\right)\right]$$

For the linear boundary we can represent $U(\chi, X)$ as a convolution:

$$U(\chi, X) = e^{-\alpha Y}\int_0^\chi \frac{(Y+\alpha(\chi-\chi'))e^{-Y^2/2(\chi'-\chi')-\alpha^2(\chi-\chi')/2}}{\sqrt{2\pi(\chi-\chi')^3}}\nu(\chi')\,d\chi'.$$

where $Y = X - \alpha\chi$. A calculation exploiting the Laplace transform (which is left to the reader as an exercise) yields

$$U(\chi, X) = e^{\mu\chi-\alpha Y}\left\{e^{\sqrt{2\mu+\alpha^2}Y}N\left(-\frac{Y}{\sqrt{\chi}}-\sqrt{(2\mu+\alpha^2)\chi}\right)\right. \quad (12.17)$$
$$\left. e^{-\sqrt{2\mu+\alpha^2}Y}N\left(-\frac{Y}{\sqrt{\chi}}+\sqrt{(2\mu+\alpha^2)\chi}\right)\right\}.$$

Formula (12.17) is useful for testing purposes.

It goes without saying that the method of heat potentials can be used to price a large variety of options in addition to one-touch options considered above. For the general single-barrier option we can write the nondimensional pricing equation in the form

$$U_\chi - \frac{1}{2}U_{XX} = 0, \quad X > a(\chi),$$

$$U(0,X) = u(X), \quad X \geq 0,$$

$$U(\chi, a(\chi)) = \eta(\chi).$$

To solve this problem via the method of heat potentials, we decompose $U(\chi, X)$ into the sum of the standard Black-Scholes price $U^{(1)}(\chi, X)$ which solves the heat equation in the entire space supplied with the initial condition

$$U^{(1)}(0,X) = \begin{cases} u(X), & X \geq 0 \\ 0, & X < 0 \end{cases},$$

and appropriate regularity conditions (we emphasize that $U^{(1)}$ does not satisfy the boundary condition at the barrier), and a correction $U^{(2)}(\chi, X)$ (which accounts for the boundary conditions). We consider $U^{(1)}$ as known and obtain the following problem for $U^{(2)}$:

$$U^{(2)}_\chi - \frac{1}{2}U^{(2)}_{XX} = 0, \tag{12.18}$$

$$U^{(2)}(0,X) = 0, \quad X \geq 0, \tag{12.19}$$

$$U^{(2)}(\chi, a(\chi)) = \eta^{(2)}(\chi), \quad U^{(2)}(\chi, X \to \infty) \to 0, \tag{12.20}$$

where

$$\eta^{(2)}(\chi) = \eta(\chi) - U^{(1)}(\chi, a(\chi)).$$

Now we are on a familiar ground since problem (12.18) - (12.20) is the pricing problem for the one-touch option with the generalized rebate.

We mention in passing that the so-called method of envelopes is a viable complement to the method of heat potentials but we do not describe it here due to the lack of space.

12.3   Static hedging

Our analysis of up-and-out calls and down-and-out puts suggests that their conventional delta-hedging is impossible because the corresponding Deltas become unlimited when the time to maturity tends to zero and the FXR approaches the barrier. Because of this fact, it is important to find alternative hedging schemes. One possibility is to hedge the barrier option statically by creating it synthetically from vanilla calls, puts, bets, and calendar spreads. We already encountered a few examples of static hedging in Section 12.2, equations (12.3), (12.6). In this section we study the general case.

To be concrete, we consider an up-and-out call. For simplicity we assume that $r^0 = r^1 = 0$. Since below we consider general time-dependent barriers, this assumption is not restrictive since we can always write the problem in forward terms. The corresponding pricing problem has the form

$$V_t + \frac{1}{2}\sigma^2 S^2 V_{SS} = 0, \quad 0 < S < B(t),$$

$$V(T,S) = (S-K)_+, \quad 0 < S < B(T),$$

$$V(t,0) = 0, \quad V(t,B(t)) = Q(t).$$

Here $B(t)$ is the (possibly time-dependent) barrier level, and $Q(t)$ is the rebate paid at maturity if the barrier is hit at time $t \leq T$.[2]

It is our intention to construct the static hedge for the above option. To this end we use Duhamel's principle described in Section 4.4. We introduce the function $W(t,S)$ defined for $0 \leq t \leq T$, $0 \leq S < \infty$ by the following formula[3]:

$$W(t,S) = V(t,S)\,\theta\,(B(t) - S) + Q(t)\,\theta\,(S - B(t)),$$

where θ is the Heaviside function. More precisely, the first term is understood as follows

$$V(t,S)\,\theta\,(B(t) - S) = \begin{cases} V(t,S), & 0 \leq S \leq B(t) \\ 0, & B(t) \leq S < \infty \end{cases}.$$

Thus, below the barrier W coincides with V, while above the barrier it has a constant value. Differentiation of this function yields:

$$W_t(t,S) = V_t(t,S)\,\theta\,(B(t) - S) + Q_t(t)\,\theta\,(S - B(t)),$$

---

[2] If need occurs, we can consider the general local volatility $\sigma(t,S)$.

[3] A similar function was used by Andersen *et al.* in their construction of the static hedge via the Meyer-Tanaka formula.

$$W_S(t, S) = V_S(t, S) \theta (B(t) - S),$$

$$W_{SS}(t, S) = V_{SS}(t, S) \theta (B(t) - S) - V_S(t, B(t)) \delta (B(t) - S).$$

We use these formulas to derive the following inhomogeneous pricing problem for W:

$$W_t + \frac{1}{2}\sigma^2 S^2 W_{SS} = \Upsilon^{(1)}(t, S) + \Upsilon^{(2)}(t, S),$$

$$W(T, S) = w(S),$$

$$W(t, 0) = 0, \quad W(t, S > B(t)) = Q(t).$$

Here

$$\Upsilon^{(1)}(t, S) = Q_t(t) \theta (S - B(t)),$$

$$\Upsilon^{(2)}(t, S) = -\frac{1}{2}\sigma^2 B^2(t) V_S(t, B(t)) \delta (B(t) - S),$$

$$w(S) = (S - K)_+ \theta (B(T) - S) + Q(T) \theta (S - B(T)).$$

We represent the solution of the above pricing problem in the form

$$W(t, S) = W^{(0)}(t, S) + W^{(1)}(t, S) + W^{(2)}(t, S),$$

where $W^{(0)}(t, S)$ solves the homogeneous pricing problem supplied with the final condition $w(S)$, while $W^{(\alpha)}(t, S), \alpha = 1, 2$, solve the inhomogeneous pricing problems supplied with the homogeneous final condition:

$$W_t^{(\alpha)} + \frac{1}{2}\sigma^2 S^2 W_{SS}^{(\alpha)} = \Upsilon^{(\alpha)}(t, S), \tag{12.21}$$

$$W^{(\alpha)}(T, S) = 0. \tag{12.22}$$

It is clear that

$$W^{(0)}(t, S) = \int_0^\infty p(t, S, T, S') w(S') dS',$$

where $p(t, S, t', S')$ is the t.p.d.f. associated with the stochastic process for S. As we know,

$$p(t, S, T, K) = C_{KK}(t, S, T, K),$$

so that

$$
\begin{aligned}
W^{(0)}(t, S) &= \int_0^\infty C_{KK}(t, S, T, S')\, w(S')\, dS' \\
&= \int_K^{B(T)} C_{KK}(t, S, T, S')\, (S' - K)\, dS' \\
&\quad + Q(T) \int_{B(T)}^\infty C_{KK}(t, S, T, S')\, dS' \\
&= (B(T) - K - Q(T))\, C_K(t, S, T, B(T)) \\
&\quad - C(t, S, T, B(T)) + C(t, S, T, B(T)).
\end{aligned}
$$

We solve problems (12.21), (12.22) via Duhamel's principle which yields:

$$
W^{(\alpha)}(t, S) = -\int_t^T \int_0^\infty p(t, S, t', S')\, \Upsilon^{(\alpha)}(t', S')\, dt'\, dS',
$$

A simple calculation yields

$$
\begin{aligned}
W^{(1)}(t, S) &= -\int_t^T \int_0^\infty p(t, S, t', S')\, Q_t(t')\, \theta(S' - B(t'))\, dt'\, dS' \\
&= -\int_t^T \int_0^\infty C_{KK}(t, S, t', S')\, Q_t(t')\, \theta(S' - B(t'))\, dt'\, dS' \\
&= \int_t^T C_K(t, S, t', B(t'))\, Q_t(t')\, dt',
\end{aligned}
$$

where we use the fact that the integral with respect to S' can be found explicitly. Similarly,

$$
W^{(2)}(t, S)
$$

$$
= \frac{1}{2} \int_t^T \int_0^\infty p(t, S, t', S') \sigma^2 B^2(t') V_S(t', B(t')) \delta(B(t') - S') dt' dS'
$$

$$
= \frac{1}{2} \int_t^T p(t, S, t', B(t')) \sigma^2 B^2(t') V_S(t', B(t')) dt'
$$

$$
= \frac{1}{2} \int_t^T C_{KK}(t, S, t', B(t')) \sigma^2 B^2(t') V_S(t', B(t')) dt'
$$

$$
= \int_t^T C_T(t, S, t', B(t')) V_S(t', B(t')) dt',
$$

where we use the Dupire formula (10.11) to perform the last transformation. Below the barrier we have

$$
V(t, S) = W(t, S) = W^{(0)}(t, S) + W^{(1)}(t, S) + W^{(2)}(t, S). \tag{12.23}
$$

Representation (12.23) is the one we are looking for since all three terms in the above sum are expressed as linear combinations of vanilla options with different strikes and maturities.

We emphasize that although the hedge which is constructed above is static, it is almost as unrealistic as the conventional dynamic hedge. The reason is that the weight $V_S(t', B(t')) \to \infty$ when $t' \to T$, so that we need to buy an infinite number of the corresponding calendar spreads.

12.4 Single-factor, double-barrier options

12.4.1 Introduction

Above we considered several representative single-barrier options. Their natural generalizations are double-barrier options which we study in this section. Such options attract buyers who are exposed to both upside and downside deviations of the FXR from its spot level and to speculators having specific views concerning the magnitude of these deviations. We consider the generic double-barrier, one-factor pricing problem and find its semi-analytic solution. The mathematical apparatus required for solving such a problem is relatively involved, however, once developed, it can be used with relative ease.

12.4.2 Formulation

For the generic single-factor, straight-double-barrier contract the pricing problem has the form

$$V_t + \frac{1}{2}\sigma^2 S^2 V_{SS} + r^{01} S V_S - r^0 V = 0, \tag{12.24}$$

$$V(T, S) = v(S), \tag{12.25}$$

$$V(t, A) = P(t), \qquad V(t, B) = Q(t), \tag{12.26}$$

where A, B are barrier levels, $\bar{S}$ is a representative FXR level such that $A < \bar{S} < B$, $v(S) = \bar{S}v(S/\bar{S})$ is the terminal payoff, and P, Q are rebates paid when the corresponding barrier is hit. Problem (12.24) - (12.26) describes double-barrier calls with no rebate

$$v(S) = (S - K)_+, \qquad P(t) = Q(t) = 0,$$

double-no-touch options

$$v(S) = 1, \qquad P(t) = Q(t) = 0,$$

double-one-touch options

$$v(S) = 0, \qquad P(t) = P, Q(t) = Q,$$

and many other options having double-barrier features.

We apply the standard change of independent and dependent variables (9.12) and obtain the following pricing problem for $U(\chi, X)$:

$$U_\chi - \frac{1}{2}U_{XX} = 0, \tag{12.27}$$

$$U(0, X) = e^{\hat{\gamma} - X}v(X) = u(X), \tag{12.28}$$

$$U(\chi, a) = \tilde{P}(\chi), \qquad U(\chi, b) = \tilde{Q}(\chi), \tag{12.29}$$

where

$$
\begin{aligned}
U(\chi, X) &= e^{\left(\hat{r}^0 + \hat{\gamma}_-^2/2\right)x + \hat{\gamma}_- X} V(t, S)/\bar{S}, \\
a &= \log(A/\bar{S}) < 0, \qquad b = \log(B/\bar{S}) > 0, \\
\tilde{P}(\chi) &= e^{\left(\hat{r}^0 + \hat{\gamma}_-^2/2\right)x} \left(A/\bar{S}\right)^{\hat{\gamma}_-} P\left(T - \sigma^2 x\right)/\bar{S}, \\
\tilde{Q}(\chi) &= e^{\left(\hat{r}^0 + \hat{\gamma}_-^2/2\right)x} \left(B/\bar{S}\right)^{\hat{\gamma}_-} P\left(T - \sigma^2 x\right)/\bar{S}.
\end{aligned}
$$

12.4.3   The pricing problem without rebates

At first we concentrate on the problem with no rebates and assume that

$$P(\chi) = Q(\chi) = 0.$$

The first thing we need to do it to construct Green's function $G(\chi, X, X')$ for problem (12.27) - (12.29) which solves equation (12.27) supplied with the initial condition

$$G(0, X, X') = \delta(X - X'),$$

and zero boundary conditions. Once this task is accomplished, any other option can be priced by a simple integration. Green's function can be constructed in two complementary ways, namely, via the methods of images and Fourier series.

We start with the method of images. The idea is to construct Green's function for the barrier problem $G(\chi, X, X')$ as a linear combination of Green's functions (heat kernels) for the no-barrier problem $G_H(\chi, X, X_n'^{\pm})$ with sources $X_n'^+$ and sinks $X_n'^-$ chosen in such a way that this combination vanishes at the barriers. We choose sources at $X_n'^+ = X - 2n(b-a)$ and sinks at $X_n'^- = -X' - 2n(b-a) + 2a$, and represent Green's function in the form

$$G(\chi, X, X') = \sum_{n=-\infty}^{\infty} \left\{ G(\chi, X, X_n'^+) - G(\chi, X, X_n'^-) \right\} \qquad (12.30)$$

$$= \sum_{n=-\infty}^{\infty} \left\{ \frac{e^{-\left(X-X'+2n(b-a)\right)^2/2\chi}}{\sqrt{2\pi\chi}} - \frac{e^{-\left(X+X'+2n(b-a)-2a\right)^2/2\chi}}{\sqrt{2\pi\chi}} \right\},$$

Taking the convolution of the Green's function with the initial data we obtain the solution of problem (12.27) - (12.29):

$$U(\chi, X) = \int_a^b G(\chi, X, X')u(X')\,dX' \qquad (12.31)$$

$$= \sum_{n=-\infty}^{\infty} \int_a^b \left\{ \frac{e^{-\left(X-X'+2n(b-a)\right)^2/2\chi}}{\sqrt{2\pi\chi}} - \frac{e^{-\left(X+X'+2n(b-a)-2a\right)^2/2\chi}}{\sqrt{2\pi\chi}} \right\}$$

$$\times u(X')\,dX'.$$

The number of terms we need to keep in order to get a good approximation for $U(\chi, X)$ depends on the time to maturity χ and distance between barriers

$b - a$. Very few terms are needed when χ is small and (or) $b - a$ is large. As χ increases, more and more terms have to be computed.

In general, representation (12.30) obtained via the method of images is less convenient than representation obtained via the method of Fourier series which we now describe. This method is a version of the eigenfunction expansion method discussed in Section 4.10. The corresponding eigenfunction problem has the form

$$-\frac{1}{2}g_{XX}(X) = \lambda g(X),$$

$$g(a) = g(b) = 0.$$

It has a nonzero solution if and only if

$$\lambda = \lambda_n = \frac{1}{2}k_n^2,$$

where

$$k_n = \frac{\pi n}{b - a}, \qquad n = 1, 2, \dots .$$

This solution has the form

$$g_n(X) = \psi_n \sin(k_n(X - a)),$$

where ψ_n is an arbitrary constant. We leave it to the reader to check that functions g_n are orthogonal on the interval (a, b);

$$\int_a^b g_m(X) g_n(X) dX = \begin{cases} 0, & m \neq n \\ \psi_n^2(b - a)/2, & m = n \end{cases}.$$

The corresponding particular solutions of the time-dependent problem have the form

$$G_n(\chi, X) = \psi_n e^{-k_n^2 \chi/2} \sin(k_n(X - a)),$$

its general solution can be represented as a linear combination of these particular solutions:

$$U(\chi, X) = \sum_{n=1}^{\infty} e^{-k_n^2 \chi/2} \psi_n \sin(k_n(X - a)).$$

The coefficients ψ_n are determined by the relation

$$u(X) = \sum_{n=1}^{\infty} \psi_n \sin(k_n(X-a)).$$

Orthogonality conditions yield

$$\psi_n = \frac{2 \int_a^b u(X) \sin(k_n(X-a)) \, dX}{(b-a)}.$$

For Green's function the initial condition is $\delta(X-X')$, so that

$$\psi_n = \frac{2 \sin(k_n(X'-a))}{(b-a)}.$$

Thus, we can represent the Green's function for problem (12.27) - (12.29) in the form

$$G(\chi, X, X') = \frac{2}{b-a} \sum_{n=1}^{\infty} e^{-k_n^2 \chi/2} \sin(k_n(X'-a)) \sin(k_n(X-a)). \quad (12.32)$$

Taking the convolution of the Green's function with the initial data, we write the solution of the pricing problem in the form

$$U(\chi, X) = \int_a^b G(\chi, X, X') u(X') \, dX' \quad (12.33)$$

$$= \frac{2}{b-a} \sum_{n=1}^{\infty} e^{-k_n^2 \chi/2} \left(\int_a^b \sin(k_n(X'-a)) u(X') \, dX' \right) \sin(k_n(X-a)).$$

The convergence properties of series (12.32) complement convergence properties of series (12.30). Namely, in converges very rapidly when either χ is large or $(b-a)$ is small and slowly otherwise. For practical applications the Fourier series method is by far superior compared to the method of images. The Fourier series expansion should be applied when $b-a$ is relatively small, while χ is relatively large; the image expansion should be used in the opposite case. Assuming that $b-a \sim 1$ we should use the Fourier series expansion until $\chi \sim 0.1$ say (roughly a few days to maturity) and switch to the image expansion afterwards.

Below we show how to use general expressions (12.31), (12.33) in order to price particular types of options.

12.4.4 Pricing of no-rebate calls and puts and double-no-touch options

We start with a call. The corresponding payoff is

$$v(S) = (S - K)_+,$$

or, equivalently,

$$u(X) = \left(e^{\hat{\gamma}_+ X} - e^{\hat{\gamma}_- X}\right)_+.$$

To price a call via the method of images we use formula (12.31):

$$U^{(C)}(\chi, X) = \int_0^b G(\chi, X, X') \left(e^{\hat{\gamma}_+ X'} - e^{\hat{\gamma}_- X'}\right) dX'$$

$$= \sum_{n=-\infty}^{\infty} \left\{K_+(\chi, X_n) - K_-(\chi, X_n) - L_+(\chi, X_n) + L_-(\chi, X_n)\right\},$$

where $X_n = X + 2n(b - a)$, and

$$K_\pm(\chi, X) = \int_0^b \frac{e^{-(X-X')^2/2\chi + \hat{\gamma}_\pm X'}}{\sqrt{2\pi\chi}} dX',$$

$$L_\pm(\chi, X) = \int_0^b \frac{e^{-(X+X'-2a)^2/2\chi + \hat{\gamma}_\pm X'}}{\sqrt{2\pi\chi}} dX' = K_\pm(\chi, 2a - X).$$

A simple calculation yields

$$K_\pm(\chi, X)$$

$$= e^{\hat{\gamma}_\pm^2 \chi/2 + \hat{\gamma}_\pm X} \left\{N\left(\frac{X}{\sqrt{\chi}} + \hat{\gamma}_\pm \sqrt{\chi}\right) - N\left(\frac{X - b}{\sqrt{\chi}} + \hat{\gamma}_\pm \sqrt{\chi}\right)\right\}$$

$$= M(\chi, X_n, \hat{\gamma}_+) - e^{\hat{\gamma}_+ b} M(\tau, X - b, \hat{\gamma}_+).$$

Accordingly, we can represent $U^{(C)}(\chi, X)$ as

$$U^{(C)}(\chi, X) = \sum_{n=-\infty}^{\infty} U_n^{(C)}(\chi, X),$$

where

$$
\begin{aligned}
U_n^{(C)}(\chi, X) &= M\left(\chi, X_n, \hat{\gamma}_+\right) - e^{\hat{\gamma}+b} M\left(\chi, X_n - b, \hat{\gamma}_+\right) \\
&\quad - M\left(\chi, X_n, \hat{\gamma}_-\right) + e^{\hat{\gamma}-b} M\left(\chi, X_n - b, \hat{\gamma}_-\right) \\
&\quad - M\left(\chi, 2a - X_n, \hat{\gamma}_+\right) + e^{\hat{\gamma}+b} M\left(\chi, 2a - b - X_n, \hat{\gamma}_+\right) \\
&\quad + M\left(\chi, 2a - X_n, \hat{\gamma}_-\right) - e^{\hat{\gamma}-b} M\left(\chi, 2a - b - X_n, \hat{\gamma}_-\right),
\end{aligned}
$$

The corresponding $V^{(C)}(\tau, S)$ has the form

$$
V^{(C)}(\tau, S) = e^{-r^0\tau} \sum_{n=-\infty}^{\infty} V_n^{(C)}(\tau, S), \tag{12.34}
$$

where

$$
\begin{aligned}
V_n^{(C)}(\tau, S) &= F q^{n\hat{\gamma}_+} \left[N\left(\frac{\ln(S_n/K) + \hat{\gamma}_+\sigma^2}{\sigma\sqrt{\tau}}\right) - N\left(\frac{\ln(S_n/B) + \hat{\gamma}_+\sigma^2}{\sigma\sqrt{\tau}}\right) \right] \\
&\quad - K q^{n\hat{\gamma}_-} \left[N\left(\frac{\ln(S_n/K) + \hat{\gamma}_-\sigma^2\tau}{\sigma\sqrt{\tau}}\right) - N\left(\frac{\ln(S_n/B) + \hat{\gamma}_-\sigma^2\tau}{\sigma\sqrt{\tau}}\right) \right] \\
&\quad - F\left(A/S\right)^{2\hat{\gamma}_+} q^{n\hat{\gamma}_+} \left[N\left(\frac{\ln\left(A^2/S_n K\right) + \hat{\gamma}_+\sigma^2}{\sigma\sqrt{\tau}}\right) - N\left(\frac{\ln\left(A^2/S_n B\right) + \hat{\gamma}_+\sigma^2}{\sigma\sqrt{\tau}}\right) \right] \\
&\quad + K\left(A/S\right)^{2\hat{\gamma}_-} q^{n\hat{\gamma}_-} \left[N\left(\frac{\ln\left(A^2/S_n K\right) + \hat{\gamma}_-\sigma^2\tau}{\sigma\sqrt{\tau}}\right) - N\left(\frac{\ln\left(A^2/S_n B\right) + \hat{\gamma}_-\sigma^2\tau}{\sigma\sqrt{\tau}}\right) \right],
\end{aligned}
$$

where $q = (B/A)^2$, and $S_n = S q^n$.

The price of a double-barrier put has a similar form

$$
V^{(P)}(\tau, S) = e^{-r^0\tau} \sum_{n=-\infty}^{\infty} V_n^{(P)}(\tau, S), \tag{12.35}
$$

where

$$
\begin{aligned}
V_n^{(P)}(\tau, S) &= F q^{n\hat{\gamma}_+} \left[N\left(\frac{\ln(S_n/K) + \hat{\gamma}_+\sigma^2}{\sigma\sqrt{\tau}}\right) - N\left(\frac{\ln(S_n/A) + \hat{\gamma}_+\sigma^2}{\sigma\sqrt{\tau}}\right) \right] \\
&\quad - K q^{n\hat{\gamma}_-} \left[N\left(\frac{\ln(S_n/K) + \hat{\gamma}_-\sigma^2\tau}{\sigma\sqrt{\tau}}\right) - N\left(\frac{\ln(S_n/A) + \hat{\gamma}_-\sigma^2\tau}{\sigma\sqrt{\tau}}\right) \right] \\
&\quad - F\left(A/S\right)^{2\hat{\gamma}_+} q^{n\hat{\gamma}_+} \left[N\left(\frac{\ln\left(A^2/S_n K\right) + \hat{\gamma}_+\sigma^2}{\sigma\sqrt{\tau}}\right) - N\left(\frac{\ln\left(A/S_n\right) + \hat{\gamma}_+\sigma^2}{\sigma\sqrt{\tau}}\right) \right] \\
&\quad + K\left(A/S\right)^{2\hat{\gamma}_-} q^{n\hat{\gamma}_-} \left[N\left(\frac{\ln\left(A^2/S_n K\right) + \hat{\gamma}_-\sigma^2\tau}{\sigma\sqrt{\tau}}\right) - N\left(\frac{\ln\left(A/S_n\right) + \hat{\gamma}_-\sigma^2\tau}{\sigma\sqrt{\tau}}\right) \right].
\end{aligned}
$$

Finally, the price of the double-no-touch option which pays the buyer a dollar provided that FXR never crosses the barriers, can be written as

$$V^{(DNT)}(\tau, S) = e^{-r^0\tau} \sum_{n=-\infty}^{\infty} V_n^{(DNT)}(\tau, S), \qquad (12.36)$$

where

$$
\begin{aligned}
V_n^{(DNT)}(\tau, S) &= q^{n\hat{\gamma}_-} \left[N\left(\frac{\ln(S_n/A) + \hat{\gamma}_- \sigma^2 \tau}{\sigma\sqrt{\tau}}\right) - N\left(\frac{\ln(S_n/B) + \hat{\gamma}_- \sigma^2 \tau}{\sigma\sqrt{\tau}}\right) \right] \\
&\quad - (A/S)^{2\hat{\gamma}_-} q^{n\hat{\gamma}_-} \left[N\left(\frac{\ln(A/S_n) + \hat{\gamma}_- \sigma^2 \tau}{\sigma\sqrt{\tau}}\right) - N\left(\frac{\ln(A^2/S_n B) + \hat{\gamma}_- \sigma^2 \tau}{\sigma\sqrt{\tau}}\right) \right].
\end{aligned}
$$

The prices of bets and calls and puts with strikes between the barriers can be combined in order to price calls with strikes below the lower barrier or puts with strikes above the upper barrier (see below).

Terms in expansions (12.34), (12.35), and (12.36) are rather complex and it is necessary to sum a lot of them to get the answer with satisfactory accuracy. Fortunately, the Fourier series method provides an elegant and refreshing alternative. Taking the convolution of Green's function (12.32) with the initial data, we write the solution of the call pricing problem in the form

$$
\begin{aligned}
U^{(C)}(\chi, X) &= \int_0^b G(\chi, X, X') \left(e^{\hat{\gamma}_+ X'} - e^{\hat{\gamma}_- X'} \right) dX' \\
&= \frac{2}{b-a} \sum_{n=1}^{\infty} e^{-k_n^2 \chi/2} \psi_n^{(C)} \sin[k_n(X - a)],
\end{aligned}
$$

where

$$\psi_n^{(C)} = \psi_{n+}^{(C)} - \psi_{n-}^{(C)},$$

$$\psi_{n\pm}^{(C)} = \int_0^b e^{\hat{\gamma}_\pm X'} \sin[k_n(X' - a)] dX'.$$

Evaluation of the integrals $\psi_{n\pm}^{(C)}$ by parts yields

$$\psi_{n\pm}^{(C)} = \frac{(-1)^{n+1} k_n e^{\hat{\gamma}_\pm b} + k_n \cos(k_n a) + \hat{\gamma}_\pm \sin(k_n a)}{\hat{\gamma}_\pm^2 + k_n^2}.$$

Returning back to the financial variables, we write $V^{(C)}(\tau, S)$ as

$$V^{(C)}(\tau, S) = \frac{2Ke^{-(\hat{r}^0+\hat{\gamma}_-^2/2)\sigma^2\tau}(K/S)^{\hat{\gamma}_-}}{\ln(B/A)} \sum_{n=1}^{\infty} \psi_n^{(C)} e^{-k_n^2\sigma^2\tau/2} \sin[k_n \ln(S/A)].$$

Puts can be valuated in a similar way,

$$V^{(P)}(\tau, S) = \frac{2Ke^{-(\hat{r}^0+\hat{\gamma}_-^2/2)\sigma^2\tau}(K/S)^{\hat{\gamma}_-}}{\ln(B/A)} \sum_{n=1}^{\infty} \psi_n^{(P)} e^{-k_n^2\sigma^2\tau/2} \sin[k_n \ln(S/A)],$$

where

$$\psi_n^{(P)} = \psi_{n+}^{(P)} - \psi_{n-}^{(P)},$$

$$\psi_{n\pm}^{(P)} = \frac{-k_n e^{\hat{\gamma}_+ + a} + k_n \cos(k_n a) + \hat{\gamma}_\pm \sin(k_n a)}{\hat{\gamma}_\pm^2 + k_n^2}.$$

We also can valuate double-no-touches. Only the expression for ψ_n has to be changed. The corresponding ψ_n have the form

$$\psi_n^{(DNT)} = \frac{k_n\left((-1)^{n+1}e^{\hat{\gamma}_- b} + e^{\hat{\gamma}_- a}\right)}{\hat{\gamma}_-^2 + k_n^2}. \tag{12.37}$$

Accordingly, the value of a double-no-touch option can be written as

$$V^{(DNT)}(\tau, S) = \frac{2e^{-(\hat{r}^0+\hat{\gamma}_-^2/2)\sigma^2\tau}(B/S)^{\hat{\gamma}_-}}{\ln(B/A)} \sum_{n=1}^{\infty} \psi_n^{(DNT)} e^{-k_n^2\sigma^2\tau/2} \sin[k_n \ln(S/A)].$$

Typical profiles $V^{(C)}(\tau, S)$ and $V^{(DNT)}(\tau, S)$ are shown in Figures 12.3 and 12.4, respectively.

It is clear that the standard put-call parity is not valid for double-barrier options. However, we can prove the following generalized formula

$$V^{(C)}(\tau, S, K) - V^{(P)}(\tau, S, K) = V^{(C)}(\tau, S, A) + (A - K)V^{(DNT)}(\tau, S).$$

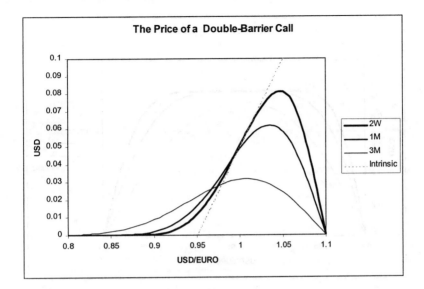

Figure 12.3: The price of a typical double-barrier call as a function of the spot FXR for three representative maturities. The relevant parameters are the same as in Figure 12.1. The lower and upper barriers are at $A = 0.80$ and $B = 1.10$.

At the same time, put-call symmetry does hold for such options. The relation between puts and calls has the form

$$
\begin{aligned}
& V^{(P,C)}(\tau, S, K, \sigma, r^0, r^1; A, B) \\
&= \frac{S}{K} V^{(C,P)}(\tau, \frac{K^2}{S}, K, \sigma, r^1, r^0; \frac{K^2}{B}, \frac{K^2}{A}) \\
&= V^{(C,P)}(\tau, K, S, \sigma, r^1, r^0; \frac{K^2}{B}, \frac{K^2}{A}).
\end{aligned}
$$

A more general relation can be established as well

$$
\begin{aligned}
& V^{(P,C)}\left(\tau, K^{1-\nu}S^{\nu}, K, \sigma, r^0, r^1; A_{-\nu}, B_{-\nu}\right) \\
&= V^{(C,P)}\left(\tau, K, K^{1-\nu}S^{\nu}, \sigma, \bar{r}^0_{\nu}, \bar{r}^1_{\nu}; A_{\nu}, B_{\nu}\right),
\end{aligned}
$$

where ν is an arbitrary power, and

$$
\left\{ \begin{array}{c} A_{\pm\nu} \\ B_{\pm\nu} \end{array} \right\} = \left\{ \begin{array}{c} \min \\ \max \end{array} \right\} \left\{ K^{1\pm1/\nu} A^{\mp1/\nu}, K^{1\pm1/\nu} B^{\mp1/\nu} \right\}, \tag{12.38}
$$

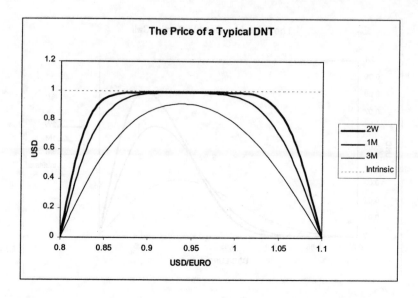

Figure 12.4: The price of a typical DNT as a function of the spot FXR for three representative maturities. The relevant parameters are the same as in Figure 12.1. The lower and upper barriers are at $A = 0.80$ and $B = 1.10$.

$$\bar{r}_\nu^0 = (1 - \nu) r^0 + \nu r^1 + \nu (1 - \nu) \sigma^2/2,$$
$$\bar{r}_\nu^1 = (2 - \nu) r^0 - (1 - \nu) r^1 - (2 - \nu) (1 - \nu) \sigma^2/2. \tag{12.39}$$

So far we have assumed that $A < K < B$. It is clear that

$$V^{(C)}(\tau, S, K) = \begin{cases} V^{(C)}(\tau, S, A) + (A - K) V^{(DNT)}(\tau, S), & \text{if } K < A \\ V^{(C)}(\tau, S, K) = 0, & \text{if } K > B \end{cases},$$
$$\tag{12.40}$$

$$V^{(P)}(\tau, S, K) = \begin{cases} V^{(P)}(\tau, S, B) + (K - B) V^{(DNT)}(\tau, S), & \text{if } K > B \\ V^{(P)}(\tau, S, K) = 0, & \text{if } K < A \end{cases}.$$
$$\tag{12.41}$$

12.4.5 Pricing of calls and puts with rebate

Consider now options with rebate. For both calls and puts the price has the usual component plus an additional rebate premium. To find this premium we have to solve the following problem

$$V_\tau - \frac{1}{2}\sigma^2 S^2 V_{SS} - r^{01} S V_S + r^0 V = 0,$$

$$V(0, S) = 0,$$

$$V(\tau, A) = e^{-\varrho\tau} P, \qquad V(\tau, B) = e^{-\varrho\tau} Q.$$

Here P, Q are rebates paid if the FXR crosses the lower and upper barriers, respectively, and ϱ is parameter which shows if the corresponding payment occurs right away $(\varrho = 0)$ or is postponed until maturity of the option $(\varrho = r^0)$. We represent the solution of this problem in the form

$$V(\tau, S) = \tilde{V}(\tau, S) + e^{-\varrho\tau}\left(\frac{Q-P}{B-A}S + \frac{PB-QA}{B-A}\right),$$

where $\tilde{V}(\tau, S)$ solves the problem

$$\tilde{V}_\tau - \frac{1}{2}\sigma^2 S^2 \tilde{V}_{SS} - r^{01} S \tilde{V}_S + r^0 \tilde{V}$$

$$= e^{-\varrho\tau}\left((r^1 + \varrho)\frac{Q-P}{B-A}S + (-r^0 + \varrho)\frac{PB-QA}{B-A}\right),$$

$$\tilde{V}(0, S) = -\left(\frac{Q-P}{B-A}S + \frac{PB-QA}{B-A}\right),$$

$$\tilde{V}(\tau, A) = 0, \qquad \tilde{V}(\tau, B) = 0.$$

By the same token as before we can write $\tilde{V}$ as

$$V(\tau, S) = \frac{2Ae^{-(\hat{r}^0 + \hat{\gamma}_-^2/2)\sigma^2\tau}(A/S)^{\hat{\gamma}_-}}{\ln(B/A)} \sum_{n=1}^{\infty} \psi_n\left(\sigma^2\tau\right)\sin[k_n \ln(S/A)].$$

Here $\psi_n(\chi)$ satisfy the following ODE

$$\frac{d\psi_n}{d\chi} + \frac{1}{2}k_n^2 \psi_n = e^{(\hat{r}^0 + \hat{\gamma}_-^2/2 - \hat{\varrho})\chi}$$

$$\times \left[(\hat{r}^1 + \hat{\varrho})\frac{Q-P}{B-A}\psi_{n+} - (\hat{r}^0 - \hat{\varrho})\frac{PB-QA}{A(B-A)}\psi_{n-}\right],$$

$$\psi_n(0) = -\left(\frac{Q-P}{B-A}\psi_{n+} + \frac{PB-QA}{A(B-A)}\psi_{n-}\right),$$

where $\hat{\varrho} = \varrho/\sigma^2$, and

$$\psi_{n\pm} = \frac{k_n\left((-1)^{n+1}e^{\hat{\gamma}_\pm \ln(B/A)} + 1\right)}{\hat{\gamma}_\pm^2 + k_n^2}.$$

Accordingly

$$\psi_n(\chi) = \frac{e^{\left(\hat{r}^0 + \hat{\gamma}_-^2/2 - \hat{\varrho}\right)\chi} - e^{-k_n^2\chi/2}}{\hat{r}^0 + \hat{\gamma}_-^2/2 - \hat{\varrho} + k_n^2/2}$$
$$\times \left[\left(\hat{r}^1 + \hat{\varrho}\right)\frac{Q-P}{B-A}\psi_{n+} - \left(\hat{r}^0 - \hat{\varrho}\right)\frac{PB-QA}{A(B-A)}\psi_{n-}\right]$$
$$-e^{-k_n^2\chi/2}\left(\frac{Q-P}{B-A}\psi_{n+} + \frac{PB-QA}{A(B-A)}\psi_{n-}\right).$$

The method of heat potentials (which can be generalized to the double-barrier case) also can be used for pricing options with rebates. We do not dwell on this possibility for the sake of brevity.

12.5 Deviations from the Black-Scholes paradigm

12.5.1 Introduction

We already know that in real markets some of the key Black-Scholes assumptions do not hold. When these assumptions are modified in order to account for market irregularities, the pricing of both vanilla and exotic options becomes considerably more involved. In Chapter 10 we described pricing and hedging of vanilla options. Here we briefly discuss pricing and hedging of barrier options. We emphasize that the impact of non-Black-Scholes effects on prices of barrier options can be tremendous (much greater than for plain vanilla options) and should never be underestimated.

12.5.2 Barrier options in the presence of the term structure of volatility

It was shown above that for vanilla options the presence of the term structure of volatility and interest rates does not pose a serious problem. By switching from spot to forward rates and prices, and rescaling the time to maturity

$$t \rightarrow \chi = \int_t^T \sigma^2(t') \, dt', \tag{12.42}$$

$$S_t \rightarrow F_{t,T} = e^{\int_t^T r^{01}(t')dt'} S_t,$$

$$C_t \rightarrow \check{C}_{t,T} = e^{\int_t^T r^0(t')dt'} C_t,$$

we obtain the pricing equation with time-independent coefficients:

$$\check{C}_\chi - \frac{1}{2} F^2 \check{C}_{FF} = 0,$$

which can be further reduced to the standard heat equation.

Unfortunately, the above transformations do not work too well for barrier options. The reason is simple: the switch $S \rightarrow F$ transforms initially flat barriers into curvilinear ones. Consider, for example, the simplest up-and-out call knocking out when the spot FXR hits the barrier level B. Transformation (12.42) yields the following pricing problem:

$$\check{C}_\chi - \frac{1}{2} F^2 \check{C}_{FF} = 0,$$

$$\check{C}(0, K) = (F - K)_+,$$

$$\check{C}(\chi, 0) = \check{C}(\chi, B(\chi)) = 0,$$

where

$$B(\chi) = e^{\int_{t(\chi)}^T r^{01}(t')dt'} B.$$

The logarithmic transformation

$$\chi \rightarrow \chi, \quad F \rightarrow X = \ln(F/K), \quad \check{C} \rightarrow U = e^{\chi/8 - X/2} \check{C}/K,$$

yields the standard heat equation with curvilinear (moving) boundary

$$U_\chi - \frac{1}{2} U_{XX} = 0,$$

$$U(0, X) = \left(e^{X/2} - e^{-X/2} \right)_+,$$

$$U(\chi, 0) = U(\chi, b(\chi)) = 0,$$

where

$$b(\chi) = \int_{t(\chi)}^{T} r^{01}(t') dt' + \ln\left(\frac{B}{K}\right).$$

As we know, this problem is rather difficult to solve. Whether we use the heat potential method, or apply numerical methods based on finite differences, or finite elements, we have to overcome considerable obstacles. Accordingly, in the presence of the term structure accurate pricing of barrier options requires a lot of effort. Very seldom it can be done analytically. When this problem is solved numerically, it is advantageous not to switch to forwards and solve the problem with time-dependent coefficients and flat barriers.

However, there is at least one case when pricing barrier options with term structure is straightforward. Namely, the pricing problems are easily solvable when the barrier level is imposed on forward rather than spot FXRs. (Unfortunately, such problems are rarely interesting in practice.) Then transformations (12.42) make the originally curvilinear barrier flat so that the valuation problem is straightforward.

12.5.3   Barrier options in the presence of constant elasticity of variance

As we know, the interest rate differential does not complicate pricing of vanilla options in the CEV framework, however, it does make pricing of barrier options rather involved. In order to avoid unnecessary complications and concentrate on the essence of the problem at hand, initially we assume that the market is symmetric, i.e., $r^0 = r^1$, $r^{01} = 0$.

We consider the following pricing problem for up-and-out calls in the CEV framework:

$$V_t + \frac{1}{2}\sigma^2 \left(\frac{S}{\bar{S}}\right)^{-2\beta} S^2 V_{SS} - r^0 V = 0,$$

$$V(T, S) = (S - K)_+,$$

$$V(t, S \to 0) \to 0, \quad V(t, B) = 0.$$

As we know, the power β, characterizes the elasticity of variance of the random process S_t. To be concrete, we assume that $0 \le \beta \le 1$. For $\beta = 0$ and

$\beta = 1$ we deal with the standard geometric and arithmetic Brownian motions, respectively.

In order to reduce this pricing problem to the Bessel form we introduce the following nondimensional variables:

$$\chi = \sigma^2 (T - t), \quad \xi = \frac{S}{\bar{S}}, \quad U = \frac{e^{r^0(T-t)}V}{\bar{S}}.$$

In these variables the pricing problem assumes the form

$$U_\chi - \frac{1}{2}\xi^{2-2\beta}U_{\xi\xi} = 0,$$

$$U(0, \xi) = (\xi - \kappa)_+,$$

$$U(\chi, \xi \to 0) \to 0, \quad U(\chi, b) = 0,$$

where $\kappa = K/\bar{S}$, $b = B/K > 1$. Next, we introduce $X = \xi^\beta/\beta$ and obtain the Lommel parabolic equation

$$U_\chi - \frac{1}{2}U_{XX} - \frac{(1 - 1/\beta)}{2X}U_X = 0,$$

$$U(0, X) = \left((\beta X)^{1/\beta} - \kappa\right)_+,$$

$$U(\chi, X \to 0) \to 0, \quad U\left(\chi, b^\beta/\beta\right) = 0.$$

Finally, the transformation

$$W(\chi, X) = X^{-1/2\beta}U(\chi, X)$$

yields the Bessel parabolic equation for $W(\chi, X)$:

$$W_\chi - \frac{1}{2}\left(W_{XX} + \frac{1}{X}W_X - \frac{1}{4\beta^2 X^2}W\right) = 0, \tag{12.43}$$

$$W(0, X) = \left((\beta X)^{1/2\beta} - \kappa(\beta X)^{-1/2\beta}\right)_+, \tag{12.44}$$

$$W\left(\chi, X \to 0\right) \to 0, \quad W\left(\chi, b^\beta/\beta\right) = 0. \tag{12.45}$$

The order of the relevant Bessel equations is $\nu = 1/2\beta$.

We solve the pricing problem via the Fourier-Bessel series method. First, we look for separable solutions of the boundary value problem:

$$W_n\left(\chi, X\right) = e^{-\lambda_n \chi/2} W_n\left(X\right),$$

and write the spectral problem for $W_n\left(X\right)$ as follows:

$$W_{n,XX}\left(X\right) + \frac{1}{X} W_{n,X}\left(X\right) + \left(\lambda_n - \frac{\nu^2}{X^2}\right) W_n\left(X\right) = 0, \tag{12.46}$$

$$W_n\left(X \to 0\right) \to 0, \quad W_n\left(b^\beta/\beta\right) = 0. \tag{12.47}$$

We notice that equation (12.46) can be written in a symmetric form:

$$\left(X W_{n,X}\left(X\right)\right)_X - \frac{\nu^2}{X} W_n\left(X\right) + \lambda_n X W_n\left(X\right) = 0,$$

so that the spectrum of problem (12.46), (12.47) is real (and positive). The regular solution of the above equation has the form

$$W_n\left(X\right) = J_\nu\left(\sqrt{\lambda_n} X\right),$$

where J_ν is the Bessel function of the first kind of order ν. This solution automatically satisfies the boundary condition at $X = 0$, however, in order to satisfy the boundary condition at $X = b^\beta/\beta$ we have to choose λ_n in the form

$$\lambda_n = \frac{\beta^2 \theta_{\nu,n}^2}{b^{2\beta}},$$

where $\theta_{\nu,n}$ is the nth root of the Bessel function J_ν. Thus,

$$W_n\left(X\right) = J_\nu\left(\frac{\beta \theta_{\nu,n} X}{b^\beta}\right).$$

We leave it to the reader to verify that these functions are orthogonal with weight X on the interval $\left(0, b^\beta/\beta\right)$, i.e.,

$$\int_0^{b^\beta/\beta} W_m\left(X\right) W_n\left(X\right) X dX = \begin{cases} 0, & \text{if} \quad m \neq n \\ J_{\nu+1}^2\left(\theta_{\nu,n}\right) b^{2\beta}/2\beta^2, & \text{if} \quad m = n \end{cases}.$$

The solution of the pricing problem (12.43) - (12.45) can be expanded into the Fourier-Bessel series of the form

$$W(\chi, X) = \sum_{n=1}^{\infty} e^{-\beta^2 \theta_{\nu,n}^2 X/2b^{2\beta}} \psi_n J_\nu \left(\frac{\beta \theta_{\nu,n} X}{b^\beta} \right),$$

where the coefficients ψ_n are defined as follows:

$$
\begin{aligned}
\psi_n &= \frac{2\beta^2}{J_{\nu+1}^2(\theta_{\nu,n}) b^{2\beta}} \int_0^{b^\beta/\beta} \left((\beta X)^\nu - \kappa (\beta X)^{-\nu} \right)_+ J_\nu \left(\frac{\beta \theta_{\nu,n} X}{b^\beta} \right) X dX \\
&= \frac{2}{J_{\nu+1}^2(\theta_{\nu,n})} \int_0^1 \left(b^{1/2} y^\nu - \kappa b^{-1/2} y^{-\nu} \right)_+ J_\nu(\theta_{\nu,n} y) y dy.
\end{aligned}
$$

A relatively straightforward algebra yields:

$$
\begin{aligned}
\psi_n &= \frac{2b^{1/2}}{J_{\nu+1}^2(\theta_{\nu,n})} \int_\varpi^1 y^{\nu+1} J_\nu(\theta_{\nu,n} y) dy \\
&\quad - \frac{2\kappa b^{-1/2}}{J_{\nu+1}^2(\theta_{\nu,n})} \int_\varpi^1 y^{-\nu+1} J_\nu(\theta_{\nu,n} y) dy \\
&= \frac{2b^{1/2} \left(J_{\nu+1}(\theta_{\nu,n}) - \varpi^{\nu+1} J_{\nu+1}(\theta_{\nu,n} \varpi) \right)}{J_{\nu+1}^2(\theta_{\nu,n}) \theta_{\nu,n}} \\
&\quad + \frac{2\kappa b^{-1/2} \left(J_{\nu-1}(\theta_{\nu,n}) - \varpi^{-\nu+1} J_{\nu-1}(\theta_{\nu,n} \varpi) \right)}{J_{\nu+1}^2(\theta_{\nu,n}) \theta_{\nu,n}} \\
&= \frac{2b^{1/2} J_{\nu+1}(\theta_{\nu,n}) + 2\kappa b^{-1/2} J_{\nu-1}(\theta_{\nu,n})}{J_{\nu+1}^2(\theta_{\nu,n}) \theta_{\nu,n}} \\
&\quad - \frac{2\kappa^{1/2} \varpi \left(J_{\nu+1}(\theta_{\nu,n} \varpi) + J_{\nu-1}(\theta_{\nu,n} \varpi) \right)}{J_{\nu+1}^2(\theta_{\nu,n}) \theta_{\nu,n}} \\
&= -\frac{2 \left(b^{1/2} - \kappa b^{-1/2} \right) \theta_{\nu,n} J_\nu'(\theta_{\nu,n}) + 4\nu \kappa^{1/2} J_\nu(\theta_{\nu,n} \varpi)}{J_{\nu+1}^2(\theta_{\nu,n}) \theta_{\nu,n}^2},
\end{aligned}
$$

where $\varpi = (\kappa/b)^{1/2\nu}$. Thus, all we need to do in order to compute $W(\chi, X)$ is to analyze the behavior of the function J_ν including the location of its zeroes. Since the corresponding expansion converges very rapidly, we need to find the first few roots only, say ten or so. They can easily be found via standard methods. After that, the series expansion $W(\chi, X)$ can be evaluated, and $U(\chi, X)$ and $V(\tau, S)$ be recovered.

Now we consider the asymmetric case when $r^{01} \neq 0$. We the sake of variety we study the pricing problem for a double-barrier call:

$$V_t + \frac{1}{2}\sigma^2 \left(\frac{S}{\bar{S}}\right)^{-2\beta} S^2 V_{SS} + r^{01}SV_S - r^0 V = 0,$$

$$V(T,S) = (S - K)_+,$$

$$V(t,A) = V(t,B) = 0.$$

The nondimensional pricing problem has the form

$$U_\chi - \frac{1}{2}\xi^{2-2\beta}U_{\xi\xi} - \hat{r}^{01}\xi U_\xi = 0,$$

$$U(0,\xi) = (\xi - \kappa)_+,$$

$$U(\chi,a) = U(\chi,b) = 0,$$

where

$$U = \frac{e^{r^0(T-t)}V}{\bar{S}}, \quad \xi = \frac{S}{\bar{S}}, \quad \kappa = \frac{K}{\bar{S}}, \quad a = \frac{A}{\bar{S}}, \quad b = \frac{B}{\bar{S}}.$$

We have to reduce the nondimensional pricing equation to the confluent hypergeometric form rather that the Bessel form. To this end we introduce the new independent variable

$$Z = -\frac{\hat{r}^{01}\xi^{2\beta}}{\beta}.$$

and rewrite the pricing problem as

$$\frac{1}{2\hat{r}^{01}\beta}U_\chi + ZU_{ZZ} + \left(1 - \frac{1}{2\beta} - Z\right)U_Z = 0,$$

$$U(0,Z) = u(Z) = \left(\left(-\frac{\beta Z}{\hat{r}^{01}}\right)^{1/2\beta} - \kappa\right)_+,$$

$$U\left(\chi,\zeta_b\right)=U\left(\chi,\zeta_a\right)=0,$$

where

$$\zeta_a=\left(-\frac{\beta a}{\hat{r}^{01}}\right)^{1/2\beta},\quad \zeta_b=\left(-\frac{\beta b}{\hat{r}^{01}}\right)^{1/2\beta}.$$

The spectral problem assumes the form

$$ZU_{n,ZZ}\left(Z\right)+\left(1-\frac{1}{2\beta}-Z\right)U_{n,Z}\left(Z\right)-\lambda U_n\left(Z\right)=0, \qquad (12.48)$$

$$U_n\left(\zeta_b\right)=U_n\left(\zeta_a\right)=0,$$

with the corresponding particular solution of the form

$$U\left(\chi,Z\right)=e^{-2\hat{r}^{01}\beta\lambda_n\chi}U_n\left(Z\right).$$

This spectral equation can be written in a symmetric form

$$\left(|Z|^{1-1/2\beta}\,e^{-Z}U_{n,Z}\left(Z\right)\right)_Z+\lambda|Z|^{-1/2\beta}\,e^{-Z}U_n\left(Z\right)=0,$$

so that its eigenvalues are real (and positive). The general solution of equation (12.48) can be written as

$$U\left(Z\right)=\Phi M\left(\lambda,1-\frac{1}{2\beta},Z\right)+\Psi|Z|^{1/2\beta}\,e^Z M\left(1-\lambda,1+\frac{1}{2\beta},-Z\right),$$

where $M\left(a,b,Z\right)$ is Kummer's function. The spectrum is defined by the dispersion relation

$$\det\begin{pmatrix} M\left(\lambda,1-\frac{1}{2\beta},\zeta_a\right) & |\zeta_a|^{1/2\beta}\,e^{\zeta_a}M\left(1-\lambda,1+\frac{1}{2\beta},-\zeta_a\right) \\ M\left(\lambda,1-\frac{1}{2\beta},\zeta_b\right) & |\zeta_a|^{1/2\beta}\,e^{\zeta_b}M\left(1-\lambda,1+\frac{1}{2\beta},-\zeta_b\right) \end{pmatrix}=0.$$

After eigenvalues λ_n and the corresponding (normalized) eigenvectors (Φ_n,Ψ_n), $\Phi_n^2+\Psi_n^2=1$, are found, the solution $U\left(\chi,X\right)$ is represented as Kummer's series expansion:

$$U\left(\chi,Z\right)=\sum_{n=0}^{\infty}e^{-2\hat{r}^{01}\beta\lambda_n\chi}\psi_n U_n\left(Z\right),$$

where

$$U_n(Z) = \Phi_n M\left(\lambda_n, 1 - \frac{1}{2\beta}, Z\right) + \Psi_n |Z|^{1/2\beta} e^Z M\left(1 - \lambda_n, 1 + \frac{1}{2\beta}, -Z\right),$$

$$\psi_n = \frac{\int_{\zeta_b}^{\zeta_a} u(Z) U_n(Z) |Z|^{-1/2\beta} e^{-Z} dZ}{\int_{\zeta_b}^{\zeta_a} U_n(Z) U_n(Z) |Z|^{-1/2\beta} e^{-Z} dZ}.$$

12.5.4 Barrier options in the presence of stochastic volatility

In the previous two subsections we showed how to price barrier options on FXRs with deterministic local volatility. We saw that analytical methods for solving the pricing problem are rather involved. However, it can easily be solved via numerical methods. In this subsection we consider the pricing problem for barrier options on FXRs with stochastic volatility. It turns out that this problem is difficult to solve both analytically and numerically. A general semi-analytical pricing methodology was developed by the present author. However, it goes well beyond the scope of this book and will be discussed elsewhere.

For the purposes of illustration, in the present subsection we study the simplest barrier problem with stochastic volatility which can be solved explicitly. We consider the mean-reverting square-root stochastic volatility model with constant parameters introduced in Section 7.7 and assume that the volatility of the FXR and the volatility of volatility are uncorrelated, $\rho = 0$, and the interest rate differential is zero $r^{01} = 0$. We show how to price the double-barrier call under the above assumptions.

Basic equations

The corresponding pricing problem is

$$V_\tau - \frac{1}{2}vS^2 V_{SS} - \frac{1}{2}\varepsilon^2 v V_{vv} - \kappa(\theta - v) V_v + r^0 V = 0,$$

$$V(0, S, v) = (S - K)_+,$$

$$V(\tau, A, v) = V(\tau, B, v) = 0,$$

$$V_\tau - \kappa\theta V_v + r^0 V = 0, \qquad V(\tau, S, v \to \infty) \to 0,$$

where $A < K < B$.

To simplify the problem as much as possible, we introduce new dependent and independent variables:

$$X = \ln\left(\frac{S}{K}\right), \qquad U = \frac{e^{r^0\tau - X/2}V}{K}.$$

We emphasize that the standard transformation $\tau \to \chi = \sigma^2\tau$ is not possible since the volatility is no longer a constant or a known function of time. The basic pricing problem written in terms of $U(\tau, X)$ assumes the form

$$U_\tau - \frac{1}{2}v\left(U_{XX} - \frac{1}{4}U\right) - \frac{1}{2}\epsilon^2 v U_{vv} - \kappa(\theta - v)U_v = 0, \qquad (12.49)$$

$$U(0, X, v) = \left(e^{X/2} - e^{-X/2}\right)_+, \qquad (12.50)$$

$$U(\tau, a, v) = 0, \qquad U(\tau, b, v) = 0, \qquad (12.51)$$

$$U_\tau(\tau, X, 0) - \kappa\theta U_v(\tau, X, 0) = 0, \qquad U(\tau, X, v \to \infty, \tau) \to 0, \qquad (12.52)$$

where $a = \ln(A/K) < 0$, $b = \ln(B/K) > 0$. It is clear that equation (12.49) does not contain first derivatives with respect to X and for this reason is invariant with respect to the transformation $X \to -X$. Among other things, this fact implies that we can solve the barrier problem in two complementary ways, namely, via the methods of images and Fourier series. In this respect the problem under consideration is similar to the classical single-factor, double-barrier problem considered in Section 12.4.

Green's function

As usual, the difficult part is to find the aggregated Green's function

$$G^B(\tau, X, v, X') = \int_0^\infty G(\tau, X, v, X', v')\,dv',$$

for the pricing problem. Green's function solves equation (12.49) supplied with boundary conditions (12.51), (12.52) and the initial condition

$$G^B(0, X, v, X') = \delta(X - X'), \qquad (12.53)$$

where $a < X' < b$. Once this task is accomplished, the call price can be found via integration with respect to X'. Green's function for equation (12.49) on the entire X-line is denoted by $G(\tau, X, v, X')$. This function satisfies equation (12.49), boundary conditions (12.52) and the initial condition (12.53). Equation (10.70) yields,

$$G(\tau, X, v, X') = G(\tau, Y, v) = \frac{1}{2\pi} \int_{-\infty}^{\infty} e^{ikY + 2(\mathsf{A}(\tau,k) - \mathsf{B}(\tau,k)v)/\varepsilon^2}\, dk, \qquad (12.54)$$

where $Y = X' - X$. Here A, B have the form

$$\mathsf{A}(\tau, k) = -\kappa\theta\,(\mu + \zeta)\,\tau - \kappa\theta \ln\left(\frac{-\mu + \zeta + (\mu + \zeta)\,e^{-2\zeta\tau}}{2\zeta}\right),$$

$$\mathsf{B}(\tau, k) = \frac{\varepsilon^2(k^2 + 1/4)\left(1 - e^{-2\zeta\tau}\right)}{4\left(-\mu + \zeta + (\mu + \zeta)\,e^{-2\zeta\tau}\right)},$$

with μ, ζ given by the following real-valued expressions,

$$\mu = -\frac{1}{2}\kappa,$$

$$\zeta = \frac{1}{2}\sqrt{\varepsilon^2(k^2 + \frac{1}{4}) + \kappa^2}.$$

It is clear that $G(\tau, Y, v)$ is an even function of its second argument since integral (12.54) is invariant with respect to reflections $Y \to -Y$, $k \to -k$. We emphasize that G^B depends on X and X' per se rather than on their difference Y.

In the framework of the method of images we represent G^B as an infinite linear combination of no-barrier Green's functions G with sources at $X_n'^{+} = X' - 2n\,(b - a)$ and sinks at $X_n'^{-} = -X' - 2n\,(b - a) + 2a$:

$$G^B(\tau, X, v, X') \qquad\qquad\qquad\qquad (12.55)$$

$$= \sum_{n=-\infty}^{\infty} \left\{ G(\tau, X_n'^{+} - X, v) - G(\tau, X_n'^{-} - X, v) \right\}$$

$$= \sum_{n=-\infty}^{\infty} \left\{ G(\tau, X' - X_n, v) - G(\tau, X' + X_n - 2a, v) \right\},$$

where $X_n = X + 2n\,(b - a)$.

In the framework of the Fourier series method we proceed by analogy with the classical case and write G^B in the form

$$G^B(\tau, X, v, X') = \frac{2}{b-a} \sum_{n=1}^{\infty} e^{2(\mathbf{A}(\tau,k_n)-\mathbf{B}(\tau,k_n)v)/\varepsilon^2} \qquad (12.56)$$
$$\times \sin(k_n(X'-a)) \sin(k_n(X-a)),$$

where, as before, $k_n = \pi n/(b-a)$.

Pricing of calls and puts

Knowing Green's function for the barrier problem, we can easily solve problem (12.49) - (12.52). Symbolically this solution $U^{(C)}(\tau, X, v)$ can be written as

$$U^{(C)}(\tau, X, v) = \int_a^b G^B(\tau, X, v, X')U(0, X', v)dX' \qquad (12.57)$$
$$= \int_0^b G^B(\tau, X, v, X')\left(e^{X'/2} - e^{-X'/2}\right)dX'.$$

First, we evaluate integral (12.57) by using formula (12.55) obtained via the method of images. We can write the solution of the pricing problem as

$$U^{(C)}(\tau, X, v) = \sum_{n=-\infty}^{\infty} \{\mathcal{I}^+(\tau, X_n, v) - \mathcal{I}^-(\tau, X_n, v) \qquad (12.58)$$
$$-\mathcal{I}^+(\tau, 2a - X_n, v) + \mathcal{I}^-(\tau, 2a - X_n, v)\},$$

where

$$\mathcal{I}^{\pm}(\tau, X, v) = \frac{1}{2\pi} \int_{-\infty}^{\infty} \frac{e^{-ikX+2(\mathbf{A}(\tau,k)-\mathbf{B}(\tau,k)v)/\varepsilon^2}\left(e^{(ik\pm 1/2)b}-1\right)}{(ik \pm 1/2)}dk.$$

A simple calculation yields

$$\mathcal{I}^{\pm}(\tau, X, v) = e^{\pm b/2}\mathcal{H}^{\pm}(\tau, X-b, v) - \mathcal{H}^{\pm}(\tau, X, v),$$

where

$$\mathcal{H}^{\pm}(\tau, X, v) = \frac{1}{2\pi} \int_{-\infty}^{\infty} \frac{e^{-ikX+2(\mathbf{A}(\tau,k)-\mathbf{B}(\tau,k)v)/\varepsilon^2}}{(ik \pm 1/2)}dk$$
$$= \frac{1}{2\pi} \int_{-\infty}^{\infty} \frac{e^{-ikX+2(\mathbf{A}(\tau,k)-\mathbf{B}(\tau,k)v)/\varepsilon^2}(-ik \pm 1/2)}{(k^2+1/4)}dk$$
$$= \frac{1}{\pi} \int_0^{\infty} \Re\left\{\frac{e^{ikX+2(\mathbf{A}(\tau,k)-\mathbf{B}(\tau,k)v)/\varepsilon^2}(-ik \pm 1/2)}{(k^2+1/4)}\right\}dk.$$

Substituting the above expressions in equation (12.58) we obtain the following expression for $U^{(C)}$:

$$U^{(C)}(\tau, X, v) = \sum_{n=-\infty}^{\infty} U_n^{(C)}(\tau, X, v),$$

where

$$U_n^{(C)}(\tau, X, v) = e^{b/2}\mathcal{H}^+(\tau, X_n - b, v) - \mathcal{H}^+(\tau, X_n, v)$$
$$-e^{-b/2}\mathcal{H}^-(\tau, X_n - b, v) + \mathcal{H}^-(\tau, X_n, v)$$
$$-e^{-b/2}\mathcal{H}^+(\tau, X_n - 2a + b, v) + \mathcal{H}^+(\tau, X_n - 2a, v)$$
$$+e^{b/2}\mathcal{H}^-(\tau, X_n - 2a + b, v) - \mathcal{H}^-(\tau, X_n - 2a, v).$$

The corresponding expression for $V^{(C)}(\tau, S, v)$ has the form

$$V^{(C)}(\tau, S, v) = e^{-r^0\tau} \sum_{n=-\infty}^{\infty} V_n^{(C)}(\tau, S, v),$$

where

$$V_n^{(C)}(\tau, S, v) \tag{12.59}$$
$$= \sqrt{SB}\mathcal{H}^+(\tau, \ln(S_n/B), v) - \sqrt{SK}\mathcal{H}^+(\tau, \ln(S_n/K), v)$$
$$-K\sqrt{S/B}\mathcal{H}^-(\tau, \ln(S_n/B), v) + \sqrt{SK}\mathcal{H}^-(\tau, \ln(S_n/K), v)$$
$$-K\sqrt{S/B}\mathcal{H}^+(\tau, \ln(S_n B/A^2), v) + \sqrt{SK}\mathcal{H}^+(\tau, \ln(S_n K/A^2), v)$$
$$+\sqrt{SB}\mathcal{H}^-(\tau, \ln(S_n B/A^2), v) - \sqrt{SK}\mathcal{H}^-(\tau, \ln(S_n K/A^2), v),$$

and $S_n = SB^{2n}/A^{2n}$. As usual, equation (12.59) is particularly useful close to maturity when τ is small since then the price is accurately reproduced by very few terms of the corresponding sums. However, when τ is large, the "domain of influence" of an individual source becomes so large that one has to use many terms to find the price with confidence.

We now turn our attention to the Fourier series method. Substituting expression (12.56) in equation (12.57) and performing the required integration, we obtain the following expression for U,

$$U^{(C)}(\tau, X, v) = \sum_{n=1}^{\infty} e^{2(A(\tau, k_n) - B(\tau, k_n)v)/\varepsilon^2} \psi_n \sin(k_n(x - a)),$$

where

$$
\begin{aligned}
\psi_n &= \frac{2\{(-1)^{n+1}k_n \left(e^{b/2} - e^{-b/2}\right) + \sin(k_n a)\}}{(k_n^2 + 1/4)(b-a)} \\
&= \frac{2\{(-1)^{n+1}k_n \left(\sqrt{B/K} - \sqrt{K/B}\right) + \sin(k_n \ln(A/K))\}}{(k_n^2 + 1/4)\log(B/A)}.
\end{aligned}
$$

Finally, we return to the original variables and write the price of a call as follows,

$$
V^{(C)}(\tau, S, v) = e^{-r^0 \tau}\sqrt{SK} \sum_{n=1}^{\infty} e^{2(\mathtt{A}(\tau,k_n) - \mathtt{B}(\tau,k_n)v)/\varepsilon^2} \psi_n \sin(k_n \ln(S/A)).
$$

$$(12.60)$$

This series becomes ever more accurate as τ becomes large or the barriers a, b move closer to each other. However, for small τ, i.e., close to maturity, or for distant barriers we have to sum up relatively many terms (although in practice this does not constitute a problem). In this respect representations (12.60) and (12.59) are complementary.

We show the price of a double-barrier call on the FXR with stochastic volatility in Figure 12.5.

For the barrier problem put-call parity is no longer valid. For this reason the price of a put has to be found separately. Calculations similar to the ones outlined above yield the following expressions for the price of a put,

$$
V^{(P)}(\tau, S, v) = e^{-r^0 \tau} \sum_{n=-\infty}^{\infty} V_n^{(P)}(\tau, S, v),
$$

where

$$
\begin{aligned}
&V_n^{(P)}(\tau, S, v) \\
&= \sqrt{SA}\mathcal{H}^+ (\tau, \ln(S_n/A), v) - \sqrt{SK}\mathcal{H}^+ (\tau, \ln(S_n/K), v) \\
&\quad - K\sqrt{S/A}\mathcal{H}^- (\tau, \ln(S_n/A), v) + \sqrt{SK}\mathcal{H}^- (\tau, \ln(S_n/K), v) \\
&\quad - K\sqrt{S/A}\mathcal{H}^- (\tau, \ln(S_n/A), v) + \sqrt{SK}\mathcal{H}^- (\tau, \ln(S_n/K), v) \\
&\quad + \sqrt{SA}\mathcal{H}^- (\tau, \ln(S_n B/A^2), v) - \sqrt{SK}\mathcal{H}^- (\tau, \ln(S_n K/A^2), v),
\end{aligned}
$$

or, equivalently,

$$
V^{(P)}(\tau, S, v) = e^{-r^0 \tau}\sqrt{SK} \sum_{n=1}^{\infty} e^{2(\mathtt{A}(\tau,k_n) - \mathtt{B}(\tau,k_n)v)/\varepsilon^2} \tilde{\psi}_n \sin(k_n \ln(S/A)),
$$

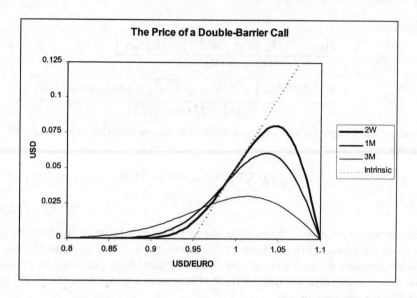

Figure 12.5: The price of a typical double-barrier call in the stochastic volatility framework as a function of the spot FXR in the stochastic volatility framework. The relevant parameters are $v = (15\%)^2$, $\theta = (20\%)^2$, $\varepsilon = 0.40$, $\kappa = 3$, $K = 0.95$, $A = 0.80$, $B = 1.10$.

where

$$
\begin{aligned}
\tilde{\psi}_n &= \frac{2\{k_n\left(e^{-a/2} - e^{a/2}\right) + \sin(k_n a)\}}{(k_n^2 + 1/4)(b - a)} \\
&= \frac{2\{k_n\left(\sqrt{K/A} - \sqrt{A/K}\right) + \sin(k_n \ln(A/K))\}}{(k_n^2 + 1/4)\log(B/A)}.
\end{aligned}
$$

12.6   Multi-factor barrier options

The number of barrier options in multi-country markets is very large and growing. They are distinguished by terminal payoffs and boundary conditions. In the opinion of the author, the most popular contracts include options on one currency with one or two barriers on some other currency, two-currency options with one barrier for each currency, two-currency quadruple-no-touch options, and some of their variations.

As well as their no-barrier counterparts, multi-factor barrier options depend not only on volatilities of the underlying FXRs but also on their correlations.

Multi-currency barrier options naturally appeal to international corporations who need to hedge some of their exposure to currency risks but do not want to pay too much for such a protection because they can count on cancellation effects of different exposures. They also attract sophisticated speculators having particular views on correlated movements of different FXRs.

Below we illustrate some salient features of multi-currency barrier options by considering in detail a few representative examples.

12.7 Options on one currency with barriers on the other currency

12.7.1 Introduction

One-factor knockout barrier options, which were considered above, have payoffs depending on some FXR and disappear when this FXR crosses a given barrier level. It is natural to generalize them by considering options with payoffs depending on one currency and knockout features on some other currency. In this section we show how to price options of this kind. Both single- and double-barrier options are considered.

12.7.2 Formulation

In this section we formulate the pricing problem for calls on one currency knocking on a second currency. Other options, such as puts and bets, can be considered by the same token. The dimensional pricing problem describing a call on the FXR S^{02} knocking out on the FXR S^{01} has the form

$$V_\tau - \frac{1}{2} \left(\sigma^{01}\right)^2 \left(S^{01}\right)^2 V_{S^{01}S^{01}} - \rho^{012}\sigma^{01}\sigma^{02}S^{01}S^{02}V_{S^{01}S^{02}} \quad (12.61)$$

$$-\frac{1}{2} \left(\sigma^{02}\right)^2 \left(S^{02}\right)^2 V_{S^{02}S^{02}} - r^{01}S^{01}V_{S^{01}} - r^{02}S^{02}V_{S^{02}} + r^0 V = 0,$$

$$V(0, S^{01}, S^{02}) = \left(S^{02} - K^{02}\right)_+ .$$

In the presence of a single barrier (say an upper barrier B^{01}) the corresponding boundary conditions are

$$V\left(\tau, 0, S^{02}\right) = V^{(C)}\left(\tau, S^{02}\right), \quad V(\tau, B^{01}, S^{02}) = 0,$$

$$V(\tau, S^{01}, 0) = 0, \qquad V(\tau, S^{01}, S^{02} \to \infty) \to e^{-r^{02}\tau} V^{SNT}\left(\tau, S^{01}\right) S^{02},$$

where $V^{(C)}\left(\tau, S^{01}\right)$, $V^{SNT}\left(\tau, S^{01}\right)$ are the prices of a one-factor call and a single-no-touch option, respectively. In the presence of two barriers, A^{01} and B^{01}, the boundary conditions assume the form

$$V(\tau, A^{01}, S^{02}) = 0, \qquad V(\tau, B^{01}, S^{02}) = 0,$$

$$V(\tau, S^{01}, 0) = 0, \qquad V(\tau, S^{01}, S^{02} \to \infty) \to e^{-r^{02}\tau} V^{(DNT)}\left(\tau, S^{01}\right) S^{02},$$

where $V^{(DNT)}\left(\tau, S^{01}\right)$ is the value of a one-factor double-no-touch option.

Below we concentrate on pricing double-barrier options. Pricing of single-barrier options, which is significantly simpler, is left to the reader as a very useful exercise.

We use A^{01} and K^{02} for nondimensionalization purposes and apply the standard change of independent and dependent variables given by formulas (9.26). The pricing problem for $U(\tau, X^1, X^2)$ is

$$U_\tau - \frac{1}{2}\left(\sigma^{01}\right)^2 U_{X^1 X^1} - \rho\sigma^{01}\sigma^{02} U_{X^1 X^2} - \frac{1}{2}\left(\sigma^{02}\right)^2 U_{X^2 X^2} = 0, \qquad (12.62)$$

$$U(0, X^1, X^2) = \left(e^{-\beta^1 X^1 + (1-\beta^2)X^2} - e^{-\beta^1 X^1 - \beta^2 X^2}\right)_+, \qquad (12.63)$$

$$U(\tau, 0, X^2) = 0, \qquad U(\tau, b, X^2) = 0, \qquad (12.64)$$

$$\begin{aligned}
&U(\tau, X^1, X^2 \to -\infty) \to 0, \\
&U(\tau, X^1, X^2 \to \infty) \to e^{-\beta^1 X^1 + (1-\beta^2)X^2} U^{(DNT)}\left(\tau, X^1\right),
\end{aligned} \qquad (12.65)$$

where $b = \log(B^{01}/A^{01}) > 0$, and $U^{(DNT)}$ it the non-dimensional double-no-touch value. For the sake of brevity we use the notation $\rho = \rho^{012}$, $\bar{\rho} = \sqrt{1 - (\rho^{012})^2}$.

The pricing problem (12.62)-(12.65) is still complicated. To rewrite it in the simplest possible form we introduce new independent variables χ, Y^1, Y^2 such that

$$\begin{aligned}
\chi &= \sigma^{01}\sigma^{02}\tau, \qquad Y^1 = \sqrt{\sigma^{02}/\sigma^{01}}X_1, \qquad (12.66) \\
Y^2 &= -\rho\sqrt{\sigma^{02}/\sigma^{01}}X_1/\bar{\rho} + \sqrt{\sigma^{01}/\sigma^{02}}X_2/\bar{\rho},
\end{aligned}$$

and write the pricing problem for $U(\chi, Y^1, Y^2)$ as

$$U_\chi - \frac{1}{2}U_{Y^1Y^1} - \frac{1}{2}U_{Y^2Y^2} = 0, \tag{12.67}$$

$$U(0, Y^1, Y^2) = \left(e^{v_+^1 Y^1 + v_+^2 Y^2} - e^{v_-^1 Y^1 + v_-^2 Y^2}\right)_+,$$

$$U(\chi, 0, Y^2) = 0, \qquad U(\chi, c, Y^2) = 0,$$

$$U(\chi, Y^1, Y^2 \to -\infty) \to 0,$$

$$U(\chi, Y^1, Y^2 \to \infty) \to e^{\left((v_+^1)^2 + (v_+^2)^2\right)\chi/2 + v_+^1 Y^1 + v_+^2 Y^2} W\left(\chi, Y^1\right),$$

where $c = \sqrt{\sigma^{02}/\sigma^{01}}b > 0$, and

$$
\begin{aligned}
v_+^1 &= -\sqrt{\sigma^{01}/\sigma^{02}}\beta^1 + \rho\sqrt{\sigma^{02}/\sigma^{01}}(1-\beta^2), \\
v_+^2 &= \bar{\rho}\sqrt{\sigma^{02}/\sigma^{01}}(1-\beta^2), \\
v_-^1 &= -\sqrt{\sigma^{01}/\sigma^{02}}\beta^1 - \rho\sqrt{\sigma^{02}/\sigma^{01}}\beta^2, \\
v_-^2 &= -\bar{\rho}\sqrt{\sigma^{02}/\sigma^{01}}\beta^2.
\end{aligned}
$$

We also use $\bar{c} = \rho c/\bar{\rho}$.

12.7.3 Solution via the Fourier method

Green's function for equation (12.67) with homogeneous boundary conditions at $Y^1 = 0, c$ and $Y^2 = \pm\infty$ can be written in the form similar to (12.32):

$$
\begin{aligned}
&G(\chi, Y^1, Y^2, \mu^1, \mu^2) \\
&= \frac{2}{c}\sum_{n=1}^{\infty} e^{-k_n^2\chi/2}\sin(k_n\mu^1)\sin(k_n Y^1)\frac{e^{-(Y^2-\mu^2)^2/2\chi}}{\sqrt{2\pi\chi}} \\
&= G^{(1)}\left(\chi, Y^1, \mu^1\right)G^{(2)}\left(\chi, Y^2, \mu^2\right),
\end{aligned}
$$

where $k_n = \pi n/c$. Thus, this function separates into a product of two one-dimensional Green's functions, one for the heat equation considered on the finite interval $[0, c]$, the other for the heat equation on the whole axis. Accordingly, the solution of the pricing problem can be written as

$$U(\chi, Y^1, Y^2) = \int\!\!\int_D G(\chi, Y^1, Y^2, \mu^1, \mu^2) \qquad (12.68)$$
$$\times \left(e^{v_+^1 \mu^1 + v_+^2 \mu^2} - e^{v_-^1 \mu^1 + v_-^2 \mu^2} \right) d\mu^1 d\mu^2,$$

where D is the part of the strip $0 \le \mu^1 \le c$ lying above the line defined by the equation

$$\rho\mu^1 + \bar\rho\mu^2 = 0.$$

When the correlation coefficient ρ is zero, the domain of integration coincides with the upper half-strip $0 \le \mu^1 \le c,\ 0 \le \mu^2 < \infty$. When this coefficient is positive the domain of integration D consists of the upper half-strip plus the triangle defined by the inequalities

$$-\bar\rho\mu^2/\rho \le \mu^1 \le c, -\bar c \le \mu^2 \le 0.$$

When this coefficient is negative the domain of integration consists of the upper half-strip minus the triangle

$$-\bar\rho\mu^2/\rho \le \mu^1 \le c, 0 \le \mu^2 \le -\bar c.$$

We emphasize that the order of integration is rather important, and that we integrate with respect to μ^2 first, and μ^1 second. Accordingly, we can write expression (12.68) as

$$U(\chi, Y^1, Y^2)$$
$$= \int_0^c \int_{-\rho\mu^1/\bar\rho}^\infty G(\chi, Y^1, Y^2, \mu^1, \mu^2) \left(e^{v_+^1 \mu^1 + v_+^2 \mu^2} - e^{v_-^1 \mu^1 + v_-^2 \mu^2} \right) d\mu^2 d\mu^1$$
$$= \int_0^c G^{(1)}\left(\chi, Y^1, \mu^1\right) \left(e^{v_+^1 \mu^1} \left(\int_{-\rho\mu^1/\bar\rho}^\infty G^{(2)}\left(\chi, Y^2, \mu^2\right) e^{v_+^2 \mu^2} d\mu^2 \right) \right.$$
$$\left. - e^{v_-^1 \mu^1} \left(\int_{-\rho\mu^1/\bar\rho}^\infty G^{(2)}\left(\chi, Y^2, \mu^2\right) e^{v_-^2 \mu^2} d\mu^2 \right) \right) d\mu^1.$$

It is easy to compute the integrals with respect to μ^2. A relatively straightforward algebra yields

$$\left(\int_{-\rho\mu^1/\bar{\rho}}^{\infty} G^{(2)}\left(\chi, Y^2, \mu^2\right) e^{v_{\pm}^2 \mu^2} d\mu^2 \right)$$
$$= e^{\left(v_{\pm}^2\right)^2 \chi/2 + v_{\pm}^2 Y^2} \mathfrak{N}\left(\frac{Y^2 + \rho\mu^1/\bar{\rho}}{\sqrt{\chi}} + v_{\pm}^2\sqrt{\chi} \right),$$

$$U(\chi, Y^1, Y^2) = \int_0^c G^{(1)}\left(\chi, Y^1, \mu^1\right) e^{-\sqrt{\sigma^{01}/\sigma^{02}}\beta^1 \mu^1}$$
$$\times \left(M\left(\chi, Y^2 + \rho\mu^1/\bar{\rho}, v_+^2\right) - M\left(\chi, Y^2 + \rho\mu^1/\bar{\rho}, v_-^2\right) \right) d\mu^1,$$

where, as usual, $M\left(\chi, Y, v\right)$ is defined by equation (8.29). We see that for "frozen" χ and Y^2 we can think of $U(\chi, Y^1, Y^2)$ as the price of a one-factor barrier option with the payoff of the form

$$U\left(0, Y^1\right) = e^{-\sqrt{\sigma^{01}/\sigma^{02}}\beta^1 \mu^1} \left(M\left(\chi, Y^2 + \rho\mu^1/\bar{\rho}, v_+^2\right) \right.$$
$$\left. - M\left(\chi, Y^2 + \rho\mu^1/\bar{\rho}, v_-^2\right) \right).$$

Numerical evaluation of the corresponding option is relatively straightforward. For the sake of completeness, however, we show how to price this option analytically.

We start with the case of zero correlation. In this case we have

$$U\left(\chi, Y^1, Y^2\right)$$
$$= \int_0^c G^{(1)}\left(\chi, Y^1, \mu^1\right) e^{\sqrt{\sigma^{01}/\sigma^{02}}\hat{\gamma}_-^{01} \mu^1}$$
$$\cdot \times \left(M\left(\chi, Y^2, \sqrt{\sigma^{02}/\sigma^{01}}\hat{\gamma}_+^{02}\right) - M\left(\chi, Y^2, \sqrt{\sigma^{02}/\sigma^{01}}\hat{\gamma}_-^{02}\right) \right) d\mu^1$$
$$= \int_0^c G^{(1)}\left(\chi, Y^1, \mu^1\right) e^{\sqrt{\sigma^{01}/\sigma^{02}}\hat{\gamma}_-^{01}\mu^1} d\mu^1$$
$$\times \left(M\left(\chi, Y^2, \sqrt{\sigma^{02}/\sigma^{01}}\hat{\gamma}_+^{02}\right) - M\left(\chi, Y^2, \sqrt{\sigma^{02}/\sigma^{01}}\hat{\gamma}_-^{02}\right) \right)$$
$$= \frac{2}{c} \sum_{n=1}^{\infty} \left(\int_0^c \sin(k_n\mu^1) e^{\sqrt{\sigma^{01}/\sigma^{02}}\hat{\gamma}_-^{01}\mu^1} d\mu^1 \right) e^{-k_n^2\chi/2} \sin(k_n Y^1)$$
$$\times \left(M\left(\chi, Y^2, \sqrt{\sigma^{02}/\sigma^{01}}\hat{\gamma}_+^{02}\right) - M\left(\chi, Y^2, \sqrt{\sigma^{02}/\sigma^{01}}\hat{\gamma}_-^{02}\right) \right).$$

We leave it to the reader to check that

$$
\int_0^c \sin(k_n\mu^1)e^{l\mu^1}\,d\mu^1 = \left. \frac{\left(l\sin(k_n\mu^1) - k_n\cos(k_n\mu^1)\right)e^{l\mu^1}}{k_n^2 + l^2} \right|_0^c \quad (12.69)
$$

$$
= \frac{\left((-1)^{n+1}e^{lc} + 1\right)k_n}{k_n^2 + l^2}.
$$

By using this formula, we can represent the solution of the pricing problem as

$$
\begin{aligned}
&U\left(\chi, Y^1, Y^2\right) \\
&= \left(\frac{2}{c}\sum_{n=1}^{\infty} \frac{\left((-1)^{n+1}e^{\sqrt{\sigma^{01}/\sigma^{02}}\hat{\gamma}_-^{01}c} + 1\right)k_n}{k_n^2 + \sigma^{01}\left(\hat{\gamma}_-^{01}\right)^2/\sigma^{02}}e^{-k_n^2\chi/2}\sin(k_nY^1) \right) \\
&\quad \times \left(M\left(\chi, Y^2, \sqrt{\sigma^{02}/\sigma^{01}}\hat{\gamma}_+^2\right) - M\left(\chi, Y^2, \sqrt{\sigma^{02}/\sigma^{01}}\hat{\gamma}_-^2\right)\right).
\end{aligned}
$$

Thus, the price is separable in the sense that it is a product of a function of Y^1, χ and a function of Y^2, χ.

In order to rewrite this expression in the financial variables, we need to invert the transformations $t, S^{01}, S^{02} \to \chi, Y^1, Y^2$. Although the corresponding formulas are easy to derive, they are quite cumbersome and we omit them for the sake of brevity. Besides, to apply the above formula in practice we recommend to do change of variables (9.26), (12.66), anyway.

In the case of nonzero(say, positive) correlation, $\rho > 0$, we need to evaluate the following integrals:

$$
\mathcal{I}_n = \int_0^c \mathfrak{N}\left(\rho\mu^1/\bar{\rho} + m\right)\sin\left(k_n\mu^1\right)e^{l\mu^1}\,d\mu^1,
$$

which reduce to the form (12.69) when $\rho = 0$. A simple integration by parts yields

$$
\begin{aligned}
\mathcal{I}_n &= \int_0^c \mathfrak{N}\left(\rho\mu^1/\bar{\rho} + m\right)d\left(\frac{\left(l\sin(k_n\mu^1) - k_n\cos(k_n\mu^1)\right)e^{l\mu^1}}{k_n^2 + l^2}\right) \\
&= \frac{\left(\mathfrak{N}\left(\rho c/\bar{\rho} + m\right)(-1)^{n+1}e^{lc} + \mathfrak{N}\left(m\right)\right)k_n}{k_n^2 + l^2} - \frac{\rho/\bar{\rho}}{\sqrt{2\pi}\left(k_n^2 + l^2\right)} \\
&\quad \times \int_0^c e^{-\left(\rho\mu^1/\bar{\rho} + m\right)^2/2 + l\mu^1}\left(l\sin(k_n\mu^1) - k_n\cos(k_n\mu^1)\right)d\mu^1.
\end{aligned}
$$

Thus, the problem reduces to the evaluation of two integrals:

$$\left\{ \begin{matrix} \mathcal{J}_n^c \\ \mathcal{J}_n^s \end{matrix} \right\} = \int_0^c e^{-\left(\rho\mu^1/\bar\rho + m\right)^2/2 + l\mu^1} \left\{ \begin{matrix} \cos \\ \sin \end{matrix} \right\} (k_n\mu^1) d\mu^1,$$

which are the real and imaginary parts of the integral

$$\mathcal{J}_n = \int_0^c e^{-\left(\rho\mu^1/\bar\rho + m\right)^2/2 + (l+ik_n)\mu^1} d\mu^1,$$

respectively. We complete the squares and obtain

$$\mathcal{J}_n = e^{\bar\rho^2(l+ik_n)^2/2\rho^2 - \bar\rho(l+ik_n)m/\rho} \int_0^c e^{-\left(\rho\mu^1/\bar\rho + m - \bar\rho(l+ik_n)/\rho\right)^2/2} d\mu^1$$

$$= \frac{\sqrt{2\pi}\bar\rho}{\rho} e^{\bar\rho^2(l+ik_n)^2/2\rho^2 - \bar\rho(l+ik_n)m/\rho} \int_{m-\bar\rho(l+ik_n)/\rho}^{\rho c/\bar\rho + m - \bar\rho(l+ik_n)/\rho} \frac{e^{-\nu^2/2}}{\sqrt{2\pi}} d\nu$$

$$= \frac{\sqrt{2\pi}\bar\rho}{\rho} e^{\bar\rho^2(l+ik_n)^2/2\rho^2 - \bar\rho(l+ik_n)m/\rho}$$

$$\times \left[\mathfrak{N}\left(\frac{\rho c}{\bar\rho} + m - \frac{\bar\rho(l+ik_n)}{\rho} \right) - \mathfrak{N}\left(m - \frac{\bar\rho(l+ik_n)}{\rho} \right) \right].$$

By using the above expressions we obtain the solution of the pricing problem written in terms of χ, Y^1, Y^2:

$$U(\chi, Y^1, Y^2) = \frac{2}{c} \sum_{n=1}^\infty e^{-k_n^2\chi/2} \sin(k_n Y^1) U_n\left(\chi, Y^2\right), \qquad (12.70)$$

where

$$U_n\left(\chi, Y^2\right)$$
$$= \frac{k_n\left[(-1)^{n+1} e^{-\sqrt{\sigma^{01}/\sigma^{02}}\beta^1 c} M\left(\chi, Y^2 + \bar c, v_+^2\right) + M\left(\chi, Y^2, v_+^2\right)\right]}{\left(v_+^1\right)^2 + k_n^2}$$
$$- \frac{k_n\left[(-1)^{n+1} e^{-\sqrt{\sigma^{01}/\sigma^{02}}\beta^1 c} M\left(\chi, Y^2 + \bar c, v_-^2\right) + M\left(\chi, Y^2, v_-^2\right)\right]}{\left(v_-^1\right)^2 + k_n^2}$$
$$+ \Im\left\{ \left(\frac{v_+^1 + ik_n}{\left(v_+^1\right)^2 + k_n^2} - \frac{v_-^1 + ik_n}{\left(v_-^1\right)^2 + k_n^2} \right) \right.$$
$$\left. \left[e^{-(\sqrt{\sigma^{01}/\sigma^{02}}\beta^1 + ik_n)c} M\left(\chi, Y^2 + \bar c, v_n^3\right) - M\left(\chi, Y^2, v_n^3\right) \right] \right\},$$

$$v_n^2 = v^2 - \bar{\rho}(v^1 - ik_n)/\rho = \bar{\rho}(\sqrt{\sigma^{01}/\sigma^{02}}\beta^1 + ik_n)/\rho.$$

We see that formula (12.70) for U involves the evaluation of the cumulative normal distribution with a complex argument $\mathfrak{N}(z)$. For this reason, it is somewhat inconvenient for coding since the cumulative normal distribution function grows very rapidly when the imaginary part of its complex argument grows. To obviate this difficulty we introduce the auxiliary error function which we denote by $\mathfrak{N}_{aux}(z)$ (it seems that the standard notation does not exist) such that

$$\mathfrak{N}_{aux}(z) = \exp(\frac{1}{2}z^2)\mathfrak{N}(z),$$

and rewrite the expression for $U(\chi, Y^1, Y^2)$ in the form

$$U(\chi, Y^1, Y^2) = \frac{2}{c}\sum_{n=1}^{\infty} e^{-k_n^2\chi/2}\sin(k_n Y^1)U_n\left(\chi, Y^2\right),$$

where

$$
\begin{aligned}
&U_n\left(\chi, Y^2\right) \\
&= \frac{k_n\left[(-1)^{n+1}e^{-\sqrt{\sigma^{01}/\sigma^{02}}\beta^1 c}M\left(\chi, Y^2+\bar{c}, v_+^2\right) + M\left(\chi, Y^2, v_+^2\right)\right]}{\left(v_+^1\right)^2 + k_n^2} \\
&\quad - \frac{k_n\left[(-1)^{n+1}e^{-\sqrt{\sigma^{01}/\sigma^{02}}\beta^1 c}M\left(\chi, Y^2+\bar{c}, v_-^2\right) + M\left(\chi, Y^2, v_-^2\right)\right]}{\left(v_-^1\right)^2 + k_n^2} \\
&\quad + \Im\left\{\left(\frac{v_+^1 + ik_n}{\left(v_+^1\right)^2 + k_n^2} - \frac{v_-^1 + ik_n}{\left(v_-^1\right)^2 + k_n^2}\right)\right. \\
&\quad \times \left[e^{-(Y^2+\bar{c})^2/2\chi-(\sqrt{\sigma^{01}/\sigma^{02}}\beta^1+ik_n)c}\mathfrak{N}_{aux}\left(\frac{Y^2+\bar{c}}{\sqrt{\chi}} + \sqrt{\chi}v_n^3\right)\right. \\
&\quad \left.\left.- e^{-Y^2/2\chi}\mathfrak{N}_{aux}\left(\frac{Y^2}{\sqrt{\chi}} + \sqrt{\chi}v_n^3\right)\right]\right\}.
\end{aligned}
$$

We introduce the notation

$$
\begin{aligned}
U_\pm^1(\chi, Y^1) &= \frac{2}{c}\sum_{n=1}^{\infty}\frac{(-1)^{n+1}k_n e^{-k_n^2\chi/2}\sin(k_n Y^1)}{v_{1\pm}^2 + k_n^2}, \\
U_\pm^2(\chi, Y^1) &= \frac{2}{c}\sum_{n=1}^{\infty}\frac{k_n e^{-k_n^2\chi/2}\sin(k_n Y^1)}{v_{1\pm}^2 + k_n^2},
\end{aligned}
$$

and write $U(\chi, Y^1, Y^2)$ in the following final form

$$U^{(C)}(\chi, Y^1, Y^2) = e^{-\sqrt{\sigma^{01}/\sigma^{02}}\beta^1 c}U^1_+(\chi, Y^1)M\left(\chi, Y^2 + \bar{c}, v^2_+\right)(12.71)$$
$$+U^2_+(\chi, Y^1)M\left(\chi, Y^2, v^2_+\right)$$
$$-e^{-\sqrt{\sigma^{01}/\sigma^{02}}\beta^1 c}U^1_+(\chi, Y^1)M\left(\chi, Y^2 + \bar{c}, v^2_-\right)$$
$$-U^2_+(\chi, Y^1)M\left(\chi, Y^2, v^2_-\right)$$
$$+\frac{2}{c}\sum_{n=1}^{\infty}e^{-k_n^2\chi/2}\sin(k_n Y^1)\Im\left\{\left(\frac{v^1_+ + ik_n}{\left(v^1_+\right)^2 + k_n^2} - \frac{v^1_- + ik_n}{\left(v^1_-\right)^2 + k_n^2}\right)\right.$$
$$\left[e^{-(Y^2+\bar{c})^2/2\chi-(\sqrt{\sigma^{01}/\sigma^{02}}\beta^1+ik_n)c}\mathfrak{M}_{aux}\left(\frac{Y^2+\bar{c}}{\sqrt{\chi}} + \sqrt{\chi}v_n^3\right)\right.$$
$$\left.\left.-e^{-Y^2/2\chi}\mathfrak{M}_{aux}\left(\frac{Y^2}{\sqrt{\chi}} + \sqrt{\chi}v_n^3\right)\right]\right\}.$$

Inverting the mapping $t, S^{01}, S^{02}, V \to \chi, Y^1, Y^2, U$ we can write the price of a call in the financial variables.

By the same token as before we can find the price of a put:

$$U^{(P)}(\chi, Y^1, Y^2) = -e^{-\sqrt{\sigma^{01}/\sigma^{02}}\beta^1 c}U^1_+(\chi, Y^1) \qquad (12.72)$$
$$\times M\left(\chi, -\left(Y^2 + \bar{c}\right), -v^2_+\right) - U^2_+(\chi, Y^1)M\left(\chi, -Y^2, -v^2_+\right)$$
$$+e^{-\sqrt{\sigma^{01}/\sigma^{02}}\beta^1 c}U^1_+(\chi, Y^1)M\left(\chi, -\left(Y^2 + \bar{c}\right), -v^2_-\right)$$
$$-U^2_+(\chi, Y^1)M\left(\chi, -Y^2, -v^2_-\right)$$
$$+\frac{2}{c}\sum_{n=1}^{\infty}e^{-k_n^2\chi/2}\sin(k_n Y^1)\Im\left\{\left(\frac{v^1_+ + ik_n}{\left(v^1_+\right)^2 + k_n^2} - \frac{v^1_- + ik_n}{\left(v^1_-\right)^2 + k_n^2}\right)\right.$$
$$\times\left[e^{-(Y^2+\bar{c})^2/2\chi-(\sqrt{\sigma^{01}/\sigma^{02}}\beta^1+ik_n)c}\mathfrak{M}_{aux}\left(\frac{Y^2+\bar{c}}{\sqrt{\chi}} + \sqrt{\chi}v_n^3\right)\right.$$
$$\left.\left.-e^{-Y^2/2\chi}\mathfrak{M}_{aux}\left(\frac{Y^2}{\sqrt{\chi}} + \sqrt{\chi}v_{3n}\right)\right]\right\}.$$

In the two-factor case the price of a bet can be found as well but we do not present it here.

In case when a rebate is paid when barriers are hit the corresponding correction solves the one-factor problem and can be found by virtue of the method described above (correlation does not affect this observation).

There are two ways of relating the price of puts and calls: (A) via put-call parity; (B) via put-call symmetry. To describe put-call parity we notice that

$$V^{(C)}(0, S^{01}, S^{02}) - V^{(P)}(0, S^{01}, S^{02}) = S^{02} - K^{02},$$

where $A^{01} < S^{01} < B^{01}$. Thus, in order to understand the behavior of $V^{(C)} - V^{(P)}$ we need to solve equation (12.61) with the initial condition

$$V\left(0, S^{01}, S^{02}\right) = S^{02} - K^{02}.$$

This can be done by virtue of the affine ansatz

$$V(\tau, S^{01}, S^{02}) = E(\tau, S^{01})S^{02} - F\left(\tau, S^{01}\right) K^{02}.$$

Substituting this expression into the governing equation and the boundary conditions we obtain the following problems for $E(\tau, S^{01}), F\left(\tau, S^{01}\right)$:

$$E_\tau - \frac{1}{2}\left(\sigma^{01}\right)^2 \left(S^{01}\right)^2 E_{S^{01}S^{01}} - \left(\rho\sigma^{01}\sigma^{02} + r^{01}\right) S^{01} E_{S^{01}} + r^2 E = 0,$$

$$E(0, S^{01}) = 1,$$

$$E(\tau, A^{01}) = 0, \qquad E(\tau, B^{01}) = 0,$$

and

$$F_\tau - \frac{1}{2}\left(\sigma^{01}\right)^2 \left(S^{01}\right)^2 F_{S^{01}S^{01}} - r^{01} S^{01} F_{S^{01}} + r^0 F = 0,$$

$$F(0, S^{01}) = 1,$$

$$F(\tau, A^{01}) = 0, \qquad F(\tau, B^{01}) = 0.$$

It is clear that E and F are two familiar one-factor bet options (the first one is a quanto option, though,) which can be priced via equation (12.36). Accordingly, we can write put-call parity relation as

$$V^{(C)}(\tau, S^{01}, S^{02}) - V^{(P)}(\tau, S^{01}, S^{02}) = E(\tau, S^{01})S^{02} - F(\tau, S^{01})K. \quad (12.73)$$

We leave it to the reader as an exercise to verify that formulas (12.71), (12.72) and (12.73) are in agreement.

To describe put-call symmetry we apply the change of variables

$$S^{02} \to \frac{\left(K^{02}\right)^2}{S^{02}},$$

in equation (12.61). A relatively complicated calculation which is left to the reader as an exercise yields

$$V^{(P,C)}(\tau, S^{01}, S^{02}, K^{02}; \sigma^{01}, \sigma^{02}, \rho, r^0, r^1, r^2; A^{01}, B^{01})$$
$$= V^{(C,P)}(\tau, S^{01}, K^{02}, S^{02}; \sigma^{01}, \sigma^{02}, -\rho, r^2, r^1 + \rho\sigma^{01}\sigma^{02}, r^0; A^{01}, B^{02}).$$

For completeness we give one more identity which is useful for checking the accuracy of numerical solutions

$$V^{(C,P)}(\tau, S^{01}, S^{02}, K^{02}; \sigma^{01}, \sigma^{02}, \rho, r^0, r^1, r^2; A^{01}, B^{01})$$
$$= V^{(C,P)}\left(\tau, L^{1-\nu}\left(S^{01}\right)^\nu, S^{02}, K^{02}; \nu\sigma^{01}, \sigma^{02}, \rho, r^0, \bar{r}_\nu^0, r^2, A_\nu^{01}, B_\nu^{01}\right),$$

where L is an arbitrary scale, ν is a nondimensional power, and $\bar{r}_\nu^0, A_\nu^{01}, B_\nu^{01}$ are given by equations (12.38), (12.39).

We leave it to the reader as an exercise to show that the value of a barrier spread option with the payoff

$$V^{(SPRD)}\left(0, S^{01}, S^{02}\right) = (S_1^{01} - K^{21}S_2)_+,$$

is given by the following formula:

$$V^{(SPRD)}(\tau, S^{01}, S^{02}; \sigma^{01}, \sigma^{02}, \rho, r^0, r^1, r^2; A^{01}, B^{01})$$
$$= V^{(C)}(\tau, S^{01}, S^{01}, K^{21}S^{02}; \sigma^{01}, \sigma^{12}, \left(\sigma^{01} - \rho\sigma^{02}\right)/\sigma^{12}, r^2,$$
$$-r^0 + r^1 + r^2 - \rho\sigma^{01}\sigma^{02}, r^1; A^{01}, B^{01}),$$

where $\sigma^{12} = \sqrt{\left(\sigma^{01}\right)^2 - 2\rho\sigma^{01}\sigma^{02} + \left(\sigma^{02}\right)^2}$.

12.7.4 Solution via the method of images

Since the expressions for the call and put values obtained via the Fourier series method are rather involved it is of some interest to obtain similar expressions via the method of images. As before, the Fourier series expressions are of greater financial interest but the image expansions can be useful in their own right.

In order to obtain the simplest formulas possible we return back to problem (12.62) - (12.65) and introduce new variables Z^1, Z^2 such that

$$Z^1 = \sqrt{\sigma^{02}/\sigma^{01}}X^1, \qquad Z^2 = \sqrt{\sigma^{01}/\sigma^{02}}X^2. \qquad (12.74)$$

The pricing problem for $U(\chi, Z^1, Z^2)$ is

$$U_\chi - \frac{1}{2}U_{Z^1 Z^1} - \rho U_{Z^1 Z^2} - \frac{1}{2}U_{Z^2 Z^2} = 0, \qquad (12.75)$$

$$U(0, Z^1, Z^2) = \left(e^{\delta^1_+ Z^1 + \delta^2_+ Z^2} - e^{\delta^1_- Z^1 + \delta^2_- Z^2}\right)_+, \qquad (12.76)$$

$$U(\chi, 0, Z^2) = 0, \qquad U(\chi, d, Z^2) = 0, \quad U(\chi, Z^1, Z^2 \to -\infty) \to 0,$$

$$U(\chi, Z^1, Z^2 \to \infty) \to e^{((\delta^1_+)^2 + 2\rho\delta^1_+ \delta^2_+ + (\delta^2_+)^2)\chi/2 + \delta^1_+ Z^1 + \delta^2_+ Z^2},$$

where $d = \sqrt{\sigma^{02}/\sigma^{01}}b > 0$, and

$$\begin{aligned} \delta^1_+ &= -\sqrt{\sigma^{01}/\sigma^{02}}\beta^1, \quad \delta^2_+ = \sqrt{\sigma^{02}/\sigma^{01}}(1 - \beta^2), \qquad (12.77) \\ \delta^1_- &= -\sqrt{\sigma^{01}/\sigma^{02}}\beta^1, \quad \delta^2_- = -\sqrt{\sigma^{02}/\sigma^{01}}\beta^2. \end{aligned}$$

As before, we start with the evaluation of Green's function localized at a certain point (ν^1, ν^2) such that $0 < \nu^1 < d$. The images of this point in the vertical boundaries $Z^1 = 0$ and $Z^1 = d$ can be combined into two groups and represented as

$$\begin{aligned} (\nu_n^{1\prime}, \nu_n^{2\prime}) &= (\nu^1, \nu^2) - (2nd, 2\rho nd), \\ (\nu_n^{1\prime\prime}, \nu_n^{2\prime\prime}) &= (-\nu^1, -2\rho\nu^1 + \nu^2) - (2nd, 2\rho nd). \end{aligned}$$

Accordingly, Green's function can be written as

$$G(\chi, Z^1, Z^2, \nu^1, \nu^2)$$

$$= \sum_{n=-\infty}^{\infty} \left[H(\chi, Z_n^1 - \nu^1, Z_n^2 - \nu^2) - H(\chi, Z_n^1 + \nu^1, Z_n^2 + 2\rho\nu^1 - \nu^2) \right],$$

where

$$Z_n^1 = Z^1 + 2nd, \qquad Z_n^2 = Z^2 + 2\rho nd,$$

and H is the standard two-dimensional Green's function for equation (12.75), i.e.,

$$H(\chi, Z^1, Z^2) = \frac{1}{2\pi\bar{\rho}\chi}e^{-\left((Z^1)^2-2\rho Z^1 Z^2+(Z^2)^2\right)/2\bar{\rho}^2\chi}.$$

For future reference we need to compute the following double integral

$$\eta(\chi, \kappa^1, \kappa^2) = \int_0^d \int_0^\infty H(\chi, \nu^1, \nu^2)e^{\kappa^1\nu^1+\kappa^2\nu^2}\,d\nu^1\,d\nu^2.$$

A sequence of transformations yields

$$\eta(\chi, \kappa^1, \kappa^2) = \frac{e^{\chi\left((\kappa^1)^2+2\rho\kappa^1\kappa^2+(\kappa^2)^2\right)/2}}{2\pi\bar{\rho}\chi}$$

$$\times \int_0^d \int_0^\infty e^{-\left[(\bar{\nu}^1)^2-2\rho\bar{\nu}^1\bar{\nu}^2+(\bar{\nu}^2)^2\right]/2\bar{\rho}^2\chi}\,d\nu^1\,d\nu^2$$

$$= \frac{e^{\chi\left((\kappa^1)^2+2\rho\kappa^1\kappa^2+(\kappa^2)^2\right)/2}}{2\pi\bar{\rho}\chi}$$

$$\times \int_{-\chi(\kappa^1+\rho\kappa^2)}^{d-\chi(\kappa^1+\rho\kappa^2)} \int_{-\chi(\rho\kappa^1+\kappa^2)}^\infty e^{-\left((\bar{\nu}^1)^2-2\rho\bar{\nu}^1\bar{\nu}^2+(\bar{\nu}^2)^2\right)/2\bar{\rho}^2\chi}\,d\bar{\nu}^1\,d\bar{\nu}^2$$

$$= \frac{e^{\chi\left((\kappa^1)^2+2\rho\kappa^1\kappa^2+(\kappa^2)^2\right)/2}}{2\pi\bar{\rho}}$$

$$\times \int_{-\sqrt{\chi}(\kappa^1+\rho\kappa^2)}^{d/\sqrt{\chi}-\sqrt{\chi}(\kappa^1+\rho\kappa^2)} \int_{-\sqrt{\chi}(\rho\kappa^1+\kappa^2)}^\infty e^{-\left((\hat{\nu}^1)^2-2\rho\hat{\nu}^1\hat{\nu}^2+(\hat{\nu}^2)^2\right)/2\bar{\rho}^2}\,d\hat{\nu}^1\,d\hat{\nu}^2$$

$$= e^{\chi\left((\kappa^1)^2+2\rho\kappa^1\kappa^2+(\kappa^2)^2\right)/2}$$

$$\times \left[\mathfrak{N}_2(\sqrt{\chi}(\kappa^1+\rho\kappa^2), \sqrt{\chi}(\rho\kappa^1+\kappa^2), \rho)\right.$$

$$\left. -\mathfrak{N}_2(-d/\sqrt{\chi}+\sqrt{\chi}(\kappa^1+\rho\kappa^2), \sqrt{\chi}(\rho\kappa^1+\kappa^2), \rho)\right],$$

where $\mathfrak{N}_2(h, k, \rho)$ is the cumulative bivariate normal distribution, and

$$\tilde{\nu}^1 = \nu^1 - \chi(\kappa^1+\rho\kappa^2), \qquad \tilde{\nu}^2 = \nu^2 - \chi(\rho\kappa^1+\kappa^2).$$

Reasonably accurate approximations for this function (for example, the one due to Drezner) are readily available, so that we can consider $\eta(\chi, \kappa^1, \kappa^2)$ as known.

Taking the convolution of the Green's function with the initial condition (12.76) we represent the solution of the pricing equation as

$$U(\chi, Z^1, Z^2)$$

$$= \sum_{n=-\infty}^{\infty} \left\{ \int_0^d \int_0^\infty H(\chi, Z_n^1 - \nu^1, Z_n^2 - \nu^2) e^{\delta_+^1 \nu^1 + \delta_+^2 \nu^2} d\nu^1 d\nu^2 \right.$$

$$- \int_0^d \int_0^\infty H(\chi, Z_n^1 - \nu^1, Z_n^2 - \nu^2) e^{\delta_-^1 \nu^1 + \delta_-^2 \nu^2} d\nu^1 d\nu^2$$

$$- \int_0^d \int_0^\infty H(\chi, Z_n^1 + \nu^1, Z_n^2 + 2\rho\nu^1 - \nu^2) e^{\delta_+^1 \nu^1 + \delta_+^2 \nu^2} d\nu^1 d\nu^2$$

$$\left. + \int_0^d \int_0^\infty H(\chi, Z_n^1 + \nu^1, Z_n^2 + 2\rho\nu^1 - \nu^2) e^{\delta_-^1 \nu^1 + \delta_-^2 \nu^2} d\nu^1 d\nu^2 \right\}.$$

A relatively simple calculation yields

$$\int_0^d \int_0^\infty H(\chi, Z_n^1 - \nu^1, Z_n^2 - \nu^2) e^{\delta_\pm^1 \nu^1 + \delta_\pm^2 \nu^2} d\nu^1 d\nu^2$$

$$= e^{-\left((Z_n^1)^2 - 2\rho Z_n^1 Z_n^2 + (Z_n^2)^2\right)/2\bar{\rho}^2 \chi}$$

$$\times \eta \left(\chi, \delta_\pm^1 + (Z_n^1 - \rho Z_n^2)/\bar{\rho}^2 \chi, \delta_\pm^2 - (\rho Z_n^1 - Z_n^2)/\bar{\rho}^2 \chi\right)$$

$$= e^{-((\delta_\pm^1)^2 + 2\rho\delta_\pm^1 \delta_\pm^2 + (\delta_\pm^2)^2)\chi/2 + (\delta_\pm^1 p_{\pm n}^1 + \delta_\pm^2 p_{\pm n}^2)\sqrt{\chi}}$$

$$\times \left[\mathfrak{N}_2 \left(p_{\pm n}^1, p_{\pm n}^2, \rho\right) - \mathfrak{N}_2 \left(p_{\pm n}^1 - d/\sqrt{\chi}, p_{\pm n}^2, \rho\right)\right],$$

where

$$p_{\pm n}^1 = \frac{Z_n^1}{\sqrt{\chi}} + \sqrt{\chi}(\delta_\pm^1 + \rho\delta_\pm^2), \quad p_{\pm n}^2 = \frac{Z_n^2}{\sqrt{\chi}} + \sqrt{\chi}(\rho\delta_\pm^1 + \delta_\pm^2),$$

and, similarly,

$$\int_0^d \int_0^\infty H(\chi, Z_n^1 + \nu^1, Z_n^2 + 2\rho\nu^1 - \nu^2) e^{\delta_\pm^1 \nu^1 + \delta_\pm^2 \nu^2} d\nu^1 d\nu^2$$

$$= e^{-\left((Z_n^1)^2 - 2\rho Z_n^1 Z_n^2 + (Z_n^2)^2\right)/2\bar{\rho}^2 \chi}$$

$$\times \eta \left(\chi, \delta_\pm^1 - ((1 - 2\rho^2)Z_n^1 + \rho Z_n^2)/\bar{\rho}^2 \chi, \delta_\pm^2 - (\rho Z_n^1 - Z_n^2)/\bar{\rho}^2 \chi\right)$$

$$= e^{-((\delta_\pm^1)^2 + 2\rho\delta_\pm^1 \delta_\pm^2 + (\delta_\pm^2)^2)\chi/2 + (\delta_\pm^1 q_{\pm n}^1 + \delta_\pm^2 q_{\pm n}^2)\sqrt{\chi}}$$

$$\times \left[\mathfrak{N}_2 \left(q_{\pm n}^1, q_{\pm n}^2, \rho\right) - \mathfrak{N}_2 \left(q_{\pm n}^1 - d/\sqrt{\chi}, q_{\pm n}^2, \rho\right)\right],$$

where

$$q^1_{\pm n} = -\frac{Z^1_n}{\sqrt{\chi}} + \sqrt{\chi}(\delta^1_\pm + \rho\delta^2_\pm),$$

$$q^2_{\pm n} = -\frac{2\rho Z^1_n - Z^2_n}{\sqrt{\chi}} + \sqrt{\chi}(\rho\delta^1_\pm + \delta^2_\pm).$$

Finally, we obtain the following representation for U:

$$U(\chi, Z^1, Z^2)$$

$$= e^{-((\delta^1_+)^2 + 2\rho\delta^1_+\delta^2_+ + (\delta^2_+)^2)\chi/2} \sum_{n=-\infty}^{\infty} e^{(\delta^1_+ p^1_{+n} + \delta^2_+ p^2_{+n})\sqrt{\chi}}$$

$$\times \left[\mathfrak{N}_2 \left(p^1_{+n}, p^2_{+n}, \rho \right) - \mathfrak{N}_2 \left(p^1_{+n} - d/\sqrt{\chi}, p^2_{+n}, \rho \right) \right]$$

$$- e^{-((\delta^1_-)^2 + 2\rho\delta^1_-\delta^2_- + (\delta^2_-)^2)\chi/2} \sum_{n=-\infty}^{\infty} e^{(\delta^1_- p^1_{-n} + \delta^2_- p^2_{-n})\sqrt{\chi}}$$

$$\times \left[\mathfrak{N}_2 \left(p^1_{-n}, p^2_{-n}, \rho \right) - \mathfrak{N}_2 \left(p^1_{-n} - d/\sqrt{\chi}, p^2_{-n}, \rho \right) \right]$$

$$- e^{-((\delta^1_+)^2 + 2\rho\delta^1_+\delta^2_+ + (\delta^2_+)^2)\chi/2} \sum_{n=-\infty}^{\infty} e^{(\delta^1_+ q^1_{+n} + \delta^2_+ q^2_{+n})\sqrt{\chi}}$$

$$\times \left[\mathfrak{N}_2 \left(q^1_{+n}, q^2_{+n}, \rho \right) - \mathfrak{N}_2 \left(q^1_{+n} - d/\sqrt{\chi}, q^2_{+n}, \rho \right) \right]$$

$$+ e^{-((\delta^1_-)^2 + 2\rho\delta^1_-\delta^2_- + (\delta^2_-)^2)\chi/2} \sum_{n=-\infty}^{\infty} e^{(\delta^1_- q^1_{-n} + \delta^2_- q^2_{-n})\sqrt{\chi}}$$

$$\times \left[\mathfrak{N}_2 \left(q^1_{-n}, q^2_{-n}, \rho \right) - \mathfrak{N}_2 \left(q^1_{-n} - d/\sqrt{\chi}, q^2_{-n}, \rho \right) \right].$$

12.7.5 An alternative approach

We know that Green's function for the pricing problem written in terms of Y_1, Y_2 is separable,

$$G \left(\chi, Y^1, Y^2, \mu^1, \mu^2 \right) = G^{(1)} \left(\chi, Y^1, \mu^1 \right) G^{(2)} \left(\chi, Y^2, \mu^2 \right),$$

while the corresponding initial data are "almost" separable,

$$U(0, Y_1, Y_2) = e^{v^1_- Y^1 + v^2_- Y^2} \left(e^{\sqrt{\sigma_2/\sigma_1}(\rho Y^1 + \bar{\rho} Y^2)} - 1 \right)_+.$$

We can capitalize on this fact and represent $U \left(\chi, Y^1, Y^2 \right)$ in the form

$$U \left(\chi, Y^1, Y^2 \right) = \int_0^c G^{(1)} \left(\chi, Y^1, \mu^1 \right) e^{v^1_- \mu^1} H^{(12)} \left(\chi, \mu^1, Y^2 \right) d\mu^1, \quad (12.78)$$

where

$$H^{(12)} \left(\chi, \mu^1, Y^2 \right) = \int_{-\infty}^{\infty} G^{(2)} \left(\chi, Y^2, \mu^2 \right) e^{v_-^2 \mu^2} \left(e^{\sqrt{\sigma_2/\sigma_1} \left(\rho \mu^1 + \bar{\rho} \mu^2 \right)} - 1 \right)_+ .$$

(12.79)

We leave it to the reader to find an explicit expression for $H^{(12)} \left(\chi, Y^2, \mu^1 \right)$. We can interpret equations (12.78), (12.79) as follows: $H^{(12)} \left(\chi, Y^2, \mu^1 \right)$ can be thought of as the price of a single-factor European option with the payoff of the form

$$\text{payoff} = e^{v_-^2 Y^2} \left(e^{\sqrt{\sigma_2/\sigma_1} \left(\rho Y^1 + \bar{\rho} Y^2 \right)} - 1 \right)_+ ,$$

(12.80)

where Y^1 is considered as a parameter; $U \left(\chi, Y^1, Y^2 \right)$ can be thought of the price of the double-no-touch option with the payoff of the form

$$\text{payoff} = e^{v_-^1 Y^1} H^{(12)} \left(\chi, Y^1, Y^2 \right),$$

(12.81)

where χ, Y^1 are considered as parameters.

Thus, in order to find $U \left(\chi, Y^1, Y^2 \right)$ we can proceed in two steps. First, we price the one-factor European option on Y^2 with payoff (12.80). Next, we price the one-factor double-no-touch option with payoff (12.81). The first problem can be solved analytically even in the presence of term structure of volatilities. The second problem can be solved analytically when all the profiles are time-independent, otherwise it has to be solved numerically. We emphasize that this procedure, although very appealing, generates the correct price of the two-factor option only for a single time χ, so that all intermediate calculations have to be discarded and redone for a different time horizon.

12.8   Options with one barrier for each currency

12.8.1   General considerations

In the previous section we showed that the pricing equation for the general two-factor option can be written in the form

$$U_\chi - \frac{1}{2} U_{Z^1 Z^1} - \rho U_{Z^1 Z^2} - \frac{1}{2} U_{Z^2 Z^2} = 0,$$

where ρ is the correlation between the assets. This equation is supplied with the deal specific boundary and initial conditions. In the previous section we studied the case when the barriers are imposed on the first FXR, while the payout depends on the second one, i.e., we assumed that

$$U(0, Z^1, Z^2) = u(Z^2),$$

$$U(\chi, 0, Z^2) = 0, \qquad U(\chi, d, Z^2) = 0.$$

Now we consider the complementary case and assume that there is a barrier for each FXR, while the payout is a general function of Z^1, Z^2, so that

$$U(0, Z^1, Z^2) = u(Z^1, Z^2),$$

$$U(\chi, 0, Z^2) = 0, \qquad U(\chi, Z^1, 0) = 0.$$

Thus, the option is knocked out when either Z^1 or Z^2 reaches the corresponding lower barrier which, without loss of generality, are put to zero. Other possibilities can be studied in a completely analogous fashion.

In order to simplify the pricing equation, we introduce the new variables

$$\eta^1 = Z^1, \qquad \eta^2 = -\frac{\rho}{\bar\rho} Z^1 + \frac{1}{\bar\rho} Z^2. \tag{12.82}$$

Transformation (12.82) turns the original domain (which coincides with the positive quadrant) into a wedge with the vertex located at the origin, one side parallel to the vertical axis, and the other side parallel to the line

$$\eta^2 + \frac{\rho}{\bar\rho}\eta^1 = 0.$$

The vertex angle, which we denote by α, can be expressed in terms of the correlation ρ as follows $\cos\alpha = -\rho$. This angle is acute when $\rho \leq 0$ and blunt when $\rho \geq 0$.

In the new variables the pricing problem can be written as

$$U_\chi - \frac{1}{2}U_{\eta^1\eta^1} - \frac{1}{2}U_{\eta^2\eta^2} = 0,$$

$$U(0, \eta^1, \eta^2) = u(\eta^1, \eta^2),$$

$$U(\chi, 0, \chi) = 0, \qquad U(\chi, \chi, -\rho\chi/\bar\rho) = 0,$$

where $\chi \geq 0$. We see that the problem is reduced to solving the heat equation in a wedge with zero Dirichlet's boundary conditions on the sides.

12.8.2   The Green's function

Since we want to make our discussion as general as possible, we restrict ourselves to finding the Green's function for this classical problem leaving it to
the reader to perform the necessary integration in order to account for specific
initial conditions $u(\eta^1, \eta^2)$. In other words, we show how to find the solution
to the heat equation in an angle corresponding to the initial condition

$$U(0, \eta^1, \eta^2) = \delta(\eta^1 - \eta^{1'})\delta(\eta^2 - \eta^{2'}).$$

In order to fully capitalize on the symmetry of the domain in question we
introduce the polar coordinates ϱ, φ in such a way that the first (slanted) side
of the wedge corresponds to $\varphi = 0$, while the second (vertical) side corresponds
to $\varphi = \alpha$,

$$\eta^1 = -\varrho \sin(\phi - \alpha), \qquad \eta^2 = \varrho \cos(\phi - \alpha).$$

In polar coordinates the pricing problem assumes the form

$$U_\chi - \frac{1}{2}\left(U_{\varrho\varrho} + \frac{1}{\varrho}U_\varrho + \frac{1}{\varrho^2}U_{\varphi\varphi}\right) = 0, \tag{12.83}$$

$$U(0, \varrho, \varphi) = \frac{1}{\varrho'}\delta(\varrho - \varrho')\delta(\varphi - \varphi'), \tag{12.84}$$

$$U(\chi, \varrho, 0) = 0, \qquad U(\chi, \varrho, \alpha) = 0, \tag{12.85}$$

where the point (ϱ', φ') corresponds to the point (η_1', η_2'). We find the Green's
function for the problem (12.83) - (12.85) via a combination of the Laplace and
Fourier transforms. First, we do the Laplace transform in time and rewrite the
problem as

$$sW - \frac{1}{2}\left(W_{\varrho\varrho} + \frac{1}{\varrho}W_\varrho + \frac{1}{\varrho^2}W_{\varphi\varphi}\right) = \frac{1}{\varrho'}\delta(\varrho - \varrho')\delta(\varphi - \varphi'), \tag{12.86}$$

$$W(s, \varrho, 0) = 0, \qquad W(s, \varrho, \alpha) = 0.$$

Next, we account for the presence of the δ function in φ by expanding $W(s, \varrho, \varphi)$
in Fourier series in φ and representing it in the form

$$W(s, \varrho, \varphi) = \frac{2}{\alpha} \sum_{n=1}^{\infty} W_n(s, \varrho, \varrho') \sin\left(\frac{n\pi\varphi}{\alpha}\right) \sin\left(\frac{n\pi\varphi'}{\alpha}\right),$$

where $W_n(s, \varrho, \varrho')$ satisfies the following equation

$$\left(\left(\frac{n\pi}{\alpha\varrho} \right)^2 + 2s \right) W_n - \left(W_{n\varrho\varrho} + \frac{1}{\varrho} W_{n\varrho} \right) = \frac{2}{\varrho'} \delta(\varrho - \varrho'),$$

and the usual regularity conditions at $\varrho = 0$ and $\varrho = \infty$. The solution of this equation has the form

$$W_n(s, \varrho, \varrho') = 2K_{\frac{n\pi}{\alpha}}(\sqrt{2s}\varrho_>) I_{\frac{n\pi}{\alpha}}(\sqrt{2s}\varrho_<),$$

where K, I are the modified Bessel functions of order $n\pi/\alpha$, and

$$\varrho_> = \max\{\varrho, \varrho_0\}, \varrho_< = \min\{\varrho, \varrho_0\}.$$

To compute the inverse Laplace transform of W_n we use the same MacDonald's formula (10.50) as in Section 10.7, which shows that W_n is the inverse Laplace transform of

$$U_n(\chi, \varrho, \varrho') = \frac{e^{-(\varrho^2 + \varrho'^2)/2\chi}}{\chi} I_{\frac{n\pi}{\alpha}}\left(\frac{\varrho\varrho'}{\chi} \right).$$

Finally, we obtain the following expression for the Green's function in the wedge

$$U(\chi, \varrho, \varphi, \varrho', \varphi') = \frac{2e^{-(\varrho^2 + \varrho'^2)/2\chi}}{\alpha\chi} \sum_{n=1}^{\infty} I_{\frac{n\pi}{\alpha}}\left(\frac{\varrho\varrho'}{\chi} \right) \qquad (12.87)$$

$$\times \sin\left(\frac{n\pi\varphi}{\alpha} \right) \sin\left(\frac{n\pi\varphi'}{\alpha} \right).$$

For fixed $\varrho\varrho'/\chi$ and $n \to \infty$ we can use the asymptotic expression for the modified Bessel function of large order to obtain

$$I_{\frac{n\pi}{\alpha}}\left(\frac{\varrho\varrho'}{\chi} \right) \approx \sqrt{\frac{\alpha}{2n\pi^2}} \left(\frac{\alpha e \varrho\varrho'}{2n\pi\chi} \right)^{\frac{n\pi}{\alpha}}.$$

This expression shows that the terms of the series (12.87) decay sufficiently fast. However, since this decay is not uniform with respect to $\varrho\varrho_0$, it is relatively difficult to deal with this series.

For this reason alone it might be beneficial to construct Green's function via the method of images. In order to do so we need to find the solution of equation (12.86) which is a rapidly decaying (rather than periodic) function of

φ. It means that we need to construct the Green's function on the Riemann surface covering the physical plane rather than on the physical plane itself. To this end we need to use the integral Fourier transform rather than the Fourier series transform in φ. By combining the Laplace and Fourier transforms we represent the Green's function as

$$W^R(s,\varrho,\varphi,\varrho',\varphi') = \frac{1}{\sqrt{2\pi}} \int_{-\infty}^{\infty} W^R(s,\varrho,\xi,\varrho')e^{i\xi(\varphi-\varphi_0)}d\xi,$$

where $W^R(s,\varrho,\xi,\varrho')$ satisfies the equation

$$\left(\xi^2 + 2s\right)W^R - \left(W^R_{\varrho\varrho} + \frac{1}{\varrho}W^R_{\varrho}\right) = \frac{2}{\varrho'}\delta\left(\varrho - \varrho'\right), \tag{12.88}$$

and the regularity conditions at $\varrho = 0$, $\varrho = \infty$. The regular solution of equation (12.88) has the same form as before, namely,

$$W^R(s,\varrho,\xi,\varrho') = 2K_{|\xi|}(\sqrt{2s}\varrho_>)I_{|\xi|}(\sqrt{2s}\varrho_<).$$

The inverse Laplace transform of $W^R(s,\varrho,\xi,\varrho')$ yields

$$U^R(\chi,\varrho,\xi,\varrho') = \frac{e^{-(\varrho^2+\varrho'^2)/2\chi}}{\chi}I_{|\xi|}\left(\frac{\varrho\varrho_0}{\chi}\right),$$

so that

$$U^R(\chi,\varrho,\varphi,\varrho',\varphi') = \frac{e^{-(\varrho^2+\varrho'^2)/2\chi}}{\sqrt{2\pi\chi}} \int_0^{\infty} I_{|\xi|}\left(\frac{\varrho\varrho'}{\chi}\right)\cos\left(\xi\left(\varphi-\varphi'\right)\right)d\xi.$$

In order to construct the periodic Green's function U^P in the physical space out of the aperiodic Green's function U^R on the Riemann surface, we have to sum up U^R corresponding to the points $\varphi' + 2m\pi$,

$$U^P(\chi,\varrho,\varphi,\varrho',\varphi') = \sum_{m=-\infty}^{\infty} U^R(\chi,\varrho,\varphi,\varrho',\varphi'+2m\pi).$$

We can sum up this series explicitly and obtain the following expression for U^P,

$$U^P(\chi,\varrho,\varphi,\varrho',\varphi') = \frac{e^{-(\varrho^2-2\varrho\varrho'\cos(\varphi-\varphi')+\varrho'^2)/2\chi}}{2\pi\chi}.$$

Unfortunately, in order to construct the Green's function in the wedge by the method of images, we have to use U^R rather than U^P. Reflecting the point (ϱ', φ') in the ϱ, φ half-plane with respect to the half-lines $\varphi = 0$ and $\varphi = \alpha$ and locating sources at the points $(\varrho, \varphi' + 2m\alpha)$ and sinks at the points $(\varrho, -\varphi' + 2m\alpha)$, we represent the Green's function for the wedge U^W as

$$U^W(\chi, \varrho, \varphi, \varrho', \varphi')$$
$$= \sum_{m=-\infty}^{\infty} \left\{ U^R(\chi, \varrho, \varphi, \varrho', \varphi' + 2m\alpha) - U^R(\varrho, \varphi, \varrho_0, -\varphi_0 + 2m\alpha) \right\}.$$

In general, using this series expansion is impractical because the terms of the series are not known explicitly (recall that we sum up the Green's functions on the Riemann surface which are expressed as complicated integrals, rather than the Green's functions in the physical plane which are expressed in terms of elementary functions). However, for special values of α, we can find U^W explicitly. Let us assume, for example, that $\alpha = \pi/2$ which means that $\rho = 0$. Then we can represent U^W as

$$U^W(\chi, \varrho, \varphi, \varrho', \varphi') = \sum_{m=-\infty}^{\infty} \left\{ U^R(\chi, \varrho, \varphi, \varrho', \varphi' + 2 \cdot 2m\alpha) \right. \qquad (12.89)$$
$$-U^R(\chi, \varrho, \varphi, \varrho', -\varphi' + 2 \cdot 2m\alpha) + U^R(\chi, \varrho, \varphi, \varrho', \varphi' + 2 \cdot (2m+1)\alpha)$$
$$\left. -U^R(\chi, \varrho, \varphi, \varrho', -\varphi' + 2 \cdot (2m+1)\alpha) \right\}$$
$$= U^P(\chi, \varrho, \varphi, \varrho', \varphi') - U^P(\chi, \varrho, \varphi, \varrho', -\varphi')$$
$$+U^P(\chi, \varrho, \varphi, \varrho', \varphi' + \pi) - U^P(\chi, \varrho, \varphi, \varrho', -\varphi' + \pi).$$

It is clear that the Green's function in the wedge is a combination of four Green's functions in the whole physical space of which only one is centered inside the corresponding wedge. Likewise, for $\alpha = \pi/3, (\rho = -1/2)$, we have

$$U^W(\chi, \varrho, \varphi, \varrho', \varphi') = U^P(\chi, \varrho, \varphi, \varrho', \varphi') - U^P(\chi, \varrho, \varphi, \varrho', -\varphi') \qquad (12.90)$$
$$+U^P(\varrho, \varphi, \varrho', \varphi' + 2\pi/3) - U^P(\varrho, \varphi, \varrho', -\varphi' + 2\pi/3)$$
$$+U^P(\varrho, \varphi, \varrho', \varphi' + 4\pi/3) - U^P(\varrho, \varphi, \varrho', -\varphi' + 4\pi/3),$$

so that U^W is a combination of six functions U^P of which only one is centered inside the wedge. Similar expressions can be obtained for $\alpha = \pi/(N+1)$, $\rho = -\cos[\pi/(N+1)]$. Although formulas (12.89), (12.90) are mere curiosities, they are useful for checking more general expressions. In addition, they can be used for the purposes of extrapolation in the interval $-1 \leq \rho \leq 1$.

12.8.3   Two-factor, double-no-touch option

For the purposes of illustration, we show how to price two-factor, double-no-touch options which pay a dollar provided that two FXRs do not cross given barriers. The corresponding payoff written in polar coordinates has the form

$$u\left(\varrho,\varphi\right) = e^{p\varrho\cos(\varphi+q)} = I_0\left(p\varrho\right) + 2\sum_{k=1}^{\infty} I_k\left(p\varrho\right)\cos\left(k\left(\varphi+q\right)\right),$$

where

$$p \;=\; \sqrt{\left(\delta_-^1\right)^2 + \left(\delta_-^2\right)^2},$$

$$q \;=\; \arctan\left(\frac{\delta_-^1 + \rho\delta_-^2}{\bar{\rho}\delta_-^2}\right) - \alpha,$$

with $\delta_-^{1,2}$ given by (12.77), and $I_k\left(.\right)$ is the modified Bessel function of order k. By using the Green's function we can represent the solution $U\left(\chi,\varrho,\varphi\right)$ as

$$U\left(\chi,\varrho,\varphi\right) \tag{12.91}$$

$$= \int_0^{\infty}\int_0^{\alpha} G\left(\chi,\varrho,\varphi,\varrho',\varphi'\right) e^{p\varrho'\sin(\varphi'+q)} \varrho' d\varrho' d\varphi'$$

$$= \frac{2e^{-\varrho^2/2\chi}}{\alpha\chi}\left\{\sum_{n=1}^{\infty}\left[A_{n0}B_{n0} + 2\sum_{k=1}^{\infty} A_{nk}B_{nk}\right]\sin\left(\frac{n\pi\varphi}{\alpha}\right)\right\},$$

where

$$A_{nk} = \int_0^{\infty} e^{-\varrho'^2/2\chi} I_{\frac{n\pi}{\alpha}}\left(\frac{\varrho\varrho'}{\chi}\right) I_k\left(p\varrho'\right)\varrho' d\varrho', \tag{12.92}$$

$$B_{nk} = \int_0^{\alpha}\cos\left(k\left(\varphi'+q\right)\right)\sin\left(\frac{n\pi\varphi'}{\alpha}\right)d\phi'. \tag{12.93}$$

Substituting expressions (12.92), (12.93) in equation (12.91) we obtain an "explicit" formula for $U\left(\chi,\varrho,\varphi\right)$.

12.9   Four-barrier options

In this section we consider a particular example of a two-factor option with four barriers, namely, the so-called quadruple-no-touch option. Such an option pays the buyer a dollar provided that two FXRs S^{01}, S^{02} stay within given barriers between the inception of the option and its maturity. In other words, the buyer receives a dollar provided that

$$A^{01} < S_t^{01} < B^{01}, \quad A^{02} < S_t^{02} < B^{02}, \quad 0 \le t \le T. \tag{12.94}$$

We use transformations (9.26), (12.74) and reduce the pricing problem to the standard form

$$U_\chi - \frac{1}{2}U_{Z^1 Z^1} - \rho U_{Z^1 Z^2} - \frac{1}{2}U_{Z^2 Z^2} = 0, \quad 0 \le Z^i \le d^i, \tag{12.95}$$

$$U\left(0, Z^1, Z^2\right) = e^{\delta^1 Z^1 + \delta^2 Z^2}, \tag{12.96}$$

$$U\left(\chi, 0, Z^2\right) = U\left(\chi, d^1, Z^2\right) = U\left(\chi, Z^1, 0\right) = U\left(\chi, Z^1, d^2\right). \tag{12.97}$$

Here

$$\delta^i = -\sqrt{\sigma^{0i}/\sigma^{0(3-i)}}\beta^i, \quad d^i = \sqrt{\sigma^{0(3-i)}/\sigma^{0i}} \ln\left(B^{0i}/A^{0i}\right),$$

where β^i are given by equation (9.27).

This problem can be solved by the same eigenfunction expansion method as we used in Section 12.4 for pricing for pricing one-factor double-barrier options. The difficulty is that for $\rho \ne 0$ exact eigenvalues and eigenfunctions are not known. This issue will be addressed shortly, for now we assume that $\rho = 0$. In this case the normalized eigenfunctions can be chosen in the form

$$u^{m_1 m_2}\left(Z^1, Z^2\right) = \frac{2}{\sqrt{d^1 d^2}} \sin\left(k_{m^1}^1 Z^1\right) \sin\left(k_{m^2}^2 Z^2\right). \tag{12.98}$$

where $k_{m^i}^i = m^i \pi / d^i$, and m^i are independent positive integers. Indeed, a straightforward calculation yields

$$\frac{1}{2}u_{Z^1 Z^1}^{m_1 m_2} + \frac{1}{2}u_{Z^2 Z^2}^{m_1 m_2} = \Lambda^{m_1 m_2} u^{m_1 m_2},$$

where

$$\Lambda^{m_1 m_2} = -\frac{1}{2}\left(\left(k^1\right)^2 + \left(k^2\right)^2\right) = -\frac{\pi^2}{2}\left(\left(\frac{m^1}{d^1}\right)^2 + \left(\frac{m^2}{d^2}\right)^2\right).$$

These functions form an orthonormal basis in the space of all functions of two variables.

Thus, particular solutions of problem (12.95), (12.97) can be chosen in the form

$$U^{m^1 m^2} \left(\chi, Z^1, Z^2 \right) = e^{\Lambda^{m^1 m^2} \chi} u^{m^1 m^2} \left(Z^1, Z^2 \right)$$

Any solution of this problem can be represented as a linear combination of these particular solutions:

$$U \left(\chi, Z^1, Z^2 \right) = \sum_{1 \leq m^1, m^2 < \infty} c^{m^1 m^2} U^{m^1 m^2} \left(\chi, Z^1, Z^2 \right), \qquad (12.99)$$

where $c^{m^1 m^2}$ are arbitrary constants. In order to satisfy initial condition (12.96), we have to choose these constants in such a way that

$$e^{\delta^1 Z^1 + \delta^2 Z^2} = \sum_{1 \leq m^1, m^2 < \infty} c^{m^1 m^2} u^{m^1 m^2} \left(Z^1, Z^2 \right).$$

Due to orthonormality, we can represent $c^{m^1 m^2}$ as follows

$$c^{m^1 m^2} = \iint_{0 \leq Z^1 \leq d^1, 0 \leq Z^2 \leq d^2} e^{\delta^1 Z^1 + \delta^2 Z^2} u^{m^1 m^2} \left(Z^1, Z^2 \right) dZ^1 dZ^2 = h^{m^1} h^{m^2},$$

$$(12.100)$$

where

$$h^{m^i} = \sqrt{\frac{2}{d^i}} \int_{0 \leq Z^i \leq d^i} e^{\delta^i Z^i} \sin \left(k_{m^i}^i Z^i \right) dZ^i.$$

By using equation (12.37) we obtain

$$h^{m^i} = \sqrt{\frac{2}{d^i}} \frac{\left((-1)^{m^i+1} e^{\delta^i d^i} + 1 \right) k_{m^i}^i}{\left(\delta^i \right)^2 + \left(k_{m^i}^i \right)^2}.$$

By using formulas (12.99), (12.100) we solve the initial value problem in its entirety. The beauty and efficiency of the above method, which was developed by the present author, stems from the fact that eigenvalues $\Lambda^{m^1 m^2}$ decay very rapidly. Accordingly, in realistic situations, very few terms in the sum (12.99) need to be evaluated. The price of a typical quadruple-no-touch option for the case of zero correlation is shown in Figure 12.6.

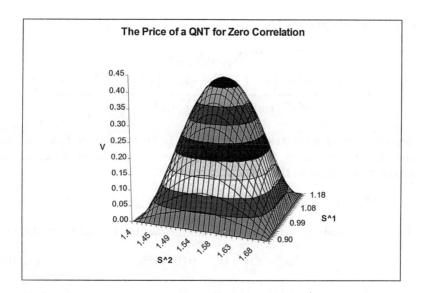

Figure 12.6: The price of a typical quadruple-no-touch with one year to maturity in the case of $\rho = 0$. The relevant parameters are $A^{01} = 0.9$, $B^{01} = 1.2$, $A^{02} = 1.4$, $B^{02} = 1.7$, $\sigma^{01} = 15\%$, $\sigma^{02} = 10\%$, $r^0 = 4.5\%$, $r^1 = 5.5\%$, $r^2 = 6\%$.

It was already mentioned that the case $\rho \neq 0$ is slightly more complex because for the spectral problem

$$\mathcal{L}u \equiv \frac{1}{2}u_{Z^1 Z^1} + \rho u_{Z^1 Z^2} + \frac{1}{2}u_{Z^2 Z^2} = \Lambda u,$$

$$u\left(0, Z^2\right) = u\left(d^1, Z^2\right) = u\left(Z^1, 0\right) = u\left(Z^1, d^2\right) = 0, \qquad (12.101)$$

the exact form of eigenfunctions and eigenvalues is not known. However, Lipton and Little showed that one can easily overcome this difficulty by using the Galerkin-Ritz method which replaces the exact spectral problem by an approximate problem which is easier to handle. As usual, in order to use the Galerkin-Ritz method we need to choose an appropriate basis in the space of functions $u\left(Z^1, Z^2\right)$ which satisfy boundary conditions (12.101). It is clear that functions $u^{m^1 m^2}\left(Z^1, Z^2\right)$ given by equation (12.98) form such a basis. A simple but tedious algebra which is left to the reader as a pleasant reminder of his high school years yields

$$\mathcal{L}^{m^1,m^2,\bar{m}^1,\bar{m}^2} = \Lambda^{m_1 m_2} \delta_{m_1,\bar{m}^1} \delta_{m^2,\bar{m}^2} \qquad (12.102)$$

$$+ \frac{4\rho m^1 m^2 \bar{m}^1 \bar{m}^2 \left(1 - (-1)^{m^1}(-1)^{\bar{m}^1}\right)\left(1 - (-1)^{m^2}(-1)^{\bar{m}^2}\right)}{d^1 d^2 \left((m^1)^2 - (\bar{m}^1)^2\right)\left((m^2)^2 - (\bar{m}^2)^2\right)}.$$

To proceed further we restrict ourselves to a finite set of basis functions and assume that $1 \leq m^1, m^2 \leq M$, so that there are M^2 basis functions in all. We count them according to the rule

$$\left(m^1, m^2\right) \rightarrow n = \left(m^1 - 1\right)M + \left(m^2 - 1\right), \qquad 0 \leq n \leq M^2 - 1.$$

The approximate initial value problem which we need to solve has the form

$$\boldsymbol{v}_\chi - \hat{\mathcal{L}}\boldsymbol{v} = \boldsymbol{0}, \qquad \boldsymbol{v}(0) = \boldsymbol{v}_0, \qquad (12.103)$$

where $\boldsymbol{v} = \left(v^0(\chi), ..., v^{M^2-1}(\chi)\right)$ is the M^2-component vector function of χ, $\hat{\mathcal{L}}$ is the $M^2 \times M^2$ symmetric matrix whose elements are given by expression (12.102), and $\boldsymbol{v}_0$ is the M^2-component vector whose elements are given by expression (12.100). Problem (12.103) can be solved in a straightforward fashion. Since $\hat{\mathcal{L}}$ is a symmetric matrix, we can represent it in the form

$$\hat{\mathcal{L}} = \mathcal{O}\mathcal{D}\mathcal{O}^T,$$

where $\mathcal{D}$ is a diagonal matrix consisting of the eigenvalues of the matrix $\hat{\mathcal{L}}$ (which are negative),

$$\mathcal{D} = diag\left(\tilde{\Lambda}^0, ..., \tilde{\Lambda}^{M^2-1}\right),$$

$\mathcal{O}$ is an orthogonal matrix, and $\mathcal{O}^T$ is the transpose of $\mathcal{O}$. By introducing $\boldsymbol{\nu} = \mathcal{O}\boldsymbol{v}$, or, equivalently, $\boldsymbol{v} = \mathcal{O}^T\boldsymbol{\nu}$, we can rewrite problem (12.103) in the form

$$\boldsymbol{\nu}_\chi - \mathcal{D}\boldsymbol{\nu} = \boldsymbol{0}, \qquad \boldsymbol{\nu}(0) = \boldsymbol{\nu}_0 = \mathcal{O}\boldsymbol{v}_0.$$

The corresponding solution is given by

$$\boldsymbol{\nu}(\chi) = \left(e^{\tilde{\Lambda}^0\chi}\nu^0, ..., e^{\tilde{\Lambda}^{M^2-1}\chi}\nu^{M^2-1}\right),$$

so that

$$v(\chi) = \mathcal{O}^T \nu(\chi).$$

Once $v(\chi)$ is found, an approximate solution of problem (12.95) - (12.97) can be represented in the form

$$U(\chi, Z^1, Z^2) = \sum_{0 \le n \le M^2 - 1} v^n(\chi) u^n(Z^1, Z^2).$$

It was mentioned earlier that $\tilde{\Lambda}^n$ are negative. It is easy to see that $\tilde{\Lambda}^n \to -\infty$ when $n \to \infty$. For realistic parameter values this convergence is very rapid. Thus we can choose a relatively small M, say $M = 10$, and obtain a very accurate approximation for $U(\chi, Z^1, Z^2)$, provided that χ is not small. We show the price of a typical quadruple-no-touch option for the case of nonzero correlation in Figure 12.7.

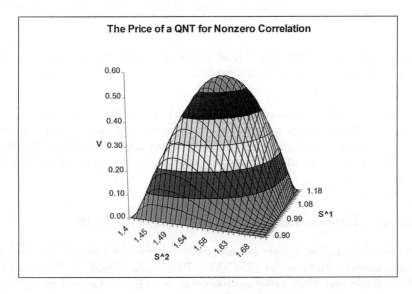

Figure 12.7: The price of a typical quadruple-no-touch in the case of $\rho = 0.90$. The relevant parameters are the same as in Figure 12.6.

In addition, in Figure 12.8 we show the expected exit time from the domain described by conditions (12.94) for the process (S_t^{01}, S_t^{02}).

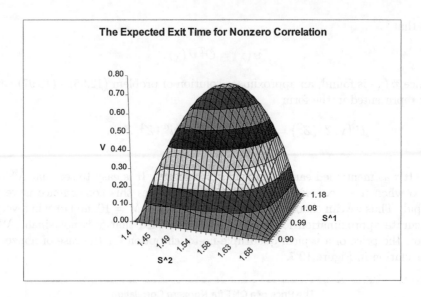

Figure 12.8: The expected exit time in the case of $\rho = 0.90$. The relevant parameters are the same as in Figure 12.6.

The eigenfunction expansion method which is described in this section can also be used for solving a variety of three-dimensional problems. For instance, one can use it for pricing barrier options on three correlated FXRs. However, since these options are of little practical interest, we do not consider them for the sake of brevity.

12.10   References and further reading

The following original papers are especially relevant for the material covered in this chapter: Andersen *et al.* (2000), Beaglehole (1993), Bowie and Carr (1994), Boyle and Tian (1999), Broadie *et al.* (1997), Carr *et al.* (1998), Davydov and Linetsky (2000), Derman *et al.* (1997), Figlewski and Gao (1999), He *et al.* (1998), Kunitomo and Ikeda (1992), Lipton (1997 b,c, 1998 a,b, 2000), Lipton and Little (2000), Merton (1973), Reiner (1998), Roberts and Shortland (1997), Rubinstein and Reiner (1991), Schmok *et al.* (1999), Schroder (1999 a). The following books contain useful mathematical insights: Morse and Feschbach (1953), Tikhonov and Samarskiji (1963).

Chapter 13

Path-dependent options II: lookback, Asian and other options

13.1 Introduction

In the previous chapter we studied barrier options whose payoffs depend on the FXR evolution in a very simple way. More general path-dependent options represent a very important class of modern derivative products.

On the face of it, they have very different descriptions and address very different financial needs. However, as we will show below, in reality almost all of them can be studied from a unified viewpoint. This observation not only allows us to find some order in the sea of chaos but also to use one exotic product to proxy hedge another one, etc. The main technical instrument we develop in order to achieve this unification is the theory of augmented (one-factor several-state-variables) SDEs which captures the essence of the pricing and hedging problem for path-dependent options. This theory complements the classical theory of local time due to Levy. Often the similarity reduction method can be used for solving one-factor several-state-variables PDEs describing path-dependent options. This method is very useful for establishing common features of different path-dependent options.

It is often argued that certain path-dependent options are ill-suited for the analysis via the PDE method and can be priced via the Monte Carlo method alone. We will show below that for the vast majority of path-dependent options which are important in practice this is not the case. In fact, specially designed PDE methods can be quite efficient for both pricing and hedging of path-dependent options.

Specific classes of path-dependent options which we study in this Chapter include lookback, timer, fader, Asian, passport, and similar options. We also discuss generic options on the trading account. In addition, we show how to price and hedge volatility and variance swaps and options on volatility.

The Chapter is organized as follows. In Section 2 we introduce functionals in the space of FXR trajectories and use them to define the main classes of path-dependent options (including barrier options studied in the previous Chapter). Next, we describe the augmentation procedure which is used below to develop a unified description of path-dependent options. In Section 3 we briefly discuss risk-neutral valuation of path-dependent options. In Section 4 we discuss probabilistic pricing of special classes of path-dependent options. In Section 5 we study lookback calls and puts. Different approaches to pricing and hedging of Asian options are discussed in Section 6. Timers, faders, and Parisian options are considered in Section 7. Sections 8 and 9 are devoted to standard and generalized passport options, respectively. In Section 10 we discuss variance and volatility swaps in the Black-Scholes framework. In Section 11 we develop techniques for pricing path-dependent options on FXRs with stochastic volatility. In Section 12 we apply these techniques to pricing forward starting options (cliquets). Section 13 is devoted to pricing options on variance and volatility in the stochastic volatility framework. References are given in Section 14.

13.2   Path-dependent options and augmented SDEs

13.2.1   Description of path dependent options

As usual, we start with the simplest possible case of the standard two-country market and assume that the FXR follows the geometrical Brownian motion,

$$\frac{dS_t}{S_t} = r^{01}dt + \sigma dW_t.$$

We observe the evolution of the price between $t = 0$ (today) and $t = T$ (maturity) and describe options whose payoffs depend on the values of S_t along the entire trajectory $S_t, 0 \leq t \leq T$, rather than on its end point S_T alone (as is the case for European calls and puts). Such options include barrier, look-back, Asian, timer, fader, passport and other classes of options on the FXR, as well as volatility swaps and related volatility-dependent products. All of these options can be defined and traded in the continuous- and discrete-time settings.

First, we consider barrier options which were studied directly in the previous chapter. In the continuous case, payoffs of such options depend on S_T and the following functionals of the price trajectory

$$M_{0,T} = \sup_{0 \leq t \leq T} S_t, \qquad m_{0,T} = \inf_{0 \leq t \leq T} S_t,$$

or more generally, in the case when partial barriers are considered,

$$M_{\Xi_{0,T}} = \sup_{t \in \Xi_{0,T}} S_t, \qquad m_{\Xi_{0,T}} = \inf_{t \in \Xi_{0,T}} S_t,$$

where $\Xi_{0,T}$ is a given observation window. By considering different possible dependencies of the payoff on $S_T, M_{0,T}, m_{0,T}$ we can construct all the barrier options considered in the previous chapter (and many others). For instance, an option with the payoff of the form

$$\text{payoff}^{(UOC)} = \theta \left(B - M_{0,T} \right) \left(S_T - K \right)_+, \qquad K < B,$$

which depends on S_T and $M_{0,T}$, is the familiar up-and out (or knock-out) call (UOC) which pays the buyer the value of the standard call with the strike K provided that the price of the stock never crosses the upper barrier B. A complementary option, which is the up-and-in (knock-in) call (UIC) has the payoff of the form

$$\text{payoff}^{(UIC)} = \theta \left(M_{0,T} - B \right) \left(S_T - K \right)_+, \qquad K < B.$$

Along similar lines, we can study double-barrier calls with payoffs depending on $S_T, M_{0,T}, m_{0,T}$,

$$\text{payoff}^{(DBC)} = \theta \left(B - M_{0,T} \right) \theta \left(m_{0,T} - A \right) \left(S_T - K \right)_+, \qquad A < K < B.$$

As we know, such an option pays the intrinsic value of the standard call provided that the FXR breaches neither the lower nor the upper barrier.

In the discrete setting we observe the FXR at discrete moments $t_0 < t_1 < \ldots < t_{N-1} < t_N$, where $t_0 = 0, t_N = T$, and define the discrete maximum and minimum:

$$M_{0,N} = \max_{n, 0 \leq n \leq N} S_{t_n}, \qquad m_{0,N} = \inf_{n, 0 \leq n \leq N} S_{t_n}.$$

The corresponding payoffs are modified in an obvious way, for example, the modified payoff of a UOC has the form

$$\text{payoff}^{(UOC)} = \theta \left(M_{0,N} - B \right) \left(S_T - K \right)_+,$$

etc.

A different kind of options which involve $M_{0,T}, m_{0,T}$, and S_T, are the so-called lookback options which give the buyer the right to acquire the foreign currency at the lowest price realized between the inception of an option and its maturity (a lookback call (LBC) with floating strike), or to sell the foreign currency at the maximum realized price (a lookback put (LBP) with floating strike). The corresponding payoffs have the form

$$\text{payoff}^{(LBC)} = S_T - m_{0,T}, \quad \text{payoff}^{(LBP)} = M_{0,T} - S_T,$$

respectively. In the discrete framework these payoffs are

$$\text{payoff}^{(LBC)} = S_T - m_{0,N}, \quad \text{payoff}^{(LBP)} = M_{0,N} - S_T.$$

Strictly speaking, LBCs and LBPs are not options since they have payoffs which are (almost) always positive and hence are always exercised.

Other lookbacks which are traded in the market have fixed strikes, for example, call (put) options on the realized maximum (minimum) of the FXR with the payoffs of the form

$$\text{payoff}^{\left(\widetilde{LBC} \right)} = \left(M_{0,T} - K \right)_+, \ \text{payoff}^{\left(\widetilde{LBP} \right)} = \left(K - M_{0,T} \right)_+, \quad (13.1)$$

etc.

Occasionally, one has to deal with the so-called partial lookback calls and puts with the payoffs of the form

$$\text{payoff}^{(PLBC)} = \left(S_T - \frac{m_{0,T}}{\Lambda} \right)_+, \quad \text{payoff}^{(PLBP)} = \left(\Lambda M_{0,T} - S_T \right)_+, \quad (13.2)$$

where $0 < \Lambda < 1$ is a reduction factor. Such options are exercised only when

$$\frac{S_T}{m_{0,T}} > \frac{1}{\Lambda}, \quad \frac{M_{0,T}}{S_T} > \frac{1}{\Lambda}.$$

It is clear that many other functionals on the realized FXR trajectory can be of financial interest. For instance, we can consider calls and puts on the average FXR observed between their inception and maturity which are called Asian calls (AsC) and Asian puts (AsP), respectively. The corresponding average is defined by

$$A_{0,t} = \frac{1}{t} \int_0^t S_{t'} \, dt',$$

so that the payoffs of AsCs and AsPs with fixed strikes K have the form

$$\text{payoff}^{(AsC)} = (A_{0,T} - K)_+ , \quad \text{payoff}^{(AsP)} = (K - A_{0,T})_+ .$$

Asian calls and puts with floating strikes are defined by the following payoffs:

$$\text{payoff}^{(\widetilde{AsC})} = (A_{0,T} - S_T)_+ , \quad \text{payoff}^{(\widetilde{AsP})} = (S_T - A_{0,T})_+ .$$

They give the buyer the right to buy (sell) the foreign currency at the average FXR prevailing between $t = 0$ and $t = T$. Integration by parts gives an alternative expression for $A_{0,t}$ which is useful in some cases:

$$\begin{aligned}
A_{0,t} &= \frac{1}{t} \int_0^t [d\,(t' S_{t'}) - t' dS_{t'}] &\text{(13.3)}\\
&= S_t - \frac{1}{t} \int_0^t t' dS_{t'} \\
&= S_0 + \int_0^t \left(1 - \frac{t'}{t}\right) dS_{t'}.
\end{aligned}$$

Often it is useful to deal with the cumulative FXR defined by

$$I_{0,t} = \int_0^t S_{t'} \, dt', \tag{13.4}$$

instead of $A_{0,t}$. Payoffs of Asian calls and puts written in terms of $I_{0,T}$ have the form

$$\text{payoff}^{(AsC)} = \left(\frac{I_{0,T}}{T} - K\right)_+ , \quad \text{payoff}^{(AsP)} = \left(K - \frac{I_{0,T}}{T}\right)_+ .$$

One of the drawbacks of barrier options (for the buyer and the seller alike) is their discontinuous dependence on the FXR trajectory. From the buyer's prospective this leads to the possibility of loosing a valuable protection if the rate breaks the barrier even for a very short period of time. From the seller's viewpoint, this discontinuity results in unacceptably large Deltas and Gammas which have to be maintained when the price approaches the barrier. These drawbacks can be rectified if the discontinuous factor $\theta\left(M_{0,T} - B\right)$, say, is replaced by a different factor depending on the occupational time, i.e., the time which the rate spends above the barrier, or the excursion time, i.e., the longest continuous time the rate spends above the barrier, etc. In addition, one can consider options depending only on the occupational time. The occupational time which the FXR spends above some level B is defined as follows

$$\vartheta_{0,t}\left(B\right) = \int_0^t \theta(S_{t'} - B) dt',$$

while the excursion time has the form

$$\varpi_{0,t}\left(B\right) = \left(t - \gamma_{0,t}\left(B\right)\right)\theta\left(S_t - B\right),$$

where $\gamma_{0,t}\left(B\right)$ is the last time before t at which S_t hit the level B, i.e.,

$$\gamma_{0,t}\left(B\right) = \sup\left\{t' \le t | S_{t'} = B\right\}.$$

In the discrete setting we define the corresponding times according to

$$\vartheta_{0,t_n}\left(B\right) = \sum_{n'=1}^{n} \theta(S_{t_{n'}} - B)\left(t_{n'} - t_{n'-1}\right),$$

$$\varpi_{0,t_n}\left(B\right) = \left(t_n - \gamma_{0,t_n}\left(B\right)\right)\theta\left(S_{t_n} - B\right),$$

where

$$\gamma_{0,t_n}\left(B\right) = \max\left\{n' \le n | \left(S_{n'} - B\right)\left(S_{n'-1} - B\right) \le 0\right\}.$$

There are several ways of constructing options depending on S_T, $\vartheta_{0,T}\left(B\right)$ which are economically relevant. For example, we can define the so-called timer options with payoffs of the form

$$\text{payoff}^{(TMR)} = F(\vartheta_{0,T}\left(B\right)), \tag{13.5}$$

where Φ is an appropriately chosen function. Two cases are particularly interesting: (A) a simple timer option with the payoff of the form

$$F(\vartheta) = \alpha\vartheta,$$

(B) a timer option floored at L and capped at U with the following payoff

$$F(\vartheta) = \min\{\max\{\alpha\vartheta, L\}, U\}.$$

In addition, we can introduce the so-called fader options with payoffs of the form

$$\text{payoff}^{(FDR)} = \Xi(S_T, \vartheta_{0,T}(B)). \tag{13.6}$$

Particularly interesting fader options have the following separable payoffs

$$
\begin{aligned}
\text{payoff}^{(FDRC)} &= F(\vartheta_{0,T}(B))(S_T - K)_+, \\
\text{payoff}^{(FDRP)} &= F(\vartheta_{0,T}(B))(K - S_T)_+,
\end{aligned}
$$

where

$$F(\vartheta) = 1 - \vartheta/T.$$

We can think of such options as calls and puts whose notional diminishes proportionally to the time spent above (say) some barrier level B.

It is clear that by appropriately choosing F we can approximate barrier options by faders. For example, it is easy to see that UOC can be represented as a limit of fader options with the following payoffs

$$\text{payoff} = e^{-\rho\vartheta_{0,T}(B)}(S_T - K)_+,$$

when $\rho \to \infty$.

Payoffs of Parisian options depend on the terminal value of the FXR, S_T, and the maximum of the excursion time $\varpi_{0,t}$ the FXR rate spends above (or below) a given barrier B. For instance, the payoffs of the Parisian call and put with strike K and knock-out period D have the form

$$
\begin{aligned}
\text{payoff}^{(PRSNC)} &= (S_T - K)_+ \, \theta\left(D - \max_{0 \le t \le T} \varpi_{0,t}\right), \tag{13.7} \\
\text{payoff}^{(PRSNP)} &= (K - S_T)_+ \, \theta\left(D - \max_{0 \le t \le T} \varpi_{0,t}\right).
\end{aligned}
$$

We can also combine some of the building blocks introduced above and design custom-made options, for instance, an Asian call with averaging occurring only when the price is above a certain barrier. At maturity such a call pays

$$
\text{payoff} = \begin{cases} \frac{\int_0^T S_t \theta(S_t - B)dt}{\int_0^T \theta(S_t - B)dt}, & \text{if} \quad M_{0,T} > B \\ 0, & \text{if} \quad M_{0,T} < B \end{cases}.
$$

One more class of derivatives which depend on the entire price trajectory are the so-called passport options. In the simplest case the payoff of a passport option is defined as follows

$$\text{payoff}^{(PO)} = \left(\int_0^T e^{r^0(T-t)} q_t S_t \sigma dW_t \right)_+ ,$$

where q_t is a trading strategy chosen by the buyer of the option in order to maximize the expected payoff. In order to guarantee that such an option has a finite value, the strategy q_t has to satisfy some constraints, for instance, $|q_t| \leq 1$, or, more generally, $-\alpha \leq q_t \leq \beta$. These constraints mean that the buyer of a passport option can buy (sell) foreign currency in the amount not exceeding β (α). Passport options, originally developed at Bankers trust by Hyer, Pugachevsky, and the author, dramatically increase the concept of optionality and allow the buyer to participate in the trading process actively.

The discounted and projected values of a trading account corresponding to a particular choice of the trading strategy q_t are given by

$$\hat{\Pi}_{0,t} = \int_0^t e^{-r^0 t'} q_{t'} dS_{t'}, \qquad \check{\Pi}_{0,t} = \int_0^t e^{r^0(t-t')} q_{t'} dS_{t'},$$

It is clear that passport options are a particular class of options on the trading account. Many other options can be considered as options on the trading account. For instance, in view of relation (13.3) Asian options can be considered as options on the trading account generated by a deterministic trading strategy (provided that discounting is done properly).

In general, the payoff of an option on the trading account has the form

$$\text{payoff}^{(PO)} = F\left(\check{\Pi}_{0,T} \right).$$

Options on variance and volatility constitute one more important class of path-dependent options.

13.2.2 The augmentation procedure

It is useful to describe various functionals of the realized FXR in terms of SDEs. It turns out that for all the functionals introduced in the previous subsection (which between them more or less exhaust functionals which appear in practice) can be described using the concept of a system of one-factor several-state-variables SDEs, or, more or less equivalently, a higher-order SDE. This unifying viewpoint is very illuminating, however it does require a certain technical proficiency since in many cases the corresponding SDEs have singular coefficients. Once the corresponding SDEs are constructed, we can use the backward Kolmogoroff equation formalism in order to price path-dependent options.

We start with the most obvious case and consider the average FXR. The governing SDEs are

$$\frac{dS_t}{S_t} = r^{01}dt + \sigma dW_t,$$

$$dA_{0,t} = \frac{1}{t}\left(S_t - A_{0,t}\right)dt,$$

$$S_0 \text{ is given}, \quad A_{0,0} = S_0.$$

An equivalent form of the governing SDE is

$$\frac{dS_t}{S_t} = r^{01}dt + \sigma dW_t, \tag{13.8}$$

$$dI_{0,t} = S_t dt,$$

$$S_0 \text{ is given}, \quad I_{0,0} = 0.$$

The coupled system of SDEs describing the evolution of the pair $S_t, M_{0,t}$ has the form

$$\frac{dS_t}{S_t} = r^{01}dt + \sigma dW_t,$$

$$dM_{0,t} = \theta(S_t - M_{0,t})\left(dS_t\right)_+,$$

$$S_0 \text{ is given}, \quad M_{0,0} = S_0,$$

where we assume that $\theta(0) = 1$. In contrast to the previous case, these SDEs have to be dealt with some care since the coefficient in the second equation is discontinuous.

Similarly, for the pair $S_t, m_{0,t}$ the corresponding equations are

$$\frac{dS_t}{S_t} = r^{01}dt + \sigma dW_t,$$

$$dm_{0,t} = \theta(m_{0,t} - S_t)\left(dS_t\right)_-,$$

$$S_0 \text{ is given}, \quad m_{0,0} = S_0.$$

For the occupational time the governing SDEs can be written in the form

$$\frac{dS_t}{S_t} = r^{01}dt + \sigma dW_t,$$

$$d\vartheta_{0,t} = \theta(S_t - B)dt,$$

$$S_0 \text{ is given,} \quad \vartheta_{0,0} = 0. \tag{13.9}$$

For the excursion time the corresponding SDEs can be written as

$$\frac{dS_t}{S_t} = r^{01}dt + \sigma dW_t,$$

$$d\varpi_{0,t} = \theta(S_t - B)dt + \varpi_{0,t}\delta(S_t - B)dS_t,$$

$$S_0 \text{ is given,} \quad \varpi_{0,0} = 0. \tag{13.10}$$

It is clear that the occupational time is closely related to the local time $\lambda_{0,t}(B)$ which shows (broadly speaking) how much time the FXR spends at a given level B. The augmented system of SDEs for $S_t, \lambda_{0,t}$ has the form

$$\frac{dS_t}{S_t} = r^{01}dt + \sigma dW_t,$$

$$d\lambda_{0,t} = \delta(S_t - B)dt,$$

$$S_0 \text{ is given,} \quad \lambda_{0,0} = 0.$$

Since B is a parameter, we can obtain a useful relation between $\vartheta_{0,T}(B)$ and $\lambda_{0,T}(B)$, namely,

$$\frac{d}{dB}\vartheta_{0,T}(B) = -\lambda_{0,T}(B).$$

As we will see later, local times appear in a natural way when one describes the distribution of P&L corresponding to some imperfect hedging strategies.

Finally, for passport options the augmented system of SDEs reads

$$\frac{dS_t}{S_t} = r^{01}dt + \sigma dW_t,$$

$$d\Pi_{0,t} = r^0\Pi_{0,t}dt + q_t\left(dS_t - r^{01}Sdt\right) = r^0\Pi_{0,t}dt + q_tS_t\sigma dW_t,$$

$$S_0 \text{ is given,} \quad \Pi_{0,0} \text{ is given,} \tag{13.11}$$

where we assume that trading gains accrue interest (while trading losses have to be financed) at the "natural" risk-neutral rates r^0, r^{01}.

The general augmented system of SDEs can be written in the form

$$\frac{dS_t}{S_t} = r^{01} dt + \sigma dW_t,$$
$$dJ_{0,t} = f\left(t, S_t, J_{0,t}\right) dt + g\left(t, S_t, J_{0,t}\right) dS_t,$$
$$S_0 \text{ is given}, \quad J_{0,0} \text{ is given},$$

or, equivalently,

$$\frac{dS_t}{S_t} = r^{01} dt + \sigma dW_t,$$
$$dJ_{0,t} = \left(f\left(t, S_t, J_{0,t}\right) + r^{01} S_t g\left(t, S_t, J_{0,t}\right)\right) dt + \sigma S_t g\left(t, S_t, J_{0,t}\right) dW_t,$$
$$S_0 \text{ is given}, \quad J_{0,0} \text{ is given}.$$

It is not difficult to extend the augmentation procedure to cover discretely monitored path-dependent options. This extension is left to the reader to think about.

13.2.3 The pricing problem for augmented SDEs

The main advantage of the augmentation procedure is that it opens the possibility of pricing path-dependent options via PDE methods. The corresponding pricing equation is the familiar backward Kolmogoroff equation with killing:

$$V_t\left(t, S, J\right) + \frac{1}{2}\sigma^2 S^2 \left(V_{SS} + 2g\left(t, S, J\right) V_{SJ} + g^2\left(t, S, J\right) V_{JJ}\right)$$
$$+ \quad r^{01} S V_S\left(t, S, J\right) + \left(f\left(t, S, J\right) + r^{01} S g\left(t, S, J\right)\right) V_J - r^0 V\left(t, S, J\right) = 0.$$

This equation is supplied with the terminal condition

$$V\left(T, S, J\right) = v\left(S, J\right),$$

and the regularity conditions. Of course, the fact that we are dealing with path-dependent options has to manifests itself somehow. Its hallmark is the fact that the pricing PDE is degenerate since there are two state variables, namely, S and J, but only one source of uncertainty. This fact makes it difficult to solve the corresponding problem directly. However, often it can be done indirectly. Besides, as we will see in a due course, in many cases similarity reductions can be used in order to transform the pricing problem to the one-state-variable form.

13.3   Risk-neutral valuation of path-dependent options

We can formally evaluate path-dependent options via the risk-neutral valuation principle. Consider such an option. Assume, for simplicity, that the payoff of this option depends on the FXR observed at discrete times $t_0 = 0, ..., t_N = T$, so that

$$\text{payoff} = F\left(S_0, S_1, ..., S_{N-1}, S_N\right),$$

where $S_n = S_{t_n}$. By analogy with the path-independent case, we can represent the value of the option in question as the discounted risk-neutral expectation of the payoff,

$$V\left(0, S_0\right) = e^{-r^0 T} \mathbb{E}\left\{F\left(S_0, S_1, ..., S_{N-1}, S_N\right)\right\},$$

or, explicitly,

$$V\left(0, S_0\right) \tag{13.12}$$

$$= e^{-r^0 T} \int \cdots \int_{0 < S_1 < \infty, ..., 0 < S_N < \infty} F\left(S_0, S_1, ..., S_{N-1}, S_N\right)$$

$$\times \pi\left(0, S_0, t_1, S_1\right) ... \pi\left(t_{N-1}, S_{N-1}, T, S_N\right) dS_1 ... dS_N,$$

where π is the standard lognormal t.p.d.f. It is clear that the latter N-dimensional integral is much more difficult to evaluate than its path-independent one-dimensional counterpart which reduces to

$$V\left(0, S_0\right) = e^{-r^0 T} \int_{0 < S_T < \infty} F\left(S_T\right) \pi\left(0, S_0, T, S_T\right) dS_T.$$

In the continuous limit we obtain the expression for the value of a path-dependent option as an integral in the functional space of trajectories starting at S_0 at time 0:

$$V\left(0, S_0\right) = e^{-r^0 T} \int_{\Omega} \mathcal{F}\left(\omega\right) d\mathcal{D}\left(\omega\right). \tag{13.13}$$

Here $\mathcal{F}\left(\omega\right)$ is a functional mapping trajectories into payoffs, and $d\mathcal{D}\left(\omega\right)$ is a risk-neutral probability measure in the space of trajectories. Usually it is easy to define $\mathcal{F}\left(\omega\right)$. For instance, for a fixed-strike Asian call we have

$$\mathcal{F}\left(\omega\right) = \left(\frac{1}{T} \int_0^T S_t dt - K\right)_+,$$

etc. At the same time, the formal definition of $dD(\omega)$ is rather involved and is beyond the scope of this book. Integrals of the form (13.13) have been studied by Wiener, Feynman and many others, however, they are difficult to define properly and deal with efficiently. Accordingly, risk-neutral valuation of path-dependent options is seldom done in practice. The only notable exception is their approximate Monte-Carlo valuation based on formula (13.12).

13.4 Probabilistic pricing

For barrier and lookback options it is possible to reduce the general formula (13.13) to a simpler form of two- or three-dimensional integrals. For instance, the value of an up-and-out can be written as

$$V^{(UOC)}(0, S_0) = e^{-r^0 T} \int_{S_0}^{B} \int_{K}^{M} (S_T - K) q(0, S_0, T, S_T, M_{0,T}) \, dS_T dM_{0,T},$$

where $q(0, S_0, T, S_T, M_{0,T})$ is the joint distribution of $S_T, M_{0,T}$ conditional on the given value of S_0.

The joint distributions for the FXR and its maximum and minimum are readily available. Here we show how to derive some of the relevant formulas. As usual, it is more convenient to use the logarithmic change of variables. We define

$$X_{t,T} = \ln(S_T/S_t), \quad y_{t,T} = \min_{t \le t' \le T} X_{t'}, \quad Y_{t,T} = \max_{t \le t' \le T} X_{t'}.$$

Our aim is to compute the following probabilities:

$$P(X_{t,T} \in dX, Y_{t,T} \le Y) = f(\tau, X, Y) \, dX,$$

$$P(X_{t,T} \in dX, y_{t,T} \ge y) = g(\tau, X, y) \, dX,$$

$$P(X_{t,T} \in dX, y_{t,T} \ge y, Y_{t,T} \le Y) = h(\tau, X, y, Y) \, dX,$$

where $y \le X \le Y$, $y \le 0$, $Y \ge 0$.

Once these probabilities are found, others can be obtained via simple integration and differentiation. For instance,

$$P(y_{t,T} \ge y, Y_{t,T} \le Y) = \int_{y}^{Y} h(\tau, X, y, Y) \, dX,$$

$$P\left(X_{t,T} \in dX, y_{t,T} \in dy, Y_{t,T} \in dY\right) = -\partial_{yY}^2 h\left(\tau, X, y, Y\right) dX dy dY,$$

etc.

We show how to compute $f\left(\tau, X, Y\right)$, $X \le Y$. This function satisfies the standard Fokker-Planck equation

$$f_\tau - \frac{1}{2}\sigma^2 f_{XX} + \left(r^{01} - \frac{1}{2}\sigma^2\right) f_X = 0,$$

which is supplied with the initial condition

$$f\left(0, X, Y\right) = \delta\left(x\right),$$

and the absorbing boundary conditions

$$f\left(\tau, -\infty, Y\right) = f\left(\tau, Y, Y\right) = 0.$$

Here Y is considered as a parameter. A straightforward application of the method of images, which is left to the reader as an exercise, yields

$$f\left(\tau, X, Y\right) = \frac{e^{-\left(X - \hat{\gamma}_- \sigma^2 \tau\right)^2 / 2\sigma^2 \tau} - e^{2\hat{\gamma}_- Y - \left(X - 2Y - \hat{\gamma}_- \sigma^2 \tau\right)^2 / 2\sigma^2 \tau}}{\sqrt{2\pi\sigma^2 \tau}}.$$

We differentiate $f\left(\tau, X, Y\right)$ with respect to Y and obtain

$$P\left(X_{t,T} \in dX, Y_{t,T} \in dY\right) = f_Y\left(\tau, X, Y\right) dX dY \qquad (13.14)$$

$$= \frac{2\left(2Y - X\right) e^{2\hat{\gamma}_- Y - \left(X - 2Y - \hat{\gamma}_- \sigma^2 \tau\right)^2 / 2\sigma^2 \tau}}{\sqrt{2\pi\sigma^2 \tau}\sigma^2 \tau} dX dY.$$

We integrate $f\left(\tau, X, Y\right)$ with respect to X, $X < Y$, and obtain

$$P\left(Y_{t,T} \le Y\right) = \int_{-\infty}^{Y} f\left(\tau, X, Y\right) dX$$

$$= \mathfrak{N}\left(\frac{Y}{\sigma\sqrt{\tau}} - \hat{\gamma}_- \sigma\sqrt{\tau}\right) - e^{2\hat{\gamma}_- Y}\mathfrak{N}\left(-\frac{Y}{\sigma\sqrt{\tau}} - \hat{\gamma}_- \sigma\sqrt{\tau}\right).$$

By the same token we can find $g\left(\tau, X, y\right)$:

$$g\left(\tau, X, y\right) = \frac{e^{-\left(X - \hat{\gamma}_- \sigma^2 \tau\right)^2 / 2\sigma^2 \tau} - e^{2\hat{\gamma}_- y - \left(X - 2y - \hat{\gamma}_- \sigma^2 \tau\right)^2 / 2\sigma^2 \tau}}{\sqrt{2\pi\sigma^2 \tau}}.$$

The evaluation of $h(\tau, X, y, Y)$ is a little more involved. It is clear that $h(\tau, X, y, Y)$ solves the boundary value problem

$$h_\tau - \frac{1}{2}\sigma^2 h_{XX} + \left(r^{01} - \frac{1}{2}\sigma^2\right)h_X = 0,$$

$$h(0, X, y, Y) = \delta(x),$$

$$h(\tau, y, y, Y) = h(\tau, Y, y, Y) = 0.$$

Accordingly, $h(\tau, X, y, Y)$ can be represented in two equivalent forms. The first representation is obtained by virtue of the method of images,

$$h(\tau, X, y, Y) = \sum_{k=-\infty}^{k=\infty}\left(P_I^{(k,+)}(\tau, X, y, Y) - P_I^{(k,-)}(\tau, X, y, Y)\right),$$

where

$$P_I^{(k,\pm)}(\tau, X, y, Y) = \frac{e^{-\hat{\gamma}_-^2\sigma^2\tau/2 + \hat{\gamma}_- X - (2kY - 2k_\pm y - X)^2/2\sigma^2\tau}}{\sqrt{2\pi\sigma^2\tau}},$$

and $k_+ = k$, $k_- = k+1$. The second representation is obtained via the method of Fourier series,

$$h(\tau, X, y, Y) = \sum_{k=1}^{k=\infty} P_F^{(k)}(\tau, X, y, Y), \tag{13.15}$$

where

$$P_F^{(k)}(\tau, X, y, Y) = \frac{2e^{-\hat{\gamma}_-^2\sigma^2\tau/2 + \hat{\gamma}_- X - k^2\pi^2\sigma^2\tau/2(Y-y)^2}}{Y - y}$$
$$\times \sin\left(\frac{-k\pi y}{Y - y}\right)\sin\left(\frac{k\pi(X - y)}{Y - y}\right).$$

As always, the first representation should be used for short-dated options and (or) wide barriers, while the second representation should be used for long-dated options and narrow barriers.

We can use the above formulas in order to revisit the pricing problem for barrier options. For instance, for an up–and–out call we can rewrite the valuation formula as

$$V^{(UOC)}(0, S_0) \tag{13.16}$$

$$= e^{-r^0 T} \int_0^{\ln(B/S_0)} \int_{\ln(K/S_0)}^{Y} \left(S_0 e^X - K\right) f_Y\left(T, X, Y\right) dX dY$$

$$= \frac{2e^{-r^0 T}}{\sqrt{2\pi\sigma^2 T}\sigma^2 T} \int_0^{\ln(B/S_0)} \int_{\ln(K/S_0)}^{Y} \left(S_0 e^X - K\right)$$

$$\times (2Y - X) \, e^{2\hat{\gamma}_- Y - \left(X - 2Y - \hat{\gamma}_- \sigma^2 \tau\right)^2 / 2\sigma^2 \tau} dX dY.$$

We leave it to the reader as an exercise to demonstrate that formulas (13.16) and (12.5) are in agreement.

13.5   Lookback calls and puts

13.5.1   Description

In the previous section we discussed barrier options whose popularity is due to the fact that they are cheaper than their vanilla counterparts and (under favorable circumstances) have the same payoffs. In this section we describe much more expensive options which, for a price, provide the buyer with the peace of mind. Very popular instruments of this kind are lookback calls (puts) which give the buyer the right to buy (sell) the foreign currency at the lowest (highest) FXR realized between the inception of a lookback option and its maturity. Floating lookback calls and puts have no prearranged strikes, their payoffs are

$$V^{(LBC)}(T, S, m, T) = S - m, \quad V^{(LBP)}(T, S, M, T) = M - S, \tag{13.17}$$

respectively. As before, we concentrate on the valuation of calls. Puts can be valued in a similar way, although there is no simple put-call parity for lookback options.

    Mathematical analysis of lookback calls combines the method of images and the method of symmetry reductions. At time t the price of a LBC depends on S_t, $m_{0,t}$, and $\tau = T - t$, i.e., on the spot FXR, the minimum FXR achieved to date, and the time to maturity. As a function of S_t the price is governed by the standard Black-Scholes pricing equation which is considered on the (time-dependent) interval $[\, m_{0,t}, \infty)$ with final condition (13.17) and the boundary conditions of the form

$$V_m^{(LBC)}(t, S = m, m, T) = 0, \qquad V^{(LBC)}(t, S \to \infty, m, T) \sim e^{-r'(T-t)} S,$$

where the subscript m denotes the partial derivative with respect to the third argument. Here the first condition expresses the fact that the price of LBC for $S = m$ cannot be linearly proportional to small variations in m because the realized minimum value at time t is larger than the realized minimum value at time T with probability one, while the second condition has the usual meaning.

As before, it is very useful to rewrite the pricing problem in the nondimensional form. This can be done by replacing K by m in equations introduced in Section 9.2. It is clear that $X = \ln(S/m) \geq 0$. The heat equation for $U(\chi, X)$,

$$U_X(\chi, X) - \frac{1}{2} U_{XX}(\chi, X) = 0, \tag{13.18}$$

is supplied with the initial and boundary conditions of the form

$$U(0, X) = e^{\hat{\gamma}_+ X} - e^{\hat{\gamma}_- X}, \qquad X \geq 0, \tag{13.19}$$

$$U_X(\chi, 0) - \hat{\gamma}_+ U(\chi, 0) = 0, \qquad U(\chi, X \to \infty) \sim e^{\hat{\gamma}_+^2 \chi/2 + \hat{\gamma}_+ X}. \tag{13.20}$$

13.5.2 Pricing via the method of images

To solve the pricing problem we follow Sommerfeld and use the following substitution:

$$W(\chi, X) = U_X(\chi, X) - \hat{\gamma}_+ U(\chi, X).$$

The pricing problem for W has the form

$$W_\tau - \frac{1}{2} W_{XX} = 0,$$

$$W(0, X) = e^{\hat{\gamma}_- X},$$

$$W(\chi, 0) = 0, \qquad W(\chi, X \to \infty) \to e^{\hat{\gamma}_-^2 \chi/2 + \hat{\gamma}_- X}.$$

We can express U in terms of W as follows:

$$U(\chi, X) = e^{\hat{\gamma}_+^2 \chi/2 + \hat{\gamma}_+ X} - \int_X^\infty e^{\hat{\gamma}_+(X-Y)} W(\chi, Y)\, dY.$$

It is very easy to find W via the familiar method of images:

$$
\begin{aligned}
&W(\chi, Y) \\
&= \frac{1}{\sqrt{2\pi\chi}} \left(\int_0^\infty e^{-(\xi-Y)^2/2\chi + \hat{\gamma}_- \xi}\, d\xi - \int_0^\infty e^{-(\xi+Y)^2/2\chi + \hat{\gamma}_- \xi}\, d\xi \right) \\
&= \frac{1}{\sqrt{2\pi\chi}} \left(e^{\hat{\gamma}_-^2 \chi/2 + \hat{\gamma}_- Y} \int_0^\infty e^{-\left((\xi-Y)/\sqrt{\chi} - \hat{\gamma}_- \sqrt{\chi}\right)^2/2}\, d\xi \right. \\
&\qquad \left. - e^{\hat{\gamma}_-^2 \chi/2 - \hat{\gamma}_- Y} \int_0^\infty e^{-\left((\xi+Y)/\sqrt{\chi} - \hat{\gamma}_- \sqrt{\chi}\right)^2/2}\, d\xi \right) \\
&= M(\chi, Y, \hat{\gamma}_-) - M(\chi, -Y, \hat{\gamma}_-).
\end{aligned}
$$

Once we know W we can determine U via a simple integration by parts:

$$
\begin{aligned}
&U(\chi, X) \hspace{4cm} (13.21)\\
&= e^{\hat{\gamma}_+^2 \chi/2 + \hat{\gamma}_+ X} - \int_X^\infty e^{\hat{\gamma}_+(X-Y)} \left(M(\chi, Y, \hat{\gamma}_-) - M(\chi, -Y, \hat{\gamma}_-) \right) dY
\end{aligned}
$$

$$= e^{\hat{\gamma}_+^2 \chi/2 + \hat{\gamma}_+ X} - e^{\hat{\gamma}_-^2 \chi/2 + \hat{\gamma}_+ X} \int_X^\infty e^{-Y} \mathfrak{N}\left(\frac{Y}{\sqrt{\chi}} + \hat{\gamma}_- \sqrt{\chi}\right) dY$$

$$+ e^{\hat{\gamma}_-^2 \chi/2 + \hat{\gamma}_+ X} \int_X^\infty e^{-2r^{01}Y} \mathfrak{N}\left(-\frac{Y}{\sqrt{\chi}} + \hat{\gamma}_- \sqrt{\chi}\right) dY$$

$$= e^{\hat{\gamma}_+^2 \chi/2 + \hat{\gamma}_+ X} + e^{\hat{\gamma}_-^2 \chi/2 + \hat{\gamma}_+ X} \int_X^\infty \mathfrak{N}\left(\frac{Y}{\sqrt{\chi}} + \hat{\gamma}_- \sqrt{\chi}\right) d\left(e^{-Y}\right)$$

$$- \frac{1}{2r^{01}} e^{\hat{\gamma}_-^2 \chi/2 + \hat{\gamma}_+ X} \int_X^\infty \mathfrak{N}\left(-\frac{Y}{\sqrt{\chi}} + \hat{\gamma}_- \sqrt{\chi}\right) d\left(e^{-2r^{01}Y}\right)$$

$$= e^{\hat{\gamma}_+^2 \chi/2 + \hat{\gamma}_+ X} - e^{\hat{\gamma}_-^2 \chi/2 + \hat{\gamma}_- X} \mathfrak{N}\left(\frac{X}{\sqrt{\chi}} + \hat{\gamma}_- \sqrt{\chi}\right)$$

$$- \frac{1}{\sqrt{2\pi\chi}} e^{\hat{\gamma}_-^2 \chi/2 + \hat{\gamma}_+ X} \int_X^\infty e^{-\left(Y/\sqrt{\chi} + \hat{\gamma}_- \sqrt{\chi}\right)^2/2 - Y} dY$$

$$+ \frac{1}{2r^{01}} e^{\hat{\gamma}_-^2 \chi/2 - \hat{\gamma}_- X} \mathfrak{N}\left(-\frac{X}{\sqrt{\chi}} + \hat{\gamma}_- \sqrt{\chi}\right)$$

$$- \frac{1}{2r^{01}\sqrt{2\pi\chi}} e^{\hat{\gamma}_-^2 \chi/2 + \hat{\gamma}_+ X} \int_X^\infty e^{-\left(-Y/\sqrt{\chi} + \hat{\gamma}_- \sqrt{\chi}\right)^2/2 - 2r^{01}Y} dY$$

$$= M\left(\chi, X, \hat{\gamma}_+\right) - M\left(\chi, X, \hat{\gamma}_-\right)$$

$$+ \frac{1}{2r^{01}} M\left(\chi, -X, \hat{\gamma}_-\right) - \frac{1}{2r^{01}} M\left(\chi, -X, -\hat{\gamma}_+\right).$$

We leave it to the reader as an exercise to obtain the following expression for the Green's function for problem (13.18) - (13.20):

$$G(\chi, X, Y) = H(\chi, X - Y) + H(\chi, X + Y) - 2\hat{\gamma}_+ M\left(\chi, -(X + Y), -\hat{\gamma}_+\right),$$

where H is the heat kernel. This expression generalizes the classical formula due to Sommerfeld.

In financial variables, the price of a LBC assumes the form

$$V^{(LBC)}(\tau, S, m) = C(\tau, S, m) \tag{13.22}$$
$$+ \frac{1}{2\hat{r}^{01}} \left\{ e^{-r^0\tau} \left(\frac{m}{S}\right)^{2\hat{\gamma}_-} m\mathfrak{N}\left(-\frac{\ln(S/m) - \gamma_-\tau}{\sigma\sqrt{\tau}}\right) \right.$$
$$\left. - e^{-r^1\tau} S\mathfrak{N}\left(-\frac{\ln(S/m) + \gamma_+\tau}{\sigma\sqrt{\tau}}\right) \right\}.$$

The price of typical lookback calls at inception are shown in Figure 13.1.

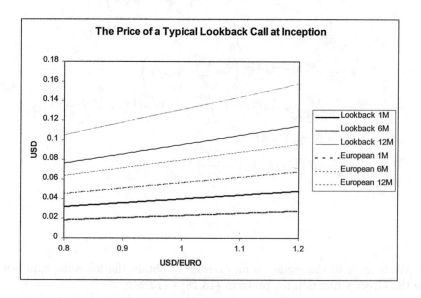

Figure 13.1: The prices of typical lookback calls at inception as functions of the spot FXR for three representative maturities, $T = 1, 6, 12$ months. The prices of European ATM calls are shown for comparison. The relevant parameters are $\sigma = 15\%$, $r^0 = 5.5\%$, $r^1 = 4.5\%$.

We leave it to the reader as an exercise to derive the valuation formula for a lookback put:

$$V^{(LBP)}(\tau, S, M) = P(\tau, S, M) \tag{13.23}$$

$$+ \frac{1}{2\hat{r}^{01}} \left\{ -e^{-r^0\tau} \left(\frac{M}{S} \right)^{2\hat{\gamma}_-} M\mathfrak{N} \left(\frac{\ln(S/M) - \gamma_-\tau}{\sigma\sqrt{\tau}} \right) \right.$$

$$\left. + e^{-r^1\tau} S\mathfrak{N} \left(\frac{\ln(S/M) + \gamma_+\tau}{\sigma\sqrt{\tau}} \right) \right\}.$$

When $r^0 = r^1 = r$, so that $r^{01} = 0$, equations (13.21), (13.22) assume the form

$$U(\chi, X) = M(\chi, X, 1/2) - M(\chi, X, -1/2)$$
$$- (X + \chi/2) M(\chi, -X, -1/2) + e^{\chi/8 + X/2} \sqrt{\chi} \mathfrak{n} (X/\sqrt{\chi} + \sqrt{\chi}/2),$$

$$V^{(LBC)}(\tau, S, m) = C(\tau, S, m)$$

$$- \left(\ln \left(\frac{S}{m} \right) + \frac{\sigma^2\tau}{2} \right) e^{-r\tau} S\mathfrak{N} \left(\frac{\ln(S/m) - \sigma^2\tau/2}{\sigma\sqrt{\tau}} \right)$$

$$+ \sigma\sqrt{\tau} e^{-r\tau} S\mathfrak{n} \left(\frac{\ln(S/m) + \sigma^2\tau/2}{\sigma\sqrt{\tau}} \right).$$

Similarly,

$$V^{(LBP)}(\tau, S, M) = P(\tau, S, M) \tag{13.24}$$

$$- \left(\ln \left(\frac{M}{S} \right) - \frac{\sigma^2\tau}{2} \right) e^{-r\tau} S\mathfrak{N} \left(-\frac{\ln(M/S) - \chi/2}{\sqrt{\chi}} \right)$$

$$+ \sigma\sqrt{\tau} e^{-r\tau} S\mathfrak{n} \left(\frac{\ln(M/S) - \sigma^2\tau/2}{\sigma\sqrt{\tau}} \right).$$

Thus, for a LBC (LBP) the price consists of the price of a plain vanilla call (put) struck at the achieved lowest (highest) FXR and a "strike bonus option." As a rule of thumb, the latter option is worth roughly as much as at the money forward call (put). That is why LBCs (LBPs), while providing the piece of mind, are rather expensive.

13.5.3 Similarity reductions

In this subsection we show how to value lookback puts (LBPs) by virtue of self-similarity. In contrast to our usual practice we concentrate on puts rather than calls since, as we will see later, they are closely related to passport options. The valuation formula which we established in the previous subsection is rederived from a different prospective in order to facilitate subsequent developments. We know that the dimensional price of a *LBP* depends on both S and M. In view of the previous discussion, one can treat M as a moving strike and represent this price in the form

$$V^{(LBP)}(\tau, S, M, \sigma, r^0, r^1) = M\Phi^{(LBP)}\left(\chi, \xi, \hat{r}^0, \hat{r}^1\right),$$

where $\xi = S/M$, $0 < \xi \leq 1$, is the corresponding moneyness. However, for our purposes, it is more convenient to consider a LBP as a call option on M struck at S and write the price in the form (9.7):

$$V^{(LBP)}(\tau, S, M, \sigma, r^0, r^1) = S\Psi^{(LBP)}\left(\chi, \eta, \hat{r}^0, \hat{r}^1\right),$$

where $\eta = M/S$, $1 \leq \eta < \infty$, is the inverse moneyness. The pricing problem for $\Psi^{(LBP)}$ can be written as

$$\Psi_\chi^{(LBP)} - \frac{1}{2}\eta^2\Psi_{\eta\eta}^{(LBP)} - \hat{r}^{10}\eta\Psi_\eta^{(LBP)} + \hat{r}^1\Psi^{(LBP)} = 0, \quad 1 \leq \eta < \infty, \quad (13.25)$$

$$\Psi^{(LBP)}(0, \eta) = \eta - 1, \tag{13.26}$$

$$\Psi_\eta^{(LBP)}(\chi, 1) = 0, \qquad \Psi_\eta^{(LBP)}(\chi, \eta \to \infty) \to e^{-\hat{r}^1\chi}. \tag{13.27}$$

The above derivation is straightforward and is left to the reader as an exercise.

13.5.4   Pricing via the Laplace transform

It is clear that pricing problems for LBPs and DOCs are similar in nature. The biggest distinction between them is in the boundary conditions. One can consider a LBP as a barrier option with the (financially nonstandard) Neumann boundary condition at the barrier $\eta = 1$. It was mentioned earlier that the solution of the valuation problem can be found by virtue of the generalized method of images due to Sommerfeld. Here we present an alternative derivation based on the Laplace transform technique which seems to be new. This derivation will help the reader to appreciate the future developments. The Laplace transform in time

$$\Psi^{(LBP)}(\chi, \eta) \to \Xi^{(LBP)}(\lambda, \eta) = \int_0^\infty e^{-\lambda\chi}\Psi^{(LBP)}(\chi, \eta)d\chi,$$

yields

$$(\lambda + \hat{r}^1)\Xi^{(LBP)} - \frac{1}{2}\eta^2\Xi_{\eta\eta}^{(LBP)} - \hat{r}^{10}\eta\Xi_\eta^{(LBP)} = \eta - 1, \quad 1 \le \eta < \infty,$$

$$\Xi_\eta^{(LBP)}(1, \lambda) = 0, \quad \Xi_\eta^{(LBP)}(\lambda, \eta \to \infty) \to \frac{1}{(\lambda + \hat{r}^0)}.$$

We represent Ξ in the form

$$\Xi^{(LBP)}(\lambda, \eta) = \tilde{\Xi}^{(LBP)}(\lambda, \eta) + \frac{\eta}{(\lambda + \hat{r}^0)} - \frac{1}{(\lambda + \hat{r}^1)},$$

and obtain the following problem for $\Xi^{(LBP)}$

$$(\lambda + \hat{r}^1)\tilde{\Xi}^{(LBP)} - \frac{1}{2}\eta^2\tilde{\Xi}_{\eta\eta}^{(LBP)} - \hat{r}^{10}\eta\tilde{\Xi}_\eta^{(LBP)} = 0, \quad 1 \le \eta < \infty,$$

$$\tilde{\Xi}_\eta^{(LBP)}(1, \lambda) = -\frac{1}{(\lambda + \hat{r}^0)}, \quad \tilde{\Xi}_\eta^{(LBP)}(\lambda, \eta \to \infty) \to 0.$$

Since Ξ satisfies a homogeneous Euler equation, it can be chosen in the form

$$\tilde{\Xi}^{(LBP)}(\lambda, \eta) = \Delta^{(LBP)}\eta^{-\alpha},$$

where

$$\alpha = -\hat{\gamma}_+ + \sqrt{\hat{\gamma}_+^2 + 2(\lambda + \hat{r}^1)}, \quad \Delta^{(LBP)} = \frac{1}{(\lambda + \hat{r}^0)\alpha}. \tag{13.28}$$

In order to compute the inverse Laplace transform of $\tilde{\Xi}$ we represent this function in the form

$$\tilde{\Xi}^{(LBP)}(\lambda, \eta) = \frac{2\eta^{\hat{\gamma}_+}e^{-\ln(\eta)\sqrt{\mu}}}{(\sqrt{\mu} - \hat{\gamma}_+)(\mu - \hat{\gamma}_-^2)}$$

$$= \frac{2\eta^{\hat{\gamma}_+}e^{-\ln(\eta)\sqrt{\mu}}}{(\hat{\gamma}_+ + \hat{\gamma}_-)(\sqrt{\mu} - \hat{\gamma}_+)} - \frac{\eta^{\hat{\gamma}_+}e^{-\ln(\eta)\sqrt{\mu}}}{\hat{\gamma}_-(\sqrt{\mu} - \hat{\gamma}_-)} + \frac{\eta^{\hat{\gamma}_+}e^{-\ln(\eta)\sqrt{\mu}}}{\hat{\gamma}_-(\hat{\gamma}_+ + \hat{\gamma}_-)(\sqrt{\mu} + \hat{\gamma}_-)},$$

where

$$\mu = \hat{\gamma}_+^2 + 2(\lambda + \hat{r}^1).$$

By using the standard inversion formulas for the Laplace transform, we obtain

$$
\mathcal{L}^{-1}\left[\tilde{\Xi}^{(LBP)}(\lambda,\eta)\right] = \frac{2\hat{\gamma}_+ e^{-\hat{r}^1 x}}{(\hat{\gamma}_+ + \hat{\gamma}_-)}\mathfrak{N}\left(-\frac{\ln(\eta)-\hat{\gamma}_+\chi}{\sqrt{\chi}}\right)
$$

$$
-\eta e^{-\hat{r}^0 x}\mathfrak{N}\left(-\frac{\ln(\eta)-\hat{\gamma}_-\chi}{\sqrt{\chi}}\right) - \frac{\eta^{(\hat{\gamma}_++\hat{\gamma}_-)}e^{-\hat{r}^0 x}}{(\hat{\gamma}_++\hat{\gamma}_-)}\mathfrak{N}\left(-\frac{\ln(\eta)+\hat{\gamma}_-\chi}{\sqrt{\chi}}\right).
$$

Accordingly,

$$
\Psi^{(LBP)}(\chi,\eta) = \mathcal{L}^{-1}\left[\tilde{\Xi}^{(LBP)}(\lambda,\eta) + \frac{\eta}{(\lambda+\hat{r}^0)} - \frac{1}{(\lambda+\hat{r}^1)}\right]
$$

$$
= \mathcal{L}^{-1}\left[\tilde{\Xi}^{(LBP)}(\lambda,\eta)\right] + e^{-\hat{r}^0 x}\eta - e^{-\hat{r}^1 x}
$$

$$
= e^{-\hat{r}^0 x}\eta\left(\mathfrak{N}\left(\frac{\ln(\eta)-\hat{\gamma}_-\chi}{\sqrt{\chi}}\right) + \frac{\eta^{-2\hat{r}^{10}-1}}{2\hat{r}^{10}}\mathfrak{N}\left(-\frac{\ln(\eta)+\hat{\gamma}_-\chi}{\sqrt{\chi}}\right)\right)
$$

$$
-e^{-\hat{r}^1 x}\left(\mathfrak{N}\left(\frac{\ln(\eta)-\hat{\gamma}_+\chi}{\sqrt{\chi}}\right) + \frac{1}{2\hat{r}^{10}}\mathfrak{N}\left(-\frac{\ln(\eta)-\hat{\gamma}_+\chi}{\sqrt{\chi}}\right)\right).
$$

It is easy to check that this formula is equivalent to the standard one. In the special case when $\hat{r}^0 = \hat{r}^1 = \hat{r}$ the above formula assumes the form

$$
\Psi^{(LBP)}(\chi,\eta) = e^{-\hat{r}x}\left(\eta\mathfrak{N}\left(\frac{\ln(\eta)+\chi/2}{\sqrt{\chi}}\right) - \mathfrak{N}\left(\frac{\ln(\eta)-\chi/2}{\sqrt{\chi}}\right)\right.
$$

$$
\left. - (\ln(\eta)-\chi/2)\,\mathfrak{N}\left(-\frac{\ln(\eta)-\chi/2}{\sqrt{\chi}}\right) + \sqrt{\chi}\mathfrak{n}\left(\frac{\ln(\eta)-\chi/2}{\sqrt{\chi}}\right)\right).
$$

13.5.5 Probabilistic pricing

By using formula (13.14) we can represent the price of a LBP in the form

$$
V^{(LBP)}(\tau,S,M) = e^{-r^0\tau}\mathbb{E}\left\{\max\left\{Se^Y,M\right\} - Se^X\right\} \tag{13.29}
$$

$$
= e^{-r^0\tau}\mathbb{E}\left\{\max\left\{Se^Y,M\right\}\right\} - e^{-r^1\tau}S
$$

$$
= e^{-r^0\tau}M\int_0^{\ln(M/S)}d\left[\mathfrak{N}\left(\frac{Y-\gamma_-\tau}{\sigma\sqrt{\tau}}\right) - e^{2\hat{\gamma}_-Y}\mathfrak{N}\left(-\frac{Y+\gamma_-\tau}{\sigma\sqrt{\tau}}\right)\right]
$$

$$
+e^{-r^0\tau}S\int_{\ln(M/S)}^{\infty}e^Y d\left[\mathfrak{N}\left(\frac{Y-\gamma_-\tau}{\sigma\sqrt{\tau}}\right) - e^{2\hat{\gamma}_-Y}\mathfrak{N}\left(-\frac{Y+\gamma_-\tau}{\sigma\sqrt{\tau}}\right)\right]
$$

$$
-e^{-r^1\tau}S.
$$

We leave it to the reader to compute the corresponding integrals and to verify that expressions (13.29) and (13.23) are equivalent.

It is not difficult to price other options incorporating lookback features via probabilistic methods. We mention just two examples: (A) a fixed strike call $(\widehat{LBC})$ (put $(\widehat{LBP})$) on the maximum (minimum) FXR; (B) a partial lookback call $(PLBC)$ and a put $(PLBP)$. The corresponding payoffs are given by (13.1), (13.2).

Consider, for example, a call on the maximum. We have

$$V^{\left(\widehat{LBC}\right)}(\tau, S, M, K) = e^{-r^0 \tau} \mathbb{E}\left\{\left(\max\left\{M, Se^Y\right\} - K\right)_+\right\}. \qquad (13.30)$$

Assuming, for simplicity, that $M < K$ we can rewrite formula (13.30) as

$$V^{\left(\widehat{LBC}\right)}(\tau, S, M, K) = e^{-r^0 \tau} \mathbb{E}\left\{\left(S^Y - K\right)_+\right\},$$

so that

$$\begin{aligned}
&V^{\left(\widehat{LBC}\right)}(\tau, S, M, K)\\
&= e^{-r^0 \tau} S \int_{\ln(K/S)}^{\infty} e^Y d\left[\mathfrak{N}\left(\frac{Y - \gamma_- \tau}{\sigma\sqrt{\tau}}\right) - e^{2\hat{\gamma}_- Y}\mathfrak{N}\left(-\frac{Y + \gamma_- \tau}{\sigma\sqrt{\tau}}\right)\right]\\
&= C(\tau, S, K) - \frac{1}{2\hat{r}^{01}}\left[e^{-r^0 \tau}\left(\frac{K}{S}\right)^{2\hat{\gamma}_-} K\mathfrak{N}\left(\frac{\ln(S/K) - \gamma_- \tau}{\sigma\sqrt{\tau}}\right)\right.\\
&\qquad \left. - e^{-r^1 \tau} S\mathfrak{N}\left(\frac{\ln(S/K) + \gamma_+ \tau}{\sigma\sqrt{\tau}}\right)\right].
\end{aligned}$$

We leave it to the reader to derive the following formulas:

$$\begin{aligned}
&V^{\left(\widehat{LBP}\right)}(\tau, S, m, K)\\
&= P(\tau, S, K) + \frac{1}{2\hat{r}^{01}}\left[e^{-r^0 \tau}\left(\frac{K}{S}\right)^{2\hat{\gamma}_-} K\mathfrak{N}\left(-\frac{\ln(S/K) + \gamma_- \tau}{\sigma\sqrt{\tau}}\right)\right.\\
&\qquad \left. - e^{-r^1 \tau} S\mathfrak{N}\left(-\frac{\ln(S/K) + \gamma_+ \tau}{\sigma\sqrt{\tau}}\right)\right]
\end{aligned}$$

where $K < m$,

$$V^{(PLBC)}(\tau, S, m) = C\left(\tau, S, \frac{m}{\Lambda}\right) + \frac{1}{2\hat{r}^{01}\Lambda^{2\hat{r}^{01}}}$$

$$\times \left[e^{-r^0\tau}\left(\frac{\Lambda m}{S}\right)^{2\hat{\gamma}_-} m\mathfrak{N}\left(-\frac{\ln(S/\Lambda m) - \gamma_-\tau}{\sigma\sqrt{\tau}}\right)\right.$$

$$\left. -e^{-r^1\tau}\frac{S}{\Lambda}\mathfrak{N}\left(-\frac{\ln(S/\Lambda m) + \gamma_+\tau}{\sigma\sqrt{\tau}}\right)\right]$$

$$V^{(PLBP)}(\tau, S, M) = P(\tau, S, \Lambda M) - \frac{\Lambda^{2\hat{r}^{01}}}{2\hat{r}^{01}}$$

$$\times \left[e^{-r^0\tau}\left(\frac{M}{\Lambda S}\right)^{2\hat{\gamma}_-} M\mathfrak{N}\left(\frac{\ln(\Lambda S/M) - \gamma_-\tau}{\sigma\sqrt{\tau}}\right)\right.$$

$$\left. -e^{-r^1\tau}\Lambda S\mathfrak{N}\left(\frac{\ln(\Lambda S/M) + \gamma_+\tau}{\sigma\sqrt{\tau}}\right)\right].$$

13.5.6 Barriers

It is relatively easy to incorporate barrier features in our analysis of lookbacks. Consider, for instance, the double-barrier lookback put which disappears if the FXR crosses either the lower barrier A or the upper barrier B. The payoff of such an option can be written as

$$V^{(BLBP)}(0, S, m, M, A, B) = (M - S)\,\theta\,(m - A)\,\theta\,(B - M),$$

where θ is the Heaviside function.

The risk-neutral valuation principle yields

$$V^{(BLBP)}(\tau, S, m, M, A, B) \tag{13.31}$$

$$= e^{-r^0\tau}S\int_X^\beta\int_\alpha^X\int_y^Y\left(e^{X'} - \max\left\{\frac{M}{S}, e^Y\right\}\right)\partial_{yY}^2 h(\tau, X', y, Y)\,dX'dydY$$

$$= e^{-r^0\tau}S\int_X^{\ln(M/S)}\int_\alpha^X\int_y^Y\left(e^{X'} - \frac{M}{S}\right)\partial_{yY}^2 h(\tau, X', y, Y)\,dX'dydY$$

$$+ e^{-r^0\tau}S\int_{\ln(M/S)}^\beta\int_\alpha^X\int_y^Y\left(e^{X'} - e^Y\right)\partial_{yY}^2 h(\tau, X', y, Y)\,dX'dydY,$$

where $\alpha = \ln(A/S) < 0$, $\beta = \ln(B/S) > 0$, and h is defined by formula (13.15). The computation of integral (13.31) is left to the reader as an exercise useful for building the computational stamina (be tough!).

13.6 Asian options

13.6.1 Description

It was mentioned earlier that payoffs of Asian options depend on the average value of the underlying FXR rather than the FXR itself. Needless to say that it is always possible to extend this definition and consider Asian options with barrier features, etc. By construction, Asian calls (puts) give the buyer the right to buy (sell) the foreign currency at the average rate prevailing between the inception of the option and its maturity. Although, in principle, the averaging can be done in a variety of ways, the arithmetic averaging is prevalent in practice. Since it is relatively difficult to price such options, we start our discussion with calls and puts on the geometrically averaged FXR which can be priced in the closed form. Once these options are analyzed in some detail, we address the real problem and develop several complementary approaches to pricing options on arithmetically averaged FXR.

13.6.2 Geometric averaging

To start with, we consider a call on the FXR geometrically averaged between the inception of the call and its maturity. For the sake of brevity we deal only with the cumulative logarithmic FXR $I_{0,t}$ given by

$$I_{0,t} = \int_0^t \ln S_{t'} dt',$$

although the average logarithmic FXR $A_{0,t} = I_{0,t}/t$ can be used as well. We represent the payoff of the corresponding call option in the form

$$\text{payoff} = \left(e^{I_{0,T}/T} - K \right)_+.$$

We denote the value of this call at time t by $V^{(C)}(t, S, I)$, where S is the spot FXR rate, and I is the cumulative rate between 0 and t.

The augmented SDEs governing the evolution of $S_t, I_{0,t}$ are

$$\frac{dS_t}{S_t} = r^{01}dt + \sigma dW_t,$$
$$dI_{0,t} = \ln S_t dt,$$
$$S_0 \text{ is given}, \quad I_{0,0} = 0.$$

As we know,

$$S_t = e^{\left(r^{01} - \sigma^2/2\right)t + \sigma W_t} S_0.$$

Accordingly,

$$
\begin{aligned}
I_{0,T} &= \int_0^T \left[\left(r^{01} - \frac{\sigma^2}{2} \right) t + \sigma W_t \right] dt + (\ln S_0) T \\
&= \left(r^{01} - \frac{\sigma^2}{2} \right) \frac{T^2}{2} + \sigma \int_0^T W_t dt + (\ln S_0) T \\
&= \left(r^{01} - \frac{\sigma^2}{2} \right) \frac{T^2}{2} - \sigma \int_0^T d\left[(T - t) W_t \right] \\
&\quad + \sigma \int_0^T (T - t) \, dW_t + (\ln S_0) T \\
&= \left(r^{01} - \frac{\sigma^2}{2} \right) \frac{T^2}{2} + \sigma \int_0^T (T - t) \, dW_t + (\ln S_0) T,
\end{aligned}
$$

$$\frac{I_{0,T}}{T} = \left(r^{01} - \frac{\sigma^2}{2} \right) \frac{T}{2} + \sigma \int_0^T \left(1 - \frac{t}{T} \right) dW_t + (\ln S_0).$$

This relation shows that $I_{0,T}/T$ is a normal variable,

$$\frac{I_{0,T}}{T} \sim \mathfrak{N} \left(\left(r^{01} - \frac{\sigma^2}{2} \right) \frac{T}{2} + \ln S_0, \frac{\sigma^2 T}{3} \right).$$

Thus, we can consider the corresponding Asian call as the standard call on a fictitious FXR with forward and volatility given by

$$\tilde{F}_{0,T} = e^{\left(r^{01} - \sigma^2/6 \right) T/2} S_0, \qquad \tilde{\sigma} = \sigma/\sqrt{3}.$$

We can use an appropriately modified Black-Scholes formula and obtain the following expression for $V^{(AsC)}(0, S, 0)$:

$$V^{(AsC)}(0, S, 0) = e^{-\left(r^0 + r^1 + \sigma^2/6 \right) T/2} S \mathfrak{N}(d_+) - e^{-r^0 T} K \mathfrak{N}(d_-),$$

where

$$d_\pm = \frac{\ln(S/K) + \left(r^{01} - \sigma^2/6 \pm \sigma^2/3 \right) T/2}{\sigma \sqrt{T/3}}.$$

We leave it to the reader as a useful exercise to find $V^{(AsC)}(t, S, I)$ for an intermediate time t, $0 < t < T$.

The corresponding expression for a put has the form

$$V^{(AsP)}(0, S, 0) = e^{-r^0 T} K \mathfrak{N}(-d_-) - e^{-(r^0 + r^1 + \sigma^2/6)T/2} S \mathfrak{N}(-d_+).$$

It is not difficult to prove put-call parity relation

$$V^{(AsC)}(0, S, 0) - V^{(AsP)}(0, S, 0) = e^{-(r^0 + r^1 + \sigma^2/6)T/2} S - e^{-r^0 T} K.$$

It is easy to derive closed form solutions for calls and puts on geometrically averaged FXR because the geometric average of a lognormal process is lognormal.

An alternative approach to finding $V^{(AsC)}$ is based on solving the pricing problems directly. The pricing equation can be written in the form

$$V_t + \frac{1}{2}\sigma^2 S^2 V_{SS} + r^{01} S V_S + \ln S V_I - r^0 V = 0.$$

It is supplied with the final data

$$V^{(AsC)}(T, S, I) = \left(e^{I/T} - K\right)_+,$$

and the usual boundary conditions. We leave it to the reader as an exercise to check that $V^{(C)}$ solves the pricing problem. In principle, one can solve the corresponding pricing problem by reducing it to the Black-Scholes form. Since both the pricing equation and the final condition are invariant with respect to the transformations

$$t \to t', \quad S \to e^\theta S', \quad I \to I' - \theta(T - t),$$

so is the solution. Accordingly, we can use the following ansatz:

$$V(t, S, I) = \Phi(t, \eta),$$

where

$$\eta = \frac{I + (T - t) \ln S}{T}.$$

A simple calculation yields the following one-factor pricing problem for $\Phi(t, \eta)$:

$$\Phi_t + \frac{1}{2}\sigma^2 \left(1 - \frac{t}{T}\right)^2 \Phi_{\eta\eta} + \left(r^{01} - \frac{1}{2}\sigma^2\right)\left(1 - \frac{t}{T}\right)\Phi_\eta - r^0\Phi = 0,$$

$$\Phi\left(T,\eta\right)=\left(e^{\eta}-1\right)_{+}.$$

This problem is a time-dependent Black-Scholes problem written in the log space. Its solution can be found by using standard transformations described in Section 10.2. We leave the corresponding calculation to the reader for the sake of brevity.

13.6.3 Arithmetic averaging

Payoffs of continuously monitored Asian options involve the cumulative FXR $I_{0,T}$ defined by equation (13.4) and, possibly, the terminal value of FXR S_T, as well. The augmented system of SDEs for $S_t, I_{0,t}$ is given by (13.8). While it is not possible to find the distribution of $I_{0,T}/T$ is a closed form, its moments are not difficult to compute. In order to do so, we use Ito's lemma and obtain the following system of SDEs for S, I, S^2, SI, I^2:

$$
\begin{aligned}
dS &= r^{01} S dt + \sigma S dW_t, \\
dI &= S dt, \\
dS^2 &= \left(2r^{01} + \sigma^2\right) S^2 dt + 2\sigma S^2 dW, \\
d\left(SI\right) &= \left(r^{01} SI + S^2\right) dt + \sigma SI dW, \\
d\left(I^2\right) &= 2SI dt, \\
S_0 &\text{ is given,} \quad I_{0,0} = 0, \quad \text{etc.}
\end{aligned}
$$

Next, we use the martingale property of the Wiener process and obtain the following system of ODEs for the expected values $\bar{S}, \bar{I}, \overline{S^2}, \overline{SI}, \overline{I^2}$:

$$
\begin{aligned}
d\bar{S} &= r^{01} \bar{S} dt, \\
d\bar{I} &= \bar{S} dt, \\
d\overline{S^2} &= \left(2r^{01} + \sigma^2\right) \overline{S^2} dt, \\
d\overline{SI} &= \left(r^{01} \overline{SI} + \overline{S^2}\right) dt, \\
d\overline{I^2} &= 2\overline{SI} dt, \\
\bar{S}_0 &= S_0, \quad \bar{I}_{0,0} = 0, \quad \text{etc.}
\end{aligned}
$$

Accordingly,

$$\bar{S} = e^{r^{01}t}S_0,$$

$$\bar{I} = \frac{e^{r^{01}t} - 1}{r^{01}}S_0,$$

$$\overline{S^2} = e^{(2r^{01}+\sigma^2)t}S_0,$$

$$\overline{SI} = \frac{e^{(2r^{01}+\sigma^2)t} - e^{r^{01}t}}{r^{01} + \sigma^2}S_0^2,$$

$$\overline{I^2} = \frac{2\left(r^{01}e^{(2r^{01}+\sigma^2)t} - (2r^{01} + \sigma^2)e^{r^{01}t} + r^{01} + \sigma^2\right)}{(r^{01} + \sigma^2)(2r^{01} + \sigma^2)r^{01}}S_0^2.$$

Thus, the first and second moments of the random variable $\xi = I_{0,T}/T$ are

$$\mathrm{M}_1\{\xi\} = \frac{e^{r^{01}T} - 1}{r^{01}T}S_0,$$

$$\mathrm{M}_2\{\xi\} = \frac{2\left(r^{01}e^{(2r^{01}+\sigma^2)T} - (2r^{01} + \sigma^2)e^{r^{01}T} + r^{01} + \sigma^2\right)}{(r^{01} + \sigma^2)(2r^{01} + \sigma^2)r^{01}T^2}S_0^2.$$

We approximate ξ by the lognormal variable with the same first and second moments as ξ,

$$\xi \sim Ae^{-B^2/2+B\eta}, \qquad \eta \sim \mathfrak{N}(0,1). \tag{13.32}$$

Equations (13.32) show that

$$\mathrm{M}_1\{\xi\} = A, \qquad \mathrm{M}_2\{\xi\} = A^2e^{B^2}.$$

Thus,

$$A = \frac{e^{r^{01}T} - 1}{r^{01}T}S_0,$$

$$B = \left\{\ln\left[\frac{2r^{01}\left(r^{01}e^{(2r^{01}+\sigma^2)T} - (2r^{01} + \sigma^2)e^{r^{01}T} + r^{01} + \sigma^2\right)}{(r^{01} + \sigma^2)(2r^{01} + \sigma^2)(e^{r^{01}T} - 1)^2}\right]\right\}^{1/2}.$$

We can think of A, B as a fictitious forward FXR and deannualized volatility, respectively, and use the standard Black-Scholes formula in order to approximately price an arithmetically averaged Asian call at inception:

$$V^{(AsC)}(0, S, 0) = e^{-r^0 T} (A\mathfrak{N}(d_+) - K\mathfrak{N}(d_-)),$$

where

$$d_\pm = \frac{\ln(A/K) \pm B^2/2}{B}.$$

For Asian calls with short maturities $(T \to 0)$ we have

$$A \to S_0, \quad B \to \frac{\sigma\sqrt{T}}{3},$$

so that prices of arithmetically and geometrically averaged calls are in agreement. Similarly,

$$V^{(AsP)}(0, S, 0) = e^{-r^0 T}(-A\mathfrak{N}(-d_+) + K\mathfrak{N}(-d_-)).$$

Put-call parity relation has the form

$$V^{(AsC)}(0, S, 0) - V^{(AsP)}(0, S, 0) = \frac{e^{-r^1 T} - e^{-r^0 T}}{r^{01} T} S - e^{-r^0 T} K. \quad (13.33)$$

We emphasize that, although the expressions for $V^{(AsC)}, V^{(AsP)}$ are approximate, put-call parity relation is exact. The reader is invited to find an explanation for this curious fact.

We leave it to the reader as an exercise to obtain a more accurate approximation based on the three moment matching.

13.6.4   Exact solution via similarity reductions

If we want to derive an exact expression for the value of an Asian call we have to solve the pricing problem for $V(t, S, I)$. We can write the corresponding pricing equation as follows:

$$V_t + \frac{1}{2}\sigma^2 S^2 V_{SS} + r^{01} S V_S + S V_I - r^0 V = 0. \quad (13.34)$$

This equation is supplied with the final condition

$$V(T, S, I) = \left(\frac{I}{T} - K\right)_+,$$

and appropriate boundary conditions. For an Asian put the pricing equation is the same while the final condition is

$$V(T, S, I) = \left(K - \frac{I}{T}\right)_+.$$

It was already mentioned that exact pricing of Asian calls and puts is very difficult. However, establishing put-call parity is not. In order to find put-call parity relation we need to solve equation (13.34) supplied with the final condition

$$V(T, S, I) = \frac{I}{T} - K, \tag{13.35}$$

where $V = V^{(AsC)} - V^{(AsP)}$, which is linear in I. We can look for the solution of problem (13.34), (13.35) in the affine form:

$$V(t, S, I) = \alpha(t) I + \beta(t) S + \gamma(t) K.$$

A simple algebra which is left to the reader yields

$$V(t, S, I) = \frac{e^{-r^0(T-t)}}{T} I + \frac{\left(e^{-r^1(T-t)} - e^{-r^0(T-t)}\right)}{r^{01}T} S - e^{-r^0(T-t)} K.$$

In particular, at inception we have

$$V^{(AsC)}(0, S, 0) - V^{(AsP)}(0, S, 0) = \frac{\left(e^{-r^1 T} - e^{-r^0 T}\right)}{r^{01}T} S - e^{-r^0 T} K,$$

in agreement with formula (13.33).

In the previous section we showed how to value LBPs by combining self-similarities and Laplace transforms. It turns out that the same technique can be used in order to value AsCs, or, in other words, to solve problem (13.34), (13.34). As before, we can use the self-similarity reduction and represent the price of an AsC in the form

$$V^{(AsC)}(t, S, I, T, K, \sigma, r^0, r^1) = S\Psi^{(AsC)}\left(\chi, \eta, \hat{r}^0, \hat{r}^1\right),$$

where

$$\eta = \frac{1}{S}\left(\frac{I}{T} - K\right).$$

This reduction can be used in order to establish a useful relation between the time t value of an Asian call issued at time 0 and maturing at time T, and the value of an Asian call newly issued at time t and maturing at time T. This relation has the form

$$V(t, S, I, T, K, \sigma, r^0, r^1) = \frac{T-t}{T} V\left(0, S, 0, T-t, \frac{TK-I}{T-t}, \sigma, r^0, r^1\right).$$

A simple calculation which is left to the reader shows that the pricing problem for $\Psi^{(AsC)}$ has the form

$$\Psi_\chi^{(AsC)} - \frac{1}{2}\eta^2 \Psi_{\eta\eta}^{(AsC)} - \left(\hat{r}^{10}\eta + \frac{1}{\hat{T}}\right) \Psi_\eta^{(AsC)} + \hat{r}^1 \Psi^{(AsC)} = 0, \quad -\infty < \eta < \infty,$$

$$(13.36)$$

$$\Psi^{(AsC)}(0, \eta) = \eta_+,$$

$$\Psi^{(AsC)}(\chi, \eta \to -\infty) \to 0, \quad \Psi_\eta^{(AsC)}(\chi, \eta \to \infty) \to e^{-\hat{r}^0 \chi},$$

where $\hat{T} = \sigma^2 T$ is the nondimensional maturity of the option. This problem is difficult to handle directly because it has to be considered on the whole axis including the origin where the diffusion coefficient vanishes. Fortunately, the pricing problem can be split into two weakly dependent problems. Namely, it can be shown that due to a singularity at $\eta = 0$, one can study the pricing problem separately for $\eta \geq 0$ and $\eta \leq 0$ as long as the corresponding solutions $\Psi_\pm^{(AsC)}$ match at $\eta = 0$. (Derivatives of these solutions need not match.) For $\eta \geq 0$ the solution can be chosen in the affine form (this ansatz is similar in nature to the one used by Vasicek, Cox *et al.*, and others),

$$\Psi_+^{(AsC)}(\chi, \eta) = e^{-\hat{r}^0 \chi} \eta - \frac{e^{-\hat{r}^1 \chi} - e^{-\hat{r}^0 \chi}}{\hat{r}^{10} \hat{T}}.$$

Unfortunately, for negative η the corresponding $\Psi_-^{(AsC)}$ has a much more complicated form. The pricing problem for $\Psi_-^{(AsC)}$ is [1]

$$\Psi_{-,\chi}^{(AsC)} - \frac{1}{2}\eta^2 \Psi_{-,\eta\eta}^{(AsC)} - \left(\hat{r}^{10}\eta + \frac{1}{\hat{T}}\right) \Psi_\eta^{(AsC)} + \hat{r}^1 \Psi^{(AsC)} = 0, \quad -\infty < \eta < 0,$$

---

[1] There is an interesting similarity between the above pricing problem and Merton's pricing problem for call options on stocks paying *constant* dividend. However, it is beyond the scope of this book.

$$\Psi_-^{(AsC)}(0,\eta) = 0,$$

$$\Psi_-^{(AsC)}(\chi, \eta \to -\infty) \to 0, \quad \Psi_-^{(AsC)}(\chi, 0) = \frac{e^{-\hat{r}^1\chi} - e^{-\hat{r}^0\chi}}{\hat{r}^{01}\hat{T}}.$$

13.6.5 Pricing via the Laplace transform

As before, the Laplace transform in time $\Psi_-^{(AsC)}(\chi, \eta) \to \Xi_-^{(AsC)}(\lambda, \eta)$ makes this problem analytically tractable (up to a point). The transformed problem has the form

$$(\lambda + \hat{r}^1)\Xi_-^{(AsC)} - \frac{1}{2}\eta^2 \Xi_{-,\eta\eta}^{(AsC)} - \left(\hat{r}^{10}\eta + \frac{1}{\hat{T}}\right)\Xi_{-,\eta}^{(AsC)} = 0, \quad -\infty < \eta < 0, \tag{13.37}$$

$$\Xi_-^{(AsC)}(\lambda, \eta \to -\infty) \to 0, \quad \Xi_-^{(AsC)}(\lambda, 0) = \frac{1}{(\lambda + \hat{r}^0)(\lambda + \hat{r}^1)\hat{T}}. \tag{13.38}$$

The pricing equation turns out to be a general confluent equation. Recall that the general confluent equation has the form

$$\Xi_{\eta\eta} + \left(\frac{2A}{\eta} + 2f_\eta + \frac{bh_\eta}{h} - h_\eta - \frac{h_{\eta\eta}}{h_\eta}\right)\Xi_\eta \tag{13.39}$$

$$+ \left(\left(\frac{bh_\eta}{h} - h_\eta - \frac{h_{\eta\eta}}{h_\eta}\right)\left(\frac{A}{\eta} + f_\eta\right)\right.$$

$$\left. + \frac{A(A-1)}{\eta^2} + \frac{2Af_\eta}{\eta} + f_{\eta\eta} + f_\eta^2 - \frac{ah_\eta^2}{h}\right)\Xi = 0,$$

where f, h are functions of η, and A, a, b are constants. In order to represent equation (13.37) in the form (13.39) we rewrite this equation as

$$\Xi_{-,\eta\eta}^{(AsC)} + \left(\frac{2}{\hat{T}\eta^2} + \frac{2\hat{r}^{10}}{\eta}\right)\Xi_{-,\eta}^{(AsC)} - \frac{2(\lambda + \hat{r}^1)}{\eta^2}\Xi_-^{(AsC)} = 0, \tag{13.40}$$

and choose the corresponding parameters as follows

$$f = 0, \quad h = \frac{2}{\hat{T}\eta}, \quad A = a = \alpha, \quad b = \beta = 2(\alpha + 1 + \hat{r}^{01}), \tag{13.41}$$

where α is given by expression (13.28). Accordingly, the regular solution of problem (13.40) has the form

$$\Xi_-^{(AsC)}(\lambda,\eta) = \Delta^{(AsC)}(-\eta)^{-\alpha} M\left(\alpha,\beta,\frac{2}{\hat{T}\eta}\right),$$

where M is Kummer's function,

$$\Delta^{(AsC)} = \frac{2^\alpha\Gamma(\beta-\alpha)}{(\lambda+\hat{r}^0)(\lambda+\hat{r}^1)\hat{T}^{\alpha+1}\Gamma(\beta)},$$

and Γ is Gamma function. The complete solution has the form

$$\Psi^{(AsC)}(\chi,\eta) = \begin{cases} e^{-\hat{r}^0\chi}\eta - \left(e^{-\hat{r}^1\chi} - e^{-\hat{r}^0\chi}\right)/\hat{r}^{10}\hat{T}, & \text{if} \quad \eta \geq 0 \\ \mathcal{L}^{-1}\left[\Xi_-^{(AsC)}(\lambda,\eta)\right] & \text{if} \quad \eta \leq 0 \end{cases},$$

where $\mathcal{L}^{-1}$ is the inverse Laplace transform. Although the numerical implementation of the inverse Laplace transform is relatively difficult to achieve, it is feasible. The price of a typical Asian option is shown in Figure 13.2.

13.6.6 Approximate pricing of Asian calls revisited

Above we used the Laplace transform method for finding an explicit (but rather complex) expression for the price of an Asian call. In this subsection we derive an approximation for this price via a probabilistic method based on self-similarity. This method nicely complements the direct method described above. To this end we notice that equation (13.36) can be interpreted as the backward Kolmogoroff equation with killing associated with the generalized linear stochastic SDE of the form

$$d\eta = \left(r^{10}\eta + \frac{1}{T}\right)dt' + \sigma\eta dW_{t'}, \qquad \eta_t \text{ is given.} \tag{13.42}$$

The idea is to find the distribution of η at time T conditional on its known value at time t. To this end, we evaluate the moments of η_T and approximate η_T by a shifted lognormal variable which has the same first three moments as η_T. We denote $\mathbb{E}\{\eta^k\} = \mu^{(k)}$. We are interested in $k = 1,2,3$. By using Ito's lemma we obtain the following equations for η^2, η^3:

$$d(\eta^2) = 2\left(\left(r^{10} + \frac{\sigma^2}{2}\right)\eta^2 + \frac{1}{T}\eta\right)dt' + 2\sigma\eta^2 dW_{t'},$$

$$d(\eta^3) = 3\left(\left(r^{10} + \sigma^2\right)\eta^3 + \frac{1}{T}\eta^2\right)dt' + 3\sigma\eta^3 dW_{t'}.$$

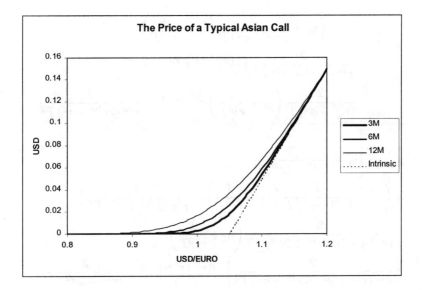

Figure 13.2: The price of typical Asian calls at inception as a function of the spot FXR for three representative maturities, $T = 3, 6, 12$ months. The relevant parameters are the same as in Figure 13.1. The strike level is $K = 1.05$.

We take the relevant expectations and obtain the following coupled system of ODEs for the moments:

$$d\mu^{(1)} = \left(r^{10}\mu^{(1)} + \frac{1}{T} \right) dt', \quad \mu_t^{(1)} = \eta_t,$$

$$d\mu^{(2)} = 2 \left(\left(r^{10} + \frac{\sigma^2}{2} \right) \mu^{(2)} + \frac{1}{T}\mu^{(1)} \right) dt', \quad \mu_t^{(2)} = \eta_t^2,$$

$$d\mu^{(3)} = 3 \left(\left(r^{10} + \sigma^2 \right) \mu^{(3)} + \frac{1}{T}\mu^{(2)} \right) dt', \quad \mu_t^{(2)} = \eta_t^2.$$

Straightforward calculation yields

$$\mu_T^{(1)} = \left(\eta_t + \frac{1}{r^{10}T} \right) e^{r^{10}(T-t)} - \frac{1}{r^{10}T},$$

$$\mu_T^{(2)} = \left(\eta_t^2 + \frac{2}{(r^{10} + \sigma^2)\,T}\left(\eta_t + \frac{1}{r^{10}T}\right)\right.$$

$$\left. - \frac{2}{r^{10}\,(2r^{10} + \sigma^2)\,T^2}\right) e^{(2r^{10} + \sigma^2)(T-t)}$$

$$- \frac{2}{(r^{10} + \sigma^2)\,T}\left(\eta_t + \frac{1}{r^{10}T}\right) e^{r^{01}(T-t)} + \frac{2}{r^{10}\,(2r^{10} + \sigma^2)\,T^2},$$

$$\mu_T^{(3)} = \left[\eta_t^3 + \frac{3}{(r^{10} + 2\sigma^2)\,T}\right.$$

$$\times \left(\eta_t^2 + \frac{2}{(r^{10} + \sigma^2)\,T}\left(\eta_t + \frac{1}{r^{10}T}\right) - \frac{2}{r^{10}\,(2r^{10} + \sigma^2)\,T^2}\right)$$

$$- \frac{6}{(r^{10} + \sigma^2)\,(2r^{10} + 3\sigma^2)\,T^2}\left(\eta_t + \frac{1}{r^{10}T}\right)$$

$$\left. + \frac{2}{r^{10}\,(r^{10} + \sigma^2)\,(2r^{10} + \sigma^2)\,T^3}\right] e^{3(r^{10} + \sigma^2)(T-t)} - \frac{3}{(r^{10} + 2\sigma^2)\,T}$$

$$\times \left[\eta_t^2 + \frac{2}{(r^{10} + \sigma^2)\,T}\left(\eta_t + \frac{1}{r^{10}T}\right) - \frac{2}{r^{10}\,(2r^{10} + \sigma^2)\,T^2}\right] e^{(2r^{10} + \sigma^2)(T-t)}$$

$$+ \frac{6}{(r^{10} + \sigma^2)\,(2r^{10} + 3\sigma^2)\,T^2}\left(\eta_t + \frac{1}{r^{10}T}\right) e^{r^{01}(T-t)}$$

$$- \frac{2}{r^{10}\,(r^{10} + \sigma^2)\,(2r^{10} + \sigma^2)\,T^3}.$$

We assume that η_T has a shifted lognormal distribution, or, equivalently, that

$$\eta_T = Ae^{-B^2/2 + B\eta} + E,$$

where η is the standard normal variable and A, B, E are unknown parameters. These parameters can be determined by solving the system of algebraic equations which we introduced in Section 8.8 when we discussed the basket approximation.

Once these parameters are determined, the price of an Asian call can be represented in the form

$$V\left(t, S, I, T, K, \sigma, r^0, r^1\right) = SC\left(t, e^{-r^{01}(T-t)}A, -E, \frac{B}{\sqrt{T-t}}, r^1, r^0\right),$$

where C is the Black-Scholes price of the standard call.

13.6.7 Discretely sampled Asian options

In this subsection we describe an algorithm for pricing discretely sampled Asian options and discuss similarities and differences between the continuous and discrete cases. The governing system of augmented SDEs for $S_t, I_{0,t}$ has the form

$$\frac{dS_t}{S_t} = r^{01} dt + \sigma dW_t,$$

$$dI_{0,t} = S_t \delta(t - t_n) dt,$$

$$S_0 \text{ is given, } I_{0,0} = 0.$$

where $0 < t_1 < ... < t_N < T$. The payoff of a discretely sampled Asian call is

$$V(T, S, I) = \left(\frac{I_{0,T}}{N} - K \right)_+. \tag{13.43}$$

It is clear that between the sampling dates the price $V(t, S, I)$ with I considered as a parameter solves the standard Black-Scholes equation. At time $t = t_n$ the price has to be continuous along the path $(S_t, I_{0,t})$ (which, by itself, is discontinuous) in order to avoid arbitrage opportunities. Accordingly,

$$V(t_{n-}, S, I) = V(t_{n+}, S, I + S),$$

where t_{n-}, t_{n+} denote times immediately before and after the sampling date t_n, respectively. Thus, in order to price a discretely sampled Asian call (say) we can work backwards in time starting at maturity and using final condition (13.43). Between sampling dates we solve (many) standard Black-Scholes problems. To cross a sampling date we use the matching condition. The process is repeated until the valuation date is reached.

As before, we can reduce the computational by using self-similarity. To this end, we introduce the following self-similar variable

$$\eta_t = \frac{I_{0,t}/N - K}{S_t},$$

and represent $V(t, S, I)$ in the form

$$V(t, S, I) = S\Psi(\chi, \eta).$$

It is clear that η_t has deterministic jumps at $t = t_n$ of magnitude $1/N$. Between sampling dates $\chi_n = \sigma^2(T - t_{N-n})$ the function $\Psi(\chi, \eta)$ solves the familiar problem

$$\Psi_\chi - \frac{1}{2}\eta^2 \Psi_{\eta\eta} - \hat{r}^{10}\eta\Psi_\eta + \hat{r}^1\Psi = 0,$$

$$\Psi\left(\chi,\eta\to-\infty\right)\to 0,\qquad\Psi\left(\chi,\eta\to\infty\right)\to e^{-\hat{r}^0\chi}.$$

The corresponding initial and matching conditions are

$$\Psi\left(0,\eta\right)=\eta_+,\qquad\Psi\left(\chi_{n+},\eta\right)=\Psi\left(\chi_{n-},\eta+\frac{1}{N}\right).$$

This pricing problem is similar in nature to its continuous counterpart. The most convenient way of solving this problem is to consider it separately on each interval $[\chi_{n-1},\chi_n]$ and to solve it by induction via the standard Crank-Nicolson method.

13.7 Timer, fader and Parisian options

13.7.1 Introduction

Options with payoffs depending either on occupational times (timers, faders, etc.), or excursion times (Parisians) are very popular in the market. While sharing many attractive features with standard barrier options, timers, faders, and (to a lesser degree) Parisians do not have their discontinuous character. In particular, Parisian options can be considered as generalized barrier options with knock-out or knock-in features triggered by the length of a consecutive time the FXR spends above (or below) a given barrier. Thus, we can think of timers, faders, and Parisians as "diluted" barrier options.

Financial rational for this class of options is clear. For example, timers which pay a coupon for every day the FXR spends below (above) some level, provide a useful cushion for exporters (importers) of goods and services.

In this section we show how to use the augmentation procedure for pricing options on occupational and excursion times.

13.7.2 Timer options

In this subsection we study the pricing problem for timer options with payoffs of the form (13.5), namely

$$\text{Payoff}^{(TMR)}=F\left(\vartheta_{0,T}\right),$$

where $\vartheta_{0,T}$ is the total time between $t=0$ and $t=T$ which the FXR S_t spends above a certain barrier B (say). (The time which S_t spends below the barrier is simply $T-\vartheta_{0,T}$.) Using similar ideas one can also value fader options with payoffs of the form (13.6). The reader should keep in mind the close connection of the present development and the Levy theory of local and occupational times. In addition, there are direct links between the problem discussed below and the P&L distribution analysis for the stop-loss start-gain strategy which we present in Chapter 14.

The augmented system of SDEs describing the evolution of the pair $S_t, \vartheta_{0,t}$ has the form (13.9). The corresponding pricing problem is

$$V_t + \frac{1}{2}\sigma^2 S^2 V_{SS} + r^{01} S V_S + \theta (S - B) V_\vartheta - r^0 V = 0,$$

$$V (T, S, \vartheta) = F (\vartheta),$$

$$V (t, S \to 0, \vartheta) \to e^{-r^0(T-t)} F (\vartheta), \ V (t, S \to \infty, \vartheta) \to e^{-r^0(T-t)} F (\vartheta + T - t).$$

We introduce the following nondimensional variables [2]

$$\chi = \sigma^2 (T - t), \ X = \ln \left(\frac{S}{B} \right), \ Y = \sigma^2 \vartheta, \ U (\chi, X, Y) = e^{\hat{r}^0 \chi} V (t, S, \vartheta),$$

and write the pricing problem for U in form

$$U_\chi - \frac{1}{2} U_{XX} - \hat{\gamma}_- U_X - \theta(X) U_Y = 0, \tag{13.44}$$

$$U(0, X, Y) = u(Y),$$

$$U (\chi, X \to -\infty, Y) \to u (Y), \ U (\chi, X \to \infty, Y) \to u (Y + \chi),$$

where

$$u (Y) = F (\vartheta), -\infty < X < \infty, \ 0 \le Y \le \hat{T} = \sigma^2 T.$$

Without loss of generality, we can extend the interval $\left[0, \hat{T} \right]$ to the entire axis $-\infty < Y < \infty$ and assume that outside of the original interval the payoff function is chosen in the most convenient fashion.

---

[2] The usual drift-removing transformation is not advantageous for the problem under consideration because it changes a simple nature of the initial condition.

Timers with linear payoffs

To start with, we consider the simplest possible payoff and assume that

$$u(Y) = \alpha Y,$$

so that the buyer receives a coupon for every day the FXR spends above the barrier. In the case in question we can use the affine ansatz

$$U(\chi, X, Y) = \alpha\left(Y + B(\chi, X)\right). \tag{13.45}$$

We substitute expression (13.45) in equation (13.44) and obtain the following inhomogeneous one-factor pricing problem for $B(\chi, X)$:

$$B_\chi - \frac{1}{2}B_{XX} - \hat{\gamma}_- B_X = \alpha\theta(X),$$

$$B(0, X) = 0.$$

To solve this problem we introduce

$$C(\chi, X) = e^{\hat{\gamma}_-^2 \chi/2 + \hat{\gamma}_- X} B(\chi, X),$$

and obtain the following inhomogeneous initial-value problem for the heat equation:

$$C_\chi - \frac{1}{2}C_{XX} = e^{\hat{\gamma}_-^2 \chi/2 + \hat{\gamma}_- X}\theta(X),$$

$$C(0, X) = 0.$$

The application of Duhamel's principle introduced in Section 4.4. yields

$$
\begin{aligned}
C(\chi, X) &= \int_0^\infty \int_0^\chi \frac{e^{-(X-X')^2/2(\chi-\chi') + \hat{\gamma}_-^2 \chi'/2 + \hat{\gamma}_- X'}}{\sqrt{2\pi(\chi-\chi')}} dX' d\chi' \\
&= e^{\hat{\gamma}_-^2 \chi/2 + \hat{\gamma}_- X} \int_0^\chi \mathfrak{N}\left(\frac{X}{\sqrt{\chi-\chi'}} + \hat{\gamma}_-\sqrt{\chi-\chi'}\right) d\chi' \\
&= e^{\hat{\gamma}_-^2 \chi/2 + \hat{\gamma}_- X} \int_0^\chi \mathfrak{N}\left(\frac{X}{\sqrt{\chi'}} + \hat{\gamma}_-\sqrt{\chi'}\right) d\chi'.
\end{aligned}
$$

Accordingly,

$$B(\chi, X) = \int_0^\chi \mathfrak{N}\left(\frac{X}{\sqrt{\chi'}} + \hat{\gamma}_-\sqrt{\chi'}\right) d\chi',$$

which can also be verified directly. By using integration by parts, we can find the above integral explicitly. A relatively involved algebra which is left to the reader as an exercise yields

$$\mathrm{B}(\chi, X) = \left\{ \begin{array}{ll} \mathrm{B}^{(+)}(\chi, X), & X > 0 \\ \mathrm{B}^{(-)}(\chi, X), & X < 0 \end{array} \right., \qquad (13.46)$$

where

$$
\begin{aligned}
&\mathrm{B}^{(+)}(\chi, X) \\
&= \chi \mathfrak{N}(d_-) + \frac{1 - 2\hat{\gamma}_- X}{2\hat{\gamma}_-^2} \mathfrak{N}(-d_-) - \frac{e^{-2\hat{\gamma}_- X}}{2\hat{\gamma}_-^2} \mathfrak{N}\left(-d_+'\right) + \frac{\sqrt{\chi}}{\hat{\gamma}_-} \mathfrak{n}(d_-),
\end{aligned}
$$

$$
\begin{aligned}
&\mathrm{B}^{(-)}(\chi, X) \\
&= \chi \mathfrak{N}(d_-) - \frac{1 - 2\hat{\gamma}_- X}{2\hat{\gamma}_-^2} \mathfrak{N}(d_-) + \frac{e^{-2\hat{\gamma}_- X}}{2\hat{\gamma}_-^2} \mathfrak{N}\left(d_+'\right) + \frac{\sqrt{\chi}}{\hat{\gamma}_-} \mathfrak{n}(d_-),
\end{aligned}
$$

$$ d_- = \frac{X}{\sqrt{\chi}} + \hat{\gamma}_- \sqrt{\chi}, \qquad d_+' = \frac{X}{\sqrt{\chi}} - \hat{\gamma}_- \sqrt{\chi}. $$

Returning to the original variables, we represent the price of a timer as follows

$$ V(t, S, \vartheta) = \alpha e^{-r^0(T-t)} \left(\sigma^2 \vartheta + \mathrm{B}\left(\sigma^2 (T - t), \ln\left(\frac{S}{B} \right) \right) \right). $$

Timers with general payoffs

Now we study more general timers with payoffs $u(Y)$. Due to the fact that coefficients of equation (13.44) are Y-independent, it is sufficient to consider the timer option with the localized payoff

$$ u(Y) = \delta(Y), $$

and construct the corresponding Green's function $G(\chi, X, Y)$. Once this function is found, the price of the general timer can be represented in the form

$$ U(\chi, X, Y) = \int_{-\infty}^{\infty} G(\chi, X, Y - Y') u(Y') dY'. $$

To start with, we write G in the form

$$G(\chi, X, Y) = e^{-\hat{\gamma}_-^2 \chi/2 - \hat{\gamma}_- X} H(\chi, X, Y),$$

where H solves the following two-factor problem

$$H_\chi - \frac{1}{2} H_{XX} - \theta(X) H_Y = 0,$$

$$H(0, X, Y) = e^{\hat{\gamma}_- X} \delta(Y).$$

The corresponding problem can be solved explicitly. We apply the Laplace transform in χ and the Fourier transform in Y:

$$H(\chi, X, Y) \to h(\lambda, X, \mu) = \int_0^\infty \int_{-\infty}^\infty e^{-\lambda\chi + i\mu Y} H(\chi, X, Y) d\chi dY,$$

and obtain an ODE for h:

$$-\frac{1}{2} h_{XX} + (\lambda + i\mu\theta(X)) h = e^{\hat{\gamma}_- X}.$$

This ODE can be solved separately on positive and negative semi-axes, provided that the matching conditions are satisfied at $X = 0$. We have

$$h(\lambda, X, \mu) = \begin{cases} h^{(+)}(\lambda, X, \mu), & X > 0 \\ h^{(-)}(\lambda, X, \mu), & X < 0 \end{cases},$$

where

$$h^{(+)}(\lambda, X, \mu) = \frac{2e^{\hat{\gamma}_- X}}{2(\lambda + i\mu) - \hat{\gamma}_-^2} + pe^{-\sqrt{2(\lambda + i\mu)}X},$$

$$h^{(-)}(\lambda, X, \mu) = \frac{2e^{\hat{\gamma}_- X}}{2\lambda - \hat{\gamma}_-^2} + qe^{\sqrt{2\lambda}X}.$$

The matching (continuity) conditions yield

$$\frac{2}{2(\lambda + i\mu) - \hat{\gamma}_-^2} + p = \frac{2}{2\lambda - \hat{\gamma}_-^2} + q,$$

$$\frac{2\hat{\gamma}_-}{2(\lambda + i\mu) - \hat{\gamma}_-^2} - \sqrt{2(\lambda + i\mu)}p = \frac{2\hat{\gamma}_-}{2\lambda - \hat{\gamma}_-^2} + \sqrt{2\lambda}q,$$

so that

$$p = \frac{1}{\sqrt{\lambda + i\mu} - \hat{\gamma}_-/\sqrt{2}} \left(\frac{1}{\sqrt{\lambda} + \hat{\gamma}_-/\sqrt{2}} - \frac{1}{\sqrt{\lambda + i\mu} + \hat{\gamma}_-/\sqrt{2}} \right),$$

$$q = \frac{1}{\sqrt{\lambda} + \hat{\gamma}_-/\sqrt{2}} \left(\frac{1}{\sqrt{\lambda + i\mu} - \hat{\gamma}_-/\sqrt{2}} - \frac{1}{\sqrt{\lambda} - \hat{\gamma}_-/\sqrt{2}} \right).$$

The inverse Laplace transform yields

$$h(\chi, X, \mu) = \begin{cases} h^{(+)}(\chi, X, \mu), & X > 0 \\ h^{(-)}(\chi, X, \mu,), & X < 0 \end{cases},$$

where

$$h^{(+)}(\chi, X, \mu) = e^{-i\mu\chi + \hat{\gamma}_-^2 \chi/2} \left(e^{\hat{\gamma}_- X} - A(\chi, X) \right)$$
$$+ 2 \int_0^\chi e^{-i\mu\chi'} B^{(+)}(\chi - \chi', 0) B^{(-)}(\chi', X) d\chi',$$

$$h^{(-)}(\chi, X, \mu) = e^{\hat{\gamma}_-^2 \chi/2} \left(e^{\hat{\gamma}_- X} - A(\chi, |X|) \right)$$
$$+ 2 \int_0^\chi e^{i\mu\chi'} B^{(+)}(\chi - \chi', |X|,) B^{(-)}(\chi', 0) d\chi',$$

$$A(\chi, X) = e^{-\hat{\gamma}_-^2 \chi/2} \left(M\left(\chi, -X, -\hat{\gamma}_-\right) + M\left(\chi, -X, \hat{\gamma}_-\right) \right),$$

$$B_\pm(\chi, X) = \frac{e^{-X^2/2\chi}}{\sqrt{2\pi\chi}} \mp \hat{\gamma}_- M\left(\chi, -X, \mp\hat{\gamma}_-\right).$$

The inverse Fourier transform yields

$$H(\chi, X, Y) = \begin{cases} H^{(+)}(\chi, X, Y), & X > 0 \\ H^{(-)}(\chi, X, Y), & X < 0 \end{cases},$$

where

$$H^{(+)}(\chi, X, Y) = e^{\hat{\gamma}_-^2 \chi/2} \delta(Y + \chi) \left(e^{\hat{\gamma}_- X} - A(\chi, X,) \right)$$
$$+ 2\theta(-Y)\theta(Y + \chi) B^{(+)}(Y + \chi, 0) B^{(-)}(-Y, X),$$

$$H^{(-)}(\chi, X, Y) = e^{\hat{\gamma}_-^2 x/2}\delta(Y)\left(e^{\hat{\gamma}_- X} - A(\chi, |X|)\right)$$
$$+2\theta(-Y)\theta(Y + \chi)B^{(+)}(Y + \chi, |X|)B^{(-)}(-Y, 0).$$

It is relatively easy to verify directly that H is the Green's function we seek (and, in particular, to check that the corresponding singularities cancel each other).[3]

The corresponding expression for G has the form

$$G(\chi, X, Y) = \begin{cases} G^{(+)}(\chi, X, Y), & X > 0 \\ G^{(-)}(\chi, X, Y), & X < 0 \end{cases},$$

where

$$G^{(+)}(\chi, X, Y) = \delta(Y + \chi)\left(1 - e^{-\hat{\gamma}_- X}A(\chi, X)\right)$$
$$+2e^{-\hat{\gamma}_-^2 x/2 - \hat{\gamma}_- X}\theta(-Y)\theta(Y + \chi)B^{(+)}(Y + \chi, 0)B^{(-)}(-Y, X),$$

$$G^{(-)}(\chi, X, Y) = \delta(Y)\left(1 - e^{-\hat{\gamma}_- X}A(\chi, |X|)\right)$$
$$+2e^{-\hat{\gamma}_-^2 x/2 - \hat{\gamma}_- X}\theta(-Y)\theta(Y + \chi)B^{(+)}(Y + \chi, |X|)B^{(-)}(-Y, 0).$$

In order to solve the pricing problem for the general payoff $u(Y)$ we evaluate the convolution of G and u and obtain

$$U(\chi, X, Y) = \begin{cases} U^{(+)}(\chi, X, Y), & X > 0 \\ U^{(-)}(\chi, X, Y), & X < 0 \end{cases},$$

where

$$U^{(+)}(\chi, X, Y) = \left(1 - e^{-\hat{\gamma}_- X}A(\chi, X)\right)u(Y + \chi) \tag{13.47}$$
$$+2e^{-\hat{\gamma}_-^2 x/2 - \hat{\gamma}_- X}\int_0^X B^{(+)}(\chi - \chi', 0)B^{(-)}(\chi', X)u(Y + \chi')d\chi',$$

$$U^{(-)}(\chi, X, Y) = \left(1 - e^{-\hat{\gamma}_- X}A(\chi, |X|)\right)u(Y) \tag{13.48}$$
$$+2e^{-\hat{\gamma}_-^2 x/2 - \hat{\gamma}_- X}\int_0^X B^{(+)}(\chi - \chi', |X|)B^{(+)}(\chi', 0)u(Y + \chi')d\chi'.$$

It is easy to check that for $u(Y) = \alpha Y$ formulas (13.47), (13.48) and (13.45), (13.46) agree with each other. We note in passing that for the so-called capped

---

[3] As an aside, we note that for $\hat{\gamma}_- = 0$ we recover the celebrated arcsine law of Lévy (1939).

and floored timers (which are particularly popular in the market) with payoffs of the form

$$u(Y) = \min\{\max\{\alpha Y, L\}, U\},$$

formulas (13.47), (13.48) can be considerably simplified. However, we do not pursue this possibility here.

We leave it to the reader to represent the price of the general timer option in the financial variables.

13.7.3 Fader options

In order to price a fader option efficiently, we need to construct the general Green's function $G(\chi, X, X', Y)$ which solves equation (13.44) supplied with the localized initial condition

$$G(0, X, X', Y) = \delta(X - X')\delta(Y),$$

and appropriate boundary conditions. This can be done by the same token as before. Details are left to the reader as a useful exercise.

13.7.4 Parisian options

It was already mentioned that knock-out or knock-in features of Parisian options are triggered by the length of a consecutive time the FXR spends above (or below) a given barrier rather than by the fact that the barrier is breached. For instance, the payoff of a Parisian call with strike K and knockoff period D is given by formula (13.7) which we repeat here for convenience:

$$\text{payoff}^{(PRSNC)} = (S_T - K)_+\, \theta\left(D - \max_{0 \le t \le T} \varpi_{0,t}\right),$$

where $\varpi_{0,t}$ is the excursion time which the FXR spends above a given barrier level B.

We know that the pair $(S_t, \varpi_{0,t})$ is governed by the augmented system of SDEs (13.10). The pricing problem for the Parisian call naturally splits into two: (A) the one-factor pricing equation for $0 < S < B$; (B) the two-factor pricing equation for $B < S < \infty, 0 < \varpi < D$. The corresponding equations and the final conditions are:

$$V_t^{(-)} + \frac{1}{2}\sigma^2 S^2 V_{SS}^{(-)} + r^{01} S V_S^{(-)} - r^0 V^{(-)} = 0, \quad 0 < S < B,$$

$$V^{(-)}(T,S) = (S-K)_+,$$

$$V_t^{(+)} + \frac{1}{2}\sigma^2 S^2 V_{SS}^{(+)} + r^{01} S V_S^{(+)} + \theta(S-U)V_{\varpi}^{(+)} - r^0 V^{(+)} = 0 \quad (13.49)$$
$$B < S < \infty, 0 < \varpi < D,$$

$$V^{(+)}(T,S,\varpi) = (S-K)_+.$$

The key peculiarity of the problem is in the matching conditions at $S = B$. For $T - t < D$ and $S < B$ or $S > B$, $D - \varpi > T - t$ (case A) the situation is simple:

$$V^{(-)}(t,S) = V^{(+)}(t,S,\varpi) = C(t,S,T,K).$$

The reason is that there is no time for the option to knock-out. For $T - t < D$ and $S > B, D - \varpi < T - t$ (case B) the function $V^{(+)}$ solves equation (13.49) and satisfies the matching condition

$$V^{(+)}(t,B,\varpi) = V^{(-)}(t,B) = C(t,S,T,K).$$

Finally, for $T - t > D$ (case C) two matching conditions have to be satisfied:

$$V^{(+)}(t,B,\varpi) = V^{(-)}(t,B), \qquad (13.50)$$

$$V_S^{(+)}(t,B,0) = V_S^{(-)}(t,B). \qquad (13.51)$$

Condition (13.50) shows that for all ϖ the value $V^{(+)}(\tau,B,\varpi)$ is the same. Condition (13.51) shows that the matching across the barrier $S = B$ is smooth.

After the usual change of variables

$$t \to \chi = \sigma^2(T-t),$$
$$S \to X = \ln(S/B), \quad \varpi \to Y = \sigma^2(D-\varpi),$$
$$V(t,S,\varpi) \to U(\chi,X,Y) = Be^{(\hat{r}^0+\hat{\gamma}_-^2/2)x+\hat{\gamma}_- X}V(t,S,\varpi),$$

we can formulate the pricing problem as follows:

$$U_\chi^{(-)}(\chi,X) - \frac{1}{2}U_{XX}^{(-)}(\chi,X) = 0,$$

$$U^{(-)}(0,X) = u(X),$$

for $X < 0$, and

$$U_\chi^{(+)}(\chi,X,Y) - \frac{1}{2}U_{XX}^{(+)}(\chi,X,Y) + U_Y^{(+)}(\chi,X,Y) = 0,$$

$$U^{(+)}(0,X,Y) = u(X),$$

$$U^{(+)}(\chi,X,0) = 0,$$

for $X > 0$, $0 \leq Y \leq \hat{D} = \sigma^2 D$. Here

$$u(X) = \left(e^{\hat{\gamma}_+ X} - \kappa e^{\hat{\gamma}_- X}\right)_+, \qquad \kappa = \frac{K}{B} < 1.$$

For $\chi < \hat{D} = \sigma^2 D$ and $X < 0$ or $X > 0$, $Y > \chi$ (case A) the solution can be written right away:

$$U^{(-)}(\chi,X) = U^{(+)}(\chi,X,Y) = U(\chi,X),$$

where $U(\chi,X)$ is the nondimensional value of a European call with strike κ. For $\chi < \hat{D}$ and $X > 0$, $Y < \chi$ (case B) the matching condition has the form

$$U^{(+)}(\chi,0,Y) = U^{(-)}(\chi,0) = U(\chi,0).$$

Finally, for $\chi > \hat{D}$ (case C) there are two matching conditions:

$$U^{(+)}(\chi,0,Y) = U^{(-)}(\chi,0),$$

$$U_X^{(+)}\left(\chi,0,\hat{D}\right) = U_X^{(-)}(\chi,0). \tag{13.52}$$

In case (B) we represent $U^{(+)}(\chi,X,Y)$ in the form

$$U^{(+)}(\chi,X,Y) = \int_{\chi-Y}^{\chi} \frac{Xe^{-X^2/2(\chi-\chi')}}{(\chi-\chi')^{3/2}} v(\chi')\,d\chi' + \theta(Y-\chi)U^{(DOC)}(\chi,X),$$

where

$$v(\chi) = U(\chi,0), \tag{13.53}$$

and $U^{(DOC)}(\chi, X)$ is the nondimensional value of the down-and-out call with strike κ and unit barrier.

In case (C) we represent $U^{(\pm)}$ as

$$U^{(-)}(\chi, X) = U^{(UOC)}(\chi, X) - \frac{1}{\sqrt{2\pi}} \int_0^\chi \frac{X e^{-X^2/2(\chi-\chi')}}{(\chi-\chi')^{3/2}} v(\chi') d\chi'$$

$$= U^{(UOC)}(\chi, X) + 2 \int_0^\chi \mathfrak{N}\left(\frac{X}{(\chi-\chi')^{1/2}}\right) v_\chi(\chi') d\chi' + 2\mathfrak{N}\left(\frac{X}{\chi^{1/2}}\right) v(0),$$

$$U^{(+)}\left(\chi, X, \hat{D}\right) = \frac{1}{\sqrt{2\pi}} \int_{\chi-\hat{D}}^\chi \frac{X e^{-X^2/2(\chi-\chi')}}{(\chi-\chi')^{3/2}} v(\chi') d\chi'$$

$$= 2 \int_{\chi-\hat{D}}^\chi \mathfrak{N}\left(-\frac{X}{(\chi-\chi')^{1/2}}\right) v_\chi(\chi') d\chi' + 2\mathfrak{N}\left(-\frac{X}{\hat{D}^{1/2}}\right) v\left(\chi-\hat{D}\right),$$

where $U^{(UOC)}(\chi, X)$ is the nondimensional value of the up-and-out call. Here $v(\chi)$ is given by expression (13.53) for $0 \leq \chi \leq \hat{D}$, and has to be determined for $\chi > \hat{D}$ in such a way that the matching condition (13.52) is satisfied. Differentiation with respect to X at $X = 0$ yields

$$U_X^{(-)}(\chi, 0) = U_X^{UO}(\chi, 0) + \frac{2}{\sqrt{2\pi}} \left(\int_0^\chi \frac{v_\chi(\chi')}{(\chi-\chi')^{1/2}} d\chi' + \frac{v(0)}{\chi^{1/2}}\right),$$

$$U_X^{(+)}\left(\chi, 0, \hat{D}\right) = -\frac{2}{\sqrt{2\pi}} \left(\int_{\chi-\hat{D}}^\chi \frac{v_\chi(\chi')}{(\chi-\chi')^{1/2}} d\chi' + \frac{v\left(\chi-\hat{D}\right)}{\hat{D}^{1/2}}\right).$$

Thus, the equation for $v(\chi)$, $\chi > \hat{D}$, which we are after, can be written as

$$-\int_0^{\chi-\hat{D}} \frac{v_\chi(\chi')}{(\chi-\chi')^{1/2}} d\chi' + 2 \int_0^\chi \frac{v_\chi(\chi')}{(\chi-\chi')^{1/2}} d\chi'$$

$$+ \frac{v(0)}{\chi^{1/2}} + \frac{v\left(\chi-\hat{D}\right)}{\hat{D}^{1/2}} + \frac{\sqrt{2\pi}}{2} U_X^{UO}(\chi, 0) = 0,$$

or, after integration by parts,

$$\frac{1}{2} \quad \int_0^{x-\hat{D}} \frac{v(\chi')}{(\chi-\chi')^{3/2}} d\chi' + 2 \int_0^{\chi} \frac{v_\chi(\chi')}{(\chi-\chi')^{1/2}} d\chi'$$

$$+ \quad \frac{2v(0)}{\chi^{1/2}} + \frac{\sqrt{2\pi}}{2} U_\chi^{UO}(\chi,0) = 0.$$

After rearrangement we can rewrite this equation in the form

$$\int_0^{\chi} \frac{v_\chi(\chi')}{(\chi-\chi')^{1/2}} d\chi' = \Upsilon(\chi), \qquad (13.54)$$

where

$$\Upsilon(\chi) = \begin{cases} \Upsilon^{(+)}(\chi), & \chi > \hat{D} \\ \Upsilon^{(-)}(\chi), & \chi < \hat{D} \end{cases},$$

$$\Upsilon^{(+)}(\chi) = -\frac{1}{4} \int_0^{\chi-\hat{D}} \frac{v(\chi')}{(\chi-\chi')^{3/2}} d\chi' - \frac{\sqrt{2\pi}}{4} U_\chi^{UO}(\chi,0) - \frac{v(0)}{\chi^{1/2}},$$

$$\Upsilon^{(-)}(\chi) = \frac{\sqrt{2\pi}}{2} \left(U(\chi,0) - U^{UO}(\chi,0) \right)_\chi - \frac{v(0)}{\chi^{1/2}}.$$

Equation (13.54) is the so-called Abel equation. It can be solved via the Laplace transform method which yields

$$v_\chi(\chi) = \frac{1}{\pi} \frac{d}{d\chi} \left(\int_0^{\chi} \frac{\Upsilon(\chi')}{(\chi-\chi')^{1/2}} d\chi' \right),$$

$$v(\chi) = \frac{1}{\pi} \int_0^{\chi} \frac{\Upsilon(\chi')}{(\chi-\chi')^{1/2}} d\chi' + v(0).$$

Once $v(\chi)$ is determined, $U^{(\pm)}$ (and hence $V^{(\pm)}$) can be found via a straightforward integration.

13.8   Standard passport options

13.8.1   Description

In this section we consider passport options (POs) originally introduced by Hyer, Lipton and Pugachevsky (1997), Recall that a PO allows the buyer to select a strategy of his choice (within certain limits) and gives him the right to keep all the gains generated by this strategy while obligating the seller to absorb all the losses. Let q_t, be the strategy function chosen by the buyer; it shows the amount of foreign currency which he buys or sells at time t, and let Π_t be the value of the corresponding trading account. It is clear that q_t has to be bounded. In this section we assume that constraints are symmetric:

$$|q_t| \leq 1.$$

We impose more general constraints for q_t in the next section. It is clear that we can think of a PO as a call option on the value of the trading account with zero strike.

In principle, q_t can depend on all the information available at time t, but without loss of generality one can assume that it is a function of S_t, Π_t. The evolution of the pair (S_t, Π_t) is governed by the augmented system of SDEs (13.11). The degenerate two-factor pricing problem for a given strategy is

$$V_t^{(PO;q)} + \frac{1}{2}\sigma^2 S^2 \left(V_{SS}^{(PO;q)} + 2qV_{S\Pi}^{(PO;q)} + q^2 V_{\Pi\Pi}^{(PO;q)} \right) \tag{13.55}$$

$$+r^{01}SV_S^{(PO;q)} + r^0\Pi V_\Pi^{(PO;q)} - r^0 V^{(PO;q)} = 0,$$

$$V^{(PO;q)}(T, S, \Pi) = \Pi_+, \tag{13.56}$$

where $V^{(PO;q)}$ denotes the instantaneous value of the option.

Problem (13.55), (13.56) explicitly depends on the choice of strategy. There are plenty of reasons for the buyer to choose a sub-optimal strategy. However, the seller of the option has to price it assuming that the buyer chooses the optimal strategy. Accordingly, in order to price a PO it is necessary to solve the so-called Hamilton-Jacobi-Bellman (HJB) problem [4] for $V^{(PO)} = \max_q \left\{ V^{(PO;q)} \right\}$:

$$V_t^{(PO)} + \max_q \left\{ \begin{array}{c} \frac{1}{2}\sigma^2 S^2 \left(V_{SS}^{(PO)} + 2qV_{S\Pi}^{(PO)} + q^2 V_{\Pi\Pi}^{(PO)} \right) \\ +r^{01}SV_S^{(PO)} + r^0\Pi V_\Pi^{(PO)} - r^0 V^{(PO)} \end{array} \right\} = 0,$$

---

[4]Recall that we deal with the HJB problem in Section 8.5 when we studied optimal investment problem.

$$V^{(PO)}(T, S, \Pi) = \Pi_+.$$

HJB problems are always difficult to solve because of their nonlinearity. However, when the optimal strategy can be determined a priori, the pricing equation becomes linear.

We note in passing that most of the options described in this book can be considered as options on the trading account corresponding to a particular choice of the trading strategy. For example, to represent a call with strike K as an option on the trading account we can choose

$$q = 1, \quad \Pi_0 = S_0 - K.$$

Similarly, for an Asian call we can choose

$$q = 1 - \frac{t}{T}, \quad \Pi_0 = S_0 - K.$$

13.8.2 Similarity reductions and splitting

Dimensional reductions which we used in order to price calls and puts can be used for pricing POs, too. For a given strategy q the value $V^{(PO;q)}$ can be represented in the form

$$V^{(PO;q)}(T - t, S, \Pi, \sigma, r^0, r^1) = S\Psi^{(PO;q)}\left(\chi, \eta, \hat{r}^0, \hat{r}^1\right),$$

where $\eta = \Pi/S$, $-\infty < \eta < \infty$, is the relative value of the trading account. The corresponding pricing problem has the form

$$\Psi_\chi^{(PO;q)} - \frac{1}{2}(\eta - q)^2 \Psi_{\eta\eta}^{(PO;q)} - \hat{r}^1\eta\Psi_\eta^{(PO;q)} + \hat{r}^1\Psi^{(PO;q)} = 0,$$

$$\Psi^{(PO;q)}(0, \eta) = \eta_+.$$

A similar representation is valid for the value of the passport option $V^{(PO)}$:

$$V^{(PO)}(t, S, \Pi) = S\Psi^{(PO)}(\chi, \eta), \tag{13.57}$$

The Hamilton-Jacobi-Bellman problem for $\Psi(\chi, \eta)$ has the form

$$\Psi_\chi^{(PO)} - \frac{1}{2}\max_{|q|\leq 1}\left\{(\eta - q)^2 \Psi_{\eta\eta}^{(PO)}\right\} - \hat{r}^1\eta\Psi_\eta^{(PO)} + \hat{r}^1\Psi^{(PO)} = 0,$$

$$\Psi^{(PO)}(0, \eta) = \eta_+.$$

The pricing problem is independent of $\hat{r}^0$ (as might be expected). As parabolic problems tend to do, it preserves convexity, so that $\Psi_{\eta\eta}^{(PO)} \geq 0$. Accordingly, the optimization bit becomes trivial:

$$q = -\text{sign}(\eta). \tag{13.58}$$

Thus, the buyer of a passport option should go long when he is in the red and go short when he is in the black. The corresponding reduced Hamilton-Jacobi-Bellman pricing problem for $\Psi^{(PO)}$ can be written as

$$\Psi_\chi^{(PO)} - \frac{1}{2}\left(|\eta| + 1\right)^2 \Psi_{\eta\eta}^{(PO)} - \hat{r}^1 \eta \Psi_\eta^{(PO)} + \hat{r}^1 \Psi^{(PO)} = 0, \quad -\infty < \eta < \infty, \tag{13.59}$$

$$\Psi^{(PO)}(0, \eta) = \eta_+, \tag{13.60}$$

$$\Psi^{(PO)}(\chi, \eta \to -\infty) \to 0, \quad \Psi_\eta^{(PO)}(\chi, \eta \to \infty) \to 1. \tag{13.61}$$

We emphasize that $\Psi^{(PO)}$ is independent of $\hat{r}^0$. Although the pricing problem is linear, it is still difficult to solve because the domain of η covers the entire axis. The corresponding diffusion coefficient does not vanish, so that the naive splitting which we used to price Asian calls cannot be used here. Fortunately, the following observation comes to the rescue. The pricing equation is invariant with respect to the transformation $\eta \to -\eta$, i.e., it preserves parity. Accordingly, the split of the initial data into the odd and even components,

$$\eta_+ = \frac{1}{2}\eta + \frac{1}{2}|\eta|,$$

is preserved for all $\chi > 0$. Thus, the pricing equation supplied with the initial data $\eta/2$ and $|\eta|/2$ can be solved separately. We denote the corresponding solutions by $\Psi_O^{(PO)}$ and $\Psi_E^{(PO)}$, respectively. It is clear that

$$\Psi_O^{(PO)} = \frac{1}{2}\eta.$$

For $\eta \geq 0$ it is convenient to deal with the adjusted even solution

$$\bar{\Psi}_E^{(PO)} = \Psi_E^{(PO)} - \frac{1}{2}\eta,$$

rather than with $\Psi_E^{(PO)}$ itself. The function $\bar{\Psi}_E^{(PO)}$ solves the problem

$$\bar{\Psi}_{E,\chi}^{(PO)} - \frac{1}{2}(\eta+1)^2 \bar{\Psi}_{E,\eta\eta}^{(PO)} - \hat{r}^1 \eta \bar{\Psi}_{E,\eta}^{(PO)} + \hat{r}^1 \bar{\Psi}_E^{(PO)} = 0, \quad 0 \le \eta < \infty, \quad (13.62)$$

$$\bar{\Psi}_E^{(PO)}(0,\eta) = 0, \quad (13.63)$$

$$\bar{\Psi}_{E,\eta}^{(PO)}(0,\chi) = -\frac{1}{2}, \quad \bar{\Psi}_E^{(PO)}(\chi, \eta \to \infty) \to 0. \quad (13.64)$$

13.8.3 Pricing via the Laplace transform

By using the Laplace transform in time

$$\bar{\Psi}_E^{(PO)}(\chi,\eta) \to \bar{\Xi}_E^{(PO)}(\lambda,\eta),$$

we obtain the following problem for $\bar{\Xi}_E^{(PO)}$:

$$\left(\lambda+\hat{r}^1\right)\bar{\Xi}_E^{(PO)} - \frac{1}{2}(\eta+1)^2\bar{\Xi}_{E,\eta\eta}^{(PO)} - \hat{r}^1\eta\bar{\Xi}_{E,\eta}^{(PO)} = 0, \quad 0 \le \eta < \infty,$$

$$\bar{\Xi}_{E,\eta}^{(PO)}(\lambda,0) = -\frac{1}{2\lambda}, \quad \bar{\Xi}_E^{(PO)}(\lambda, \eta \to \infty) \to 0,$$

The shift $\eta \to \zeta = \eta+1$ yields the pricing problem of the form

$$\left(\lambda+\hat{r}^1\right)\bar{\Xi}_E^{(PO)} - \frac{1}{2}\zeta^2\bar{\Xi}_{E,\zeta\zeta}^{(PO)} - \hat{r}^1\left(\zeta-1\right)\bar{\Xi}_{E,\zeta}^{(PO)} = 0, \quad 1 \le \zeta < \infty,$$

$$\bar{\Xi}_{E,\zeta}^{(PO)}(\lambda,1) = -\frac{1}{2\lambda}, \quad \bar{\Xi}_E^{(PO)}(\lambda, \zeta \to \infty) \to 0,$$

which is analogous to problem (13.37), (13.38). Its regular solution can be written as

$$\bar{\Xi}_E^{(PO)}(\zeta,\lambda) = \Delta^{(PO)}\zeta^{-\alpha}M\left(\alpha,\beta,-\frac{2\hat{r}^1}{\zeta}\right),$$

where

$$\Delta^{(PO)} = \frac{\beta}{2\lambda\alpha\left(\beta M(\alpha,\beta,-2\hat{r}^1) - 2\hat{r}^1 M(\alpha+1,\beta+1,-2\hat{r}^1)\right)},$$

and α, β are given by expressions (13.28), (13.41) with $\hat{r}^0 = 0$. Thus,

$$\Xi_E^{(PO)}(\lambda, \eta) = \Delta^{(PO)}(\eta + 1)^{-\alpha} M\left(\alpha, \beta, -\frac{2\hat{r}^1}{\eta + 1}\right),$$

$$\Psi_E^{(PO)}(\chi, \eta) = |\eta|/2 + \mathcal{L}^{-1}\left[\Xi_E^{(PO)}(|\eta|, \lambda)\right].$$

Finally, $\Psi^{(PO)}$ can be represented as

$$\Psi^{(PO)}(\chi, \eta) = \eta_+ + \mathcal{L}^{-1}\left[\Xi_E^{(PO)}(|\eta|, \lambda)\right]. \tag{13.65}$$

13.8.4   Explicit solution for zero foreign interest rate

When $\hat{r}^1 = 0$ the function $\Psi^{(PO)}$ can be found explicitly. We have

$$\Xi_E^{(PO)}(\lambda, \eta) = \frac{\sqrt{\eta + 1}e^{-\ln(\eta+1)\sqrt{\mu}}}{(\mu - 1/4)(\sqrt{\mu} - 1/2)}$$

$$= \frac{\sqrt{\eta + 1}e^{-\ln(\eta+1)\sqrt{\mu}}}{(\sqrt{\mu} + 1/2)} - \frac{\sqrt{\eta + 1}e^{-\ln(\eta+1)\sqrt{\mu}}}{(\sqrt{\mu} - 1/2)} + \frac{\sqrt{\eta + 1}e^{-\ln(\eta+1)\sqrt{\mu}}}{(\sqrt{\mu} - 1/2)^2},$$

where $\mu = 2\lambda + 1/4$. A tedious calculation yields

$$\Psi^{(PO)}(\chi, \eta) = \frac{1}{2}\left(\eta + (|\eta| + 1)\,\mathfrak{N}(d_+) - \mathfrak{N}(d_-)\right) \tag{13.66}$$
$$-\sqrt{\chi}d_-\mathfrak{N}(-d_-) + \sqrt{\chi}\mathfrak{n}(d_-)\Big),$$

where

$$d_\pm = \frac{\ln(|\eta| + 1)}{\sqrt{\chi}} \pm \frac{\sqrt{\chi}}{2}.$$

It can be checked that expression (13.65) approaches expression (13.66) when $r^1 \to 0$.

For $\chi \to 0$ (i.e., for either short maturities or low volatilities) we have

$$\Psi^{(PO)}(\chi, 0) = \frac{1}{2}\left(1 + \frac{\chi}{2}\right)\mathfrak{N}\left(\frac{\sqrt{\chi}}{2}\right) - \frac{1}{2}\mathfrak{N}\left(-\frac{\sqrt{\chi}}{2}\right) + \frac{\sqrt{\chi}}{2}\mathfrak{n}\left(\frac{\sqrt{\chi}}{2}\right)$$

$$\approx \frac{\sqrt{\chi}}{\sqrt{2\pi}} + \frac{\chi}{8} - \frac{(\sqrt{\chi})^3}{12\sqrt{2\pi}} + \dots.$$

Recall that the price of an ATMF call is given by

$$\Psi^{(C)}(\chi, 0) = \mathfrak{N}\left(\frac{\sqrt{\chi}}{2}\right) - \mathfrak{N}\left(-\frac{\sqrt{\chi}}{2}\right) \approx \frac{\sqrt{\chi}}{\sqrt{2\pi}} - \frac{(\sqrt{\chi})^3}{24\sqrt{2\pi}} + \ldots$$

Thus, for $\chi \to 0$ passport options are only marginally more expensive than ATMF calls. The price of a typical passport option is shown in Figure 13.3.

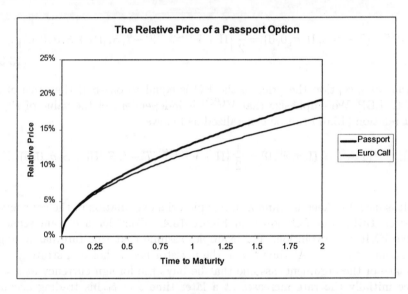

Figure 13.3: The relative price (in percent) of a passport option as a function of time to maturity. Initial value of the trading account is zero, $\sigma = 30\%$, $r^0 = r^1 = 0$. The relative price of an ATM European call is shown for comparison.

Comparison of formulas (13.66), (13.24) shows that at inception when $\eta = 0$ the price of a passport option is equal to one half of the price of a lookback put,

$$\Psi^{(PO)}(\chi, 0) = \frac{1}{2}\Psi^{(LBP)}(\chi, 1).$$

In general, the relation between $\Psi^{(LBP)}$ and $\Psi^{(PO)}$ can be written as

$$\Psi^{(PO)}(\chi, \eta) = \frac{1}{2}\left[\eta + \Psi^{(LBP)}(\chi, |\eta| + 1)\right].$$

These relations can be explained by observing that problem (13.62) - (13.64) can be transformed into problem (13.25) - (13.27) by virtue of a simple shift and scaling.

The dimensional relations between POs and LBPs are as follows:

$$V^{(PO)}(T - t, S, 0, \sigma, 0, 0) = \frac{1}{2} V^{(LBP)}(T - t, S, S, \sigma, 0, 0),$$

$$V^{(PO)}(T - t, S, \Pi, \sigma, 0, 0) = \frac{1}{2} \left[\Pi + V^{(LBP)}(T - t, S, |\Pi| + S, \sigma, 0, 0) \right],$$
(13.67)

so that at inception the price of the PO is equal to one-half the price of an ATMF LBP. We emphasize that $V^{(PO)}$ is independent of the value of r^0, so that relation (13.67) can be generalized as follows

$$V^{(PO)}(T - t, S, \Pi, \sigma, r^0, 0) = \frac{1}{2} \left[\Pi + V^{(LBP)}(T - t, S, |\Pi| + S, \sigma, 0, 0) \right].$$

It is useful to keep in mind a simple pictorial explanation of the connection between LBPs and POs given in Figure 13.4. Consider a certain scenario of the FXR rate evolution. For example, assume that this rate has a single maximum at $t = t_*$. At time $t = t_0$ the investor has a choice of strategy. For the sake of the argument, assume that he buys the foreign currency at $t = 0$. Since initially the rate increases at a later time $t = t_1$ his trading account becomes positive, so that his optimal strategy is to sell the currency. Sooner or later his trading account becomes negative and he has to buy the currency. This oscillatory pattern of buying and selling will repeat itself until $t = t_*$. Depending on the value of the trading account (which hovers near zero) two outcomes are possible. If $\Pi(t_*) > 0$ then between $t = t_*$ and $t = t_N$ the investor has to sell the currency thus accumulating a profit $\Pi(t_N) \sim M(S_{t_*} - S_{t_N})$. If $\Pi(t_*) < 0$ then he has to go buy the currency which produces a loss $\Pi(t_N) \sim -M(S_{t_*} - S_{t_N})$ (which has to be absorbed by the seller of the option). It is clear that the value of $\Pi(t_*)$ depends on the initial choice of strategy and fine details of the rate evolution between t_0 and t_*. Accordingly, it can be both positive and negative with equal probability, so that the price of the PO should be equal to one-half the price of the corresponding LBP.

In the general case when $\hat{r}^1 \neq 0$ the pricing problem cannot be simplified any further and has to be solved by the brute force method. However, due to the fact that the diffusion coefficient always stays positive (so that the

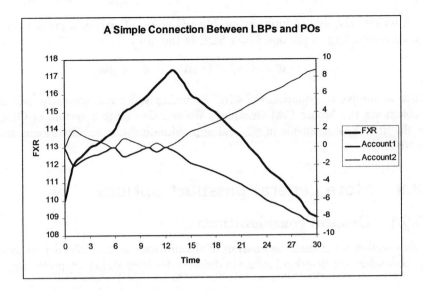

Figure 13.4: A simple pictorial explanation of the connection between LBPs and POs. This figure shows the behavior of a hypothetical FXR (left scale) and two trading accounts (right scale). Account 1 (2) corresponds to a small negative (positive) initial wealth.

problem is non-degenerate) this can be achieved with little effort by applying the standard Crank-Nicolson scheme. The cautious reader who (rightfully) dislikes dealing with advection terms can use the following change of variables

$$\tau, \eta, \Psi \rightarrow \tau, \tilde{\eta} = e^{\hat{r}^1 \chi} \eta, \tilde{\Psi} = e^{\hat{r}^1 \chi} \Psi,$$

and rewrite the pricing problem as follows

$$\tilde{\Psi}_\chi - \frac{1}{2} \left(|\tilde{\eta}| + e^{\hat{r}^1 \chi} \right)^2 \tilde{\Psi}_{\tilde{\eta}\tilde{\eta}} = 0,$$

$$\tilde{\Psi}(0, \tilde{\eta}) = \tilde{\eta}_+,$$

$$\tilde{\Psi}(\chi, \tilde{\eta} \rightarrow -\infty) \rightarrow 0, \quad \tilde{\Psi}_{\tilde{\eta}}(\chi, \tilde{\eta} \rightarrow \infty) \rightarrow 1.$$

Alternatively, we can interpret problem (13.59) - (13.61) as a pricing problem corresponding to the one-factor SDE of the form

$$d\eta = r^1 \eta dt' + \sigma \left(|\eta| + 1\right) dW_{t'}, \quad \eta_t \text{ is given.}$$

which is similar to equation (13.42). Accordingly, we can solve the pricing problem via the Monte Carlo method. We can also write a system of ODEs for the first three moments of $\eta_{t'}$, and approximate η_T by a shifted lognormal variable.

13.9   More general passport options

13.9.1   General considerations

In this section we extend the analysis of the previous section in order to cover the case when the position limits are different for long and short positions:

$$-a \leq q_t \leq b,$$

where $a, b > 0$. For notational simplicity below we write $\alpha = (b - a)/2$, $\beta = (b + a)/2 > 0$. When $a = b = 1$ we have $\alpha = 0$, $\beta = 1$. For $a = 0, b = 1$ and $a = 1, b = 0$ the corresponding passport options are called vacation calls and puts, respectively.

As in the symmetric case, the optimal strategy $q = q(\eta)$ should be chosen in such a way that the squared difference $(\eta - q)^2$ is maximized in the class of q belonging to the interval $[-a, b]$. The corresponding solution is

$$q = \begin{cases} -a, & \eta \geq \alpha \\ b, & \eta < \alpha \end{cases},$$

or, equivalently,

$$q = \alpha - \text{sign}\left(\eta - \alpha\right)\beta,$$

where the sign function is assumed to be right-continuous. When $\alpha = 0$, $\beta = 1$ ($a = b = 1$) we obtain the familiar expression (13.58). We can represent the pricing problem in the form

$$\Psi_\chi^{(PO)} - \frac{1}{2}\left(|\eta - \alpha| + \beta\right)^2 \Psi_{\eta\eta}^{(PO)} - \hat{r}^1 \eta \Psi_\eta^{(PO)} + \hat{r}^1 \Psi^{(PO)} = 0,$$

$$\Psi^{(PO)}(0,\eta) = \eta_+.$$

This problem is considered on the entire axis, and natural boundary conditions for $\eta \to \pm\infty$ are imposed:

$$\Psi^{(PO)}(\chi, \eta \to -\infty) \to 0, \qquad \Psi_\eta^{(PO)}(\chi, \eta \to \infty) \to 1.$$

13.9.2 Explicit solution for zero foreign interest rate

In this section we show how the method of splitting can be used in order to simplify the solution of the pricing problem in the special case when $\alpha > 0$, $\hat{r}^1 = 0$. This case is not only interesting in its own right but can also be used as a useful check for the general case. The pricing equation reduces to the form

$$\Psi_\chi^{(PO)} - \frac{1}{2}\left(|\eta - \alpha| + \beta\right)^2 \Psi_{\eta\eta}^{(PO)} = 0.$$

It is clear that the pricing equation is invariant with respect to the parity transform

$$\eta \to 2\alpha - \eta,$$

which has the fixed point at $\eta = \alpha$, accordingly, we can study the problem on the semi-axis $\alpha \le \eta < \infty$ provided that we adjust the initial and boundary conditions appropriately. To this end we decompose η_+ into the even and odd parts with respect to the above parity transform:

$$\eta_+ = \frac{\eta_+ + (2\alpha - \eta)_+}{2} + \frac{\eta_+ - (2\alpha - \eta)_+}{2}.$$

The pricing problems for $\Psi_{E,O}^{(PO)}$ on the semi-axis $\alpha \le \eta < \infty$ are

$$\Psi_{E,\chi}^{(PO)} - \frac{1}{2}\left(\eta - \alpha + \beta\right)^2 \Psi_{E,\eta\eta}^{(PO)} = 0,$$

$$\Psi_E^{(PO)}(0,\eta) = \frac{\eta_+ + (2\alpha - \eta)_+}{2} = \begin{cases} \alpha, & \alpha \le \eta \le 2\alpha \\ \eta/2, & 2\alpha \le \eta < \infty \end{cases},$$

$$\Psi_{E,\eta}^{(PO)}(\chi, \alpha) = 0, \qquad \Psi_{E,\eta}^{(PO)}(\chi, \eta \to \infty) \to \frac{1}{2};$$

$$\Psi_{O,\chi}^{(PO)} - \frac{1}{2}\left(\eta - \alpha + \beta\right)^2 \Psi_{O,\eta\eta}^{(PO)} = 0,$$

$$\Psi_O^{(PO)}\left(0,\eta\right) = \frac{\eta_+ - (2\alpha - \eta)_+}{2} = \begin{cases} \eta - \alpha, & \alpha \le \eta \le 2\alpha \\ \eta/2, & 2\alpha \le \eta < \infty \end{cases},$$

$$\Psi_O^{(PO)}\left(\chi,\alpha\right) = 0, \qquad \Psi_{O,\eta}^{(PO)}\left(\chi,\eta \to \infty\right) \to \frac{1}{2}.$$

We represent $\Psi_{E,O}^{(PO)}$ as follows

$$\Psi_E^{(PO)}\left(\chi,\eta\right) = \alpha + \tilde{\Psi}_E^{(PO)}\left(\chi,\eta\right),$$

$$\Psi_O^{(PO)}\left(\chi,\eta\right) = \eta - \alpha - \tilde{\Psi}_O^{(PO)}\left(\chi,\eta\right),$$

where $\tilde{\Psi}_{E,O}^{(PO)}$ satisfy the same pricing equations and boundary conditions as $\Psi_{E,O}^{(PO)}$ but supplied with the initial conditions

$$\tilde{\Psi}_{E,O}^{(PO)}\left(0,\eta\right) = \frac{1}{2}\left(\eta - 2\alpha\right)_+.$$

Finally, we introduce the shifted variable $\tilde{\eta} = \eta - \alpha + \beta$, $\beta \le \tilde{\eta} < \infty$, and write the pricing problems for $\tilde{\Psi}_{E,O}^{(PO)}$ as

$$\tilde{\Psi}_{E,O,\chi}^{(PO)} - \frac{1}{2}\tilde{\eta}^2 \tilde{\Psi}_{E,O,\tilde{\eta}\tilde{\eta}}^{(PO)} = 0,$$

$$\tilde{\Psi}_{E,O}^{(PO)}\left(0,\tilde{\eta}\right) = \frac{1}{2}\left(\tilde{\eta} - \alpha - \beta\right)_+,$$

$$\tilde{\Psi}_{E,\tilde{\eta}}^{(PO)}\left(\chi,\beta\right) = 0, \qquad \tilde{\Psi}_{E,\tilde{\eta}}^{(PO)}\left(\chi,\tilde{\eta} \to \infty\right) \to \frac{1}{2},$$

$$\tilde{\Psi}_O^{(PO)}\left(\chi,\beta\right) = 0, \qquad \tilde{\Psi}_{O,\tilde{\eta}}^{(PO)}\left(\chi,\tilde{\eta} \to \infty\right) \to \frac{1}{2}.$$

It is clear that $\tilde{\Psi}_O^{(PO)}$ is $1/2$ times the price of the down-and-out call with strike $\alpha + \beta$ and barrier at β:

$$\tilde{\Psi}_O^{(PO)}(\chi, \tilde{\eta}) = \frac{1}{2} \Psi^{(DOC)}(\chi, \tilde{\eta}).$$

The interpretation of $\tilde{\Psi}_E^{(PO)}$ is a bit more complex. After looking at the pricing equation for a long enough time one can realize that $\tilde{\Psi}_E^{(PO)}$ is $(\alpha + \beta)/2$ times the price of the partial lookback put with the reduction factor of $\beta/(\alpha + \beta)$:

$$\tilde{\Psi}_E^{(PO)}(\chi, \tilde{\eta}) = \frac{(\alpha + \beta)}{2} \Psi^{(PLBP)}\left(\chi, \frac{\tilde{\eta}}{\beta}\right).$$

Since the prices of barrier and partial lookback options are readily available, we can price the passport option under consideration explicitly. For $\alpha = 0$, $\beta = 1$ the price assumes the familiar form (13.66).

The final expression for $\Psi(\chi, \eta)$ has the form

$$\Psi(\chi, \eta) = \begin{cases} \left[\eta + \frac{(\alpha + \beta)}{2} \Psi^{(PLBP)}\left(\chi, \frac{\eta - \alpha + \beta}{\beta}\right)\right. \\ \left. - \frac{1}{2} \Psi^{(DOC)}(\chi, \eta - \alpha + \beta)\right], & \eta \geq \alpha \\ \left[\eta + \frac{(\alpha + \beta)}{2} \Psi^{(PLBP)}\left(\chi, \frac{-\eta + \alpha + \beta}{\beta}\right)\right. \\ \left. + \frac{1}{2} \Psi^{(DOC)}(\chi, -\eta + \alpha + \beta)\right], & \eta < \alpha \end{cases}$$

It is clear that $\Psi(\chi, \eta)$ is continuous at $\eta = \alpha$ by construction.

As we know, the price of a down-and-out call with strike $\alpha + \beta$ and barrier at β is

$$\Psi^{(DOC)}(\chi, \eta)$$
$$= \eta \Psi^{(C)}\left(\chi, \frac{(\alpha + \beta)}{\eta}\right) - \frac{(\alpha + \beta)\eta}{\beta} \Psi^{(P)}\left(\chi, \frac{\beta^2}{(\alpha + \beta)\eta}\right)$$
$$= \eta \mathfrak{N}(d_{+,+}) - (\alpha + \beta)\mathfrak{N}(d_{+,-}) + \frac{(\alpha + \beta)\eta}{\beta}\mathfrak{N}(-d_{-,+}) - \beta\mathfrak{N}(-d_{-,-}),$$

where

$$d_{\pm,\pm} = \frac{1}{\sqrt{\chi}}\ln\left(\frac{\eta}{\beta}\right) \pm \frac{1}{\sqrt{\chi}}\ln\left(\frac{\beta}{\alpha + \beta}\right) \pm \frac{\sqrt{\chi}}{2}.$$

The price of a partial lookback with the reduction factor of $\beta/(\alpha + \beta)$ is less well-known, nevertheless,

$$\Psi^{(PLBP)}(\chi, \eta)$$
$$= \frac{\beta}{(\alpha + \beta)}\eta\mathfrak{N}(f_{+,+}) - \mathfrak{N}(f_{+,-}) + \frac{\beta\sqrt{\chi}}{(\alpha + \beta)}\left(-f_{-,-}\mathfrak{N}(-f_{-,-}) + \mathfrak{n}(f_{-,-})\right),$$

where

$$f_{\pm,\pm} = \frac{1}{\sqrt{\chi}} \ln(\eta) \pm \frac{1}{\sqrt{\chi}} \ln\left(\frac{\beta}{\alpha+\beta}\right) \pm \frac{\sqrt{\chi}}{2}.$$

Combining the above formulas we get an explicit expression for η. For $\eta \geq \alpha$ we have

$$\Psi(\chi,\eta) = \eta + \frac{\beta(1-\sqrt{\chi}p_-)}{2}\mathfrak{N}(-p_-,-)$$
$$-\frac{(\alpha+\beta)(\eta-\alpha+\beta)}{2\beta}\mathfrak{N}(-p_-,+) + \frac{\beta\sqrt{\chi}}{2}\mathfrak{n}(p_-,-).$$

For $\eta < \alpha$ we have

$$\Psi(\tau,\eta) = \eta + (-\eta+\alpha+\beta)\mathfrak{N}(q_+,+)$$
$$-(\alpha+\beta)\mathfrak{N}(q_+,-) - \frac{\beta(1+\sqrt{\chi}q_-,-)}{2}\mathfrak{N}(-q_-,-)$$
$$+\frac{(\alpha+\beta)(-\eta+\alpha+\beta)}{2\beta}\mathfrak{N}(-q_-,+) + \frac{\beta\sqrt{\chi}}{2}\mathfrak{n}(q_-,-).$$

Here

$$p_{\pm,\pm} = \frac{1}{\sqrt{\chi}} \ln\left(\frac{\eta-\alpha+\beta}{\beta}\right) \pm \frac{1}{\sqrt{\chi}} \ln\left(\frac{\beta}{\alpha+\beta}\right) \pm \frac{\sqrt{\chi}}{2},$$

$$q_{\pm,\pm} = \frac{1}{\sqrt{\chi}} \ln\left(\frac{-\eta+\alpha+\beta}{\beta}\right) \pm \frac{1}{\sqrt{\chi}} \ln\left(\frac{\beta}{\alpha+\beta}\right) \pm \frac{\sqrt{\chi}}{2}.$$

The above formulas become particularly simple at inception when $\eta = 0$. Since, by assumption, $\alpha > 0$ we have

$$q_{+,\pm} = \pm\frac{\sqrt{\chi}}{2},$$

$$q_{-,\pm} = \frac{2}{\sqrt{\chi}} \ln\left(\frac{\alpha+\beta}{\beta}\right) \pm \frac{\sqrt{\chi}}{2},$$

$$\Psi\left(\chi,0\right) = \left(\alpha+\beta\right)\left(\mathfrak{N}\left(\frac{\sqrt{\chi}}{2}\right) - \mathfrak{N}\left(-\frac{\sqrt{\chi}}{2}\right)\right)$$

$$-\frac{\beta}{2}\left(1+2\ln\left(\frac{\alpha+\beta}{\beta}\right) - \frac{\chi}{2}\right)\mathfrak{N}\left(-\frac{2}{\sqrt{\chi}}\ln\left(\frac{\alpha+\beta}{\beta}\right) + \frac{\sqrt{\chi}}{2}\right)$$

$$+\frac{\left(\alpha+\beta\right)^2}{2\beta}\mathfrak{N}\left(-\frac{2}{\sqrt{\chi}}\ln\left(\frac{\alpha+\beta}{\beta}\right) - \frac{\sqrt{\chi}}{2}\right)$$

$$+\frac{\beta\sqrt{\chi}}{2}\mathfrak{n}\left(\frac{2}{\sqrt{\chi}}\ln\left(\frac{\alpha+\beta}{\beta}\right) - \frac{\sqrt{\chi}}{2}\right).$$

For $\chi \to 0$ we have, with exponential accuracy,

$$\Psi\left(\chi,0\right) \approx \left(\alpha+\beta\right)\left(\frac{\sqrt{\chi}}{\sqrt{2\pi}} - \frac{\left(\sqrt{\chi}\right)^3}{24\sqrt{2\pi}}\right) + \dots$$

Thus, for $\alpha > 0$ the value of a PO can be approximated by the value of $(\alpha + \beta)$ ATMF calls much more accurately than in the symmetric case.

13.10   Variance and volatility swaps

13.10.1   Introduction

Variance and volatility swaps (and, more generally, options on realized variance and volatility) are convenient tools which allow market participants to express their views on the evolution of the FXR. Buyers and sellers of such contracts are directly exposed to the realized variance and volatility of the FXR *per se*. In this section we develop simple tools for analyzing variance and volatility swaps. We continue our investigation in Section 13.13.

13.10.2   Description of swaps

We denote by S_n, $n = 0, .., N$, a series of consecutive FXRs rates observed at times $t_0 = 0$ (today),..., $t_N = T$ (maturity). Returns on holding a unit of foreign currency over a period between t_{n-1} and t_n are denoted by $x_n = \ln(S_{t_n}/S_{t_{n-1}})$. Returns on holding a unit of foreign currency forward are denoted by $x_n^F = \ln(F_{t_n,T}/F_{t_{n-1},T})$. We are interested in the realized variance υ (υ^F) and volatility σ (σ^F) of returns x_n (x_n^F). The standard statistical definitions of these quantities are as follows

$$
\begin{aligned}
\upsilon &= \frac{\left(\sum_{1\leq n\leq N} x_n^2 - \frac{1}{N}\left(\sum_{1\leq n\leq N} x_n\right)^2\right)}{N-1} \\
&= \frac{(\mathcal{J}^1 x, x)}{N-1} = \frac{(x,x)-(e_N,x)^2}{N-1},
\end{aligned}
\tag{13.68}
$$

$$
\begin{aligned}
\sigma &= \sqrt{\frac{\left(\sum_{1\leq n\leq N} x_n^2 - \frac{1}{N}\left(\sum_{1\leq n\leq N} x_n\right)^2\right)}{N-1}} \\
&= \sqrt{\frac{(\mathcal{J}^1 x, x)}{N-1}} = \sqrt{\frac{(x,x)-(e_N,x)^2}{N-1}},
\end{aligned}
\tag{13.69}
$$

and similarly for υ^F, σ^F. Here e_N is a unit vector, and $\mathcal{J}^\alpha$ is a projection matrix of the form

$$
e_N = \frac{1}{\sqrt{N}}(1,...,1), \quad \mathcal{J}^\alpha = \mathcal{I} - \alpha e_N \otimes e_N.
$$

However, often simpler definitions are used:

$$
\tilde{\upsilon} = \frac{\sum_{1\leq n\leq N}\left(x_n^F\right)^2}{N-1} = \frac{(x^F, x^F)}{N-1},
\tag{13.70}
$$

$$
\tilde{\sigma} = \sqrt{\frac{\sum_{1\leq n\leq N}\left(x_n^F\right)^2}{N-1}} = \sqrt{\frac{(x^F, x^F)}{N-1}},
$$

and similarly for υ^F, σ^F.

Accordingly, we can define variance swaps (VRSs) and volatility swaps (VLSs) of several kinds, depending of which definition of variance and volatility we use. A typical VRS involves a single cash flow at maturity, its normalized payoff is defined by the following expression:

$$
\text{payoff}^{(VRS)} = K - \upsilon',
$$

where υ' is an appropriately chosen realized variance, and K is the strike. The normalized payoff of a VLS is defined in a similar way:

$$
\text{payoff}^{(VLS)} = K - \sigma'.
$$

Our objective is to find the correct values of $K^{(VRS)}$, $K^{(VLS)}$ and an appropriate hedging strategy such that the corresponding P&Ls are made as small as possible.

It is clear that VRS and VLS can be considered as special classes of discretely sampled path-dependent options. In this section we analyze these options in the Black-Scholes framework. We study them in a more general setting in Section 13.13.

13.10.3 Pricing and hedging of swaps via convexity adjustments

To be concrete, we use statistical definitions (13.68), (13.69). Our objective is to find the risk-neutral expectations of v and σ which are the fair values of $K^{(VRS)}$ and $K^{(VLS)}$.

Assume that we evaluate the variance and volatility of the FXR after L observations are made and $M = N - L$ are left. In other words, the valuation time is t, $\sum_{l \leq L} \tau_l \leq t < \sum_{l \leq L+1} \tau_l$. We denote the vector of known values of x by X_L, and the vector of its unknown future values by x_M. By using this notation we can write v and σ as follows

$$
\begin{aligned}
v &= \frac{\left\{ (X_L, X_L) + (x_M, x_M) - \left[\frac{\sqrt{L}}{\sqrt{N}}(e_L, X_L) + \frac{\sqrt{M}}{\sqrt{N}}(e_M, x_M) \right]^2 \right\}}{N - 1} \\
&= \frac{\left\{ (\mathcal{J}^{M/N} x_M, x_M) + (\tilde{b}, x_M) + \tilde{d} \right\}}{N - 1},
\end{aligned}
$$

$$
\sigma = \sqrt{\frac{(\mathcal{J}^{M/N} x_M, x_M) + (\tilde{b}, x_M) + \tilde{d}}{N - 1}},
$$

where

$$
\tilde{b} = -\frac{2\sqrt{LM}}{N}(e_L, X_L)e_M, \quad \tilde{d} = (\mathcal{J}^{L/N} X_L, X_L).
$$

We assume that the unknown values x_M can be represented in the form

$$
x_M = \mathcal{D}\lambda_M + \delta_M,
$$

where λ_M are independent standard normal vectors, $\mathcal{D} = diag(\sigma_m)$ is the volatility matrix (representing the term structure of volatilities), and δ is the drift vector. After some algebra we get

$$v = \frac{(\mathcal{P}\lambda_M, \lambda_M) + (b, \lambda_M) + d}{N - 1},$$

$$\sigma = \sqrt{\frac{(\mathcal{P}\lambda_M, \lambda_M) + (b, \lambda_M) + d}{N - 1}},$$

where

$$\begin{aligned}
\mathcal{P} &= \mathcal{D}\mathcal{J}^{M/N}\mathcal{D}, \\
b &= 2\mathcal{D}\mathcal{J}^{M/N}\delta_M + \mathcal{D}\tilde{b}, \\
d &= (\mathcal{J}^{M/N}\delta_M, \delta_M) + (\tilde{b}, \delta_M) + \tilde{d}.
\end{aligned}$$

In order to simplify the notation, we denote the random variables $(\mathcal{P}\lambda_M, \lambda_M)$, (b, λ_M) by p, b, respectively, and split them into their expected values and deviations, $p = \bar{p} + \hat{p}$, $b = \hat{b}$, where

$$\bar{p} = Tr(\mathcal{P}) = \left(1 - \frac{1}{N}\right) \sum \sigma_m^2.$$

Here Tr stands for the trace of a matrix. By taking the expectation of v, we get

$$\begin{aligned}
\mathbb{E}\{v\} &= \frac{Tr(\mathcal{P}) + d}{N - 1} \\
&= \frac{\left(1 - \frac{1}{N}\right) \sum \sigma_m^2 + \sum X_l^2 + \sum \delta_m^2 - \frac{1}{N} \left(\sum X_l + \sum \delta_m\right)^2}{N - 1}.
\end{aligned}$$

In order to find the expected value of volatility, we represent σ the form

$$\sigma = \sqrt{\frac{\bar{p} + d + \hat{p} + \hat{b}}{N - 1}} = \sqrt{\mathbb{E}\{v\}} \left[1 + \frac{1}{2}U - \frac{1}{8}U^2 + \cdots\right],$$

where

$$U = \frac{\hat{p} + \hat{b}}{\bar{p} + d},$$

and dots stand for higher order terms. By taking the expectation we get

$$
\begin{aligned}
\mathbb{E}\{\sigma\} &= \sqrt{\mathbb{E}\{v\}} \left[1 - \frac{1}{8}\mathbb{E}\{U^2\}\right] \\
&= \sqrt{\mathbb{E}\{v\}} \left[1 - \frac{\mathbb{E}\{\hat{p}^2\} + \mathbb{E}\{\hat{b}^2\}}{8(N-1)^2[\mathbb{E}\{v\}]^2}\right] \\
&= \sqrt{\mathbb{E}\{v\}} \left[1 - \frac{Tr(\mathcal{P}\mathcal{P}^* + \mathcal{P}^2) + (b,b)}{8(N-1)^2[\mathbb{E}\{v\}]^2}\right].
\end{aligned}
$$

After some (considerable) amount of algebra we get

$$
Tr(\mathcal{P}\mathcal{P}^* + \mathcal{P}^2) = 2\left(1 - \frac{2}{N}\right)\sum \sigma_m^4 + \frac{2}{N^2}\left[\sum \sigma_m^2\right]^2,
$$

$$
\begin{aligned}
(b,b) &= 4\left(\sum \delta_m^2 \sigma_m^2 - \frac{2}{N}\left[\sum X_l + \sum \delta_m\right]\sum \delta_m \sigma_m^2 \right. \\
&\quad \left. + \frac{1}{N^2}\left[\sum X_l + \sum \delta_m\right]^2 \sum \sigma_m^2\right),
\end{aligned}
$$

which completes the derivation.

If we denote the value of a volatility swap at inception by Υ,

$$
\begin{aligned}
\Upsilon(\sigma_1, ..., \sigma_N, \delta_1, ..., \delta_N) &= \sqrt{\frac{(N-1)\Sigma(\sigma^2) + N\Sigma(\delta^2) - [\Sigma(\delta)]^2}{N(N-1)}} \\
&\times \left[1 - \frac{N(N-2)\Sigma(\sigma^4) + [\Sigma(\sigma^2)]^2 + 2N^2\Sigma(\sigma^2\delta^2) - 4N\Sigma(\delta)\Sigma(\sigma^2\delta) + 2\Sigma(\sigma^2)[\Sigma(\delta)]^2}{4((N-1)\Sigma(\sigma^2) + N\Sigma(\delta^2) - [\Sigma(\delta)]^2)^2}\right],
\end{aligned}
$$

where $\Sigma(x) = \sum_{n=1}^{N} x_n$, then we can represent its value after L observations as

$$
\Upsilon(0, ..., 0, \sigma_{L+1}, ..., \sigma_N, X_1, ..., X_L, \delta_{L+1}, ..., \delta_N).
$$

The above expressions can be written in a more transparent form if we introduce

$$
\hat{\delta} = (\hat{\delta}_1, ..., \hat{\delta}_N), \quad \hat{\delta}_m = \delta_m - \frac{1}{N}\Sigma(\delta).
$$

Then we have

$$\Upsilon(\sigma_1, ..., \sigma_N, \hat{\delta}_1, ..., \hat{\delta}_N) = \sqrt{\frac{(N-1)\Sigma(\sigma^2) + N\Sigma(\hat{\delta}^2)}{N(N-1)}}$$

$$\times \left[1 - \frac{N(N-2)\Sigma(\sigma^4) + \left[\Sigma(\sigma^2)\right]^2 + 2N^2\Sigma(\sigma^2\hat{\delta}^2)}{4\left((N-1)\Sigma(\sigma^2) + N\Sigma(\hat{\delta}^2)\right)^2} \right],$$

and similarly for the expected value of volatility after L fixings,

$$\Upsilon(0, ..., 0, \sigma_{L+1}, ..., \sigma_N, \hat{X}_1, ..., \hat{X}_L, \hat{\delta}_{L+1}, ..., \hat{\delta}_N),$$

where

$$\hat{X}_l = X_l - \frac{1}{N}\left[\Sigma(X) + \Sigma(\delta)\right], \quad \hat{\delta}_m = \delta_m - \frac{1}{N}\left[\Sigma(X) + \Sigma(\delta)\right].$$

It is very easy to evaluate the corresponding Greeks of the deal by virtue of the above formula. Indeed, it can be seen that the only quantities depending on the current time t and the value of the FXR S_t are σ_{L+1}, δ_{L+1},

$$\sigma_{L+1} = \frac{\tilde{\sigma}_{L+1}\sqrt{t_{L+1} - t}}{\sqrt{\tau_{L+1}}}, \quad \delta_{L+1} = \ln\left(\frac{S_t}{S_{t_L}}\right) + \tilde{\delta}_{L+1}(t_{L+1} - t),$$

where $\tilde{\sigma}_{L+1}, \tilde{\delta}_{L+1}$ are values of the volatility and drift obtained from the term structure. Accordingly,

$$\Delta = \frac{\partial \Upsilon}{\partial \delta_{L+1}} \frac{1}{S_t}, \quad \Gamma = \left(\frac{\partial^2 \Upsilon}{\partial^2 \delta_{L+1}} - \frac{\partial \Upsilon}{\partial \delta_{L+1}}\right) \frac{1}{S_t^2},$$

etc.

In order to get a better feel for these formulas, let us consider the simplest possible case end evaluate the expected variance and volatility at the beginning of the swap ($L = 0$, $M = N$) assuming that the term structure is flat, so that $\sigma_m = \breve{\sigma}$, $\delta_m = \breve{\delta}$. In this case

$$Tr(\mathcal{P}\mathcal{P}^* + \mathcal{P}^2) = 2(N-1)\breve{\sigma}^4,$$

$$(b, b) = 0,$$

so that

$$\mathbb{E}\{v\} = \breve{\sigma}^2,$$

$$\mathbb{E}\{\sigma\} = \left[1 - \frac{1}{4(N-1)}\right] \breve{\sigma}.$$

After L observations are made, we can represent the corresponding expectations as follows

$$\mathbb{E}\{v\} = \frac{M}{N}\breve{\sigma}^2 + \frac{\sum X_l^2 + M\breve{\delta}^2 - \frac{1}{N}\left(\sum X_l + M\breve{\delta}\right)^2}{N-1},$$

where the second term represents the variance of the sequence $X_1, ..., X_L$, $\breve{\delta}, ..., \breve{\delta}$, and

$$\mathbb{E}\{\sigma\} = \sqrt{\mathbb{E}\{v\}} \left(1 - \frac{\left[\left(1-2/N+M/N^2\right)\breve{\sigma}^2 + 2\left(\breve{\delta} - \left(\sum X_l + M\breve{\delta}\right)/N\right)^2\right]M\breve{\sigma}^2}{4(N-1)^2[\mathbb{E}\{v\}]^2}\right).$$

In the homogeneous case it is not difficult to find the exact distributions of v and σ. At inception we can represent the variance and volatility in the form

$$v = \frac{(\mathcal{J}^1\lambda, \lambda)}{N-1}\breve{\sigma}^2,$$

$$\sigma = \sqrt{\frac{(\mathcal{J}^1 x, x)}{N-1}}\breve{\sigma}.$$

A rotation of the standard basis in the λ-space such that the last basis vector of the new basis coincides with e_N transforms λ into $\tilde{\lambda}$ and the quadratic form $(\mathcal{J}^1\lambda, \lambda)$ into the form $\sum_{n=1}^{N-1} \tilde{\lambda}^2$. The random variable $\zeta_{N-1} = \sum_{n=1}^{N-1} \tilde{\lambda}^2$ is described by the well-known χ^2 distribution with $N-1$ degrees of freedom, while its square root $\psi_{N-1} = \sqrt{\zeta_{N-1}}$ is described by the χ distribution with $N-1$ degrees of freedom. Accordingly,

$$v = \frac{\zeta_{N-1}}{N-1}\breve{\sigma}^2,$$

$$\sigma = \frac{\psi_{N-1}}{\sqrt{N-1}}\breve{\sigma},$$

where the p.d.f.'s for ζ_{N-1}, ψ_{N-1} have the form

$$g(\zeta) = \frac{1}{2^{(N-1)/2}\Gamma[(N-1)/2]}\zeta^{(N-3)/2} \exp\left[-\frac{\zeta}{2}\right],$$

$$g(\sigma) = \frac{1}{2^{(N-3)/2}\Gamma[(N-1)/2]}\psi^{N-3}\exp\left[-\frac{\psi^2}{2}\right].$$

It is easy to check that

$$\mathbb{E}\{v\} = \breve{\sigma}^2,$$

$$\mathbb{E}\{\sigma\} = \frac{\sqrt{2}\Gamma(N/2)}{\sqrt{N-1}\Gamma[(N-1)/2]}\breve{\sigma} \approx \left[1 - \frac{1}{4(N-1)}\right]\breve{\sigma}.$$

Thus, there is no convexity adjustment for v but there is one for σ.

If L observations are already made we can use a similar rotation and represent v, σ as follows

$$v = \frac{\breve{\sigma}^2\zeta + \frac{L}{N}\breve{\sigma}^2\xi^2 + 2\Phi\xi + \Psi}{N-1},$$

$$\sigma = \sqrt{\frac{\breve{\sigma}^2\zeta + \frac{L}{N}\breve{\sigma}^2\xi^2 + 2\Phi\breve{\sigma}\xi + \Psi}{N-1}},$$

where ζ and ξ are independent random variables with the chi-squared and normal distributions, respectively, while

$$\Phi = \left(\frac{\sum X_l + M\breve{\delta}}{N} - \breve{\delta}\right)\sqrt{M},$$

$$\Psi = \sum X_l^2 + M\breve{\delta}^2 - \frac{1}{N}\left(\sum X_l + M\breve{\delta}\right)^2.$$

Thus,

$$\mathbb{E}\{v\} = \frac{M-1}{N-1}\breve{\sigma}^2 + \frac{L}{N(N-1)}\breve{\sigma}^2$$

$$+\frac{\sum X_l^2 + M\breve{\delta}^2 - \frac{1}{N}\left(\sum X_l + M\breve{\delta}\right)^2}{N-1}$$

$$= \frac{M}{N}\breve{\sigma}^2 + \frac{\sum X_l^2 + M\breve{\delta}^2 - \frac{1}{N}\left(\sum X_l + M\breve{\delta}\right)^2}{N-1},$$

as before. The expectation of σ is represented by the integral

$$\mathbb{E}\{\sigma\} = \frac{1}{2^{(N-1)/2}\Gamma[(N-1)/2]\sqrt{2\pi}}$$

$$\times \int_0^\infty \int_{-\infty}^\infty \sqrt{\frac{\breve{\sigma}^2\zeta + \frac{L}{N}\breve{\sigma}^2\xi^2 + 2\Phi\breve{\sigma}\xi + \Psi}{N-1}}\, \zeta^{(M-3)/2} \exp\left[-\frac{\zeta+\xi^2}{2}\right] d\zeta d\xi.$$

This integral is difficult to evaluate explicitly. However, the convexity adjustment produces the same formula as before.

13.10.4   Log contracts and robust pricing and hedging of variance swaps

In this subsection we develop an alternative approach to the valuation of variance swaps. We define the realized variance of the forward FXR via formula (13.70). Accordingly, the payoff of the swap is given by

$$\text{payoff}^{(VRS)} = K^{(VRS)} - \tilde{v}^F.$$

We proceed in two steps. First, we introduce a European option which we call a modified log contract (MLC) and show that P&L of such an option (provided that it is hedged dynamically) is very close to (but not identical with) P&L of the VRS. Second, we demonstrate how to replace MLC by a strip of puts and calls. As a result, we find a set of tradeables which replicates the VRS. The most attractive feature of this approach is that it is independent on the dynamics of the underlying FXR and can be used in the presence of the smile as easily as in the Black-Scholes world. It is clear that going into a VRS of the first kind and an offsetting MLC would result in a dramatically reduced P&L.

Recall (see Section 8.4) that a MLC is a European option with the payoff of the form

$$\text{payoff}^{(MLC)} = F(S_T) = \left[\ln\left(\frac{\varkappa}{S_T}\right) + \frac{S_T}{\varkappa} - 1\right],$$

where $\varkappa$ is a given strike. When the forward price of the FXR follows the standard lognormal process, i.e., $\sigma_t \equiv \sigma$, the price of the MLC can be found explicitly. A straightforward algebra shows that the forward price $\check{V}^{(MLC)}(t,F)$ of this contract has the form

$$\check{V}^{(MLC)}(t,F) = F(F) + \frac{1}{2}\sigma^2(T-t),$$

In general, the price of a MLC can be written as

$$\check{V}^{(MLC)}(t, F) = F(F) + \frac{1}{2}\hat{\sigma}_{t,T}^2(T - t), \tag{13.71}$$

where $\hat{\sigma}_{t,T}$ is the implied volatility of the FXR between t and T. It is shown below how this volatility can be determined from the market data.

The hedging strategy for a MLC is suggested by equation (13.71). It also takes into account our desire to replicate the P&L of a VRS as closely as possible. Accordingly, the strategy consists of buying Δ_n shares of the underlying at discrete times t_n, where

$$\Delta_n = \left(\frac{1}{\kappa} - \frac{1}{F}\right). \tag{13.72}$$

We emphasize that this Δ is not the true Δ of a MLC in the presence of the smile. Let us evaluate the P&L of a discretely hedged MLC. By using equation (13.72) we obtain

$$
\begin{aligned}
P\&L^{(MLC)} &= F(F_0) - F(F_T) + \frac{1}{2}\hat{\sigma}_{0,T}^2 T + \sum_{n=1}^{N} \Delta_n(F_n - F_{n-1}) \\
&= \ln\left(\frac{F_T}{F_0}\right) + \frac{F_0 - F_T}{\kappa} + \frac{1}{2}\hat{\sigma}_{0,T}^2 T + \sum_{n=1}^{N} \Delta_{n-1}(F_n - F_{n-1}) \\
&= \ln\left(\frac{F_T}{F_0}\right) + \frac{1}{2}\hat{\sigma}_{0,T}^2 T - \sum_{n=1}^{N} \frac{1}{F_{n-1}}(F_n - F_{n-1}) \\
&= \ln\left(\frac{F_T}{F_0}\right) + \frac{1}{2}\hat{\sigma}_{0,T}^2 T - \sum_{n=1}^{N} \left(e^{x_n^F} - 1\right) \\
&= \ln\left(\frac{F_T}{F_0}\right) + \frac{1}{2}\hat{\sigma}_{0,T}^2 T - \sum_{n=1}^{N} \left(x_n^F + \frac{1}{2}\left(x_n^F\right)^2 + \frac{1}{6}\left(x_n^F\right)^3 + ...\right) \\
&= \frac{1}{2}\hat{\sigma}_{0,T}^2 T - \frac{1}{2}\sum_{n=1}^{N} x_n^2 - \frac{1}{6}\sum_{n=1}^{N} \left(x_n^F\right)^3 + ... \,.
\end{aligned}
$$

At the same time,

$$P\&L^{(VRS)} = K^{(VRS)} - \frac{1}{N-1}\sum_{n=1}^{N} \left(x_n^F\right)^2.$$

Accordingly, the P&L of the difference between $(N-1)/2$ VRSs and a MLC is given by

$$\delta P\&L \approx \frac{(N-1)}{2} K^{(VRS)} - \frac{1}{2}\hat{\sigma}_{0,T}^2 T + \frac{1}{6}\sum_{n=0}^{N-1} x_n^3.$$

Accordingly, by choosing

$$K^{(VRS)} = \frac{\hat{\sigma}_{0,T}^2 T}{N-1}, \tag{13.73}$$

we can make this difference sufficiently small. Thus, by entering into one side of a VRS and the opposite side of the appropriately hedged MLC we can reduce the unhedgeable P&L of the combined deal to

$$\delta P\&L \approx \frac{1}{6}\sum_{n=0}^{N-1} \left(x_n^F\right)^3.$$

We emphasize that equation (13.73) is ostensibly independent of the choice of κ which determines the exact payoff for the MLC. However, in the non-Black-Scholes world this dependence still exists due to the fact that $\hat{\sigma}_{0,T}^2$ implicitly depends on κ.

It is important to note that the close relation between the P&L of VRSs and MLCs holds not only at inception but at any subsequent moment as well. Thus, the valuation and hedging of VRSs can be reduced (modulo small unhedgeable terms) to the valuation and hedging of MLCs. Accordingly, in order to deal with VRSs it is necessary to replicate MLCs in terms of calls and puts. For MLCs replication formula (8.34) yields

$$\check{V}^{(MLC)}(t,F) = \int_0^\kappa \frac{\check{P}(t,F,T,X)}{X^2} dX + \int_\kappa^\infty \frac{\check{C}(t,F,T,X)}{X^2} dX. \tag{13.74}$$

We emphasize that relation (13.74) is valid regardless of the validity of the classical Black-Scholes assumptions. Indeed, all it says is that the r.h.s. and l.h.s. both satisfy the pricing equation (which is obvious) and, in addition, are equal at maturity (which can be verified via a simple calculation), so that the r.h.s. and l.h.s. are equal at any time t, $0 \le t \le T$. We can use this relation in order to find the implied volatility $\hat{\sigma}_{t,T}$,

$$\hat{\sigma}_{t,T} = \sqrt{\frac{2}{(T-t)}\left[\int_0^\kappa \frac{\check{P}(t,F_{t,T},T,X)}{X^2} dX + \int_\kappa^\infty \frac{\check{C}(t,F_{t,T},T,X)}{X^2} dX - \Xi(F_{t,T})\right]}.$$

Thus, theoretically, a MLC can be replicated by a strip of an appropriately weighted calls and puts. In order to replicate such a contract in practice, we choose a discrete set of strikes centered at the break FXR κ (this will necessarily introduce an additional error into our replication and hedging scheme). The choice of κ remains somewhat arbitrary. Perhaps, the best choice is $\kappa = F_{0,T}$, since it guarantees that $\overset{\wedge}{\sigma}_{0,T}$ has a simple form

$$\overset{\wedge}{\sigma}_{0,T} = \sqrt{\frac{2}{T} \left[\int_0^{F_{0,T}} \frac{\check{P}(0, F_{0,T}, T, X)}{X^2} dX + \int_{F_{0,T}}^{\infty} \frac{\check{C}(0, F_{0,T}, T, X)}{X^2} dX \right]}.$$

13.11 The impact of stochastic volatility on path-dependent options

13.11.1 The general valuation formula

We already know that deviations from the Black-Scholes paradigm have strong impact on pricing and hedging of vanilla options. This impact is even more profound for (some classes) of path-dependent options. In this section we develop the general technique for pricing options on forex with stochastic volatility. Specific applications of this technique to forward starting options and options on volatility and variance are considered in Sections 13.12 and 13.13, respectively.

To be concrete, we choose the standard square-root process for the variance and write the governing system of SDEs for S_t, v_t in the form:

$$\frac{dS}{S} = r^{01} dt + \sqrt{v} dW, \tag{13.75}$$

$$dv = \kappa(\theta - v)dt + \varepsilon\sqrt{v} d\Omega,$$

where $corr\,(dW, d\Omega) = \rho$. The corresponding SDEs written in forward terms are

$$\frac{dF}{F} = \sqrt{v} dW, \tag{13.76}$$

$$dv = \kappa(\theta - v)dt + \varepsilon\sqrt{v} d\Omega.$$

Our objective is to price a European path-dependent option with the general payoff

$$\text{Payoff} = F(S_0, S_1, ..., S_N),$$

where $S_n = S_{t_n}$ is the FXR at time t_n. We evaluate the price of this option as the discounted expected value (under risk-neutral measure) of the payoff. Accordingly, we can write today's value of this option as:

$$V(0, S_0, v_0) = e^{-r^0 T} \int \cdots \int_{0 < S_n < \infty, 0 < v_n < \infty} F(S_0, S_1, ..., S_N) \quad (13.77)$$
$$\times \pi(0, S_0, v_0, t_1, S_1, v_1) ... \pi(t_{N-1}, S_{N-1}, v_{N-1}, T, S_N, v_N)$$
$$\times dS_1 ... dS_N dv_1 ... dv_N,$$

where $\pi(t_n, S_n, v_n, t_{n+1}, S_{n+1}, v_{n+1})$ is the t.p.d.f. for the vector process governed by SDEs (13.75).

It is clear that it is much more difficult to evaluate integral (13.77) than integral (13.12). (As we know, the evaluation of integral (13.12) is difficult in its own right.) We develop a suitable approach to studying integral (13.77) in the next subsection.

13.11.2   Evaluation of the t.p.d.f.

To start with, we simplify the situation by introducing the logarithmic forward FXR $X_{t,T} = \ln(F_{t,T}/F_{0,T})$, and rewriting the governing SDEs as

$$dX = -\frac{1}{2}v dt + \sqrt{v} dW, \quad (13.78)$$
$$dv = \kappa(\theta - v)dt + \varepsilon\sqrt{v} d\Omega.$$

To avoid unnecessary complications we assume that

$$\vartheta = \frac{2\kappa\theta}{\varepsilon^2} - 1 > 0,$$

so that the process v_t never crosses zero.

We need to find the t.p.d.f. for the vector process governed by SDEs (13.78), which is denoted by $p(t, X, v, t', X', v')$. Since the coefficients of the corresponding SDEs are independent on t, X, the density p depends on the differences $\tau = t' - t$, $Y = X' - X$, rather than the arguments themselves, so that

$$p(t, X, v, t', X', v') = p(\tau, Y, v, v').$$

In order to remove undesirable drift terms, it is convenient to introduce

$$\hat{p}(\tau, Y, v, v') = e^{Y/2} p(\tau, Y, v, v').$$

It is easy to check that $\hat{p}$ as a function of t', X', v' is governed by the forward Fokker-Planck equation with killing, while as a function of t, X, v it is governed by the backward Kolmogoroff equation with killing. These equations can be written as follows

$$\hat{p}_\tau - \frac{1}{2}\frac{\partial^2}{\partial Y^2}(v'\hat{p})_{YY} - (\varepsilon\rho v'\hat{p})_{Yv'} - \frac{1}{2}\left(\varepsilon^2 v'\hat{p}\right)_{v'v'} + \left(\hat{\kappa}(\hat{\theta} - v')\hat{p}\right)_{v'} + \frac{1}{8}v'\hat{p} = 0,$$

$$\hat{p}_\tau - \frac{1}{2}v\hat{p}_{YY} - \varepsilon\rho v\hat{p}_{Yv} - \frac{1}{2}\varepsilon^2 v\hat{p}_{vv} - \hat{\kappa}(\hat{\theta} - v)\hat{p}_v + \frac{1}{8}v\hat{p} = 0,$$

where $\hat{\kappa} = (\kappa - \varepsilon\rho/2)$, $\hat{\theta} = \kappa\theta/\hat{\kappa}$. The corresponding initial conditions are the same in both cases, namely,

$$\hat{p}(\tau, Y, v, v') \longrightarrow \delta(Y)\delta(v' - v) \text{ as } \tau \longrightarrow 0.$$

Due to the fact that the dynamics of v is independent on the dynamics of X (but not *vice versa*) it does make sense to study the transition probability density

$$q(t, v, t', v') = q(\tau, v, v'),$$

which can be used for pricing options on volatility and for other purposes. The governing equations for q have the form

$$q_\tau + (\kappa(\theta - v')q)_{v'} - \frac{1}{2}\left(\varepsilon^2 v'q\right)_{v'v'} = 0,$$

$$q_\tau - \kappa(\theta - v)q_v - \frac{1}{2}\varepsilon^2 v q_{vv} = 0,$$

$$q(\tau, v, v') \longrightarrow \delta(v' - v) \text{ as } \tau \longrightarrow 0.$$

We start with the more general and complex case and show how to evaluate $\hat{p}$, not surprisingly, we obtain a formula for q as a by-product. [5] We use the same methodology as in Section 10.9, where we priced European options on FXRs with stochastic volatility. To be concrete, we consider the backward

---

[5] It is also possible to evaluate q directly by reducing the scalar SDE for v to the Bessel form.

Kolmogoroff equation. Due to the fact that its coefficients are linear functions of v, we can write p in the affine form as follows:

$$\hat{p}(\tau, Y, v, v') = \frac{2}{(2\pi)^2 \, \varepsilon^2} \int_{-\infty}^{\infty} \int_{-\infty}^{\infty} e^{ikY + 2[A(\tau,k,l) - B(\tau,k,l)v + ilv']/\varepsilon^2} \, dk dl.$$

This representation suggests that solutions of the stochastic pricing equation might behave irregularly when $\epsilon \to 0$. However, it can be checked that both $A \to 0$ and $B \to 0$ when $\epsilon \to 0$, so that the corresponding transition is smooth. Substituting this expression into the governing equation we obtain the following system of ODEs and initial conditions for A, B:

$$\frac{d}{d\tau} B + B^2 + (ik\varepsilon\rho + \hat{\kappa})B - \frac{1}{4}\varepsilon^2 (k^2 + \frac{1}{4}) = 0, \quad B(0, k, l) = il, \qquad (13.79)$$

$$\frac{d}{d\tau} A + \kappa\theta B = 0, \quad A(0, k, l) = 0$$

We linearize equation (13.79) via the familiar substitution

$$B = C_\tau / C. \qquad (13.80)$$

and represent A in the form

$$A = -\kappa\theta \ln C. \qquad (13.81)$$

The linear second-order ODE and appropriate initial conditions for C are:

$$\frac{d^2}{d\tau^2} C + (ik\varepsilon\rho + \hat{\kappa}) \frac{d}{d\tau} C - \frac{1}{4}\varepsilon^2 (k^2 + \frac{1}{4}) C = 0,$$

$$C(0, k, l) = 1, \quad \frac{d}{d\tau} C(0, k, l) = il.$$

The solution of the above problem can be written as

$$C(\tau, k, l) = \frac{e^{(\mu+\zeta)\tau} \left(-\mu + \zeta + il + (\mu + \zeta - il)e^{-2\zeta\tau} \right)}{2\zeta},$$

where μ and ζ are given by formulas (10.75) and (10.76), respectively. We emphasize the fact that all the formulas we have to deal with are defined in the complex plane. Accordingly, we have to be careful when we define such functions as $\sqrt{Z}$ and $\log(Z)$, where Z is a complex number. As before, we consider the branches of the square root and the logarithm defined in the complex plane with a branch cut along the negative semi-axis, such that $\sqrt{1} = 1$ and $\ln(1) = 0$. It is very important to understand that these functions are discontinuous along the negative semi-axis where we have a branch cut; however, the discontinuity of the square root is irrelevant for our purposes, while the discontinuity of the logarithm can easily be accounted for. (We omit details for brevity.) Formulas (13.80), (13.81) yield

$$
\mathsf{B}(\tau,k,l) = \frac{\varepsilon^2(k^2+1/4)(1-e^{-2\zeta\tau}) + 4il(\mu+\zeta+(-\mu+\zeta)e^{-2\zeta\tau})}{4\left(-\mu+\zeta+il+(\mu+\zeta-il)e^{-2\zeta\tau}\right)},
$$

$$
\mathsf{A}(\tau,k,l) = -\kappa\theta\left(\mu+\zeta\right)\tau
$$
$$
-\kappa\theta\left[\ln\left(\frac{-\mu+\zeta+il+(\mu+\zeta-il)e^{-2\zeta\tau}}{2\zeta}\right) + 2\pi iN\right].
$$

Finally, we obtain the following expression for $\hat{p}$:

$$
\hat{p}(\tau,Y,v,v') \tag{13.82}
$$
$$
= \frac{2}{(2\pi)^2\varepsilon^2} \int_{-\infty}^{\infty}\int_{-\infty}^{\infty} \exp\left\{ \frac{\hat{\kappa}\kappa\theta}{\varepsilon^2}\tau + ik\left(Y+\frac{\rho\kappa\theta}{\varepsilon}\tau\right) + \frac{2ilv'}{\varepsilon^2} \right.
$$
$$
-\frac{2\kappa\theta}{\varepsilon^2}\left[\zeta\tau + \ln\left(\frac{-\mu+\zeta+il+(\mu+\zeta-il)e^{-2\zeta\tau}}{2\zeta}\right) + 2\pi iN\right]
$$
$$
\left. -\frac{v\left[(k^2+1/4)(1-e^{-2\zeta\tau}) + 4il(\zeta+\mu+(-\mu+\zeta)e^{-2\zeta\tau})/\varepsilon^2\right]}{2\left(-\mu+\zeta+il+(\mu+\zeta-il)e^{-2\zeta\tau}\right)} \right\} dk\,dl.
$$

All we need to do in order to obtain an expression for q is to assume (somewhat informally) that $k = -i/2$ in the above derivation and postmultiply the result by $e^{-Y/2}$. After some algebra we obtain the following expression for q:

$$
q(\tau,v,v') = \frac{2}{2\pi\varepsilon^2} \int_{-\infty}^{\infty} \exp\left\{ \frac{2ilv'}{\varepsilon^2} - \frac{2\kappa\theta}{\varepsilon^2}\ln\left(\frac{\kappa+il-ile^{-\kappa\tau}}{\kappa}\right) \right. \tag{13.83}
$$
$$
\left. -\frac{2il\kappa e^{-\kappa\tau}v}{\varepsilon^2\left(\kappa+il-ile^{-\kappa\tau}\right)} \right\} dl.
$$

Integrals (13.82), (13.83) can be computed by virtue of the FFT. In both cases integration with respect to l can be done explicitly in terms of the modified Bessel functions, or, equivalently, in terms of the noncentral chi-squared distributions. For $\hat{p}$ we have:

$$\hat{p}(\tau, Y, v, v') = \frac{1}{2\pi} \int_{-\infty}^{\infty} \exp\left\{ \frac{\hat{\kappa}\kappa\theta}{\varepsilon^2}\tau + ik\left(Y + \frac{\rho\kappa\theta}{\varepsilon}\tau\right)\right. \tag{13.84}$$

$$\left. - \frac{2\kappa\theta}{\varepsilon^2}\left[\zeta\tau + \ln\left(\frac{-\mu + \zeta + (\mu+\zeta)e^{-2\zeta\tau}}{2\zeta}\right)\right] - \frac{v(k^2 + 1/4)}{\varepsilon^2 \widetilde{M}}\right\} dk$$

$$\times \frac{2\widetilde{M}}{2\pi} \int_{-\infty}^{\infty} \exp\left\{ -2\widetilde{M}v'i\eta - \frac{2\kappa\theta}{\varepsilon^2}\ln(1 - 2i\eta) + \frac{2\widetilde{M}\widetilde{v}i\eta}{1 - 2i\eta}\right\} d\eta$$

$$= \frac{1}{2\pi} \int_{-\infty}^{\infty} \exp\left\{ \frac{\hat{\kappa}\kappa\theta}{\varepsilon^2}\tau + ik\left(Y + \frac{\rho\kappa\theta}{\varepsilon}\tau\right)\right.$$

$$\left. - \frac{2\kappa\theta}{\varepsilon^2}\left[\zeta\tau + \ln\left(\frac{-\mu + \zeta + (\mu+\zeta)e^{-2\zeta\tau}}{2\zeta}\right)\right]\right.$$

$$\left. - \frac{2v\left[(\mu + \zeta + (-\mu+\zeta)e^{-2\zeta\tau})\right]}{\varepsilon^2 (1 - e^{-2\zeta\tau})} - \widetilde{M}v'\right\} \widetilde{M}\left(\frac{v'}{\widetilde{v}}\right)^{\vartheta/2} I_\vartheta\left(2\widetilde{M}\sqrt{\widetilde{v}v'}\right) dk$$

$$\equiv \frac{1}{2\pi} \int_{-\infty}^{\infty} e^{ikY} \hat{\Pi}(\tau, k, v, v')\, dk,$$

where

$$\eta = -\frac{l}{\varepsilon^2\widetilde{M}}, \qquad \widetilde{v} = \frac{4\zeta^2 e^{-2\zeta\tau}v}{(-\mu + \zeta + (\mu+\zeta)e^{-2\zeta\tau})^2},$$

$$\widetilde{M} = \frac{2\left(-\mu + \zeta + (\mu+\zeta)e^{-2\zeta\tau}\right)}{\varepsilon^2 (1 - e^{-2\zeta\tau})}.$$

Thus, $\hat{p}(\tau, Y, v, v')$ is the inverse Fourier transform of $\hat{\Pi}(\tau, k, v, v')$ evaluated at the point $-Y$. Similarly, for q we have:

$$q(\tau, v, v')$$

$$= \frac{2\overline{M}}{(2\pi)} \int_{-\infty}^{\infty} \exp\left\{ -2\overline{M}v'i\xi - \frac{2\kappa\theta}{\varepsilon^2}\ln(1 - 2i\xi) + \frac{2\overline{M}\,\overline{v}i\xi}{1 - 2i\xi}\right\} d\xi$$

$$= \overline{M}e^{-\overline{M}(\overline{v}+v')}\left(\frac{v'}{\overline{v}}\right)^{\vartheta/2} I_\vartheta\left[2\overline{M}\sqrt{\overline{v}v'}\right],$$

where

$$\xi = -\frac{l}{\varepsilon^2\overline{M}}, \qquad \overline{v} = e^{-\kappa\tau}v, \qquad \overline{M} = \frac{2\kappa}{\varepsilon^2 (1 - e^{-\kappa\tau})}.$$

In both formulas I_ϑ is the modified Bessel function of order ϑ.

13.11.3   A transformed valuation formula

In this subsection we revisit the general valuation formula (13.77). Based on the discussion of the previous subsection, we represent this formula in the form

$$
V(0, S_0, v_0) = \int \cdots \int_{-\infty < Y_n < \infty,\, 0 < v_n < \infty} \Lambda(S_0, Y_1, ..., Y_n, ...Y_N)
$$
$$
\times \hat{p}\left(\tau_1, Y_1, v_0, v_1\right) ... \hat{p}(\tau_N, Y_N, v_{N-1}, v_N)
$$
$$
\times dY_1 ... dY_N dv_1 ... dv_N,
$$

where $Y_n = \ln\left(F_{t_n, T} / F_{t_{n-1}, T}\right)$, $\tau_n = t_n - t_{n-1}$, and

$$
\Lambda(S_0, Y_1, ..., Y_n, ...Y_N) = e^{-r^0 T - \frac{1}{2}\sum_{n \le N} Y_n} F\left(S_0, e^{r^{01}\tau_1 + Y_1} S_0, ...,\right.
$$
$$
\times \left. e^{\sum_{n' \le n}\left(r^{01}\tau_{n'} + Y_{n'}\right)} S_0, ..., e^{\sum_{n' \le N}\left(r^{01}\tau_{n'} + Y_{n'}\right)} S_0\right).
$$

By using expression (13.84) we represent $V(0, S_0, v_0)$ in the form

$$
V(0, S_0, v_0) = \frac{1}{(2\pi)^N} \int \cdots \int_{-\infty < k_n < \infty,\, 0 < v_n < \infty} \Xi(S_0, k_1, ..., k_n, ...k_N)
$$
$$
\times \hat{\Pi}\left(\tau_1, k_1, v_0, v_1\right) ... \hat{\Pi}\left(\tau_N, k_N, v_{N-1}, v_N\right)
$$
$$
\times dk_1 ... dk_N dv_1 ... dv_N,
$$

where $\Xi(S_0, k_1, ..., k_n, ...k_N)$ is the Fourier transform of $\Lambda(S_0, Y_1, ..., Y_n, ...Y_N)$:

$$
\Xi(S_0, k_1, ..., k_n, ...k_N) = \int \cdots \int_{-\infty < Y_n < \infty} \Lambda(S_0, Y_1, ..., Y_n, ...Y_N)
$$
$$
\times e^{ik_1 Y_1 + ... + ik_n Y_n + ... + ik_N Y_N} dY_1 ... dY_N.
$$

13.12   Forward starting options (cliquets)

It is natural to apply the formalism developed in the previous section to studying options on volatility. However, to warm up the reader, we first consider simpler (but closely related) options which are called non-dimensional and dimensional cliquets. The payoffs of these options have the form

$$
F^{(ND)}(S_0, S_1, S_2) = \left(\frac{S_2}{S_1} - \Lambda e^{r^{01}\tau_2}\right)_+, \tag{13.85}
$$

$$F^{(D)}(S_0, S_1, S_2) = \left(S_2 - \Lambda e^{r^{01}\tau_2} S_1\right)_+ = S_1 F^{(NDC)}(S_0, S_1, S_2),$$

respectively. Here $S_1 = S_{t_1}$, $S_2 = S_T$, where $0 < t_1 < T$. These options have a transparent financial meaning. They can be interpreted as calls whose strike is not known in advance and is determined at time t_1 as a multiple of the forward FXR at this time. (In the nondimensional case the relative call price is considered.) By using the expressions for the t.p.d.f. derived in the previous section we can obtain relatively simple expressions for the prices of dimensional and non-dimensional cliquets which are intuitive and easily implementable.

We start with the non-dimensional case which are easier to handle than its dimensional counterpart. We substitute expression (13.85) in formula (13.77) and, after some algebra which is left to the reader, obtain the following transparent representation for $V^{(ND)}$:

$$V^{(ND)}(0, S_0, v_0) = e^{-r^0\tau_1} \int_0^\infty \left[\int_0^\infty \pi(\tau_1, S_0, v_0, S_1, v_1) \, dS_1 \right]$$

$$\times \left[e^{-r^0\tau_2} \iint_{0 < S_2 < \infty, 0 < v_2 < \infty} \left(\frac{S_2}{S_1} - \Lambda e^{r^{01}\tau_2} \right)_+ \pi(\tau_2, S_1, v_1, S_2, v_2) \, dS_2 dv_2 \right]$$

$$= e^{-r\tau_1} \int_0^\infty q(\tau_1, v_0, v_1) \Phi\left(\tau_2, \frac{1}{\Lambda}, v_1\right) dv_1$$

$$= e^{-r^0\tau_1} \int_0^\infty \overline{M} e^{-\overline{M}(\bar{v}_0 + v_1)} \left(\frac{v_1}{\bar{v}_0}\right)^{\vartheta/2} I_\vartheta\left(2\overline{M}\sqrt{\bar{v}_0 v_1}\right) \Phi\left(\tau_2, \frac{1}{\Lambda}, v_1\right) dv_1,$$

where $\Phi(\tau_2, 1/\Lambda, v_1)$ is the nondimensional price of a call in the stochastic volatility framework given by formula (10.80). Here we use the fact that

$$\mathcal{I}_0 = \int_0^\infty \pi(\tau_1, S_0, v_0, S_1, v_1) \, dS_1 = q(\tau_1, v_0, v_1).$$

Thus,

$$V^{(ND)}(0, S_0, v_0) = e^{-r^0\tau_1} \mathbb{E}\left\{ \Phi\left(\tau_2, \frac{1}{\Lambda}, v_1\right) \right\},$$

where the expectation is taken with respect to the p.d.f. q.

For dimensional cliquets we have

$$V^{(D)}(0, S_0, v_0) = e^{-r^0\tau_1} S_0 \int_0^\infty \left[\int_0^\infty \frac{S_1}{S_0} \pi(\tau_1, S_0, v_0, S_1, v_1)\, dS_1 \right]$$

$$\times \left[e^{-r^0\tau_2} \iint_{0 < S_2 < \infty, 0 < v_2 < \infty} \left(\frac{S_2}{S_1} - \Lambda e^{r^{01}\tau_2} \right)_+ \pi(\tau_2, S_1, v_1, S_2, v_2)\, dS_2 dv_2 \right]$$

$$= e^{-r\tau_1} \int_0^\infty \mathcal{I}_1(\tau_1, v_0, v_1) \Phi\left(\tau_2, \frac{1}{\Lambda}, v_1 \right) dv_1,$$

where

$$\mathcal{I}_1 = \int_0^\infty \frac{S_1}{S_0} \pi(\tau_1, S_0, v_0, S_1, v_1)\, dS_1.$$

In order to evaluate this integral we use the formalism developed in the previous section. We write

$$\mathcal{I}_1 = e^{r^{01}\tau_1} \int_{-\infty}^\infty \hat{p}(\tau_1, Y, v_0, v_1) e^{Y/2} dY.$$

Even though this integral looks formidable, it can be evaluated in the closed form. The key observation is that

$$\frac{1}{2\pi} \int_{-\infty}^\infty e^{ikY} e^{Y/2} dY = \delta\left(k - \frac{i}{2} \right).$$

It is difficult to derive this formula (and its sister formula (8.28)) properly, and we are not going to do so here. By using this formula we get

$$\mathcal{I}_1 = e^{r^{01}\tau_1} \hat{\Pi}\left(\tau, \frac{i}{2}, v_0, v_1 \right)$$

$$= e^{r^{01}\tau_1} \widetilde{M} e^{-\widetilde{M}(\tilde{v}_0 + v_1)} \left(\frac{v_1}{\tilde{v}_0} \right)^{\vartheta/2} I_\vartheta\left(2\widetilde{M}\sqrt{\tilde{v}_0 v_1} \right)$$

where

$$\tilde{v}_0 = e^{-(\kappa - \varepsilon\rho)\tau} v_0, \qquad \widetilde{M} = \frac{2(\kappa - \varepsilon\rho)}{\varepsilon^2 \left(1 - e^{-(\kappa - \varepsilon\rho)\tau} \right)}.$$

Accordingly,

$$V^{(D)}(0, S_0, v_0) = e^{-r^1\tau_1} S_0$$

$$\times \int_0^\infty \widetilde{M} e^{-\widetilde{M}(\tilde{v}_0 + v_1)} \left(\frac{v_1}{\tilde{v}_0} \right)^{\vartheta/2} I_\vartheta\left(2\widetilde{M}\sqrt{\tilde{v}_0 v_1} \right) \Phi\left(\tau_2, \frac{1}{\Lambda}, v_1 \right) dv_1,$$

or, equivalently

$$V^{(D)}(0, S_0, v_0) = e^{-r^1 \tau_1} S_0 \mathbb{E} \left\{ \Phi \left(\tau_2, \frac{1}{\Lambda}, v_1 \right) \right\}, \tag{13.86}$$

where the expectation is taken with respect to the p.d.f. $\tilde{q}$. It is clear that the price of the dimensional cliquet can be obtained from the price of the non-dimensional cliquet via a simple change of parameters $\kappa \to \kappa - \varepsilon \rho$, $r^0 \to r^1$ and multiplication by S_0.

It is remarkable that the price of both non-dimensional and dimensional cliquets can be accurately reproduced by means of a simple convexity adjustment. For the non-dimensional cliquet we have

$$V^{(ND)}(0, S_0, v_0) \approx e^{-r^0 \tau_1} \left[\Phi \left(\tau_2, \frac{1}{\Lambda}, \bar{v}_0 + \frac{\vartheta + 1}{\overline{M}} \right) \right.$$
$$\left. \times + \frac{1}{2} \frac{1}{\overline{M}} \left(2\bar{v}_0 + \frac{\vartheta + 1}{\overline{M}} \right) \frac{\partial^2}{\partial v_1^2} \Phi \left(\tau_2, \frac{1}{\Lambda}, \bar{v}_0 + \frac{\vartheta + 1}{\overline{M}} \right) \right],$$

where

$$\bar{v}_0 + \frac{\vartheta + 1}{\overline{M}} = e^{-\kappa \tau_1} v_0 + \left(1 - e^{-\kappa \tau_1} \right) \theta = \mathbb{E} \left\{ v_1 \right\},$$

$$\frac{1}{\overline{M}} \left(2\bar{v}_0 + \frac{\vartheta + 1}{\overline{M}} \right) = \frac{\varepsilon^2}{\kappa} \left(1 - e^{-\kappa \tau_1} \right) \left[e^{-\kappa \tau_1} v_0 + \frac{1}{2} \left(1 - e^{-\kappa \tau_1} \right) \theta \right] = \mathbb{V} \left\{ v_1 \right\}.$$

The corresponding dimensional formula is

$$V^{(D)}(0, S_0, v_0) \approx e^{-r^1 \tau_1} S_0 \left[\Phi \left(\tau_2, \frac{1}{\Lambda}, \tilde{v}_0 + \frac{q + 1}{\widetilde{M}} \right) \right.$$
$$\left. \times + \frac{1}{2} \frac{1}{\widetilde{M}} \left(2\tilde{v}_0 + \frac{q + 1}{\widetilde{M}} \right) \frac{\partial^2}{\partial v_1^2} \Phi \left(\tau_2, \frac{1}{\Lambda}, \tilde{v}_0 + \frac{q + 1}{\widetilde{M}} \right) \right].$$

13.13 Options on volatility

13.13.1 The pricing problem

In this section we show how to price futures and options on volatility and variance in the stochastic volatility framework. We assume that the evolution of the pair $(F_{t,T}, v_t)$ is governed by SDEs (13.76). We are interested in

European-style derivatives on the realized variance and the realized volatility of the underlying. Putting aside effects of discretization, we define the corresponding quantities as

$$\Upsilon_{0,t} = \frac{1}{t} \int_0^t v(t')dt',$$

$$\Sigma_{0,t} = \sqrt{\frac{1}{t} \int_0^t v(t')dt'} = \sqrt{\Upsilon_{0,t}}.$$

Typical options, which we are interested in, are called variance and volatility swaps and swaptions. These options have the following non-dimensional payoffs:

$$V^{(VRS)}(T, F, v, \Upsilon) = \Upsilon T - K,$$
$$V^{(VLS)}(T, F, v, \Sigma) = \Sigma \sqrt{T} - K,$$
$$V^{(VRSN)}(T, F, v, \Upsilon) = (\Upsilon T - K)_+,$$
$$V^{(VLSN)}(T, F, v, \Sigma) = (\Sigma \sqrt{T} - K)_+.$$

In order to price these products we use the augmentation technique and introduce the cumulative variance

$$I_{0,t} = \int_0^t v(t')dt'.$$

We write the pricing equation for the forward price $\check{V}(t, F, v, I)$ of a typical option as follows:

$$\check{V}_t + \frac{1}{2}vF^2\check{V}_{FF} + \varepsilon\rho vF\check{V}_{Fv} + \frac{1}{2}\varepsilon^2 v\check{V}_{vv} + \kappa(\theta - v)\check{V}_v + v\check{V}_I = 0.$$

Thus, we have to deal with a degenerate three-factor pricing equation. This equation is supplied with the final conditions

$$\check{V}^{(VRS)}(T, F, v, I) = I - K,$$
$$\check{V}^{(VLS)}(T, F, v, I) = \sqrt{I} - K,$$
$$\check{V}^{(VRSN)}(T, F, v, I) = (I - K)_+,$$
$$\check{V}^{(VLSN)}(T, F, v, I) = \left(\sqrt{I} - K\right)_+,$$

and natural boundary conditions.

As always, it is advantageous to rewrite the pricing problems in terms of $\tau = T - t$:

$$\check{V}_\tau - \frac{1}{2}vF^2\check{V}_{FF} - \varepsilon\rho vF\check{V}_{Fv} - \frac{1}{2}\varepsilon^2 v\check{V}_{vv} - \kappa(\theta - v)\check{V}_v - v\check{V}_I = 0. \quad (13.87)$$

The general initial condition which we need to consider is

$$\check{V}(0, F, v, I) = F(I).$$

13.13.2 Pricing of variance swaps

Here we discuss the simplest problem and show how to price variance swaps. To start with, we notice that the pricing equation has a particular time-independent solution of the form

$$\check{V}^{(0)}(\tau, F, v, I) = 2\ln F + I.$$

Accordingly, we can represent the price of a VRS as

$$\check{V}^{(VRSWP)}(\tau, F, v, I) = \check{V}^{(0)}(\tau, F, v, I) - \check{V}^{(LC)}(\tau, F, v),$$

where $\check{V}^{(LC)}(\tau, F, v)$ is the price of a log contract with the payoff of the form

$$\check{V}^{(LC)}(0, F, v) = 2\ln F + K.$$

The price of the latter contract is governed by the two-factor nondegenerate pricing equation

$$\check{V}_\tau^{(LC)} - \frac{1}{2}vF^2\check{V}_{FF}^{(LC)} - \varepsilon\rho vF\check{V}_{Fv}^{(LC)} - \frac{1}{2}\varepsilon^2 v\check{V}_{vv}^{(LC)} - \kappa(\theta - v)\check{V}_v^{(LC)} = 0.$$

We use the affine ansatz and represent $\check{V}^{(LC)}$ as follows

$$\check{V}^{(LC)}(\tau, F, v) = 2\ln F + K + \alpha(\tau) - \beta(\tau)v,$$

where α, β satisfy the equations

$$\beta_\tau + \kappa\beta - 1 = 0, \quad \beta(0) = 0,$$
$$\alpha_\tau + \kappa\theta\beta = 0, \quad \alpha(0) = 0.$$

These equations can be solved explicitly. The corresponding solution is

$$\alpha(\tau) = \theta\frac{(1 - e^{-\kappa\tau} - \kappa\tau)}{\kappa}, \qquad \beta(\tau) = \frac{(1 - e^{-\kappa\tau})}{\kappa}.$$

Accordingly, we can represent the price of a variance swap as

$$\check{V}^{(VRS)}(\tau, F, v, I) = I - K - \theta\frac{(1 - e^{-\kappa\tau} - \kappa\tau)}{\kappa} + v\frac{(1 - e^{-\kappa\tau})}{\kappa}.$$

As might be expected, the price of the variance swap is independent of the forward FXR F. At inception this price has the form

$$\check{V}^{(VRS)}(T, F, v, 0) = -K - \theta\frac{(1 - e^{-\kappa T} - \kappa T)}{\kappa} + v\frac{(1 - e^{-\kappa T})}{\kappa}.$$

In order for this price to be zero the strike should be chosen as follows

$$K = -\theta\frac{(1 - e^{-\kappa T} - \kappa T)}{\kappa} + v\frac{(1 - e^{-\kappa T})}{\kappa} \equiv \gamma(T, v, \kappa, \theta).$$

By using the relation between VRSs and LCs we can establish the following useful identity

$$\frac{\gamma}{2} = \int_0^\varkappa \frac{\check{P}(T, \varkappa, X)}{X^2}dX + \int_\varkappa^\infty \frac{\check{C}(T, \varkappa, X)}{X^2}dX.$$

13.13.3 Pricing of general swaps and swaptions

In general, however, we have to deal with more complex solutions of the augmented pricing equation (13.87). Since the initial data are F-independent so are the solutions. Accordingly, the pricing equation can be simplified to the form

$$\check{V}_\tau - \frac{1}{2}\epsilon^2 v\check{V}_{vv} - \kappa(\theta - v)\check{V}_v - v\check{V}_I = 0. \qquad (13.88)$$

This is a two-factor (albeit degenerate) equation. We formally extend the range of I to the whole axis $-\infty < I < \infty$ from the positive semi-axis by assuming that the payoff vanishes for negative I. Instead of solving equation (13.88) in four different cases corresponding to four different choices of the payoff, we develop a procedure for finding the corresponding Green's function $g(\tau, v, J)$, satisfying the initial condition of the form

$$g(0, v, J) = \delta(J).$$

Once g is found, the general solution of the pricing problem can be represented in the form

$$\check{V}(\tau, v, I) = \int_0^\infty g(\tau, v, I - I') F(I') dI'.$$

It is easy to show that the Green's function can be can be chosen in the affine form:

$$g(\tau, v, J) = \frac{1}{2\pi} \int_{-\infty}^\infty \exp\left\{ ikJ + \frac{2}{\varepsilon^2} [A(\tau, k) - B(\tau, k)v] \right\} dk,$$

where we temporarily set aside issues related to the boundary conditions for J. (Because of the degenerate character of the pricing equation only one condition at $J = \infty$ is needed.) As before, we can find a system of ordinary differential equations which govern the dynamics of A and B. This system has the form

$$B_\tau + B^2 + \kappa B + \frac{1}{2} i\varepsilon^2 k = 0, \qquad B(0, k) = 0,$$

$$A_\tau + \kappa\theta B = 0, \qquad A(0, k) = 0.$$

It can be solved in the same way as the corresponding system of equations (10.71), (10.72). Namely, we can write A, B as

$$A = -\kappa\theta \ln(C), \qquad B = C_\tau/C,$$

where C satisfies the equation

$$C_{\tau\tau} + \kappa C_\tau + \frac{1}{2} i\varepsilon^2 k C = 0, \qquad C(k, 0) = 1, \qquad C_\tau(k, 0) = 0.$$

A simple algebra yields

$$C = \frac{e^{(-\kappa/2+\zeta)\tau}\left(\kappa/2 + \zeta + (-\kappa/2 + \zeta)e^{-2\zeta\tau}\right)}{2\zeta},$$

$$B = -\frac{i\varepsilon^2 k\left(1 - e^{-2\zeta\tau}\right)}{2\left(\kappa/2 + \zeta + (-\kappa/2 + \zeta)e^{-2\zeta\tau}\right)},$$

$$A = -\kappa\theta(-\kappa/2 + \zeta)\tau - \kappa\theta \ln\left(\frac{\kappa/2 + \zeta + (-\kappa/2 + \zeta)e^{-2\zeta\tau}}{2\zeta}\right),$$

where

$$\zeta = \frac{1}{2}\sqrt{\kappa^2 - 2i\varepsilon^2 k}.$$

By using the above formulas, we obtain the following expression for the Green's function, which is very similar to, but somewhat simpler than, the corresponding expression (10.78):

$$
\begin{aligned}
g\left(\tau, v, J\right) \;=\; & \frac{1}{2\pi} \int_{-\infty}^{\infty} \exp\left\{ ikJ - \frac{2\kappa\theta}{\varepsilon^2}\left(-\frac{\kappa}{2} + \zeta\right)\tau \right. \\
& - \frac{2\kappa\theta}{\varepsilon^2}\ln\left(\frac{\kappa/2 + \zeta + \left(-\kappa/2 + \zeta\right)e^{-2\zeta\tau}}{2\zeta}\right) \\
& \left. + \frac{ik\left(1 - e^{-2\zeta\tau}\right)v}{\left(\kappa/2 + \zeta + \left(-\kappa/2 + \zeta\right)e^{-2\zeta\tau}\right)} \right\}.
\end{aligned}
$$

We emphasize that the Green's function can be evaluated numerically via the FFT. Once the Green's function is found, all the swaps and swaptions, which we are interested in, can be evaluated via a simple integration.

13.14 References and further reading

There are numerous papers devoted to path-dependent options. The following papers are particularly relevant for our presentation: Ahn *et al. (1998)*, Andersen *et al. (1998)*, Andreasen (1998), Chesney *et al. (1997)*, Carr and Madan (1998), Conze and Viswanathan (1991), Delbaen and Yor (1999), Demeterfi *et al. (1999)*, Garbade (1999), Geman and Eydeland (1995), Geman and Yor (1993), Goldman *et al. (1979)*, Graversen and Peskir (1997), Henderson and Hobson (1999, 2000), Hobson (1998), Hyer, Lipton and Pugachevsky (1997), Levy (1992), Linetsky (1998, 1999), Lipton (1997 a, 1998 c, 1999, 2000 b), Lipton and McGhee (1999, 2000), Lipton and Pugachevsky (1998 b,c), Matytsin (1999), Nagayama (1998), Neuberger (1996), Rogers and Shiu (1995), Schroder (1999 b,c), Shepp and Shiryaev (1993), Shreve and Večeř (2000), Turnbull and Wakeman (1991), Večeř and Shreve (2000), Vorst (1996), Whaley (1993). Some useful approaches to pricing path-dependent options can be found in the books by Wilmott *et al.* (1993), Wilmott *et al.* (1995). A helpful table of Laplace transforms in given by Abramowitz and Stegun (1972).

Chapter 14

Deviations from the Black-Scholes paradigm II: market frictions

14.1 Introduction

In this chapter we briefly discuss effects of imperfect hedging, and market frictions, such as transaction costs, liquidity constraints, default risk, etc., on pricing and hedging of derivatives. To start with, we develop a formalism for dealing with imperfectly hedged options. Not surprisingly, it is not possible to find a unique price for such an option. Instead, we can derive a degenerate Kolmogoroff equation (very similar in nature to equations used in the previous chapter in order to study path-dependent options) which provides a probabilistic distribution of the profit and loss (P&L) associated with a given hedging strategy. Once this distribution is found, we can price options in accordance with our utility function. We show how to derive the P&L distribution for the popular stop-loss start-gain hedging strategy. We discuss the uncertain volatility model which provided worst-case scenario bounds for derivative prices. Next, we turn our attention to transaction costs in the form of bid-ask spreads and show how to modify the basic theory to account for these costs. If taken seriously, these costs make continuous hedging prohibitively expensive, so that we are forced to consider imperfect hedging in this context. We also discuss liquidity issues with a particular emphasis on the impact of hedging of large positions in options on the FXR itself. Finally, we analyze the impact of default of one of the counterparties on the price of a derivative contract between them. For options which give rights to the buyer and impose obligations on the seller only the possibility of seller's default has to be taken into account. In principle, for forward and futures contracts the possibility of default of both the seller and buyer has to be considered. However, for brevity we study only the implications of the seller's default and leave it to the reader to analyze the case of a default prone buyer.

This chapter is organized as follows. In Section 2 we develop a formalism for studying imperfectly hedged options. In Section 3 we discuss the uncertain volatility model. In Section 4 we study the impact of transaction costs on option prices. We deal with effects of liquidity in Section 5. In Section 6 we discuss the impact of seller's default on prices of options and forward contracts. In Section 7 we give the relevant references.

14.2 Imperfect hedging

14.2.1 P&L distributions

In this section we develop techniques for studying imperfectly hedged European options. We analyze the situation from the viewpoint of a seller of a European call who chooses a certain imperfect hedging strategy q. For simplicity we assume that both domestic and foreign interest rates are zero. We also assume that the hedging strategy is Markovian and depends only on t, S, although it is not difficult to consider a more general case. There are many reasons for not hedging according to the Black-Scholes strategy. The seller can deviate from this strategy either by choice (for example, because he follows efficient mean-variance or utility maximizing hedging strategies), or by chance (because continuous hedging is impossible, or the actual volatility of S is not known, or for many other reasons). Deviations from the Black-Scholes strategy cause P&L ϑ which is equal to the difference between the final value of the trading account Π_T and the final value of a European call $(S_T - K)_+$,

$$\vartheta = \Pi_T - (S_T - K)_+,$$

to be a random variable. Accordingly, it is necessary to study the p.d.f. for this random variable.

The coupled system of SDEs describing the evolution of S, Π has the familiar form

$$\frac{dS}{S} = \mu dt + \sigma dW, \qquad (14.1)$$

$$d\Pi = q(t, S)dS,$$

which is similar to system (13.11), except for the fact that the drift μ of S is not necessarily equal to r^{01} (which, by our current assumption, is zero). The t.p.d.f. $\Theta(t, S_t, \Pi_t, T, S_T, \Pi_T)$ for system (14.1) is governed by the standard forward Fokker-Planck equation. In terms of Θ one can represent the p.d.f. $\theta(t, S_t, \Pi_t, ; \vartheta)$ for the random variable ϑ as

$$
\begin{aligned}
\theta(t, S_t, \Pi_t; \vartheta) &= \int_0^\infty \int_{-\infty}^\infty \Theta(t, S_t, \Pi_t, T, S_T, \Pi_T) \\
&\quad \times \delta \left[\Pi_T - (S_T - K)_+ - \vartheta \right] dS_T d\Pi_T, \\
&= V^{(q)}(t, S_t, \Pi_t - \vartheta),
\end{aligned}
$$

where $V^{(q)}(t, S, \Pi)$ solves the backward Kolmogoroff problem

$$V_t^{(q)} + \frac{1}{2}\sigma^2 S^2 \left(V_{SS}^{(q)} + 2q V_{S\Pi}^{(q)} + q^2 V_{\Pi\Pi}^{(q)} \right) + \mu S V_S^{(q)} + \mu q S V_\Pi^{(q)} = 0, \qquad (14.2)$$

$$V^{(q)}(T, S, \Pi) = \delta \left[\Pi - (S - K)_+ \right],$$

and δ is the Dirac delta function. Equation (14.2) is practically identical to the unoptimized pricing problem (13.55) for the PO, as can be expected.

It is convenient to represent the trading strategy in the form

$$q(t, S) = Q_S(t, S),$$

where $Q(t, S)$ is the corresponding potential function, introduce the adjusted trading account

$$\tilde{\Pi} = \Pi - Q(t, S),$$

and represent P&L as

$$\vartheta = \tilde{\Pi}_T + Q(T, S_T) - (S_T - K)_+.$$

The evolution of the pair $S, \tilde{\Pi}$ is governed by the system of SDEs of the form

$$dS = \mu S dt + \sigma S dW,$$

$$d\tilde{\Pi} = \varkappa(t, S)dt,$$

where

$$\varkappa(t, S) = - \left[Q_t(t, S) + \frac{1}{2}\sigma^2 S^2 Q_{SS}(t, S) \right].$$

Note that for the standard Black-Scholes trading strategy $\varkappa(S, t) = 0$ and $Q(S_T, T) = (S_T - K)_+$, so that both $\tilde{\Pi}_T$ and ϑ are nonrandom and the corresponding P&L is identically equal to zero, or, in other words, the p.d.f. for ϑ is $\delta(\vartheta)$.

It is easy to show that

$$\theta(t, S_t, \tilde{\Pi}_t; \vartheta) = \tilde{V}^{(q)}(t, S_t, \tilde{\Pi}_t - \vartheta),$$

where $\tilde{V}^{(q)}(t, S, \tilde{\Pi})$ solves the backward Kolmogoroff problem

$$\tilde{V}_t^{(q)} + \frac{1}{2}\sigma^2 S^2 \tilde{V}_{SS}^{(q)} + \mu S \tilde{V}_S^{(q)} + \varkappa(t, S)\tilde{V}_{\tilde{\Pi}}^{(q)} = 0, \qquad (14.3)$$

$$\tilde{V}^{(q)}(T, S, \tilde{\Pi}) = \delta[\tilde{\Pi} + Q(T, S) - (S - K)_+],$$

which strongly resembles the valuation problem for Asian calls. Unfortunately, for this problem a simple self-similar reduction is not possible, so that it has to be treated as a degenerate two-factor parabolic problem. Fortunately, several established numerical schemes can be used in order to solve it. A viable alternative is to exploit the technique developed by Landau (in order to solve the Vlasov equation) and apply the Fourier transform in $\tilde{\Pi}$,

$$\tilde{V}^{(q)}(t, S, \tilde{\Pi}) \rightarrow \tilde{W}^{(q)}(t, S, k) = \int_{-\infty}^{\infty} e^{ik\tilde{\Pi}} \tilde{V}^{(q)}(t, S, \tilde{\Pi}) d\tilde{\Pi},$$

in order to replace the original two-factor problem by a family of one-factor problems

$$\tilde{W}_t^{(q)} + \frac{1}{2}\sigma^2 S^2 \tilde{W}_{SS}^{(q)} + \mu S \tilde{W}_S^{(q)} - ik\varkappa(t, S)\tilde{W}^{(q)} = 0,$$

$$\tilde{W}^{(q)}(T, S, k) = e^{-ik[Q(T,S)-(S-K)_+]},$$

parametrized by k. Once $\tilde{W}^{(q)}(t, S, k)$ is found, one can construct $\tilde{V}^{(q)}(t, S, \tilde{\Pi})$ by virtue of the inverse Fourier transform.

14.2.2 Stop-loss start-gain hedging and local times

In order to illustrate the ideas outlined above, we discuss the stop-loss start-gain (SLSG) strategy. For this strategy

$$q(t, S) = \theta(S - K), \quad Q(S, t) = (S - K)_+,$$

where θ is the Heaviside function. The hedger who follows this strategy buys one unit of the FC every time the FXR hits the strike level K from below, and sells the same amount of the FC whenever this level is hit from above. Intuitively this looks like a perfect hedge; however, as was explained in Section 8.3, the SLSG strategy results in a random P&L with a nontrivial p.d.f. (which nonetheless does have a δ-function component). Broadly speaking, the hedger who follows the SLSG strategy assumes (whether he appreciates it or not) that for hedging purposes the volatility of the FXR is zero. In the case in question problem (14.3) has the form

$$\tilde{V}_t^{(SLSG)} + \frac{1}{2}\sigma^2 S^2 \tilde{V}_{SS}^{(SLSG)} + \mu S \tilde{V}_S^{(SLSG)} - \frac{1}{2}\sigma^2 K^2 \delta(S - K)\tilde{V}_{\tilde{\Pi}}^{(SLSG)} = 0,$$

$$\tilde{V}^{(SLSG)}(T, S, \tilde{\Pi}) = \delta(\tilde{\Pi}).$$

First, we use the dimensional reduction and rewrite the pricing problem as follows

$$\Phi_\chi^{(SLSG)} - \frac{1}{2}\xi^2 \Phi_{\xi\xi}^{(SLSG)} - \hat{\mu}\xi\Phi_\xi^{(SLSG)} + \frac{1}{2}\delta(\xi - 1)\Phi_\varpi^{(SLSG)} = 0,$$

$$\Phi^{(SLSG)}(0, \xi, \varpi) = \delta(\varpi),$$

where

$$\Phi^{(SLSG)} = K\tilde{V}^{(SLSG)}, \ \xi = S/K, \ \varpi = \tilde{\Pi}/K, \ \chi = \sigma^2(T - t), \ \hat{\mu} = \mu/\sigma^2.$$

Next, we combine the Laplace transform in time and the Fourier transform in space and represent the pricing problem in the form

$$\lambda\Theta^{(SLSG)} - \frac{1}{2}\xi^2\Theta_{\xi\xi}^{(SLSG)} - \hat{\mu}\xi\Theta_\xi^{(SLSG)} - \frac{1}{2}ik\delta(\xi - 1)\Theta^{(SLSG)} = 1,$$

where $-\infty < \xi < \infty$, and

$$\Theta^{(SLSG)}(\lambda, \xi, \kappa) = \int_0^{\infty} \int_{-\infty}^{\infty} \Phi^{(SLSG)}(\chi, \xi, \varpi) e^{-\lambda\chi + ik\varpi} d\chi d\varpi.$$

This equation is similar in nature to the Laplace-transformed pricing equation for the passport option and can be solved by virtue of the technique described in Section 13.8. Omitting the corresponding algebra for the sake of brevity, we simply present the final solution of the original problem

$$\tilde{V}^{(SLSG)}(T-t, S, \tilde{\Pi}) = \left[1 - \frac{1}{\sqrt{2\pi}} 1 \, |\ln \xi| \, \xi^{(1-\hat{\mu})/2} \mathcal{I}_1\right] \frac{\delta(\varpi)}{K}$$

$$+\sqrt{\frac{2}{\pi}} \xi^{(1-\hat{\mu})/2} \mathcal{I}_2 \frac{\theta(\varpi)}{K},$$

where

$$\mathcal{I}_1 = \int_0^{\chi} \exp\left[-\frac{(\ln \xi)^2}{2\eta} - \frac{(1-\hat{\mu})^2 \eta}{8}\right] \eta^{-3/2} d\eta,$$

$$\mathcal{I}_2 = \int_0^{\chi} \exp\left[-\frac{(|\ln \xi| + 2\varpi)^2}{2\eta} - \frac{(1-\hat{\mu})^2 \eta}{8}\right]$$

$$\times \left[\frac{(|\ln \xi| + 2\varpi)^2}{\eta} - 1\right] \eta^{-3/2} d\eta.$$

It is clear that this p.d.f. contains both localized and delocalized components.

14.2.3 Parameter misspecification

In the previous subsection we analyzed the impact of the ultimate parameter misspecification (i.e., of assuming that $\sigma = 0$) on the P&L distribution for a European call. In this subsection we consider this problem for a more general standpoint. For simplicity we further assume that $\mu = 0$.

General considerations

We are interested in the case of parameter (specifically, volatility) misspecification when we delta-hedge an option with the payoff

$$\text{payoff} = v(S),$$

by assuming that its price is

$$Q(t, S) = V^{(\Sigma)}(t, S),$$

where $V^{(\Sigma)}(t, S)$ solves the problem

$$V_t^{(\Sigma)} + \frac{1}{2}\Sigma^2 S^2 V_{SS}^{(\Sigma)} = 0,$$

$$V(T, S) = v(S).$$

By using the trivial identity

$$-\left(V_t^{(\Sigma)} + \frac{1}{2}\sigma^2 S^2 V_{SS}^{(\Sigma)}\right) = \frac{1}{2}\left(\Sigma^2 - \sigma^2\right) S^2 V_{SS}^{(\Sigma)},$$

we can rewrite the equation for $V\left(t, S, \tilde{\Pi}\right)$ in the form

$$P_t + \frac{1}{2}\sigma^2 S^2 P_{SS} + \frac{1}{2}\left(\Sigma^2 - \sigma^2\right) S^2 V_{SS}^{(\Sigma)} P_{\tilde{\Pi}} = 0.$$

It is relatively difficult (but not impossible) to solve the backward Kolmogoroff problem for P. Instead of doing so, we solve the system of equations for the first two central moments of the corresponding p.d.f. We introduce the first two noncentral moments

$$\mathrm{M}^{(i)}(t, S) = \int_{-\infty}^{\infty} P\left(t, S, \tilde{\Pi}\right) \tilde{\Pi}^i d\tilde{\Pi}, \quad i = 1, 2,$$

and integrate the governing equation and the final condition in order to obtain the following system of equations for $\mathrm{M}^{(1)}, \mathrm{M}^{(2)}$:

$$\mathcal{L}^\sigma \mathrm{M}^{(1)}(t, S) = \frac{1}{2}\left(\Sigma^2 - \sigma^2\right) S^2 V_{SS}^{(\Sigma)}(t, S), \quad \mathrm{M}^{(1)}(T, S) = 0,$$

$$\mathcal{L}^\sigma \mathrm{M}^{(2)}(t, S) = \left(\Sigma^2 - \sigma^2\right) S^2 V_{SS}^{(\Sigma)}(t, S) \mathrm{M}^{(1)}(t, S), \quad \mathrm{M}^{(2)}(T, S) = 0.$$

Here

$$\mathcal{L}^\sigma = \partial_t + \frac{1}{2}\sigma^2 S^2 \partial_S^2.$$

We introduce the first two central moments

$$\mu^{(1)} = \mathbb{M}^{(1)}, \qquad \mu^{(2)} = \mathbb{M}^{(2)} - \left(\mathbb{M}^{(1)}\right)^2,$$

and rewrite the governing equations as follows

$$\mathcal{L}^\sigma \mu^{(1)}(t, S) = \frac{1}{2}\left(\Sigma^2 - \sigma^2\right) S^2 V_{SS}^{(\Sigma)}(t, S), \qquad \mu^{(1)}(T, S) = 0,$$

$$\mathcal{L}^\sigma \mu^{(2)}(t, S) = -\sigma^2 \left(S\mu_S^{(1)}(t, S)\right)^2, \qquad \mu^{(2)}(T, S) = 0.$$

The equation for $\mu^{(1)}$ can be solved explicitly:

$$\mu^{(1)}(t, S) = V^{(\sigma)}(t, S) - V^{(\Sigma)}(t, S),$$

while the equation for $\mu^{(2)}$ can be solved via Duhamel's principle:

$$\mu^{(2)}(t, S) = \sigma^2 \int_t^T \int_0^\infty p^{(\sigma)}(t, S, t', S') \left(S'V^{(\sigma)}(t', S') - S'V^{(\Sigma)}(t', S')\right) dt'dS',$$

where

$$
\begin{aligned}
p^{(\sigma)}(t, S, t', S') &= \frac{e^{-\left(\ln(S/S') - \sigma^2(t'-t)/2\right)^2/2\sigma^2(t'-t)}}{\sqrt{2\pi}\sigma\sqrt{(t'-t)}S'} \\
&= \frac{\mathrm{n}\left(\frac{\ln(S/S') - \sigma^2(t'-t)/2}{\sigma\sqrt{t'-t}}\right)}{\sigma\sqrt{(t'-t)}S'},
\end{aligned}
$$

is the standard lognormal t.p.d.f.

The bet option

In this subsection we specify the general equations derived in the previous section to the special case of a call bet. The corresponding payoff is

$$v(S) = \theta(S - K).$$

The prices $V^{(\sigma)}$ and $V^{(\Sigma)}$ can be written as

$$V^{(\sigma)}(t, S) = \mathfrak{N}\left(\frac{\ln(S'/K) - \sigma^2(T - t')/2}{\sigma\sqrt{T - t'}}\right),$$

$$V^{(\Sigma)}(t, S) = \mathfrak{N}\left(\frac{\ln\left(S'/K\right) - \Sigma^2\left(T - t'\right)/2}{\Sigma\sqrt{T - t'}}\right).$$

A simple calculation yields

$$\mu^{(2)}(t, S)$$

$$= \sigma^2 \int_t^T \int_0^\infty \frac{\mathfrak{n}\left(\frac{\ln\left(S/S'\right) - \sigma^2\left(t' - t\right)/2}{\sigma\sqrt{t' - t}}\right)}{\sigma\sqrt{(t' - t)}} \left(\frac{\mathfrak{n}\left(\frac{\ln\left(S'/K\right) - \sigma^2\left(T - t'\right)/2}{\sigma\sqrt{T - t'}}\right)}{\sigma\sqrt{T - t'}}\right.$$

$$\left. - \frac{\left(\mathfrak{n}\left(\frac{\ln\left(S'/K\right) - \Sigma^2\left(T - t'\right)/2}{\Sigma\sqrt{T - t'}}\right)\right)^2}{\Sigma\sqrt{T - t'}}\right) dt' \frac{dS'}{S'}$$

$$= \int_t^T \left(\mathcal{I}_1\left(t'\right) + \mathcal{I}_2\left(t'\right) + \mathcal{I}_3\left(t'\right)\right) dt',$$

where

$$\mathcal{I}_1\left(t'\right) = \int_{-\infty}^{\infty} \frac{\exp\left(-\frac{\left(X' + \frac{1}{2}\sigma^2\left(t' - t\right)\right)^2}{2\sigma^2\left(t' - t\right)} - \frac{\left(X' - \kappa - \frac{1}{2}\sigma^2\left(T - t'\right)\right)^2}{\sigma^2\left(T - t'\right)}\right)}{2\pi\sqrt{2\pi}\sigma\sqrt{(t' - t)(T - t')}} dX',$$

$$\mathcal{I}_2\left(t'\right) = -2 \int_{-\infty}^{\infty}$$

$$\times \frac{\exp\left(-\frac{\left(X' + \frac{1}{2}\sigma^2\left(t' - t\right)\right)^2}{2\sigma^2\left(t' - t\right)} - \frac{\left(X' - \kappa - \frac{1}{2}\sigma^2\left(T - t'\right)\right)^2}{2\sigma^2\left(T - t'\right)} - \frac{\left(X' - \kappa - \frac{1}{2}\Sigma^2\left(T - t'\right)\right)^2}{2\Sigma^2\left(T - t'\right)}\right)}{2\pi\sqrt{2\pi}\Sigma\sqrt{(t' - t)(T - t')}} dX',$$

$$\mathcal{I}_3\left(t'\right) = \sigma \int_{-\infty}^{\infty} \frac{\exp\left(-\frac{\left(X' + \frac{1}{2}\sigma^2\left(t' - t\right)\right)^2}{2\sigma^2\left(t' - t\right)} - \frac{\left(X' - \kappa - \frac{1}{2}\Sigma^2\left(T - t'\right)\right)^2}{\Sigma^2\left(T - t'\right)}\right)}{2\pi\sqrt{2\pi}\Sigma^2\sqrt{(t' - t)(T - t')}} dX',$$

and $X' = \ln\left(S'/S\right)$, $\kappa = \ln\left(K/S\right)$.

We can find the corresponding integrals by completing the squares. We have

$$\mathcal{I}_1 = \int_{-\infty}^{\infty} \frac{\exp\left(-\left(a_1 X'^2 + 2b_1 X' + c_1\right)\right)}{2\pi\sqrt{2\pi}\sigma\sqrt{(t' - t)(T - t')}} dX'$$

$$= \frac{\exp\left(b_1^2/a_1 - c_1\right)}{2\pi\sqrt{2a_1}\sigma\sqrt{(t' - t)(T - t')}},$$

where

$$a_1 = \frac{1}{2\sigma^2 (t' - t)} + \frac{1}{\sigma^2 (T - t')},$$

$$b_1 = -\frac{1}{4} - \frac{\kappa}{\sigma^2 (T - t')},$$

$$c_1 = \frac{\sigma^2 (t' - t)}{8} + \frac{\sigma^2 (T - t')}{4} + \kappa + \frac{\kappa^2}{\sigma^2 (T - t')}.$$

Similarly,

$$\mathcal{I}_2 = -\frac{\exp\left(b_2^2/a_2 - c_2\right)}{\pi\sqrt{2a_2}\Sigma\sqrt{(t' - t)(T - t')}},$$

$$a_2 = \frac{1}{2\sigma^2 (t' - t)} + \frac{1}{2\sigma^2 (T - t')} + \frac{1}{\Sigma^2 (T - t')},$$

$$b_2 = -\frac{1}{4} - \frac{\kappa}{2\sigma^2 (T - t')} - \frac{\kappa}{2\Sigma^2 (T - t')},$$

$$c_2 = \frac{\sigma^2 (t' - t)}{8} + \frac{\sigma^2 (T - t')}{8} + \frac{\Sigma^2 (T - t')}{8}$$
$$+ \kappa + \frac{\kappa^2}{2\sigma^2 (T - t')} + \frac{\kappa^2}{2\Sigma^2 (T - t')},$$

and

$$\mathcal{I}_3 = \frac{\sigma \exp\left(b_3^2/a_3 - c_3\right)}{2\pi\sqrt{2a_3}\Sigma^2\sqrt{(t' - t)(T - t')}},$$

$$a_3 = \frac{1}{2\sigma^2 (t' - t)} + \frac{1}{\Sigma^2 (T - t')},$$

$$b_3 = -\frac{1}{4} - \frac{\kappa}{\Sigma^2 (T - t')},$$

$$c_3 = \frac{\sigma^2 (t' - t)}{8} + \frac{\Sigma^2 (T - t')}{4} + \kappa + \frac{\kappa^2}{\Sigma^2 (T - t')}.$$

The remaining integration with respect to t' is performed numerically. The results are shown in Figure 14.1.

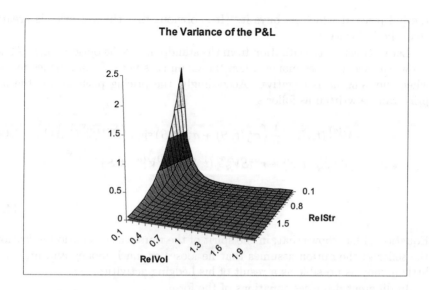

Figure 14.1: The variance of the P&L caused by the parameter misspecification for the bet option. Here $RelVol = \Sigma/\sigma$, $RelStr = \ln(K/S)$.

14.3 The uncertain volatility model

The uncertain volatility model nicely complements the local and stochastic volatility models which are described in Chapter 10. In a nutshell, the idea is as follows. Suppose that we do not know the actual volatility path, but we do know that σ is always sandwiched between some deterministic bounds:

$$\sigma_{\min}(t, S) \le \sigma \le \sigma_{\max}(t, S),$$

where $\sigma_{\min}(t, S)$, $\sigma_{\max}(t, S)$, are given. Below we use the notation

$$\sigma_0^2(t, S) = \frac{1}{2}\left(\sigma_{\max}^2(t, S) + \sigma_{\min}^2(t, S)\right),$$

$$\sigma_1^2(t, S) = \frac{1}{2}\left(\sigma_{\max}^2(t, S) - \sigma_{\min}^2(t, S)\right).$$

In this case, we obviously cannot find a unique price of an option. Instead, we should look for its worst-case price. In fact, every option has two worst-case prices, the ask price at which a risk-averse market maker sells the option, and the bid price at which he buys it. (It is obvious that the ask price is greater than the bid price.)

Let us consider the situation from the standpoint of the option seller. As we know, the seller looses money when the Gamma is positive and makes money when the Gamma is negative. Accordingly, the pricing problem for the ask price can be written as follows

$$V_t^{(a)}(t, S) + \frac{1}{2} \left\{ \sigma_0^2(t, S) + \sigma_1^2(t, S) \operatorname{sign}\left(S^2 V_{SS}^{(a)}(t, S)\right) \right\} \quad (14.4)$$
$$\times \quad S^2 V_{SS}^{(a)}(t, S) + r^{01} S V_S^{(a)}(t, S) - r^0 V^{(a)}(t, S) = 0,$$

$$V^{(a)}(T, S) = v(S). \quad (14.5)$$

Equation (14.4) shows that, in the spirit of the worst-case scenario replication, the seller of the option assumes that he looses as much money and makes as little money as possible as a result of his hedging activities.

In different disguises equations of the form

$$V_t + \frac{1}{2} F(t, S, V_{SS}) S^2 V_{SS} + r^{01} S V_S - r^0 V = 0, \quad (14.6)$$

appear in our analysis of transaction costs and liquidity effects presented below. Such equations were originally studied in the hydrodynamic context by Barenblatt and his co-workers.

Similarly, the pricing problem for the bid price has the form

$$V_t^{(b)}(t, S) + \frac{1}{2} \left\{ \sigma_0^2(t, S) - \sigma_1^2(t, S) \operatorname{sign}\left(S^2 V_{SS}^{(b)}(t, S)\right) \right\} \quad (14.7)$$
$$\times \quad S^2 V_{SS}^{(b)}(t, S) + r^{01} S V_S^{(b)}(t, S) - r^0 V^{(b)}(t, S) = 0,$$

$$V^{(b)}(T, S) = v(S). \quad (14.8)$$

It is very easy to find the bid and ask prices for options with convex payoffs, for instance, for standard calls and puts, since their Gammas do not change sign. For a European call we have

$$C_t^{(a)}(t, S) + \frac{1}{2} \sigma_{\max}^2(t, S) S^2 C_{SS}^{(a)}(t, S) + r^{01} S C_S^{(a)}(t, S) - r^0 C^{(a)}(t, S) = 0,$$

$$C_t^{(b)}(t,S) + \frac{1}{2}\sigma_{\min}^2(t,S)S^2 C_{SS}^{(b)}(t,S) + r^{01}SC_S^{(b)}(t,S) - r^0 C^{(b)}(t,S) = 0,$$

$$C^{(a)}(T,S) = C^{(b)}(T,S) = (S-K)_+,$$

and similarly for a put.

The situation becomes very different when the payoff of the option in question is not convex, for instance, for call and put bets. Since their Gammas are not sign-definite, we have to solve nonlinear pricing problems (14.4), (14.5) and (14.7), (14.8) in order to determine the corresponding bid and ask prices. This task is demanding, because it involves the determination of the free boundary separating the domains of positive and negative Gammas, and can only be done numerically. (This valuation problem has more than a passing similarity with the valuation problem for American options which is considered in Chapter 11.) Standard finite-difference methods can be used for this purpose. We omit details for the sake of brevity.

When the gap between $\sigma_{\min}^2(t,S)$ and $\sigma_{\max}^2(t,S)$ is small, i.e.,

$$\frac{\sigma_1^2(t,S)}{\sigma_0^2(t,S)} = \varepsilon \ll 1,$$

we can find $V^{(a)}, V^{(b)}$ via the method of linearization. Consider, for example $V^{(aks)}$ and expand it in a series in powers of ε:

$$V^{(a)} = V^{(a,0)} + \varepsilon V^{(a,1)} + \dots.$$

It is obvious that $V^{(a,0)}$ solves the standard homogeneous pricing problem

$$V_t^{(a,0)}(t,S) + \frac{1}{2}\sigma_0^2(t,S)S^2 V_{SS}^{(a,0)}(t,S) + r^{01}SV_S^{(a,0)}(t,S) - r^0 V^{(a,0)}(t,S) = 0,$$

$$V^{(a,0)}(T,S) = v(S),$$

while $V^{(a,1)}$ solves the inhomogeneous pricing problem of the form

$$V_t^{(a,1)}(t,S) + \frac{1}{2}\sigma_0^2(t,S)S^2 V_{SS}^{(a,1)}(t,S) + r^{01}SV_S^{(a,1)}(t,S) - r^0 V^{(a,1)}(t,S)$$

$$= -\frac{1}{2}\sigma_1^2(t,S)\,\text{sign}\left(S^2 V_{SS}^{(a,0)}(t,S)\right)S^2 V_{SS}^{(a,0)}(t,S),$$

$$V^{(a,1)}(T, S) = 0.$$

Thus, the valuation problem for $V^{(a)}$ becomes linear (as the name of the method suggests). We leave it to the reader to derive the corresponding pricing problem for $V^{(b)}$.

We finish this section with a word of warning. Under normal circumstances, the estimates provided by the uncertain volatility model in its crude form described above are too wide to be used in practice.

14.4   Transaction costs

Transaction costs have profound effect on derivative prices for several reasons, the most important of which is that they make continuous hedging impossible and, consequently, destroy the very essence of the Black-Scholes approach. In this section we discuss some simple techniques for accounting for transaction costs.

We assume that the midmarket FXR S_t follows the usual geometric Brownian motion

$$\frac{dS}{S} = \mu dt + \sigma dW_t,$$

while the corresponding bid and ask prices are given by

$$S_t^{(a)} = \left(1 + \frac{\kappa}{2}\right) S_t, \qquad S_t^{(b)} = \left(1 - \frac{\kappa}{2}\right) S_t,$$

where κ is a given (small) constant.

We consider an option from the standpoint of the option seller and evaluate its ask price. To avoid the accumulation of infinite transaction costs we (have to) assume that the positive time interval between rehedgings, which is denoted by δt, is fixed. Our objective is to price the option in question by constructing an appropriate nonanticipating, self-financing, replicating strategy. We form the familiar portfolio Π by assuming that we sell the option and buy Δ units of the foreign bond maturing at time T. The value of this portfolio at time t is

$$\Pi_t = \Pi(t, S_t) = -V^{(a)}(t, S_t) + \Delta^{(a)}(t, S_t) S_t.$$

The change in its value between two adjacent rehedging moments t and $t + \delta t$

can be approximated as

$$\Pi_{t+\delta t} - \Pi_t$$

$$\approx - \left(V_t^{(a)} \delta t + V_S^{(a)} \left(S_{t+\delta t} - S_t \right) + \frac{1}{2} \sigma^2 S^2 V_{SS}^{(a)} \delta t \right)$$

$$+ \Delta^{(a)} \left(\left(S_{t+\delta t} - S_t \right) + r^1 S_t \delta t \right) - \frac{1}{2} \kappa \left| \Delta_{t+\delta t}^{(a)} - \Delta_t^{(a)} \right| S_t + ...,$$

where terms of order $\delta t^{3/2}$ and higher are omitted. The third term on the right represents the transaction cost of rehedging, i.e., of changing the number of foreign bonds from $\Delta_t^{(a)}$ to $\Delta_{t+\delta t}^{(a)}$. We use the discrete delta-hedging strategy which makes our portfolio approximately risk-free, and choose $\Delta_t^{(a)}$, $\Delta_{t+\delta t}^{(a)}$, in the form

$$\Delta_t^{(a)} = V_S^{(a)} (t, S_t), \qquad \Delta_{t+\delta t}^{(a)} = V_S^{(a)} (t + \delta t, S_{t+\delta t}).$$

Accordingly, we can approximate the difference $\Delta_{t+\delta t}^{(a)} - \Delta_t^{(a)}$ as

$$\Delta_{t+\delta t}^{(a)} - \Delta_t^{(a)} \approx V_{SS}^{(a)} (t, S_t) \left(S_{t+\delta t} - S_t \right) + ...$$

$$\approx V_{SS}^{(a)} (t, S_t) \sigma S_t \left| W_{t+\delta t} - W_t \right| + ...,$$

where we omit terms of order δt and higher. Thus,

$$\Pi_{t+\delta t} - \Pi_t \approx - \left(V_t^{(a)} + \frac{1}{2} \sigma^2 S^2 V_{SS}^{(a)} - r^1 S V_S^{(a)} \right) \delta t$$

$$- \frac{1}{2} \kappa \sigma S^2 \left| V_{SS}^{(a)} \right| \left| W_{t+\delta t} - W_t \right| + ...$$

After taking the expectation and using formula (4.30), we obtain

$$\mathbb{E} \{ \Pi_{t+\delta t} - \Pi_t \} \approx - \left(V_t^{(a)} + \frac{1}{2} \sigma^2 S^2 V_{SS}^{(a)} - r^1 S V_S^{(a)} \right) \delta t$$

$$- \frac{1}{2} \kappa \sigma S^2 \left| V_{SS}^{(a)} \right| \sqrt{\frac{2 \delta t}{\pi}}.$$

On the other hand,

$$\mathbb{E} \{ \Pi_{t+\delta t} - \Pi_t \} \approx r^0 \Pi_t \delta t.$$

Thus, the pricing equation for $V^{(a)}$ has the form

$$V_t^{(a)} + \frac{1}{2} \left\{ 1 + \text{Asign} \left(V_{SS}^{(a)} \right) \right\} \sigma^2 S^2 V_{SS}^{(a)} + r^{01} S V_S^{(a)} - r^0 V^{(a)} = 0, \quad (14.9)$$

where

$$A = \sqrt{\frac{2\kappa^2}{\pi\sigma^2\delta t}},$$

is the so-called Leland number. Equation (14.9) is supplied with the standard final condition

$$V^{(a)}(T, S) = v(S).$$

The Leland number is a key nondimensional parameter in the theory of transaction costs. When $A \to 0$ (which means either a small bid-ask spread or infrequent rehedgings) transaction costs can be neglected; in the opposite limit they are paramount.

We leave it to the reader to derive the corresponding pricing problem for $V^{(b)}$.

Thus, in general, in the presence of transaction costs the pricing equation is a nonlinear equation of the Barenblatt type. However, for options with convex payoffs this equation is the standard Black-Scholes equation with increased implied volatility

$$\sigma_I = \sqrt{1 + A}\sigma,$$

so that

$$C^{(a)}\left(t, S, K, T, \sigma, r^0, r^1\right) = C\left(t, S, T, K, \sqrt{1 + A}\sigma, r^0, r^1\right).$$

The Black-Scholes formula yields

$$C\left(t, S, T, K, \sigma \to \infty, r^0, r^1\right) \to e^{-r^1(T-t)}S.$$

Thus, if we keep κ fixed and let $\delta t \to 0$, we obtain the following disappointing result

$$C^{(a)}\left(t, S, K, T, \sigma, r^0, r^1\right) \to e^{-r^1(T-t)}S,$$

which means that the only acceptable hedging strategy for a call is to buy a foreign bond with the face value of one and keep it to maturity. Of course, it is not possible to sell a call for $e^{-r^1(T-t)}S$, which explains why selling calls (and other options) in the presence of transaction costs is not a risk-free activity.

For options with convex payoffs (such as calls) equation (14.9) never looses its backward parabolic character. For options with nonconvex payoffs (for example, bets) this equation is backward parabolic provided that $A < 1$. If $A \geq 1$ the situation is more complex, however, with some modifications, which we do not describe here, equation (14.9) is still valid.

14.5 Liquidity risk

In this section we analyze the impact of liquidity effects on pricing and hedging of derivatives. First of all, we need to quantify the concept of liquidity. We define the liquidity L of a foreign currency (which is measured in the units of the foreign currency) as the marginal change in the notional amount traded in the market N (which is measured in the units of the domestic currency) caused by the marginal change of its spot FXR:

$$L = \frac{\partial N}{\partial S}.$$

It is clear that L is positive, $L > 0$, since the FXR increase attracts additional currency sellers. For very liquid (illiquid) currencies L approaches infinity (zero).

The liquidity adjusted SDE governing the evolution of the FXR can be written in the form

$$dS = \mu S dt + \sigma S dW_t + \frac{1}{L} dN.$$

In order to find liquidity adjusted derivative prices we need to modify the Black-Scholes hedging strategy described in Section 9.2 by taking into account the third term in the above equation. As usual, we consider the situation from the standpoint of the option seller and form the delta-hedged portfolio

$$\Pi(t, S) = -V^{(a)}(t, S) + \Delta^{(a)}(t, S) S = -V(t, S) + N,$$

where

$$\Delta^{(a)}(t, S) S = N = S V_S^{(a)}(t, S).$$

(We only consider changes in the notional amount of foreign currency caused by hedging of the derivative in question.) Accordingly,

$$\begin{aligned} dS &= \mu S dt + \sigma S dW_t + \frac{1}{L} d\left[S V_S^{(a)}(t, S) \right] \\ &= \sigma S dW_t + \frac{(S V_S)_S}{L} dS + ..., \end{aligned}$$

where we omit terms of order dt and higher, so that

$$dS = \frac{\sigma S dW_t}{\left(1 - \frac{1}{L} \left(S V_S^{(a)} \right)_S \right)},$$

$$(dS)^2 = \frac{\sigma^2 S^2 dt}{\left(1 - \frac{1}{\mathsf{L}}\left(SV_S^{(a)}\right)_S\right)^2}.$$

A simple calculation yields

$$d\Pi = -\left(V_t^{(a)} dt + V_S^{(a)} dS + \frac{1}{2}V_{SS}^{(a)}(dS)^2\right) + V_S^{(a)}\left(dS + r^1 Sdt\right)$$

$$= -\left(V_t^{(a)} + \frac{1}{2}\frac{\sigma^2 S^2 V_{SS}^{(a)}}{\left(1 - \frac{1}{\mathsf{L}}\left(SV_S^{(a)}\right)_S\right)^2} - r^1 SV_S^{(a)}\right) dt.$$

On the other hand,

$$d\Pi = r^0 \Pi dt.$$

Thus, the modified Black-Scholes equation has the form

$$V_t^{(a)} + \frac{1}{2}\frac{\sigma^2 S^2 V_{SS}^{(a)}}{\left(1 - \frac{1}{\mathsf{L}}\left(SV_S^{(a)}\right)_S\right)^2} + r^{01} SV_S^{(a)} - r^0 V^{(a)} = 0.$$

As advertised, this equation has the form (14.6). It is supplied with the standard final condition

$$V^{(a)}(T, S) = v(S).$$

For $\mathsf{L} = \infty$ the modified pricing problem coincides with the corresponding Black-Scholes problem. Thus, for derivatives with payoffs convex with respect to $\ln S$ liquidity magnifies volatility and hence increases the ask price of such derivatives. For derivatives with nonconvex payoffs the situation is more complicated.

We leave it to the reader to verify that the liquidity-adjusted pricing problem for $V^{(b)}$ has the form

$$V_t^{(b)} + \frac{1}{2}\frac{\sigma^2 S^2 V_{SS}^{(b)}}{\left(1 + \frac{1}{\mathsf{L}}\left(SV_S^{(b)}\right)_S\right)^2} + r^{01} SV_S^{(b)} - r^0 V^{(b)} = 0,$$

$$V^{(b)}(T, S) = v(S).$$

It is clear that under normal circumstances liquidity reduces volatility and, hence, the bid price.

Since the pricing problems are nonlinear, derivative prices depend on their notional amounts in a complicated way. These problems have to be solved numerically. In order to avoid undesirable behavior of the bid and ask prices, we have to limit the magnitude of the local volatility above and below.

14.6 Default risk

14.6.1 Introduction

So far, we studied the valuation problem for options and forward contracts without taking into account the possibility of seller's default. However, spectacular failures which occurred during the Asian and Russian crises make it imperative to understand how to value forex options and forward contracts with a default prone counterparty. The quest to solve this problem has a long and convoluted history. Nevertheless, the definite answer to the valuation problem is still lacking. In this section we discuss a very simple model for describing options and forwards with default risk and present some explicit pricing formulas for them.

We assume that default happens when the value of the counterparty's stock which follows the usual geometrical Brownian motion hits a certain threshold level. The value of the FXR follows the geometrical Brownian motion as well. In the event of default the buyer looses the marked-to-market value of the corresponding option or the value of a forward contract if this value is positive (we assume that the buyer has to pay in full if the value of a forward contract is negative).

14.6.2 The pricing model

In the present section we introduce a very simple model for describing options and forward contracts with default risk. The model itself is relatively crude and leaves a lot to be desired. However, it gives a taste of things to be expected once a more general and accurate model is built. Consider a party which buys an option on a certain underlying asset from a default prone counterparty. Denote the value of the counterparty's stock by ϖ and the FXR by S. Since the buyer of an option or a forward contract is in danger of not being able to execute it because of the seller's default, they are entitled to pay less than the full no-default price. Our objective is to find the corresponding discount.

In mathematical terms our model can be formulated as follows. The value of the seller's stock follows the standard geometrical Brownian motion

$$\frac{d\varpi_t}{\varpi_t} = r^{\varpi} dt + \sigma_{\varpi} dW_t^{\varpi},$$

while the value of the FXR follows a correlated geometrical Brownian motion

$$\frac{dS_t}{S_t} = r^{01} dt + \sigma_S dW_t^S,$$

where the Brownian motions W^{ϖ} and W^S are correlated, $corr(dW_v, dW_s) = \rho$.

There are two critical issues which we need to address in order to construct a sensible model: (a) what constitutes a default; (b) what happens in the case of default. The simplest answer to the first question is that the counterparty defaults when the value ϖ of its stock falls below a certain critical level D. The answer to the second question is a little more subtle. We can assume, for example, that the buyer gets nothing in the case of default. More generally, we can assume that the buyer recovers a fraction of the market value of the non-default option. With the above assumptions in mind, we can write the standard pricing equation for the price $C^*(t, S, \varpi)$ of the defaultable call option with strike K,

$$C_t^* + \frac{1}{2}\sigma_S^2 S^2 C_{SS}^* + \rho\sigma_S\sigma_{\varpi} S\varpi C_{S\varpi}^* + \frac{1}{2}\sigma_{\varpi}^2 \varpi^2 C_{\varpi\varpi}^*$$
$$+ \quad r^{01} S C_S^* + r^{\varpi}\varpi C_{\varpi}^* - r^0 C^* = 0.$$

When we deal with plane vanilla calls this equation is considered in the quarter-plane $S \geq 0, \varpi \geq D$, and is supplied with the following boundary and final conditions

$$C^*(t, S, D) = pC(t, S),$$

$$C^*(T, S, \varpi) = (S - K)_+,$$

where $C(t, S)$ is the standard Black-Scholes price of the non-defaultable call, and p, $0 \leq p < 1$, is the recovery coefficient. When $p = 0$ there is no recovery in the case of default. If we deal with a barrier option (a down-and-out call with a given barrier level A, say), the pricing equation remains unchanged. However, the domain where it has to be solved shrinks to the quadrant $S \geq A, \varpi \geq D$, and an additional boundary condition is introduced,

$$C^*(t, B, \varpi) = 0.$$

We can consider both European and American options in the above framework.

For the defaultable forward contract whose value is denoted by $FO^*(t, S, \varpi)$ the pricing problem has the form

$$FO_t^* + \frac{1}{2}\sigma_S^2 S^2 FO_{SS}^* + \rho\sigma_S\sigma_\varpi S\varpi FO_{S\varpi}^* + \frac{1}{2}\sigma_\varpi^2 \varpi^2 FO_{\varpi\varpi}^* \quad (14.10)$$
$$+ \quad r^{01} SFO_S^* + r^\varpi \varpi FO_\varpi^* - r^0 FO^* = 0,$$

$$FO^*(t, S, D) \quad (14.11)$$
$$= \left(e^{-r^1(T-t)} S - e^{-r^0(T-t)} K\right)_- + p\left(e^{-r^1(T-t)} S - e^{-r^0(T-t)} K\right)_+,$$

$$FO^*(T, S, \varpi) = S - K. \quad (14.12)$$

In general, the barrier value D is difficult to estimate. Traditionally, as a proxy to this value one can use the so-called credit spread, i.e. the excess yield on bonds issued by the counterparty compared to the yield of the government bonds, say. Below we will see how to relate this excess yield to the value of D.

14.6.3 Pricing of defaultable European calls

In this section we show how to use techniques developed in Chapter 12 for pricing barrier options in order to evaluate explicitly defaultable European calls.

The case of zero correlation

We start with the case of zero correlation. In this case the pricing equation assumes the form

$$C_t^* + \frac{1}{2}\sigma_S^2 S^2 C_{SS}^* + \frac{1}{2}\sigma_\varpi^2 \varpi^2 C_{\varpi\varpi}^* + r^{01} SC_S^* + r^\varpi \varpi C_\varpi^* - r^0 C^* = 0.$$

The price $C(t, S, V)$ of a European call (as well as a barrier call) can be presented in the form

$$C^*(t, S, \varpi) = f(t, \varpi)C(t, S),$$

where $f(t, V)$ solves the problem

$$f_t + \frac{1}{2}\sigma_\varpi^2 \varpi^2 f_{\varpi\varpi} + r^\varpi \varpi f_\varpi = 0,$$

$$f(t, D) = p,$$

$$f(T, \varpi) = 1.$$

The solution $f(t, \varpi)$, which can easily be found explicitly by the method of images (see Section 12.2 for details), has the form

$$f(t, \varpi) = p + (1 - p)\left[\mathfrak{N}(e_+) - \left(\frac{\varpi}{D}\right)^{1 - 2r^\varpi/\sigma_\varpi^2} \mathfrak{N}(e_-)\right],$$

where

$$e_\pm = \frac{\pm\log(\varpi/D) + r_\varpi(T - t)}{\sigma_\varpi\sqrt{T - t}} - \frac{\sigma_\varpi\sqrt{T - t}}{2}.$$

Thus, the possibility of default results is the decrease of the price of a call by a factor of f. This is true for any other option (but not necessarily a forward contract) as well.

It is important to relate f to some financially observable quantities. The most obvious one is the credit spread. Under our assumptions the price $B_{t,T}$ of the no-default bond has the form

$$B_{t,T} = e^{-r^0(T-t)}.$$

It is clear that the price $B_{t,T}^*(\varpi)$ of the defaultable bond is

$$B_{t,T}^*(\varpi) = f(t, \varpi)B_{t,T} = e^{-y(\varpi)(T-t)}.$$

According to the definition of the excess yield

$$\Delta y = y(\varpi) - r^0,$$

we have

$$f(t, \varpi) = e^{-\Delta y(T-t)}.$$

This relation in nothing more that an oblique way of saying what the current value of ϖ/D is. Inverting this relation we can write

$$\frac{\varpi}{D} = g(t, \Delta y).$$

The connection we have established is less relevant for the case of zero correlation than for the case of nonzero correlation considered below. It is clear that for $p > 0$ there is an upper limit to the magnitude of Δy at a given t. Keeping the definition of the excess yield in mind, we can represent the price of the defaultable call as

$$C^*(t, S, \varpi) = e^{-\Delta y(T-t)} C(t, S).$$

For American options the variables are no longer separable, but the pricing problem can be solved numerically via the ADI method. We emphasize that the value of an American option is less affected by the possibility of default that the value of the corresponding European one. Nevertheless, the decline in value is not negligible because the seller's default can force the buyer to exercise his call suboptimally.

The case of non-zero correlation

In the case of non-zero correlation the variables can no longer be separated. We represent the price of the defaultable call in the form

$$C^*(t, S, \varpi) = pC(t, S) + (1 - p)C^{**}(t, S, \varpi),$$

where $C^{**}(t, S, \varpi)$ satisfies the usual pricing equation and no-recovery boundary conditions. By using the method of images we can represent $C^{**}(t, S, \varpi)$ as follows,

$$
\begin{aligned}
&C^{**}(t, S, \varpi) \\
&= e^{-r^1(T-t)} S \left[\mathfrak{N}_2 \left(d_{+,+}, e_{+,+}, \rho \right) - \left(\frac{\varpi}{D} \right)^{1 - 2r^\varpi/\sigma_\varpi^2 - 2\rho\sigma_S/\sigma_\varpi} \mathfrak{N}_2 \left(d_{+,-}, e_{-,+}, \rho \right) \right] \\
&\quad - e^{-r^0(T-t)} K \left[\mathfrak{N}_2 \left(d_{-,+}, e_{+,-}, \rho \right) - \left(\frac{\varpi}{D} \right)^{1 - 2r^\varpi/\sigma_\varpi^2} \mathfrak{N}_2 \left(d_{-,+}, e_{-,-}, \rho \right) \right],
\end{aligned}
$$

where

$$d_{\pm,\pm} = \frac{\log(S/K) + r^{01}(T - t)}{\sigma_S\sqrt{T - t}} \pm \frac{\sigma_S\sqrt{T - t}}{2} + \frac{(-1 \pm 1)\rho\log(\varpi/D)}{\sigma_\varpi\sqrt{T - t}},$$

$$e_{\pm,\pm} = \frac{\pm \log(\varpi/D) + r^\varpi(T-t)}{\sigma_\varpi\sqrt{T-t}} - \frac{\sigma_\varpi\sqrt{T-t}}{2} + \frac{(1\pm 1)\rho\sigma_S\sqrt{T-t}}{2}.$$

Here $\mathfrak{N}_2$ is the cumulative bivariate normal distribution. It is easy to show that for $\rho = 0$ the above formula reduces to the one derived in the previous subsection. By substituting into the pricing formula ϖ expressed as a function of Δy, we obtain the price of a risky option in the case of non-zero correlation. As before, in order to find the value of a risky American option we have to use the ADI method.

14.6.4   Pricing of defaultable forward contracts

In order to price a defaultable forward contract we need to solve problem (14.10) - (14.12). It is convenient to split $FO^*(t, S, \varpi)$ as follows

$$FO^*(t, S, \varpi) = FO(t, S) - (1-p)FO^{**}(t, S, \varpi),$$

where $FO^{**}(t, S, \varpi)$ solves equation (14.10) supplied with the boundary condition

$$FO^{**}(t, S, D) = \left(e^{-r^1(T-t)}S - e^{-r^0(T-t)}K\right)_+,$$

and zero final condition.

It is natural to solve the pricing problem for $FO^{**}(t, S, \varpi)$ via the method of heat potentials described in Section 12.2. However, for the sake of variety, we develop a direct approach to solving this problem. It is clear that we can represent $FO^{**}(t, S, \varpi)$ in the form

$$
\begin{aligned}
&FO^{**}(t, S, \varpi)\\
&= \mathbb{E}_t\left\{\int_t^T e^{-r^0(t'-t)}\left(e^{-r^1(T-t')}S_{t'} - e^{-r^0(T-t')}K\right)_+ 1_{\{T_\varpi \in dt'\}}dt'\right\}\\
&= \mathbb{E}_t\left\{e^{-r^0(T-t)}\int_t^T \left(e^{r^{01}(T-t')}S_{t'} - K\right)_+ 1_{\{T_\varpi \in dt'\}}dt'\right\}\\
&= e^{-r^0(T-t)}\int_t^T \mathbb{E}_t\left\{\left(e^{r^{01}(T-t')}S_{t'} - K\right)_+ 1_{\{T_\varpi \in dt'\}}\right\}dt',
\end{aligned}
$$

where T_ϖ is the time of the first hitting of the barrier D by the stock price ϖ. Next, we write $\varpi_{t'}$, $S_{t'}$ as

$$\varpi_{t'} = \exp\left\{\left(r^\varpi - \frac{\sigma_\varpi^2}{2}\right)(t'-t) + \sigma_\varpi\left(W_{t'}^\varpi - W_t^\varpi\right)\right\}\varpi_t,$$

$$S_{t'} = \exp\left\{\left(r^{01} - \frac{\sigma_S^2}{2}\right)(t'-t) + \rho\sigma_S\left(W_{t'}^{\varpi} - W_t^{\varpi}\right) + \bar\rho\,\sigma_S\left(W_{t'}^{S,\perp} - W_t^{S,\perp}\right)\right\} S_t,$$

where $\bar\rho = \sqrt{1-\rho^2}$, and $corr\left(dW_t^{\varpi}, dW_t^{S,\perp}\right) = 0$. Since we only need to know the distribution of $S_{t'}$ when $\varpi_{t'}$ hits the barrier, i.e., when

$$W_{t'}^{\varpi} - W_t^{\varpi} = \frac{1}{\sigma_{\varpi}}\left[\ln\left(\frac{D}{\varpi_t}\right) - \left(r^{\varpi} - \frac{\sigma_{\varpi}^2}{2}\right)(t'-t)\right],$$

we can rewrite S_t in the form

$$S_{t'} = \exp\left\{\left(r^{01} - \frac{\bar\rho^2\sigma_S^2}{2}\right)(t'-t) + \bar\rho\,\sigma_S\left(W_{t'}^{S,\perp} - W_t^{S,\perp}\right)\right\} Q_{t'},$$

where

$$Q_{t'} = \left(\frac{D}{\varpi_t}\right)^{\rho\sigma_S/\sigma_{\varpi}} \exp\left\{-\left(\frac{\rho\sigma_S r^{\varpi}}{\sigma_{\varpi}} + \frac{1}{2}\rho^2\sigma_S^2 - \frac{1}{2}\rho\sigma_S\sigma_{\varpi}\right)(t'-t)\right\} S_t.$$

Accordingly, we can represent $FO^{**}\left(t, S_t, \varpi_t\right)$ as

$$
\begin{aligned}
&FO^{**}\left(t, S_t, \varpi_t\right) \\
={}& \int_t^T \mathbb{E}_t\left\{\left(e^{-r^1(T-t)-\bar\rho^2\sigma_S^2(t'-t)/2+\bar\rho\,\sigma_S\left(W_{t'}^{S,\perp}-W_t^{S,\perp}\right)}Q_{t'} - e^{-r^0(T-t)}K\right)_+\right. \\
&\left. 1_{\{T_{\varpi}\in dt'\}}dt'\right\} \\
={}& \int_t^T \mathbb{E}_t\left\{\left(e^{-r^1(T-t)-\bar\rho^2\sigma_S^2(t'-t)/2+\bar\rho\,\sigma_S\left(W_{t'}^{S,\perp}-W_t^{S,\perp}\right)}Q_{t'} - e^{-r^0(T-t)}K\right)_+\right\} \\
&\times P_{\{T_{\varpi}\in dt'\}}.
\end{aligned}
$$

Here we use the fact that W_t^{ϖ} and $W_t^{S,\perp}$ are independent Brownian motions. By using the probabilistic interpretation of the Black-Scholes formula we can show that

$$
\begin{aligned}
&\mathbb{E}_t\left\{\left(e^{-r^1(T-t)-\bar\rho^2\sigma_S^2(t'-t)/2+\bar\rho\,\sigma_S\left(W_{t'}^{S,\perp}-W_t^{S,\perp}\right)}Q_{t'} - e^{-r^0(T-t)}K\right)_+\right\} \\
={}& e^{-r^1(T-t)}Q_{t'}\mathfrak{N}(d_+) - e^{-r^0(T-t)}K\mathfrak{N}(d_-),
\end{aligned}
$$

where

$$d_\pm = \frac{\ln(e^{r^{01}(T-t)}Q_{t'}/K)}{\bar\rho\sigma_S\sqrt{t'-t}} \pm \frac{1}{2}\bar\rho\sigma_S\sqrt{t'-t}.$$

The probability of the stock price $\varpi_{t'}$ hitting the barrier D at time t' is

$$P(T_\varpi \in dt') = \frac{|\ln(D/\varpi_t)| \, e^{-[\ln(D/\varpi_t)-(r^\varpi-\sigma_\varpi^2/2)(t'-t)]^2/2\sigma_\varpi^2(t'-t)}}{\sqrt{2\pi\sigma_\varpi^2(t-t')^3}} \, dt'.$$

By using the above formulas, we can represent FO^{**} in the final form

$$FO^{**}(t, S_t, \varpi_t) = \int_t^T \left[e^{-r^1(T-t)} Q_{t'} \mathfrak{N}(d_+) - e^{-r^0(T-t)} K \mathfrak{N}(d_-) \right]$$
$$\times \frac{|\ln(D/\varpi_t)| \, e^{-[\ln(D/\varpi_t)-(r^\varpi-\sigma_\varpi^2/2)(t'-t)]^2/2\sigma_\varpi^2(t'-t)}}{\sqrt{2\pi\sigma_\varpi^2(t-t')^3}} \, dt'.$$

In this formula the ratio D/ϖ_t is determined by the excess yield Δy. Thus

$$FO^*(t, S_t, \varpi_t) = e^{-r^1(T-t)} S - e^{-r^0(T-t)} K \qquad (14.13)$$
$$- (1-p) \int_t^T \left[e^{-r^1(T-t)} Q_{t'} \mathfrak{N}(d_+) - e^{-r^0(T-t)} K \mathfrak{N}(d_-) \right]$$
$$\times \frac{|\ln(D/\varpi_t)| \, e^{-[\ln(D/\varpi_t)-(r^\varpi-\sigma_\varpi^2/2)(t'-t)]^2/2\sigma_\varpi^2(t'-t)}}{\sqrt{2\pi\sigma_\varpi^2(t-t')^3}} \, dt'.$$

In order to find $F_{t,T}^*$ we need to solve the equation

$$FO^*(t, S_t, \varpi_t) = 0, \qquad (14.14)$$

with respect to K. It is clear that $F_{t,T}^* < F_{t,T}$. Although expression (14.13) cannot be computed explicitly, it can easily be found numerically. Due to the possibility of default, the nonrisky forward price has to be reduced accordingly. It is interesting to note that this reduction is negligible not only when the default probability is small (as one would expect) but also when it is large (since in the latter case default occurs very quickly and its consequences are insignificant). Accordingly, the reduction attains its maximum value for intermediate probabilities of default. It is clear that this reduction should not be neglected under realistic conditions.

14.7   References and further reading

The original papers devoted to the topics covered in this chapter are as follows: Avellaneda *et al.* (1995), Avellaneda and Paras (1994), Bestimas *et al.* (1998), Boyle and Vorst (1992), Carr and Jarrow (1990), Davis *et al.* (1993), Esipov and Vaysburd (1999), Gallus (1999), Hodges and Neuberger (1989), Johnson and Stulz (1987), Hull and White (1995), Karpoff (1987), Krakovsky (1999), Leland (1985), Lipton and Pugachevsky (1998 a), Lyons (1995), Lyons and Smith (1999), Merton (1974), Schweizer (1991), Soner *et al.* (1995). The book by Wilmott (1998) contains an interesting alternative discussion of market imperfections.

Chapter 15

Future directions of research and conclusions

15.1 Introduction

In this short final chapter we outline some future research directions which, in our opinion, are particularly promising, and briefly summarize the main contributions which we make in this book.

The organization of this chapter is very simple. In Section 2 we outline future research directions. In Section 3 we draw conclusions. Finally, in Section 3 we give relevant references.

15.2 Future directions

It is well known that it is notoriously hard to make reliable predictions of future directions of scientific research. Financial engineering is not an exception from this rule. However, some directions in which it is going to develop are less obscure than others and can be identified with confidence. In the spirit of this book, we restrict ourselves to the forex issues.

It is clear that in addition to standard Wiener and Poisson processes which are used throughout this book as conventional "stochastic engines" for modelling the behavior of financial variables, more general Levy processes will be widely used as well. In fact, in various forms, their usage had been advocated by leading researchers in the field for some time in order to account for the fact that short-term returns on investment in forex (as well as many other financial instruments) are strongly non-Gaussian.

In addition, a much greater attention will be paid to the related issue of how to determine the spot FXR *per se* and to predict its short-term evolution. In order to address this very important issue in earnest, an adequate formalism for studying the market microstructure including the supply and demand and liquidity effects will be developed.

The future will see an inevitable convergence of different techniques for assessing and mitigating financial risks in forex markets. Before too long, one can expect a merger of financial engineering, actuarial science and game theory.

Besides, due to a great practical need, new powerful techniques for solving the asset allocation problem, which take a full advantage in the latest developments in stochastic control, will be developed.

15.3   Conclusions

By now we feel that our main objectives are fulfilled and it is time for us to let the reader go. In this book we make three contributions. First, we introduce the reader to the key problems of contemporary financial engineering in the forex context with a particular emphasis on pricing and risk management of derivative instruments. Second, we describe and develop a whole spectrum of mathematical tools which are needed for solving these problems. Finally, we demonstrate how to use these tools in a variety of practically important situations. We hope that this book will help the readers to solve their own modelling problems. Good luck.

15.4   References and further reading

Barndorff-Nielsen (1998), Bertoin (1996), Clark (1973), Eberlein and Keller (1995), Esscher (1932), Fama (1965), Gerber and Shiu (1994), de Grauwe *et al.* (1993), Levy (1948), Lipton (2000), Lo and MacKinlay (1999), Malkiel (1990), Mandelbrot (1963), Mantegna and Stanley (1995), Schmidt (2000), Zolotarev (1989).

Bibliography

[1] M. Abramowitz and I. A. Stegun, *Handbook of Mathematical Functions*, Dover, New York, 1972.

[2] H. Ahn, A. Penaud and P. Wilmott, "Various passport options and their valuation", MFG Working Paper, Oxford Univ., 1998.

[3] K. I. Amin and V. K. Ng, "Option valuation with systematic stochastic volatility", *Journal of Finance* **48** (1993), 881-910.

[4] L. Andersen and J. Andreasen, "Jump-diffusion processes: volatility smile fitting and numerical methods for pricing", Working Paper, 1999.

[5] L. Andersen, J. Andreasen and R. Brotherton-Ratcliffe, "The passport option", *Journal of Computational Finance* **1** (1998), no. 3, 15-36.

[6] L. Andersen, J. Andreasen and D. Eliezer, "Static replication of barrier options: some general results", Working Paper, 2000.

[7] L. Andersen and R. Brotherton-Ratcliffe, "The equity option volatility smile: a finite difference approach", *Journal of Computational Finance* **1** (1998), no. 2, 5-38.

[8] J. Andreasen, "The pricing of discretely sampled Asian and lookback options: a change of numeraire approach", *Journal of Computational Finance* **2** (1998), no. 1, 5-30.

[9] L. Arnold, *Stochastic Differential Equations: Theory and Applications*, Wiley, New York, 1974.

[10] K. J. Arrow, *Essays in the Theory of Risk Bearing*, Markham, Chicago, 1971.

[11] M. Avellaneda and P. Laurence, *Quantitative Modeling of Derivative Securities. From Theory to Practice,* Chapman & Hall/CRC, Boca Raton, FL, 2000.

[12] M. Avellaneda, A. Levy and A. Paras, "Pricing and hedging derivative securities in markets with uncertain volatilities", *Applied Mathematical Finance* **2** (1995), 73-88.

[13] M. Avellaneda and A. Paras, "Dynamic hedging portfolios for derivative securities in the presence of large transaction costs", *Applied Mathematical Finance* **1** (1994), 165-194.

[14] L. Bachelier, "Théorie de la spéculation", *Annales de l'Ecole Normale Supérieure* **17** (1900), 21-86. Translated in *The Random Character of Stock Market Prices,* P. Cootner, editor, MIT Press, Cambridge, MA, 1965.

[15] C. T. H. Baker, *The Numerical Treatment of Integral Equations.* Oxford Univ. Press, Oxford, 1977.

[16] C. A. Ball. "A review of stochastic volatility models with application to option pricing", *Financial Markets, Institutions and Instruments* **2** (1993), no. 5, 55-69.

[17] C. A. Ball and A. Roma, "Stochastic volatility option pricing", *Journal of Financial and Quantitative Analysis* **29** (1994), 589-607.

[18] P. Balland and L. P. Hughston, "Pricing and hedging with a sticky-delta smile", Working Paper, 2000.

[19] O. E. Barndorff-Nielsen, "Processes of normal inverse Gaussian type", *Finance and Stochastics* **2** (1998), no. 1, 41-68.

[20] G. Barone-Adesi and R. Elliott, "Approximations for the values of American options", *Stochastic Analysis and Applications* **9** (1991), no. 2, 115-131.

[21] G. Barone-Adesi and R. E. Whaley, "Efficient analytic approximation of American option values", *Journal of Finance* **42** (1987), no. 2, 301-320.

[22] G. I. Barenblatt, *Scaling, Self-similarity, and Intermediate Asymptotics,* Cambridge Univ. Press, Cambridge, 1996.

[23] G. Barles, J. Burdeau, M. Romano and N. Samsen, "Critical stock price near expiration", *Mathematical Finance* **5** (1995), 77-95.

[24] D. S. Bates, "Jumps and stochastic volatility: exchange rate processes implicit in Deutsche mark options", *Review of Financial Studies* **9** (1996), no. 1, 69-107.

[25] M. Baxter and A. Rennie, *Financial Calculus. An Introduction to Derivative Pricing,* Cambridge Univ. Press, Cambridge, 1996.

[26] D. R. Beaglehole, "Down and out, up and out options", Working Paper, 1993.

[27] R. M. Beam and R. F. Warming, "Alternating direction implicit methods for parabolic equations with a mixed derivative", *SIAM Journal of Scientific and Statistical Computing* **1** (1980), no. 1, 131-159.

[28] S. Beckers, "The constant elasticity of variance model and its implications for option pricing", *Journal of Finance* **35** (1980), no. 3, 661-673.

[29] D. Bertsimas, L. Kogan and A. W. Lo, "When time is continuous", Working Paper, 1998.

[30] J. Bertoin, *Lévy Processes,* Cambridge Univ. Press, Cambridge, 1996.

[31] F. Black, "The pricing of commodity contracts", *Journal of Financial Economics* **3** (1976), 167-179.

[32] F. Black, "The holes in Black-Scholes", *Risk Magazine* **1** (1988), no. 3.

[33] F. Black, E. Derman and W. Toy, "A one-factor model of interest rate and its application to Treasury bond options", *Financial Analysts Journal* **46** (1990), 33-39.

[34] F. Black and P. Karasinski, "Bond and option pricing when short rates are lognormal", *Financial Analysts Journal* **47** (1991), 52-59.

[35] F. Black and M. Scholes, "The pricing of options and corporate liabilities", *Journal of Political Economy* **81** (1973), no.3, 637-659.

[36] G. Bluman and S. Kumei, *Symmetries and Differential Equations,* Springer, Berlin, 1989.

[37] A. J. Boness, "Elements of a theory of a stock option value", *Journal of Political Economy* **72** (1964), no. 2, 163-175.

[38] A. N. Borodin and P. Salminen, *Handbook of Brownian Motion - Facts and Formulae,* Birkhauser, Basel, 1996.

[39] I. Bouchouev and V. Isakov, "The inverse problem of option pricing", *Inverse Problems* **13** (1997), L11-L17.

[40] J. Bowie and P. Carr, "Static simplicity", *Risk Magazine* **7** (1994), no. 9, 45-49.

[41] P. P. Boyle, "Options: a Monte Carlo approach", *Journal of Financial Economics* **4** (1977), 323-338.

[42] P. P. Boyle and Y. S. Tian, "Pricing lookback and barrier options under the CEV process", *Journal of Financial and Quantitative Analysis* **34** (1999), no. 2, 241-264.

[43] P. P. Boyle and T. Vorst, "Option replication in discrete time with transaction costs", *Journal of Finance* **47** (1992), 271-293.

[44] A. Brace, D. Gatarek and M. Musiela, "The market model of interest rate dynamics", *Mathematical Finance* **7** (1997), 127-154.

[45] D. T. Breeden and R. H. Litzenberger, "Prices of state-contingent claims implicit in options prices", *Journal of Business* **5** (1978), 621-652.

[46] M. Brennan and E. Schwartz, "Finite-difference methods and jump processes arising in the pricing of contingent claims: a synthesis", *Journal of Financial and Quantitative Analysis* **13** (1978), 462-474.

[47] M. Britten-Jones and A. Neuberger, "Option prices, implied prices processes, and stochastic volatility", Working Paper, 2000.

[48] M. Britten-Jones and S. M. Schaefer, "Non-linear value-at-risk", Working Paper, 1997.

[49] M. Broadie and P. Glasserman, "Monte Carlo methods for pricing high-dimensional American options: an overview", Working Paper, 1997.

[50] M. Broadie and J. Detemple, "American option valuation: new bounds, approximations, and a comparison of existing methods", *Review of Financial Studies* **9** (1996), 1211-1250.

[51] M. Broadie, P. Glasserman and S. Kou, "A continuity correction for discrete barrier options", *Mathematical Finance* **7** (1997), no. 4, 325-349.

[52] P. W. Buchen and M. Kelly, "The Maximum entropy distribution of an asset inferred from option prices", *Journal of Financial and Quantitative Analysis* **31** (1996), 143-159.

[53] R. H. Cameron and W. T. Martin, "Transformation of Wiener integrals under a general class of linear transformations", *Transactions of the American Mathematical Society* **58** (1945), 184-219.

[54] P. Carr, "Randomization and the American Put", *Review of Financial Studies* **11** (1998), 597–626.

[55] P. Carr, K. Ellis and V. Gupta, "Static hedging of exotic options", *Journal of Finance* **53** (1998), 1165-1190.

[56] P. Carr and R. Jarrow, "The stop-loss start-gain strategy and option valuation", *Review of Financial Studies* **3** (1990), no. 3, 469-492.

[57] P. Carr, R. Jarrow and R. Myneni, "Alternative characterization of American put options", *Mathematical Finance* **2** (1992), 87-105.

[58] P. Carr, A. Lipton and D. B. Madan, "The reduction method for valuing derivative securities", Working Paper, 2000.

[59] P. Carr, D. B. Madan, "Towards a Theory of Volatility Trading", in *Volatility*, R. Jarrow, editor, Risk Publications, London, 1998.

[60] P. Carr, D. B. Madan, "Option pricing the fast Fourier transform", *Journal of Computational Finance* **2** (1999), 61-73.

[61] M. Chesney, J. Cornwall, M. Jeanblanc-Picqué, G. Kentwell and M. Yor, "Parisian pricing", *Risk Magazine* **10** (1997), no. 1.

[62] M. Chesney and L. O. Scott, "Pricing European options: a comparison of the modified Black-Scholes model and a random variance model", *Journal of Financial and Quantitative Analysis* **24** (1989), 267-284.

[63] R. V. Churchill and J. W. Brown, *Fourier Series and Boundary Value Problems*, 4th edition, McGraw-Hill, New York, 1987.

[64] P. K. Clark, "A subordinated stochastic process model with finite variance for speculative prices", *Econometrica* **41** (1973), 135-155.

[65] A. Conze and Viswanathan, "Path-dependent options - the case of lookback options", *Journal of Finance* **46** (1991), 1893-1907.

[66] J. C. Cox, "Notes on option pricing I: constant elasticity of variance diffusions", Working Paper, 1975.

[67] J. C. Cox, J. E. Ingersoll and S. A. Ross, "The relationship between forward prices and futures prices", *Journal of Financial Economics* **9** (1981), 321-346.

[68] J. C. Cox, J. E. Ingersoll and S. A. Ross, "A theory of term structure of interest rates", *Econometrica* **53** (1985), 385-467.

[69] J. C. Cox and S. A. Ross, "The valuation of options for alternative stochastic processes", *Journal of Financial Economics* **3** (1976), 145-166.

[70] J. C. Cox, S. A. Ross and M. Rubinstein, "Option pricing: a simplified approach", *Journal of Financial Economics* **7** (1979), 229-263.

[71] J. C. Cox and M. Rubinstein, *Options Markets*, Prentice-Hall, Englewood Cliffs, NJ, 1985.

[72] J. Crank, *Free and Moving Boundary Problems*, Clarendon Press, Oxford, 1984.

[73] J. Crank, *Mathematics of Diffusion*, Oxford Univ. Press, Oxford, 1989.

[74] J. Crank and P. Nicolson, "A practical method for numerical evaluation of solutions of partial differential equations of the heat conduction type", *Proceedings of the Cambridge Philosophical Society* **43** (1947), 50-67.

[75] S. R. Das and R. K. Sundaram, "On smiles and smirks: a term structure perspective", *Journal of Financial and Quantitative Analysis* **34** (1999), no. 2, 211-239.

[76] M. H. A. Davis, V. G. Panas and T. Zariphopoulou, "European option pricing with transaction costs", *SIAM Journal of Control and Optimization* **31** (1993), 470-493.

[77] D. Davydov and V. Linetsky, "Pricing options on scalar diffusions: an eigenfunction expansion approach", Working Paper, 2000.

[78] G. Debreu, *Theory of Value*, Yale Univ. Press, New Haven, 1959.

[79] F. Delbaen and W. Schachermayer, "A general version of the fundamental theorem of asset pricing", *Mathematische Annalen* **300** (1994), 463-520.

[80] F. Delbaen and M. Yor, "Passport options", Working Paper, 1999.

[81] K. Demeterfi, E. Derman, M. Kamal and J. Zou, "More than you ever wanted to know about volatility swaps", Working Paper, 1999.

[82] M. A. H. Dempster and J. P. Hutton, "Fast numerical valuation of American exotic and complex options", *Applied Mathematical Finance* **4** (1997), 1-20.

[83] E. Derman, "Regimes of volatility", *Risk Magazine* **12** (1999), no. 4, 55-59.

[84] E. Derman and I. Kani, "Riding on a smile", *Risk Magazine* **7** (1994), no. 2, 32-39.

[85] E. Derman, D. Ergener and I. Kani, "Static options replication", In *Frontiers in Derivatives*, A Konishi and R.E. Dattatreya, Editors, Irwin, Homewood, 1997.

[86] A. K. Dixit and R. S. Pindyck, *Investment Under Uncertainty*, Princeton Univ. Press, Princeton, NJ, 1994.

[87] M. U. Dothan, *Prices in Financial Markets*, Oxford Univ. Press, Oxford, 1990.

[88] J.-C. Duan, "The GARCH option pricing model", *Mathematical Finance* **5** (1995), 13-32.

[89] D. Duffie, *Dynamic Asset Pricing Theory*, 2nd edition, Princeton Univ. Press, Princeton, 1996.

[90] D. Duffie and J. Pan, "An overview of value at risk", *Journal of Derivatives* **4** (1997), no. 3, 7-49.

[91] B. Dumas, J. Fleming and R. E. Whaley, "Implied volatility functions: empirical tests", *Journal of Finance* **53** (1998), 2059-2106.

[92] B. Dupire, "Pricing with a smile", *Risk Magazine* **7** (1994), no. 1, 18-20.

[93] B. Dupire, "A unified theory of volatility", Working Paper, 1996.

[94] R. Durrett, *Stochastic Calculus: A Practical Introduction*, CRC Press, Boca Raton, FL, 1996.

[95] E. Eberlein and U. Keller, "Hyperbolic distributions in finance", *Bernoulli* **1** (1995), no.3, 281-299.

[96] D. C. Emanuel and J. D. MacBeth, "Further results on the constant elasticity of variance call option pricing model", *Journal of Financial and Quantitative Analysis* **17** (1982), no.4, 531-554.

[97] A. Erdelyi (Editor), *Bateman Manuscript Project, Higher Transcendental Functions, I,* McGraw-Hill, New York, 1953.

[98] S. Esipov and I. Vaysburd, "On the profit and loss distribution of dynamic hedging strategies", *International Journal of Theoretical and Applied Finance,* **2** (1999), 131-152.

[99] F. Esscher, "On the probability function in the collective theory of risk", *Skandinavisk Aktuarietidskrift* **15** (1932), 175-195.

[100] E. F. Fama, "The behavior of stock market prices", *Journal of Business* **38** (1965), 34-105.

[101] E. F. Fama and M. H. Miller, *The Theory of Finance,* Dryden Press, Hinsdale, IL, 1972.

[102] W. Feller, *An Introduction to Probability Theory and its Applications,* vol. 1, 3rd edition, Wiley, New York, 1968.

[103] W. Feller, *An Introduction to Probability Theory and its Applications,* vol. 2, 2nd edition, Wiley, New York, 1971.

[104] W. Feller, "Two singular diffusion problems", *Annals of Mathematics* **55** (1952), 468-519.

[105] R. J. Feynman, "Space-time approach to nonrelativistic quantum mechanics", *Reviews of Modern Physics* **20** (1948), 367-387.

[106] W. H. Fleming and R. W. Rishel, *Deterministic and Stochastic Optimal Control,* Springer, Berlin, 1975.

[107] S. Figlewski and B. Gao, "The adaptive mesh model: a new approach to efficient option pricing", *Journal of Financial Economics* **53** (1999), 313-351.

[108] R. Frey and C. A. Sin, "Bounds on European option prices under stochastic volatility", *Mathematical Finance* **9** (1999), 97-116.

[109] C. Gallus, "Exploding hedging errors for digital options", *Finance and Stochastics* **3** (1999), 187-201.

[110] K. Garbade, "Managerial discretion and the contingent valuation of corporate securities", *Journal of Derivatives* **6** (1999), no. 4.

[111] J. Gatheral, "Rational shapes of the volatility surface", *Risk's 6th Annual Congress,* Boston, June 2000.

[112] M. B. Garman and S. W. Kohlhagen, "Foreign currency option values", *Journal of International Money and Finance* **2** (1983), 231-237.

[113] R. Gazizov and N. Ibragimov, "Lie symmetry analysis of differential equations in finance", *Nonlinear Dynamics* **17** (1998), 387-407.

[114] H. Geman and A. Eydeland, "Asian options revisited: inverting the Laplace transform", *Risk Magazine* **8** (1995), no. 4, 65-67.

[115] H. Geman and M. Yor, "Bessel processes, Asian options, and perpetuities", *Mathematical Finance* **3** (1993), no. 4, 349-375.

[116] H. U. Gerber and E. S. W. Shiu, "Martingale approach to pricing perpetual American options on two stocks", *Mathematical Finance* **6** (1996), no. 3, 303-322.

[117] H. U. Gerber and E. S. W. Shiu, "Option pricing by Esscher transforms", *Transactions of the Society of Actuaries* **46** (1994), 99-191.

[118] R. Geske and H. E. Johnson, "The American put option valued analytically", *Journal of Finance* **39** (1984), 1511-1524.

[119] R. Geske and K. Shastri, "The early exercise of American puts", *Journal of Banking and Finance* **9** (1985), 207-219.

[120] I. I. Gihman and A. V. Skorohod, *Stochastic Differential Equations,* Springer, Berlin, 1972.

[121] I. V. Girsanov, "On transforming a certain class of stochastic processes by absolutely continuous substitution of measures", *Theory of Probability and its Applications* **5** (1962), no. 3, 285-301.

[122] D. H. Goldenberg, "A unified method for pricing options on diffusion processes", *Journal of Financial Economics* **29** (1991), 3-34

[123] M. B. Goldman, H. Sosin and M. Gatto, "Path dependent options: buy at the low, sell at the high", *Journal of Finance* **34** (1979), 1111-1128.

[124] J. O. Grabbe, "The pricing of call and put options on foreign exchange", *Journal of International Money and Finance* **2** (1983), 239-253.

[125] P. de Grauwe, H. Dewachter and M. Embrechts, *Exchange Rate Theory: Chaotic Models of Foreign Exchange*, Blackwell, Cambridge, MA, 1993.

[126] S. E. Graversen and G. Peskir, "On the Russian option: the expected waiting time", *Theory of Probability and its Applications* **42** (1997), no. 3, 416-425.

[127] R. C. Green and R. A. Jarrow, "Spanning and completeness in markets with contingent claims", *Journal of Economic Theory* **41** (1987), 202-210.

[128] P. S. Hagan and D. E. Woodward, "Equivalent Black Volatilities", Working Paper, 1998.

[129] J. M. Harrison and D. M. Kreps, "Martingales and arbitrage in multiperiod securities markets", *Journal of Economic Theory* **20** (1979), 381-408.

[130] J. M. Harrison and S. R. Pliska, "Martingales and stochastic integrals in the theory of continuous trading", *Stochastic Processes and Their Applications* **11** (1981), 215-260.

[131] H. He, W. P. Keirstead and J. Rebholz, "Double lookbacks", *Mathematical Finance* **8** (1998), no. 3, 201-228.

[132] D. Heath, R. A. Jarrow and A. Morton, "Bond pricing and the term structure of interest rates: a new methodology for contingent claims valuation", *Econometrica* **60** (1992), 77-105.

[133] V. Henderson, D. Hobson, "Passport options with stochastic volatility", Working Paper, 2000.

[134] V. Henderson, D. Hobson, "Local time, coupling and the passport options", *Finance and Stochastics* **4** (1999), no. 1.

[135] S. L. Heston, "A closed-form solution for options with stochastic volatility with applications to bond and currency options", *Review of Financial Studies* **6** (1993), 327-343.

[136] T. Ho and S. Lee, "Term structure movements and pricing interest rate contingent claims", *Journal of Finance* **41** (1986), 1011-1029.

[137] D. G. Hobson, "Stochastic volatility", in *Statistics in Finance*, D. J. Hand and S. D. Jacka (editors), Arnold, London, 1998.

[138] D. G. Hobson, "Robust hedging of the lookback option", *Finance and Stochastics* **2** (1998), 329-347.

[139] S. D. Hodges and A. Neuberger, "Optimal replication of contingent claims under transaction costs", *Review of Futures Markets* **8** (1989), 222-239.

[140] J. K. Hoogland and C. D. D. Neumann, "Local scale invariance and contingent claim pricing", *International Journal of Theoretical and Applied Finance,* to appear.

[141] N. Hoffman, E. Platten and M. Schweizer, "Option pricing under incompleteness and stochastic volatility", *Mathematical Finance* **2** (1992), no. 2., 153-187.

[142] C. Huang and R. H. Litzenberger, *Foundations for Financial Economics*, North-Holland, Amsterdam, 1988.

[143] L. P. Hughston, "Geometric analysis of arbitrage and market completeness", Conference Presentation, 1997.

[144] J. Hull, *Options, Futures, and Other Derivatives,* 4th edition, Prentice-Hall, Upper Saddle River, 2000.

[145] J. Hull and A. White, "The pricing of options on assets with stochastic volatilities", *Journal of Finance* **42** (1987), 281-300.

[146] J. Hull and A. White, "An analysis of the bias in option pricing caused by a stochastic volatility", *Advances in Futures and Options Research* **3** (1988), 29-61.

[147] J. Hull and A. White, "Pricing interest rate derivative securities", *Review of Financial Studies* **3** (1990), 573-592.

[148] J. Hull and A. White, "The impact of default on the prices of options and other derivative securities", *Journal of Banking and Finance* **19** (1995), 299-322.

[149] P. J. Hunt and J. Kennedy, *Financial Derivatives in Theory and Practice*, Wiley, New York, 2000.

[150] T. Hyer, A. Lipton-Lifschitz and D. Pugachevsky, "Passport to success", *Risk Magazine* **10** (1997), no. 9, 127-131.

[151] T. Hyer and A. Lipton, "The perturbative valuation of contingent claims", Working Paper, 1998.

[152] T. Hyer and D. Pugachevsky, "Marking European options with skew", Working Paper, 1998.

[153] J. E. Ingersoll, *Theory of Financial Decision Making,* Rowman and Littlefield Publishers, Savage, MD, 1987.

[154] J. E. Ingersoll, "Valuing foreign exchange options with a bounded exchange rate process", *Review of Derivatives Research* **1** (1996), no. 2, 159-181.

[155] S. W. Inglis, "The volatility smile: a PDE approach", in *Equity Derivatives Handbook*, 2nd edition, Euromoney, London, 1998.

[156] S. W. Inglis and D. Pugachevsky, "The 'Three Moments' method for pricing basket and Asian options", Working Paper, 1998.

[157] K. Ito, "Stochastic integrals", *Proceedings of the Imperial Academy of Tokyo* **20** (1944), 519-524.

[158] K. Ito and H. P. McKean, *Diffusion Processes and Their Sample Paths,* Springer, New York, 1965.

[159] S. D. Jacka, "Optimal stopping and the American put", *Mathematical Finance* **1** (1991), no. 2, 1-14.

[160] F. Jamshidian, "An exact bond option pricing formula", *Journal of Finance* **64** (1989), 205-209.

[161] F. Jamshidian, "Forward induction and construction of yield curve diffusion models", *Journal of Fixed Income* **1** (1991), 62-74.

[162] R. Jarrow and A. Rudd, "Approximate option valuation for arbitrary stochastic processes", *Journal of Financial Economics* **10** (1982), 347-369.

[163] R. Jarrow and A. Rudd, *Option Pricing,* Richard D. Irwin, Homewood, 1983.

[164] H. Johnson, "Options on the maximum or the minimum of several assets", *Journal of Financial and Quantitative Analysis* **22** (1987), 277-283.

[165] H. Johnson and D. Shanno, "Option pricing when the variance is changing", *Journal of Financial and Quantitative Analysis* **22** (1987), 143-151.

[166] H. Johnson and R. Stulz, "The pricing of options with default risk", *Journal of Finance* **42** (1987), 267-280.

[167] I. Karatzas and S. E. Shreve, *Brownian Motion and Stochastic Calculus*, Springer, New York, 1991.

[168] I. Karatzas and S. E. Shreve, *Methods of Mathematical Finance*, Springer, New York, 1998.

[169] S. Karlin and H. M. Taylor, *A First Course in Stochastic Processes*, Academic Press, New York, 1975.

[170] S. Karlin and H. M. Taylor, *A Second Course in Stochastic Processes*, Academic Press, New York, 1981.

[171] J. M. Karpoff, "The relation between price changes and trading volume", *Journal of Financial and Quantitative Analysis* **22** (1987), 109-126.

[172] J. Kevorkian, *Partial Differential Equations. Analytical Solution Techniques*, Chapman & Hall, New York, 1993.

[173] V. A. Kholodnyi and J. F. Press, *Foreign Exchange Option Symmetry*, World Scientific, Singapore, 1998.

[174] I. J. Kim, "The analytic valuation of American options", *Review of Financial Studies* **3** (1990), 547-572.

[175] P. E. Kloeden and E. Platen, *Numerical Solution of Stochastic Differential Equations*, Springer, Berlin, 1992.

[176] A. Kocić, "Numeraire invariance and generalized risk neutral valuation", *Advances in Futures and Options Research* **9** (1997), 157-173.

[177] A. N. Kolmogoroff, "Uber die analytischen Methoden in der Wahrscheinlichkeitsrechnung", *Mathematische Annalen* **104** (1931), 415-458.

[178] R. Korn and E. Korn, *Option Pricing and Portfolio Optimization. Modern Methods of Financial Mathematics*, American Mathematical Society, Providence, 2001.

[179] V. S. Korolyk, N. I. Portenko, A. V. Skorokhod and A. F. Turbin, *Spravochnik po teorii veroyatnostey i matematicheskoi statistike*, Nauka, Moskva, 1985 (in Russian).

[180] S. G. Kou, "A jump diffusion model for option pricing with three properties: leptokurtic feature, volatility smile, and analytical tractability", Working Paper, 2000.

[181] A. Krakovsky, "Pricing liquidity into derivatives", *Risk Magazine* **12** (1999), no. 12, 65-67.

[182] N. Kunitomo and M. Ikeda, "Pricing options with curved boundaries", *Mathematical Finance* **2** (1992), no. 4, 275-298.

[183] D. Lamberton and B. Lapeyre, *Introduction to Stochastic Calculus Applied to Finance*, Chapman and Hall, London, 1996.

[184] P. Langevin, "Sur la théorie du mouvement brownien", *Comptes Rendus de l'Académie des Sciences, Paris* **146** (1908), 530-533.

[185] H. E. Leland, "Option pricing and replication with transaction costs", *Journal of Finance* **40** (1985), 1283-1301.

[186] E. Levy, "The valuation of average rate currency options", *Journal of International Money and Finance* **11** (1992), 474-491.

[187] P. Lévy, *Processes Stochastiques et Mouvement Brownien*, Gauthier-Villars, Paris, 1948.

[188] A. L. Lewis, *Option Valuation under Stochastic Volatility with Mathematica Code*, Finance Press, 2000.

[189] V. Linetsky, "Steps to the barrier", *Risk Magazine* **11** (1998), no. 4.

[190] V. Linetsky, "Step options", *Mathematical Finance* **9** (1999), 55-96.

[191] J. Lintner, "The valuation of risky assets and the selection of risky investments on stock portfolios and capital budgets", *Review of Economics and Statistics* **47** (1965), 13-34.

[192] A. Lipton, "Analytical valuation of passport option", Working Paper, 1997 a.

[193] A. Lipton, "Analytical valuation of barrier options on assets with stochastic volatility", Working Paper, 1997 b.

[194] A. Lipton, "Analytical valuation of double-barrier options", Working Paper, 1997 c.

[195] A. Lipton, "The analytical valuation of two-factor barrier options with one barrier for each factor", Working Paper, 1998 a.

[196] A. Lipton, "The heat potential method for solving one-factor parabolic equations with moving boundary", Working Paper, 1998 b.

[197] A. Lipton, "How to evaluate path-dependent options on assets with stochastic volatility", Working Paper, 1998 c.

[198] A. Lipton-Lifschitz, "Predictability and unpredictability in finance", *Physica D* **133** (1999), 321-347.

[199] A. Lipton, "Similarities via self-similarities", *Risk Magazine* **12** (1999), no. 9, 101-105.

[200] A. Lipton, "Group theoretical methods for option pricing", *Risk's 6th Annual Congress,* Boston, June 2000.

[201] A. Lipton, "Interactions between mathematics and finance: past, present, and future", Keynote Address, *Math Week, Risk's 2nd Annual Conference on Innovative Research in Derivatives Modelling and Analysis,* New York - London, November 2000 a.

[202] A. Lipton, "Pricing and risk managing exotics on assets with stochastic volatility", *ICBI 7th Annual Conference on Risk Management,* Geneva, December 2000 b.

[203] A. Lipton and T. Little, "A general eigenfunction approach", *Math Week, Risk's 2nd Annual Conference on Innovative Research in Derivatives Modelling and Analysis,* New York - London, November 2000.

[204] A. Lipton and W. McGhee, "Volatility and correlation swaps", Working Paper, 1999.

[205] A. Lipton and W. McGhee, "How to price a passport option efficiently", Working Paper, 2000.

[206] A. Lipton and D. Pugachevsky, "The valuation of VAR and exotic options via universal distribution functions", Working Paper, 1997.

[207] A. Lipton and D. Pugachevsky, "The valuation of risky options and forward contracts", Working Paper, 1998 a.

[208] A. Lipton and D. Pugachevsky, "The variance and volatility swaps", Working Paper, 1998 b.

[209] A. Lipton and D. Pugachevsky, "Pricing of volatility sensitive products in the Heston model framework", Working Paper, 1998 c.

[210] T. Little, V. Pant and C. Hou, "A new integral representation of the early exercise boundary for American put options", *Journal of Computational Finance* **3** (2000), no. 3, 73-96.

[211] A. W. Lo and A. C. MacKinlay, *A Non-random Walk Down Wall Street*, Princeton Univ. Press, Princeton, NJ, 1999.

[212] J. B. Long, "The numeraire portfolio", *Journal of Financial Economics* **26** (1990), 29-69.

[213] F. A. Longstaff and E. S. Schwartz, "Valuing American options by simulation: a simple least-squares approach", Working Paper, 2000.

[214] D. Luenberger, *Investment Science,* Oxford Univ. Press, Oxford, 1998.

[215] T. J. Lyons, "Uncertain volatility and the risk-free synthesis of derivatives", *Applied Mathematical Finance* **2** (1995), 117-133.

[216] T. J. Lyons, A. T. Smith, "Uncertain volatility", *Risk Magazine* **12** (1999), no. 9, 106-109.

[217] B. G. Malkiel, *A Random Walk Down Wall Street,* Norton, New York, 1990

[218] B. B. Mandelbrot, "The variation of certain speculative prices", *Journal of Business* **36** (1963), 394-416.

[219] S. R. Mane, "The early exercise boundary of American options near expiry", Working Paper, 1999.

[220] R. N. Mantegna and H. E. Stanley, "Scaling behavior in the dynamics of an economic index", *Nature* **376** (1995), 46-49.

[221] W. Margrabe, "The value of an option to exchange one asset for another", *Journal of Finance* **33** (1978), 177-186.

[222] H. Markowitz, *Mean-Variance Analysis in Portfolio Choice and Capital Markets,* Blackwell, Cambridge, MA, 1990.

[223] G. Maruyama, "Continuous Markov processes and stochastic equations", *Rend. Circolo Math. Palermo* **4** (1955), 48-90.

[224] A. Matytsin, "Modelling volatility and volatility derivatives", Conference Presentation, 1999.

[225] H. P. McKean, "A free boundary problem for the heat equation arising from a problem of mathematical economics", *Industrial Management Review* **6** (1965), 32-39.

[226] R. C. Merton, "Optimum consumption and portfolio rules in a continuous time model", *Journal of Economic Theory* **3** (1971), 373-413.

[227] R. C. Merton, "Theory of rational option pricing", *Bell Journal of Economics and Management Science* **4** (1973), 141-183.

[228] R. C. Merton, "On the pricing of corporate debt: the risk structure of interest rates", *Journal of Finance* **29** (1973), 449-470.

[229] R. C. Merton, "Option pricing when underlying stock returns are discontinuous", *Journal of Financial Economics* **3** (1976), 125-144.

[230] R. C. Merton, *Continuous-Time Finance,* Blackwell, Cambridge, MA, 1990.

[231] G. N. Milstein, "Approximate integration of stochastic differential equations", *Theory of Probability and its Applications* **19** (1974), 557-563.

[232] G. N. Milstein, *Approximate integration of stochastic differential equations,* Kluwer, Boston, MA, 1995.

[233] A. R. Mitchell and D. F. Griffiths, *The Finite Elements Method in Partial Differential Equations,* Wiley, Chichester, 1980.

[234] F. Modigliani and M. H. Miller, "The cost of capital, corporation finance, and the theory of investment", *American Economic Review* **48** (1958), 261-297.

[235] E. Mordecki, "Optimal stopping for a diffusion with jumps", *Finance and Stochastics* **3** (1999), 227-236.

[236] P. M. Morse and H. Feschbach, *Methods of Theoretical Physics, Parts I, II,* McGraw-Hill, New York, 1953.

[237] K. W. Morton and D. F. Mayers, *Numerical Solution of Partial Differential Equations,* Cambridge Univ. Press, Cambridge, 1994.

[238] J. Mossin, "Equilibrium in a capital asset market", *Econometrica* **34** (1966), 768-783.

[239] M. Musiela and M. Rutkowski, *Martingale Methods in Financial Modelling,* Springer, Berlin, 1997.

[240] R. Myneni, "The pricing of the American option", *Annals of Applied Probability* **2** (1992), 1-23.

[241] D. Nachman, "Spanning and completeness with options", *Review of Financial Studies* **3** (1988), 311-328.

[242] I. Nagayama, "Pricing of passport option", *Journal of Mathematical Sciences of the University of Tokyo* **5** (1998), 747-785.

[243] A. Neuberger, "The log contract and other power contracts", in *The Handbook of Exotic Options,* I. Nelken (editor), Irwin, Chicago, 1996.

[244] L. T. Nielsen, *Pricing and Hedging of Derivative Securities,* Oxford Univ. Press, New York, 2000.

[245] B. Oksendal, *Stochastic Differential Equations,* 3rd edition, Springer, Berlin, 1992.

[246] D. W. Peaceman and H. H. Rachford, "The numerical solution of parabolic and elliptic differential equations", *Journal of Society of Industrial and Applied Mathematics* **3** (1955), 28-41.

[247] I. de Pinto, *Traité de la Circulation et du Crédit,* Marc Michel Rey, Amsterdam, 1771.

[248] S. R. Pliska, *Introduction to Mathematical Finance. Discrete Time Models,* Blackwell, Cambridge, MA, 1997.

[249] W. Press, S. Teukolsky, W. Vetterling and B. Flannery, *Numerical Recipes in C - The Art of Scientific Computing,* Cambridge Univ. Press, Cambridge, 1992.

[250] R. Rabinovitch, "Pricing stock and bond options when the default free rate is stochastic", *Journal of Financial and Quantitative Analysis* **24** (1989), 447-457.

[251] S. Rady, "Option pricing in the presence of natural boundaries and a quadratic diffusion term", *Finance and Stochastics* **1** (1997), 331-344.

[252] E. Reiner, "Classifying, identifying and using mathematical symmetries to reduce the complexity of pricing and hedging exotic options", Conference Presentation, 1997.

[253] E. Reiner, "Convolution methods for exotic options", *Conference on Computational Intelligence for Financial Engineering,* March 1998.

[254] E. Reiner, "Volatility rules and implied processes", *Risk Conference on New Advances in Derivatives Modelling and Analysis,* October 1998.

[255] E. Renault and N. Touzi, "Option hedging and implied volatilities in a stochastic volatility model", *Mathematical Finance* **6** (1996), 279-302.

[256] G. O. Roberts and C. F. Shortland, "Pricing barrier options with time-dependent coefficients", *Mathematical Finance* **7** (1997), no. 1, 83-93.

[257] L. C. G. Rogers and Z. Shi, "The value of an Asian option", *Journal of Applied Probability* **32** (1995), 1077-1088.

[258] L. C. G. Rogers and D. Williams, *Diffusions, Markov Processes and Martingales: Ito Calculus,* vol. 2, Wiley, Chichester, 1987.

[259] L. I. Rubinstein, *The Stefan Problem,* American Mathematical Society, Providence, RI, 1971.

[260] M. Rubinstein, "Displaced diffusion option pricing", *Journal of Finance* **38** (1983), 213-217.

[261] M. Rubinstein, "Implied binomial trees", *Journal of Finance* **49** (1994), 771-818.

[262] M. Rubinstein and E. Reiner, "Breaking down the barriers", *Risk Magazine* **4** (1991), no. 8, 28-35.

[263] P. A. Samuelson, "Rational theory of warrant pricing", *Industrial Management Review* **6** (1965), 13-32.

[264] M. Schroder, "Computing the constant elasticity of variance option pricing formula", *Journal of Finance* **44** (1989), 211-219.

[265] M. Schroder, "On the valuation of double-barrier options: computational aspects", Working Paper, 1999.

[266] M. Schroder, "On the valuation of Paris barrier options: the first standard case", Working Paper, 1999.

[267] M. Schroder, "On the valuation of arithmetic-average Asian options: integral representations", Working Paper, 1999.

[268] A. B. Schmidt, "Modeling the demand-price relations in a high-frequency foreign exchange market", *Physica A* **271** (1999), 507-514.

[269] W. M. Schmidt, "On a general class of one-factor models for the term structure of interest rates", *Finance and Stochastics* **1** (1997), no. 1, 3-24.

[270] U. Schmock, S. E. Shreve and U. Wystup, "Valuation of exotic options under shortselling constraints", Working Paper, 1999.

[271] E. Schwartz, "The valuation of warrants: implementing a new approach", *Journal of Financial Economics* **4** (1977), 79-93.

[272] M. Schweizer, "Option hedging for semimartingales", *Stochastic Processes and Applications* **37** (1991), 339-363.

[273] L. O. Scott, "Option pricing when variance changes randomly: theory, estimation and an application", *Journal of Financial and Quantitative Analysis* **22** (1987), 419-438.

[274] W. F. Sharpe, *Investments,* Prentice-Hall, Englewood Cliffs, 1985.

[275] L. A. Shepp and A. N. Shiryaev, "The Russian option: Reduced regret", *Annals of Applied Probability* **3** (1993), 631-640.

[276] D. C. Shimko, *Finance in Continuous Time. A Primer,* Kolb, Miami, 1992.

[277] A. N. Shiryaev, *Essentials of Stochastic Finance. Facts, Models, Theory,* World Scientific, Singapore, 1999.

[278] S. E. Shreve and J. Večeř, "Options on a traded account: vacation calls, vacation puts and passport options", *Finance and Stochastic* **4** (2000), no. 3, 255-274.

[279] G. D. Smith, *Numerical Solution of Partial Differential Equations: Finite Difference Methods,* Oxford Univ. Press, Oxford, 1985.

[280] C. Sprenkle, "Warrant prices as indications of expectations", *Yale Economic Essays* **1** (1961), 132-179.

[281] H. Soner, S. Shreve and J. Cvitanic, "There is no nontrivial hedging portfolio for option pricing with transaction costs", *Annals of Applied Probability* **5** (1995), 327-355.

[282] E. M. Stein and J. C. Stein, "Stock price distributions with stochastic volatility: an analytic approach", *Review of Financial Studies* **4** (1991), 727-752.

[283] D. Stirzaker, *Elementary Probability,* Cambridge Univ Press, Cambridge, 1994.

[284] G. Strang, *Linear Algebra and Its Applications,* Harcourt, Brace, and Jovanovich, San Diego, CA, 1988.

[285] J. C. Strikwerda, *Finite Difference Schemes and Partial Differential Equations,* Wadsworth & Brooks/Cole, Pacific Grove, CA, 1989.

[286] R. M. Stulz, "Options on the minimum or maximum of two risky assets", *Journal of Financial Economics* **10** (1982), 161-185.

[287] A. A. Sveshnikov, *Problems in Probability Theory, Mathematical Statistics and Theory of Random Functions,* Dover, New York, 1978.

[288] D. Tavella and C. Randall, *Pricing Financial Instruments. The Finite Difference Method,* Wiley, New York, 2000.

[289] S. J. Taylor, "Modelling stochastic volatility: a review and comparative study", *Mathematical Finance* **4** (1994), 183-204.

[290] A. N. Tikhonov and A. A. Samarskiji, *Equations of Mathematical Physics,* Pergamon Press, Oxford, 1963.

[291] J. A. Tilley, "Valuing American options in a path simulation model", *Transactions of the Society of Actuaries* **45** (1993), 83-104.

[292] S. M. Turnbull and L. M. Wakeman, "A quick algorithm for pricing European average options", *Journal of Financial and Quantitative Analysis* **26** (1991), no. 3, 177-188.

[293] G. E. Uhlenbeck and L. S. Ornstein, "On the theory of Brownian motion", *Physical Review* **36** (1930), 823-841.

[294] P. L. G. van Moerbecke, "On optimal stopping and free boundary problems", *Archive for Rational Mechanics and Analysis* **60** (1976), no. 2, 101-148.

[295] O. A. Vasicek, "An equilibrium characterization of the term structure", *Journal of Financial Economics* **5** (1977), 177-188.

[296] J. Večeř and S. Shreve, "Upgrading your passport", *Risk Magazine* **13** (2000), no. 7, 81-83.

[297] T. C. F. Vorst, "Averaging options", in *The Handbook of Exotic Options*, I. Nelken (editor), Irwin, Chicago, 1996.

[298] R. E. Whaley, "Derivatives on market volatility: hedging tools long overdue", *Journal of Derivatives* **1** (1993), 71-84.

[299] J. B. Wiggins, "Option values under stochastic volatility: theory and empirical evidence", *Journal of Financial Economics* **19** (1987), 351-372.

[300] P. Wilmott, *Derivatives. The Theory and Practice of Financial Engineering*, Wiley, Chichester, 1998.

[301] P. Wilmott, J. Dewynne and S. Howison, *Option Pricing: Mathematical Models and Computation*, Oxford Financial Press, Oxford, 1993.

[302] P. Wilmott, S. Howison and J. Dewynne, *The Mathematics of Financial Derivatives. A Student Introduction*, Cambridge Univ. Press, Cambridge 1995.

[303] X. Xu and S. J. Taylor, "The term structure of volatility implied by foreign exchange options", *Journal of Financial and Quantitative Analysis* **29** (1994), 57-74.

[304] G. Yu, "Valuation of American options for alternative diffusion processes", Working Paper, 1992.

[305] P. G. Zhang, *Exotic Options*, World Scientific, Singapore, 1997.

[306] V. M. Zolotarev, *One-dimensional Stable Distributions*, American Mathematical Society, Providence, 1986.

[307] C. Zuhlsdorff, "The pricing of derivatives on assets with quadratic volatility", Working Paper, 1999.

[308] D. Zwillinger, *Handbook of Differential Equations*, Academic Press, San Diego, 1989.

Index